FOUNDATION COURSE in BIOLOGY

with CASE STUDY Approach
for NEET / Olympiad

Corporate Office

DISHA PUBLICATION

45, 2nd Floor, Maharishi Dayanand Marg, Corner Market, Malviya Nagar, New Delhi - 110017
Tel : 49842349 / 49842350

© Copyright Disha

No part of this publication may be reproduced in any form without prior permission of the publisher. The author and the publisher do not take any legal responsibility for any errors or misrepresentations that might have crept in. We have tried and made our best efforts to provide accurate up-to-date information in this book.

All Right Reserved

Disha Experts

Neha Upadhyay

Typeset by Disha DTP Team

www.dishapublication.com
Books & ebooks for School & Competitive Exams

www.mylearninggraph.com
e-tests for Competitive Exams

Write to us at **info@dishapublication.com**

CONTENTS

1 Crop Production & Management

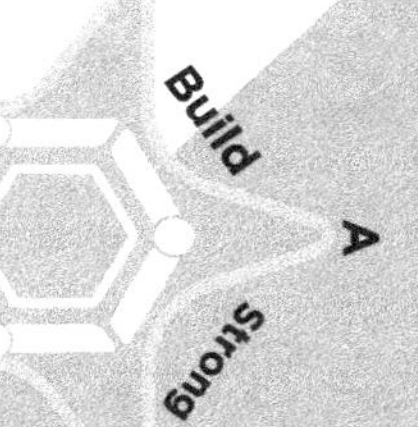

CONCEPT MAP

CROP : It is a plant or plant product that can be grown or cultivated and harvested extensively for profit or subsistence.

KHARIF CROP : Grown in rainy season during the month of June to September. They require short day length for flowering. Example- Soyabean, maize.

RABI CROP : Grown in winter season during the month of October to March. They require long day length for flowering. Example- wheat, barley.

ADDITION OF MANURE AND FERTILIZERS: The substances that are added to the soil in the form of nutrients for healthy growth of plants are called manure and fertilizer.

AGRICULTURAL PRACTICES: The production of crops by cultivation of land is called agriculture.

PREPARATION OF SOIL : Ideal soil should be balanced, well-drained, fertile and with pH between 6 and 7.

SOWING OF SEEDS : Process of placing seeds in the ground for growing the crop plants.

IRRIGATION: The process of supplying water to crops in the fields at different intervals.

PROTECTION FROM WEEDS & CROP PROTECTION: The unwanted plants that grow along with crops and compete with crop for water, nutrient, light and space are called weeds. Example- Parthenium, Amaranthus.

HARVESTING: Process of cutting and gathering of matured food crop. It is done by using sickle, for age harvesters and combines.

STORAGE OF FOOD GRAINS: Food grains obtained by harvesting the crops are dried in sunshine and are stored. Small scale storage uses jute bag and metallic bins, while large scale storage uses silos and granaries.

PLOUGHING: The process of loosening and turning the soil.

BY MANUAL HAND: Seeds are scattered in field by farmers called broad casting method.

LEVELLING: Ploughed soil is levelled by pressing it with leveller to prevent soil erosion by wind.

BY SEED DRILL: Seed drill are sown at right intervals and proper depth using drill.

THRESHING: Process of separating grain seeds from pods or chaff or plant.

MANURING: Process of applying organic minerals and adding nutrients to soil.

TRADITIONAL METHOD: This method was used earlier, they are cheap but less efficient. Types- Moat, Dhekli, Rahat, Chain pump.

MODERN METHOD: Includes sprinkler and drip system water is supplied using pipes and provides efficient coverage.

WINNOWING: Process of separating grain from the mixture of thrashed chaff.

CROP

Crop is a plant or plant product that can be grown or cultivated and harvested extensively for profit or subsistence. For example, if all the plants of maize are grown in a field, then it is called a maize crop. Similarly, if all the plants of wheat are grown, then it is called a wheat crop.

Crop can be used as:

- *food crops*, for human consumption (e.g., wheat, potatoes).
- *feed crops*, for livestock consumption (e.g., oats, alfalfa).
- *fibre crops*, for ropes and textiles (e.g., cotton, hemp).
- *oil crops*, for consumptions or industrial uses (e.g., cottonseed, corn).
- *ornamental crops*, for landscape gardening (e.g., dogwood, azalea); and industrial uses.
- *secondary crops*, for various personal and industrial uses (e.g., rubber, tobacco).

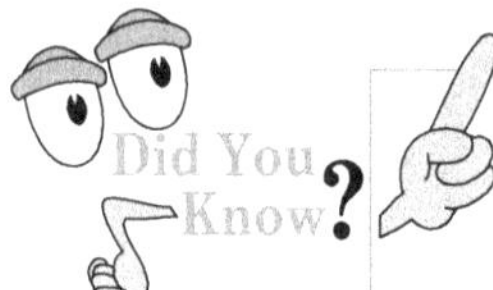

The first cultivated crop plants were cereals such as wheat, barley, rice and maize. Their seeds are rich in carbohydrates and therefore form the staple diet almost everywhere in the world. Wheat is the most important cereal in the world, followed by paddy and maize.

Table : Some other examples of crops

Crops	Examples
Cereal crops	Wheat, Paddy, Millet, etc
Pulses	Gram, Peas, Beans
Oil seeds	Mustard, Groundnut, Sunflower
Vegetables	Tomato, Cabbage, Spinach
Fruits	Banana, Mango, Orange etc.

All the crops are grown in their specific seasons. Paddy, for example, is grown during rainy season while maize is grown during winter season. Therefore, **on the basis of seasons, all the crops are categorised into two main groups** —kharif crops and rabi crops.

(i) **Kharif crops :** The crops grown in rainy season during the months of June to September are called Kharif crops. They are also known as summer or monsoon crop. These crops require warm, wet weather at major period of crop growth and also required short day length for flowering. Soyabean, maize, sugarcane, groundnut, paddy and cotton are the examples of Kharif crops.

(ii) **Rabi crops :** The crops grown in winter season from October to March are called rabi crops. They are also known as winter crop. These crops grow well in cold and dry weather and require longer day length for flowering. Wheat, barley, mustard, peas gram, linseed etc. are some examples of rabi crops.

Another type of crop is **summer/zaid crops**. These crops are grown in summer month from March to June. They require warm day weather for major growth period and longer day length for flowering. E.g. groundnuts, watermelon, pumpkins, gourds.

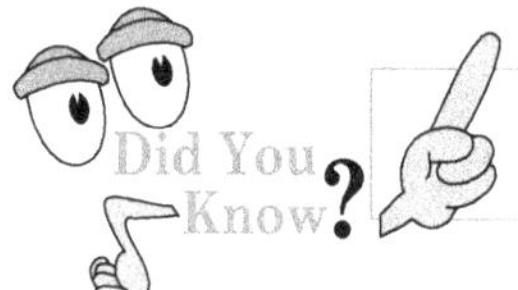

Worms helps plants by mixing the soil, so gardeners love them because they are "free" help.

1. Why we classify crop plants?
2. What will happen if the farmer grows Rabi crops during rainy season instead of winter?
3. Why crops such as paddy are grown only in rainy season?

SOLUTION :

1. We classify crop plants:
   - To get acquainted with crops.
   - To know the adaptability of crops.
   - To know the growing habit of crops.

-   To know the growing season of the crop
-   To understand the climatic requirement of different crops.
-   To know the economic products of the crop plant and its use.
-   To understand the requirement of soil & water for different crops.
-   Overall to know the actual condition required for the cultivation of plant.

2. If Rabi crops are sown in rainy season i.e. from June to September, then the whole plant crop will get destroyed. This could be because of absence of factors required to maintain the crops such as lack of optimum temperature, adaptability, availability of pests and many more. Hence, Rabi crops such as wheat, mustard etc. should be sown only in winter season

3. It is because crops such as paddy require large quantity of water. Therefore, they are grown in the rainy season to fulfil their excessive water requirement.

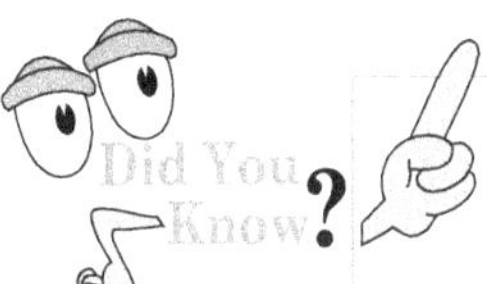

Agriculture forms a complex web of product, producer, distributor and consumer. All of them are interconnected and dependent upon each other for survival.

AGRICULTURAL PRACTICES

The growing of crops in the fields by the farmer for obtaining food like wheat, rice etc, is called *agriculture*. About 70% of the India's population is dependent on agriculture. India is also ranked second in terms of agricultural output.

Agriculture was the key development in the rise of sedentary human civilization, whereby farming of domesticated species created food surpluses that nurtured the development of civilization. The study of agriculture is known as **agricultural science**. The reason for the increased agricultural output is the steady improvement in irrigation methods, new agricultural technology and modern agricultural practices. Farmers carry out certain activities in a particular sequence till the crops matures at harvest. These activities are known as *agricultural practices*. These practices increases the overall yield of a crop.

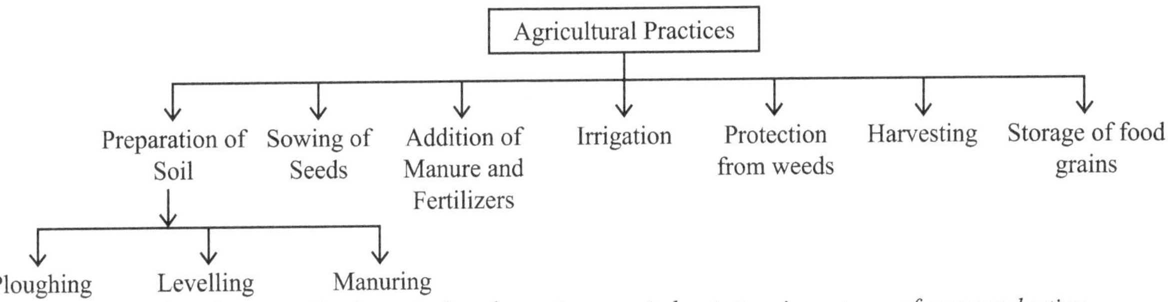

Outline classification of basic agricultural practices carried out at various stages of crop production

PREPARATION OF SOIL

Crop quality greatly depends on the soil composition. The ideal soil is balanced, well-drained, fertile and with a pH (acidity level) ranging between 6 and 7. It is important to add decomposed manure or compost which, in addition to improving soil structure and composition, will supply nutritive elements required by the plants. Preparation of soil is the first step to be followed before growing a crop. It is usually employed to loosen the soil. Plants absorb water, nutrients and salts from the soil. Therefore, it is important to prepare soil for a healthy produce.

Methods of Soil Preparation

The soil is prepared for sowing the seeds of the crop by ploughing, levelling and manuring.

Ploughing

The process of loosening and turning the soil is called ploughing or tilling. A properly set up plough will break and turn the soil so that all the weeds, (grass), crop residue and debris are buried without any scrap of waste present in the field. It also provides a seed free medium for planting an alternative crop.

The loosening of soil plays an important role in crop production because –

(i)   It allows the plant roots to penetrate freely and deeper into the soil so that plants are held firmly to the ground.
(ii) It also allows the roots of the plant to breathe easily. It is because loose soil can hold a lot of air in its spaces.
(iii) It helps in the growth of microbes and worms present in soil.
(iv) It helps to remove weeds and other undesirable plants in the field.
(v)   It helps in breaking down big soil crunches to get better yields.

Friendly Earthworms

Earthworms are called best friends of farmers. They can consume practically all kinds of organic matter. They pull down any organic matter that is deposited on the soil surface such as leaf fall, debris etc. This organic matter then undergoes biochemical change in the intestine of earthworm. Hence, earthworm converts the dead organic matter into rich humus, thereby enriching the Soil's nutritional value.

Earthworms are important to farmers in the following respects :-
(i)   It improves the soil fertility.
(ii)   It maintains the physical condition of the soil.
(iii)   It helps in mixing of sub soil and top soil.
(iv)   It helps in providing required nutrients to plants.
(v)   It helps in recycling of waste materials in the surroundings.

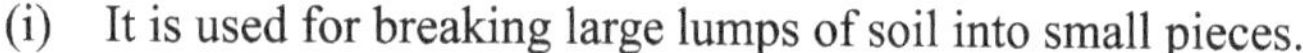

Tools used for ploughing are : plough, hoe and cultivator.

(i) Plough : It is the most ancient method for ploughing the seed. Ploughs were traditionally drawn by working animals such as horses or cattle, but in modern times they may be drawn by tractors. A plough are made of wood, iron, or steel. It contains a triangular iron rod which is called ploughshare. Then there is a long log of wood called ploughshaft.

The one end of the shaft has a handle and the other end is attached to a beam which is placed on a pair of bulls or other animals such as camel, horse etc.

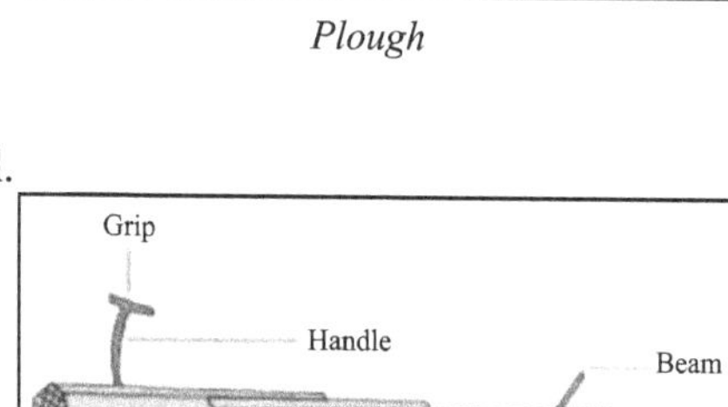

Plough

Importance of plough
(i)   It is used for breaking large lumps of soil into small pieces.
(ii)   It is used for removal of weeds, grass, crop residues, debris etc. from soil.
(iii) It is used for adding manure or fertilizers to the soil.

(ii) Hoe : Hoe are bladed tools that have a long rod of wood or iron. The one end of wood has a fixed strong blade and a bent plate of iron that works like a blade. The other end is attached to a beam that is placed on a pair of bull during ploughing the field.

Hoe

Importance of hoe
(i)   To agitate surface of soil so as to remove weeds and other unwanted plants.
(ii)   To dig and move the soil upside down.
(iii) To chop roots and other crop residues.

(iii) Cultivator : It is the modern method of ploughing used these days. It is an instrument equipped with shovels, blades etc. and used to break up soil and remove seeds. Cultivators are very similar to harrows in their function but are generally used to work large clods of soil while harrows tend to be used afterwards to create finer tilth. While the terms cultivator and harrow are sometimes used interchangeably, cultivators are determined by their ability to penetrate large depths in order to sufficiently break up the soil for seedbed preparation. Tractors are used to drive cultivator.

The tractor type cultivator tiller is suitable for large scale farming especially when you want to plant grain crops like wheat, corn and others. If you have a few acres of land to cultivate, you should invest in this type of cultivator tiller. With the help of a tractor, you can till and cultivate large acres of land in a short period of time.

Cultivator driven by a tractor

Importance of cultivator
(i)   It removes and destroys weeds, as well as fertilizes the soil and covers seeds with soil.
(ii)   It saves labour and time involved during ploughing.

Levelling

Unevenness of the soil surface has a significant impact on the germination and yield of crops. After ploughing, the field is levelled with the help of a leveller. It is because the ploughed soil is quite loose, so it is liable to be carried away by strong wind or washed away by rain water. The ploughed soil is levelled by pressing it with a wooden leveller.

Importance of levelling

(i) It prevents the top fertile soil from being carried away by strong wind or washed away by rain water.

(ii) It helps in uniform distribution of water in fields during irrigation.

(iii) It prevents the loss of moisture from ploughed soil.

(iv) For better crop establishment.

(v) It reduces irrigation time.

(vi) Less effort in crop management.

(vii) It increases the yield and quality.

(viii) Optimization of water use efficiency.

Levelling of agricultural land

Manuring

Manure is an organic matter used as fertilizer in agriculture. Sometimes before ploughing, the manure is added to the soil. The process of applying organic minerals and adding nutrients to the soil is called **manuring**. This is done for proper mixing of manure with soil. Manuring is done to increase the fertility of the soil before seed is sown in field. Manures improve the fertility of the soil by adding organic matter and nutrients, such as nitrogen that is trapped by bacteria in the soil. Higher organisms then feed on the fungi and bacteria in a chain of life.

Manuring

SOWING OF SEEDS

Sowing of seeds is the second important step of crop production. Once the soil in the fields has been prepared by ploughing, levelling and manuring, the seeds of the crop can be sown in it. *Sowing is the process of placing the seeds in the ground soil for future growth of crop plants.*

However seeds those are to be selected for growing should be of good quality. The quality of seed depends on the plants that are used for collecting seeds.

Characteristic of plants that are used for collecting the seeds

(i) Plants should be healthy and of vigorous growth.

(ii) Plants resistant to pests and diseases. So that they will produce healthy seeds.

(iii) Seeds should be collected from matured, well formed plants that produce sweet tasting fruit.

(iv) Always collect healthy seeds from high yielding plants. This will ensure the good yield of plants in subsequent generation.

Methods of Sowing Seeds

There are two methods of sowing the seeds in the soil. These are sowing by hand and by seed drill.

Sowing by Hand

The scattering of seed by hand is the simplest and ancient method of delivering seed to the soil. This process is known as *broadcasting*. In this method, the seeds are scattered in the field by the farmer in standing position. This method, however has few disadvantages like the seeds may not be properly distributed in field and may fall in clusters at one place and at another place there may be none.

Sowing by a Seed Drill

Sowing of seeds by drill is a better method of sowing than broadcasting. The seeds sown with this method are sown at right intervals and at a proper depth.

Tools Used for Sowing Seeds

Traditional Tool

It is a funnel shaped tool and is driven by plough. The seeds are filled into the funnel that has a long pipe with sharp ends. The seeds from the funnel moves into the pipe placed into the soil as plough move.

Modern Method (Seed drill)

Seed drill is a machine for planting seed at a controlled depth and in specified amounts. These days seed drills are used (for sowing seed) that involves the use of tractors.

Traditional method of sowing

A seed drill is a long iron tube having a funnel at the top. It is tied to back of the plough andseeds are put into the funnel of the seed drill. As the plough makes furrows in the soil, the seeds from the seed drill are gradually released and sown into the soil furrow made by plough.

Importance of seed drill tool

(i)   It allows uniform distribution of seeds into the soil at a proper depth.

(ii)   It also protects the seeds from birds.

(iii) It saves time and labour.

*Modern method of sowing
(Seed drill)*

Precautions to be taken while Sowing Seeds in Soil

(i)   **The seeds should be sown at right intervals or spacing**. It is because sowing seeds at proper distance avoids the competition among the plants. All plants in the field require optimum light, water and nutrients for their normal growth and development. So if they are grown nearby they will compete with each other and in turn would reduce the yield of crop. Therefore, it is advised to sow seeds at uniform distance.

(ii)   **Seeds should be sown at right depth in soil**. If the seeds are sown too deep, then they may not germinate because they cannot breathe due to insufficient air at greater depth. Also, if you just spread the seeds on the surface of the soil, then the seeds will be easily picked and can be eaten by birds. *Hence*, seeds should be sown at proper depth in the soil.

(iii) The seeds used for sowing should be clean, healthy and free from diseases.

Let's Do Activity

How can you find whether the given sample of seeds are healthier or not?

Take a clean jar half filled with water. Put some seeds (damaged and healthy) into the jar and stir it well.

Now observe the seeds present in jar.

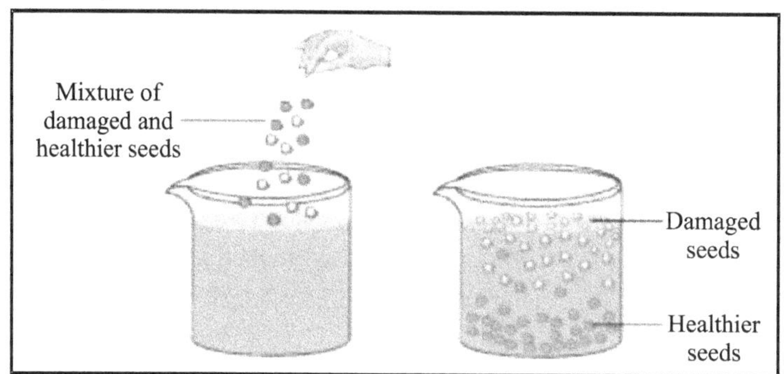

What do you observe?

You can see some of the seeds are floating on the surface while some of them settle down at the bottom.

The seeds that float on water surface are actually damaged seeds. They are hollow from inside. Hence, they are lighter in weight and floats at the top. Whereas healthier seeds sink to the bottom of jar. Healthy seeds are heavier and healthy in all respects.

Time to Check Your Knowledge

☛   **Why seeds are not sown in dry and highly wet soil?**

SOLUTION :

Moisture in the soil is necessary for germination. So, if seeds are sown in dry soil, they may not germinate. Similarly, if the seeds are sown in a highly wet soil, then on drying, the soil surface becomes too hard that the germinating seedling might not be able to come out of ground.

CONNECTING TOPIC

TRANSPLANTATION

Sometimes some seeds (for example, rice, tomato, chilli, cabbage, brinjal etc) are not directly planted in the fields, instead they are planted in the seed beds called nurseries and when they grow into seedlings they are transferred in the field.

You must have seen farmers transplanting paddy (rice) seedlings in the fields. This method is known as **transplantation**.

In case of paddy (rice) crops, the seeds are first sown in a small plot of land and are allowed to grow into tiny plants called seedlings. After the seeds have grown into tiny plants (called seedling) in the nursery, only the healthy and well-developed seedlings are then picked out and transferred to the regular field for further growth. *This process of transferring the seedlings from the nursery to the main field by hand is called transplantation.* During transplantation, farmers keep the proper distance between various seedlings and also between rows of seedling. This is done to ensure that each and every plant gets the sufficient sunlight, water and other nutrients for normal and healthy growth of plants. This process of transplantation has several advantages over the direct sowing.

Paddy seedling transplantation

Advantages of Transplantation

(i)   It enables us to select only the better and healthy seedlings for the cultivation of crops.

(ii)   It allows better and deeper penetration of roots in the soil.

(iii) It promotes better development of shoot system of plants.

(iv)   It allows seedlings to be transplanted at the right spacings so that each and every plantlet gets uniform dose of sunlight, water and nutrients and reduces competition between the plants.

Time to Check Your Knowledge

☛ **Find out more examples of crops that are cultivated by transplantation method ?**

SOLUTION :

Tomatoes and chillies

ADDITION OF MANURE AND FERTILIZERS

The plants require number of essential nutrients for their growth and development. All the nutrients required by plants can be obtained from air, water and soil. Deficiency of any of these nutrients might affect the life activities of plant, which in turn can reduce the net yield of the crop.

You must have seen that in an area, some of the plants show weak growth while some of them show vigorous growth. Can you guess, why such variations are seen?

It is because of the lack of certain nutrients required by plant for normal growth and development. Lack of nutrients makes the soil infertile. So, unless the depleted plant nutrients are put back into the soil from time to time the growth of crops would be poor. Hence, deficiency of plant nutrients in the soil is compensated by adding **manures** and **fertilizers** to the soil.

Manure

Manure is a natural fertilizer. It is prepared by the decomposition of plant and animal waste. It is known to have a large quantity of organic materials and little amount of plant nutrients. Thus, manures provide a lot of organic matter like humus to the soil. The humus improves the physical and chemical properties of the soil. It also improves the soil texture for better retention of water and aeration of soil. Since manure is produced by decomposition of animal's excreta and plant waste, it protects the environment from harmful chemicals. Thus, it helps in recycling of farm wastes.

Farmers may add manure directly to the soil in the fields or after converting it into compost by burying it in pits.

Note

Types of Manure

There are three types of manure: animal manure (farm yard manure), compost and plant manure.

Animal manure: This is the combination of animal faeces or dungs, urine and plant products used as beddings for the animals. Dung, farm refuse, fallen leaves, twigs etc are dumped in heaps to undergo decomposition and form dark amorphous manure. The faeces of poultry, goat, sheep, cattle, pigs and rabbits are essential for farmyard preparation. The period of decomposition varies with the type of animal dung used. Before applying the manure, it must be allowed to decompose fully so as to avoid burning the roots of the crops.

Plant (Green) manure: Green manure refers to crops which have already been uprooted (and have often already been stuffed under the soil). Typically, plant manures are crops that are grown for the purpose of plowing them in and using it as nutrients and organic matter.

Green manure crops are commonly associated with organic farming, and are considered essential for annual cropping systems that wish to be sustainable.

Compost manure: Compost is rotten vegetable matter, garbage, sewage, sludge and animal remains often enriched with small amounts of chemical fertilizers during decomposition stage.

What is composting?

Composting is the process of converting dead organic matter into rich humus. The waste materials such as cow dung, vegetable waste, sewage waste etc are dumped into a pit. The pit is then covered with mud to prevent air and light entering it. It is then left undisturbed for few months. During this process, the microbes decompose the animal and plant waste and convert it into inorganic materials. These inorganic materials are excellent nutrients for plants.

Sometimes, the process of composting is done with the help of earthworm. Then this process is known as vermi-composting. Earthworms can consume practically all kinds of organic matter. This organic matter undergoes biochemical change in the intestine of earthworm. Hence, earthworm converts organic matter into rich humus, thereby enriching the soil with nutrients. The process of composting ensures the continuance of fertility cycle. Composting is considered as the best recycler in nature.

Advantages of Manure

(i) It enriches the soil with organic material.

(ii) It increases the water holding capacity of soil.

(iii) It aerates the soil by making it porous.

(iv) It helps in the growth of micro-organisms.

(v) It improves the soil texture.

(vi) It increases the crop production.

(vii) It replenishes the soil with all manures.

FERTILIZERS

Fertile soil contains minerals, organic matter and a number of microscopic forms of plant and animal life. The soil should also contain soluble minerals. If the soil is deficient in these minerals, fertilizers must be added to ensure healthy crop production.

Fertilizers are commercially available plant nutrients. They can be organic or inorganic in nature. They ensure healthy growth and development of plants by providing required nutrients such as nitrogen(N), phosphorous(P), potassium(K), sulphur(S) etc., to the plant. They have nutrients in a concentrated form. So they provide quick replenishment of plant nutrients in the soil and restore its fertility. They also have high solubility in water, so are easily absorbed by the plants.

Fertilizers are good only for short term use, as it is harmful to the symbiotic microorganism that lives in soil. The excess use of fertilizers also causes water pollution.

Excessive use of fertilizers degrades the quality of soil in the long run, for example, excessive use of nitrogenous fertilizers makes the soil and water rich in nitrates. Nitrogen-rich water is not good for drinking. Nitrates from the soil also flow into rivers and lakes with rainwater and enhance the growth of weeds and algae. This decreases the oxygen content of water leading to death of aquatic life. Excessive use of fertilizers can change the nature of the soil making it either too acidic or too alkaline.

Note

Types of Fertilizers

Nitrogenous fertilizers : Urea, Ammonium sulphate, Ammonium nitrate, Sodium nitrate.

Phosphatic fertilizers : Calcium hydrogen phosphate or superphosphate, Ammonium hydrogen phosphate, Ammonium phosphate.

Potassium fertilizers: Potassium nitrate, Potassium chloride, Potassium sulphate.

☞ **How NPK helps plants in their growth?**

SOLUTION :

Nitrogen is extremely important for leaf growth; phosphorus promotes development of roots, flowers and seeds or fruit; and potassium is necessary for the growth of strong stems and movement of water in plants, in addition to promoting flowering and fruiting.

Let us perform an activity to find out how fertilizers and manure affects the plant growth.
Take some healthy gram seeds and allow them to germinate in a pot.

Then take three empty jars and label them as A, B and C.
In jar A, add little amount of soil mixed with urea, a fertilizer.
In jar B, add similar amount of soil but mixed green manure.
In jar C, add similar amount of soil without any manure or fertilizer.
Now water all these vessels bearing soil.

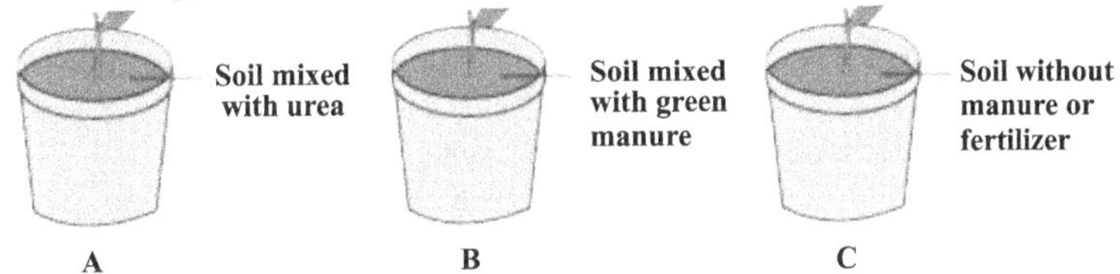

Now from the pot, select three equal sized seedlings and plant them in jar A, B and C. Keep the vessel in a safe and lighted place. Water them regularly and observe the growth.
What did you observe after few weeks?

You can observe that seedlings develop into small plantlets in all the three jars after few days. However, their growth varies in all the three.
Jar A shows maximum growth while jar C showed the least growth.
Plantlets in jar A showed the maximum growth because urea is readily soluble in water and acts quickly. When it is supplied to the soil, nitrogen is rapidly changed into ammonia. Later seeds use this ammonia for its growth and development.
The plantlets in jar B also show the growth but less compared to jar A.
The growth of plantlet in jar C is least because soil is infertile as it lacks certain essential soil nutrients.

Table : Difference between manure and fertilizers

	Manure	Fertilizers
(i)	Manure is a natural substance that is prepared by decomposition of animal excreta and plant wastes.	They are commercially available plant nutrients produced from chemical substances.
(ii)	They have large quantity of organic material and little amount of plant nutrients.	They can be organic or inorganic in nature.
(iii)	They help in enriching the soil with organic matter and nutrients.	They help in enriching the soil with organic matter and nutrients in concentrated form.
(iv)	It provides humus to the soil.	It does not provide any humus to soil.
(v)	It protects the environment and helps in recycling of waste.	Its excessive use can cause pollution.
(vi)	It is slowly absorbed by the plants.	It is readily absorbed by the plants.
(vii)	Example– animal excreta, plant waste, sewage waste etc.	Example– sodium nitrates, urea, ammoniam sulphate etc.

CONNECTING TOPIC

CROP ROTATION

Crop rotation is the practice of growing two or more varieties of crops on the same land in sequential seasons.

The continuous growing of same crop over and over again might reduce the particular nutrient from the soil. Hence, farmers employ crop rotation so that they can replenish the lost nutrients from the soil.

In crop rotation, the cereal crops like wheat, maize etc are grown alternately with leguminous crops like pulses, beans, peas, etc. Legumes have nitrogen fixing bacteria in their root nodules that can fix atmospheric nitrogen.

For example, when maize crop is grown first, it takes away a lot of nitrogen from soil for its growth and development and makes the soil nitrogen deficient. And next, when leguminous crops are grown in the same field, leguminous crops with its nitrogen fixing bacteria enriches the soil with nitrogen compounds and increases its fertility. When another cereal crop like wheat is grown after that, then wheat can utilize this extra nitrogen from soil for its growth and produce a crop with increased yield. In this way, rotating different crops (leguminous and non-leguminous crops) in the same field replenishes the soil with nitrogen naturally and thereby increases the crop production.

Advantages of Crop Rotation

(i)   It improves the fertility of soil and hence brings about an increase in food production.

(ii)   It reduces the need of fertilizers.

(iii)   It reduces the build up of pests & diseases that affect different group of plants.

(iv)   They ensure that enough nutrient are available to different crops each year.

(v)   It aids in building and maintaining healthy soil by maintaining level of its organic matter content and soil structure.

(vi)   It controls weeds.

Note

Monoculture is the repeated planting of the same crop in the field year after year.

Intercropping is the growth of two or more crops in proximity in the same field during a growing season to promote interaction between them. Available growth resources, such as light, water and nutrients are more completely absorbed and converted to crop biomass by intercropping as a result of differences in competitive ability for growth factors between intercrop components. The more efficient utilization of growth resources leads to yield advantages and increased stability compared to sole cropping.

Mixed cropping, also known as multiple cropping, is growing of two or more crops simultaneously on the same piece of land. It leads to an improvement in the fertility of the soil and increase in crop yield. The products and refuse from one crop plant help in the growth of the other crop plant and vice-versa. Mixed cropping is an insurance against crop failure in abnormal weather conditions. It also helps the farmer to improve its yield and avoid crop failure which is very common in India and Asian countries.

☛   **Study the given sequence of pictures and then answer the questions.**

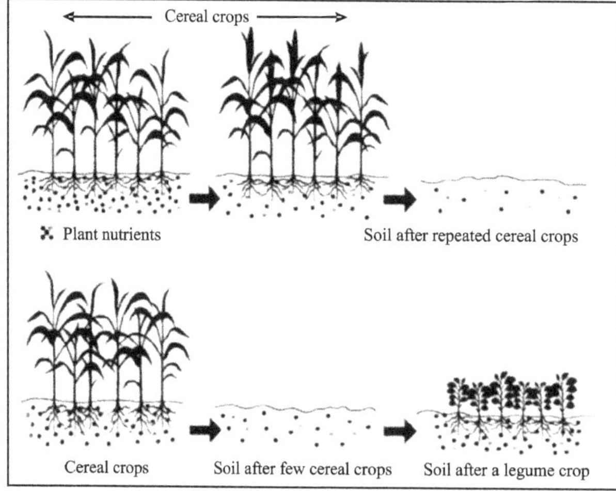

1.   **What happens to plant nutrients in the soil after growing cereals repeatedly in the same field for many years?**

2.   **Does soil fertility decreases when only cereal crops are grown again and again?**

3.   **What happens to plant nutrients in soil after growing leguminous crops?**

SOLUTION :

1. The continuous plantation of crops in a field makes the soil poor in certain nutrients such as nitrogen, phosphorus, potassium etc. As a result, the soil fertility decreases and hence the crop yield.
2. The soil fertility decreases when crop with similar requirements are grown again and again. For example, when a crop like maize is grown repeatatively, it takes up a lot of nitrogen from soil for its growth and makes the soil nitrogen deficient. If now, the same kind of crop or crop with similar requirement is grown then it would further make the soil nutrient deficient. Thus, the continuous plantation of any crop in field makes the soil poor in certain nutrients.
3. Legumes have nitrogen fixing bacteria in their root nodules that can fix atmospheric nitrogen. When the leguminous crop is grown in the same field, then the leguminous crop with its nitrogen fixing bacteria enriches the soil with nitrogen compounds and increases its fertility.

IRRIGATION

Water is essential for the growth of plants. It transports all nutrients required by the plant to each and every part of the plant body. It also maintains the moisture content of soil and prevents soil from drying.

It is therefore, necessary to supply water to crop plants in the fields, periodically. *The process of supplying water to crops in the fields is called* **irrigation**. Irrigation is used to assist in the growing of agricultural crops, maintenance of landscapes, and revegetation of disturbed soils in dry areas and during periods of inadequate rainfall. It also protects plants against frost, suppressing weed growth in grain fields and preventing soil consolidation. The time and frequency of irrigation varies according to different seasons, crops and soil types. The various sources of irrigation are wells, canals, rivers, dams, ponds and lakes. Even rain is a source of irrigation of crops.

Importance of Irrigation

(i) Irrigation before ploughing makes the soil soft due to which ploughing becomes easier.
(ii) It provides moisture for germination of seeds.
(iii) It is important for the absorption of nutrient elements by plants from soil. The water dissolves the nutrient present in the soil to form a solution. This solution of nutrients is then absorbed by the roots for the development of plants.

Methods of Irrigation

Two methods of irrigation that helps in conservation of water are : **traditional method** and **modern method**.

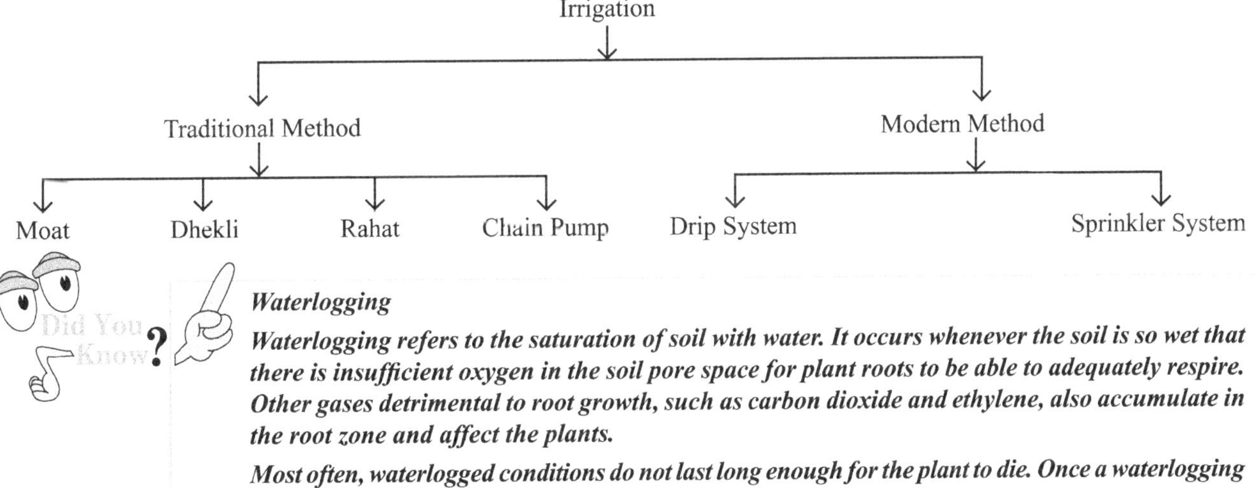

Waterlogging

Waterlogging refers to the saturation of soil with water. It occurs whenever the soil is so wet that there is insufficient oxygen in the soil pore space for plant roots to be able to adequately respire. Other gases detrimental to root growth, such as carbon dioxide and ethylene, also accumulate in the root zone and affect the plants.

Most often, waterlogged conditions do not last long enough for the plant to die. Once a waterlogging event has passed, plants recommence respiring. As long as soil conditions are moist, the older roots close to the surface allows the plant to survive.

Traditional Method

This method was used earlier for irrigation. They are cheaper but less efficient. It often includes pulley system that are used to deliver water to soil, vegetation, flowers and/or other forms of plant life. Types of traditional methods are moat, dhekli, rahat and chain pump.

(i) **Moat:** It is based on pulley system. Moat is a deep, wide ditch that is usually filled with water and that goes around the walls of a place (such as a castle) to protect it from being attacked. It has been used to collect water that was then taken directly to the fields *via* buckets and placed over the field. In other forms wells were used to keep water contained to draw on it.

(ii) **Dhekli:** Dhekli is mainly seen in rural areas. It is done manually. The person takes out water through a bucket and pour it into the field. This causes a lot of water wastage and now with water scarcity problem, people don't use this method of irrigation.

(iii) **Rahat:** It is based on lever system. The rahat system of irrigation was used in older times as a way to get water from a well by using oxen. The Rahat System of irrigation requires a large well in which a wheel is used. The wheel is turned by oxen, buffalo or cows to get the water out of the well and then spread out over the crops.

(iv) **Chain pump:** It is based on pumps. Chain pump is a type of water pump. The pump consists of a pipe connected to a water supply, a circular chain and flat platters that are the same size and shape as the pipe. These platters are connected to the chain, which is then drawn up through the pipe. Water is caught on the platter and brought up to the surface. The chain is circular, so as the platters rise on one side of the chain and then drops back into the water.

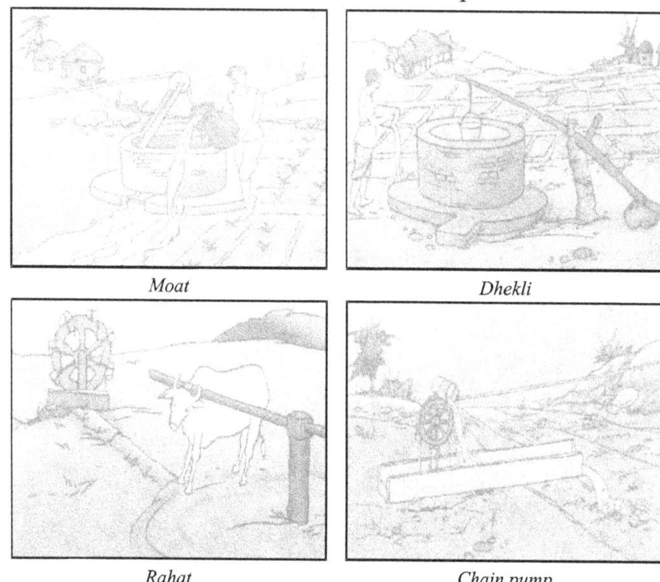

Traditional methods of irrigation

Modern Methods

Modern methods of irrigation are used for supplying water to fields economically. Types of modern method of irrigation are : sprinkler system of irrigation and drip system of irrigation.

(i) **Sprinkler system :** This system of irrigation supplies water to plants (crops) in the form of rain. It consists of perpendicular pipe which has a rotating nozzle on to and is joined to main pipeline. Water escapes from the rotating nozzles when it passes through the main pipe under pressure with the help of a pump. In this method, water is supplied using pipes to one or more central locations within the field. Sprinkler are useful for lawns and coffee plantations.

This method is more useful on uneven land that have fewer water supplies. Most of the crops such as wheat, grain, vegetable, pulses etc are irrigated by this method of irrigation.

Advantages of sprinkler system of irrigation

(i) It provides efficient coverage of water from small to large areas.

(ii) It has a wide range of water capacity. Hence, they are used for nearly all soils.

(ii) **Drip system :** Drip irrigation systems are methods of microirrigation wherein water is applied through emitters to the soil surface as drops or small streams. The discharge rate of the emitters is low so this irrigation method can be used on all soil types. This method of irrigation is more efficient for irrigating fruits and vegetables. In this method, water is delivered at or near the roots of the plant drop by drop. Water is passed through plastic pipes that have holes in it. These plastic pipes are then laid along the rows of crop. This is the most efficient method of irrigation as there is no wastage of water at all.

Advantages of drip system of irrigation

(i) It saves water, as water is delivered at or near the roots of the plant.

(ii) It avoids random watering of crops.

(iii) It improves water holding capacity of soil and reduces soil erosion.

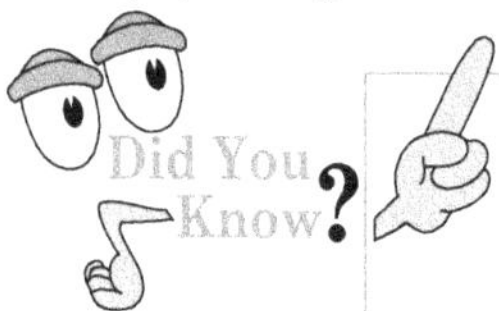

Net irrigation water requirement (NIWR) is defined as the quantity of water which is necessary for crop growth. It is expressed in millimetres per year or in m3/ha per year (1mm = 10m3/ha). It can be supplied through rainwater or through irrigation methods.

The water requirement of any crop depends on crop factors, soil factors, climatic factors and crop management practices.

☞ **Why gardeners need to give more water to plants in summers?**

SOLUTION :

Gardeners give more water to plants in summers because in summers, the evaporation rate is high from soil and leaves. This makes the soil deficient of important nutrients required for the growth of plant. Hence, we need to give more water to plants to prevent drying of plants.

CONNECTING TOPIC

EFFECT OF EXCESSIVE IRRIGATION OF WATER

The crops need to be irrigated with just the right amount of water, neither too little nor too much. Excessive irrigation of water is harmful to crops because,

(i) Excessive supply of irrigation water to crop fields reduces the air trapped in the spaces between soil particles. As a result the roots of crop plants do not get sufficient air to breathe and hence they die.

(ii) Also, excess of water in the fields increases the amount of salt on the surface of soil, which is formed due to excessive evaporation. The accumulation of salt in the field lower the fertility of soil and hence reduces the crop growth and development.

It takes 100 pounds of rain water to produce a single pound of food from the crops.

Between 10 and 20 tons of water must pass through the roots of an acre of corn before one bushel of corn will be produced.

☞ **Why potted plants in our homes do not grow well if they are watered excessively?**

SOLUTION :

It is because, excess of water expels most of the air from the spaces between soil particles. As a result, plant roots do not get sufficient air to breathe and hence they do not grow well.

What is lodging?

The falling of mature crop plants in the fields due to action of strong winds is called lodging. The correct timing of irrigation is very important for a good crop yield. For example, if the irrigation of a wheat field is done when the crop has fully matured or if there is heavy rainfall during harvesting season, then the wheat plants are unable to resist strong winds. In such cases, a strong wind blowing over the fields makes the matured wheat plants fall on the ground. As a result, the quantity and quality of wheat crop decreases. It also reduces yield and quality of straw. There are many external factors that have a influence on lodging including: wind, rain, topography, soil type, fore crop, tillage, nitrogen fertilizers, diseases, sowing date, seed rate, and variety. Lodging has a negative influence on both the yield and the yield quality.

PROTECTION FROM WEED

When you grow a food crop in the field, you must have noticed the growth of certain other plants along with major cultivated crops. What are these? These undesirable plant that grow along with crop are called **weeds**. Weeds compete with the crop for water, nutrient, space and light. As a result of competition, crops gets lesser amount of nutrients, space and light then that are required for survival. *Hence,* the productivity of crop reduces. Therefore, it is necessary to remove the weeds from the cultivated field. Wild oat, Grass, *Amaranthus*, *Xanthium*, *Parthenium* are common weeds.

(a) Harrow   *(b) Trowel (Khurpi)*

Implements used for weeding

The process of removing weeds from the cultivated field is called **weeding**. The best time to remove weeds is when the soil is damp and moist, *for example*, the day after it has rained during spring time. Damp soils are loose and make it easier to remove weeds along with their roots. Otherwise, it may run the risk of cutting off the roots because they are stuck in the soil. If the soil is hard and there is no rain in the next few days, consider hosing down the area with water and let the water soak overnight before you start removing weeds.

Manual weeding   *Spraying weedicide*   *Sickle (Used in harvesting)*

Various Ways of Weeding

(i)   Removal of weeds by pulling them out with hand is the traditional method of weeding.

(ii) Proper ploughing before sowing seeds helps in uprooting weeds.

(iii) Removal of weeds by using a trowel (khurpi) and harrow. *You must have seen farmers sitting in the field and uprooting certain plant with Khurpi. What are they doing?* Any guesses!! Farmers are uprooting the undesirable plants that are grown along with main crops. This is a manual method of removing weeds.

(iv) Crop rotation is another method for controlling the growth of weed. The weeds are very choosy about the crops with which they grow. *Hence,* by rotating the crops that have different nutrient requirements in the same field, disturbs the weed's life cycle and reduces their growth in the field.

(v)   Weeds can also be destroyed by spraying special chemicals called **weedicides** on them. Benthiocarb, butachlor, 2, 4-D (2, 4 Dichlorophenoxy acetic acid) etc are some examples of weedicides. They are not harmful to crops but they can be harmful to farmers. Hence, these chemical should be carefully used and sprayed. Farmers are advised to cover their nose and mouth with a piece of cloth while spraying the weedicides on crops.

Time to Check Your Knowledge

☛ **Why should weeding be done before flowering?**

SOLUTION :

Weeding is done before flowering so that weeds cannot produce seeds to multiply their number and to prevent the mixing of their seeds with grains.

HARVESTING

The process of cutting and gathering of the matured food crop is called **harvesting**. Most of the crops are harvested in autumn season. In harvesting, the crops like wheat or rice are cut close to the ground by hand using a tool called **sickle**. It is the manual method of harvesting crops. In large fields, the crops are harvested using a machine called **harvester**.

In India, harvesting is done mostly by sickle. Sickle is made up of a curved, plain blade of carbon steel. It has a wooden handle to hold the sickle. The tang of the blade is lightly fixed into the handle with a ferrule.

Other methods of harvesting are – forage harvesters and combines.

(i)   **Forage harvesters :** These are tractor drawn self propelled machines that are used to collect chop and then discharge the crop into field as it moves through.

(ii)   **Combines :** They are farm machines that are used to harvest seed crops and grains. Combines perform cutting, threshing, separating, cleaning and grain handling operations in the field.

Forage harvesters

Combine

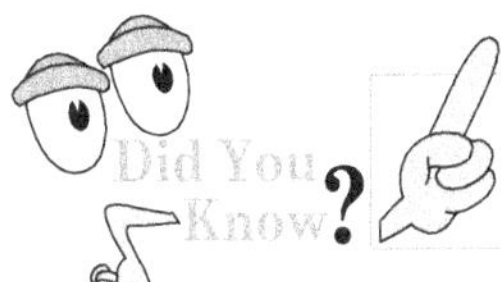

The first combine harvester was designed in 1836 by America's Hiram Moore and John Hascall. It was pulled by horses.

☛   **Can you name some of the festivals associated with the harvest season?**

SOLUTION :

The harvesting of crop is considered as an important celebration for farmers. It fills the heart of all farmers with happiness and a sense of well being. Pongal, Baisakhi, Holi, Diwali, Nabanya, Bihu etc are the festivals associated with the harvest season. These festivals are celebrated by farmers with great enthusiasm.

THRESHING

After harvesting, the next step is threshing. *You must have seen farmers rubbing the grain betweenpalms or beating the crops with a hard object. What are they doing?* They are separating the grain seeds from pods or chaff or plant. This process is known as **threshing**.

Threshing is the process of separating the grain seeds from the scaly, inedible chaff that surrounds it. Threshing does not remove the bran from the grain. It may be done by beating the grain using a flail on a threshing floor. It is a slow and time consuming process if done manually. Hence, it is carried out with a machine called *"combine"*. Combine is actually a harvester as well as a thresher.

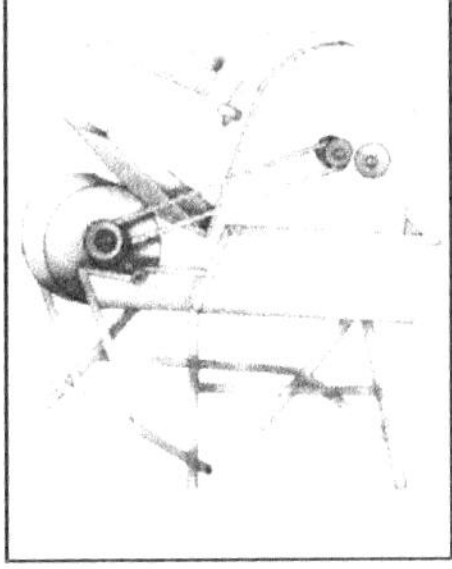

Thresher

Winnowing

After grains are threshed, the chaff is removed from the grains. This process is known as winnowing. Hence, *winnowing is the process of separating grain from the mixture of threshed chaff.*

When the grain mixed with chaff and hay is made to fall from a height in blowing wind, the grain being heavy, falls straight to the ground, whereas chaff and hay, being much lighter, are carried away to some distance by the wind. In this way, the grains forms a separate heap and can be collected and packed in a gunny bag.

The machine that is used for doing winnowing is called *winnower*. It is efficient, quick and easy operable machine to separate grain from chaff.

Winnowing

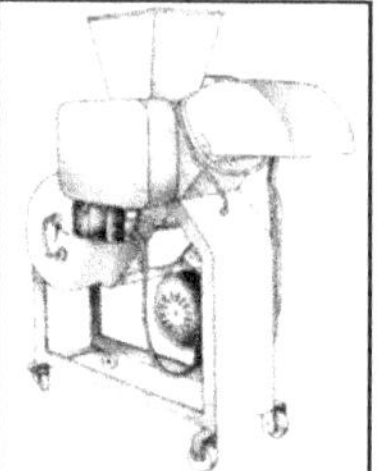

Winnower

Storage of Food Grains

Storage is the most important agricultural activity. The food grains obtained by harvesting the crops are dried in the sunlight before storing. This is because higher moisture content in grain promotes the growth of fungus and moulds on them, which later damages the stored grains. *Hence*, drying crops in sunlight before storing reduces the moisture content of grains and prevents their spoilage during storage.

The farmers store the dried grains in metal bins and jute bags. The Government agencies like FCI (Food Corporation of India) buy grains from farmers and store it in big godowns. It is done so that it can be supplied throughout the country, round the year. The large scale storage of food grains is done in gunny bags and in grain silos.

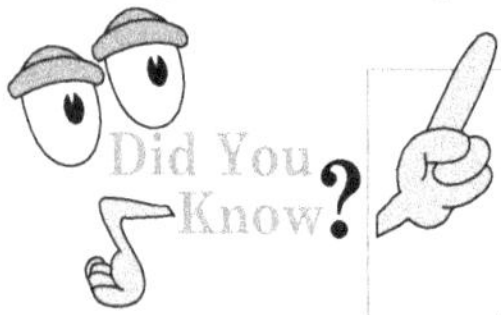

Chemical Treatment : Pesticides are sprayed in the storage structure before storing food grain. This kills the pests before the arrival of stocks and also eliminates chances of contamination of food grain with pesticides. The pesticides which can be sprayed are – BHC (benzene hexachloride), malathion and pyrethrum.

(1) Fumigation is a method by which pests are exposed to fumes or vapours of chemicals, without contaminating the stored food grains.

(2) Care should be taken that the grains for human consumption are not treated with poisonous chemicals.

How the viability of seed can be checked?

Take few stored seeds from the godowns. Count them and place then in a tray that contains fresh compost. Water the compost and keep the tray in a warm lighted place.

Observe the growth of seeds.

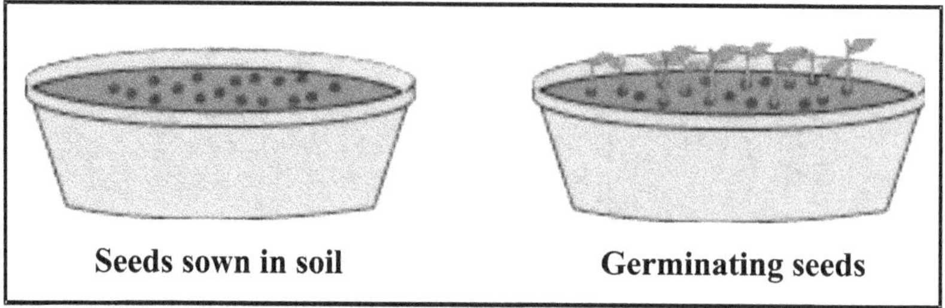

What did you observe?

You can see that more than half of the seeds sprout. It means that these stored seeds are viable and has good chances of germinating in the garden or field.

The ability of the plant to produce new plants depends on the time of harvest and the conditions of seed storage. Hence, it is important to take all necessary precautions while storing the seeds.

Precautions to be taken while storing seeds

(i) Well-dried seeds should be stored. The viability of seeds depend on temperature and moisture. *Hence*, seeds should be stored at proper temperature and with proper moisture, otherwise it will deteriorate quickly.

(ii) At homes or shops the seeds should be stored in a sealed, water resistant, air tight container. The container should be kept in a cool and dark place.

(iii) Protect the seed from the insects. The seeds can be protected from insects/pests by —

    (a) storing the seed with wood ash. Wood ash prevents the entry of insect inside container.

    (b) store seeds with lime. Lime has an insect repelling property.

    (c) mix the seeds with vegetable or coconut oil.

(iv) The seeds that are in bulk quantity should be stored in **silos** and **granaries**. Silos and granaries are store house for storing threshed grain that is present in large quantity. Silos are tall cylindrical containers for bulk storage of grains. Granaries are often built above the ground. The distance of granaries from the ground protects the grains from mice and other pest.

(v) Sometimes, the dried neem leaves are added along with grain to protect it from insects or pests. The leaves and oil of the neem are very effective against a wide range of storage pests.

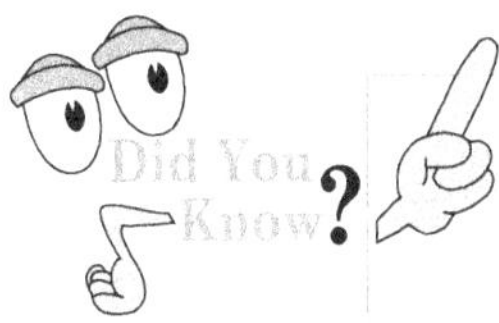

One of the most controversial scientific discoveries of the 20th century is the genetic modification (GM) of food. The genes of every living organism can be altered to change its characteristics. For example, farmers can add anti-pest genes to crops, which enable them to survive longer or grow unusually large, without being affected by pests.

CONNECTING TOPIC

CROP IMPROVEMENT

The improvement in crop plants is necessary for increasing the crop yield and their quality.

Crop improvement can be done by breeding new varieties of crops having higher yields and resistance to pests and diseases. The agricultural scientists or plant breeders can achieve this by artificial cross-breeding or hybridization.

For example, if you want to obtain an improved variety of a crop that has higher yield as well as is disease resistant, then you should select two existing crops varieties, one having higher yield and other having more resistance to diseases. When higher yielding plant is crossed with disease resistant plant, then a new variety of plant is produced that contains qualities of both parents plants.

Thus, the new plant (hybrid) will produce higher yield and will be disease resistant.

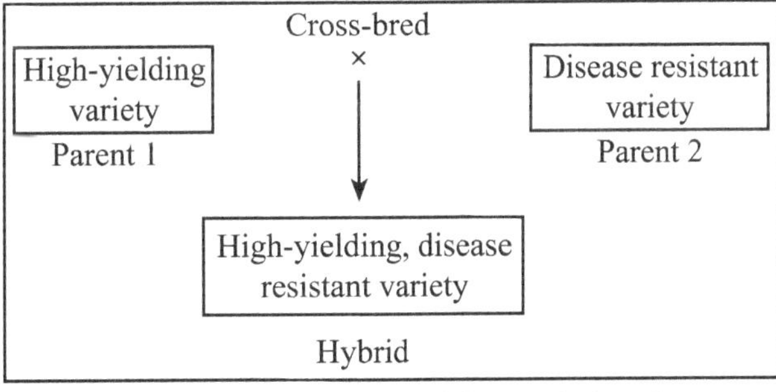

Table : Examples of high-yielding varieties of crops

Crops	High yielding varieties in India
Wheat	Sonalika, Kalyan sona, Sharbati Hira Moti Sonara
Paddy	Jaya, Padma, Pusa 215
Maize	Ganga 101, Rajit, Deccan hybrid

M. S. Swaminathan is known as "Indian Father of Green Revolution" for his leadership and success in introducing and further developing high-yielding varieties of wheat in India.

What is hybridization?

Hybridization is the process of cross-breeding two different varieties of crop plant each having a desired characteristics to obtain a new crop that has both the desired characteristics. It is used extensively in agriculture, where new forms of disease resistant plants are produced commercially.

THE GREEN REVOLUTION

The average production of most of the crop in our country, India, has doubled during the last 30 years. But the production of wheat crop has tripled during the last 30 years. This great increase in the production of food - grain crops (especially the wheat crop) in India during the last 30 years is called green revolution. This is a sort of revolution taking place in Indian agriculture, leading to enormous food grain production.

Green revolution is a large increase in crop production in developing countries achieved by the use of artificial fertilizers, pesticides, and high-yield crop varieties. The beginning of the Green Revolution is often attributed to Norman Borlaug, an American scientist. In the 1940s, he began conducting research in Mexico and developed new disease resistance high-yield variety of wheat. By combining Borlaug's wheat varieties with new mechanized agricultural technologies, Mexico was able to produce more wheat than was needed by its own citizens, leading to it becoming an exporter of wheat by the 1960s. Prior to the use of these varieties, the country was importing almost half of its wheat supply.

Due to the success of the Green Revolution in Mexico, its technologies spread worldwide in the 1950s and 1960s.

Note

White revolution

The introduction of growth of milk production and encouraging Indian dairy farmers to keep more animals for increasing production of milk and become self sufficient is called white revolution.

Livestock

Livestock are those domesticated or farm animals that are kept for use or profit. The most important livestock of India are cattle, buffaloes which yield milk and help in agriculture. On the basis of their utility animals are categorised as:
– Milk giving animals (Cows, buffaloes, goats)
– Meat and egg giving animals (Sheep, goat, pig, duck)
– Animals utilized as motive power (Buffaloes, horse, donkey, bullock, camel)
– Wool giving animals (Sheep)

Why green revolution is called green?

It is called green because it led to unprecedented greenery of crops everywhere in country. It has made our country self sufficient in food production and even created buffer stocks of food grains for use in times of natural calamities like drought and flood, when food production is reduced.

FOOD OBTAINED FROM ANIMALS

Like plants, animal also provide us different types of food. The food provided by animals consists of milk, egg and meat. They are rich source of proteins. In fact, animal food provides certain proteins that are not present in plant foods.

Hence, it is important to maintain the population of livestock as they provide various kinds of food to us. Maintaining lifestock includes various aspects like feeding, breeding and disease control of various animals. This process is known as **animal husbandry**. *Animal husbandry is the science of caring, feeding, breeding and raising the livestock on a large scale.* It includes animals like cattle, goat, sheep, poultry and fish.

Objectives of animal husbandry are —
(i)   To improve the breeds of domestic animals
(ii)   To provide better nutrition and atmosphere to animals so that the yield of their product (like meat, eggs, milk etc) can be increased.

Poultry farming:

The raising of domesticated birds such as chicken, turkey, duck, and geese, commercially for the purpose of producing meat or eggs for food is called poultry farming. Poultry are farmed in great numbers with chickens being the most numerous. More than 50 billion chickens are raised annually as a source of food, for both their meat and their eggs.

Bee keeping or Apiculture:

Beekeeping is the maintenance of honey bee colonies, commonly in hives, by humans. A beekeeper (or apiarist) keeps bees in order to collect their honey and other products that the hive produces (like beeswax, propolis, pollen, and royal jelly), to pollinate crops, or to produce bees for sale to other beekeepers. A location where bees are kept is called an apiary or "bee yard".

Fish farming:

Fish farming is the principal form of aquaculture, while other methods may fall under mariculture. It involves raising fish commercially in tanks or enclosures, usually for food. A facility that releases juvenile fish into the wild for recreational fishing or to supplement a species' natural numbers is generally referred to as a fish hatchery.

Fish species raised by fish farms include salmon, catfish, tilapia, cod and others.

Basically, there are two kinds of aquaculture: extensive aquaculture based on local photosynthetical production and intensive aquaculture, in which the fishes are fed with external food supply.

Cattle farming:

It is the act of raising and breeding cattle for the production of meat or milk. Beef farming is raising beef cattle for slaughter (meat), and dairy farming is raising cows for milk.

Let us perform an activity to find out various types of animal food and their sources.

Collect the information from your surroundings to complete the given table.

Sl. No.	Category of Animal Products	Types of food/material	Sources
1.	Meat yielding	Meat	Sheep, Coat, Fish
2.	Milk yielding	Milk	Cow, Buffalo, Goat
3.	Egg yielding	Egg	Hen
4.	Honey and wax producing insects		
5.	Fibre yielding animals		
6.	Silk producing animals		

SUMMARY

- Plants of same kind that grow on a large scale in an area is known as crop. E.g. rice, wheat, maize etc.
- The production of crops by cultivation of land is called agriculture.
- In India, crop can be categorised into two types based on seasons – Rabi and Kharif crops.
  - Kharif crops – Crops grown in rainy season (June – September). Example – Paddy, Maize Groundnuts, etc.
  - Rabi crops – Crops grown in winter season (October– March). Examples – Wheat, Peas, Mustard, Barley etc.
- The basic activities done by farmers in the crop field in order to raise a particular crop is called agricultural practices.
- Seven agricultural practices done by the farmer to raise a particular crop are –
  1. Preparation of soil
  2. Sowing of seeds
  3. Adding manure and fertilizer
  4. Irrigation
  5. Protection from weeds and pests
  6. Harvesting, Threshing, Winnowing
  7. Storage of food grains
- The process of loosening and turning of the soil is called tilling or ploughing. This is done by plough, hoe and cultivator.
- The process of scattering seeds in the ground soil for growing the crop plants is called sowing.
- The sowing of seed by hand is called broadcasting while the instrument used for sowing is a seed drill.
- The substances that are added to the soil in the form of nutrients for healthy growth of plants are called manure and fertilizer.
- Process of converting dead organic matter into rich humus with the help of earthworm is called vermicomposting.
- Practice in which leguminous and non-leguminous crops are grown alternately in the same field is called crop rotation.
- Irrigation is the supply of water to crops at different intervals.
- The sources of irrigation are wells, tube well, ponds, lakes, rivers, dams and canals.
- The traditional methods of irrigation are moat, dhekli, rahat and chain pump.
- The modern methods of irrigation are sprinkler system and drip system.
- Process of transferring seedlings from a nursery to the main field, by hand is called transplantation.
- The unwanted plants that grow along with a cultivated crop are called weeds. E.g. Grass, Xanthium, wild oat etc.
- The process of removing unwanted plants from a crop is called weeding.
- The cutting of crop after it gets mature is called harvesting. It is done manually by sickle.
- In large fields, crops are cut by a motorised machine called harvester.
- In the harvested crop, the grain seeds need to be separated from the chaff. This process is called threshing.
- Winnowing is the process of separating grain from chaff and hay with the help of wind.
- The food grains obtained by harvesting the crops are dried in sunlight before storing.
  - Small scale – Jute bags, metallic bins
  - Large scale – Silos, granaries
- The process of rearing animals to obtain food is known as animal husbandry.

CASE STUDY : Crop Production

CASE - I : *For a farmer with a huge land, which technique is best suitable for harvesting?*

On a huge farm, manual labour will not be efficient. Therefore, the farmer needs to deploy a technique like combine which is less time consuming, and can perform the function of both harvester as well as thrasher.

CASE - II : *For a farmer with an uneven land, which methods of irrigation can be employed?*

For an uneven land, modern methods of irrigation like sprinkler and drip system are more efficient.

CASE - III : *In the month of June, Kishor grows barley on a piece of land. He later found out that the whole crop is destroyed. What can be the reason behind this?*

Barley is a rabi crop and should be sown in winter season from November to April.

Think Out of the Box

Q 1. How can a farmer prevent overcropping?

Q 2. Ram goes to the market to bring seeds. What is the best way to check the viability of seeds?

Biology

Exercise 1 — Master Boards

Multiple Choice Questions

DIRECTIONS : This section contains multiple choice questions. Each question has four choices (a), (b), (c) and (d) out of which ONLY ONE is correct.

1. Supply of water to crops at appropriate intervals is called
   (a) irrigation (b) cultivation
   (c) harvesting (d) sowing
2. Which instrument is used for spraying weedicides ?
   (a) sprayer (b) cultivator
   (c) plough (d) combine
3. The process of separation of grain from the chaff after harvesting is known as
   (a) tiling (b) threshing
   (c) spraying (d) weeding
4. The government agency responsible for purchasing grains from the farmers, safe storage and distribution is
   (a) CBI (b) FBI
   (c) FCI (d) FDI
5. In agriculture, broadcasting is used for
   (a) ploughing the fields (b) rotating the crops
   (c) removing the weeds (d) sowing the seeds

Assertion & Reason

DIRECTIONS : Each of these questions contains an Assertion followed by reason. Read them carefully and answer the question on the basis of following options. You have to select the one that best describes the two statements.

(a) If both **Assertion** and **Reason** are **correct** and Reason is the **correct explanation** of Assertion.
(b) If both **Assertion** and **Reason** are correct, but Reason is **not the correct explanation** of Assertion.
(c) If **Assertion** is **correct** but **Reason** is **incorrect**.
(d) If **Assertion** is **incorrect** but **Reason** is **correct**.

1. **Assertion :** Crop improvement can be done by breeding new varieties of crops having higher yields.
   Reason : The main aim of plant breeding is to produce new crops superior to existing one.
2. **Assertion :** Use of fertilizers enhances the crop productivity.
   Reason : Irrigation is very important in increasing crop productivity.
3. **Assertion :** Gram and cloves are Rabi crops.
   Reason : They are grown during the months of November to April.
4. **Assertion :** Ploughing soil is a pre-requisite before sowing.
   Reason : At the end of the plough, a sharp chesel like iron nail is attached, which helps in ploughing the soil.
5. **Assertion :** Manure and biofertilizers should be used in place of chemical fertilizers.
   Reason : Chemical fertilizers cause pollution by releasing excess nutrients in water bodies.

Fill in the Blanks

DIRECTIONS : Complete the following statements with an appropriate word / term to be filled in the blank space(s).

1. The excess water in the field is known as ______.
2. Crops such as ______ requires a constant supply of water.
3. ______ crop is grown during the month of June to September.
4. ______ is the first step to be followed before growing a crop.
5. The process of converting dead organic matter into rich humus with the help of earthworm is known as ______.
6. ______ are a good source of nitrogen, phosphorus and potassium but are good for only short term use.
7. Rotation of leguminous crop with wheat or maize is an example of ______.
8. In ______ system of irrigation, water is delivered at or near the roots of the plant drop by drop.
9. Weeds can be removed manually with a ______.
10. The seeds of paddy are first grown in small plots called ______.
11. The substances that are added to the soil in the form of nutrients for the healthy growth of plants are called ______ and ______.
12. ______ is a simple tool which is used for removing weeds and for loosening the soil.
13. ______ is the agricultural practice of breeding and raising livestock.
14. ______ are like artificial rainmakers.
15. Organisms that damage the crop are known as ______

True / False

DIRECTIONS : Read the following statements and write your answer as true or false.

1. Cotton is a Rabi crop.
2. The agricultural practice, called harvesting comes before weeding.
3. Groundnut enriches the soil with nitrogen.
4. Nitrogenous fertilizer is required for growing nitrogenous crops.
5. In addition to gunny bags, metal bins are also used for storing food grains on large scales.
6. Rotation of crop helps in controlling weeds.
7. Combine is a combination of harvester and thresher.
8. Plough is used for adding manure or fertilizers to the crop.
9. The excessive use of manure causes water pollution.
10. Rabi crops are grown in winter.

Match the Following

Directions : Question contain statements given in two columns which have to be matched. Statements in column I have to be matched with terms given in column II.

S.No.	Column-I	Column-II
A.	Plant that is grown in large quantities especially as food or fodder for livestock.	(p) Rabi crops
B.	Crops planted in June and harvested in September.	(q) Transplantation

C.	Crops planted in October and harvested in March	(r)	Kharif crops
D.	Undesirable plants that grow with the crops	(s)	Manure
E.	Process of transferring seedlings from a nursery to the main field	(t)	Fertilizers
F.	Process of supplying water to crops at different intervals	(u)	Weedicides
G.	Organic substance obtained from decomposition of plant and animals waste	(v)	Weeds
H.	Chemical substances that are rich in plant nutrients like nitrogen, phosphorus and potassium	(w)	Animal husbandry
I.	The chemical substance that controls the growth of weeds	(x)	Crop
J.	The process of rearing animals for food, clothing and other useful products	(y)	Irrigation

Passage Based Questions

DIRECTIONS : *Study the given paragraph(s) and answer the following questions.*

Ramesh is a small scale farmer and hold 3 acre of land. He would like to increase the wheat production in his farm. Harshit a student of M.Sc advised him to go to his agriculture department centre of his locality to get high yielding variety of wheat crop and explain the difference between Kharif and Rabi crops. He also suggested not to use chemical fertilizer.

1. Which of the following is not a Kharif crop?
   (a) paddy   (b) mustard
   (c) maize   (d) groundnut
2. Which of the following is not a Rabi crop?
   (a) soyabean   (b) wheat
   (c) peas   (d) linseed
3. Which of the following cannot be provided to the soil by chemical fertilizer?
   (a) Nitrogen   (b) Humus
   (c) Potassium   (d) Phosphorus

Very Short Answer Questions

1. Name two primary cropping pattern in India.
2. What is a crop?
3. Which is the first step in cultivation of a crop?
4. What is tilling?
5. Name the implement used for ploughing the fields.
6. Which step in the preparation of soil loosens and turns the soil in the fields?
7. What is sowing?
8. Name the implement used in sowing.
9. Name the practice used for cultivating rice.
10. Name the various sources of irrigation in our country.
11. What is meant by term "water logging" as used in agriculture?

12. Name two substances that are added to fields by farmers to maintain the fertility of soil.
13. What is a compost?
14. Name two fertilizers.
15. Which crop is grown between two cereal crops in crop rotation?
16. What is crop rotation?
17. *Xanthium*, growing in a wheat field is known as_____.
18. Give one advantage of drip system of irrigation.
19. Name two implements used for weeding.
20. What are weedicides?
21. Name the chemical substances that are sprayed on crops to protect them from damage.
22. Which agricultural practice is carried out with the help of sickle?
23. Name the process in which grains are separated from chaff and hay with the help of wind.
24. Name the two ways in which farmers store food grains.
25. Name the machine used both for harvesting and threshing.
26. Give two examples of Rabi crops.
27. Give two examples of Kharif crops.
28. What do you mean by nitrogen fixation?
29. Give two example of crop grown from June to September.
30. Name the nitrogen fixing bacteria present in root nodules of leguminous plants.

Short Answer Questions

1. How Kharif crop is different from Rabi crop?
2. Give four importance of soil loosening.
3. What are the advantages of levelling?
4. Write down differences between fertilizers and manure?
5. Why is manure better than fertilizer?
6. How are weeds removed manually? When is the best time to remove them?
7. List the steps involved in crop production in sequential order.
8. Differentiate between insecticides, rodenticides and fungicides.
9. Why grains are dried before storage?
10. Which of the following are Kharif crops and which are Rabi crops?
    Soyabean, Barley, Mustard, Peas, Cotton, Groundnut
11. What types of crops are grown :
    (i) During October to March?
    (ii) During June to September?
12. Name three steps involved in the preparation of soil for sowing the seeds.
13. Which of the following are cultivated by transplantation? Paddy, Chillies, Tomatoes, Maize, Wheat
14. State two advantages of the process of transplantation of growing crops?
15. What is the necessity of irrigating the crops?
16. How do weeds affect the growth of crops?
17. What is weeding? State the various methods of weeding.
18. Define the terms –
    (i) Harvesting   (ii) Threshing
    (iii) Winnowing
19. What do you understand by "combine" that is used in agriculture? State its function.
20. What is the advantage of storing food grains in gunny bags?
21. What is done to protect the grains stored in gunny bags in big godowns from damage?

22. Explain the irrigational methods that are used in modern times.
23. How are manure prepared?

Long Answer Questions

1. Explain how soil is affected by the continuous plantation of crops in a field? Why preparation of soil is considered to be an important step in agricultural practices.
2. What are *Rhizobium* bacteria? Why are they useful? What enables leguminous plants to fix nitrogen?
3. What precautions should be taken while sowing the seeds?
4. What are pests? What steps are taken to protect crops from pests? Why should the grains, fruits and vegetables be washed properly before use?

Reasoning Based Questions

1. Why should farmer cover the nose and mouth with cloth while spraying weedicides?
2. Explain why, the frequency of irrigation of crops is higher in summer season.
3. Why is it necessary to dry the harvested food grains before storage?
4. Why do farmers carrying out levelling of the ploughed fields?
5. Why wheat cannot be sown in the Kharif season?
6. Explain why, the seeds should be sown at right spacing?
7. Why is weeding necessary.

Hots Questions

1. Why do farmers normally use a mixture of manures and fertilizers in the fields?
2. Which method of irrigation will you use if you live in a dry area with shortage of water?
3. Discuss two methods of weeding in which poisonous chemicals are not used.

4. Why does the government maintain a buffer stock of grains?
5.

Do you agree? Give reason in support of your answer.
6. Four students proposed four different ways to fulfil the food requirement to a large number of people in our country. Which method according to you can bring about the maximum increase in crop production in our country?

Increase land under cultivation	Use more manure and fertilizers
Less wastage in storage	Use better varieties of crops plants

7. What happens if the farmer grows Mustard during rainy season instead of winter?
8. "Indian farmers gamble with the monsoon". Illustrate this statement.
9. The recent incidents of farmers' suicides in different states of our country are the result of indebtedness. Do you agree with this?
10. How do pest reduce crop productivity?
11. How does continuous rainfall affect crop production?

Exercise 2 ⭐ ## Master NCERT (Text-book & Exemplar)

Text-book Exercise

1. Select the correct word from the following list and fill in the blanks. float, water, crop, nutrients, preparation
   (a) The same kind of plants grown and cultivated on a large scale at a place is called __________.
   (b) The first step before growing crops is __________ of the soil.
   (c) Damaged seeds would __________ on top of water.
   (d) For growing a crop, sufficient sunlight, __________ and __________ from the soil are essential.
2. Match items in column A with those in column B.

A		B
(i) Kharif crops	(a)	Food for cattle
(ii) Rabi crops	(b)	Urea and super phosphate
(iii) Chemical fertilisers	(c)	Animal excreta, cow dung, urine and plant waste
(iv) Organic manure	(d)	Wheat, gram, pea
	(e)	Paddy and maize

3. Give two examples of each.
   (a) Kharif crop
   (b) Rabi crop
4. Write a paragraph in your own words on each of the following.
   (a) Preparwation of soil   (b) Sowing
   (c) Weeding   (d) Threshing
5. Explain how fertilisers are different from manure.
6. What is irrigation? Describe two methods of irrigation which conserves water.
7. If wheat is sown in the kharif season, what would happen? Discuss.
8. Explain how soil gets affected by the continuous plantation of similar crops in a field.
9. What are weeds? How can we control them?
10. Arrange the following boxes in proper order to make a flow chart of sugarcane crop production.

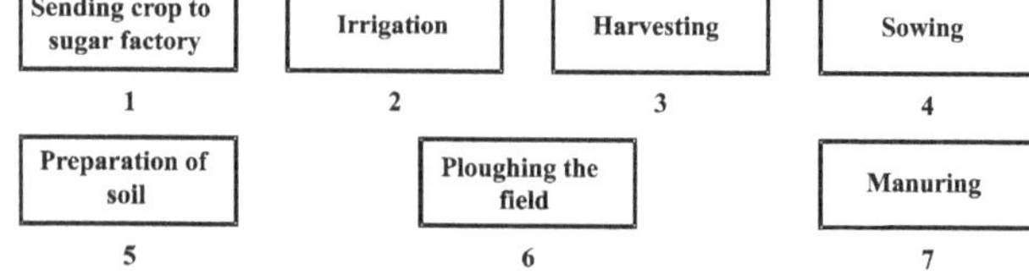

11. Complete the following word puzzle with the help of clues given below.

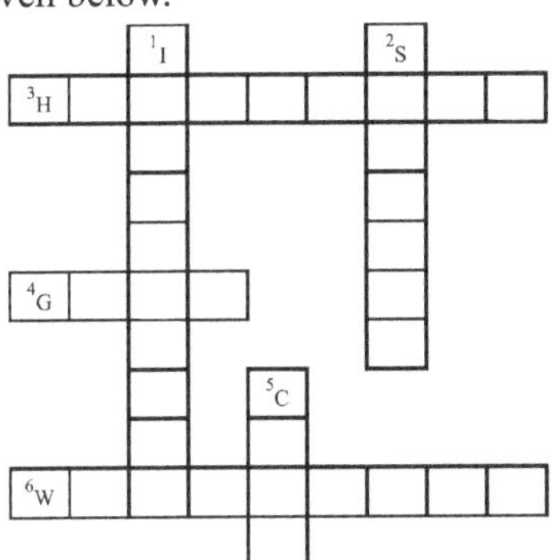

Down
1. Providing water to the crops.
2. Keeping crop grains for a long time under proper conditions.
5. Certain plants of the same kind grown on a large scale.

Across
3. A machine used for cutting the matured crop.
4. A rabi crop that is also one of the pulses.
6. A process of separating the grain from chaff.

 **Foundation Builder**

Exercise 3

Multiple Choice Questions

DIRECTIONS : This section contains multiple choice questions. Each question has four choices (a), (b), (c) and (d) out of which ONLY ONE is correct. Choose the correct option.

1. Person known for his pioneering efforts in promoting the green revolution in India is
   (a) Benjamin Franklin (b) Norman Borlang
   (c) Robert Brown (d) Albert Einstein
2. Which of the following is not a rabi crop?
   (a) Wheat (b) Mustard
   (c) Sugarcane (d) Peas
3. Which of the following crops would enrich the soil with nitrogen?
   (a) Apple (b) Beans
   (c) Paddy (d) Potato
4. The process of turning and loosening of soil is called
   (a) tilling (b) harvesting
   (c) threshing (d) irrigation
5. Threshing is the process of
   (a) separating chaff from the grain
   (b) cutting of mature crop
   (c) sowing seeds by hands
   (d) turning and loosening of soil
6. Which of the following statements is not correct about fertilizer?
   (a) It enriches the soil with organic material.
   (b) It provides nutrients to the soil immediately in concentrated from.
   (c) It increases the crop production several times
   (d) It is available in all seasons.
7. Which of the following is a modern method of Irrigation?
   (a) Rahat (b) Moat
   (c) Chain pump (d) Drip system

Exemplar Questions

1. If you are given a dry piece of land for cultivation what will you do before sowing the seeds?
2. During which months do farmers grow mustard in India?
3. Which activity of the farmer can promote growth of earthworms and microbes in the field?
4. What are organic foods?
5. (a) Name the tool used with a tractor for sowing seeds in the field.
   (b) What are the advantages of using this tool?
6. (a) Name the practice followed for large scale rearing of farm animals.
   (b) What facilities are provided to farm animals?
7. Despite favourable climatic conditions, a farmer's crop failed to give good yield. What could be the possible reason for this.
8. As a part of eco-club activity students were asked to raise a kitchen garden in the school premises. They were provided with some materials given in the box. List the other materials you would require. How will you plan the garden? Write the steps.
   khurpi, water-can, spade, shovel
   Note: You have been asked to use only environment friendly

8. Which of the following is incorrectly matched?

	Agricultural Steps	Implements Used
(a)	Ploughing	Hoe
(b)	Irrigation	Sprinklers
(c)	Weeding	Trowel
(d)	Harvesting	Harrow

9. The simple tool used for removing weeds and for loosening the soil is called.
   (a) plough (b) sickle
   (c) harrow (d) trowel
10. The process of putting seeds in the soil for germination is known as
    (a) sowing (b) manuring
    (c) weeding (d) tilling
11. Ploughing in bigger fields is done by using
    (a) hoe (b) cultivator
    (c) combine (d) sickle
12. Which of the following statements is not correct about ploughing?
    (a) It facilitates deeper penetration of soils.
    (b) It maintains fertility of soil.
    (c) It helps in proper mixing of organic matter and nutrients evenly.
    (d) It helps in enriching the soil with organic matter and nutrients.
13. The process of removing weeds from the cultivated field is known as
    (a) weeding (b) weedicide
    (c) tilling (d) crop rotation
14. An example of manure is
    (a) cow dung (b) urea
    (c) ammonium sulphate (d) super phosphate

15. The large scale storage of food grains is done in
    (a) Gunny bag + Jute bags
    (b) Jute bags + Metal bins
    (c) Metal bins + Grain silos
    (d) Grain silos + gunny bag
16. The last step in crop production is
    (a) soil preparation   (b) crop harvesting
    (c) irrigation   (d) sowing
17. An example of fertilizer is
    (a) cow dung   (b) plant waste
    (c) urea   (d) urine
18. Which of the following statement is incorrect?
    (a) Always use certified seeds to maintain the quality of crop.
    (b) Harvest the crop when grains are fully matured.
    (c) Use recommended dose of fertilizers.
    (d) Irrigate the soil with polluted water.
19. By which method was a new breed 'Hisardale' of sheep formed by using Bikaneri ewes and Marino rams? **[NTSE]**
    (a) Mutational breeding   (b) Cross breeding
    (c) Inbreeding   (d) Out crossing
20. Select the incorrect statement regarding inbreeding. **[NTSE]**
    (a) Inbreeding depression cannot be overcome by out-crossing.
    (b) Inbreeding helps in elimination of deleterious alleles from the population.
    (c) Inbreeding is necessary to evolve a pure line in any animal.
    (d) Continued inbreeding reduces fertility and leads to inbreeding depression.
21. Homozygous purelines in cattle can be obtained by: **[NTSE]**
    (a) mating of unrelated individuals of same breed.
    (b) mating of individuals of different breed.
    (c) mating of individuals of different species.
    (d) mating of related individuals of same breed.
22. Outbreeding is an important strategy of animal husbandry because it : **[NTSE]**
    (a) is useful in producing purelines of animals.
    (b) is useful in overcoming inbreeding depression.
    (c) exposes harmful recessive genes that are eliminated by selection.
    (d) helps in accumulation of superior genes.
23. A system of rotating crops with legume or grass pasture to improve soil structure and fertility is called **[NTSE]**
    (a) Ley farming   (b) Contour farming
    (c) Strip farming   (d) Shifting agriculture
24. Which one of the following is detrimental to soil fertility?
    (a) Saprophytic bacteria (b) *Nitrosomonas* **[NTSE]**
    (c) *Nitrobacter*   (d) *Pseudomonas*
25. *Bombyx mori* (silkworm) belongs to the order **[NTSE]**
    (a) Lepidoptera   (b) Diptera
    (c) Hymenoptera   (d) Coleoptera
26. An indigenous breed of chickens is : **[JSTSE]**
    (a) Plymouth rock   (b) Aseel
    (c) White leghorn   (d) Rhode Island Red
27. Causing storage losses to agricultural produce **[JSTSE]**
    (a) Insects   (b) Rodents
    (c) Mites   (d) All the above
28. In Plant hybridisation crossing is done between **[JSTSE]**
    (a) Intervarietal   (b) Interspecific
    (c) Intergeneric   (d) All the above
29. Growing of different crops on a piece of land in a pre-planned succession is known as : **[JSTSE]**
    (a) Inter cropping   (b) Crop rotation
    (c) Hybridisation   (d) None of the above
30. Leghorn is a improved variety of **[JSTSE]**
    (a) Fish   (b) Cow
    (c) Sheep   (d) Fowl
31. Which of the following is a rock bee? **[JSTSE]**
    (a) Apis dorsata   (b) Apis cerana
    (c) Apis florae   (d) Apis mellifera
32. The characteristic shown by local breeds of cow like Red Sindhi, Sahiwal is : **[JSTSE]**
    (a) Long lactation periods
    (b) Well built and strong
    (c) Excellent resistance to diseases
    (d) High milk production
33. Which of the following is the indigenous breed of chickens? **[JSTSE]**
    (a) Plymonth Rock   (b) White Leghorn
    (c) Rhode Island Red   (d) Aseel
34. A farmer made an observation in a backwater paddy field of coastal Kerala that the paddy plants wilt during noon onwards everyday but appear normal next morning. What would be the possible reason for wilting? **[NTSE]**
    (a) The rate of water absorption is less than the rate of transpiration in the afternoon.
    (b) The rate of water absorption is more than the rate of transpiration in the afternoon.
    (c) The changes in the rate of water absorption and transpiration are not associated with wilting.
    (d) The rate of water absorption is not related to the rate of transpiration.
35. Manure formed by earthworms is called as- **[NTSE]**
    (a) Organic manure   (b) Vermi compost
    (c) Manure   (d) None of these
36. Weeds not only use nutrients from the soil but are also
    (A) harmful for some organisms including human beings
    (B) useful for the crops and harmful for human beings
    (C) harmful to the crops and some animals
    (D) crop specific **[NTSE]**
    Select the alternative which includes all correct statements.
    (a) (A), (C) and (D)   (b) (B), (C) and (D)
    (c) (A), (B) and (C)   (d) (A), (B) and (D)
37. A few gram seeds were placed in each of the three pots A, B and C containing soil. The soil in Pot A is mixed with some green twigs and leaves. The soil in pot B is mixed with old cow dung while soil of pot C is mixed with urea. Pots are watered regularly. Which of the following will be observed after 10 days? **[NTSE]**
    (a) Lot of growth in A
    (b) Not much growth in B
    (c) Lot of growth in B but very little growth in C
    (d) Little growth in A and lot of growth in B and C
38. Which of the following rotation of crops will reduce dependence on the use of chemical fertilizers? **[NTSE]**
    (a) Rice and Chilli   (b) Wheat and Potato
    (c) Potato and Rice   (d) Gram and Rice
39. Rani had an uneven plot of land in which water was scarce. What system could she adopt for irrigation? **[NTSE]**
    (a) Canal   (b) Sprinkler
    (c) Drip   (d) Hand pump
40. Causing storage losses to agricultural produce **[JSTSE]**
    (a) Insects   (b) Rodents
    (c) Mites   (d) All the above

41. Growing of different crops on a piece of land in a pre-planned succession is known as : **[JSTSE]**
    (a) Inter cropping   (b) Crop rotation
    (c) Hybridisation   (d) None of the above

42. Leghorn is a improved variety of   **[JSTSE]**
    (a) Fish   (b) Cow
    (c) Sheep   (d) Fowl

43. A farmer made an observation in a backwater paddy field of coastal Kerala that the paddy plants wilt during noon onwards everyday but appear normal next morning. What would be the possible reason for wilting? **[NTSE]**
    (a) The rate of water absorption is less than the rate of transpiration in the afternoon.
    (b) The rate of water absorption is more than the rate of transpiration in the afternoon.
    (c) The changes in the rate of water absorption and transpiration are not associated with wilting.
    (d) The rate of water absorption is not related to the rate of transpiration.

Assertion & Reason

DIRECTIONS : *Each of these questions contains an Assertion followed by reason. Read them carefully and answer the question on the basis of following options. You have to select the one that best describes the two statements.*

(a) If both **Assertion** and **Reason** are **correct** and Reason is the **correct explanation** of Assertion.
(b) If both **Assertion** and **Reason** are correct, but Reason is **not the correct explanation** of Assertion.
(c) If **Assertion** is **correct** but **Reason** is **incorrect**.
(d) If **Assertion** is **incorrect** but **Reason** is **correct**.

1. **Assertion :** Gram and Barley are Rabi crops.
   Reason : They are grown during the months of November to April.
2. **Assertion :** Fertilizers provide quick replenishment of plant nutrients in the soil and restore its fertility.
   Reason : They are easily absorbed by the plants.
3. **Assertion :** A fertilizer provides a lot of organic matter like humus to the soil.
   Reason : They are very rich in plant nutrients like NPK.
4. **Assertion :** Crop improvement can be done by breeding new varieties of crops having higher yields.
   Reason : The main aim of plant breeding is to produce new crops superior to existing ones.
5. **Assertion :** When the crop is changed during crop rotation, the weeds associated with it usually disappear.
   Reason : The weeds are very choosy about the crop with which they grow.
6. **Assertion :** Earthworm are called a farmer's friends.
   Reason : The burrowing action of earthworms helps to loosen the soil particles.

Exercise 4 ⭐ **Foundation Builder ✛**

Multiple Choice Questions

DIRECTIONS (Qs.1-27): *This section contains multiple choice questions. Each question has four choices (a), (b), (c) and (d) out of which ONLY ONE is correct. Choose the correct option.*

1. The best way to increase the yield of wheat in India is
   (a) to sow seeds of improved varieties.
   (b) to use tractors.
   (c) to reduce the quantity of rational consumers.
   (d) to remove weeds from wheat fields.
2. Fowl grown only for meat is known as
   (a) hybrid   (b) broiler
   (c) milch   (d) bird culture
3. Increase in food production has been possible by the success of
   (a) green revolution   (b) white revolution
   (c) red revolution
   (d) green revolution for food grain and white revolution for milk
4. The term 'aquaculture' means
   (a) cattle breeding   (b) marine fisheries
   (c) inland fisheries   (d) Both (b) and (c)
5. Hybridization
   (a) is done to incorporate desirable characteristics into crop varieties.
   (b) refers to crossing between genetically dissimilar plants.
   (c) may be intervarietal or interspecific.
   (d) All these statements are correct.
6. Manure helps in improving soil fertility and structure by supplying small quantities of nutrients. It is also advantageous in
   (a) protecting environment from excessive use of fertilizers
   (b) recycling farm waste
   (c) disposing biological waste
   (d) All of these
7. Cattle husbandry is done for the following purposes
   (i) Milk production   (ii) Agriculture work
   (iii) Meat production   (iv) Egg production
   (a) (i), (ii) and (iii)   (b) (ii), (iii) and (iv)
   (c) (iii) and (iv)   (d) (i) and (iv)
8. Fertilizers should be used carefully because
   (a) increase in soil fertility is only short lived.
   (b) they can be harmful to the micro-organisms present in the soil.
   (c) they can lead to water pollution.
   (d) All of these
9. Organic farming is a farming system with ____________ use of chemicals such as fertilizers, herbicides or pesticides and with a ____________ input of organic manures.
   (a) almost no, minimum   (b) minimal, maximum
   (c) maximum, minimum   (d) excessive, little
10. Use of neem leaves or turmeric during grain storage serves the purpose of
    (a) bio-pesticides
    (b) providing nutrients
    (c) impart the desired colours to the grain
    (d) preparation of biofertilizers
11. Mixed cropping is
    (a) growing same crops in different seasons.
    (b) growing two or more crops simultaneously on the same piece of land in a haphazard manner.
    (c) growing two or more crops simultaneously on the same field in a definite pattern.
    (d) growing different crops on a piece of land in a preplanned succession.

12. Poultry farming is undertaken to raise following
(i) Egg production (ii) Feather production
(iii) Chicken meat (iv) Milk production
(a) (i) and (iii) (b) (i) and (ii)
(c) (ii) and (iii) (d) (iii) and (iv)

13. Insect pests damage the crop by
(a) cutting the root, stem and leaf.
(b) sucking the cell sap.
(c) boring into the stems and fruits.
(d) All of these

14. The most common activity followed by the farmers to generate additional income is
(a) part-time jobs in industries
(b) bee-keeping
(c) star gazing
(d) pumping of water

15. Eutrophication is caused by
(a) excessive use of fertilizers
(b) excessive growing of crops
(c) monocropping
(d) None of the above

16. Green manure is formed by
(a) decomposing animal residue
(b) decomposing algae
(c) ploughing of leguminous plants into the soil
(d) decomposition of the dead plants and animal wastes

17. The main source of food and fodder is
(a) lichen (b) cereals
(c) fungus (d) cotton

18. *Rhizobium* bacteria is
(a) the bacteria found in the intestines of animals which help in the digestion of cellulose present in their feed.
(b) the bacteria which are used in sewage works to break down the organic matter in sewage and make it harmless.
(c) the nitrogen fixing bacteria present in root nodules of leguminous plant convert atmospheric nitrogen gas into nitrogen compound.
(d) the bacteria that makes curd from milk.

19. On the basis of following features identify correct option.
(I) It consists of organic matter.
(II) It is prepared from animal excreta and plant waste.
(III) It causes no pollution.
(a) Manure (b) Fertilizer
(c) Vermi-compost (d) Pesticide

20. On the basis of following features identify correct option.
(I) It helps in absorption of nutrient elements by plants from soil.
(II) It provides moisture for germination of seeds as seeds do not germinate in dry soils.
(a) Nutrient management (b) Mineral replenishment
(c) Irrigation (d) Cropping patterns

21. By which method was a new breed 'Hisardale' of sheep formed by using Bikaneri ewes and Marino rams? **[NTSE]**
(a) Mutational breeding (b) Cross breeding
(c) Inbreeding (d) Out crossing

22. Select the incorrect statement regarding inbreeding. **[NTSE]**
(a) Inbreeding depression cannot be overcome by out-crossing.
(b) Inbreeding helps in elimination of deleterious alleles from the population.

(c) Inbreeding is necessary to evolve a pure line in any animal.
(d) Continued inbreeding reduces fertility and leads to inbreeding depression.

23. Select the incorrect statement. **[NTSE]**
(a) Inbreeding increases homozygosity.
(b) Inbreeding is essential to evolve purelines in any animal.
(c) Inbreeding selects harmful recessive genes that reduce fertility and productivity.
(d) Inbreeding helps in accumulation of superior genes and elimination of undesirable genes.

24. In plant breeding programmes, the entire collection (of plants/seeds) having all the diverse alleles for all genes in a given crop is called:
(a) cross-hybridisation among the selected parents.
(b) evaluation and selection of parents.
(c) germplasm collection
(d) selection of superior recombinants

25. Jaya and Ratna developed for green revolution in India are the varieties of
(a) maize (b) rice
(c) wheat (d) bajra

26. Crop plants grown in monoculture are
(a) free from intraspecific competition
(b) characterised by poor root system
(c) highly prone to pests
(d) low in yield

27. Which of the following has maximum genetic diversity in India?
(a) Rice (b) Mango
(c) Wheat (d) Groundnut

Multiple Matching Questions

DIRECTIONS (Qs.28-29) : Each question contains two columns which have to be matched. Statement/terms given in column I have to be matched with statement/terms given in column II.

28. Match Column - I with Column - II

Column-I		Column-II
A.	Hybrid variety	1. X-ray
B.	Mutation	2. Allopolyploidy
C.	Pure line	3. F_1 generation
D.	*Triticale*	4. Selection in self pollinated crops
		5. Genetic engineering

(a) A → 3; B → 2; C → 1; D → 4
(b) A → 3; B → 1; C → 4; D → 2
(c) A → 1; B → 3; C → 4; D → 2
(d) A → 2; B → 1; C → 3; D → 4

29. Match the column I and II:

Column-I		Column-II
(A)	Pusa shubhra	(i) Leaf and stripe rust
(B)	Pusa swarnim	(ii) Curl blight black rot
(C)	Pusa sadabahar	(iii) Chilly mosaic virus
(D)	Himgiri	(iv) White rust

(a) (A) – (i), (B) – (iii), (C) – (iv), (D) – (ii)
(b) (A) – (ii), (B) – (iv), (C) – (iii), (D) – (i)
(c) (A) – (iv), (B) – (iii), (C) – (ii), (D) – (i)
(d) (A) – (i), (B) – (ii), (C) – (iv), (D) – (iii)

SOLUTIONS
(Brief Explanations of Selected Questions)

Exercise 1 — Master Boards

Multiple Choice Questions

1. (a) 2. (a) 3. (b) 4. (c)
5. (d)

Assertion & Reason

1. (b) Both A and R are correct, but R is not the correct explanation of A.

   Crop improvement refes to the genetic alteration of plants to satisfy human needs. It main purpose to obtain higher yield, better quality, resistance to disease and shorter duration which are suitable to a particular environmental conditions.

2. (b) Both A and R are correct, but R is not the correct explanation of A.

   The direct application of fertilizer to crop or soils is a simple route to increase crop yield. Average yield per hectare has increased from 1.1 tons in 1950 to 2.3 tons in 1986 by the use of inorganic fertilizers. Irrigation is very important in increasing crop productivity as water is an essential component of vital activities of plant.

3. (a) Both A and R are true and R is the correct explanation of A.

   The crops grown in the winter season are called Rabi crop. Some of the examples of Rabi crop are : Wheat, Gram (Chana), Pea, Mustered etc.

4. (b) Both A and R are correct but R is not the correct explanation of A.

   Ploughing is the turning up of the soil of the field with the help of a plough. It is done before sowing of the seeds. It helps to loosen the soil, Hence improves air circulation in the soil.

5. (a) Both A and R are correct and R is the correct explanation of A.

   Manures and bio-fertilisers do not produce chemical pollutants by releasing excess nutrients in water.

Fill in the Blanks

1. Water logging
2. Paddy
3. Kharif
4. Preparation of soil
5. Vermicomposting
6. Fertilizers
7. Crop rotation
8. Drip
9. Harrow/Khurpi
10. Nurseries
11. Manure, fertilizers
12. Hoe
13. Animal husbandry
14. Sprinklers
15. Pests.

True / False

1. False. Cotton is a Kharif crop.
2. False. Harvesting comes after weeding.
3. True. Groundnut is a leguminous crop.
4. False. Nitrogenous fertilizer is not required for growing nitrogenous crops, since leguminous crops can fix the atmospheric nitrogen themselves by using nitrogen fixing bacteria present in their root nodules.
5. False. In addition to gunny bags, silos are also used for storing food grains on large scales. Metal bins are used for small scale storage.
6. True
7. True
8. True
9. False. The excessive use of fertilizer causes water pollution.
10. True

Match the Following

A – (x), **B** – (r), **C** – (p), **D** – (v), **E** – (q), **F** – (y), **G** – (s), **H** – (t), **I** – (u), **J** – (w)

Passage Based Questions

1. (b) 2. (c) 3. (b)

Very Short Answer Questions

1. Kharif and rabi crops.
2. Large scale cultivation of plants of same kind at one place is called crop.
3. Soil preparation
4. Turning and loosening of soil.
5. Plough / Hoe
6. Ploughing
7. Process of placing seed in the ground soil for growing crop plants.
8. Seed drill
9. Transplantation
10. Wells, canals, rivers, dams, ponds and lakes
11. Water logging refers to saturation of the soil with water sufficient to prevent or hinder agriculture.
12. Manure and fertilizers
13. Compost is a mixture of various decaying organic substances, like dead leaves or manure, used as a fertilizer for growing plants.
14. Urea, Ammonium sulphate
15. Leguminous crops
16. Crop rotation is a practice designed to minimise pests and diseases, reduce chemical usage, aid in building and maintaining healthy soil, and manage nutrient requirements-all which will maximise yield.
17. Weeds
18. It avoids random watering of crops.
19. Harrow and Trowel
20. Weedicides are pesticides that are used to kill weeds.
21. 2, 4 - D (2, 4 - Dichlorophenoxy acetic Acid)

22. Harvesting
23. Winnowing
24. Small scale – Jute bags, metallic bins
    Large scale – Silos, granaries
25. Combine
26. Pea, mustard
27. Paddy, Maize
28. Nitrogen fixation is the chemical processes by which atmospheric nitrogen is assimilated into organic compounds, especially by certain microorganisms as part of the nitrogen cycle.
29. Groundnut, Maize (Kharif crops)
30. *Rhizobium*

Short Answer Questions

1.

	Rabi Crop	Kharif Crop
(i)	Grown in winter season	Grown in rainy season
(ii)	Seeds are sown in October and harvested in March.	Seeds are sown in June and harvested in September.
(iii)	E.g. pea, mustard, wheat, gram etc.	E.g. paddy, maize, groundnut etc.

2. Importance of soil loosening are –
   (i) Roots penetrate deep into the soil and breathe easily, water holding capacity of soil increases.
   (ii) Helps in the growth of microbes and earthworm which help in turning the soil and add humus to itl.
   (iii) The nutrient rich soil comes up and nutrients are easily absorbed by plants.
   (iv) Proper mixing of manure in the soil.
3. Levelling is a process for ensuring that the depths and discharge variations over the field are relatively uniform and, as a result, that water distributions in the root zone are also uniform. It improves the efficiency of water, labour and energy resources utilization.
4.

	Manure	Fertilizer
(i)	Obtained by the decomposition of plant and animal waste	Obtained from inorganic salt.
(ii)	Prepared in fields	Prepared in factories
(iii)	Provides humus to soil	Does not provide humus
(iv)	Rich in plant nutrient	Less rich in plant nutrient

5. Manure is better than fertilizer because it
   (i) enhances water holding capacity of soil.
   (ii) makes soil porous due to which exchange of gases becomes easy.
   (iii) increases number of friendly microbes.
   (iv) improves texture of soil.
6. Weeds are unwanted plants that grow along with the crops. They are removed manually by using hand, khurpa, hoe or a rake in small field while in large area they are removed by ploughing, harrowing etc. The best time to remove weeds is when the soil is damp and moist.
7. Steps involved in crop production are :
   (i) Preparation of soil (ii) Seed selection and sowing
   (iii) Manuring (iv) Irrigation
   (v) Weeding
   (vi) Protection from animals, birds, pest and disease
   (vii) Harvesting, threshing and winnowing
   (viii) Storage
8. An insecticide is a substance used to kills insects. They include ovicides and larvicides used against insect eggs and larvae, respectively. Rodenticide is a chemical or other agent used to destroy rats or other rodent pests and prevent them from damaging food, crops, etc. Fungicides are chemical compounds or biological organisms used to kill or inhibit growth of fungi or fungal spores.
9. Grains are dried before storage to reduce their moisture content because moisture attracts fungus and bacteria resulting in its destruction.
10. Kharip crops : Soyabean, Cotton, Groundnut
    Rabi crops : Barley, Mustard, Pea
11. (i) Kharif crops. These crops are sown in the rainy season. Example: paddy, maize, soyabean.
    (ii) Rabi crops. These crops are grown in winter season. Example : wheat, mustard, and pea.
12. Ploughing, levelling and manuring.
13. Chillies and tomatoes are cultivated by transplantation. Transplantation usually refers to the practice of taking very young plants that have been started in pots or a nursery and moving them to a large production field.
14. The process of replanting the seedling from the nursery to the main field is called transplantation. Its advantages are :
    (i) It enables us to select only healthy seedlings.
    (ii) It promotes better penetration of roots in the soil.
15. Irrigation makes agriculture possible in areas previously unsuitable for intensive crop production. Irrigation transports water to crops to increase their yield, keep crops cool under excessive heat conditions and prevents freezing.
16. Weed affects crops by competing for water, minerals and sunlight. They also spread pests on the crops and sometimes produce poisonous substances harmful to crops. All these results in low yield of crop production.
17. Removal of unwanted plants that grow along with the crops are called weeding. Weeding can be done by
    (i) Manually removing seeds by using hand or trowel or harrow.
    (ii) Spraying weedicides which destroy weeds but not the crops.
18. (i) **Harvesting :** Cutting of crop plants after maturation is called harvesting. It is done by cutting the crop plants close to the ground or pulling out the crop plants.
    (ii) **Threshing :** Separation of grains from chaff is called threshing.
    (iii) **Winnowing :** Separation of grains from chaff with the help of wind is called winnowing.
19. Combines are farm machine that aids in the harvesting of grain crops by combining three separate functions into one piece of equipment. The combine harvester performs

the processes of reaping, threshing, and cleaning. This allows the crop to be harvested more quickly and efficiently, and enables farmers to harvest larger amounts of crop at a time. Some crops that can be harvested using this machine includes wheat, soyabeans, oats and rye.

20. Gunny bags are jute bags which protect the food grains from rodents and other damages while their storage.

21. To protect the grains stored in gunny bags in big godowns from damage, following should be done –
    (i) Fumigation with chemicals which repel pest or kill their without affecting the grains.
    (ii) Neem leaves are kept along with grains.
    (iii) Storage area can be sprayed regularly.

22. The irrigational method that are used in modern times are – Sprinkler system and drip irrigation. Sprinkler system of irrigation is useful for sandy soils and drip irrigation is best technique for watering fruit plants, gardens and trees.

23. Manure is obtained from the decomposition of plant or animal wastes. Plant and animal wastes are dumped in pits at open places and allowed to decompose by microbes. The decomposition product is manure.

Long Answer Questions

1. Continuous plantation of crops in field makes the soil poorer in important nutrients required for the growth of crops. It leads to decrease in soil fertility and hence the crop yield. Preparation of soil is considered to be an important step in agricultural practices because it helps in loosening the soil. Loosened soil allows growth of microorganisms and earthworms thus leading to its enrichment. It also helps the roots to breathe properly.

2. *Rhizobium* bacteria are soil bacteria. It forms a mutual beneficial association with plants. It plays an important role in fixing nitrogen after becoming established inside the root nodules of legumes. *Rhizobium* bacteria enable leguminous plants to fix nitrogen. It takes in atmospheric nitrogen and then converts it into a soluble form which the plant can absorb. These bacteria cannot make their own food so they provide nitrogen to the plants and in return obtains food and shelter from the host plant.

3. Precautions taken in sowing the seeds are :
    (i) Seeds should be sown at right spacing to get sufficient amount of sunlight, water and nutrients.
    (ii) Seeds should be planted at proper depth in the soil. If they are planted deep in the soil then they cannot respire properly and if planted on surface then can be eaten by birds.
    (iii) Seeds should be clean, healthy and free from disease.
    (iv) Seeds require water for germination. The soil therefore should have water in it during the process of sowing.

4. A pest is any organism that spreads disease, causes destruction or is otherwise a nuisance. Some examples of pests are mosquitoes, rodents, and weeds. Crops can be protected by using pesticides. Grains, fruits and vegetables should be washed properly before using to remove pesticides coated on them. Because pesticides are harmful poisonous chemicals which affects our health.

Reasoning Based Questions

1. Farmer must cover their nose and mouth while spraying weedicides and pesticides because they can be in it goes inside the body.

2. The frequency of irrigation is much higher in summer due to the water loss from transpiration which is much greater as compared to other seasons.

3. Food grains which are to be stored for future use should be completely dried because of the following reasons:
    (a) Presence of moisture may be favourable for the growth of micro-organisms.
    (b) Presence of moisture and favourable temperature enhance germination of stored seeds.

4. The levelling of ploughed fields prevent the top fertile soil from being carried away by strong winds or washed away be rain water.

5. If wheat is grown in Kharif season, the whole crops might get destroyed because of many factors such as lack of optimum temperature, adaptability etc.

6. Seeds should be sown at right spacing. They should be neither sown too close nor too far apart. If seeds are placed too close, then plants formed form them will be also too close and will not get enough sunlight, heats and nutrients to grow. Thus, the seeds should be sown at right spacing to proper growth.

7. Weeding can be defined as the removal of weeds (unwanted plants) from the field. Weeding is necessary because weeds compete with main crop plant for different factors such as water, sunlight etc. Due to unwanted plants there is reduction in yield also.

HOTS Questions

1. Farmer use a mixture of manures and fertilizers in the field so that the nutrients which cannot be fulfilled by the manures can be fulfilled by the plants and the nutrients which are not in the fertilizers can be fulfilled by the manures, *e.g.* -NPK [nitrogen, phosphate and potassium] fulfil the nutrients which are not present in the manures.

2. Sprinkler system of irrigation. This system is used on the uneven land where less water is available. Sprinkler irrigation is a method of applying irrigation water which is similar to natural rainfall. Water is distributed through a system of pipes usually by pumping. It is then sprayed into the air through sprinklers so that it breaks up into small water drops which fall to the ground.

3. Crop rotation and proper ploughing before sowing seeds helps in removing weeds. In these methods poisononous chemicals are not used.

4. An extra stock called buffer stock is maintained so that grains are available in plenty even if there is a short fall in production in a particular year, for example due to monsoon failure.

5. No, this is not true. Crop rotation helps replenishment of the soil with nitrogen.

6. To fulfil the food requirement of increasing population in our country we need to constantly increase the food grain production. This can be done by increasing the land under cultivation. But we cannot indefinitely go on increasing farmland, as this leads to environmental problems.

Hence, improvement in the methods of agricultural practices is the most suitable alternative to increase crop produce. Better irrigation methods, proper use of manure and fertilizers etc will help improving the crop produce. Also, by providing better storage methods, we can reduce wastage of food grain. However, recently, an increase in crop produce has come about from using better varieties of crops that have higher yield and more resistance to diseases.

Hence, these days, use of better varieties of crop plants has brought about maximum increase in crop production in our country.

7. Mustard is a Rabi crop which requires cold and dry weather. Therefore, in rainy season it will not grow well and gets destroyed in excess water.

8. (i) Uneven distribution of rainfall-spatial and temporal

   (ii) Uncertainty of monsoon.

   (iii) Lack of irrigation facilities

   (iv) Frequent flood and drought is a common phenomenon associated with the monsoon.

9. Yes, the reasons are as follows :

   (1) Less income or savings.

   (2) Crop failure

   (3) Difficult procedure of financial institution which has pushed them to borrow from private money lenders at high rate of interest.

   (4) Inadequate support price of procurement of crops

   (5) Low returns from agriculture.

   (6) Lack of implementation of land reforms.

10. Pests are organisms that attack and damage crops. They can limit crop productivity.

11. Continuous rainfall will make cultivation difficult and reduces agricultural output. All plants need at least some water to survive; therefore rain (being the most effective means of watering) is important to agriculture. While a regular rain pattern is usually vital to healthy plants, too much or too little rainfall can be harmful, even devastating to crops. Drought can kill crops and increase erosion, while overly wet weather can cause harmful fungus growth. Plants need varying amounts of rainfall to survive. For example, certain cacti require small amounts of water, while tropical plants may need up to hundreds of inches of rain per year to survive.

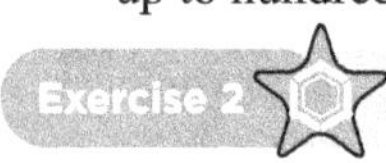

Exercise 2   Master NCERT (Text-book & Exemplar)

Text-book Exercise

1. (a) The same kind of plants grown and cultivated on a large scale at a place is called _ crop _.

   (b) The first step before growing crops is _ preparation _ of the soil.

   (c) Damaged seeds would __float__ on top of water.

   (d) For growing a crop, sufficient sunlight, _ water __ and ___ nutrients_ from the soil are essential.

2.
	A		B
(i)	Kharif crops	(e)	Paddy and maize
(ii)	Rabi crops	(d)	Wheat, gram, pea
(iii)	Chemical fertilisers	(b)	Urea and super phosphate
(iv)	Organic manure	(c)	Animal excreta, cow dung, urine and plant waste

3. (a) Kharif crop → Paddy, maize

   (b) Rabi crop → Wheat, gram

4. (a) Preparation of soil:

   It is the first **method** to be followed before growing a crop. This method includes loosening of soil so that the root can penetrate deep into it. The loosening of the soil helps in the growth of several soil microbes, earthworms etc., which enrich the soil with humus and other essential nutrients. Plants require nutrients for their proper growth and functioning. The process of loosening is called ploughing. This brings the nutrient-rich soil to the top, which helps the plants to utilize the nutrients for their growth.

   (b) Sowing:

   Sowing is an important step in crop production. In this process the seed is placed in or on the soil for future growth. The seeds that are selected should be of good quality. This improves the net yield of the crop. Sowing is usually done with the help of a traditional tool or a seed drill. The traditional tool is like a funnel and was used earlier. Nowadays, seed drills that make the use of tractors are used for sowing. This tool disperses seeds uniformly and sows seeds at proper depth and at regular intowards. This method saves time and also protects the seeds from birds.

   (c) Weeding:

   Undesirable plants that grow along with the crop are known as weeds. The process of removing these weeds is called weeding. *Xanthium*, *Parthenium*, etc. are some common weeds. Weeds compete with the crop for nutrients, light, and space. As a result, crop plants get lesser nutrients, light, and space for their development which reduces their productivity. This is why, various weeding **methods** are employed.

Some important weeding methods are:

(i) Weeds can be controlled by using weedicides. It is a chemical, which is sprayed in the fields to kill all the weeds without causing any harm to the crop.

(ii) Tilling before sowing of crops also helps in removing weeds. Tilling uproots the weeds. The best time for removal of weeds is before flowering.

(iii) The manual method of weeding is done with the help of a khurpi. It involves regular uprooting of weeds close to the ground.

(d) Threshing:

   Threshing involves the process of separating grains or seeds from chaff. It is done after harvesting. It is done with the help of a machine known as 'Combine'. This machine is a combined harvester and thresher. It harvests plants as well as cleans grains.

5. Differences between fertilisers and manure:

Fertiliser	*Manure*
Fertilisers are commercially available plant nutrients, obtained from chemical substances.	Manure is a natural substance. It is prepared by the decomposition of animal excreta and plant wastes.
They can be organic or inorganic in nature.	Manure is known to have a large quantity of organic materials and very little amount of plant nutrients.
They ensure healthy growth and development of plants by providing them with nitrogen, phosphorus, potassium, etc.	They help in enriching the soil with organic matter and nutrients.
The addition of fertilisers to the soil requires special guidelines such as dose time, post addition precautions, etc., to be followed.	The addition of manure does not require any special guidelines.
A fertiliser does not provide any humus to the soil.	Manure provides humus to the soil and increases soil fertility.
Its excessive use causes water pollution. It cannot replenish organic matter of soil.	It protects the environment and helps in recycling farm waste.

6. Irrigation is the method of supplying water to crops at different intervals. The time and frequency of irrigation varies according to different seasons, crops, and soil types. There are various sources of irrigation such as wells, canals, rivers, dams, ponds, and lakes. Two important methods of irrigation which are helpful in conserving water are:

(a) Sprinkler system:

In this method, water is supplied through pipes to one or more central locations within the field. When water is allowed to flow under high pressure with the help of a pump, it gets sprinkled on the crops. This system is more useful on uneven land, having fewer water supplies.

(b) Drip system:

In this method, water is delivered at or near the roots of plants, drop by drop. This is the most efficient method of irrigation as there is no wastage of water at all. This method is important in areas having water scarcity.

7. If wheat is sown in the kharif season (from June to September), then the whole crop might get destroyed because of many factors such as lack of optimum temperature, in appropriate day length, availability of pests, excess of rain etc. Therefore, wheat crop should not be sown during this season.

8. Continuous plantation of similar crops in a field makes the soil deficient in certain nutrients such as nitrogen, phosphorus, potassium, etc. This is because plants require nutrients for their proper growth and functioning. When a farmer continues to grow crops one after the other, all the nutrients available in the soil reduces and the crop yield decreases automatically.

9. Undesirable plants that grow along with crop plants are known as weeds. *Xanthium*, *Parthenium*, etc. are some common weeds. Weeds compete with the main crop for nutrients, light, and space. As a result, crop plants get lesser nutrients, light, and space for their development. This in turn, reduces their productivity. Thus, various weeding methods are employed.

Some important weeding methods are:

(i) Weeds can be controlled using weedicides. These are chemicals, which can be sprayed in the fields to kill all available weeds. Weedicides are not harmful to the main crops.

(ii) Tilling before sowing of crops also helps in removing weeds. Tilling uproots the weeds. The best time for the removal of weeds is before flowering.

(iii) The manual method weeding is done with the help of a khurpi. It involves regular uprooting or cutting of weeds close to the ground.

10. Flow chart of sugarcane crop production:

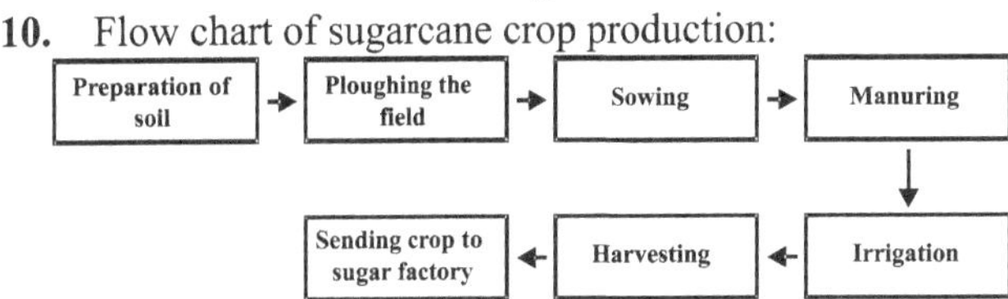

11. Down

1. Irrigation
2. Storage
5. Crop

Across

3. Harvestor
4. Gram
6. Winnowing

			¹I				²S		
³H	A	R	V	E	S	T	O	R	
			R				O		
			I				R		
			G				A		
⁴G	R	A	M				G		
			T				E		
			I		⁵C				
			O		R				
⁶W	I	N	N	O	W	I	N	G	
					P				

1. The field should watered, tilled and ploughed before sowing seeds.
2. October to March.
3. Loosening the soil/maintaining high moisture levels in soil.
4. Crops cultivated without using any chemicals like fertilisers, pesticides, weedicides etc. are called organic foods.
5. (a) Seed drill.
   (b) The advantages are:-
      (i) seeds are sown at a uniform distance and depth to avoid over crowding.
      (ii) after sowing, seeds are covered by soil which prevent them from being eaten by birds.
      (iii) It saves time and labour.
6. (a) Animal husbandry.
   (b) Animals are provided with proper food, shelter and care.
7. (i) He did not use good quality seeds.
   (ii) His field was not well irrigated.
   (iii) Manures/fertilisers were not properly applied.
   (iv) Weeds were not removed.
8. The following items are required – seeds and seedlings of vegetable plants from nursery, kitchen waste, water. Step for raising the garden:
   1. Kitchen waste will be collected and composted in a pit.
   2. A patch of land will be identified for the garden.
   3. Soil will be dug up and levelled with the help of a spade.
   4. Sowing of seeds / transplanting of seedlings.
   5. Select seeds/seedings as per the season. Water the plants regularly with a water-can.
   6. Compost will be applied.
   7. Weeds will be removed periodically with the help of khurpi.

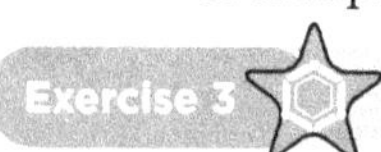

Exercise 3 — Foundation Builder

1. (b) Dr. Norman Borlang, an American agricultural scientist was the first to promote the green revolution in India.
2. (c) Sugarcane is not a Rabi crop. It is a Kharif crop. Kharif crops are grown in rainy season.
3. (b) Beans is a leguminous crop that enriches the soil with nitrogen. Leguminous crops fix the atmospheric nitrogen themselves by using nitrogen fixing bacteria present in their root nodules.
4. (a) The process of turning and loosening of soil is called ploughing or filling. Harvesting is the process of cutting the crop and gathering them to transport it to the market. Threshing is the process of separating the chaff from the grain. Irrigation is the process of watering the plants in a field.
5. (a) Threshing is the process of separating the grain seeds from pods or chaff. The process of cutting of mature crop is known as harvesting. The process of sowing seeds by hands is known as broadcasting while ploughing is the process of turning and loosening of soil.

6. (a) Manure enriches the soil with organic material (humus). A fertilizer does not provide any humus to soil.
7. (d) Drip system of irrigation is a modern method of irrigation. In this method water is delivered at or near the roots of the plant drop by drop. Moat, Rahat and chain pump are traditional methods of irrigation, they are cheaper but less efficient.
8. (d) Harrow is used for removing unwanted plants (weeds) from the crops. The implements used for harvesting are sickle and harvesting machine.
9. (a) Plough is an implement made of wood. It is drawn over soil to turn it over and cut furrows in preparation for the planting of seeds. Sickle is an implement for cutting grain, grass, etc., It consists of a curved, hook like blade mounted in a short handle. Harrow is a cultivating implement set with spikes, spring teeth, or disks and used primarily for pulverizing and smoothing the soil. Trowel is a small tool with a curved blade that is used by gardeners for digging holes.
10. (a) Manuring is addition of manure to the soils to improve its fertility. Weeding is the removal of undesirable, unattractive, or troublesome plant especially one growing where it is not wanted. Tilling is to prepare (land) for the raising of crops, as by plowing and harrowing.
11. (b) Ploughing in bigger field is done by cultivator. Cultivator is a mechanical implement for breaking up the ground and uprooting weeds. Hoe is a long-handled gardening tool with a thin metal blade, used mainly for weeding. Sickle is a hand-held agricultural tool with a variously curved blade. It is used for harvesting grain crops or cutting succulent forage chiefly for feeding livestock. Combine is a farm machine used for both threshing and harvesting.
12. (d) Manuring helps in enriching the soil with organic matter and nutrients.
13. (a) Weedicide is a chemical or organic substance which is used to remove unwanted plants mainly like weeds which effect the healthy growth of the plant. Tilling is to prepare (land) for the raising of crops, as by plowing and harrowing. Crop rotation is the practice of growing different crops in succession on the same land chiefly to preserve the productive capacity of the soil.
14. (a) Cow dung is an example of manure. Manure is organic matter used as organic fertilizer in agriculture. It contributes to the fertility of the soil by adding organic matter and nutrients, such as nitrogen, that are trapped by bacteria in the soil. Urea, ammonium phosphate and superphosphate are fertilizers.
15. (d) The large scale storage of food grains is done in grain silos and gunny bags.
16. (b) Crop harvesting is the last step in the production of crop. Harvesting is the cutting and gathering the mature crop.

17. (c) Urea is an example of fertilizer. Fertilizer is a manmade mineral salt which are added to the soil to provide nutrients like nitrogen, phosphorous and potassium.

18. (d) Appropriate supply of water to the crop is called irrigation. Soil cannot be irrigated with polluted water.

19. (b) Hisardale is a new breed of sheep developed in Punjab by crossing Bikaneri-ewe and Marino rams.
In cross-breeding, superior male of one breed are mated with superior females of another breed.

20. (a) Inbreeding depression, the reduction of fitness caused by inbreeding, is a universal phenomenon that depends on past mutation, selection, and genetic drift. Inbreeding depression can be overcome by the following ways:
- Out breeding: The breeding of animals which are unrelated to each other and do not have come ancestors for 4-6 generations.
- Out crossing: Mating done with the animals of same breed but after 4-6 generations.
- Cross breeding: Superior male mated with superior female of another breed.
- Interspecific hybridisations: Male and female animal of two different related species.

21. (d) Inbreeding increases homozygosity. So, mating of the related individuals of same breed will give homozygous purelines.

22. (b) Outbreeding is useful in the problem of inbreeding depression.

23. (a) The growing of grass or legumes in rotation with grain or tilled crops as a soil conservation measure is called Ley farming.

24. (d) *Pseudomonas* is denitrifying bacteria which converts nitrates present in soil to free atmospheric nitrogen, thus depleting soil fertility and reducing agricultural productivity.

25. (a) The silkworms belong to phylum : Arthropoda, class : Insecta, order : Lepidoptera. It is the order of insects that includes butterflies and moths. About 1,80,000 species of the Lepidoptera are described till now.

26. (b)

27. (d) Insects, Rodents and mites are the pests which damages crop shortage.

28. (d) Plant hybridization can be done between different varieties, species and genus.

29. (b) Crop rotation is a growing of crops in a pre-planned manner.

30. (d) Leghorn is a variety of fowl.

31. (a) Rock bee is a common name of Apis dorsata.

32. (c) The local breeds of cow like Red Sindhi, Sahiwal carrying high immunity power.

33. (d)

34. (a) When rate of water absorption is less than the rate of transpiration, plant cells loose water and thus plants wilt in the afternoon.

35. (b) Vermi-compost is a manure formed by earthworms.

36. (a) Weeds are unwanted plants that reduce available moisture, nutrients, sunlight and growing space needed by crop plants, e.g. dandelion, wild carrot, bermuda grass etc. Livestock can be poisoned or injured by certain unwanted plants while grazing or fed in stored feed, e.g. poison hemlock (*Conicum maculatum*).

37. (d) Very little growth in A but lot of growth in B and C because B and C have good amount of nutrients in their soil in the form of humus and fertilizers.

38. (d) If rice crop is grown along with a leguminous crop (e.g. Gram), then the usage of nitrogen from the soil by rice plant is compensated by the addition of nitrogen in the soil by nitrogen fixing legume. This in turn increases the soil fertility and ultimately the yield of crop.

39. (b) She can adopted sprinkler system which is the modern method of irrigation. In this technique, the perpendicular pipes having rotating nozzle on top are joined to the main pipeline at regular intervals and when water flows through it under pressure with the help of pump it gets sprinkled on the crop. It is useful for uneven land or where soil is sandy.

40. (d) Insects, rodents and mites are the pests which damages crop shortage.

41. (b) Crop rotation is a growing of crops in a pre-planned manner.

42. (d) Leghorn is a variety of fowl.

43. (a) When rate of water absorption is less than the rate of transpiration, plant cells loose water and thus plants wilt in the afternoon.

Assertion & Reason

1. (a) Rabi crops refers to agricultural crops sown in winter and harvested in the spring. It is the spring harvest (also known as the "winter crop") in Indian subcontinent. The Rabi crops are grown between the months mid-October to March. The water that has percolated in the ground during the rains is main source of water for these crops. Examples of Rabi crop are wheat, gram, pea, mustard, linseed and barley.

2. (a) Fertilizers are a large number of natural and synthetic materials, containing the chemical elements that improves growth and productiveness of plants. Fertilizers enhance the natural fertility of the soil or replace the chemical elements taken from the soil by previous crops. Modern chemical fertilizers include one or more of the three elements most important in plant nutrition: nitrogen, phosphorus, and potassium.

3. (d) Refer answer 2

4. (b) Crop improvement refers to the genetic alteration of plants to satisfy human needs. It proposes to obtain higher yield, better quality, resistance to diseases and pests, along with shorter duration which are suitable to a particular environmental condition.

5. (a) Weed species are typically associated with crops, and crop rotations determine their specific weed population over time. Crop rotation is the system of growing a sequence of different crops on the same ground so as to maintain or increase its fertility, to avoid depleting the soil and to control weeds, diseases, and pests.

6. **(a)** Earthworms are called farmer's friend because they play an important role in breaking down dead organic matter by a process known as decomposition. Decomposition releases nutrients locked up in dead plants and animals and makes them available for use by living plants. Earthworms are also responsible for mixing soil layers and incorporating organic matter into the soil. Charles Darwin referred to earthworms as 'nature's ploughs' because of their ability of mixing soil and organic matter. This mixing improves the fertility of the soil by allowing the organic matter to be dispersed through out the soil and the nutrients held in it to become available to bacteria, fungi and plants.

Exercise 4 ⭐ **Foundation Builder +**

1. (a)   **2.** (b)

3. **(d)** Increase in food production has been possible by the success of green revolution for food grain and white revolution for milk.

4. (d)

5. **(d)** Hybridization is done to incorporate desirable characteristics into crop varieties. It refers to crossing between genetically dissimilar plants that may be inter varietal or inter specific.

6. **(d)** Manure helps in improving soil fertility and structure by supplying small quantities of nutrients. It is also advantageous in protecting environment from excessive use of fertilizers, recycling farm waste and disposing biological waste.

7. (a)

8. **(d)** Fertilizers should be used carefully because continuous use decreases the soil fertility. They are man-made chemicals and so can be harmful to the micro-organisms present in the soil and also lead to water pollution on getting washed away in rains.

9. **(b)** Organic farming is a farming system with minimal use of chemicals such as fertilizers, herbicides or pesticides and with a maximum input of organic manures.

10. **(a)** Use of neem leaves or turmeric during grain storage serves the purpose of bio-pesticides.

11. **(b)** Mixed cropping is growing two or more crops simultaneously on the same piece of land in a haphazard manner.

12. (a)

13. **(d)** Insect pests damage the crop by cutting the root, stem and leaf; sucking the cell sap or boring into the stems and fruits.

14. **(b)** The most common activity followed by the farmers to generate additional income is bee keeping.

15. **(a)** The tremendous increase in the amount of algae and other organic matter in the waters of lakes, ponds, rivers due to the presence of nitrates and phosphate salts (fertilizers), often leading to serious depletion of dissolved oxygen in water is called eutrophication.

16. **(c)** Leguminous plants like sun hemp are sown in the soil and later ploughed back into the soil at flowering stage.

17. (b)   **18.** (c)   **19.** (a)   **20.** (c)

21. **(b)** Hisardale is a new breed of sheep developed in Punjab by crossing Bikaneri-ewe and Marino rams.
In cross-breeding, superior male of one breed are mated with superior females of another breed.

22. **(a)** Inbreeding depression, the reduction of fitness caused by inbreeding, is a universal phenomenon that depends on past mutation, selection, and genetic drift. Inbreeding depression can be overcome by the following ways:
- Out breeding: The breeding of animals which are unrelated to each other and do not have come ancestors for 4-6 generations.
- Out crossing: Mating done with the animals of same breed but after 4-6 generations.
- Cross breeding: Superior male mated with superior female of another breed.
- Interspecific hybridisations: Male and female animal of two different related species.

23. **(c)** Inbreeding exposes harmful recessive genes that are eliminated by selection. It also helps in accumulation of superior genes and elimination of less desirable genes. Therefore this is selection at each step & which increase the productivity of inbred population. Close and continued inbreeding usually reduces fertility and even productivity.

24. **(c)** Germplasm collection is the first step of plant breeding programmes. As genetic variability is the root of any breeding programme. In many crops pre-existing genetic variability is available from wild relatives of the crop.

25. **(b)** Jaya and Ratna are two rice varieties developed for green revolution in India.
- The scientific name of Jaya is IET-723. This paddy variety takes about 130 days to grow and the grain is long, bold and white. Its yield is 50-60 quintals per hectare.
- The scientific name of 'Ratna' is IET-1411. It takes about 130-135 days to grow. The grain is long, slender and white. Its yield is 45-50 quintal/hectare.

26. **(c)** Crop plants grown in monoculture are highly prone to pests.

27. **(a)** During the period 1960 to 2000 rice production went up from 35 million tonnes to 89.5 million tonnes. This was due to the development of semi-dwarf varieties of rice. there are 2,00,000 varieties of rice in India.

28. (b)

29. **(b)** Pusa shubhra, a variety of cauliflower, is resistant to a disease curl blight black rot.
Pusa swarnim (Karan rai), a variety of *Brassica*, is resistant to disease called white rust.
Pusa sadabahar, a variety of chilli, is resistant to disease chilly mosaic virus.
Himgiri a variety of wheat, is resistant to, a disease named leaf and stripe rust.

Think Out of the Box

Case Study

1. Over cropping can be prevented in a number of ways often by rotating the type of crop being produced as different crops require different types of nutrients.

2. The best way to check the viability of seeds is by Germination test.

(C O N C E P T   M A P)

MICROORGANISMS : Single celled living organisms which invisible to naked eyes.

★ **BACTERIA :** Small, single-celled organism present everywhere and heterotrophic in nature. Two types– aerobic and anaerobic. Example- *E.coli*, Streptococcus.

★ **FUNGI :** Multicellular non-green plant-like organisms, which don't contain chlorophyll and cannot synthesize their own food. Example- Mushroom.

★ **PROTOZOA:** Microscopic eukaryotic organisms that have complex internal structure. Example- Amoeba, paramecium.

★ **ALGAE:** Plant like organisms, that have chlorophyll and are autotrophs. Example- diatoms, volvox

★ **VIRUS:** Smallest microorganism, which do not show any characteristics of living things. Example- HIV, TMV

MICROORGANISMS

BENEFICIAL MICROORGANISMS: Microbes carry out about 90% of biochemical reactions occurring in our planet.

HARMFUL MICROORGANISM: Disease causing microorganism are called pathogens. Disease spread by harmful microbes from our infected person to a healthy person through air, water, food or physical contact are called communicable diseases.

FOOD POISONING : Microorganisms can grow on our food and spoil it by releasing toxic substances. If we eat such food, we may get ill or even die.

Food and beverage industry: Bacteria plays an important role in making curd, bread, cheese and pickles. Bacteria and yeast also helps in the process of fermentation.

Making Medicine and Vaccines: Antibiotics are medicines produced by certain microorganisms to kill other disease causing organisms. Vaccines are suspension of killed microbes that mimics the disease causing microorganisms.

Increasing Soil Fertility: Microorganisms decomposes dead plants and animals and break them into their component parts, thus, increasing nutrients in the soil.

Cleaning of Environment: Bacteria and fungi break down complex pollutants into simpler substances to gain energy and nutrients, thus cleaning the environment.

★ *Belongs to connecting topic.*

Build A Strong Foundation

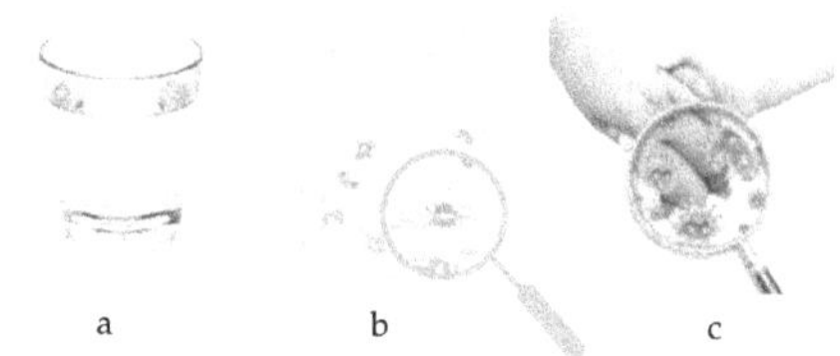

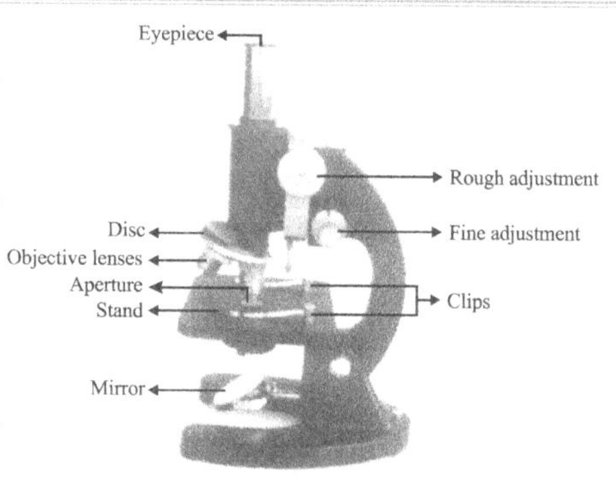

a: Clean and transparent glass of water; b and c: Glass and hand respectively showing microorganisms with magnifying glass

MICROORGANISMS

Microorganisms are microscopic, living, single celled organisms. Microorganisms have adapted to inhabit almost every corner of the world. They are invisible to naked eyes. Such small organisms can be observed through a microscope.

Microscope is a device that produces enlarged images of very small objects. The simple student's microscope that is often used in schools is called *compound microscope*. A compound microscope has two lens system — The eye piece and the objective lenses. The microscope can normally make an object look 25 to 400 times its actual size. So, while you are observing an object in a microscope, you are observing its magnified image. The lens of a compound microscope is made up of convex (magnifying) lenses. It uses light (generally sunlight) to illuminate the object and is also known as light microscope. After the invention of microscope, it was found that microorganisms occur everywhere. Microorganisms were observed for the first time by **Anton Von Leeunwenhoek** of Holland. Microorganisms are diverse and include bacteria, archae protozoa, fungi, algae etc.

A compound microscope

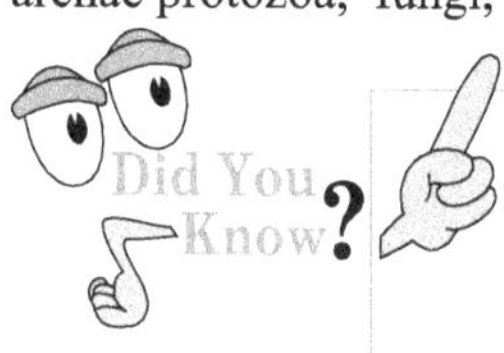

- *Microbes are the oldest form of life on earth (3.8 billion years).*
- *Most microorganisms are microscopic, but there are some bacteria such as Thiomargarita namibiensis and some protozoa such as Stentor, which are macroscopic and visible to the naked eye.*
- *Microbes comprise ~60% of the earth's biomass.*
- *Microbial cycling of such critical chemical elements as carbon and nitrogen helps keep the world habitable for all life forms.*
- *Microbes generate at least half of the oxygen we breathe.*
- *Microbes thrive in an amazing diversity of habitats in extremes of heat, cold, radiation, pressure, salinity, acidity, and darkness, and often where no other life forms could exist and where nutrients come only from inorganic matter.*
- *Microbes offer unusual capabilities reflecting the diversity of their environmental niches. These may prove useful as a source of new genes and organisms of value in addressing bioremediation, global change, biotechnology, and energy production.*
- *Diversity patterns of microorganisms can be used for monitoring and predicting environmental change*
- *The study of microorganism is called microbiology and the scientist involved in the study are called microbiologists.*

Fun Time

Name three advertisement that you see in television where germs are shown.

Let us perform an activity to observe some common microbes.
Collect some moist soil from your garden in a beaker and add little water to it. Shake the beaker to mix soil and water thoroughly. Now allow the soil particle to settle done. Then take a drop of water from the beaker and spread it over a clean glass slide. Place a coverslip over the slide and observe it under microscope.

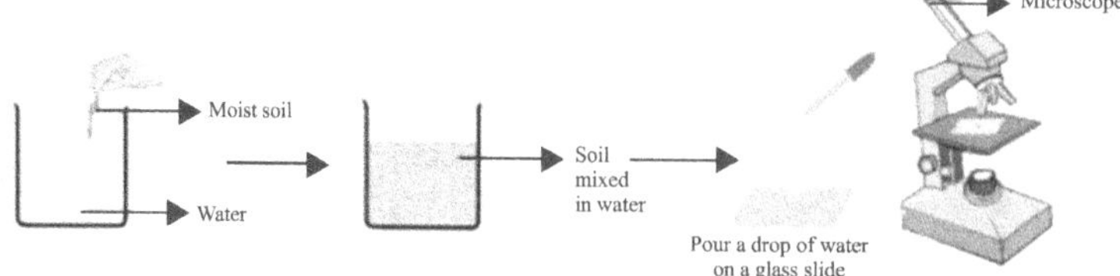

What did you observe?
You can observe several minute organisms floating in water. These tiny organism are called microbes.

Microorganisms are present everywhere in our environment, in soil, hot springs, on the ocean floor, in air, deep inside the rocks with in the earth's crust. They are also present in our house, in refrigerator, in the bathroom, in foods, floors, toys, and even in our body.

CONNECTING TOPIC

CHARACTERISTICS OF MICROORGANISMS

Some characteristics of microorganisms are:
(i) They can be unicellular or multicellular. Bacteria, some algae and protozoans are single celled organisms, while algae and fungi are multicellular organisms.
(ii) They can be solitary or colonial. A protozoan, say *Amoeba* can spend its whole life alone moving in water whereas others like fungi and bacteria live and work together in colonies to help each other.
(iii) They can be autotrophic or heterotrophic. Some algae and fungi autotrophs as they can prepare their own food by the process of photosynthesis. Some bacteria, few fungi and viruses are heterotrophs as they feed one.
(iv) Microorganisms can reproduce sexually, asexually or both. Sexual reproduction involves formation of new individual by fusion between their parent gametes while asexual reproduction involves the splitting of microbes into two identical pieces by itself. A bacterium, *for example*, reproduces asexually by binary fusion or sexually by conjugation.

CLASSIFICATION OF MICROORGANISMS

There is a huge variety of microorganisms on the earth. *Hence*, based on their size and shape they are classified into four major groups.

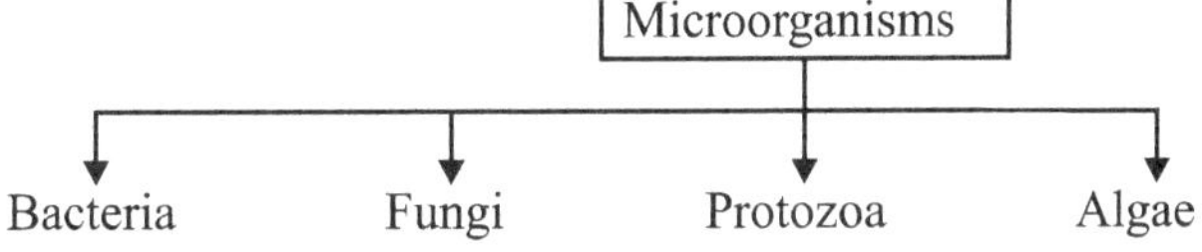

CONNECTING TOPIC

Bacteria

Bacteria are small, single-celled organism, present everywhere, on land, in water and in the air. Some live in or on other organisms including plants and animals (including humans). A lot of these bacterial cells are found in the lining of the digestive system. Bacteria are heterotrophic in nature i.e., they get their food from eating other organisms or from eating organic matter. Their size vary from 0.2 to 100μ in diameter.

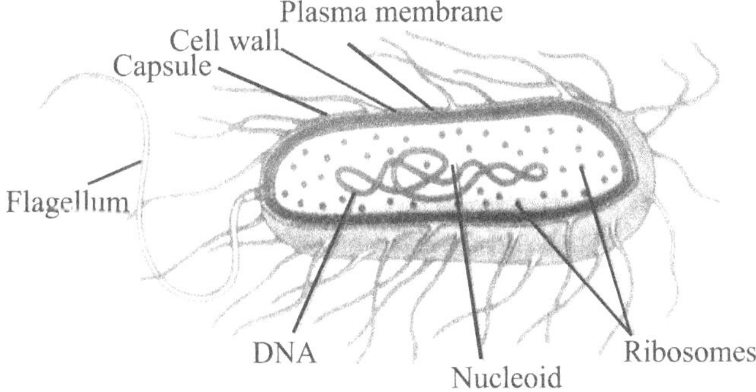

Structure of a bacteria

Aerobic & anaerobic bacteria
The bacteria which need oxygen for their respiration are called **aerobic bacteria**. Those bacteria which do not need oxygen for respiration are called **anaerobic bacteria**.

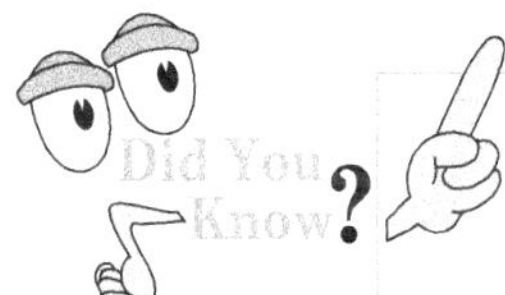

- *Bacteria play a vital role in maintaining the Earth as a suitable place for inhabitation by other forms of life, and protozoa play a vital role in controlling their numbers and biomass.*
- *Coliform bacteria are used as indicators of water pollution*

Gram Stain

Bacteria are viewed under a light microscope using a special stain. The stain that is traditionally used for this is the **Gram Stain**. In 1884, a Scientist named **Christian Gram** developed a stain or dye called "Gram stain" that showed that all bacteria are divided into two groups. They poured purple dye (Gram' stain) over bacterial smear on a microscope slide. The cell wall of the bacteria take up the colour. Now, if a solvent is applied to the slide, bacteria that have got a cell wall keep their purple colour, but bacteria that have got an extra cell membrane outside their cell wall quickly lose the purple stain and become colourless. Hence, on the basis of the response to Gram's stain, bacteria are divided into two groups –

(i) Gram positive bacteria :- Bacteria that manage to keep the original purple dye (Gram' stain) are called **gram positive bacteria**. Example – Staphylococcus, Streptococcus.

(ii) Gram negative bacteria :- Bacteria that do not retain the original purple dye (Gram' stain) are called **Gram negative bacteria**. Example – Escherichia coli, Salmonella, Pseudomonas.

CONNECTING TOPIC

FUNGI

Fungi are multicellular non-green plant-like organisms that do not contain chlorophyll and are unable to synthesize their own food. Fungi are found in just about any habitat but most live on the land, mainly in soil or on plant material rather than in sea or fresh water.

The main body of most fungi is made up of fine, branched, and usually colourless threads called **hyphae**. Each fungus will have vast numbers of these hyphae, all intertwined to make up a tangled web called the **mycelium**.

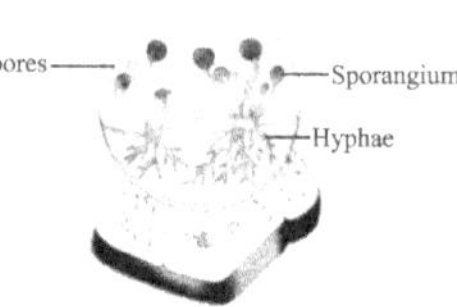

Bread mould (Rhizopus)

Mushroom

Most of the fungi are invisible to the naked eyes. For example, yeast and bread moulds. However, there are some examples of fungi that are not microscopic and hence can be seen through naked eyes. For example, mushroom. Mushroom is a fleshy fungus that comprises of a cap at the end of a stem. It arises from an underground mycelium and are used extensively in cooking.

You all must have noticed the presence of whitish grayish patch on the slice of bread. What are these? Any guesses? The whitish grayish patches are fungus, a multicellular organism that has developed on the surface of slice of bread. If you carefully observe the slice of bread under microscope or magnifying glass, you can see several tiny thread like structures called **hyphae**.

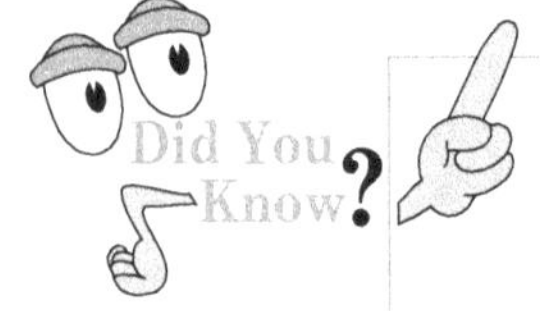

- *Some fungi look like plants, but they cannot make their food like plants do. Unlike algae or plants, fungi lack the chlorophyll necessary for photosynthesis and must therefore live as parasites or saprobes. Saprobes are organisms that derive their nourishment from dead or decayed organic matter.*

- *Rhizopus fungus is commonly known as bread mould.*

- *A huge fungus called Armillaria bulbosa is reportedly formed in Michigan, USA. It covers an area of 15 hectors, weighs around 10,000 kg and survives for 150 years. This makes it one of the oldest, largest and heaviest living things known on this planet.*

Lichen and Mycorrhiza

Some fungi are involved in symbiotic relationships. For example, lichens and mycorrhiza. Lichens show a mutualistic relationship between a fungus and an algae or a cyanobacterium. Here, the fungus helps in absorption of nutrients and provides protection, while algae prepares the food. Mycorrhiza is a symbiotic association between fungi and roots of higher plants.

Cyanobacteria

Cyanobacterium is a group of photosynthetic bacteria. They are widespread in marine and freshwater environments with some species capable of nitrogen fixation. Though classified as bacteria, they resemble the eukaryotic algae in many ways. Due to resemblance in physical appearance and similarity in ecological riches they were once treated as algae. They contain certain pigments like, chlorophyll, which given them a blue-green colour.

CONNECTING TOPIC

Protozoa

Protozoa are microscopic eukaryotic organisms that have relatively complex internal sturcture and carry out complex metabolic activities. They can be unicellular or multicellular. They are animal like, just as algae are plant like. They come in many different shapes and sizes ranging from an Amoeba (which can change its shape) to Paramecium (with its fixed shape and complex structure). They live in a wide variety of moist habitats including fresh water, marine environments and the soil. Their sizes vary from 2 to 200μ.

Protozoans are motile, nearly all possess flagella, cilia, or pseudopodia that allow them to navigate their aqueous habitats.

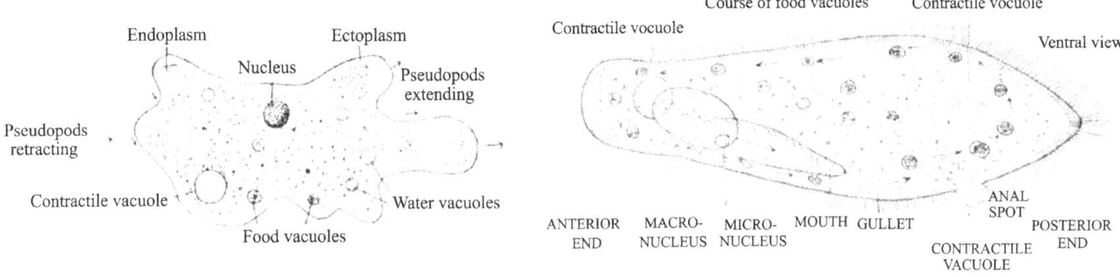

Amoeba   *Paramecium*

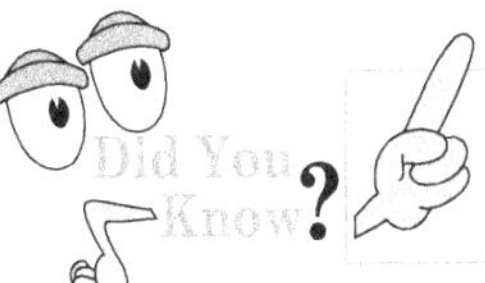

> ***Euglena is a protozoan, which contains chlorophyll and can photosynthesize.***

CONNECTING TOPIC

Algae

Algae is a large group of simple, plant like organisms. The algae have chlorophyll and can manufacture their own food through the process of photosynthesis. Algae occur in most habitats ranging from marine and freshwater to desert sands and from hot boiling springs to snow and ice. They vary from small, single-celled forms to complex multicellular forms. The simplest algae are single celled (e.g., the diatoms); the more complex forms consist of many cells grouped in a spherical colony (e.g., Volvox), in a ribbon like filament (e.g., Spirogyra), or in a branching thallus form (e.g., Fucus). The giant kelps of the eastern Pacific grow to more than 61 meters in length and form dense marine forests.

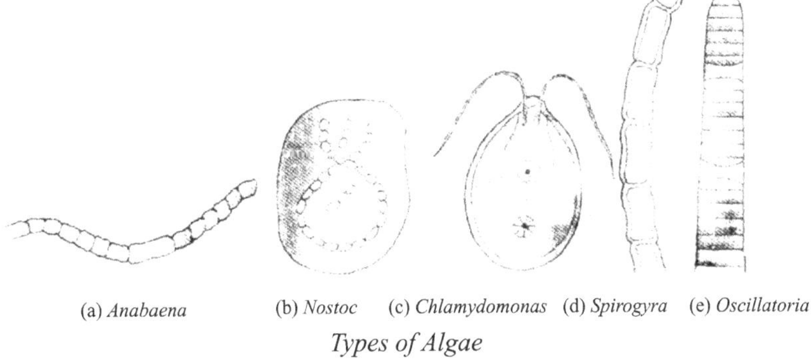

(a) *Anabaena*   (b) *Nostoc*   (c) *Chlamydomonas* (d) *Spirogyra* (e) *Oscillatoria*

Types of Algae

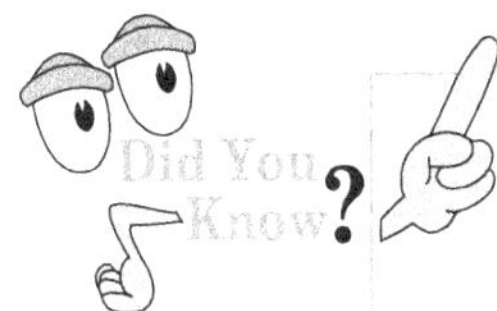

> ***Algae are important as primary producers of organic matter at the base of food chain. They also provide oxygen for the aquatic organisms.***
> ***The branch dealing with the study of algae is called phycology or aloglogy.***
> ***The gelatinous substance "agar" used in culture medium for growing microorganisms (such as bacteria) in laboratory and is made from red algae.***
> ***What is algal bloom?***
> ***An algal bloom is a rapid increase in the density of algae in an aquatic system. Algal blooms sometimes are natural phenomena, but their frequency, duration and intensity are increased by nutrient pollution. Algae can multiply quickly in waterways with an overabundance of nitrogen and phosphorus, particularly when the water is warm and the weather is calm. This proliferation causes blooms of algae that turn the water noticeably green, although other colours can occur.***

CONNECTING TOPIC

VIRUSES

Virus (means poisonous fluid) is the smallest microorganisms that is visible only through electron microscope. Viruses are distinguished from free living microbes such as bacteria and fungi with respect to their small size and relatively simple structures. They do not show most of the characteristics of living things. For example, they do not respire, feed, grow, excrete or move on their own. They are just capable of reproducing. Viruses can multiply and reproduce only inside the cells of other organisms like plant, animal and bacterial cells. The cell in which they multiply is called host-cell. The virus gets inside the host cells and makes hundred and thousand copies of itself by using the host machinery. Viruses are non-living outside the host cells but start reproducing as soon as they enter inside the host cell. Hence, viruses are said to be on the border line dividing the living things from non-living things. Rous Sarcoma virus and HIV are examples of viruses. A virus is made up of a core of genetic material, either DNA or RNA, surrounded by a protective coat called a capsid which is made up of protein. Sometimes the capsid is surrounded by an additional spikey coat called the envelope.

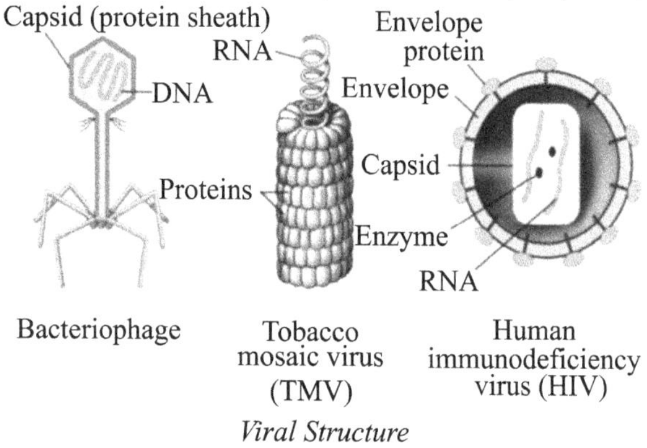

Viral Structure

MICROORGANISMS AND US

By now, we have learnt that there is a huge variety of microorganisms on Earth. These organisms play a vital role in keeping the planet running. Let us now discuss, *how Microorganisms are beneficial to mankind and how they keep the planet Earth running?*

BENEFICIAL MICROORGANISMS

Microbes or microorganisms carry out about 90% of the biochemical reactions that occur on our planet. They are useful in the following ways —
(i)   Food and beverage industry.
(ii) Making medicines and vaccines.
(iii) Increasing soil fertility.
(iv) Cleaning of environment.

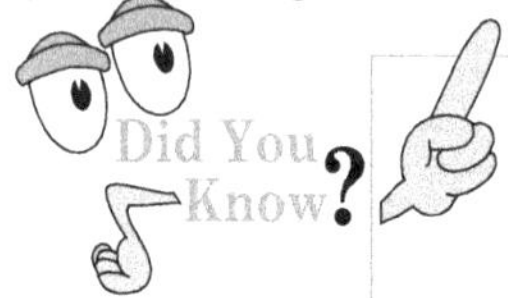

- *Curd is a nutritious food that helps in digestion. Lactobacillus bacteria inhibit the growth of disease – causing microorganism inside intestinal tract and promote beneficial bacteria needed for digestion.*
- *Streptococcus and Lactobacillus species are involved in the manufacturing of cheese.*

Food and Beverage Industry

(i)   Bacteria help us in making food. They play an important role in formation of curd and cheese. (You must have seen your mother adding a teaspoon of curd to lukewarm milk. Have you ever thought why she does so?) She adds curd to the warm milk because curd contains a bacterium called *Lactobacillus*. This bacteria multiplies and converts the milk into curd. Similarly, there is another bacterium called *Rennin* that is used for making cheese from milk. Rennin ferments the milk sugar to produce lactic acid. This lactic acid separates the milk into solid curd and liquid called milk whey. Whey is the watery part of the milk that is separated from curd during cheese formation. Later on, this separated curd from the milk is used to make cheese.

(ii) Idli, dosa and dhokla also require yeast in their preparations. Yeast makes dhokla soft and fluffy. Mixture of dal and rice for making idli and dosa is allowed to stand for few hours. As fermentation occurs, the mixture rises and becomes sour.

(iii) Bacteria and yeast also help in the process of fermentation.

Fermentation is the process of converting a complex organic substance into simpler substance with the action of bacteria or yeast. Both of these organisms can ferment the sugar present in various foods like fruits, milk, grain etc. During the process of breakdown of sugar, alcohol is formed and carbon dioxide is released.

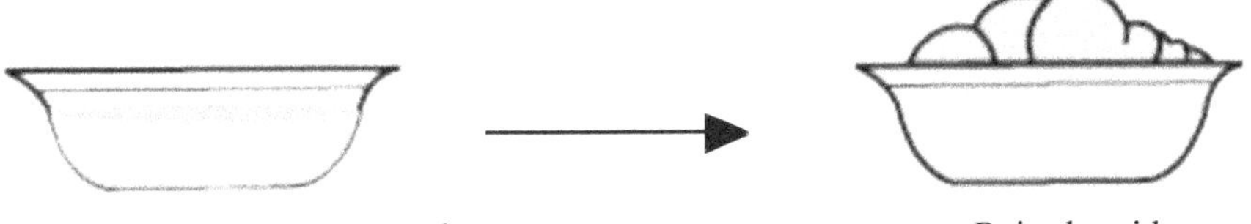

$$\text{Glucose} \xrightarrow[\text{Oxygen}]{\text{without}} \text{Alcohol} + \text{Energy} + CO_2$$

Yeast is commonly used in baking of cake or bread as it ferments the sugar present in the dough into carbon dioxide. The carbon dioxide released from the yeast fills the dough and increases its volume. When this dough is baked, more bubbles of gas are formed due to the heat. As the gas escapes, the bread rises and becomes soft and fluffy.

Maida mixed with yeast powder   Raised maida

Baking of Cake

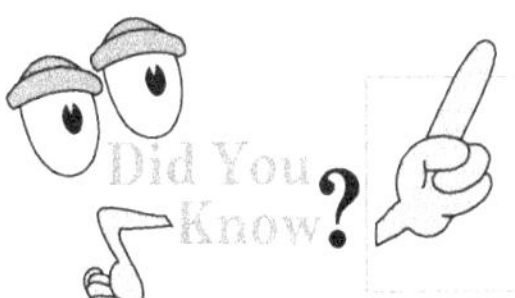

Baker's yeast (Saccharomyces cerevisiae) is used in baking industry.

Let us perform an experiment to observe the increase in volume during fermentation of sugar by yeast cells.

Take two test tubes and mark them as A and B. Clamp both the test tubes on a stand and keep it in a safer place. Pour about 4-5 drops of yeast and sugar mixture in test tube B only. Test tube A acts as control test tube, with only water in it. Now take two stretched balloons and tie them to the mouth of each test tube. Now set both the test tubes aside in a warm place and record your observations.

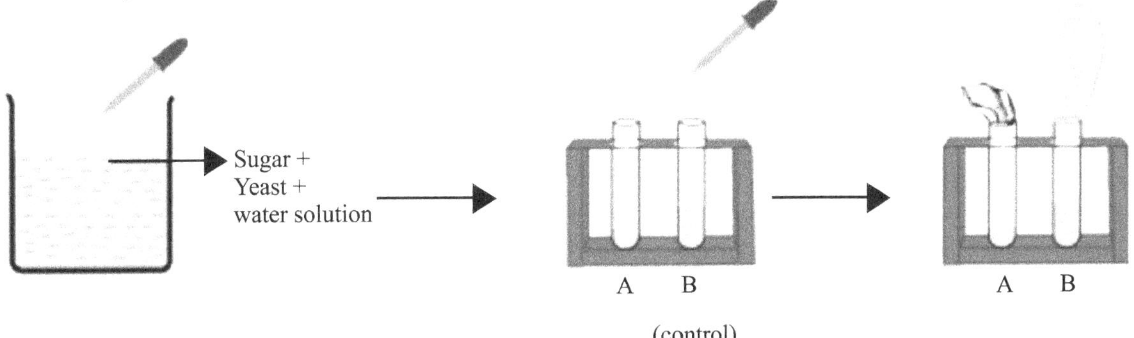

Observation : You will observe that balloon in test tube B inflates after few minutes whereas balloon in test tube A remains deflated.

Result : This happens because yeast cells present in the solution of test tube B ferments the sugar present in it. As the yeast keeps on feeding sugar, it produces carbon dioxide. Since, there is no place for carbon dioxide to go except for going up, so it fills the balloon. This process is known as fermentation.

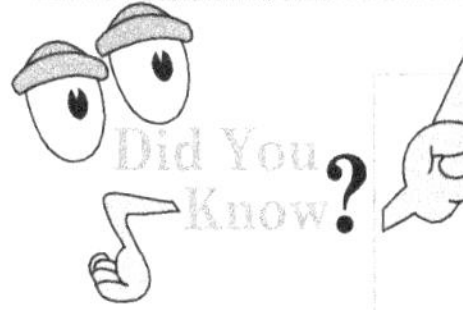

Microbes in the healthy human body
Some microbes live in the human body without causing any harm and help in keeping our body functioning normally. However, if their numbers become unbalanced, they may make us sick.

Ear (outer)	*Aspergillus (fungus)*
Skin	*Candida (fungus)*
Small intestine	*Clostridium*
Intestines	*Escherichia coli*
Vagina	*Gardnerella vaginalis*
Stomach	*Lactobacillus*
Urethra	*Mycobacterium*
Nose	*Staphlococcus aureus*
Mouth	*Streptococcus salivarius*
Large intestine	*Trichomonas hominis (protozoa)*

(iv) Microorganisms are also used for commercial production of alcohol like beer and wine. Beer is prepared by the fermentation of sugar in barley and wine by fermentation of sugar in grapes.

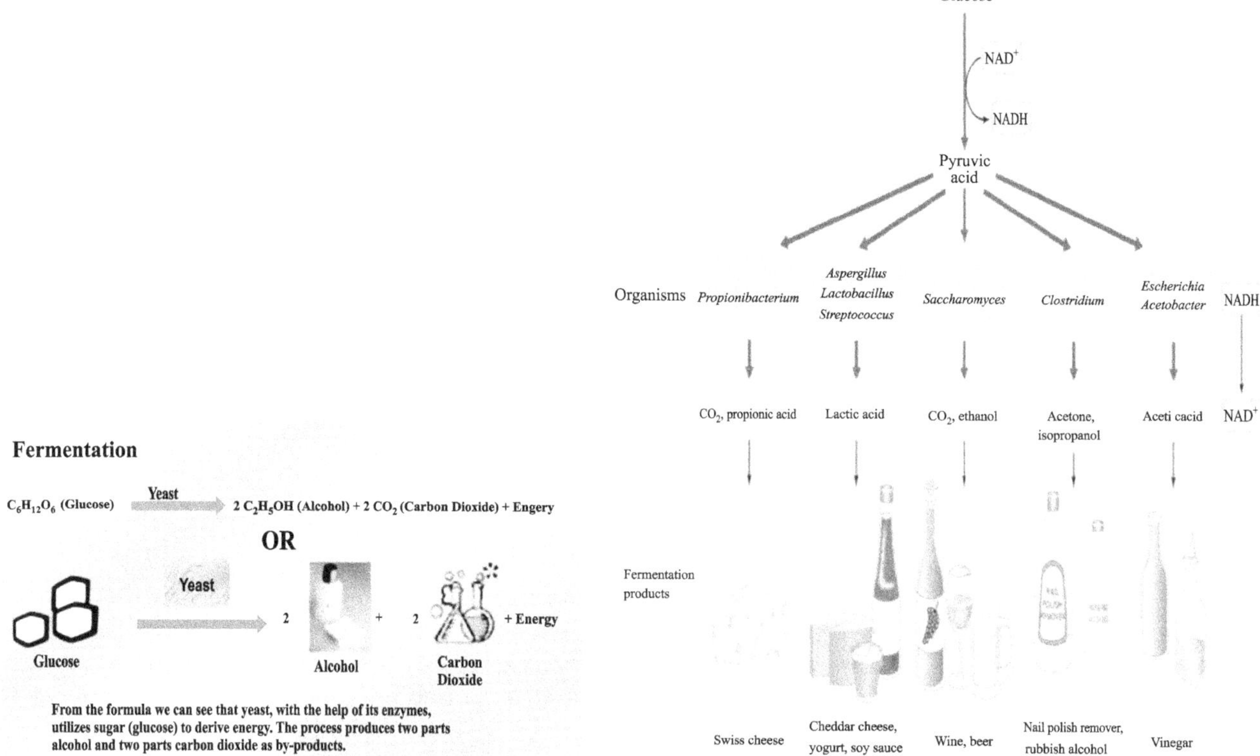

Fermentation

$$C_6H_{12}O_6 \text{ (Glucose)} \xrightarrow{\text{Yeast}} 2\ C_2H_5OH \text{ (Alcohol)} + 2\ CO_2 \text{ (Carbon Dioxide)} + \text{Engery}$$

OR

From the formula we can see that yeast, with the help of its enzymes, utilizes sugar (glucose) to derive energy. The process produces two parts alcohol and two parts carbon dioxide as by-products.

Microbes used in the process of fermentation

Let's Do Activity

Let us perform an experiment to show that fermentation of sugar by yeast produces alcohol.

Take some warm water in a flask so that it is one-third full. Then add 2-3 teaspoons of sugar into it and mix well. Now add half a teaspoon of yeast to it. Cover the flask and keep it in a warm place for 4 to 5 hours. Now smell the solution.

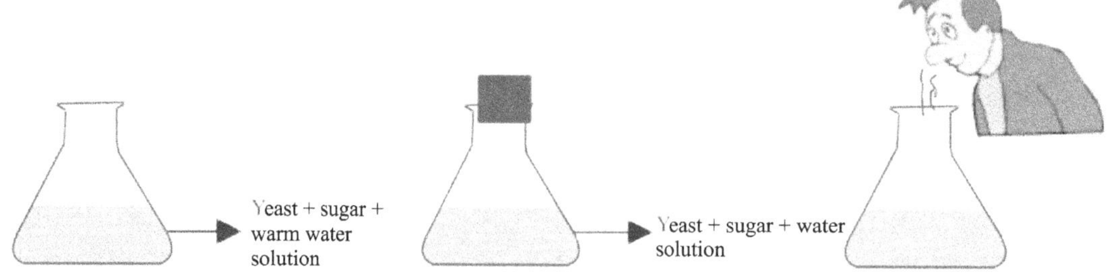

Observation : The solution smell like alcohol because the yeast in the solution converts the sugar into alcohol and releases carbon dioxide. This process is known as fermentation.

$$\text{Glucose} \xrightarrow[\text{absence of oxygen}]{\text{In the}} \text{Alcohol} + \text{Energy} + CO_2$$

Thus, yeast is used in the manufacture of alcoholic drinks such as beer and wine.

Making Medicines and Vaccines

Bacteria and fungi are used for making antibiotics and vaccines.

(i) **Antibiotics :**

   Antibiotics are produced by certain microorganisms, to kill other disease-causing microorganisms. These medicines either kill or stop the growth of disease – causing microorganisms. Penicillin, tetracycline, streptomycin and erythromycin are

some examples of antibiotics. Antibiotics destroy the bacteria by weakening their cell wall. As a result of weakened cell wall, the immune cells such as white blood cells enter into the bacterial cell and causes cell lysis. **Cell lysis** is the process of destruction of cells such as blood cell and bacteria.

Though antibiotics are used to kill disease causing microorganisms, it is still necessary to take certain precautions while using antibiotics.

- *Edward Jenner developed the smallpox vaccination method in 1796. In 1788, the English town Gloucestershire was plagued with smallpox. Jenner observed that milkmaids who suffered the mild disease of cowpox never contracted smallpox. Subsequently, Jenner proved that by being inoculated with cowpox, one could remain immune to smallpox. The invention of this method of vaccination ultimately resulted in the eradication of smallpox.*
- *Jenner coined the term "vaccination," which comes from the latin world "vaccinia" meaning 'cowpox'.*
- *The inoculation of a vaccine in the body to produce immunity is called vaccination.*

Precautions that need to be taken while using antibiotics are –

(i)   Always take antibiotics on the advice of well-qualified doctor.

(ii)   Courses of antibiotic should be completed as per the prescription given by the doctor.

(iii)   Always take antibiotics in the right amount and at the right time. An inappropriate dose of antibiotic makes it ineffective. Also, its excessive consumption may kill the useful bacteria present in our body.

(ii)   **Vaccines :**

Microorganisms are also used as vaccines. (You must have heard about pulse polio programme organised by government. Have you ever thought what are these programmes all about?) Polio drops given to children are actually vaccines. Vaccines protect humans and other animals from several diseases such as cholera, typhoid, tuberculosis, hepatitis, chicken pox, measles, polio and small pox. Vaccines are the suspension of killed microbes that mimic the disease causing microorganisms and produce immunity to a particular disease. When they are swallowed or injected into the body of patient, the body produces antibodies to fight them. *Antibodies* are body's defensive cells that fight against several infectious foreign substances. The antibodies remain in the body and protect it from any future attack of germs.

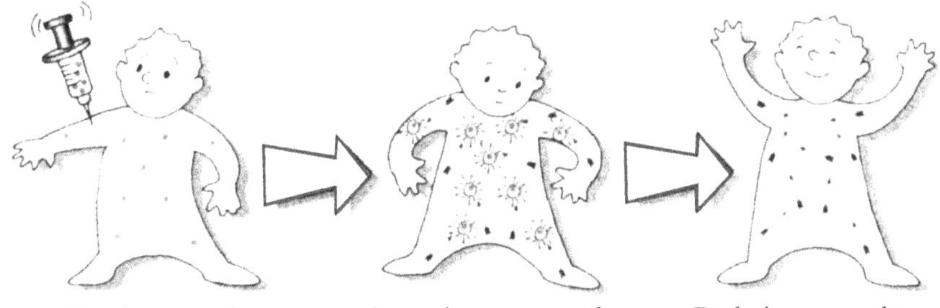

Use of vaccine

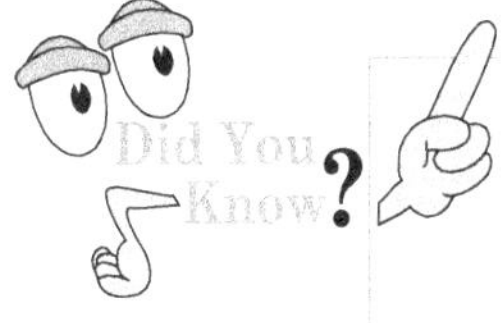

Anthrax vaccine

The anthrax vaccine was developed by Louis Pasteur in 1881. Anthrax was the first disease for which the causative agent was isolated in 1863 by C.J. Davaine, and the vaccine was developed. Pasteur studied about the bacterium that causes the disease and performed many experiments. Finally he produced a vaccine with weak and harmless anthrax bacterium and tested it on cattle and sheep.

☛ **Why do we take antibiotics?**

SOLUTION :

Antibiotics are chemicals. When these chemicals are put into the body they kill or stop the growth of certain kinds of germs. In other words, they help our body to fight diseases. The body is then said to have developed immunity against the disease. Vaccine is therefore called as **immunization**. Hence, vaccines teach our immune system to fight against that microbe. If you ever get sick with a particular disease, you will be able to fight the infection as you are vaccinated against that microbe.

It is important to get rid of the fever as quickly as possible as it destroys vital proteins in our body.

Fever

Our body has an average temperature of 98.6° Fahrenheit or 32°C when it is healthy. Some diseases make this temperature rise and we call this higher temperature fever. So, what exactly is fever?

Fever actually helps us fight sickness. Fever makes the vital processes and organs in the body work faster. The body produces more hormones, enzymes and blood cells. As our blood circulates faster, we breathe faster to get rid of wastes and poisons in our system.

How penicillin was discovered?

Penicillin was the first antibiotic discovered by Alexander Fleming in 1929 and received nobel prize in 1945.

How penicillin was discovered by Alexander Fleming?

Alexander Fleming accidently discovered penicillin. He was actually working on a culture of disease-causing microorganisms called Staphylococci. He left the culture and went for a holiday. When he returned from the holiday, he noticed that petri dishes were contaminated by a fungus and bacteria. Staphylococcus could not grow in the area because of invaded mould (fungus). The fungus invaded into the culture dish from nearby opened window. Fleming extracted the antibiotic substance from the mould and named it penicillin.

Increasing Soil Fertility

Microorganisms such as bacteria and algae enrich the soil with essential nutrients. These nutrients are required by plants for their normal growth and development.

(How microorganisms enrich the soil with nutrients?) There are trillions of tiny bacteria in soil. These bacteria feed upon dead plants and animals and break them into their component parts. Then these rotting parts of plants and animals get mixed with the soil and enrich the soil with nutrients. These nutrients are then recycled back in the atmosphere through food chains. Bacteria that helps in breaking down of dead plants and animals are called **decomposing bacteria** or **decomposers**. The decomposers convert dead organic matter into rich humus, thereby enriching the soil with nutrients.

Some bacteria such as *Rhizobium* live in the root nodules of plants such as gram, pea, etc. These bacteria can fix atmospheric nitrogen and convert it into usable nitrogenous compounds. These nitrogenous compounds can be easily absorbed and utilized by plants for synthesis of proteins and other compounds. Such type of bacteria are called **nitrogen fixers**. They produce nitrogen in exchange for carbohydrate produced by pea and bean plants. Some blue green algae can also fix atmospheric nitrogen.

Cleaning of Environment

Microbes like bacteria and fungi play an important role in cleaning the environment. Bacteria and fungi break down complex pollutants into simpler substances to gain energy and nutrients by the process called **biodegradation**. They clean up hazardous waste from industries, farms, and cities and oil spills. The Scientists also use bacteria to remove pollutants from the soil. They help recycle dead animals and plants.

Some microbes are also used in biological treatment of sewage and industrial effluents. They break down the waste material into a usable form which helps in cleaning the environment. This is nature's method of keeping the environment free from pollution.

Note:
Bioremediation

Bioremediation is the use of organisms to metabolise pollutants. It involves break down and consumption of pollutants into harmless natural substances by the help of microorganisms. The microbes used for bioremediation are called **bioremediators** which include bacteria and fungi.

Bioaugmentation

Bioaugmentation is the process of adding genetically engineered microbes to a system to act as bioremediators.

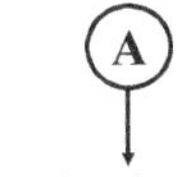

Let us perform an activity to understand how microbes help in cleaning environment

Collect the garbage from your house and separate them into two groups A and B. Group A contains wastes like dead leaves, peels of fruits and vegetable, newspaper etc. Group B contains wastes like polythene bags, glass, aluminium foil, plastic toys etc.

(A)

Plant and animal wastes, newspaper etc.

(B)

Polythene bags, glass, aluminum foil, plastic toy etc.

Put these garbage into two different bins and label them as A and B. Now cover both the pots with soil and leave them aside for 2-3 weeks.

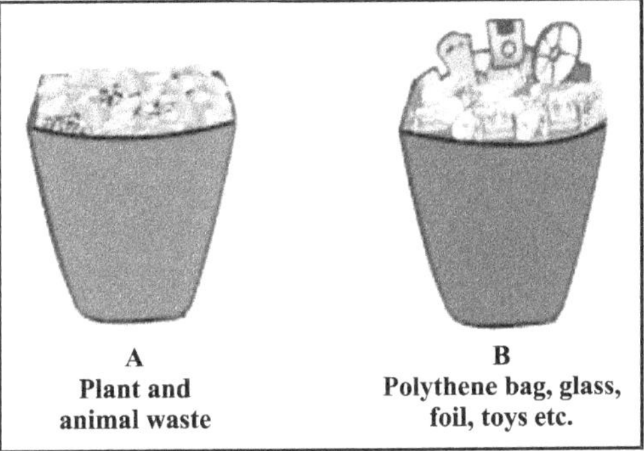

Observation after 2-3 weeks : The waste in bin A decomposes whereas waste in bin B does not get decomposed.
Explanation – The microorganism present in the soil decomposes the organic matter in waste A and turns them into dark brown manure. This manure adds nutrients to soil and increases its fertility. This process is known as decomposition. Decomposition is the process of breaking down organic matter from dead bodies of plants and animals into raw materials like carbon dioxide, water and nutrients. This process occurs with the help of decomposing organisms like bacteria and fungi. The decomposing organisms contain enzymes that are able to digest plant and animal waste. But, these bacteria are not able to digest some of the substances like polythene bag, plastic toys, aluminium foil etc. It is because they do not have enzymes for digesting these substances. Therefore the waste present in pot B does not get degraded or decomposed by decomposing bacteria and hence remains in its usual form.

CONNECTING TOPIC

Some other Uses of Microorganisms

(i) Certain bacteria and protozoan are found in the digestive system of some animals like cows, goats and sheep. These bacteria help the animals digest grass and plants.

(ii) Bacteria are useful in tobacco, leather and jute industries. Tanning, a process to make animals skin into leather by treating it with chemicals, is done with the help of bacteria.

(iii) Some bacteria decompose animal waste, leafy waste from crops etc. in the absence of oxygen to produce methane. Methane is used as a fuel and is one of the chief constituents of biogas.

CASE STUDY-1 : Friendly Microorganisms

Initially we though that all the micro-organisms are harmful and cause diseases. Later discovery showed that only few microbes are harmful. Certain micro-organisme are used for various purpose by human beings as well as in nature.

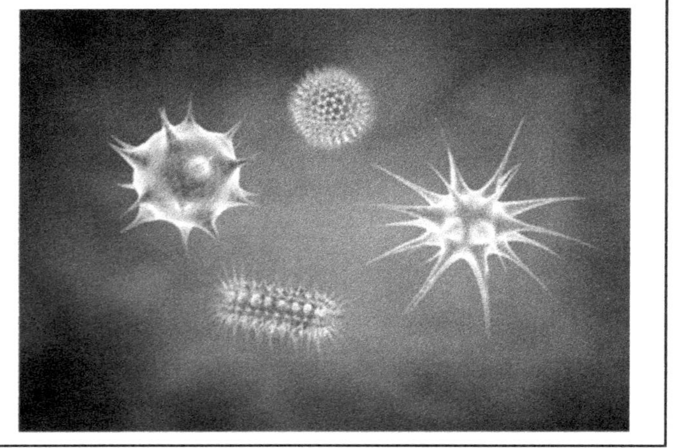

CASE - I : *Shella was observing the preparation her mom is doing in the kitchen for making Dosa and Idli. Her mother left the mixture of Dal and Rice undisturbed for few hours. After sometime, Sheela observed the mixture has resin up. Why is it so?*

As fermentation occurs, the mixture of dal and rice rises and becomes sour.

CASE - II : *During winters, sheela observes that her mother wraps a warm piece of cloth around the container with milk to make curd. Why does she do this?*

The bacteria needs high temperature to turn milk into curd. In winters a warm cloth wrapped around the container will help in setting the curd faster.

CASE - III : *After rain Pooja observed all the sewage waste was gathered near her house. She was worried that from this waste many diseases will spread. After 2-3 days she observed the decomposition of waste has started. How this would happen?*

Some microbes start acting and the sewage waste and breakdown the waste material into a usable form which helps in cleaning the environment.

 ## Think Out of the Box

Q 1. In India, it is seen that the people are scared to take COVID-19 vaccination as it contains corona virus and can cause an infection. What is the best possible explanation to clear this myth?

Q 2. Microbes will never grow in the food which kept inside the refri greater ? Do you agree?

HARMFUL MICROORGANISMS

By now, you have learnt that some microorganisms are beneficial to humans. (But are all microorganisms helpful?) Not all microorganisms are helpful as there are some microorganisms that cause diseases in humans, animals and plants. These disease causing microorganisms are called **pathogen** *or* **germs**.

At times, germs enter the human body. If the germs are present in large numbers, the person is said to be infected. These germs do not allow the body to function properly and the person becomes sick. A particular disease is caused by a specific kind of germ. *For example*, typhoid is caused by a kind of bacteria which is different from the one which causes cholera. Let us discuss about agents that spread diseases. Diseases can spread through various means such as air, water food and vector.

Means of Spread of Diseases

(i) **Air :** Certain disease causing microorganisms are expelled into air by coughing, sneezing, talking etc. When a person suffering from common cold or flu sneezes, coughs or spits, germs are released in the air. As a result, the person breathing this air can get infected. The diseases that can spread through air are common cold, flu, chicken pox, mumps, measles, tuberculosis, polio etc.

(ii) **Water :** Sometimes the causal microorganism gets mixed with water and spreads water-borne diseases like, cholera, typhoid, hepatitis etc.

(iii) **Food :** Sometimes the disease is transferred from the food that we eat. The bacteria may survive in the food that is not properly cooked and hence causes food-borne diseases.

(iv) **Vector :** Vector is an organism that carries microbes and is responsible for its transmission. Diseases such as malaria are spread by animals called vector or carrier. The vector

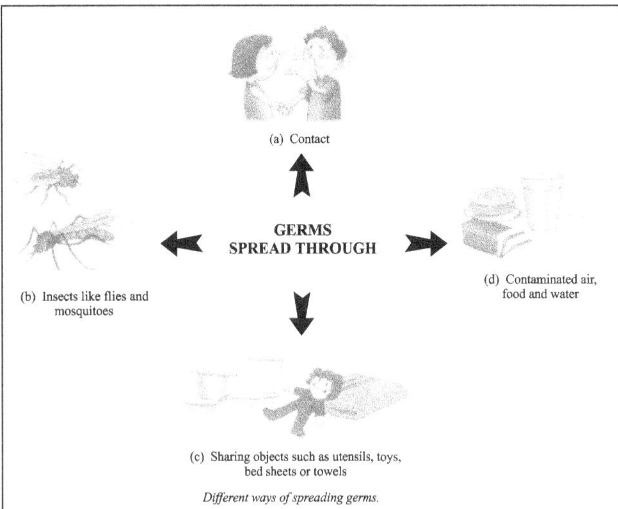

Different ways of spreading germs.

for malarial disease is female *Anopheles* mosquito. *Aedes* mosquito acts as a carrier for the dengue virus. Another example of vector that spread disease is housefly. Housefly sits on uncovered food and transfers microorganisms or pathogen to it. Hence, it is always advised not to leave the food uncovered.

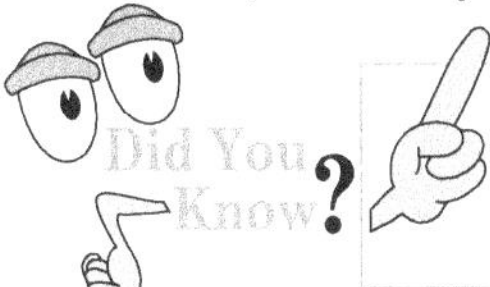

During sneezing, a germ can travel at 50 miles per hour across a room.

Aedes mosquito has small, black and white strips on its legs and back. It bites during day time in early hours of morning and late hours of afternoon.

Communicable Diseases

The diseases that can be transferred from an infected person to a healthy person through air, water, food and vector are called *communicable diseases*. Cholera, tuberculosis and common cold. Some example of communicable diseases.

☞ 1. **Why it is advised to stay away from the person who is suffering from cough and cold?**

2. **Why do people say "Do not let the water to collect anywhere in your house or locality".**

SOLUTION :

1. *Methods to prevent the spread of communicable disease*
   I. Preventive measures to be taken for air-borne diseases
   (i) Stay away from infected person.
   (ii) Keeping a handkerchief on nose while sneezing.
   (iii) Complete isolation from diseased person.
   (iv) Get vaccinated at right time.
   II. Preventive measures for water borne diseases
   (i) Ensure proper disposal of sewage.
   (ii) Ensure safe supply of drinking water.
   (iii) Maintain good sanitary habits.
   (iv) Always drink boiled water.
   (v) Get vaccinated at right time.
   III. Preventive measures for vector–borne diseases
   (i) Do not allow water to stagnate in your surroundings.
   (ii) Keep your surroundings neat and clean.
   (iii) Use mosquito repellant.
2. The stagnant water is a place for mosquito breeding and the female *Anopheles* mosquito is the carrier of malarial parasite.

There are certain Don'ts that make conditions unfavourable for growth of microorganisms and certain Do's that will help destroying diseases causing microorganisms. Find out those Don't and Do's and write your answers in the space provided below.

	"Don'ts" that make conditions unfavourable for the growth of Microorganisms		*"Do's" that destroys disease causing Microorganisms*
1.	*Do not keep your surroundings dirty.*	*1.*	*Get Vaccinated at right time.*
2.		*2.*	
3.		*3.*	
4.		*4.*	

Table : Some common human diseases caused by microorganisms

	Human Diseases	*Causative Micro-organisms*	*Transmitting agents*		*Preventive Measures (General)*
(i)	*Tuberculosis*	*Bacteria*	*Air*	*(i)*	*Isolation of the infected person.*
				(ii)	*Vaccination at suitable age.*
(ii)	*Measles*	*Virus*	*Air*		
(iii)	*Chicken Pox*	*Virus*	*Air/Contact*		
(iv)	*Polio*	*Virus*	*Air/Water*		
(v)	*Cholera*	*Bacteria*	*Water/Food*	*(i)*	*Maintaining personal hygiene.*
				(ii)	*Consuming properly cooked food.*
				(iii)	*Drinking boiled water.*
(vi)	*Typhoid*	*Bacteria*	*Water*	*(iv)*	*Vaccination*
(vii)	*Hepatitis A*	*Virus*	*Water*	*(i)*	*Drinking boiled water.*
				(ii)	*Vaccination*
(viii)	*Malaria*	*Protozoa*	*Mosquito*	*(i)*	*Using mosquito nets or repellents.*
				(ii)	*Spraying insecticides.*
				(iii)	*Destroying breeding grounds of mosquitoes such as stagnant water.*

Table : Some common plant diseases caused by microorganisms

Plant disease	Means of transmission
Bacterial diseases	
Soft Rot / Red stripe of sugarcane	Air
Citrus canker	Air / water / insects
Bacterial Blight of gram	Air
Viral diseases	
Tobacco mosaic disease	Wind / water
Yellow vein mosaic of bhindi (okra)	Insect
Tomato mosaic	Air
Fungal diseases	
Rust of wheat	Air / seeds
Late blight of potato	Rain / wind
Fungal blight of gram	Wind / water

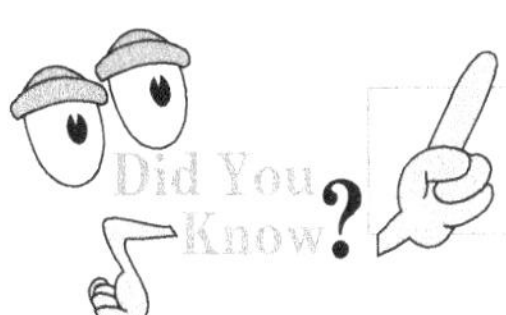

Hepatitis-B virus causes many deaths in only one day as by AIDS virus in one year. In India, about 4.30 crore people suffer from hepatitis-B. The vaccine against hepatitis-B is available.

FOOD PRESERVATION

Food which is left in the open for a few days often gets spoiled. It becomes blackish, smelly and mushy. This is because of the action of microbes like bacteria and fungi. They feed on the food and break it down into simpler substances. During the process, carbon dioxide and poisonous substances are produced. This is called **food spoilage**. Consuming such food can cause **food poisoning**. Therefore food should be preserved to avoid getting these infections. **Food preservation** is the process of treating and handling food to stop or slow down spoilage (loss of quality, edibility or nutritional value).

Preservation usually involves preventing the growth of bacteria, yeasts, fungi, and other micro-organisms (although some methods work by introducing benign bacteria, or fungi to the food), as well as reducing the oxidation of fats which causes rancidity. Food preservation also includes processes that inhibit natural discoloration which occurs during food preparation, such as the enzymatic browning reaction in apples after they are cut.

Expiry Date & Best Before !!!
You must have noticed that most of the food items that we get from market have "expiry date" or "best before" on them. What are these?
Expiry data refers to the date before which the supplier wants the food to be consumed. It is unhealthy to consume food after the expiry date because they are likely to have deteriorated either in flavour, texture, appearance or nutrional value.

☛ **Why we get very sick if we eat food that has gone bad?**

SOLUTION :

It is because of food poisoning. *Food poisoning* is a food-borne illness that occurs suddenly after you consume a contaminated food or drink. Sometimes, the food is spoiled by some microorganisms producing certain toxic substances. These toxic substances make the food poisonous. The typical symptoms of food poisoning are nausea, vomiting, abdominal cramp and diarrhea. (But how do decomposers get onto the food?) The spores of bacteria and fungi are small and light. They are blown in the air. Food left in the open is exposed to them and they start to grow. Bacteria and fungi grow and multiply quickly when there is sufficient air, water and warmth. Under these conditions, food decays very quickly.

(If you take a piece of bread, sprinkle a few drops of water and leave it undisturbed in a warm place for a few days, what do you think will happen?) You will observe a cotton like mesh growing on the surface of slice of bread. This thread like structures is a type of mould (fungus). Fungus spoils the bread and makes it unfit for consumption.

Microorganisms are one of the major causes of food spoilage. Therefore, it is advised to preserve the food properly before storing. Food preservation creates conditions unfavourable for the growth of microbes. Different food preservation techniques are employed for different types of food.

Advantages of preserving food are —

(i)   It avoids wastage of food.

(ii)   Preservation techniques facilitate the distribution of food like fruits and vegetables to other countries.

(iii) This allows the availability of food every year. For example, frozen strawberries are available in all year.

(iv) It maintains nutritional value, texture and flavor of food.

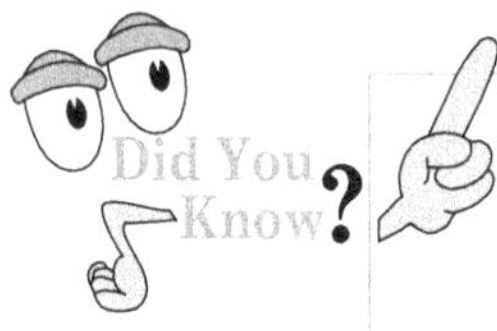

Pasteurization

Pasteurization is process in which food is heated to a temperature that kills harmful germs and then cooled quickly. Heating does not harm the flavour and quality of food. Pasteurization is also used with beer, wine, fruit juices, cheese and egg products.

French chemist and biologist Louis Pasteur (1822-1895) who invented pasteurization, developed the germ theory, founded the field of bacteriology and created the vaccines against anthrax and rabies.

COMMON METHODS OF FOOD PRESERVATION

Heating

Heating food at high temperature kills microbes. For example, milk and water are boiled to kill microbes.

(The milk stored in packets does not get spoiled as it has been pasteurized.) The pasteurized milk can be consumed directly as it is free from microbes. The milk is made sterile by heating it at 70°C for about 15 to 30 seconds. Then the boiled milk is suddenly chilled and stored inside the packets. This process is known as **pasteurization**.

Cooling

Storing of food in refrigerator slows the bacterial action because of low temperature. All food and drinks like meat, fruits and vegetables and beverages are preserved by this method. However, once the food is taken out of freezer and warmed, microbes start growing again.

Chemical preservatives

Certain chemical preservatives like sodium benzoate and sodium metabisulphite helps to control the microbial growth. These are used to preserve jams, squashes and ketch ups.

Other examples of preservatives used are –

(a)   **Salting :** It checks the growth of bacteria by forcing microorganisms to lose water by a process called osmosis. It is used to preserve meat, fish, pickles, chips etc.

(b)   **Sugar :** It inhibits the growth of bacteria and therefore is used as preservative in jams, jellies and squashes. Sugar also makes microbes lose water by osmosis.

(c)   **Pickling :** Pickling is used to preserve pickles. It uses preservative qualities of salt along with the preservative qualities of acid, such as vinegar. Vinegar provides acidic medium to pickles and inhibits the growth of bacteria. Cucumber, for example is preserved for several years when it is soaked in a 10% of salt water brine for several days.

Drying

Drying is the oldest method of food preservation. It removes all the moisture from the food. As a result, there will be no bacterial growth. Cereals, pulses, spices and dry fruits are stored by drying method.

Canning

Canning stores the food for a long time. It is a process whereby you boil the food to kill the bacteria and then store it in a can with a seal. Many canned food items are available in market. However note that after breaking the seal of the can, bacteria can enter and spoil the food. So, it is advised to refrigerate the food contents as soon as the can is opened.

Freeze drying

It is a special type of food preservation. In this, the food is frozen and then placed in a vacuum to change the ice crystals directly into vapour form. It involves the direct conversion of solid form into vapour without going into liquid stage. This method is used to make instant cooling.

Give an example of each of these preserving methods of food.

Method	How it works	Example
Pickling	The food is mixed with vinegar. The acid in vinegar stops microbes from growing	
Drying	Microbes cannot grow without water.	
Preservatives	Preservatives are chemicals that kill microbes or stop them from growing.	
Canning	Food is cooked and then sealed so that bacteria can not get in.	
Sugar	Food is cooked in sugar. The sugar is too concentrated for microbes.	
Radiation	Radiation kills microbes.	
Salting	Microbes cannot grow in salt. It is too concentrated.	

☞ **Why it is advisable to consume sweets made from milk like rasagulla within 24 hours of preparation?**

SOLUTION :

Every food item has a specific shelf life, beyond which it may become unsuitable for consumption. Shelf life is the length of time a product may be stored so that it remains suitable for consumption.

Look up the packets of food items listed in the given table. Try to fill in the required information.

Sl. No.	Type of Food	Method of Packaging (Bottles, Cans, Cartons)	Storage area	Shelf life
1.	Crispy Items (Chips, Biscuits)			
2.	Diary products (Butter, Ghee, Chocolates)			
3.	Jam, Sauce			

Based on your observation answer the following questions :–
(i) Which type of food items have the shortest "best before" or "expiry date"?
(ii) Which type of food have the longest "best before" or "expiry date"?

CASE STUDY-2 : Food Preservation

Food preservation is the process of treating food to stop or slow down spillage, loss of quality, edibility or nutritional value.

CASE - I : *Nupur observes that her mother keeps ghee at the room temperature irrespective of any season. What can be the reason behind this?*

Ghee has zero water content, so it can be kept at room temperature. The absence of water prevents the growth of microbes, and hence, the spoilage of food.

CASE - II : *Sometimes a fungal growth is observed in a home made pickle. Suggest a probable reason for this centre.*

Less oil in pickle can result in the growth of micro-organisms.

CASE - III : *Why are chips vacuum seals.*

Vacuum sealing prevents the growth of microbes due to the absence of oxygen.

CASE - IV : *Sometimes we see that the juice poches which we buy from market are bloated. Why is it so?*

Bloated juice pouches indicate the presence of microorganisms inside it. When a microbe feeds on the content of pouch, it produces gas which makes to pouch bloat.

 ## Think Out of the Box

Q 1. Why do we boil and then refrigerate the pasteurized milk?

Q 2. What is the best way to preserve sugarcane?

NITROGEN FIXATION

Nitrogen fixation is a process that causes free nitrogen, which is a relatively inert gas plentiful in air, to combine chemically with other elements and forms more reactive nitrogen compounds such as ammonia, nitrates, or nitrites.

Normally nitrogen does not react with other elements. Nitrogen is fixed or combined in nature as nitric oxide by lightning and ultraviolet rays, but more significant amounts of nitrogen are fixed as ammonia, nitrites, and nitrates by soil microorganisms, like *Rhizobium*.

Rhizobium is a soil bacterium that is involved in nitrogen fixation from atmosphere.

(Now as some of the atmospheric nitrogen is fixed by the bacteria present in soil and some by lightning, you must be wondering how this fixed nitrogen is recycled back into the atmosphere). There are certain other bacteria that convert the nitrogenous compound present in soil to nitrogen gas. To understand this process, refer nitrogen cycle.

NITROGEN CYCLE

The nitrogen cycle is a cyclic process that transforms nitrogen and nitrogen containing compounds in nature. Earth's atmosphere has about 78% of nitrogen gas. It forms essential constituent of all living organisms and is essential for many biological processes. It is present in all amino acid, proteins, nucleic acid and vitamins. In plants, nitrogen is a part of chlorophyll molecule. Fixation of nitrogen is an essential process as nitrogen cannot be directly taken by plants and animals. So it needs to be fixed and then converted into some usable compounds. Certain bacteria and some blue green algae are able to fix the nitrogen and assimilate it as organic nitrogen. An example of N_2 fixing bacteria is *Rhizobium*. This process is called **biological fixation**. Once the nitrogen is converted into usable form, it is absorbed from the soil by the plant. Animals obtain this nitrogen directly or indirectly from the plants. When a plant or animal dies, nitrifying bacteria and some fungi present in the soil converts all the organic nitrogen into ammonia, nitrites and nitrates. Another

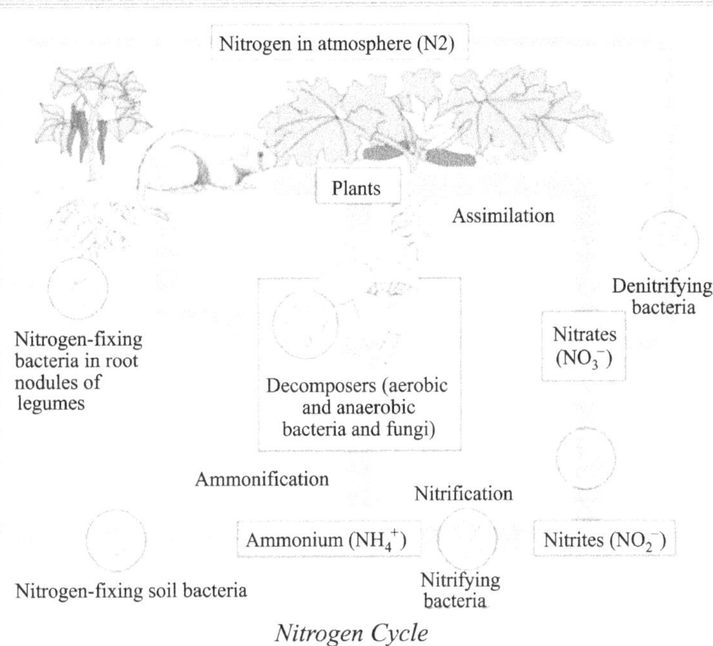

Nitrogen Cycle

type of bacteria then convert these nitrites and nitrates into elemental nitrogen which is then released into atmosphere, completing the nitrogen cycle.

Hence, nitrogen passes from atmosphere to soil and water in the form of simpler compounds and then back into the atmosphere in the form of nitrogen molecule.

Hence, nitrogen cycle involves the following steps-

(i)   *Nitrogen fixation* - It is the process of converting free nitrogen gas of atmosphere into nitrogen compunds using nitrogen fixing bacteria.

(ii) *Nitrogen assimilation :-* It is the proces of conversion of inorganic nitrogen compounds into organic compounds like proteins.

(iii) *Ammonification :* It is the process of conversion of complex organic compounds like proteins into ammonia and ammonium compounds by bacteria and fungi. *Bacillus ramosus, B. Vulgaris* and Actinomycetes are ammonifying bacteria and fungi respectively.

(iv) *Nitrification :* It is the process of conversion of ammonia into nitrates using nitrifying bacteria like *Nitrosomonas* and *Nitrobacter*.

(v)   *Denitrification :* It is the process of converting nitrates to free nitrogen gas using denitrifying bacteria like *Pseudomonas*.

Note :

Two types of nitrogen fixing bacteria

–   *Free-living (non-symbiotic) bacteria such as cyanobacteria (or blue-green algae) Anabaena and Nostoc, Azotobacter, Beijerinckia, and Clostridium*

–   *Mutualistic (symbiotic) bacteria such as Rhizobium, associated with leguminous plants, and Spirillum lipoferum, associated with cereal grasses.*

SUMMARY

- Microorganisms are too small to be seen through naked eyes.
- Bacteria, fungi, viruses, protozoa and algae are five major groups of microorganisms.
- Microbes can survive in all conditions - hot, cold, wet, dry and humid.
- Air, water and moisture are the three main requirements for microbial growth.
- Bacteria play an important role in making curd, bread, cheese and pickles.
- *Fermentation* is the process of converting a complex organic substance into simpler substance with the help of bacteria or yeast.
- *Antibiotics* are medicines that are produced by certain microorganisms, to kill other disease causing microorganisms.
- *Vaccines* are suspension of killed microbes that mimics the disease causing microorganisms.
- *Vaccination* is the protection of the body from infectious disease by administration of vaccines.
- *Antibodies* are protein molecules produced in the blood by immune system to fight against the antigen.
- Microorganisms such as bacteria and fungi enrich the soil with nutrients.
- *Decomposition* is the process of break down of organic matter from the dead bodies of plants and animals into raw materials such as CO_2, H_2O and nutrients.
- Bacteria play an important role in cleaning of environment.
- Microorganisms cannot decompose materials like polythene bags, glass, bottles etc.
- Disease causing microorganisms are called *pathogens*.
- *Communicable diseases* are diseases that spread by harmful microbes from an infected person to a heathy person through air, water or physical contact.
- *Food preservation* is the process of protecting food from the growth of microorganisms.
- *Various modes of food preservation :*
1. Salt – Meat, fish, amla, raw mangoes
2. Edible oil and vinegar – Pickels
3. Sugar – Jams, jellies, squashes
4. Chemical like sodium benzoate and sodium metabisulphite
5. Refrigeration
6. Air tight packaging
- *Pasteurization* is the process of heating milk at 70°C for about 15 to 30 seconds and then rapidly cooling it.
- The cyclic process of nitrogen being fixed, used by plants and animals and later returned to atmosphere is termed as *nitrogen cycle*.

Exercise 1 — Master Boards

Multiple Choice Questions

DIRECTIONS : *This section contains multiple choice questions. Each question has four choices (a), (b), (c) and (d) out of which ONLY ONE is correct.*

1. The vaccine for small pox was discovered by
   (a) Alexandar Fleming   (b) Edward Jenner
   (c) Lovis Pasteur   (d) Rober Koch
2. Which of the following is not a use of micro organisms?
   (a) preparation of medicine
   (b) preparation of food by photosynthesis
   (c) recycling of materials in nature
   (d) increasing the fertility of soil
3. Partial sterilization of a product such as milk at a high temperature is known as
   (a) Pasteurization   (b) Pickling
   (c) Filtration   (d) Refrigeration
4. Which of the following disease can be cured using antibiotics?
   (a) AIDS   (b) Dengue
   (c) Typhoid   (d) Malaria
5. Which among the following statement is not associated with food preservation?
   (a) Preservation of decay a spoilage
   (b) Decreased shelf life
   (c) Air-tight sealing
   (d) Storage for future use

Assertion & Reason

DIRECTIONS : *Each of these questions contains an Assertion followed by reason. Read them carefully and answer the question on the basis of following options. You have to select the one that best describes the two statements.*

(a) If both **Assertion** and **Reason** are **correct** and Reason is the **correct explanation** of Assertion.
(b) If both **Assertion** and **Reason** are correct, but Reason is **not the correct explanation** of Assertion.
(c) If **Assertion** is **correct** but **Reason** is **incorrect**.
(d) If **Assertion** is **incorrect** but **Reason** is **correct**.

1. **Assertion :** Biofertilizer are preferred to chemical fertilizer.
   Reason : Chemical fertilizer are more hazardous to environment.
2. **Assertion :** Beside curdling of milk, LAB also improve curds nutritional activity.
   Reason : LBB, when present in human stomach, check disease causing microbes.
3. **Assertion :** Newer antibiotics are required produced regularly.
   Reason : Pathogen often develop resistance to existing antibiotics.
4. **Assertion :** Atmospheric nitrogen gas is always fixed by nitrogen fixing micro organisms.
   Reason : Decomposer release nitrogen gas from dead bodies of plants and animals.
5. **Assertion :** Curdling is required in the manufacture of cheese.
   Reason : Lactic acid bacteria are used for purpose.

Fill in the Blanks

DIRECTIONS : *Complete the following statements with an appropriate word / term to be filled in the blank space(s).*

1. ______________ can reproduce and multiply only inside the host cell.
2. ______________ spreads by the bite of female *Anopheles* mosquito.
3. The protection of the body from infectious disease by administration of vaccines is called ____________.
4. ______________ accidently discovered penicillin.
5. ______________ teaches our immune system to fight against the microbes.
6. Bacteria such as ____________ can fix atmospheric nitrogen and convert it into usable nitrogenous compounds.
7. The process of breakdown of organic matter from the dead bodies of plants and animals into raw materials is known as ____________.
8. The causative microorganism of disease, measles, is a ____________.
9. Common cold is a/ an ____________ borne disease.
10. Raw mangoes and tamarind can be preserved by ________.

True / False

DIRECTIONS : *Read the following statements and write your answer as true or false.*

1. Microorganisms live only in air.
2. All the microorganisms are harmful.
3. Bacteria and fungi have the ability to decompose organic matter.
4. Amoebic dysentery is caused by a protozoan called *Entamoeba histolytica*.
5. Viruses are non-cellular organisms.
6. Rabies is a fatal disease caused by bacteria.
7. Pasteurization is a technique of preserving food especially milk.
8. Algae is able to convert sugar into alcohol and carbon dioxide.
9. All blue green algae have the ability to fix nitrogen.
10. Rennin converts milk into curd.
11. Viral fever can be treated by giving antibiotics.

Match the Following

DIRECTIONS : *Each question contains two columns which have to be matched. Statement/terms given in column I have to be matched with statement/terms given in column II.*

1.

Column-I (Microorganisms)		Column-II (Examples)
A. Bacteria	p.	*Plasmodium*
B. Protozoan	q.	Yeast
C. Fungi	r.	*Staphylococci*
D. Algae	s.	HIV
E. Viruses	t.	*Spirogyra*

2.

	Column-I (Term)		Column-II (Feature)
A.	Virus	p.	Fungus which is used to make a drug.
B.	Cyanobacteria	q.	A kind of protozoan
C.	*Plasmodium*	r.	They are bacteria having chlorophyll
D.	*Spirogyra*	s.	An ultramicroscopic organism that is visible only through electron microscope.
E.	*Penicillium*	t.	Green filamentous alga commonly found in fresh water habitats

Passage Based Questions

DIRECTIONS : *Study the given paragraph(s) and answer the following questions.*

During unfortunate corona virus lockdown, Kavita started cursing the microbes on earth. On hearing this, Deepak told Kavita that not all the microbes are harmful for us. Many microbes are useful in producing medicines, bioactive molecules and house hold products. Therefore micro-organisms show both beneficial and harmful effects.

1. What helps in the rise of bread or dosa dough?
   (a) Heat   (b) Grinding
   (c) Growth of yeast cell   (d) pressure

2. Which bacteria helps in settling of the curd?
   (a) *Laclobacillus*   (b) *Penicillin*
   (c) *Azetobactor*   (d) *Chizobuin*

3. Which of the following is not used as food preservative?
   (a) Salt   (b) Sugar
   (c) Vinegar   (d) methane

Very Short Answer Questions

1. Which term is used to refer the tiniest organisms that can only be seen through a microscope?

2. Name the instrument used to see microorganisms.

3. Name a food product prepared by the action of bacteria.

4. Which of the two is a spherical bacteria :- coccus or bacillus?

5. Name the microorganisms which are much smaller than bacteria and cause diseases.

6. To which category of microorganisms do the given organism belongs – mushroom and yeast?

7. Name the disease caused by
   (i) *Plasmodium*   (ii) *Entamoeba*
   (iii) *Trypanosoma*

8. Which *Anopheles* mosquito (male or female) transmits *Plasmodium* through its bite?

9. Which microorganism is used in the production of alcohol from sugar?

10. Name one fungus which is used as a food.

11. Name two plant diseases caused by fungi.

12. Name an antibiotic manufactured from fungi.

13. What are pathogens?

14. What do you understand by "expiry date" written on packed food items?

Short Answer Questions

1. What are the major groups of microorganisms? Give two examples of each.

2. How is nitrogen utilized by living organisms?

3. Define antibodies and antibiotics. What precautions should be taken while consuming antibiotics?

4. What is food poisoning?

5. What are preservatives? List the various methods of preservation.

6. How does bacterium *Lactobacillus* helps in curd formation?

7. Identify the types of bacteria shown in the given figure.

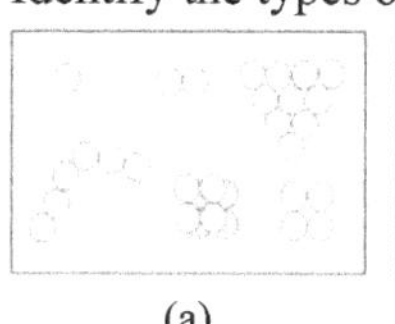 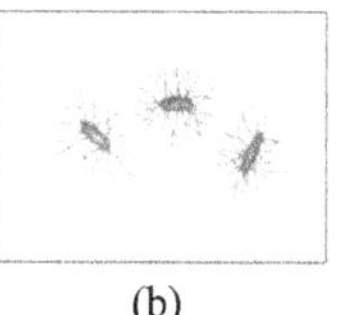 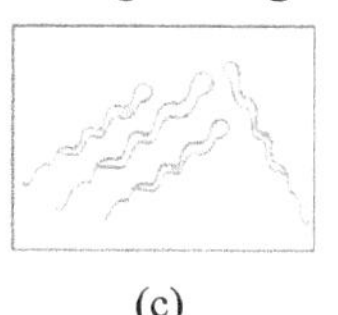

      (a)   (b)   (c)

8. Write three ways by which bacteria are useful to us and three ways by which they are harmful?

9. Which organism makes the bread soft and fluffy?

10. Name two microorganisms which act as decomposer? How is this activity useful to us?

11. How do the following help in food preservation?
   (a) Salt   (b) Sugar
   (c) Heating   (d) Drying.

12. How was penicillin discovered by Alexander Fleming?

13. How decomposers help in enriching the soil with nutrients?

14. All fungi are not microscopic. Do you agree? Explain.

15. How do fungi help in recycling of dead organic materials in nature?

16. Yeast is capable of converting sugar into two products. Name the two products and explain the process involved?

17. What are vectors ? How do they spread diseases?

18. Why is it advised to keep distance from a person suffering from tuberculosis?

19. Why is it advised to maintain good sanitary habits?

Long Answer Questions

1. How is nitrogen recycled back into the atmosphere? How *Rhizobium* helps in nitrogen fixation?

2. List down ten diseases and their causative agents.

3. Write down preventive measures for
   (a) Air–borne diseases
   (b) Water–borne diseases
   (c) Vector – borne diseases

4. Write a short note on vaccines.

5. Explain the role of bacteria in nitrogen cycle.

Reasoning Based Questions

1. Why micro-organisms are important in the environment?

2. Why are antibiotics not effective against 'common cold' and 'flu'?

3. Why are children given vaccination?

4. Why should we not let water called anywhere in the neighborhood?

5. Why all micro-organisms are not considered harmful?

6. Why do you have to use pressure canner for some food and not for others.

7. Why do curd sets faster in summer than in winter?

8. Why is it advised to wash your hands before handling food and after going to the toilet?

9. Why is virus called a mysterious microorganism?

10. Why the Garbage that includes plant and animal waste smells very bad after few days.

1. Priya wants to see the apples that are kept cold will rot or stay edible. So she places the apple in the refrigerator and records the date. What she should use as a control?

2. Sonia noticed that the milk she brought from the market is lumpy and tastes sour. What inference should Sonia make?

3. Shashi and her friends wonder if pond water has microorganisms in it because it smells bad. Describe a way they could find this out.

4. The sealed packets in which food items such as chips are sold are usually filled with nitrogen. What is the use of this nitrogen?

5. How will you determine whether or not food inside a sealed can is infected with microbes?

6. There are few indicators that tell us whether a given sample of food is suitable for consumption or not. List down five indicators of food spoilage.

7. Manish forgot his lunch box in school on Friday. His lunch box has a leftover rice and some vegetables. What do you think would have happened to the leftover food by Monday morning? Give reasons.

8. Microorganisms helps in keeping the planet Earth running. Justify, giving two examples.

9. What is food poisoning? What precautions should be taken to avoid food poisoning?

10. Mention the discoveries made by following scientists.
(i) Louis Pasteur   (ii) Alexander Fleming
(iii) Edward Jenner

11. Microbes are too many to count and too small to find. Comment.

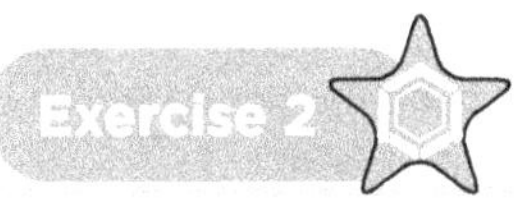

Exercise 2 Master NCERT (Text–book & Exemplar)

1. (a) Microorganisms can be seen with the help of a ______.
   (b) Blue green algae fix ______ directly from air to enhance fertility of soil.
   (c) Alcohol is produced with the help of ______.
   (d) Cholera is caused by ______.

2. Yeast is used in the production of
   (a) sugar   (b) alcohol
   (c) hydrochloric acid   (d) oxygen

3. The following is an antibiotic
   (a) Sodium bicarbonate   (b) Streptomycin
   (c) Alcohol   (d) Yeast

4. Carrier of malaria - causing protozoan is
   (a) female *Anopheles* mosquito
   (b) cockroach
   (c) housefly
   (d) butterfly

5. The most common carrier of communicable diseases is
   (a) ant   (b) housefly
   (c) dragonfly   (d) spider

6. The bread or *idli* dough rises because of
   (a) heat   (b) grinding
   (c) growth of yeast cells   (d) kneading

7. The process of conversion of sugar into alcohol is called
   (a) nitrogen fixation   (b) moulding
   (c) fermentation   (d) infection

8. Match the organisms in column-I with their action in column-II.

Column-I		Column-II
(i) Bacteria	(a)	Fixing Nitrogen
(ii) Rhizobium	(b)	Setting of curd
(iii) Lactobacillus	(c)	Baking of bread
(iv) Yeast	(d)	Causing Malaria
(v) A protozoan	(e)	Causing Cholera
(vi) A Virus	(f)	Causing Aids
	(g)	Producing antibodies

9. Can microorganisms be seen with the naked eye? If not, how can they be seen?

10. What are the major groups of microorganisms?

11. Name the microorganisms which can fix atmospheric nitrogen in the soil.

12. Write 10 lines on the usefulness of microorganisms in our lives.

13. Write a short paragraph on the harms caused by microorganisms.

14. What are antibiotics? What precautions must be taken while taking antibiotics?

1. Unscramble the jumbled words underlined in the following statements.
   (a) Cells of our body produce santiidobe to fight pathogens.
   (b) curbossulite is an air-borne disease caused by a bacterium.
   (c) Xanrhat is a dangerous bacterial disease.
   (d) Yeasts are used in the wine industry because of their property of meronettinaf.

2. Name one commercial use of yeast.

3. Name the process in yeast that converts sugars into alcohol.

4. Polio drops are not given to children suffering from diarrhoea. Why?

5. What will happen to '*pooris*' and '*unused kneaded flour*' if they are left in the open for a day or two?

6. (a) Name two diseases that are caused by virus.
   (b) Write one important characteristic of virus.

7. Give reasons for the following:
   (a) Fresh milk is boiled before consumption while processed milk stored in packets can be consumed without boiling.
   (b) Raw vegetables and fruits are kept in refrigerators whereas jams and pickles can be kept outside.
   (c) Farmers prefer to grow beans and peas in nitrogen deficient soils.
   (d) Mosquitoes can be controlled by preventing stagnation of water through they do not live in water. Why?

8. How can we prevent the following diseases?
   (a) Cholera
   (b) Typhoid
   (c) Hepatitis A

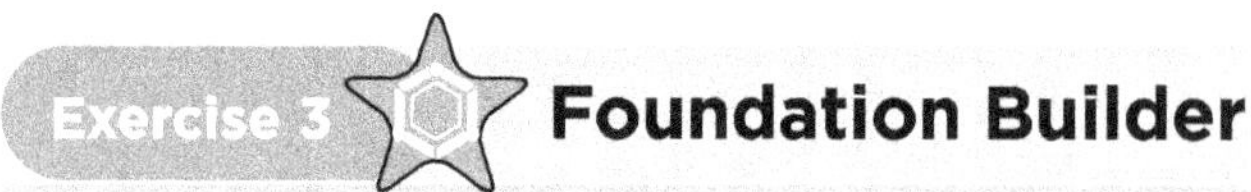

Multiple Choice Questions

DIRECTIONS : *This section contains ultiple choice questions. Each question has four choices (a), (b), (c) and (d) out of which ONLY ONE is correct. Choose the correct option.*

1. Which of the following organisms is considered to be on the borderline of living and non-living?
   (a) Bacteria   (b) Algae
   (c) Virus   (d) Fungi

2. *Amoeba* and *Paramecium* belongs to group
   (a) bacteria   (b) algae
   (c) fungi   (d) protozoan

3. Which microbe is used to make curd from milk?
   (a) Bacteria   (b) Virus
   (c) Fungi   (d) Protozoan

4. Which of the following makes bread soft and fluffy?
   (a) Finely ground flour
   (b) Alcohol given off during fermentation of sugar
   (c) Carbon dioxide gas given off during fermentation of sugar
   (d) Oxygen gas

5. The gas released during fermentation of sugar by yeast cells is
   (a) carbon dioxide   (b) carbon monoxide
   (c) hydrogen   (d) oxygen

6. Which of the following bacterium is responsible for the formation of moulds on moist bread?
   (a) *Lactobacillus*   (b) *Streptococcus*
   (c) *Rhizobium*   (d) *Rhizopus*

7. Which disease is caused by virus?
   (a) Tuberculosis   (b) Common cold
   (c) Typhoid   (d) Malaria

8. Which of the following is not the preventive measure for water borne disease?
   (a) Proper disposal of sewage
   (b) Maintenance of good sanitary habits
   (c) Drinking boiled water
   (d) Covering mouth or nose while sneezing

9. Bacteria can be seen only
   (a) in light   (b) in darkness
   (c) under a microscope   (d) under a magnifying glass

10. Which of the following microorganisms cannot multiply on their own?
    (a) Bacteria and Protozoa (b) Algae and Fungi
    (c) Fungi and Virus   (d) Viruses

11. The process that releases free nitrogen back into the air is known as
    (a) ammonification   (b) nitrification
    (c) denitrification   (d) purification

12. Which of the following is a nitrifying bacteria?
    (a) *Nitrosomonas* and *Nitrobacter*
    (b) *Nitrosomonas* and *Pseudomonas*
    (c) *Nitrobacter* and *Pseudomonas*
    (d) *Nitrobacter* and *Lactobacillus*

13. The suspension of killed microbes that mimics the disease causing microorganisms is known as
    (a) antibiotics   (b) vaccines
    (c) vector   (d) pathogen

14. Which microorganism is smaller than bacteria?
    (a) Protozoan   (b) Virus
    (c) Fungi   (d) Algae

15. Which of these elements help to increase the soil fertility?
    (a) Hydrogen   (b) Nitrogen
    (c) Carbon   (d) Oxygen

16. Which of the following describes the most ideal location for microorganisms to live?
    (a) Nearly everywhere   (b) In warm, humid places
    (c) Sunny, dry areas   (d) Underwater

17. Microbes are an important part of the environment because they
    (a) break down waste products
    (b) cause the water cycle
    (c) protect the ozone layer
    (d) block global warming

18. Infectious diseases can spread
    (a) from one person to another.
    (b) by eating only frost fruit.
    (c) from washing your hands.
    (d) by inheritance.

19. The mode of transmission of dengue is
    (a) air   (b) contact
    (c) water   (d) vector

20. What is the most important way to stop infections from being spread?
    (a) Cleanliness   (b) Heating
    (c) Eating   (d) Taking tablets

21. What does your stomach use to kill microbes?
    (a) Acid   (b) Water
    (c) Salt   (d) Alkali

22. Which of the following correctly describes the size of fungi compared to the size of bacteria?
    (a) Fungi are larger
    (b) Bacteria are larger
    (c) They are about the same size
    (d) They are of the same size but of different shapes

23. Most bacteria can be killed by
    (a) cooking   (b) refrigeration
    (c) freezing   (d) salting

24. When a person is made immune to a disease by an injection they have usually been
    (a) vaccinated   (b) infected
    (c) infectious   (d) communicable

25. How do bacteria help our bodies to function?
    (a) They make our muscles and lungs stronger.
    (b) They help to digest food in the intestines.
    (c) They circulate in our blood and help carry oxygen.
    (d) They make our skin flexible and clean.

26. Study the given diagram of the nitrogen cycle.

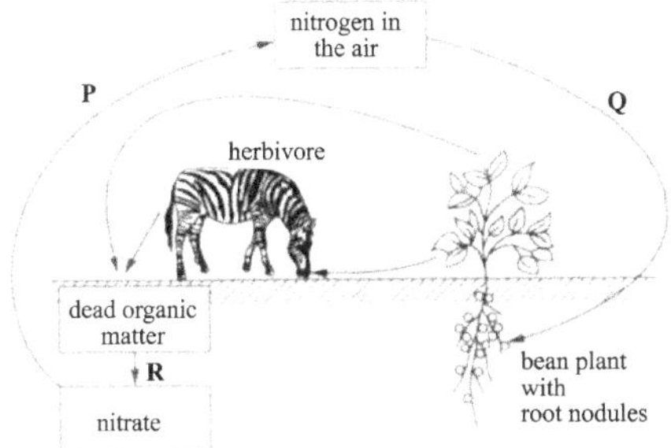

Which arrow indicates nitrogen fixation and denitrification respectively?

	Nitrogen Fixation	**Denitrification**
(a)	P	Q
(b)	P	R
(c)	Q	P
(d)	Q	R

27. Which of the following is put into Anaerobic sludge digester for further sewage treatment? **[NTSE]**
    (a) Floating debris
    (b) Effluents of primary treatment
    (c) Activated sludge
    (d) Primary sludge

28. Match the following organisms with the products they produce: **[NTSE]**
    (A) *Lactobacillus*   (i) Cheese
    (B) *Saccharomyces*   (ii) Curd
        cerevisiae
    (C) *Aspergillus niger* (iii) Citric acid
    (D) *Acetobacter aceti* (iv) Bread
                             (v) Acetic acid
    Select the correct option.
	(A)	**(B)**	**(C)**	**(D)**
(a)	(ii)	(iv)	(v)	(iii)
(b)	(ii)	(iv)	(iii)	(v)
(c)	(iii)	(iv)	(v)	(i)
(d)	(ii)	(i)	(iii)	(v)

29. Which of the following in sewage treatment removes suspended solids? **[NTSE]**
    (a) Secondary treatment
    (b) Primary treatment
    (c) Sludge treatment
    (d) Tertiary treatment

30. Which of the following is correctly matched for the product produced by them ? **[NTSE]**
    (a) *Methanobacterium* : Lactic acid
    (b) *Penicillium notatum* : Acetic acid
    (c) *Sacchromyces cerevisiae* : Ethanol
    (d) *Acetobacter aceti* : Antibiotics

31. The guts of cow and buffalo possess: **[NTSE]**
    (a) *Chlorella* spp.   (b) Methanogens
    (c) Cyanobacteria   (d) *Fucus* spp.

32. The primitive prokaryotes responsible for the production of biogas from the dung of ruminant animals, include the **[NTSE]**

(a) Halophiles
(b) Thermoacidiophiles
(c) Methanogens
(d) Eubacteria

33. Filariasis is caused by
    (a) Entamoeba histolytica
    (b) Plasmodium falciparum
    (c) Trypanosoma brucei
    (d) Wuchereria bancrofti

34. Which one of the following conversions does not happen under anaerobic conditions?
    (a) Glucose to ethanol by Saccharomyces
    (b) Lactose to lactic acid by Lactobacillus
    (c) Glucose to CO_2 and H_2O by Saccharomyces
    (d) Cellulose to glucose by Cellulomonas

35. A single bacterium is actively growing in a medium that supports its growth to a number of 100 million. Assuming the division time of the bacterium as 3 hours and the lifespan of non-dividing bacteria as 5 hours, which one of the following represents the maximum number of bacteria that would be present at the end of 15 hours?
    (a) 10   (b) 64
    (c) 24   (d) 32

36. The Diphtheria Pertussis Tetanus (DPT) vaccine consists of
    (a) live attenuated strains of diphtheria, pertussis, Tetanus.
    (b) toxoid of diphtheria, tetanus and heat-killed whole cells of pertussis.
    (c) whole cell lysate of diphtheria, pertussis, tetanus.
    (d) heat-killed strains of diphtheria, pertusis, tetanus.

37. Excess salt inhibits bacterial growth in pickles by
    (a) endosmosis   (b) exosmosis
    (c) oxidation   (d) denaturation

38. Widal test is prescribed to diagnose
    (a) typhoid   (b) pneumonia
    (c) malaria   (d) filaria

39. Etiology is : **[JSTSE]**
    (a) Prevention of diseases
    (b) Cause of diseases
    (c) Transmission of diseases
    (d) Treatment of diseases

40. Antibiotic do not work against viral infectons because
    (a) Viruses have hard protein coat **[JSTSE]**
    (b) Viruses do not follow bio-chemical pathways to make cell wall
    (c) Viruses are not infections
    (d) Viruses have a rigid cell wall

41. The diseases last for only very short period of time is known as **[JSTSE]**
    (a) Chronic disease
    (b) Acute disease
    (c) Infectious disease
    (d) None of the above

42. The animals carrying infecting agents from a sick person to other are called **[JSTSE]**
    (a) Vector   (b) Parasite
    (c) Host   (d) Infection

43. Kala - azar disease caused by : **[JSTSE]**
    (a) Round worm   (b) Leishmania
    (c) Amoeba   (d) Trypanosoma

44. Read the following. **[NTSE]**
(A) Malaria is transmitted by a virus.
(B) Cholera is caused by *Mycobacterium*.
(C) *Salmonella typhi* spreads through soil and water.
(D) Varicella causes chicken pox.
Which of the following is true?
(a) (A) and (C) (b) (B) and (D)
(c) (C) and (D) (d) (A) and (B)

45. Which one is not an infectious disease? **[JSTSE]**
(a) Common cold (b) Tuberculosis
(c) Cancer (d) Cholera

46. Majority of children in many parts of India are already immune to one of the disease by the time they are five years old. The disease is : **[JSTSE]**
(a) Jaundice (b) Typhoid
(c) Hepatitis A (d) Rabies

47. Who discovered the Vaccine for small pox? **[JSTSE]**
(a) Edward Jenner (b) Fleming
(c) Louis Pasteur (d) Rober Koch

48. Which one of the following pairs of causative agent and type of disease are correct ? **[NTSE]**
(I) *Leishmania* — Sleeping sickness
(II) Nematode — Elephantiasis
(III) *Trypanosoma* — Kala azar
(IV) Staphylococcus — Acne
(a) (I) and (II) (b) (II) and (III)
(c) (II) and (IV) (d) (III) and (IV)

49. Which of the following is a mismatch? **[JSTSE]**
(a) Leprosy - Bacteria (b) AIDS - Bacteria
(c) Malaria - Protozoa (d) Elephantiasis - Nematode

50. The animals carrying infecting agents from a sick person to other are called **[JSTSE]**
(a) Vector (b) Parasite
(c) Host (d) Infection

51. Barley is ground to powder. The powder is mixed with water and some yeast. The mixture is kept in a closed and moist container. Which of the following will be produced?]
(a) Sodium bicarbonate **[NTSE]**
(b) Alcohol only
(c) Carbon dioxide only
(d) Alcohol and Carbon dioxide

52. Raju was suffering from severe stomach pain and the doctor diagnosed that he was suffering from peptic ulcers and treated him with antibiotics. He was relieved of pain. What could be the reason for peptic ulcers? **[NTSE]**
(a) Reduced secretion of hormones.
(b) Reduced water content.
(c) Growth of *Helicobacter pylori*.
(d) Excess secretion of enzyme.

53. Diseases that spread by vectors such as mosquitoes are
(a) Encephalitis and Malaria **[NTSE]**
(b) Syphilis and AIDS
(c) Tuberculosis and sleeping sickness
(d) Kala-azar and SARS

54. A leguminous plant grown in an autoclaved, sterilized soil fails to produce root nodules because **[NTSE]**
(a) autoclaved soil is not good for root growth.

(b) autoclaved soil is devoid of bacteria.
(c) autoclaving reduces N_2 content of soil.
(d) plants cannot form root hairs in such a soil.

55. The causative agent of the disease 'sleeping sickness' in human beings is an **[NTSE]**
(a) intracellular parasite found in RBC.
(b) extracellular parasite found in blood plasma.
(c) intracellular parasite found in WBC.
(d) extracellular parasite found on the surface of platelets.

56. Which one is not a infectious disease? **[JSTSE]**
(a) Common cold (b) Tuberculosis
(c) Cancer (d) Cholera

57. Who discovered the Vaccine for small pox? **[JSTSE]**
(a) Edward Jenner (b) Fleming
(c) Louis Pasteur (d) Rober Koch

58. Majority of children in many parts of India are already immune to one of the disease by the time they are five years old. The disease is : **[JSTSE]**
(a) Jaundice (b) Typhoid
(c) Hepatitis A (d) Rabies

59. Antibiotic pencillin blocks a bio-chemical pathway in bacteria due to which it dies easily as they become unable to make: **[JSTSE]**
(a) Cell wall (b) Cell Membrane
(c) Nucleus (d) Golgi apparatus

Assertion & Reason

DIRECTIONS : *Each of these questions contains an Assertion followed by reason. Read them carefully and answer the question on the basis of following options. You have to select the one that best describes the two statements.*

(a) If both **Assertion** and **Reason** are **correct** and Reason is the **correct explanation** of Assertion.
(b) If both **Assertion** and **Reason** are correct, but Reason is **not the correct explanation** of Assertion.
(c) If **Assertion** is **correct** but **Reason** is **incorrect**.
(d) If **Assertion** is **incorrect** but **Reason** is **correct**.

1. **Assertion** – Viruses can be seen with the help of electron microscope.
Reason – It is much smaller than bacteria.

2. **Assertion** – Pathogens are harmful to mankind.
Reason – They either kill or prevent the growth of microorganisms.

3. **Assertion** – *Rhizobium* lives in the root nodules of leguminous plants.
Reason – It fixes nitrogen through a symbiotic relationship.

4. **Assertion** – Salting is used for preserving meat and fish by common salt.
Reason – It does not allow the growth of bacteria.

5. **Assertion** – Salt is added to chips and pickles.
Reason – Salting removes oxygen from the food item.

6. **Assertion** – Fermentation is the process of breaking down of sugar molecules by microorganisms to produce an acid or alcohol.
Reason – Cheese is prepared by the bacterial fermentation of milk.

Match the Following

DIRECTIONS : Each question contains two columns which have to be matched. Statement/terms given in column I have to be matched with statement/terms given in column II.

1. Match the items in column-I with those in column-II, and select the correct choice: **[NTSE]**

Column-I		**Column-II**
A.	Small pox	I.	Bacteria
B.	Cholera	II.	Virus
C.	Malaria	III.	Deficiency of minerals
D.	Anaemia	IV.	Female mosquito

(a) A-IV, B-II, C-III, D-I
(b) A-II, B-I, C-IV, D-III
(c) A-IV, B-III, C-II, D-I
(d) A-III, B-IV, C-I, D-II

2. Match the items in column-I with those in column-II, and select the correct choice: **[NTSE]**

Column-I		**Column-II**
A.	Small pox	I.	Bacteria
B.	Cholera	II.	Virus
C.	Malaria	III.	Deficiency of minerals
D.	Anaemia	IV.	Female mosquito

(a) A-IV, B-II, C-III, D-I   (b) A-II, B-I, C-IV, D-III
(c) A-IV, B-III, C-II, D-I   (d) A-III, B-IV, C-I, D-II

Exercise 4 — Foundation Builder +

Multiple Choice Questions

DIRECTIONS (Qs. 1-30) : This section contains multiple choice questions. Each question has 4 choices (a), (b), (c) and (d) out of which ONLY ONE is correct.

1. Vaccines are prepared from
   (a) vitamins   (b) blood
   (c) serum   (d) plasma

2. Which one of the following pairs of disease can spread through blood transfusion?
   (a) Cholera and hepatitis
   (b) Hepatitis and AIDS
   (c) Diabetes mellitus and malaria
   (d) Hay fever and AIDS

3. Antibodies are produced by
   (a) erythrocytes   (b) thrombocytes
   (c) monocytes   (d) lymphocytes

4. Conditions necessary for good individual health are
   (a) public cleanliness
   (b) good economic condition
   (c) social equality and harmony
   (d) All of the above

5. Mosquito is not a vector for which disease from following?
   (a) Malaria   (b) Typhoid
   (c) Dengu   (d) Elephantiasis

6. Diseases where microbes or micro organisms are the immediate causes are called
   (a) infectious diseases (b) genetic abnormalities
   (c) community diseases (d) chronic diseases

7. Wide range of categories of classification of organisms causing infectious diseases include
   (a) single celled organisms like protozoan
   (b) very small microbes likes virus
   (c) multi cellular organisms such as worms
   (d) All of these

8. A communicable disease is caused by
   (a) metabolic disorder (b) allergy
   (c) pathogen   (d) hormonal balance

9. Which one is a bacterial disease?
   (a) Tuberculosis   (b) Mumps
   (c) Measles   (d) Malaria

10. The bacterium that commonly lives in animal and human intestine is
    (a) Bacillus anthracis (b) Vibrio cholerae
    (c) Escherichia coli   (d) Corynebacterium

11. Which gas is responsible for the puffed-up appearance of dough ?
    (a) CO_2 (b) O_2
    (c) SO_2 (d) NO_2

12. In cheese microorganisms are required for
    (a) ripening only
    (b) souring of milk only
    (c) souring and ripening
    (d) development of resistance to spoilage

13. Glucose fermentation by yeast yields
    (a) ethanol + CO_2 (b) ethanol + H_2O
    (c) methanol + CO_2 (d) H_2O + CO_2

14. Primary treatment of sewage is
    (a) physical process   (b) biological process
    (c) chemical process   (d) biochemical process

15. Primary sludge is used for the
    (a) preparation of compost
    (b) preparation of manure
    (c) biogas production
    (d) all of these

16. Which one is used in production of alcohol/ethanol ?
    (a) *Saccharomyces cerevisiae*
    (b) *Torulopsis utilis*
    (c) *Clostridium botulinum*
    (d) *Leuconostoc citrovorum*

17. Lactobacillus mediated change of milk to curd occurs due to
    (a) coagulation and partial digestion of milk fats.
    (b) coagulation and partial digestion of milk proteins.
    (c) coagulation of milk proteins and complete digestion of milk fats.
    (d) coagulation of milk fats and complete digestion of proteins.

18. Conversion of sugar into alcohol during fermentation is due to the direct action of
    (a) temperature
    (b) micro-organisms
    (c) zymase
    (d) concentration of sugar solution

19. Sewage treatment process in which part of decomposer bacteria is recycled into starting of the process is called _________ .
(a) cyclic treatment   (b) primary treatment
(c) tertiary treatment   (d) activated sludge treatment

20. The chemical substances produced by some microbes which can kill or retard the growth of other microbes are called _________ .
(a) toddy   (b) lactic acid
(c) antibiotics   (d) ethanol

21. Match the following columns and select the correct option.

Column-I		Column-II
(a) *Clostridium butylicum*	(i)	Cyclosporin-A
(b) *Trichoderma polysporum*	(ii)	Butyric Acid
(c) *Monascus purpureus*	(iii)	Citric Acid
(d) *Aspergillus niger*	(iv)	Blood cholesterol lowering agent

	(A)	(B)	(C)	(D)
(a)	(ii)	(i)	(iv)	(iii)
(b)	(i)	(ii)	(iv)	(iii)
(c)	(iv)	(iii)	(ii)	(i)
(d)	(iii)	(iv)	(ii)	(i)

22. Which of the following is put into Anaerobic sludge digester for further sewage treatment? **[NTSE]**
(a) Floating debris
(b) Effluents of primary treatment
(c) Activated sludge
(d) Primary sludge

23. Match the following organisms with the products they produce: **[NTSE]**
(a) *Lactobacillus*   (i) Cheese
(b) *Saccharomyces cerevisiae*   (ii) Curd
(c) *Aspergillus niger*   (iii) Citric acid
(d) *Acetobacter aceti*   (iv) Bread
                     (v) Acetic acid
Select the correct option.

	(a)	(b)	(c)	(d)
(a)	(ii)	(iv)	(v)	(iii)
(b)	(ii)	(iv)	(iii)	(v)
(c)	(iii)	(iv)	(v)	(i)
(d)	(ii)	(i)	(iii)	(v)

24. Which of the following is a commercial blood cholesterol lowering agent? **[NTSE]**
(a) Cyclosporin A   (b) Statin
(c) Streptokinase   (d) Lipases

25. A good producer of citric acid is:
(a) *Pseudomonas*   (b) *Clostridium*
(c) *Saccharomyces*   (d) *Aspergillus*

26. Which of the following statements about methanogens is *not correct* ? **[NTSE]**
(a) They produce methane gas.
(b) They can be used to produce biogas.
(c) They are found in the rumen of cattle and their excreta.
(d) They grow aerobically and breakdown cellulose-rich food.

27. Among the following pairs of microbes, which pair has both the microbes that can be used as biofertilisers?
(a) *Aspergillus and Cyanobacteria*   **[NTSE]**
(b) *Aspergillus and Rhizopus*
(c) *Rhizobium and Rhizopus*
(d) *Cyanobacteria and Rhizobium*

28. A biocontrol agent to be a part of an integrated pest management should be **[NTSE]**
(a) Species-specific and inactive on nontarget organisms.
(b) Species-specific and symbiotic.
(c) Free living and broad spectrum.
(d) Narrow spectrum and symbiotic.

29. Select the correct group of biocontrol agents. **[NTSE]**
(a) Bacillus thuringiensis, Tobacco mosaic virus, Aphids
(b) Trichoderma, Baculovirus, Bacillus thuringiensis
(c) Oscillatoria, Rhizobium, Trichoderma
(d) Nostoc, Azospirillium, Nucleopolyhedrovirus

30. Which of the following can be used as a biocontrol agent in the treatment of plant disease? **[NTSE]**
(a) *Trichoderma*   (b) *Chlorella*
(c) *Anabaena*   (d) *Lactobacillus*

Match the Following

DIRECTIONS : *Each question contains two columns which have to be matched. Statement/terms given in column I have to be matched with statement/terms given in column II.*

31. Which of the following is wrongly matched in the given table ? **[NTSE]**

	Microbe	Product	Application
(a)	*Trichoderma polysporum*	Cyclosporin A	immunosuppressive drug
(b)	*Monascus purpureus*	Statins	lowering of blood cholesterol
(c)	*Streptococcus*	Streptokinase	removal of clot from blood vessel
(d)	*Clostridium butylicum*	Lipase	removal of oil stains

32. Match the following list of microbes and their importance: **[NTSE]**

(A)	Saccharomyces cerevisiae	(i)	Production of immunosuppressive agents
(B)	Monascus Purpureus	(ii)	Ripening of Swiss cheese
(C)	Trichoderma polysporum	(iii)	Commercial production of ethanol
(D)	Propionibacterium sharamanii	(iv)	Production of blood cholestrol lowering agents

	(A)	(B)	(C)	(D)
(a)	(iv)	(iii)	(ii)	(i)
(b)	(iv)	(ii)	(i)	(iii)
(c)	(iii)	(i)	(iv)	(ii)
(d)	(iii)	(iv)	(i)	(ii)

SOLUTIONS
(Brief Explanations of Selected Questions)

 **Exercise 1** ⭐ **Master Boards**

Multiple Choice Questions

1. (b)   2. (b)   3. (a)   4. (c)
5. (b)

Assertion & Reason

1. (a) Both assertion and reason are correct, and R is the correct explanation of A.
   Biofertilizer are preferred to chemical fertilizers, because they are more expensive and disturb flora and fauna, and affects soil pH.
2. (b) Both assertion and reason are correct and but R is not the correct explanation of A. LAB improve its nutritional quality by increasing vitamin B_{12} besides curdling the milk. LAB produce myrial beneficial effects for human being include alleviation of lactose intolerance peptic ulcer etc.
3. (a) Both A and R are correct, and R is the correct explanation of A.
   Pathogen ofter develop resistance to existing antibiotics, so newer antibiotics are required to produce regularly.
4. (d) Both Assertion and Reason are false.
   Nitrogen is also fixed by photochemical and electrochemical reactions of atmosphere. Dead bodies of plants and animals possess nitrogenous compounds. These dead bodies are acted upon decomposes which release ammonia and utilize organic acid for their body building.
5. (b) Both A and R are true but R it not the correct explanation of A.
   The manufacture of cheese require two main steps curdling and ripening. Curdling die milk proteins form a solid material from which the liquid is drained away. The curdling process is microbiological, since acid production of lactic acid is sufficient to coagulate milk protein.

Fill in the Blanks

1. Virus,   2. Malaria,
3. Vaccination,   4. Alexander Fleming,
5. Vaccine,   6. *Rhizobium*,
7. Decomposition,   8. Virus,
9. Air,   10. Salt.

True / False

1. False,   2. False,   3. True,   4. True,
5. True,   6. False,   7. True,   8. False,
9. False,   10. True,   11. False

Match the Following

1. A → r, B → p, C → q, D → t, E → s
2. A → s, B → r, C → q, D → t, E → p

Passage Based Questions

1. (c)   2. (a)   3. (d)

Very Short Answer Questions

1. Microbes / Microorganisms
2. Microscope
3. Curd, prepared by *Lactobacillus*.
4. Coccus
5. Virus
6. Fungi
7. *Plasmodium* – Malaria
   Entamoeba – Amoebic dysentery
   Trypanosoma – Sleeping sickness
8. Female *Anopheles*
9. Yeast, a fungus
10. Mushroom
11. Rust of wheat and Rust of rice
12. Penicillin
13. Pathogens are disease causing microorganisms.
14. Expiry date refers to the date by which the supplier intended the food to be consumed.

Short Answer Questions

1. Major group of microorganism are:
   Bacteria, eg. *E.coli* and *Diplococcus*.
   Fungi, eg. *Rhizopus* and *Penicillium*.
   Protoza, eg. *Plasmodium* and *Amoeba*.
   Algae, eg. *Spirogyra* and *Chlamydomonas*.
   Virus, eg. HIV and Rous sarcoma virus
2. Nitrogen is required by all living organisms for the synthesis of proteins, nucleic acids and other nitrogen containing compounds. The Earth's atmosphere contains almost 80 % nitrogen gas. It cannot be used in this form by most living organisms until it has been fixed, that is reduced (combined with hydrogen) to ammonia.
   The nitrogen cycle is a series of processes that convert nitrogen gas to organic substances and back to nitrogen in nature. It is a continuous cycle that is maintained by the decomposers and nitrogenous bacteria.
3. Antibodies are proteins generally found in the blood that detect and destroy invaders, like bacteria and viruses. Antibioties are chemical substance that in dilute solutions can inhibit the growth of microorganisms or destroy them with little or no harm to the infected host cell.
   The precautions that needs to be taken while consuming antibiotics are:

(i) We should take antibiotic only after consulting a doctor.

(ii) Antibiotics should not be taken empty stomach.

(iii) We should complete the dose of antibiotic as advised by the doctor.

4. Food poisoning is when someone gets sick from eating food or drink that has gone bad or is contaminated. There are two kinds of food poisoning: poisoning by toxic agent or by infectious agent. Food infection occurs when the food contains bacteria or other microbes which infects the body is consumed.

5. Preservatives are substance used to preserve foodstuffs, wood, or other materials against decay. Various method of food preservation are: heating, cooling, salting, pickling, drying, canning and freeze drying.

6. *Lactobacillus* bacteria can convert a sugar into an acid by the means of fermentation. Milk contains a sugar called lactose, a disaccharide (compound sugar) made by the glycosidic bonding between glucose and galactose (monosaccharides). When the milk is heated to a temperature of 30-40 °C and a small amount of old curd is added to it, the *Lactobacillus* in that curd sample starts to grow. These convert the lactose into lactic acid, which imparts the sour taste to curd.

7. a. cocci; b: bacilli, c: spiral

8. Useful bacteria: They are useful in cleaning the environment; making medicines and vaccines; and in combination with yeasts and fungi, have been used in the preparation of fermented foods such as cheese, curd, pickles, soy sauce, vinegar, wine, and yogurt.

Harmful bacteria: They are harmful in causing communicable diseases like cholera, typhoid, tuberculosis etc; food poisoning etc.

9. Yeast makes the bread soft and fluffy. The yeast uses sugar for its food. In the process of breaking down of sugar, alcohol is formed and carbon dioxide is given off. If the yeast is added to dough it breaks down sugar present in the dough. The bubbles of carbon dioxide given off in the process causes dough to rise.

10. Bacteria and fungi acts as decomposers. They both play an important role in nature. They break down the unused dead material and turn them into nutrients in the soil, which is used by plants to grow. Decomposers are an important part of the food chain.

11. Salt: Checks the growth of bacteria by forcing microorganisms to lose water by process called osmosis.

Sugar: By inhibiting the growth of bacteria.

Heating: Kills microbes present in the food. Eg, milk and water are boiled to kill the microbes.

Drying: Stops the growth of microorganisms by removing the water present in the food.

12. In 1926, Alexander Fleming discovered penicillin, a substance produced by fungi that was able to inhibit bacterial growth. While working on *Staphylococcus* he found that mould had developed on an accidentally contaminated *Staphylococcus* culture plate. Upon examination of the mould, he noticed that the culture prevented the growth of *Staphylococci*. He then extracted the antibiotic substance from the mould and named it as penicillin.

13. Many of the millions of organisms that live in the soil, including bacteria, fungi, insects, and earthworms, are known as decomposers. They live on the remains of dead plants and animals and break down these organic remains into simple chemicals that are released into the soil. Some of these chemicals provide nutrients for new plants to grow, so decomposers can recycle plant material.

14. No, not all fungi are microscopic. Fungi such as mushroom can be seen through naked eyes.

15. Fungi together with bacteria decompose the organic matter present in dead plants and animals remains and convert it into simple soluble minerals, water and gases, which then gets mixed into the soil, water bodies and air. Hence, fungi help in recycling dead organic materials in soil.

16. Yeast ferments the sugar present in various food and produces alcohol, with the release of carbon dioxide and little energy.

$$\text{Glucose} \xrightarrow[\text{Yeast}]{\text{without oxygen}} \text{Alcohol} + \text{Energy} + CO_2$$

The process involved is known as fermentation. Fermentation is the process of converting complex organic substances into simpler substances.

17. Vector is any agent (person, animal or microorganism) that carries and transmits an infectious pathogen into another living organism. Vector spreads diseases while feeding on infected vertebrates (e.g., birds, rodents, other larger animals, or humans), and then pass on the microbe to a susceptible person or other animal.

18. Tuberculosis (TB), caused by *Mycobacterium* bacteria, is an infectious disease. The bacteria get into the air when someone who has a tuberculosis lung infection coughs, sneezes, shouts, or spits. Therefore, it is advised to keep a distance from a person suffering from TB.

19. To prevent the communication of communicable diseases.

Long Answer Questions

1. Nitrogen is recycled in nature by a natural phenomenon called the nitrogen cycle. When animals and plants die, their nitrogen compounds are broken down by soil bacteria, fungi and other decomposers. In this way, nitrogen compounds are returned to the soil, where they may be absorbed by plants again. *Rhizobium* plays a very important role in agriculture by inducing nitrogen-fixing nodules on the roots of legumes such as peas, beans, clover and alfalfa. They use the nitrogen in the air and convert it to a form that the plants can use, like a biological fertilizer.

2. Refer inside the chapter to the table of some common humans diseases caused by microorganisms.

3. Preventive measures to be taken for air borne diseases includes washing hands, using appropriate hand disinfectant, getting regular immunizations against diseases believed to be locally present, wearing a respirator and limiting time spent in the presence of any patient likely to be a source of infection.

Preventive measures to be taken for water borne diseases includes drinking boiled water, proper disposal of sewage and maintain good sanitary habit.

Preventive measures to be taken for vector borne disease includes use of mosquito repellent, keeping surroundings neat and clean etc.

4. Vaccines are biological preparation of killed microorganisms, living attenuated organisms, or living fully virulent organisms, its toxins or one of its surface proteins that is administered to produce or artificially increase immunity for a particular disease. The agent stimulates the body's immune system to recognize the agent as foreign, destroy it, and "remember" it, so that the immune system can more easily recognize and destroy any of these microorganisms that it later encounters. (Refer examples from the chapter)

5. Bacteria present in the soil or in plant roots change nitrogen gas from the atmosphere into solid nitrogen compounds that plants can use in the soil. The symbiotic nitrogen-fixing bacteria invade the root hairs of host plants, where they multiply and stimulate formation of root nodules, enlargements of plant cells and bacteria in intimate association. Within the nodules the bacteria converts free nitrogen to nitrates, which the host plant utilizes for its development.

Reasoning Based Questions

1. The most significant effect of the micro-organism on earth is their ability to recycle the primary elements that make up all living system, especially carbon (C), oxygen (O) and nitrogen (N).

2. Because antibiotics only fight bacteria and not viruses, they're usually ineffective against colds.

3. Children are given vaccination to develop antibodies against various diseased so that they are less likely to become seriously it.

4. The main reason fragment water should be allowed to be collect in Neighborhood so that breeding ground would soon become for harmful mosquitoes that might spread deadly disease like dengue.

5. Some micro-organisms are not considered harmful because they help you to digest food, protein against infection and even maintain your reproductive health.

6. Higher pressure is required to kill the bacterial in low-acid foods like fish, meat etc therefore, only safe way to can these is by using pressure canner.

7. The bacteria needs warmth to turn the milk into curd, so in summer the temperature is higher which helps the bacteria to multiply faster. This faster division of bacteria helps to change the milk into curd, but in winter the temperature is neither warm nor favourable for bacteria that's why it takes more time in winter than in summer for the curd to set.

8. Germs easily spread through poor hygiene, cross contamination occur between raw and ready-to-eat foods and during animal handling. The number of germs on fingertips doubles after using the toilet. Therefore, washing hands properly helps prevent the spread of various forms of germs which can cause serious health problems. Use soap and warm running water to wash hands for at least 10 seconds. Liquid soap is best.

9. Viruses are mysterious because they fall on the threshold of living and non-living beings. They are tiny microorganisms, about thousand times smaller than bacterial cells. Viruses do not have enzymes or the chemicals, which are important for life sustaining chemical reactions. Thus, viruses need a host cell such as bacteria, plant or animal to exist, grow and reproduce to act like a living being.

10. Because of incomplete fermentation and bacterial processes.

HOTS Questions

1. Priya should keep another apple in a warm place for the same length of time.

2. Milk is lumpy and tastes sour so it means that milk is old or has been left in a warm place.

3. Shashi and her friend could use a microscope and look at the pond water to see if microorganisms are visible or not. Also, they can boil the pond water to kill or get rid of microorganisms to see if it still smells.

4. Nitrogen is a non-reactive gas. It has no colour, odour or taste. Potato chip packages are filled with nitrogen gas to stop oxidation, and thus spoilage of the chips. It retards bacterial growth and keeps the food from decaying.

5. Any kind of swelling of the sealed can is a cause of suspicion as this indicates the formation of gas inside the tin. This swelling could be due to the production of gaseous byproducts due to microbial growth.

6. **Indicators of food spoilage –**
   (i) **Odour :** Repulsive odours are produced when the bacteria break down the protein present in food.
   (ii) **Sliminess :** It occurs due to bacterial growth.
   (iii) **Discolouration :** Microbial growth may result in discolouration of food.
   (iv) **Souring :** Food items become sour due to production of acids by bacteria.
   (v) **Gas formation :** Bacteria and yeast produces gaseous by-products that affects the texture of food items.

7. Cooked rice gives out moisture. Since, moisture is one of the main requirements for microbial growth, so the leftover food will start producing repulsive odours, become slimy and sometimes may have coloured spores that give the food a distinctive colour.

8. Microorganisms play a vital role in the lives of plant and animals. They carry about 90% of the biochemical reaction that occurs in our planet. *For example,*
   (i) Microorganisms enrich the soil with nutrients.
   (ii) Certain microbes are also used in the biological treatment of sewage and industrial effluents.

9. Food poisoning is a food borne illness that occurs suddenly after you consume a contaminated food or drink. To avoid food poisoning –
   (i) wash fresh food items well before eating them.
   (ii) avoid eating leftovers after a long time.
   (iii) eat properly cooked and heated food items.
   (iv) check the shelf life of packaged food items.

Biology

10. Louis Pasteur: Germ theory of disease; Pasteurization
    Alexander Fleming: Antibiotic (Penicillin)
    Edward Jenner: Vaccine (small pox).

11. Microbes are single-cell organisms and too small to be seen with the unaided eye. They include bacteria, protozoa, fungi, algae and virus that are too small to be seen without the aid of a microscope. In terms of numbers, most of the diversity of life on Earth is represented by microbes. They live everywhere in the soil, air, land. They even live inside our digestive systems. Therefore, they are too many to count and too small to find.

Exercise 2 — Master NCERT (Text–book & Exemplar)

Text-book Exercise

1. (a) microscope   (b) nitrogen
   (c) yeast   (d) Bacteria
2. (b)   **3.** (b)   **4.** (a)   **5.** (b)
6. (c)   **7.** (c)
8. (i) → e, (ii) → a, (iii) → b, (iv) → c, (v) → (d), (vi) → f.
9. No, the microorganisms cannot be seen with the naked eyes. They can be seen only with the help of a microscope.
10. The major groups of microorganisms are :
    1. Virus   2. Bacteria   3. Fungi
    4. Protozoa   5. Some algae
11. The microorganisms which can fix atmospheric nitrogen includes bacteria like *Rhizobium* and some blue green algae. They are commonly called biological nitrogen fixers and helps in increasing the fertility of the soil.
12. Microorganisms play a very important role in our life. Some of their uses are mentioned below :
    1. The bacterium *Lactobacillus* promotes the formation of curd.
    2. Bacteria are also involved in the making of cheese, pickles and many other food items.
    3. Yeast is used for commercial production of alcohol like wine, for baking breads, cakes etc.
    4. Microorganisms are used for the manufacturing of antibiotics.
    5. Vaccines for various diseases are prepared from microorganism.
    6. Some bacteria like *Rhizobium* and blue green algae are able to fix nitrogen from the atmosphere and help in increasing the fertility of the soil.
    7. Some microorganism helps in decomposing the organic waste and dead plants and animals into simple substances and thus clean up the environment.
    8. The bacteria present in our intestine helps in digestion of food.
    9. Some algae provide food for aquatic animals.
    10. Microorganisms are also used to produce organic acids. Example- *Aspergillus Niger* produce citric acid.
13. Microorganisms through very useful to us may also cause harm to our lives. For instance some microorganisms cause diseases in plants, animals as well as human beings. Diseases caused in human beings include cholera, typhoid, tuberculoses, common cold, chicken pox etc. Diseases caused in Plants – Rust of wheat (caused by fungi), loose smut of sugarcane (caused by fungi), bacterial blight of citrus fruits caused by bacteria. Some microorganisms spoil food, clothing and leather. The microbes that grow on our food produce toxic chemicals which are poisonous and leads to illness.

14. The medicines produced by microorganisms that kill or stop the growth of disease causing microorganisms are called antibiotics. A number of antibiotics are produced by bacteria and fungi. Few precautions which must be takes while using antibiotics are:
    - They should be taken on the advice of a qualified doctor.
    - We must complete the course prescribed by the doctor.

Exemplar questions

1. (a) antibodies   (c) Anthrax
   (b) tuberculosis   (d) fermentation
2. Baking bread/manufacture of alcoholic drinks
3. Fermentation
4. If the child is suffering from diarrhoea, the orally given vaccine may be excreted out because of frequent motions.
5. The 'unused kneaded flour', if left in warm conditions, gets infected by microbes which cause fermentation and spoils the flour. The *pooris* would remain in relatively good condition because they were deep fried in heated oil that kills microbes.
6. (a) Polio/Chicken Pox/Influenza
   (b) Virus can reproduce only inside the host cell.
7. (a) Fresh milk is boiled before consumption to kill the microorganisms in it. But packed milk is pasteurised and does not contain any microorganisms. It can thus be consumed without boiling.
   (b) Raw vegetables and fruits get easily the infected by microorganisms and get spoilt. They are kept in refrigerator as low temperature inhibits growth of microbes. Jams and pickles contain sugar and salt as preservatives. They do not get infected by microbes easily.
   (c) Beans and peas are leguminous plants and have *Rhizobium* in their root nodules. These bacteria can fix atmospheric nitrogen to enrich the soil with nitrogen and increase its fertility.
   (d) Though mosquitoes live on land, their larvae grow in water. If water stagnation is prevented the larvae cannot survive.
8. (a) **Cholera:** By maintaining personal hygiene and good sanitation practices.
   (b) **Typhoid:** Eating properly cooked food, drinking boiled water, getting vaccinated against the diseases.
   (c) **Hepatitis A:** Drinking boiled water and getting vaccinated against the diseases.

Multiple Choice Questions

1. (c) Virus is considered to be on the borderline of living and non living.

2. (d) *Amoeba* and *Paramecium* belong to protozoa. Protozoans are microscopic eukaryotic organisms.

3. (a) A bacterium, called *Lactobacillus*, is used to make curd from sour milk.

4. (c) Yeast ferments the sugar present in the dough into carbon dioxide. The CO_2 released from the yeast fills the dough and increases its volume. Once, the bread has baked, the heat causes the bubbles to break and makes the bread soft and fluffy.

5. (a) Fermentation is the process of converting complex organic substance into simpler substance with the action of yeast or bacteria. Yeast ferments the sugar into alcohol, carbon dioxide and little energy.

6. (d) The fungus *Rhizopus* is responsible for the formation of moulds on moist bread.

7. (b) Common cold is caused by virus. Tuberculosis and typhoid are bacterial diseases and Malaria is a protozoan disease.

8. (d) Covering mouth or nose while sneezing, coughing is a preventive measure for air-borne disease.

9. (c) Bacteria are single-celled microorganisms that can exist either as independent (free-living) organisms or as parasites (dependent on another organism for life). Most bacteria are so small that they are only visible under a light microscope.

10. (d) Virus is a small infectious agent that replicates only inside the living cells of other organisms.

11. (c) Denitrification is the biological conversion of nitrate to nitrogen gas, nitric oxide or nitrous oxide. These compounds are gaseous compounds and are not readily available for microbial growth; therefore they are typically released to the atmosphere.

12. (a) Nitrifying bacteria are *Nitrosomonas, Nitrosococcus, Nitrobacter, Nitrococcus.*

13. (b) Vaccine is a biological preparation that improves immunity to a particular disease. A vaccine typically contains an agent that resembles a disease-causing microorganism and is often made from weakened or killed forms of the microbe, its toxins or one of its surface proteins.

14. (b) Virus is the smaller than bacteria. Virus is an ultramicroscopic (20 to 300 nm in diameter), metabolically inert, infectious agent that replicates only within the cells of living hosts, mainly bacteria, plants, and animals.

15. (b) Nitrogen (N) is essential for plant growth. It increases the soil fertility.

16. (c) Microbes thrive on land, in the oceans and on human skin. They even survive in extreme places like near deep-sea vents.

17. (a) Microbes are essential components of every ecosystem. They break down garbage and dead organisms. Microorganisms are important for decay process because decay recycles important nutrients for plant growth.

18. (a) Infectious diseases can spread from one person to another through air, water and food.

19. (d) A vector is a vehicle that carries and transmits a disease to its host organism. The dengue virus is transmitted to humans *via* the bite of an infected mosquito. Only a few mosquito species are vectors for the dengue virus.

20. (a) Cleanliness is the most important way to stop infection from being spread.

21. (a) The major way the stomach kills microbes is by secreting stomach acid. The acid in the stomach is important in the first stages of digesting food, but also acts to kill a lot of food-borne microbes that could potentially harm us.

22. (a) Fungi are diverse in terms of their shape, size and means of infecting humans. They are larger than bacteria.

23. (a) If the temperature is high enough and the cooking is reasonably prolonged, the majority of bacteria will be killed. Refrigeration of 4°C does not kill bacteria but slows down the rate of reproduction so that food remains safe for longer period. Freezing and salting stops bacteria from reproducing but does not kill them.

24. (a) inoculating with a vaccine in order to produce immunity to an infectious disease, is called vaccinated.

25. (b) Microorganisms inhabit various sites of the human body, including the skin, nose, mouth and the gut. Bacteria such as *Escherichia coli* and *Clostridium* are normally found in the colon. These bacterias help to digest food in intestine by breaking down the undigested fibre into glucose.

26. (c) Nitrogen fixation is the conversion of atmospheric nitrogen into nitrogenous compounds by living organisms. Eg, *Rhizobium*. Denitrification is the process in which some of the nitrates are absorbed and rest are converted to free nitrogen gas by denitrifying bacteria. Eg, *Pseudomonas, Micrococcus.*

27. (c) The sediment in settlement tank is called activated sludge. A small part of the activated sludge is pumped back into aeration tank. Remaining major part of the sludge is pumped into large tank called anaerobic sludge digesters.

28. (b) Microbes are used in production of several household and industrial products –
   • *Lactobacillus* – Production of curd
   • *Saccharomyces cerevisiae* – Bread making
   • *Aspergillus niger* – Citric acid production
   • *Acetobacter aceti* – Acetic acid

29. (b) Primary treatment is a physical process which involves two process, i.e. filtration and sedimentation of big solid waste.

30. (c) *Saccharomyces cerevisiae* commonly know as Brewer's yeast, causes fermentation of carbohydrates and produces ethanol.

31. (b) Methanogens (microorganisms producing methane) are found in the guts of ruminant animals e.g. cows and buffalloes.

32. (c) Methanogens are microorganisms that produce methane as a metabolic byproduct in anoxic conditions. They are obligate anaerobic ancient and primitive bacteria. They are involved in methanogenesis.

33. (d) Filariasis is caused by *Wuchereria bancrofti*. It lives in lymphatic vessels and causes swelling of lower limbs and scrotum.
Entamoeba histolytica causes amoebiasis.
Plasmodium falciparum causes malaria. *Trypanosoma brucei* causes African sleeping sickness.

34. (c) Conversion of glucose to CO_2 and H_2O by Saccharomyces is a aerobic reaction which takes place in the presence of oxygen.
$$C_6H_{12}O_6 + 6O_2 \rightarrow 6CO_2 + 6H_2O$$

35. (d) Each bacterium doubles up after every 3 hours, so it will divide 5 times in 15 hours.
Therefore, the number of bacteria can be calculate by the formula $= 2^n$
$\therefore \quad 2^5 = 32$
So, after 15 hours, maximum number of bacteria will be 32.

36. (b) DTP (diptheria, tetanus toxoids and pertussis) vaccine is used for active immunisation of children upto age 7 years against diptheria, tetanus and pertussis (whooping cough) simultaneously. The vaccine components include diphtheria and tetanus toxoids and heat killed whole cells of the bacterium that causes pertussis.

37. (b) Excessive salt inhibits the bacterial growth in pickles by exosmosis because external medium become hypertonic. It results in drawing water out of the cells of microbe through osmosis (more specifically exosmosis). Due to this bacteria will die by the process of plasmolysis.

38. (a) The widal test is used for diagonosis of typhoid fever. Typhoid is caused by *Salmonella typhi* bacteria. Widal test is based on demonstrating the presence of IgM and IgG antibody in the serum of an infected patient, against the 'H' (flagellar) and 'O' (somatic) antigens of *Salmonella typhi*.

39. (b)

40. (b) Antibiotic does not affects viruses because they are Acellular organism.

41. (b) Acute diseases last for short period.

42. (a) Vector are the animals helps in the transmission of diseases.

43. (c)

44. (c) **Malaria** is a mosquito borne infectious disease of human and other animals caused by protists (a type of microorganism) of the genus Plasmodium. It is transmitted by female Anopheles mosquito.

Cholera is an infection of the small intestine that causes a large amount of water diarrhoea. It is caused by Vibrio cholerae, a bacterium.

45. (c) Cancer is not a infectious disease.

46. (c) In the children of India Autiommunity develops against hepatitis - A because of water quality.

47. (a) Edward Jenner discovered vaccine for small pox in 1798.

48. (c) A nematode, *Wuchereria bancrofti* causes Elephantiasis. *Staphylococcus* is a genus of Gram-positive bacteria cansing infection in skin. *Leishmania* causes kala azar and sleeping sickness is caused by *Trypanosoma*.

49. (b) AIDS is caused by a virus.

50. (a) Vector are the animals helps in the transmission of diseases.

51. (d) The mixture show fermentation reaction which is the anaerobic (in the absence of oxygen) breakdown of carbohydrates by microorganisms(e.g. yeast) producing alcohol, carbon dioxide and energy. It is also called alcoholic fermentation.
$$C_6H_{12}O_6 \xrightarrow{\text{Yeast}} 2C_2H_5OH + 2CO_2 + \text{energy}$$
Carbohydrate
(Barley)

52. (c) A peptic ulcer generally occurs on the area of the gastrointestinal tract. It is usually acidic and extremely of the painful. These types of ulcers are associated with *Helicobacter pylori*, a helical shaped bacterium that lives in the acidic environment of the stomach.

53. (a) Encephalitis and Malaria both are caused by mosquitoes. Encephalitis is inflammation of brain tissues caused by viral infection. It starts with fever and headache. Malaria is transmitted by infected female *Anopheles* mosquito. It is caused by parasitic protozoans belonging to genus *plasmodium*. Fever, headache and vomiting are main symptoms of this disease.

54. (b) Autoclaving is a method of sterilisation which kills all the organisms. Since the soil is autoclaved, it will not have the bacteria *Rhizobium* which is essential for nodule formation, and hence the plant will fail to produce root nodules.

55. (b) Sleeping sickness is caused by *Trypanosoma sp.* which is an extracellular parasite found in blood plasma.

56. (c) Cancer is not a infectious disease.

57. (a) Edward Jenner discovered vaccine for small pox in 1798.

58. (c) In the children of India Autiommunity develops against hepatitis - A because of water quality.

59. (a) Penicillin resists the formation of cell wall in the bacteria due to which they die esily.

Assertion & Reason

1. (a) Virus do not have a cellular structure. They are so small that they can only be seen through an electron microscope.

2. (c) Pathogens are harmful to mankind as they cause death and severe fatal diseases. Antibiotics either kill or prevent the growth of microorganisms.

3. (a) *Rhizobium* are soil bacteria that lives in the root nodules of leguminous plants. It fixes nitrogen through a symbiotic relationship.

4. (a) Salting is used for preserving meat and fish by common salt as salt forces microorganisms to loose water by the process of osmosis and thus preventing their growth.

5. (c) Salt is added to chips and pickles. Salting forces micro organisms to lose water by a process known as osmosis, thus preventing their growth and reproduction. Chemical preservatives act as antioxidants and remove oxygen from the food item.

6. (b) Fermentation is a metabolic process that converts sugar to acids, gases or alcohols. It occurs in yeast and bacteria but also in oxygen starved muscle cells as in case of lactic acid fermentation. Cheese is an important product of fermentative lactic acid bacteria.

Match the Following

1. (b) Small pox is caused by 'Variola virus'. Cholera, is a bacterial disease, caused by 'Vibrio cholerae'. Malaria is a protozoan disease, caused by plasmodium and it's vector is '*Anopheles* female mosquito'. Anaemia is caused due to the deficiency of iron.

2. (b) Small pox is caused by 'Variola virus'. Cholera, is a bacterial disease, caused by '*Vibrio cholerae*'. Malaria is a protozoan disease, caused by plasmodium and it's vector is 'Anopheles female mosquito'. Anaemia is caused due to the deficiency of iron.

Exercise 4 — Foundation Builder +

1. (c)   2. (b)   3. (d)

4. (d) Conditions necessary for good individual health are public cleanliness, good economic condition, and social equality and harmony.

5. (d)

6. (a) Diseases where microbes or micro organisms are the immediate causes are called the infectious diseases.

7. (d) Wide range of categories of classification of organisms causing infectious diseases include single celled organisms like protozoan, very small microbes like virus, multi-cellular organisms such as worms.

8. (c)   9. (a)

10. (c) *Escherichia coli* is a gram-negative, facultative anaerobic, rod-shaped bacterium of the genus *Escherichia*. It is commonly found in the lower intestine of warm-blooded organisms (also called endotherms).

11. (a) The dough, which is used for making bread, is fermented by using baker's yeast (*Saccharomyces cerevisiae*). The puffed up appearance of dough is due to the production of CO_2 gas.

12. (c) Cheese is prepared by the coagulation of casein and other minor milk proteins by an enzyme rennin. Rennin is extracted from the calf gastric mucosa. *Streptococcus* and *Lactobacillus* species are involved in the manufacture of most cheese. In cheese manufacture, these microorganisms are important in both souring and ripening processes.

13. (a) Fermentation is defined as an energy yielding process whereby organic molecules serve as both electron donors and electron accepters. The molecule being metabolized does not have all its potential energy extracted from it. Beer and wine are produced by fermenting glucose with yeast. Yeast contains enzymes that catalyse the breakdown of glucose to ethanol and carbon dioxide.

14. (a) Primary treatment of sewage is a physical process and concerned mainly with the removal of coarse solid materials through filtration and sedimentation.

15. (d) Primary sludge is used for the preparation of compost, manure and biogas production. Primary sludge is a result of the capture of suspended solids and organics in the primary treatment process through gravitational sedimentation. The secondary treatment process uses microorganisms to consume the organic matter in the wastewater. The microorganisms feed on the biodegradable material in the wastewater in the aeration tank then flow into a secondary clarifier where the biomass settles out and removed as secondary sludge.

16. (a)   17. (b)

18. (c) Zymase is an enzyme complex that catalyzes the fermentation of sugar into ethanol and carbon dioxide. It occurs naturally in yeasts. Its activity varies among yeast strains.

19. (d) Activated sludge is a mass of microorganisms cultivated in the treatment process to break down organic matter into carbon dioxide, water, and other inorganic compounds. The activated sludge process has three basic components: i) a reactor in which the microorganisms are kept in suspension, aerated, and in contact with the waste they are treating; ii. liquid-solid separation and iii. a sludge recycling system for returning activated sludge back to the beginning of the process.

20. (c) Antibiotics are medicines that are produced by certain microorganisms to kill other disease causing microorganisms. These medicines are commonly obtained from bacteria and fungi.

21. (a) *Clostridium butylicum* (a bacterium) is used for the production of butyric acid. An bioactive molecule, cyclosporin A, that is used as an immunosuppressive agent in organ-transplant patients, is produced by the fungus *Trichoderma polysporum*. Statins produced by the yeast *Monascus purpureus* have been commercialized as blood-

Biology

cholesterol lowering agents. It acts by competitively inhibiting the enzyme responsible for synthesis of cholesterol. *Aspergillus niger* (a fungus) is used for the commercial production of citric acid.

22. (c) The sediment in settlement tank is called activated sludge. A small part of the activated sludge is pumped back into aeration tank. Remaining major part of the sludge is pumped into large tank called anaerobic sludge digesters.

23. (b) Microbes are used in production of several household and industrial products –
   * *Lactobacillus* – Production of curd
   * *Saccharomyces cerevisiae* – Bread making
   * *Aspergillus niger* – Citric acid production
   * *Acetobacter aceti* – Acetic acid

24. (b) Statins are drugs that can lower blood cholesterol. It is obtained from a yeast (Fungi) called *Monascus purpureus*.
   They work by blocking a substance, body needs to make cholesterol.

25. (d) A good source of citric acid is *Aspergillus niger* (a fungus). Apart from citric acid, oxalic acid, gallic acid, gluconic acid are extracted from fungus.

26. (d) Methanogens are anaerobic unicellular organisms that release methane as a waste product of cellular metabolism.

27. (d) Biofertilisers are organisms that enrich the nutrient quality of the soil. The main sources of biofertilisers are bacteria, fungi and cyanobacteria. Cyanobacteria like *Anabaena, Nostoc* etc. and *Rhizobium (which form root modules in leguminous plants)* are able to fix atmospheric nitrogen into organic forms which is used by the plant as nutrients. *Rhizopus and Aspergillus are used in production of other compounds of human benefit.*

28. (a) Biocontrol agents are natural enemies like parasitism, predation and other mechanisms for controlling the plant pests. They play an important role in controlling the plant pests like nematodes weeds, insects, and mites and also helps in maintaining and balancing the plant species along with their natural enemies. A good biocontrol agent should be species-specific and inactive on non-target organisms.

29. (b) Biocontrol agents are those natural organisms like parasitism, predation and other mechanisms which play an important role in controlling the plant pests like nematodes weeds, insects, and mites and helps in maintaining and balancing the plant species along with their natural enemies. Fungus *Trichoderma*, Baculoviruses (NPV) and *Bacillus thuringiensis* are used as biocontrol agents.
   Rhizobium, Nostoc, Azospirillum and *Oscillatoria* are used as biofertilisers, whereas TMV is a pathogen and aphids are pests that harm crop plants.

30. (a) *Trichoderma* is a very effective biological mean for plant disease management especially the soil born. It is a free-living fungus which is common in soil and root ecosystems. It reduces growth, survival or infections caused by pathogens by different mechanisms like competition, antibiosis, mycoparasitism, hyphal interactions, and enzyme secretion.

31. (d) *Clostridium butylicum* is used for butyric acid production

32. (d) A - (iii), B - (iv), C - (i), D - (ii)

Think Out of the Box :

Case Study-1

1. Vaccine is a biological preparation to improve immunity for a panticular disease. It consists of an inactive, weakened killed form of a microbe its toxins or its surface proteins. Once this cocktail is injected in an individual antibodies are produced as an immune response. These antibodies will help in fighting any future infection with COVID-19. Therefore, vaccination will not cause a disease but will help in preventing it.

2. Refrigeration only delay but do not completely rule out the possibility of food spoilage. If the food is taken out of the freezer, the microbes start growing again.

Case Study-2

1. If pasteurized milk is kept at the room temperature, then it will promote the growth of microbes. Hence, it is boiled and then stored in fridge to be used for a longer period of time.

2. Sugarcane can be best preserved in the form of jaggery or jaggery chocolates.

3 Conservation of Plants and Animals

Build A Strong Foundation

CONCEPT MAP

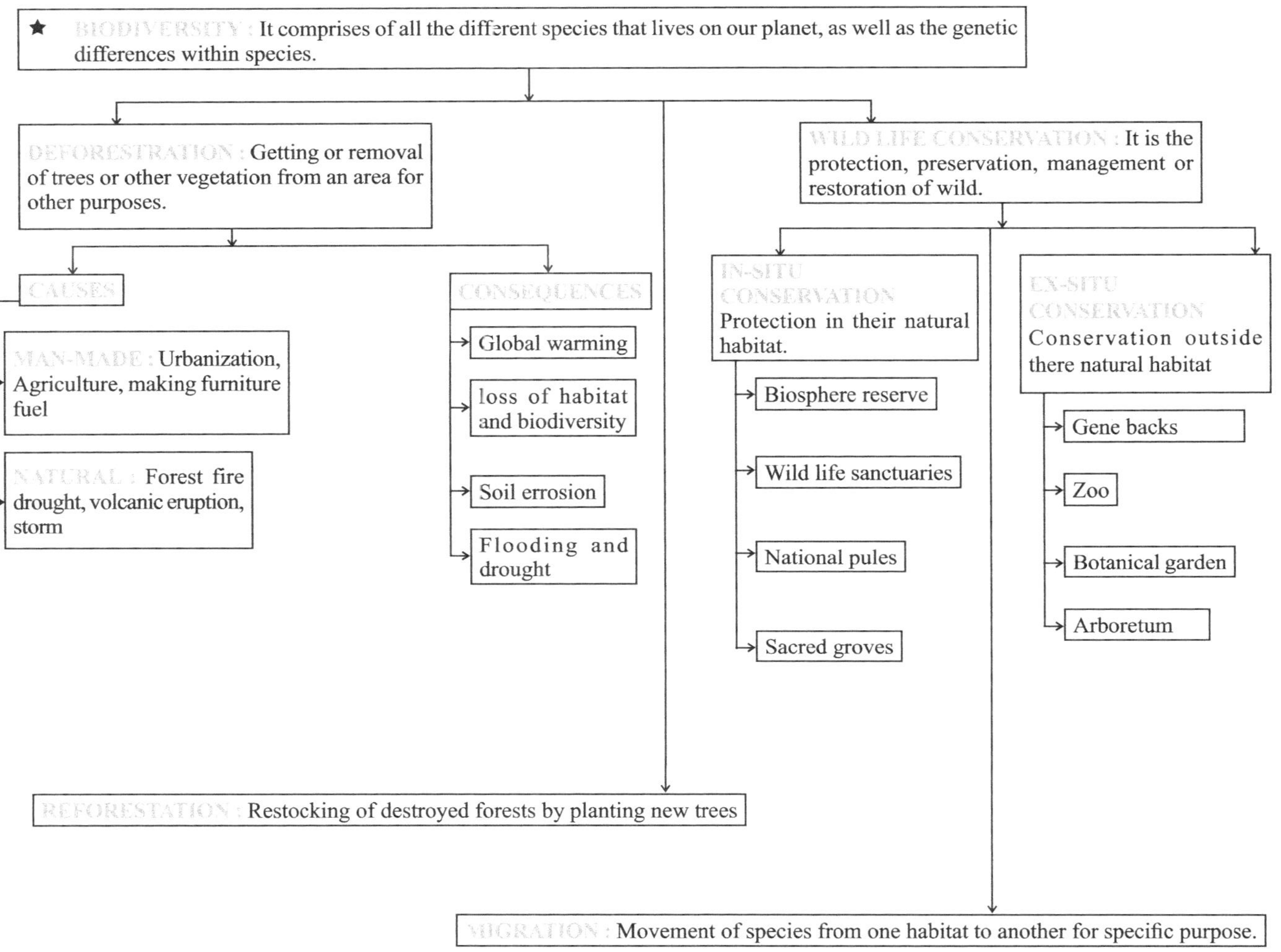
★ BIODIVERSITY : It comprises of all the diffərent species that lives on our planet, as well as the genetic differences within species.
DEFORESTRATION : Getting or removal of trees or other vegetation from an area for other purposes.
CAUSES
MAN-MADE : Urbanization, Agriculture, making furniture fuel
NATURAL : Forest fire drought, volcanic eruption, storm
CONSEQUENCES
Global warming
loss of habitat and biodiversity
Soil errosion
Flooding and drought
WILD LIFE CONSERVATION : It is the protection, preservation, management or restoration of wild.
IN-SITU CONSERVATION Protection in their natural habitat.
Biosphere reserve
Wild life sanctuaries
National pules
Sacred groves
EX-SITU CONSERVATION Conservation outside there natural habitat
Gene backs
Zoo
Botanical garden
Arboretum
REFORESTATION : Restocking of destroyed forests by planting new trees
MIGRATION : Movement of species from one habitat to another for specific purpose.

★ *Belongs to connecting topic.*

DEFORESTATION

Deforestation is the cutting or removal of trees or other vegetation from an area for industrial, agricultural or other purposes. It involves permanent end of forest cover to make that land available for residential, commercial or industrial purpose. Deforestation is considered to be one of the contributing factors to global climate change.

Causes of deforestation

The causes of deforestation can be classified into two classes :- Man made and natural causes of deforestation.

(i) Man-made causes of deforestation: These are the primary and the most common reasons of deforestation.
  (a) Forests are cleared for procuring ;and for cultivation.
  (b) Forests are destroyed for building houses and factories.
  (c) Trees are also cut down for making furniture or using wood as fuel.

(ii) Natural causes of deforestation: These include
  (a) **Forest fires:** These are caused by lightning and strong winds that help to spread the flames. Hundreds of trees are lost each year due to forest fires in various parts of the world. This happens due to extreme warm summers and milder winters.
  (b) **Severe droughts:** Drought in the forest has increased the amount of flammable bush and debris on the forest fires. As a result, the forest catches fire easily and destroys the immeasurable amount of valuable timber. Drought reduces the humidity and rainfall. If drought stays long enough, the leaf litter dries out killing off decomposers and reducing the effectiveness of nutrient cycling.
  (c) **Volcanic eruption:** It is one of the several natural forces that is capable of causing damage to forests. The ashes emitted during the eruption coat tree leaves, which in turn interfere with photosynthesis and destroy the plants.
  (d) **Typhoon or heavy storm:** These are violent storms that destroy much of the rain forest.

Note

Habitat is the natural surroundings of a plant or an animal, where it grows, multiplies and thrives naturally.

CONSEQUENCES OF DEFORESTATION

(i) Climate change & global warming : Deforestation increases the temperature and pollution level on Earth. Plants absorb CO_2 from the atmosphere to perform photosynthesis. If the plants are destroyed then the level of CO_2 in the atmosphere will rise. As a result, CO_2 will trap more radiations, thereby resulting in global warming. Global warming refers to an average increase in earth's temperature. Global warming is caused largely due to emissions of greenhouse gases like carbon dioxide into the atmosphere.

(ii) Loss of biodiversity : Deforestation leads to loss of biodiversity. If we go on cutting trees, the natural habitats of many animals will get completely destroyed. As a result the biodiversity of many areas will be severely affected.

(iii) Loss of habitat : Deforestation also destroys the habitat of many wild animals. The habitat of an animal provides shelter, food and protection. If the habitat of an animal is disturbed then it will go to other places in search of food and shelter. As a result, it could get killed easily by other animals in this process.

(iv) Soil erosion : Deforestation increases soil erosion. Roots of plants hold soil particles together. In the absence of plants, the top layer of the soil will be easily removed by the action of high speed winds or water flow.

(v) Desertification : Deforestation leads to desertification. In the absence of trees, soil erosion occurs more rapidly exposing the lower hard and rocky layer. As a result, soil loses humus and becomes less fertile. Hence, a fertile land, which acts as a source of living for farmers gets converted into a desert. This process is known as *desertification* of land.

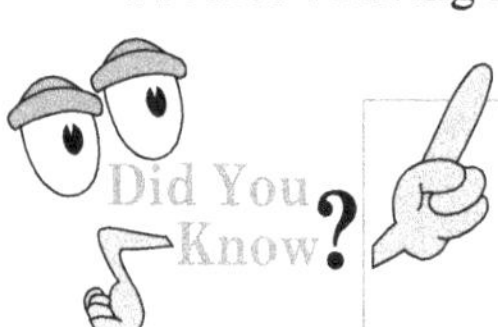

Facts on deforestation
- *Forests cover 30% of the earth's land.*
- *Agriculture is the leading cause of deforestation.*
- *Deforestation has considerably stopped in places like Europe, Pacific, North America and some parts of Asia due to lack of agricultural land.*
- *Poverty, over-population and unequal land access are the main causes of man- made deforestation.*
- *Worldwide more than 1.6 billion people rely on forests products for all or part of their livelihoods.*
- *The world's forests store 283 billion tons of carbon present in the biomass.*

(vi) Disruption of the water cycle: Trees plays an important role in maintaining the water cycle. They draw up water *via* their roots, which are then released into the atmosphere. A large part of the water that circulates in the ecosystem of rainforests, for example, remains inside the plants. When these trees are cut down, it results in the climate getting drier in that area. The level of groundwater tables are affected and soon get depleted. The trees help in prevention of running off of water and help the soil absorb the flowing water. When there are no trees, water just runs off, leaving no chance for the groundwater tables to absorb more water. This will ultimately lead to reduction in water resources.

(vii) Scarcity of product : Deforestation results in the shortage of products we get from forests.

(viii) Flooding and Drought: One of the vital functions of forests is to absorb and store great amounts of water quickly when there are heavy rains. When forests are cut down, this regulation of the flow of water is disrupted, which leads to alternating periods of flood and then drought in the affected area and thus leading in disruption of human settlements as well as loss of life in thousands.

Therefore, we need to conserve the biodiversity for our survival and to maintain the natural ecological balance.

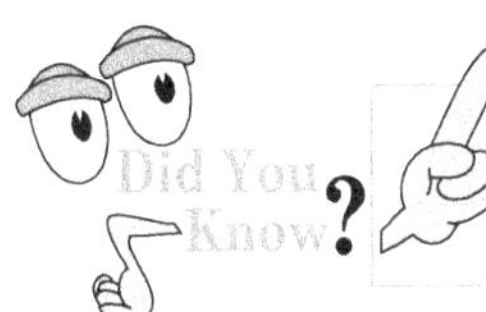

If the deforested area is left undisturbed, it re-establishes itself. This is known as natural reforestation. There is no role of human being in it.

CONNECTING TOPIC

BIODIVERSITY

Biodiversity comprises of different species that live on our planet as well as the genetic differences within species. Biodiversity of Earth includes all organisms-big and small, from an Amoeba to a blue whale and from algae to the Sequoia tree, that exist on our planet. The biodiversity of a region depends on the environment of that region. For example, plants, animals and even microorganisms living in a desert region are very different from those living in a forest. Similarly, organisms living in a grassland are entirely different from ocean. This means every different region on Earth has its own biodiversity.

Conservation of Biodiversity

Conservation is the protection, preservation, management or restoration of wild life and natural resources. Natural resources are those living and non-living resources of the Earth which have the potentiality to be used by human beings to fullfill their requirements of food, shelter and clothing etc. The common natural resources include energy, air, water, land, minerals, microorganisms, plants and animals. Wild life and Forest constitute the biotic resource of nature, while air, water, land etc. are abiotic resource of nature.

To conserve biodiversity, we need to establish protected areas for plants and animals, restoring ecosystems and managing already existing plant and animals.

Through the conservation of biodiversity the survival of many species and habitats which are threatened due to human activities can be ensured.

Importance of forests (plants) and wildlife (animals)

(i) Roots of trees help to bind the soil. It helps to prevent the top soil from getting eroded by wind, and water.

(ii) Trees and other vegetation form the habitat of many animals. Hence, destroying forest would lead to destruction of natural habitat of many species of plants and animals.

(iii) Forest maintains a balance between carbon dioxide and oxygen levels in atmosphere.

(iv) It provides us useful products such as gum, timber, medicines, etc from trees.

(v) Plants and animals form vital links in food chains and food webs.

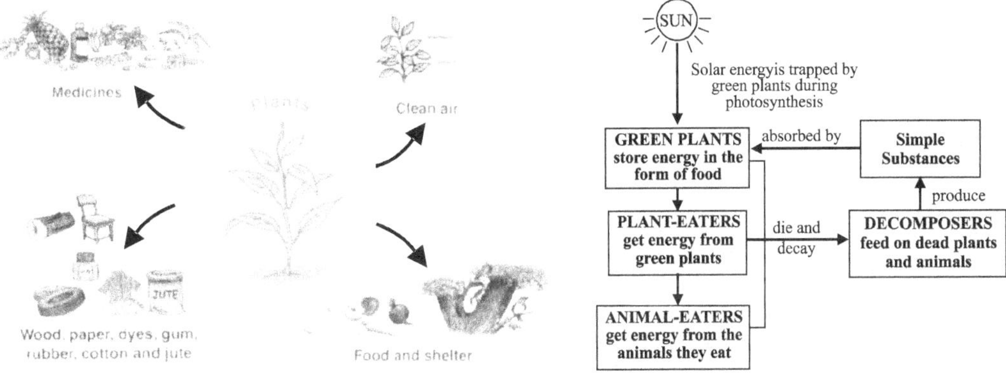

Importance of biodiversity   *Energy Pathway*

Food Webs

A food web is a system of interconnected and interdependent food chains. It can also be defined as a network of food relationships through which nutrients and energy are passed from one living organism to another.

The destruction of either of the two, plant or animal, will affect the life of other. Hence, we need to conserve biodiversity to maintain the balance of nature. But since, due to the overgrowing demands of over-population and urbanization our forest covers and wild life are under threat. One of the major threat to biodiversity is deforestation.

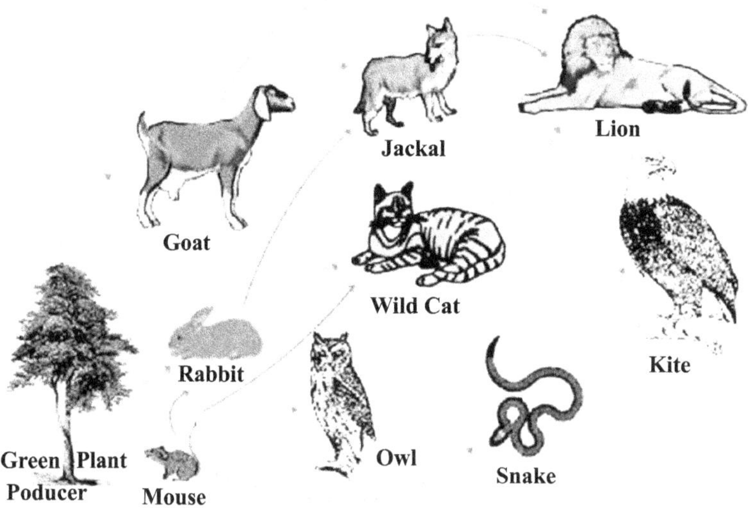

Food Web in a Forest

WILDLIFE AND ITS CONSERVATION

Wildlife includes those animals that have not been domesticated or tamed and are usually living in a natural environment. Deserts, forests, rain forests, plains, grasslands, and other areas including the most developed urban sites, all have distinct forms of wildlife. Wildlife is important because it balances population, maintain food chains, natural cycles, biodiversity, and prevents soil erosion etc. The government has also laid down several rules, methods and policies to protect and conserve the wildlife.

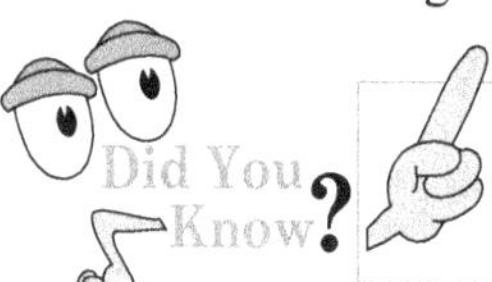

Species is a group of population that are able to reproduce offsprings only with members of a species that share common characteristics. For example, Homo sapiens or human beings form.

Endemic Species

Endemic species are those species of plants and animals that are found exclusively in that particular area and no where else in the world. For example, Bison and Indian giant squirrel are endemic flora of Pachmarhi Biosphere reserve whereas sal and wild mango are endemic fauna of this area.

The Great Indian Bustard is endemic to India. However it has been classified as endangered species that are on verge of extinction.

Threatened Species

A threatened species is a native species that is at risk of becoming endangered in the near future. A threatened species may have a declining population or be exceptionally rare. Like endangered species, the cause of its rarity is variable, but may be due to threats such as habitat destruction, climate change, or pressure from invasive species.

Extinct Species

You must have heard about dinosaurs. *Have you ever thought what happened to the dinosaurs that once existed on the Earth?* Yes, dinosaurs died and gradually disappeared from Earth because they were not able to reproduce and adapt to climate changes. When species are unable to compete with other organisms, and no longer exist on Earth then such species are called *extinct species*. Dodo, passenger pigeon etc are some examples of extinct species. *Dinosaur* got extinct due to natural reasons and *Dodo* became extinct mainly due to people hunting it for food.

Exotic species

An exotic species is any species intentionally or accidentally transported and released by man into an environment outside its present range. These plant and animal species are considered to be among the most servere agents of habitat alteration and degradation, and they are a major cause of the continuing loss of biological diversity throughout the world.

Endangered Species

Endangered species are those species that are on verge of becoming extinct. For example, blue whale, tiger, leopard etc are examples of endangered species.

Vulnerable Species

Vulnerable species are those species that already exists in low number and are likely to move into endangered category in the near future, if causal factors such as habitat destruction, over-exploitation and other environmental disturbances, continues over a period of time. Musk deer, sambhar deer, black buck etc are examples of vulnerable species.

Rare Species

Rare species includes those species whose population in the world is very small. So if they are not protected then they might fall into the category of vulnerable or endangered species. For example, Indian elephant, wild buffalo, bengal fox, gaur etc are rare species.

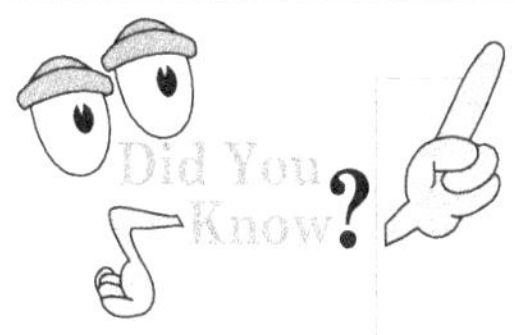

- *The black rhino has been reduced down to about 2,550 due to poaching. Most of the ones that survive today live in protected areas.*
- *Giant panda and the island fox are two examples of species whose existence on Earth has been threatened due to destruction of their habitat.*

Red Data Book

The Red Data Book is the state document established for documenting rare and endangered species of animals, plants and fungi as well as some local sub-species that exist within the territory of the state or country. This book provides central information for studies and monitoring programmes on rare and endangered species and their habits. Species are classified into different categories of perceived risk. Each Red Data Book usually deals with a specific group of animals or plants (e. reptiles, insects, mosses). Red data book has pink pages for critically endangered species.

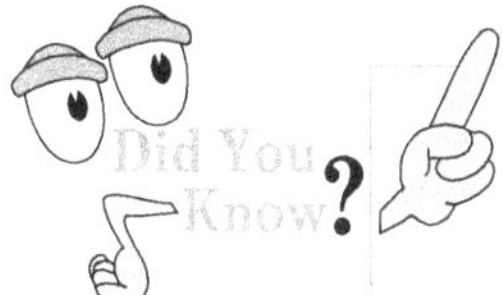

In red data book, 'red' stands for 'danger'. The 2000 Red List contains assessments of more than 18,000 species, 11,000 of which are threatened. According to the Red List, in India –

44 Plant species – Critically endangered

113 Plant species – Endangered

87 Plant species – Vulnerable

18 Animal species – Critically endangered

54 Animal species – Endangered

143 Animal species – Vulnerable

STRATEGIES FOR WILDLIFE CONSERVATION

Wildlife conservation is the practice of protecting endangered plant and animal species and their habitats. Wildlife conservation has become an increasingly important practice due to the negative effects of human activity on wildlife.

Several steps have been taken by government towards the conservation of our biodiversity (forest and wildlife). *Wildlife protection act* was passed in 1972 and amended in 1981. *Forest protection act* was passed in 1980 while *environment protection act* was passed in 1986. Under the wild life protection act, a large number of sanctuaries, national parks and biosphere reserves were established in different parts of the country.

The various strategies to conserve wildlife can be divided into two categories-

1. In-situ conservation

In-situ conservation is on-site conservation. It is the process of protecting an endangered plant or animal species in its natural habitat, either by protecting or cleaning up the habitat itself, or by defending the species from predators. It can be done through a network of protected area. It includes biological reserves, wildlife sanctuaries, National parks, sacred grooves and sacred parks.

2. Ex-situ conservation

Ex-situ conservation means literally, "off-site conservation". It is the conservation and maintenance of samples of living organisms outside their natural habitat, in the form of whole plants, seeds, pollens, vegetative propagules, and tissue or cell cultures. *Ex situ* conservation normally takes place in zoos, aquariums, botanical gardens, nurseries, wood and banks (seed, pollen, gene etc...) Moreover, they play a key role in providing material for scientific research which provides both a better understanding of the biological cycles of diverse species.

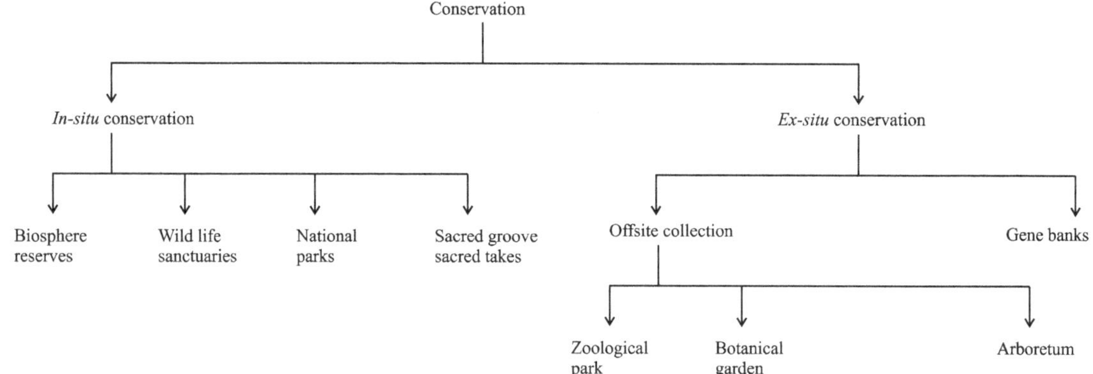

Flow chart : Categories of conservation

Important steps for wildlife conservation are:

(i) Protection of life in natural as well as artificial habitat.

(ii) Maintenance of life supporting system like air, water and land.

(iii) Protection of migratory animals by international agreements.

(iv) Preservation of an entire ecosystem rather than a single species.

(v) Discouraging the overexploitation of species of an ecosystem.

(vi) Preventing trade of rare species.

(vii) Setting up national parks, sanctuaries etc.

(viii) Integration of national conservation programmes with international ones.

In-situ Conservation

(i) **Biosphere reserves:** Biosphere reserves are multipurpose protected areas of land or water to support the conservation of ecosystems as well as the sustainability of mankind's impact on the environment. These areas were created by the United Nations Educational, Scientific, and Cultural Organization (UNESCO) under a program called Man and the Biosphere (MAB) in 1971. The first biosphere reserve in India was set up in 1986 in Nilgiri. There are about 686 biosphere reserves in 122 countries of the world. At present, 11 biosphere reserves of India have been recognised internationally under MAB programme.

Table : *Some biosphere reserves and their location in India.*

Biosphere Reserves	Location
Nilgiri	Tamil Nadu-Kerala
Gulf of Mannar	Tamil Nadu
Sunderban	West Bengal
Nanda Devi	Uttarakhand
Nokrek	Meghalaya
Pachmarhi	Madhya Pradesh
Similipal	Odisha
Achanakmar - Amarkantak	Madhya Pradesh - Chhattisgarh
Great Nicobar	Andaman & Nicobar Island
Agasthyamala	Karnataka-Tamil Nadu-Kerala
Khangchendzonga	Sikkim

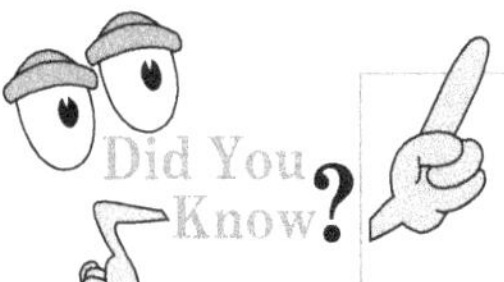

• ***The Bharatpur bird sanctuary is known as the largest bird sanctuary in Asia.***
• ***Ashoka was the first ruler to order the establishment of wildlife sanctuary.***

Biosphere reserves are divided into:

(i) **Core zone:** It is strongly protected for the conservation of biological diversity to make sure that different types of plants and animals are safe from human impact. In this area, no human activity is allowed.

(ii) **Buffer zone:** It surrounds the core zones and provides a space for environmental research, recreation, and tourism. Only limited human activity is allowed.

(iii) **Transition or manipulation zone:** This area is for local communities that have a hand in managing the resources of the area through farming, fisheries, and other non-governmental activities. Several human activities can occur in the manipulation zone.

(ii) Wildlife sanctuaries: It is an area within which animals are protected from all possible dangers such as hunting. Sanctuaries provide protection and suitable living conditions to wild animals. These sanctuaries protect some of the threatened wild animals such as black buck, Indian elephant, Pink headed duck, Gharial, Python, One horned rhinoceros etc.

At present there are 543 sanctuaries in India.

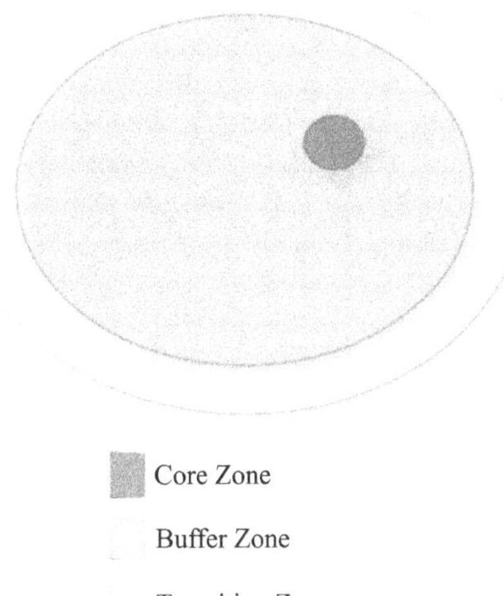

Table : *Some Wildlife sanctuaries of India*

S. No.	Name of the Sanctuary	Organisms for which they are known
(i)	Dachigam Sanctuary (J & K)	Kashmir Stag (Hangul)
(ii)	Bharatpur Bird Sanctuary (Rajasthan)	Siberian Crane, egrets herons (Famous for aquatic birds)
(iii)	Rann of Kutch Sanctuary (Gujarat)	Wild ass, the Flamingo, the Star tortoise and the Desert fox
(iv)	Gir Sanctuary (Gujarat)	Asiatic lion, Chital, Sambhar and Neelgai.
(v)	Bandipur Sanctuary (Karnataka)	Indian elephant.
(vi)	Madumalai Sanctuary (Tamil Nadu)	Indian elephant.
(vii)	Sanctuaries in Annamalai region (Tamil Nadu)	Elephant, tiger, panther, gaur etc

(iii) National parks: A national park is an area of land that is protected by the government to conserve wild life. In national park, animals can freely roam around and use the natural resources. Cultivation grazing, forestry and habitat manipulation are not allowed in the national parks. At present, there are 104 national parks in India.

Table : *Some National parks of India*

S. No.	Name of the National Park	Organisms for which they are known
(i)	Kaziranga National park (Assam)	One horned rhinoceros
(ii)	Desert National Park (Jaisalmer, Rajasthan)	Neelgai, Chinkara, Black Buck and Great Indian Bustard
(iii)	Corbett National Park (Uttarakhand)	Tiger, Elephant, Panther
(iv)	Kanha National Park (Madhya Pradesh)	Wild Tigers, Chinkara
(v)	Gir National Park (Gujarat)	Asiatic Lion, Panther, Sambar
(vi)	Sundarbans (West Bengal)	Royal Bengal Tiger

- *The World's first national park is yellow stone national park.*
- *The first national park of India was set up in the foot hills of Himalayas in Uttar Pradesh and was known as Hailey National Park. It is now known as Jim Corbett National Park.*

The main aim of establishing these protected areas is to preserve plant and animal life in their natural habitat. They are allowed to breed and multiply so that their numbers increase. The cutting down of trees and hunting animals in these protected areas are strictly prohibited.

Table : *Differences between Wild life sanctuary and Biosphere reserve*

S. No.	Wildlife sanctuary	Biosphere reserve
(i)	It is an area within which animals are protected from possible dangers such as hunting. Their habitat is also conserved in this area.	It is a large protected area constructed for the conservation of biodiversity.
(ii)	It provides protection and suitable living conditions to wild animals.	It helps in the conservation of various life forms such as plants, animals, and microorganisms.
(iii)	An example of wild life sanctuary is Gir sanctuary.	An example of biosphere reserve is Pachmarhi biosphere reserve.

(iv) Sacred groves: Sacred grove is an area with particular types of trees dedicated to local deities or ancestral spirits. They are protected by local communities through social traditions and taboos incorporating spiritual and ecological values. At present, 14,000 sacred groves have been reported from India.

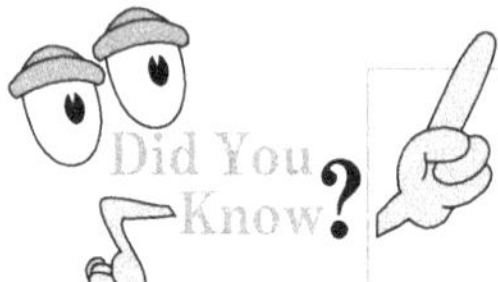

Sacred Groves of India comprise trees like Deodara (considered to be the "abode of Gods") Sal, Rudraksha, Bael, Ashok, Pipal, Neem, Banyan tree: native to India, Mango tree and bushes like, Basil (native to India and Iran) and grass like Doob or Durva etc.

Ex-Situ Conservation

(i) Zoological park (Zoo): A zoo or zoological park refers to any park, cage or an enclosure in which live animals are kept for public exhibition. It plays a major role in creating awareness among common people about the need to conserve nature. It is an artificial habitat that serves as breeding centres for some rare and endangered animals. Here, animals are bred under controlled conditions so that babies are well protected and preserved.

(ii) Botanical gardens: Botanical gardens are large protected areas established to conserve rare and threatened plants. It is a place where wide variety of plants are cultivated for scientific, educational and ornamantal purposes.
They serve as seed banks and have reserve of seeds of several species of plants. Here, seeds are preserved under controlled conditions.

(iii) Arboretum: An arboretum is a place where trees, shrubs and herbaceous plants are cultivated for scientific and educational purposes.

(iv) Gene banks: Gene banks are institutes that maintain stocks of viable seeds (seed bank), live growing plants (orchard), tissue culture and frozen germplasm with the whole range of genetic variability.

1. If a fish is to be conserved outside its habitat, where should it be kept ?
2. What is the difference between zoo and wild life sanctuary?

SOLUTION :
1. Fishes and aquatic organisms can be conserved in large aquaria.
2.

	Zoological Park (Zoo)	Wild Life Sanctuary
(i)	It is a facility where animals are kept for public exhibition	It is an area within which animals are protected from possible dangers such as hunting.
(ii)	It is an artificial habitat.	It conserves the natural habitat of animals.

Wildlife conservation refers to the practise of protecting wild species and their habitats in order to maintain healthy wildlife species or populations and to restore, protect or enhance natural ecosystem.

CASE - I : *Which conservation strategy is best for the conservation of germplasm?*

Gene banks, an *ex-situ* conservation strategy is best for the conservation of germplasm.

CASE - II : *Which in-situ conservation strategy covers the largest area?*

Biosphere reserves cover the largest area.

CASE - III : *Which in-situ conservation strategy is used for the conservation of only animals?*

Wildlife sanctuaries are only used for the conservation of wildlife i.e. wild animals.

CASE - IV : *Which zone of biosphere reserve is used for the purpose of environmental research?*

Buffer zone is used for the purpose of environmental research.

Think Out of the Box

Q 1. Which is the preferred method of wildlife conservation, *in-situ or ex-situ*?

Q 2. Write two advantages of ex-situ conservation over in-situ conservation strategies?

Q 3. Are haunting and logging permitted in sacred groves?

Try to identify the various type of flora and fauna present in your locality. Click their photo and make a scrap book.

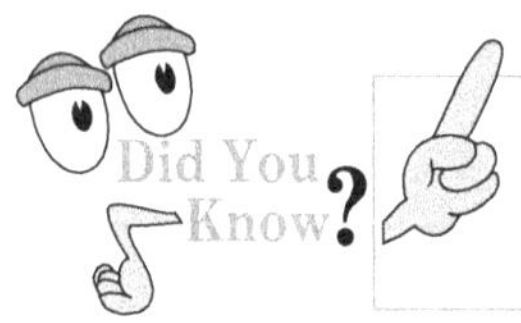

World Wide Fund for Nature (WWF) It is an organisation founded by 1961 by Sir Peter Scott. It aims at conservation of nature. It also plays a large role in raising funds towards projects concerned with saving wildlife in various parts of the globe.

PROJECT TIGER

Population of tiger is declining day by day or we can say that they have become an endangered species that are on verge of extinction and or will become extinct sooner or later. Due to this rapid decline in populations of tigers across the world, the government has started certain conservation programmes that aimed at saving tigers. For example, Project tiger.

Project Tiger is the most famous wildlife conservation project of India, which was launched on 1st April, 1973 to protect the diminishing population of Indian tigers.

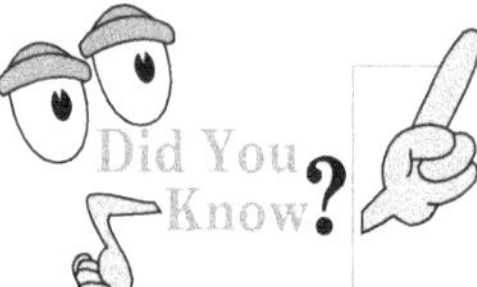

Gir Lion Project
The Gir forest in saurashtra perinsula of Gujarat is unique as it is the only surviving habitat of the Asian lion Panthera leon pressica. This lion is found only in Gir forest of Gujarat.

Objectives of Project Tiger

The main objective of Project Tiger is to ensure a viable population of tiger in India for scientific, economic, aesthetic, cultural and ecological values. Main objectives under the scheme include wildlife management, protection measures and site specific ecodevelopment to reduce the dependency of local communities on tiger reserve resources.

Then several plans were made such as –

(i)   All forms of human exploitation is removed from core areas.

(ii)   To restore the natural ecosystem of these reserves, human beings were restricted from the sites. The government decided to shift villages that came under the reserves to different areas.

(iii) The flora and fauna of these areas were monitored and were researched if they showed any change.

Achievement – You will be surprised to know that due to this programme, tiger population in Satpura tiger Reserve showed a significant increase.

☛   **How did the given animals become extinct?**

GIANT PANDA	YELLOW-EYED PENGUIN	RED WOLF
(Less than 1,000 remaining)	(About 3,000 left in the wind)	(Only 200 exist in capacity, none in the wild)

SOLUTION :

According to the theory of evolution, some animal species become extinct because they are less successful than other species that gradually replace them. These so-called "failed" animals that are unable to adapt to the changing circumstances or environment. Also, humans have acclerated this extinction by changing the environment so rapidly that animals do not have the time to adapt. Hunting is another main reason for the reduced numbers and probably extinction of animals such as tiger, the blue whale and the giant panda.

MIGRATION

The process of movement of animals in large numbers from one place to another to overcome unfavourble conditions is called migration. You must have heard of the Siberian crane that are actually endemic to Siberia. Do you know that they travel large distances and come to India in groups during winter? Why do they travel large distances and come to India? Actually, they travel long distances to escape the cold and unfavourable conditions of Siberia.

Migration is caused by the need to find food, by climatic changes during the year, and by the need to breed. Every autumn, for example, Swallows gather in large flocks to rest before they begin their long migration to Africa. Swallows and their relatives, swifts and martins migrate to Africa when the weather becomes too cold for them to catch their insect prey. They return in the spring when the weather in northern Europe begins to warm up.

The Arctic tern makes the longest known migration by travelling from the Arctic to the Antarctic and then back again. On its way, it passes through Japan, Alaska, Canada and Fiji before returning home again to breed.

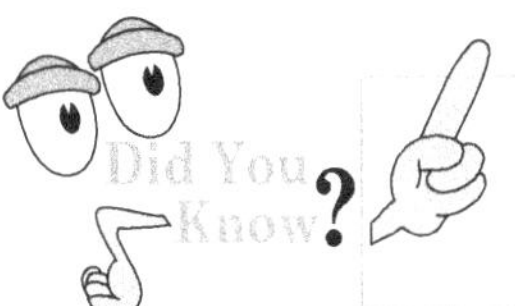

- *Many fishes migrate in both fresh water and the ocean.*
- *Tuna make some of the longest migrations. They need to migrate due to sea temperature, as fish need the correct temperature in order to breed.*

Advantages of Migration

(i) It provides migrating species more favourable conditions of temperature, food and water. For example, Siberian crane migrates to India during winters.

(ii) It also provides suitable place for reproduction that may not be available in their native place. For example, salmon migrates from salt water to freshwater to lay eggs and then comes back.

Hence, we can say organisms migrate from one place to another to avoid inhabitable climatic conditions or for breeding.

☞ **Migratory birds are susceptible to become endangered. Can you give the reason, why ?**

SOLUTION :

Migratory birds are susceptible to become endangered because many of the places they used to migrate have been altered by human actions. As a result, these animals don't have any place to go when weather conditions become harsh or food in their habitat becomes scarce.

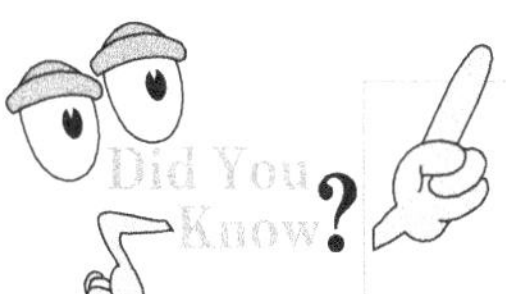

It takes seventeen full grown trees to make one ton of paper.

RECYCLING OF PAPER

Trees, as we know, are important to maintain the balance of nature. Therefore, in order to save trees and to prevent the impact of their loss, we need to use paper carefully.

Methods to save paper

(1) **Recycling of paper :** *Recycling* is the process of collecting waste paper and to regain materials in order to use them again. By recycling of paper, not only we can save trees but also can save energy and water needed for manufacturing paper. Hence, collect used paper and recycle it.

(2) Use both the sides of paper for writing.

(3) Spread awareness among people regarding the importance of paper.

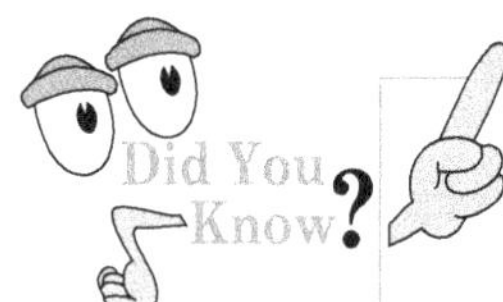

For every ton of paper that is recycled, the following are saved :
- *17 trees.*
- *275 pounds of sulphur.*
- *350 pounds of limestone.*
- *9000 pounds of steam.*
- *60,000 gallons of water.*
- *225 kilowatt hours of energy.*
- *3.3 cubic yards of landfill space.*

SUMMARY

- *Conservation* is the wise use of natural resources with an aim to preserve living and non-living resources.
- *Biodiversity* refers to variety of living organisms in a specific area.
- Plants and animals depend on each for survival.
- *Deforestation* is the process of cutting trees from an area for industrial, agricultural or other purposes.
- *Causes of deforestation are* – man-made; and natural like, forest fires, volcanic eruptions, drought etc.
- *Consequences of deforestation are* –
  - Soil erosion
  - Floods and droughts
  - Disruption of water cycle
  - Loss of biodiversity
  - Climate change due to global warming
  - Desertification
- Under the wild life protection act, a larger number of sanctuaries, national park and biosphere reserve were established in different parts of the country.
- *Sanctuaries* are areas where animals are protected from any disturbance to them and their habitat.
- *National park* are areas reserved for wild life where they can freely use the habitats and natural resources.
- *Biosphere reserves* are large protected areas for conservation of wildlife, plant and animal resources and traditional life of the tribals living on the area.
- IUCN (International Union for Conservation of Nature and Natural resources) works towards assessing the global conservation status of plants and animals.
- *Red data book* is the source book which keeps a record of all the endangered plants and animals.
- Plants and animals of a particular area are known as flora and fauna, respectively, of that area.
- *Endangered animals* are animals whose numbers are diminishing to a level that they might face extinction.
- *Endemic species* are those species of plants and animals that are found exclusively in a particular area.
- *Extinct animals* are animals that no longer exist in nature.
- *Project tiger* was launched on 1st April 1973 by government to protect the tigers of our country.
- *Migration* is the phenomenon of movement of a species from its own habitat to some other habitat for a particular time period, every year for a specific purposes like breeding.
- We should save, reuse and recycle paper to save trees, energy and water.
- *Reforestation* is the restoring of destroyed forests by planting new trees.
- If a forest area is left undisturbed for a long time, it restablishes itself.

Exercise 1 — Master Boards

Multiple Choice Questions

DIRECTIONS : *This section contains multiple choice questions. Each question has four choices (a), (b), (c) and (d) out of which ONLY ONE is correct.*

1. One of the following is not a part of the fauna of Pachmarhi Biosphere Reserve. This one is :
   (a) yak   (b) leopard
   (c) blue bull   (d) barking deer
2. Which of the following wild animals is not listed in the Red Data Book of India?
   (a) blackbuk   (b) flying squirrel
   (c) tiger   (d) leopard
3. An increase in the amount of carbon dioxide results in
   (a) winter season   (b) global warming
   (c) rainfall   (d) all of these
4. Name the sphere that supports life, and where living organism exists.
   (a) Atmosphere   (b) Lithosphere
   (c) Biosphere   (d) None of these
5. Which of the following is an endangered species of animals?
   (a) Dinosaur   (b) Asiatic lion
   (c) Irish deer   (d) Hyena

Assertion & Reason

DIRECTIONS : *Each of these questions contains an Assertion followed by Reason. Read them carefully and answer the question on the basis of following options. You have to select the one that best describes the two statements.*

(a) If both **Assertion** and **Reason** are **correct** and Reason is the **correct explanation** of Assertion.
(b) If both **Assertion** and **Reason** are correct, but Reason is **not the correct explanation** of Assertion.
(c) If **Assertion** is **correct** but **Reason** is **incorrect**.
(d) If **Assertion** is **incorrect** but **Reason** is **correct**.

1. **Assertion :** Reforestation may occur naturally in deforested area.
   Reason : This is a secondary succession.
2. **Assertion :** Critically endangered category includes the species which have sufficient population at present but is undergoing depletion due to some factors.
   Reason : Vulnerable category includes the species which are facing high risk of extinction in the wild and can becomes extinct any moment.
3. **Assertion :** A biosphere reserve is a specified area.
   Reason : No restriction on human activities has bear imposed is biosphere reserve.
4. **Assertion :** Now-a-day biodiversity is declining with an accelerated rate.
   Reason : Exotic species are considered to be major cause of extinction of species.
5. **Assertion :** Project Tiger was launched to improve the tiger population.
   Reason : Tiger is an endangered species in India.

Fill in the Blanks

DIRECTIONS : *Complete the following statements with an appropriate word / term to be filled in the blank spaces.*

1. The diverse plant species found in a particular area are known as _________.
2. In a wild life sanctuary, poaching of animals is _________.
3. _________ results in depletion of wild life.
4. Animals whose numbers are rapidly falling are called _________ species.
5. Illegal hunting of animals for their valuable body parts is called _________.
6. The natural surroundings of a plant or animal species is called _________.
7. Group of population capable of interbreeding is called _________.

True / False

DIRECTIONS : *Read the following statements and write your answer as true or false.*

1. Afforestation can cause desertification.
2. An average increase in Earth's temperature is known as global warming.
3. Tiger is an endangered species.
4. An animal that is widely distributed over the earth is said to be endemic.
5. Saving paper means saving trees.
6. Wildlife conservation and soil conservation are closely related.
7. Migratory birds fly to far away places every year during a particular time for a holiday.
8. The red data book shows species that are at the risk of extinction.

Match the Following

DIRECTIONS : *Each question contains statements/terms given in two columns which have to be matched. Statements/terms in column I have to be matched with statements/terms given in column II.*

1.

	Column-I (Terms)		Column-II (Feature)
A.	Biodiversity	(p)	Conversion of fertile land into deserts
B.	Desertification	(q)	Movement of species
C.	Deforestation	(r)	Variety of living organisms in specific area.
D.	Reforestation	(s)	Clearing of forests
E.	Biosphere reserve	(t)	Plantation of new trees.
F.	Migration	(u)	Large protected area meant for conservation of biodiversity

2.

Column-I (Terms)	Column-II (Definition)
A. Biosphere Reserve	(p) Areas where animals are protected from any disturbance to them and their habitat.
B. National parks	(q) Areas reserved for animals where they can freely use the habitats and natural resources.
C. Wildlife sanctuaries	(r) Large protected areas for conservation of wild life, plant and animal resources and traditional life of the tribals living in that area.

3.

Column-I	Column-II
A. Arctic tern	(p) Extinct species
B. *Homo sapiens*	(q) Endemic to Assam
C. Dodo	(r) Threatened species
D. Giant panda	(s) Forest reserves
E. Pachmarhi biosphere reserve	(t) A species
F. One-horned Rhino	(u) A migratory bird

Passage Based Questions

DIRECTIONS : *Study the given paragraph(s) and answer the following questions.*

Passage

Ritu is reading a topic 'Conservation of biodiversity via *in-situ* and *ex-situ*. She read about biodiversity hotspot. These area have high diversity of endemic species. She also read about Red Data Book.

1. Red Data Book keep the record of
 (a) endangered plants and animals
 (b) extinct animals and plants
 (c) endemic animals and plants
 (d) all of the above

2. The plants, animals and micro-organisms along with climate, soil, river etc., of an area referred to as
 (a) Ecosystem (b) Biosphere
 (c) Biodiversity (d) Kingdom

3. Which of the following is an endangered species of animals?
 (a) Dinosaur (b) Asiatic lion
 (c) Deer (d) Hyena

Very Short Answer Questions

1. Define biodiversity.
2. If one wants to conserve an organism outside its habitat, where should it be kept?
3. Name one endemic animal of India.
4. Are migratory animals susceptible to become endangered?
5. Name two animals that have become endangered due to poaching.
6. When is an animal said to be extinct?
7. What results in desertification, global warming and shortage of forest products?

8. Expand IUCN.
9. Give two examples of each flora and fauna of Pachmarhi biosphere reserve.
10. Why do birds migrate?
11. Who publishes the Red list of Threatened species?
12. Name three programmes that have gained recognition for conservation of nature.
13. What is conservation?
14. Which term refers to illegal hunting of animals?
15. What is the main aim of the IUCN Red list?
16. Name one international organization that aims at conservation of nature.
17. What does "Red" in Red Data book stands for?

Short Answer Questions

1. Why is biodiversity under threat?
2. How forest reserves help in conserving biodiversity?
3. Define
 (a) Sanctuaries (b) Zoological park
4. Name few sanctuaries in India along with animals they protect?
5. Write a short note on Project Tiger.
6. What is recycling of paper? How recycling of paper helps in saving trees?
7. Why it is necessary to conserve Wild Life?
8. How deforestation can lead to desertification?
9. How wild life conservation and forest conservation related to each other ?
10. Why forests are useful to us?
11. Why did IUCN prepare red data book?
12. How can governments ensure the preservation of biodiversity?
13.

Do you agree with this? Give reason.

Long Answer Questions

1. How deforestation leads to reduced rainfall?
2. List four causes and consequences of deforestation. What are the causes of extinction of wild life?
3. Define
 (1) Threatened species (2) Extinct species
 (3) Endemic species (4) Endangered species
4. Differentiate –
 (i) Flora and Fauna
 (ii) Endangered and threatened species
 (iii) Endemic and extinct species
 (iv) Wildlife sanctuary and zoological park.

Reasoning Based Questions

1. Explain how, deforestation makes the soil infertile leading to desertification.
2. Why even protected forests are not completely safe for wild animals.
3. Why does Siberian crane come from Siberia to place like Bharatpur in India every year for a few months?

4. Why should we saw, reuse and recycle paper?

5. Why should forests and wildlife be conserved?

6. Explain how, deforestation leads to frequent flooding of rivers.

HOTS Questions

1.

Is this statements correct? Explain using example.

2. Introduction of an exotic species to a habitat has a negative impact on the diversity of that region. Comment.

3. How is diversity related to environmental health?

4. Captive breeding programmes help in maintaining biodiversity. How?

5. Why are migratory animals susceptible to face extinction?

6. Suppose an animal species 'X' not normally found in your area is released where you live. If that animal has no natural enemies there, what might happen?

7. Why Indian Rhinoceros and Asian elephants are placed in the Red List. Explain, giving example.

8.

Do you agree with the statement given. Give reason in support of your answer.

9. A tiger from wildlife sanctuary was shifted in a Zoological garden. Where do you think the tiger will be happier.

10. A construction company used to cut 10 trees every month and planted 10 new saplings every month as replacement. Do you think they are successful in maintaining the number of trees in a forest. Justify.

11. State the laws that your state has for the protection of endangered wildlife. Find out if there is a state endangered species list. Report your findings in your class.

Exercise 2   ⬡ Master NCERT (Text–book & Exemplar)

Text-book Exercise

1. (a) A place where animals are protected in their natural habitat is called ______.

(b) Species found only in a particular area is known as ______.

(c) Migratory birds fly to far away places because of ______ changes.

(d) Information about endangered species is recorded in the ______.

(e) ______ is the restocking of destroyed forests by planting new trees.

2. Differentiate between the following:

(a) Wildlife sanctuary and biosphere reserve

(b) Zoo and wildlife sanctuary

(c) Endangered and extinct species

3. Discuss the effects of deforestation on the following :

(a) Wild animals   (b) Environment

(c) Villages (Rural areas) (d) Cities (Urban areas)

(e) Earth   (f) The next generation

4. What will happen if :

(a) we go on cutting trees.

(b) the habitat of an animal is disturbed.

(c) the top layer of soil is exposed.

5. **Answer in brief :**

(a) Why should we conserve biodiversity?

(b) Protected forests are also not completely safe for wild animals. Why?

(c) Some tribals depend on the jungle. How?

(d) What are the causes and consequences of deforestation?

(e) What is Red Data Book?

(f) What do you understand by the term migration?

6. In order to meet the ever-increasing demand in factories and for shelter, trees are being continually cut, is it justified to cut trees for such projects? Discuss and prepared a brief report.

7. How can you contribute to the maintenance of green wealth of your locality? Make a list of actions to be taken by you.

8. Explain how deforestation leads to reduced rainfall.

9. Find out the information about the national parks in your state. Identify and show their location on the outline map of India.

10. Why should paper be saved? Prepare a list of ways by which you can save paper.

11. **Complete the word puzzle :**

DOWN

1. Species on the verge of extinction.
2. A book carrying information about endangered species.
5. Consequence of deforestation.

ACROSS

1. Species which have vanished.
3. Species found only in a particular habitat.
4. Variety of plants, animals and microoganisms found in an area.

Exemplar Questions

1. Why is it important to conserve forests?

2. Can a forest regenerate naturally in a short period of time.

3. Name the first Reserve Forest of India.

4. Why are wildlife sanctuaries important for conservation of plants and animals?

5. Why are endemic organisms in greater danger of becoming extinct?

6. A new species X is introduced in a forest. How is it likely to affect the local species of that area?

7. Does soil erosion affect the fertility of soil? How?

8. Is deforestation associated with global warming? Explain.

9. How does deforestation lead to frequent floods and droughts?

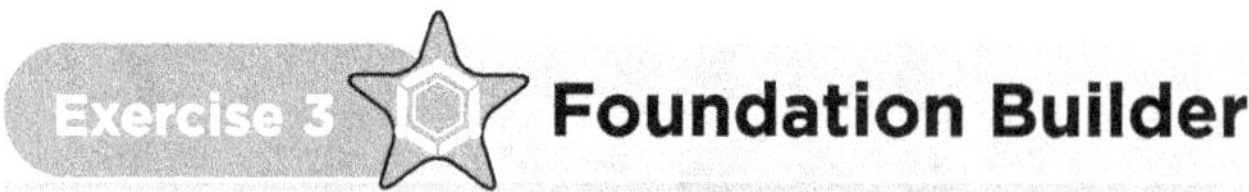

Exercise 3 — Foundation Builder

Multiple Choice Questions

DIRECTIONS : *This section contains multiple choice questions. Each question has four choices (a), (b), (c) and (d) out of which ONLY ONE is correct.*

1. The human activity that is responsible for loss of biodiversity is
   (a) urbanization
   (b) afforestation
   (c) establishment of biosphere reserve
   (d) respiration

2. Species native to a particular habitat is known as
   (a) endemic species   (b) endangered species
   (c) threatened species   (d) extinct species

3. An example of extinct species is
   (a) The Royal Bengal tiger
   (b) The Giant Panda
   (c) The African elephant
   (d) The Dinosaur

4. The Kaziranga wildlife sanctuary preserves
   (a) elephant   (b) rhinoceros
   (c) asiatic lions   (d) royal bengal tiger

5. The endangered species are listed out in
   (a) blue data book   (b) red data book
   (c) yellow data book (d) green data book

6. The diverse animal species found in their natural surroundings is called
   (a) flora   (b) fauna
   (c) endemic species   (d) endangered species

7. Which of these is not caused by deforestation?
   (a) Global warming
   (b) Desertification
   (c) Reduction in ground water
   (d) Storms

8. Which one of these is not included under Red list?
   (a) Extinct   (b) Endemic
   (c) Endangered   (d) Vulnerable

9. World wild fund for Nature Works in the field of
   (a) Wildlife conservation
   (b) Forest conservation
   (c) Water conservation
   (d) Soil conservation

10. The Indian Government launched "Project Tiger" in
    (a) 1970   (b) 1973
    (c) 1974   (d) 1975

11. The variety of forms of life found in a region is
    (a) biodiversity   (b) flora
    (c) fauna   (d) endemic

12. Decrease in population size over few years and decrease in the size of its habitat indicates that an organism is
    (a) threatened   (b) vulnerable
    (c) extinct   (d) endemic

13. An area made up of living components like plants, animals and microorganisms along with non-living component such as climate, soil etc is known as
    (a) ecosystem   (b) population
    (c) community   (d) organism

14. Which is not a consequence of deforestation?
    (a) Desertification (b) Global warming
    (c) Poaching   (d) Floods

15. Which of the following is an example of a single cell that does not function as a full-fledged organism?   **[NTSE]**
    (A) White blood cell (WBC)
    (B) *Amoeba*
    (C) WBC and *Amoeba*
    (D) *Paramecium*
    (a) (B) only   (b) (B) and (D)
    (c) (A) only   (d) (C) and (D)

16. Meena had a big farm. On Sunday she went to her farm and was surprised to see a house being constructed and a wooden almirah being made out of a tree.   **[NTSE]** This may be considered as
    (A) reforestation   (B) desertification
    (C) deforestation   (D) drought
    Which of the following is correct?
    (a) (A) and (B)   (b) (A) and (D)
    (c) (C) only   (d) (A) only

17. Select the correct statements with respect to migration in animals.   **[NTSE]**
    (A) The same Siberian Crane can be seen in Bharatpur in two consecutive winters.
    (B) Some fish lay eggs in rivers and the fingerlings gradually swim to sea.
    (C) Some fish migrate from cold climate to a warmer climate to escape cold weather.
    (D) Some butterflies migrate up to 10,000 kilometres to escape cold weather.
    Which of the following alternative has the correct statements?
    (a) (A) and (B)   (b) (B) and (C)
    (c) (C) and (D)   (d) (A) and (D)

18. A similarity among black buck, gharial, rhinoceros and marsh crocodile is that they are   **[NTSE]**
    (a) animals with thick chitinous skin
    (b) oviparous
    (c) endangered species
    (d) found in the forests of north-east India

19. Students were taken to a museum on an educational trip. Which one of the following documents will provide the information on endangered animals and plants?
    (a) Data book   (b) Atlas   **[NTSE]**
    (c) Red Data Book   (d) Dictionary

20. Which one of the following signifies *ex-situ* conservation?   **[NTSE]**
    (a) National parks and Biosphere habitats
    (b) Wild animal in their natural habitats
    (c) Inhabitants of natural ecosystems
    (d) Conservation methods practiced in Zoo and Botanical garden

21. The record of all endangered plants and animals is called as: **[JSTSE]**
(a) Flora   (b) Monograph
(c) Manual   (d) Red Data Book

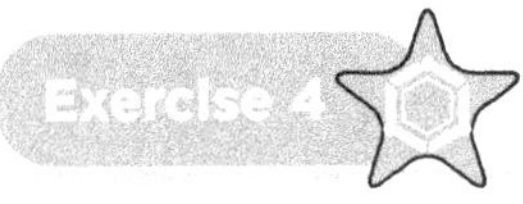

Assertion & Reason

DIRECTIONS : *Each of these questions contains an Assertion followed by Reason. Read them carefully and answer the question on the basis of following options. You have to select the one that best describes the two statements.*

(a) If both **Assertion** and **Reason** are **correct** and Reason is the **correct explanation** of Assertion.
(b) If both **Assertion** and **Reason** are correct, but Reason is **not the correct explanation** of Assertion.
(c) If **Assertion** is **correct** but **Reason** is **incorrect**.
(d) If **Assertion** is **incorrect** but **Reason** is **correct**.

1. **Assertion :** Spotted dear and black buck belongs to category of vulnerable species.
Reason : They are species whose number is declining and if not protected they can become endangered species.

2. **Assertion :** The Earth was once dominated by dinosaurs.
Reason : Dinosaurs got extinct due to natural calamities.

3. **Assertion :** The great Indian Bustard has been threatened.
Reason : It is due to introduction of new species in their habitat.

4. **Assertion :** IUCN publishes a comprehensive list known as IUCN Red list of endemic species.
Reason : IUCN Red list is to focus the attention of conservationists towards species that are under threat of becoming extinct.

5. **Assertion :** Afforestation is a positive step towards restoration of forest and wildlife.
Reason : Afforestation is a slow process.

Exercise 4 — ⭐ Foundation Builder +

Multiple Choice Questions

DIRECTIONS (Qs.1-8): *This section contains multiple choice questions. Each question has four choices (a), (b), (c) and (d) out of which ONLY ONE is correct.*

1. A species facing extremely high risk of extinction in the immediate future is called:
(a) Vulnerable   (b) Endemic
(c) Critically endangered   (d) Extinct

2. The organization which publishes the Red List of species is:
(a) ICFRE   (b) IUCN
(c) UNEP   (d) WWF

3. Tiger is **not** a resident in which one of the following national park?
(a) Sunderbans   (b) Gir
(c) Jim Corbett   (d) Ranthambhor

4. According to Robert May, the global species diversity is about **[NTSE]**
(a) 20 million   (b) 50 million
(c) 7 million   (d) 1.5 million

5. Which of the following is the most important cause of animals and plants being driven to extinction? **[NTSE]**
(a) Over - exploitation
(b) Alien species invasion
(c) Habitat loss and fragmentation
(d) Co-extinctions

6. Which of the following regions of the globe exhibits highest species diversity? **[NTSE]**
(a) Madagascar   (b) Himalayas
(c) Amazon forests   (d) Western Ghats of India

7. Which of the following is the most important cause for animals and plants being driven to extinction? **[NTSE]**
(a) Habitat loss and fragmentation
(b) Drought and floods
(c) Economic exploitation
(d) Alien species invasion

8. Which one of the following is not a method of in situ conservation of biodiversity? **[NTSE]**
(a) Biosphere Reserve   (b) Wildlife Sanctuary
(c) Botanical Garden   (d) Sacred Grove

Multiple Matching Questions

DIRECTIONS : *Each question contains two columns which have to be matched. Statement/terms given in column I have to be matched with statement/terms given in column II.*

9. Match Column-I with Column-II and choose the correct option

	Column-I		Column-II
A.	Nile Perch in Lake Victoria	1.	Obvious reasons for biodiversity conservation
B.	Narrowly utilitarian	2.	Habitat destruction
C.	Main cause for biodiversity loss	3.	High endemism
D.	Hot spots	4.	Alien species

(a) A→(2), B→(1), C→(4), D→(3)
(b) A→(4), B→(1), C→(2), D→(3)
(c) A→(1), B→(3), C→(2) , D→(4)
(d) A→(2), B→(1), C→(3), D→(4)

10. Find out the pairs, which are correctly matched

	Column-I		Column-II
A.	Rhinoceros	1.	Bharatpur
B.	Tiger project in Karnataka	2.	Tropical evergreen forest
C.	Assemblage protection	3.	Kaziranga
D.	Silent valley	4.	National park
		5.	Bandipur

(a) A→(5), B→(3), C→(1), D→(4)
(b) A→(2), B→(4), C→(3), D→(5)
(c) A→(4), B→(3), C→(2) , D→(5)
(d) A→(3), B→(5), C→(1), D→(2)

SOLUTIONS
(Brief Explanations of Selected Questions)

Multiple Choice Questions

1. (a)   2. (d)   3. (b)   4. (c)   5. (b)

Assertion & Reason

1. (b) Both Assertion and Reason are correct but Reason is not the correct explanation of Assertion.
   The planting of trees in an area in which forests were destroyed is called reforestation. It can also take place naturally. If the deforested area is left undisturbed for some time, it re-established itself by the natural growth of trees. This is also included in the secondary succession.

2. (d) Both Assertion and Reason are false.
   Critically endangered is the highest risk category assigned by the IUCN red list for wild species. 'Vulnerable' species are those whose population is sufficient at present but is undergoing depletion due to some factors so that it is facing the risk of becoming extinct in medium term future.

3. (c) Assertion is true but Reason is false.
   Biosphere reserve are multipurpose protected areas. Multiple uses of the land is permitted by dividing it into zones, each for particular activity.
   These zones are
   (i) Core (no human activity)
   (ii) Buffer (limited human activity)
   (iii) Manipulation zone (several activity occur)

4. (b) Both Assertion and Reason are true and Reason is the correct explanation of Assertion.
   Biodiversity is extinct in accelerated great because of a variety of factor like destruction of habitat, disturbance and degradation of habitat. Exotic species are the ones that enter a new graphical area and hinder the growth of native species of that particular area.

5. (a) Both Assertion and Reason are true and Reason is the correct explanation of Assertion.
   There are approx 21 tiger reserves in India. To save the tiger from extinction in India. Project Tiger was launched on April 1, 1973. This project planned to create tiger reserve in selected area of India. Due to his effort, considerable improvement has been observed in tiger population.

Fill in the Blanks

1. Fauna   2. Prohibited   3. Deforestation
4. Endangered   5. Poaching   6. Habitat
7. Species.

True / False

1. False. Deforestation can cause desertification.

2. True   3. True
4. False. Endemic species are found only in a particular area.
5. True   6. True
7. False. Migratory birds migrate to find food, escape the inhospital winter condition and reproduction.
8. True

Match the Following

1. A → (r), B → (p), C → (s), D → (t), E → (u), F → (q)
2. A → (r), B → (p), C → (q)
3. A → (u), B → (t), C → (p), D → (r), E → (s), F → (q)

Passage Based Questions

1. (a)   2. (a)   3. (b)

Very Short Answer Questions

1. The variety of life forms found on our planet in a particular area is called bidiversity.
2. Zoological park
3. Great Indian Bustard
4. Yes
5. Rhinoceros and Tiger
6. When an organism no longer exists in nature, it is said to be extinct.
7. Deforestation
8. International Union for Conservation of Nature and Natural Resources.
9. Sal and teak are the flora and chinkara and leopard are examples of fauna of Pachmarhi Biosphere Reserve.
10. Birds migrate from one place to another to beat unfavourble conditions and for breeding.
11. IUCN
12. Vanmahotsav Programme, the Chipko Andolan and Project Tiger.
13. Conservation refers to use of natural resources with an aim to preserve or protect living and non-living resources.
14. Poaching
15. Main aim of IUCN is to identify and documentation of endangered species.
16. WWF (World Wide Fund for Nature)
17. "Red" stands for "Danger".

Short Answer Questions

1. Biodiversity is under threat due to the following reasons
   (i) Increase in human population.
   (ii) Pollution of air, water and land.
   (iii) Climatic changes, for example, global warming.
   (iv) Poaching.
   (v) Natural disasters such as earthquake, floods, droughts etc.

2. Forest reserves helps in conserving biodiversity by serving the following purposes :
   (i) Prevention of deforestation.
   (ii) Replenishment of lost forest by afforestation
   (iii) Protection of food and shelter meant for wildlife.

Conservation of Plants and Animals

3. (a) A sanctuary is a protected land area where animals are brought to live and be protected for the rest of their lives. Hunting is strictly prohibited there.

   (b) Zoological park is a collection of wild animals kept in close or open confinement usually for public viewing.

4. Wildlife sanctuaries in India have been extremely successful in conserving the wildlife of India. They are the ideal place to witness the imposing beauty of the forests and their endless range of wildlife. Examples are:

   (i) Dachigham, Jammu and Kashmir : Hangul

   (ii) Bharatpur bird sanctuary, Rajasthan : Siberian crane

   (iii) Bandipur sanctuary, Karnataa ; Elephant.

5. Project Tiger was launched on 1st April, 1973 to protect the diminishing population of Indian tigers. Tiger is one of the endangered species and to preserve it, project tiger was launched. The project aims at ensuring a viable population of bengal tigers in their natural habitats and also to protect them from extinction, and preserving areas of biological importance as a natural heritage.

6. One tonne of paper requires the chopping of 17 full grown trees. Therefore, our huge need of paper would require more cutting of trees. This in turn would lead to deforestation and disruption in the balance of nature. Hence, in order to save trees, we should minimize the wastage of paper or we should use recycled paper.

7. Wild life refers to living organisms plants, animals and microorganisms other than the cultivated plants and domesticated animals. Wild life needs to be conserved for

   (i) maintaining the ecological balance for supporting life.

   (ii) preserving different kinds of species (biodiversity).

   (iii) preserving economically important plants and animals.

   (iv) conserving the endangered species.

8. Deforestation causes soil erosion or removal of fertile top layer of the soil. This leaves the soil devoid of humus and makes it infertile, gradually converting it to a desert. This process is known as desertification.

9. Wildlife and forest conservation are related because in order to protect wildlife, it is essential to protect forests which provide food and shelter to wildlife.

10. Forest is useful to us because it provides us oxygen, protects soil and provides habitat to a large number of animals, increase the amount and periodicity of rainfall and reduce drought, global warming etc.

11. IUCN prepares Red Data Book to lists rare species and those in danger of extinction.

12. Government ensures the preservation of biodiversity by enacting several legal provisions or acts related to conservation of wildlife and forests. These acts are forest conservation act (1980) and wildlife protection act (1972). Forest conservation act empowers govt and forest department to create and manage reserved forest, conserve forest as a natural heritage and control and regulate cattle grazing in forest. Objectives of Wildlife protection act are the prohibition of hunting and control and management of captive breeding.

13. No, protected forests are not completely safe for wild animals. It is because people who live nearby use the resources from those forests for their own benefits. This activities in turn disrupts the life system and also endangers the animals living there.

Long Answer Questions

1. Deforestation is the removal of trees or other vegetation from an area for industrial, agricultural, or other purpose. Plants or trees absorb CO_2 from the atmosphere. If plants are destroyed, then the level of CO_2 will rise. The high levels of CO_2 in the atmosphere will trap more heat radiations, leading to global warming. This increase in temperature of the Earth wil disturb the natural water cycle. As a result of disruption in the water cycle, there will be a change in the rainfall pattern. The reduced amount of rainwater can cause droughts.

2. *Causes of deforestation*

   (i) Procurement of land for crop production.

   (ii) Procurement of land for urban settlement.

   (iii) Use of wood for timber and fuel.

   (iv) Natural calamities such as forest fires and droughts

   Consequences of deforestation

   (i) Loss of biodiversity

   (ii) Soil erosion

   (iii) Change in climatic conditions

   (iv) Flood and droughts

   Causes of extinction of wildlife are –

   (i) Habitat loss

   (ii) Poaching

   (iii) Introduction of new species

   (iv) Natural calamities

   (v) Lack of strict wildlife laws.

3. (1) Threatened species is a native species that is at risk of becoming endangered in the near future. A threatened species may have a declining population or be exceptionally rare.

   (2) Extinct species is the species of which last remaining member has died.

   (3) Endemic species is one whose habitat is restricted to a particular area. It may be an animal, a plant, a fungus, or even a microorganism.

   (4) Endangered species is a native species that faces a significant risk of extinction in the near future throughout all or a significant portion of its range. Such species may be declining in number due to threats such as habitat destruction, climate change, or pressure from invasive species.

4. (i)

	Flora	**Fauna**
(i)	It refers to all living plants in a particular area.	It refers to all animals living in a particular area.
(ii)	Sal, teak, mango, etc. form the flora of Pachmarhi biosphere reserve.	Leaopard, wolf, wild dog, etc. form the fauna of Pachmarhi biosphere reserve.

(ii)

Endangered species	Threatened species
A species present in such small numbers that it is at risk of extinction.	A native species that is at risk of becoming endangered in the near future. It may have a declining population or be exceptionally rare. Like endangered species, the cause of its rarity is variable, but may be due to threats such as habitat destruction, climate change, or pressure from invasive species.

(iii)

	Endemic species	Extinct species
(i)	An endemic species is one whose habitat is restricted to a particular area.	The species which no more exist on the planet.
(ii)	Example : Indian giant squirrel	Example : Dinosaur, passenger pigeon

(iv)

	Wildlife sanctuary	Zoological park
(i)	It is an area within which animals are protected from possible dangers such as hunting. Their habitat is also conserved in this area.	It is a place where animals are kept for public exhibition.
(ii)	It conserves the natural habitat of animals.	It is an artificial habitat.

Reasoning Based Questions

1. Deforestation causes soil erosion or removal of fertile top layer of the soil. This leaves the soil devoid of humans and makes it infertile, gradually converting it into desert.

2. The protected forests are not also safe completely for wildlife because the poaching takes place at large scale in these areas.

3. Siberian cranes come to India during winter because in Siberia, it is cold, daylight is of shorter duration, food is scarce. So they look for better living conditions else where to rear their young ones and to come to India as it has favourable condition for their survival.

4. Recycling prevents the emission of many greenhouse gases and water pollutants and saw energy using recovered material generate less solid waste recycling helps to reduce the pollination caused by the extraction and processing of virgin materials.

5. We should conserve forests because they are essential for us in the following terms-
Forests provide us with oxygen, they cause rainfall forests prevents soil erosion. Plants are dependent on animals and birds for their pollination and seed dispersal.

6. Cutting down of trees loosens the grip of the roots holding the soil. As roots get loose then they cannot absorb water from the soil thus leading to frequent flooding of river.

HOTS Questions

1. Biodiversity is the variability among living organisms from all sources, including terrestrial, marine, and other aquatic ecosystems and the ecological complexes of which they are part. This includes diversity within species, between species, and of ecosystems.

2. Species that have been introduced or moved by human activities to a location where they do not naturally occur are termed exotic species. Exotic species are not necessarily harmful. These introduced or exotic species can adversely affect the ecosystem. Some exotic plants have turned into weeds, multiplying fast and causing harm to the ecosystem, e.g. water hyacinth and lantana. Exotics are invariably introduced without their natural enemies that control and balance their spread in their native land, and hence, grow and flourish without any hindrance and cause harm to the environment. Any disturbance in one gives rise to imbalance in others and this is what happens when an exotic species is introduced.

3. Biodiversity is the variety of life. It is extremely important to people and the health of ecosystems. A few of the reasons are:
   (i) It provides us with foods and materials and contributes to the economy. Without a diversity of pollinators, plants, and soils, our supermarkets would have a lot less produce. Hence, it allows us to live healthy and happy lives.
   (ii) Most medical discoveries to cure diseases and lengthen life spans were made because of research into plant and animal biology and genetics. Every time a species goes extinct or genetic diversity is lost, we will never know whether research would have given us a new vaccine or drug.
   (iii) Biodiversity allows for ecosystems to adjust to disturbances like extreme fires and floods.
   (iv) Genetic diversity prevents diseases and helps species adjust to changes in their environment.
   (v) It is an important part of ecological services that make life livable on Earth. They include everything from cleaning water and absorbing chemicals, which wetlands do, to providing oxygen for us to breathe- one of the many things that plants do for people.

4. Endangered plants and animals can be conserved outside their natural habitats through captive breeding programmes. For example : Animals can be taken care of in zoos, plants in botanical garden and fishes and aquatic animals in large aquaria. When the numbers of species increase sufficiently outside their natural habitat, they are then reintroduced into the wild. This helps in maintaining biodiversity.

5. Migratory animals face extinction because the places they used to migrate have been altered by human actions. As a result, these animals have no place to go anywhere (when weather conditions becomes harsh or food in their habitat become scarce).

6. The introduction of a new species into a new locality from some other area is called exotic species. But in case of species X, its population will increase.

7. The Indian rhinoceros are poached mainly for their horns that are believed to have medicinal value.
Asian elephants are threatened mainly because of habitat destruction.

8. No, I don't agree. Though it is not justified to cut trees to meet ever increasing demands of human population, but one can look for alternate ways to conserve forest or to fulfill human needs. We can plant more and more trees and encourage people to plant trees by informing them about importance of trees.

9. Tiger will be happier in its natural habitat.

10. There is no doubt that afforestation is a positive step towards restoration of forests and wildlife. But it is a slow process as new plant would take several years to grow big.

11. For self-attempt.

Exercise 2 — Master NCERT (Text-book & Exemplar)

Text-book Exercise

1. (a) wildlife sanctuary (b) Endemic species
   (c) climatic (d) Red Data Book
   (e) Reforestation

2. (a) Wildlife sanctuary and biosphere reserve:

Wildlife Sanctuary	Biosphere Reserve
A protected area where animals can live in their natural habitat is known as a wildlife sanctuary. In these sanctuaries hunting, poaching, grazing, felling trees etc. are strictly prohibited.	An area which is conserved to protect the biodiversity and culture of that area is known as biosphere reserve. A biosphere reserve consists of many protected areas like sanctuaries, national parks, lakes mountains etc.

(b) Zoo and wildlife sanctuary

Zoo	Wildlife Sanctuary
Zoo is a place where animals live in artificial habitat.	In a sanctuary animals live in natural habitat.
The animals protected live in a definite place. They are allowed to be viewed by public spread in small areas.	The animals are protected and conserved in very large areas. These areas are prohibited for hunting, grazing, felling trees etc.

(c) Endangered and extinct species

Endangered species	Extinct species
The species which are at the verge of extinction and which are required to be protected and conserved are known as endangered species.	The species that are totally finished having no living individual on the earth are known as extinct species.
Example : tiger, wild buffalo etc.	Example : dinosaurs.

3. (a) **Wild animals :** The wild animals live in forest. Deforestation destroys their natural habitat. In the natural habitat the animals have no place to live and breed. As a result of absence of their habitat, many animals reach the verge of extinction.

(b) **Environment :** The environment is adversely affected by deforestation. Global warming. Carbon dioxide gets accumulated in the atmosphere because of lack of green plants and thus causes global warming.

(c) **Villages (Rural areas) :** The rural areas largely depend on forests for their likelihood. Deforestation has reduced their resources and the uninhabited animals are also a danger for the villagers.

(d) **Cities (Urban areas) :** Cities are also affected by deforestation indirectly. The changes in the climate results in calamities like flood and droughts which affects the cities also.

(e) **Earth :** Deforestation has lead to the conversion of fertile lands into deserts. The natural calamities like floods and droughts are also the result of deforestation. The climate of earth is changing due to deforestation.

(f) **The next generation :** Deforestation has a negative impact on climate and many are at the verge of extinction some species are already extinct. The next generation may not be able to see the beautiful and attractive fauna and flora. It may have to suffer for the effects of global warming, no fuel and no paper etc.

4. (a) **We go on cutting trees :** If we continue cutting of trees, rainfall and fertility of soil will decrease and the chances of natural calamities will increase. It will also lead to decrease in water holding capacity of the soil which results in floods. Animal life will also be negatively affected.

(b) **The habitat of an animal is disturbed :** The animals are adapted to live in their natural habitat. The survival of the animals becomes difficult. If their natural habitat is disturbed. They will not have any space to live and to breed. As a result, they will not survive and also because of scarcity of food the animals have started wandering int he nearby villages and targeting domestic animals as their prey.

(c) **The top layer of soil is exposed :** The roots of trees find the soil. Deforestation exposes the top layer of soil which gets washed away with water. The removal of top layer gradually converts the fertile land into desert. Moreover the soil washed away with water gets also gets deposited in the river bed resulting in decrease in the depth of rivers. The chances of floods increased many folds.

5. (a) We should conserve biodiversity. The universe encompasses a vast variety of organism each of which plays a very important role. Every organism is unique and precious. Hence, should be saved it from becoming extinct.

(b) Protected forests are not completely safe for wild animals because poachers have found access in there areas and are killing animals and for joy. There is a need to make strict rules against poaching and trespassing.

(c) Some tribals are dependent on the jungle for their food, fuel, wood, shelter etc. They live in forests and are entirely dependent on them for their survival.

(d) The main cause of deforestation is growing population, urbanization and industrialization. Need for more land and resources have lead to the cutting down of forests. The main consequences of deforestation are desertification and natural calamities.

(e) Red Data book keeps the record of all the endangered animals and plants. It is published by IUCN.

(f) Some species of birds and animals move from their habitat to some other habitat for the purpose of breeding and specific purposes. Siberian birds move to far away areas every year during a particular time because of climatic changes and return to their original habitat when the climate become suitable for them. This periodic behaviour of some species is known as migration.

6. Trees are being continually cut so as to meet the ever increasing demand in factories and for shelter. Cutting of trees can only be justified when reforestation is done. Reforestation is the reestablishment of destroyed forests by planting new trees. The trees planted should be of the same species that are generally found in the forests. We should plant as many trees as we cut. Reforestation can take place naturally also if the land is left undisturbed. The forests will establish itself over a period of time. We have damaged our forests to such an extent that it is difficult to retain the green wealth for our future generations. So, it is very important to plant more trees and to find out ways of recycling and restoring our natural wealth.

7. The green wealth of the locality is the responsibility of every resident. We should grow more and more plants in the locality. We should work together to conserve the green belt of the locality. We should discourage cutting of trees and spread awareness about the benefit of plants teach the small children and encourage the slogan 'one man one tree' so that every individual at least has one tree and takes care of it.

8. Plants absorb water from the soil and lose water in the form of water vapour which evaporates to form clouds. Deforestation leads to cutting down of trees. As a result, less water is absorbed from the soil and it disturbs the water cycle. The formation of cloud becomes difficult which lead to reduced rainfall.

9. For self-attempt.

10. Paper is very useful in our day to day life Thousands of trees are cut to fulfill the demand of paper each day. If the trees continue to be cut for paper at the same rate, one day we will be left with no trees. So we should save paper and use it intelligently. The ways by which we can save paper are :

1. We should recycle the waste paper.
2. We should not litter paper here and there.
3. Paper should be sent for recycling.
4. We should not tear our old books and donate it to poor children so that they can reuse those books.
5. Buying recycled paper products should be encourage.
6. We should avoid taking paper bags from the shops, instead we should carry jute bags.

11.

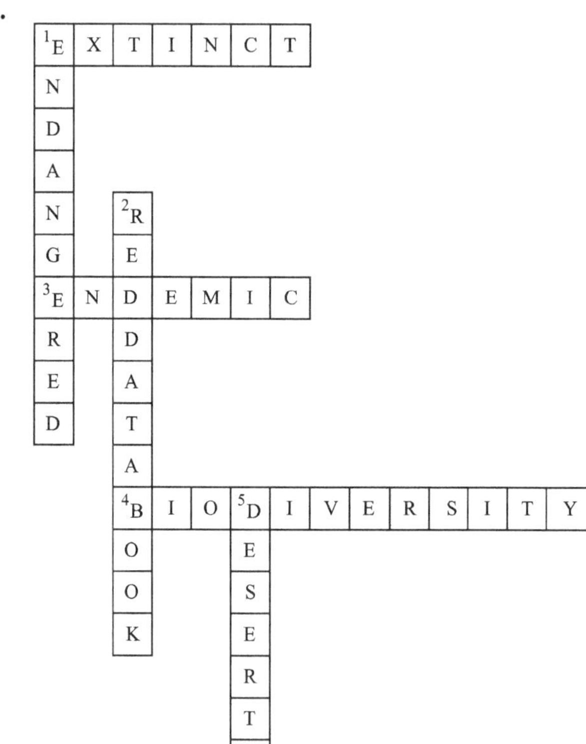

Exemplar questions

1. To maintain balance in nature/to conserve the natural ecosystem.

2. Reforestation can take place naturally by leaving the deforested area undisturbed for a long time. But this process takes a long time in terms of years.

3. Satpura national park.

4. Wildlife sanctuaries are protected areas where human activities like plantation, cultivation, grazing, falling of trees, hunting and poaching are prohibited completely.

5. Endemic organisms are confined to a limited geographical area. They cannot adapt or live outside their natural habitat. Any disturbance to their habitat will adversely affect them.

6. Introduction of a new species may affect the existence of local species due to competion.

7. Yes, Soil erosion removes the fertile top layer of the soil thereby, exposing the hard rocky lower layers which are less fertile.

8. Yes, Plants absorb carbon dioxide from the atmosphere for photosynthesis. Deforestation results in decreased number or trees leading to accumulation of carbon dioxide in the atmosphere. Carbon dioxide in the atmosphere traps heat rays reflected by the earth which results in global warming.

9. Deforestation results in decreased water holding capacity of soil. This reduces the infiltration of water into the ground which causes floods. On the other hand, deforestation leads to higher level of carbon dioxide in the atmosphere which causes global warming. Scarcity of trees disturbs the water cycle and may reduce rainfall leading to droughts.

Exercise 3 ⭐ Foundation Builder

Multiple Choice Questions

1. (a) Urban development has led to a large scale destruction of forest and loss of biodiversity.

2. (a) Endemic species are those species of plants and animals which are found exclusively in a particular area. They are not naturally found anywhere else. A particular type of animal or plant may be endemic to a zone, a state or a country.

3. (d) Endangered species are those which are facing the danger of extinction.

4. (b) Kaziranga wild life sanctuary is the name to exemplify the most popular conservation efforts to save the endangered species like one-horned rhinoceros in India. It is located in the Golaghat and Nagaon district of Assam, and declared the most notable World Heritage Site by UNESCO in the year 1985.

5. (b) The Red Data Book is the state document established for documenting rare and endangered species of animals, plants and fungi as well as some local sub-species that exist within the territory of the state or country. This book is maintained by IUCN (International Union for Conservation of Nature and Natural resources).

6. (b) All the animal life of a given place or time, especially when distinguished from the plant life (flora) is called fauna.

7. (d) Storm is a violent disturbance of the atmosphere with strong winds and usually rain, thunder, lightning, or snow. It is not caused by deforestation.

8. (b) Endemic is not included under red list because red list includes those species whose continued existence is threatened. Species are classified into different categories of perceived risk. Each Red Data Book usually deals with a specific group of animals or plants (e. reptiles, insects, mosses). Endemic species are those species of plants and animals which are found exclusively in a particular area. They are not naturally found anywhere else.

9. (a) The World Wide Fund for Nature is an international non-governmental organization founded on April 26 1961, and is working on issues regarding the conservation, research and restoration of the environment. WWF aims to preserve the life on Earth and the ecological system by: protecting wild life. It protects natural areas and wild populations of plants and animals. It also supports projects for saving/conserving endangered species; promoting sustainable approaches to the use of renewable natural resources; promoting more efficient use of resources and energy; and reducing pollution.

10. (b) Project Tiger was launched by the government of India in 1973. The project aims at ensuring a viable population of Bengal tigers in their natural habitats and also to protect them from extinction, and preserving areas of biological importance as a natural heritage forever represented as close as possible the diversity of ecosystems across the tiger's distribution in the country.

11. (a) Biodiversity is the term used to describe the variety of life found on Earth and all of the natural processes. This includes ecosystem, genetic and cultural diversity, and the connections between these and all species.

12. (a) Species which is likely to become endangered unless protective measures are taken are called vulnerable species. Extinct species is a population of species that no longer exists. Endemic species is one whose habitat is restricted to a particular area.

13. (a) An ecosystem is a community of living organisms (plants, animals and microbes) in conjunction with the non-living components of their environment (things like air, water and mineral soil), interacting as a system. These biotic and abiotic components are regarded as linked together through nutrient cycles and energy flows.

14. (c) Poaching is defined as the illegal hunting, killing or capturing of wild animals, usually associated with land use rights.

15. (c) WBCs are blood corpuscles involve in defending the body against both infectious diseases and foreign materials but they are not able to survive independently unlike Amoeba and Paramecium, which are acellular protozoans and complete their life processes like digestion, respiration, circulation, excretion etc. within a single cell.

16. (c) As the land was used for construction of house and the trees are cut for timber, it is an example of deforestation. Other examples of deforestation include conversion of forestland to farms, ranches, or urban use.

17. (d)

18. (c) Endangered species are those species of plants and animals whose numbers are diminishing to a level that they might face extinction. Black buck, gharial, rhinoceros and marsh crocodile all these are listed under endangered species.

19. (c) A Red Data Book contains list of species whose continued existence is threatened. Each Red Data Book usually deals with a specific group of animals or plants. They are now being published in many different countries and provide useful informations on the threat status of the species.

20. (d) In the process of ex-situ conservation, the diversity of species are removed from their habitat and conserved in another managed and controlled environment, ex-zoo, botanical garden, etc.

21. (d) Red Data Book have the record of all endangered plants and animals.

Assertion & Reason

1. (a) Spotted deer and black buck belongs to vulnerable species. Vulnerable species that is likely to become endangered and is often at risk is due to loss of habitat or declining population.

2. (a) Dinosaurs were a group of land animals that lived from about 230 million years ago until about 60 million years ago. These spans the era of the Earth's history known as the mesozoic era, which includes, from most ancient to most recent, the triassic, jurassic and cretaceous periods. Dinosaurs grew in population and diversity during their time on Earth before becoming extinct at the end of the Cretaceous period. Dinosaurs became extinct due to natural calamities as they did not adjust or adapt to the changed environment for their survival.

3. (c) The great Indian bustard is a bustard found in India and the adjoining regions of Pakistan. It is a large bird with a horizontal body and long bare legs and gives an ostrich like appearance. This bird is among the heaviest of the flying birds. These birds are often found associated in the same habitat as blackbuck. The great Indian bustard has been threatened because of hunting and loss of its habitat.

4. (d) Red Data Book list is the state document established for documenting rare and endangered species of animals, plants and fungi as well as some local sub-species that exist within the territory of the state or country. This book is maintained by IUCN (International Union for Conservation of Nature and Natural resources).

5. (b) Afforestation is the establishment of a forest or stand of trees in an area where there was no forest. It helps in wildlife and forest conservation. This differs from reafforestation which is the restocking of existing forests and woodlands which have been depleted.

Exercise 4 ⭐ **Foundation Builder +**

1. (c) **Critically Endangered :** The taxon facing very high risk of extinction in the wild can become extinct any moment in the immediate future, e.g. *Sus salvinus* (Pigmy Hog), *Berberis nilghiriensis*.

2. (b) IUCN or WCN maintains a red data book which is a catalogue of threatened plants and animals facing risk of extinction. The IUCN red list (2004) documents the extinction of 784 species (including 338 vertebrates, 359 invertebrates and 87 plants) in the last 500 years.

3. (b) Tiger is not resident in Gir national park. Gir has a large population of marsh crocodile or mugger, which is among the 40 species of reptiles and amphibians recorded in the sanctuary. According to official census figures, Gir has about 300 lions

and 300 leopards, making it one of the major big-cat concentrations in India. Sambar and spotted deer (chital), blue bull (nilgai), chousingha (the world's only four-horned antelope), chinkara (Indian gazelle) and wild boar thrive in Gir. Jackal, striped hyena, jungle cat, rusty-spotted cat, langur, porcupine, black-naped Indian hare are among the other mammals of Gir.

4. (c) Robert May estimated global species diversity at about 7 million. Although some extreme estimates range from 20 to 50 million.

5. (c) The primary cause of human-induced extinction events is simply human overpopulation of planet Earth. The most important causal anthropogenic activities are habitat destruction and fragmentation.

6. (c) The largely tropical Amazon rain forest in South America has the greatest biodiversity on earth.

7. (a) Habitat loss and fragmentation are the most important cause for animals and plants being driven to extinction. Habitats of various organisms are altered or destroyed by uncontrolled and unsustainable human activities (such as deforestation, slash and burn agriculture, mining, and urbanisation). This will lead to breaking up of the habitat into small pieces, which effect the movement of migratory animals and also, decrease the genetic exchange between populations leading to a declination of species.

8. (c) Botanical garden is an *ex - situ* conservation (offsite conservation) method to conserve biodiversity.

9. (b) **10.** (d)

1. *In-situ* conservation is considered to be a better method of wildlife conservation as compared to *ex-situ*. *In-situ* conservation strategy provides larger habitat area and greater mobility to the organisms as they are being safeguarded in their own habitat.

2. The two advantages of *ex-situ* conservation over *in-situ* conservation strategies are as follows –
   (a) It gives longer lifetime to the organisms as the competition for food and shelter is less.
   (b) Genetic techniques can be utilised in this strategy.

3. Hunting and logging are usually strictly prohibited within these patches. Some NGOs work with local villagers to protect such groves.

4 Cell-Structure and Functions

Build A Strong Foundation

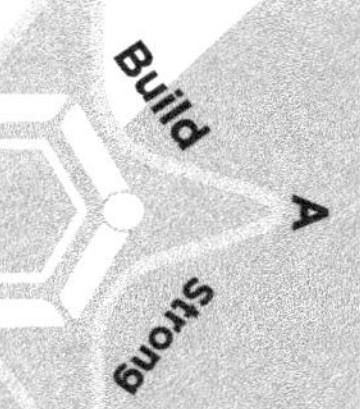

CONCEPT MAP

ORGANISM : An entire living being that can carry out all basic life processes.

↓

ORGAN SYSTEM : Group of two or more tissues that carries out a specific function.

↓

ORGANS : Made up of tissues that work together to perform a specific activity.

↓

TISSUE : A group of cells having a common origin and performing a similar but specific function.

↓

CELL : The smallest and complete expression of the fundamental structure and functions of all living organisms.

↓

- **PROKARYOTIC CELL :** Nuclear envelope and membrane bound organelles are absent. Example- Bacteria and blue green algae.
- **EUKARYOTIC CELL :** Organized nucleus with nuclear envelope and presence of membrane-bound organelles like mitochondria, lysosome, etc. Example- Plant and animal.

↓

CELL STRUCTURE

- **PLASMA MEMBRANE**
- **CYTOPLASM**
- **CELL ORGANELLES**
  - Nucleus
  - Vacuoles
  - Endoplasmic reticulum
  - Ribosomes
  - Golgi bodies
  - Mitochondria
  - Lysosomes
  - Cilia & Flagella

DISCOVERY OF CELL

The discovery of the cellular structure of organism is intimately bound up with the invention of the compound microscope. The preparation of the cells and cell parts for their study requires very specialized methods. In 1665, Robert Hooke first discovered the existence of cells during his description of the structure of cork. He used a microscope to investigate the structure of a thin slice of cork. He observed that cork had several tiny compartments in it. He called these tiny compartments as cells. However the cell discovered by Hooke, were dead and only cellulosic cell walls were visible. He actually observed only cell walls.

The first living cell was seen under microscope by Dutch discoverer Anton Von Leeuwenhoek. Years later as microscopes improved, other biologists continued the work of Hooke and Leeuwenhoek, learning more about cells. In the 1830s, two German Scientists Malthias Jacob Schleiden and Theodor Schwann, helped to convince other scientists that all living things are made of cells. They both compared their findings and proposed that cells are the units of both structure and function of organism. Their findings are now referred to as **cell theory** or **cell principle**. In 1939, Schleiden and Schwann formulated the cell theory.

According to cell theory -
(i)   All living things are composed of one or more cells.
(ii)   Cells are the basic units of structure and function in living things.
(iii) All cells arise from pre-existing cells by cell division.
(iv)   Cells have similar structure and metabolism.
(v)   The functions of an organisms are due to activities and interaction of its cells.

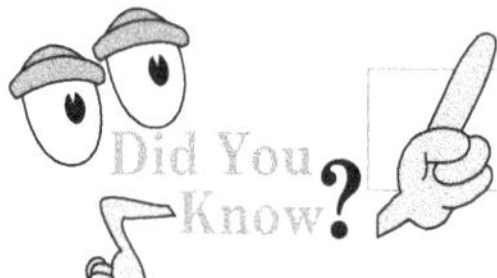

__The body of all living organisms except virus has cellular organisation.__

CONNECTING TOPIC

Exceptions to Cell Theory

Cell theory does not have universal application. All kinds of true cells share the following three basic characteristics – a set of genes, a limiting plasma membrane and a metabolic machinary. Examples which do not fit easily in these parameters of a true cells are viruses, protozoans and many thallophytes; bacteria and cyanobacteria etc.

__The given figure represents the structure of a compound microscope. This microscope is used to view smaller specimens such as cell structures which cannot be seen at lower levels of magnification.__
__Compound microscope is an optical instrument for forming magnified images of small objects. It consists of an objective lens with a very short focal length and an eyepiece with a longer focal length, both lenses mounted in the same tube.__

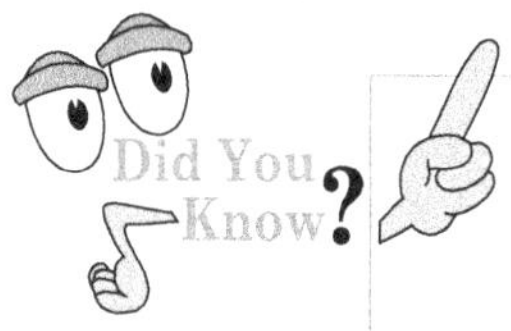

__• Microscope was invented by Anton Von Leewenhoek. It is the biggest invention in the history of science. It allowed biologists to study the microscopic organisms like bacteria, fungi etc.__
__• Microscope enable us to see the object as small as one millionth of a meter (10–6m). Such magnifying power microscopes have helped the scientists to study the minute details of cell.__

CELLS

A cell is the smallest and complete expression of the fundamental structure and functions of all living organisms. For example, building is made up of basic bricks. Here bricks are the basic structural units which make building of different designs, shapes and sizes. Similarly in living world also, organisms differ from each other in respect to their body, size and shape but all of them are made up of cells.

Cell contains all the necessities of life like water, nutrients, minerals, protein, enzymes, fats and carbohydrates.

ORGANISMS SHOW VARIETY IN CELL NUMBER, SHAPE AND SIZE

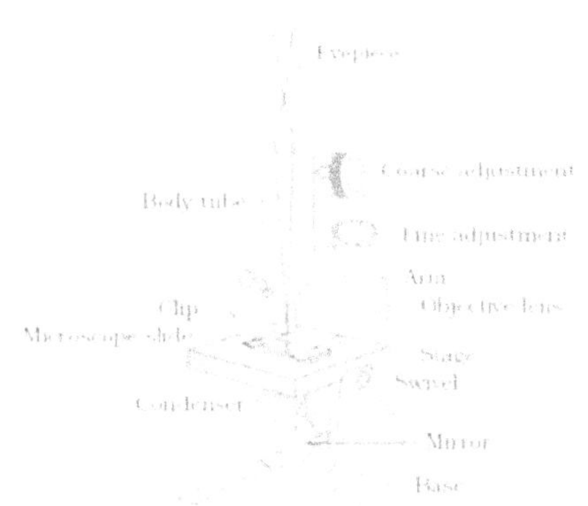

Life exhibit varying degree of organization. We know that body of all living organisms is made up of cells which carry out certain basic functions.

There are many many different kinds of cells. Even cells within the same organism show enormous diversity of size, shape and internal organization. Our body contains 10^{13} to 10^{14} cells of around 300 different cell types. Cells not only differ in size and function, but also appear different from each other.

The invention of electron microscope and staining techniques helped scientists to study the detailed structure of cell. Cells are grouped into tissues, tissues into organs and organs into organ systems.

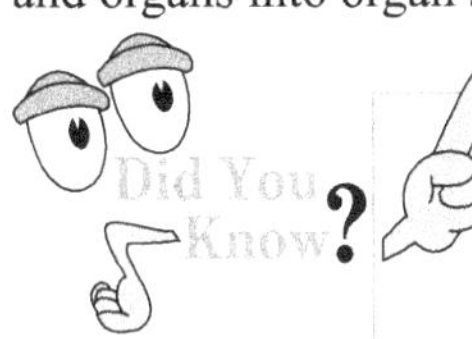

Acetabularia is a single called algae. It may measure upto 10 cm. This is why this green giant alga is used in genetic and molecular studies.

- *Tissue is a group of cells having a common origin and performing a similar but specific function.*
  Examples: Muscle tissue, which can shorten or contract to cause movement.
  - *Nerve tissue, which carries nerve signals*
  - *Connective tissues, which fills the gaps between other tissues.*
  - *Epithelial tissues, which provides protection and support.*
- *Organs are made up of tissues that work together to perform a specific activity. For example, eyes perform the function of sight, whereas lungs help in respiration. Similarly, kidney helps in excretion.*

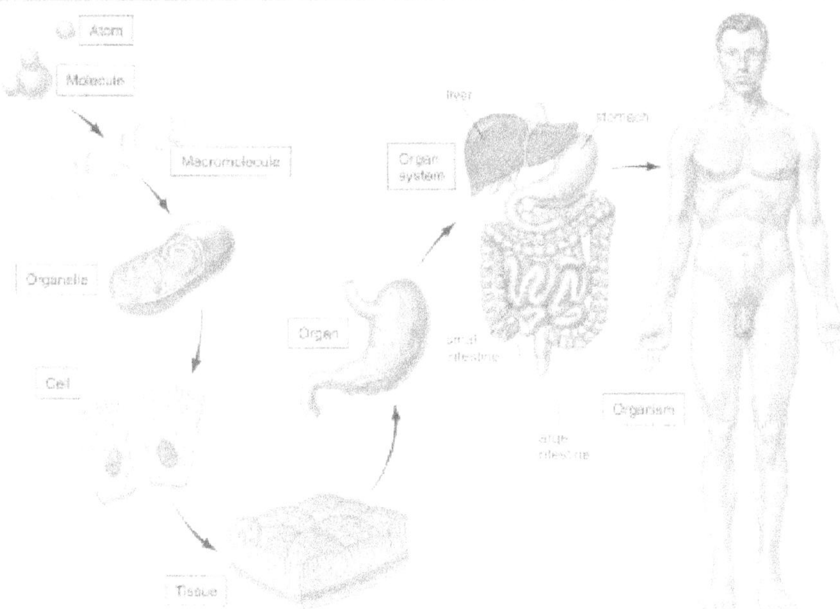

- **Organ systems** are groups of two or more organs that carries out a specific function to help keep the body live and work well.
  Human body has 11 major organ systems – circulatory, digestive, endocrine, excretory (urinary), immune (lymphatic), integumentary, muscular, nervous, reproductive, respiratory and skeletal.
  For example, the heart, blood vessels and blood make up the circulatory system. Circulatory system circulates blood all around the body and supplies every tiny part with essential substances such as oxygen, nutrients, and collects wastes for removal from body.
- **Organism** is an entire living being that can carry out all basic life processes. It means they can take in materials, release energy from food, release wastes, grow, respond to the environment and reproduce. Example - bacteria, *Amoeba*, mushroom, sunflower, human, etc.

Let us discuss variety of number, shape and size in cells.

NUMBER OF CELLS

The number of cells vary from a single cell to many cells in an organisms. Some organisms are composed of single cells (called *unicellular organisms*), like *Amoeba, Paramecium* etc. or some have many cells (called multicellular organism) like humans, dog, horse, pigeon, frog etc. Unicellular organisms are capable of independent existence. With no dependence on others for any function, material or information a single cell controls all the functions like feeding, movement, respiration, reproduction etc. Unicellular organisms are less efficient due to absence of division of labour.

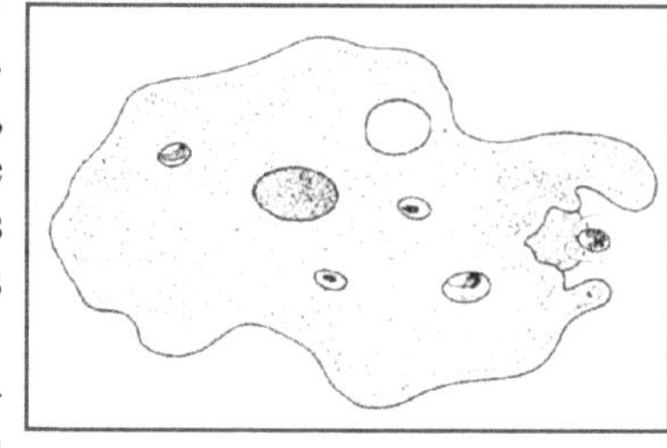

Amoeba

All multicellular organisms start their life from a single cell (called zygote). In multicellular organisms, all the life activities or different functions are divided among various cells or group of cells. *Hence*, there is division of labour in such organisms. This means that each type of cells are specialized to perform a particular job. For example, a nerve cell carries messages over long distances in the body. A muscle cells bring about movement of body parts and red blood cells carry oxygen and distribute it to all parts of the body. Hence, all the cells in a multicellular organisms work together in groups of similar cells called tissue.

Note:

WBC is a cell while *Amoeba* is a full fledge organism that is capable of independent existence.

CELL SHAPE

Cells come in a variety of shapes – depending on their function. The shape of the cells may be variable *i.e.* constantly changing for example *Amoeba*, WBC etc or fixed. Look at the structure of *Amoeba*. *What type of shape does Amoeba, have?* The shape of *Amoeba* appears to be irregular. Unlike other organisms, it does not have definite shape. It keeps on changing its shape. *Why do Amoeba change its shape?* The change in shape is due to formation of pseudopodia. Pseudopodia are finger like projections protruding out of its body. The protrusions help *Amoeba* in movement and capturing food.

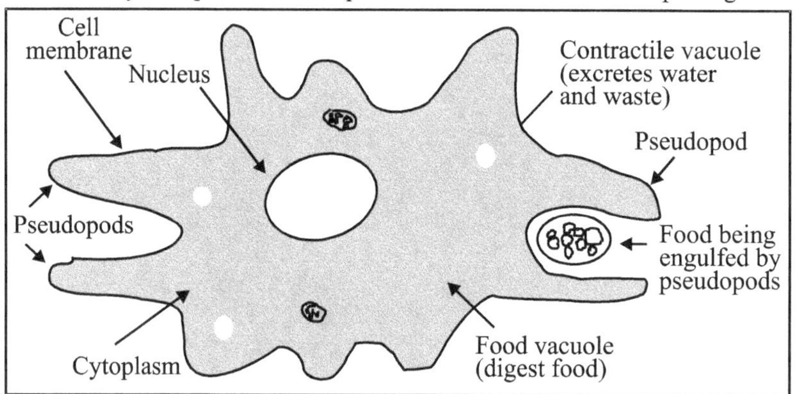

Amoeba capturing food

Similarly, in human beings white blood cell (WBC) has the ability to change its shape. They eat up or kill bacteria that enter into our blood and save us from many diseases.

The cells are different in shapes and sizes so that they can perform different functions. Or we can say, cells have specialized shape to do different jobs.

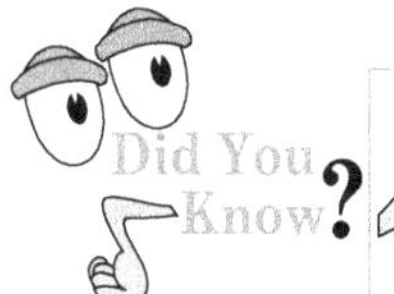

Different shapes of cells

Shape	Examples
Spindle shaped	Smooth muscle fibre
Elongated	Nerve cells
Branched	Chromatophores
Discoidal	Red blood cells

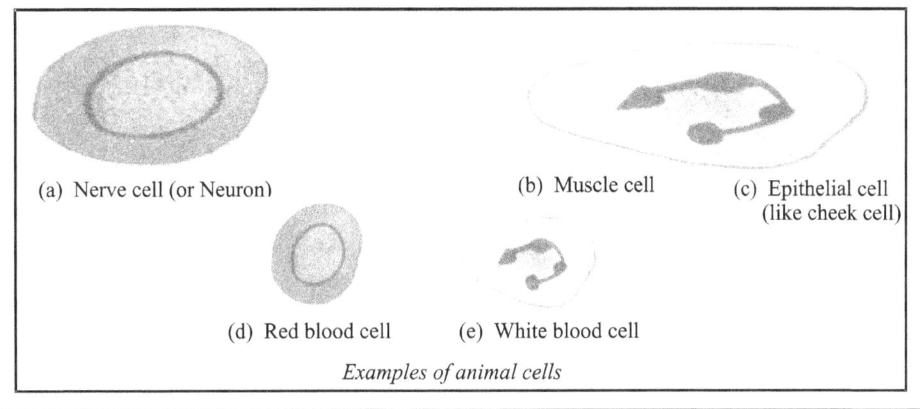

(a) Nerve cell (or Neuron)   (b) Muscle cell   (c) Epithelial cell (like cheek cell)

(d) Red blood cell   (e) White blood cell

Examples of animal cells

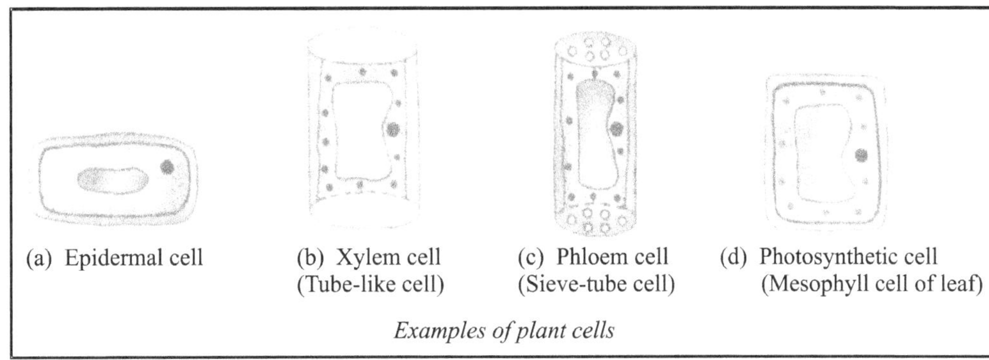

(a) Epidermal cell   (b) Xylem cell (Tube-like cell)   (c) Phloem cell (Sieve-tube cell)   (d) Photosynthetic cell (Mesophyll cell of leaf)

Examples of plant cells

Let us now discuss how shape of a cell helps in its functioning. A nerve cell (or neuron) is very long and has a wire like branches coming out of it. This large length of nerve cell helps it to carry impulses over long distances in the body. Also, the wire like branches helps it to make contact and carry messages between brain and other parts of body. *Hence*, nerve cells are specially adapted to transmit messages. Similarly, muscle cells are spindle in shape and adapted for movement. They bring about movement of the body parts by contraction and relaxation. On the contrary, in the plant, xylem cells are tube like plant cells that carry water and mineral salts from the roots of the plant and transfer to its leaves whereas phloem cells carry the food made by leaves to all other parts of the plant.

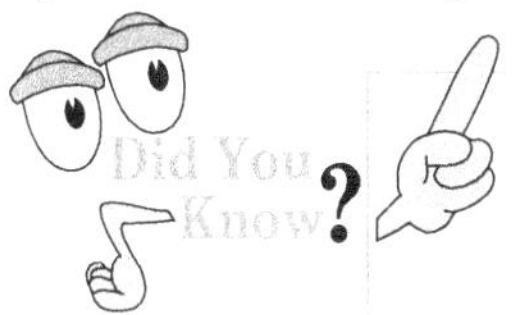

- *Metabolically active cells are smaller in size.*
- *Cells of a particular type have almost same volume.*
- *Size of cell has no relation with the size of the body of the animal or plant. It is related to its function.*

Factors governing the size of the cell
- *ratio between the volume of the nucleus and the cytoplasm (nucleocytoplasmic ratio)*
- *ratio of the cell surface to the cell volume*
- *rate of metabolism*

CELL SIZE

The size of cells vary from the very small cells of a bacteria to the largest cell which is the egg of an Ostrich. Cell are extremely small and can be seen properly only when magnified and viewed through the lenses of a microscope.

The largest cell is an egg of ostrich that measures as much as 6 inches in diameter with shell and 3 inches without shell. The smallest cell so far observed is considered to be of PPLO (Pleuropneumonia like organism) or Mycoplasma *i.e.* 0.1 mm.

The viruses are still smaller in size but cannot be considered as cell because of sub-cellular nature.

Cells are small in size because of the following facts –

(i) The cell's nucleus can only control a certain amount of active cytoplasm.

(ii) The cells are limited in size because of their surface area to volume ratio. It is an important factor. A group of small cells have a relatively more surface area than a single large cell for a given volume. A cell requires nutrients, oxygen and other materials for its survival and growth. Hence, it is necessary that all these materials should enter through its surface. As cell grows larger at some point, its surface area become too small to allow these materials to enter the cell quickly to meet the cell's need. Thus, as cell increases in size, its surface area to volume ratio decreases causing cell to function less efficiently.

How cell increases its number?

The cells in a living body increase their number by constant cell division. Cell division is a process where cell divides into two new daughter cells. These daughter cells are identical to parent cell, but are smaller in size. Hence, with time, it grows to its maximum size and then divide to produce more and more cells. The main factor that is responsible for the growth of a small plant into a big tree is the continuous process of cell division. Similary in humans, a baby grows into an adult man/ woman by continuous process of cell division.

But, do all cells grow and divide throughout life? No, not all cells in our body grow and divide throughout life. There are some cells that do not grow in number after a certain age. For example, the cells in the skin of our body grow and divide throughout life, but brain cells do not grow in number after a certain age, that is, after 18 years. Then when do cells die? Cell have a fixed lifespan and are replaced automatically as they die off. The more active the cells the shorter the time it will live.

The lifespan of certain cells are –

- Skin cells lives for 19 days
- Eyelashes lives for 3-4 months
- Liver cells lives for 2-4 years
- Sperm lives for 2 months
- RBCs lives for 4 months
- Bone cells lives for 15-25 years

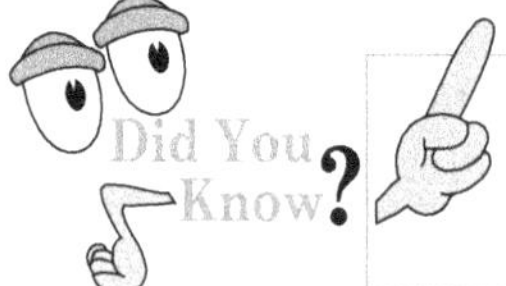

A cell without a nucleus dies in short time. Eg. human erythrocytes.
- *The biggest organ within the body is the liver, while the largest organ of the whole body is skin.*
- *Among the smallest cells in the human body are red blood cells which are only 0.007 mm across.*

1. **Why cell is called structural and functional unit of life?**
2. **Why are cells important?**
3. **The main organs of various system has been given. Identify their respective human organ system.**

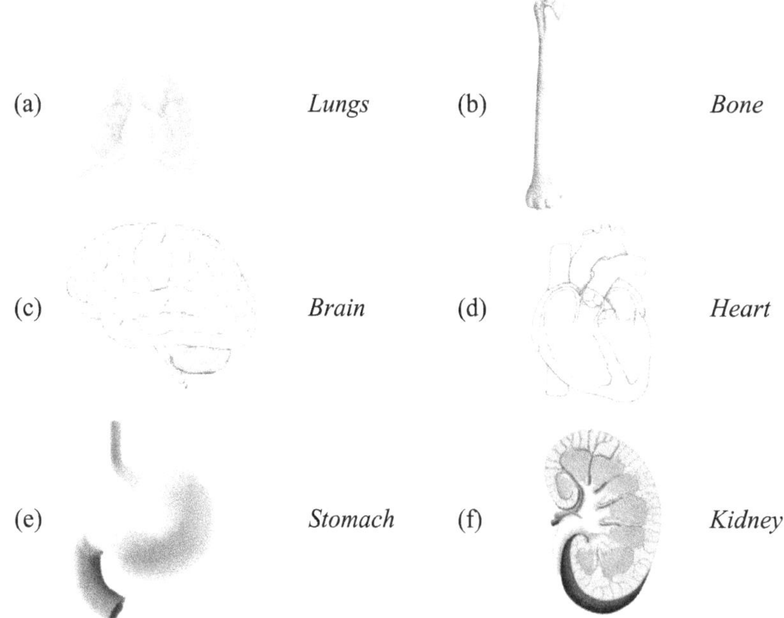

SOLUTION :

1. Cells are called structural and functional unit of life because –
   (i) All living beings are composed of cells and their products.
   (ii) Each living cell, either as a unicellular organism or as a part of multicellular organism has certain basic functions to perform in the body.

2. Cells are the basic functional and structural unit of life. All living things are made up of cells. Cells make up all the parts of an organisms and are responsible for everything that goes inside the organisms. Cells are the basis of organisms. Several kinds of tissues arrange together to form organs and perform special functions. Various organs combine to form organ systems. All organ systems coordinate together to make the body function smoothly.

3. (a) Respiratory system (b) Skeletal system (c) Nervous system
   (d) Circulatory system (e) Digestive system (f) Excretory system

CELL STRUCTURE AND FUNCTION

As we learnt that cell is the structural and functional unit of organisms so it is clear that each living organisms is made up of a large number of cells.

Each cell is an amazing world in itself. It can take in nutrients, convert these nutrients into energy, carry out specialized function and reproduce as necessary. Even more amazing is that each cell stores its own set of instructions for carrying out each of its activities. *Cells are of two types* – Plant cells and animal cells :

Though many things are common between animal cells and the plant cells but they differ in some way. Animal cells differ from plant cells in terms of structure and types of organelles (Described later).

What do you understand by the word organelle? The various structure present inside the cell are called organelles. Organelles are specialized part of a cell having some specific function like, they bring in food supplies, get rid of waste, protect and repair the cell etc.

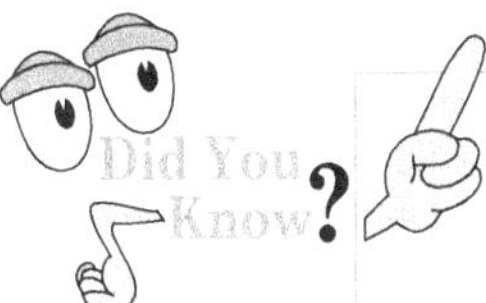

Staining
It is the use of a dye reagent or other material for producing colouration in tissues or microorganisms for microscopic examination. Examples of dyes are eosin, saffranine, haematoxylin, fast green, methylene blue etc.

Let us perform an experiment to study plant and animal cells with a microscope.
Part A : Plant cells (Onion skin mount)
Procedure :
   (i)   *Take a onion piece and peel the delicate transparent tissue from its inner surface using forceps.*
   (ii) *Place this tissue, unwrinkled in a small drop of water on a glass slide.*
   (iii) *Then add a small drop of Safranine stain to the tissue and cover it with a cover slip. While placing the coverslip ensure that there is no air bubbles under the coverslip.*
   (iv) *Now observe the slide under a microscope.*

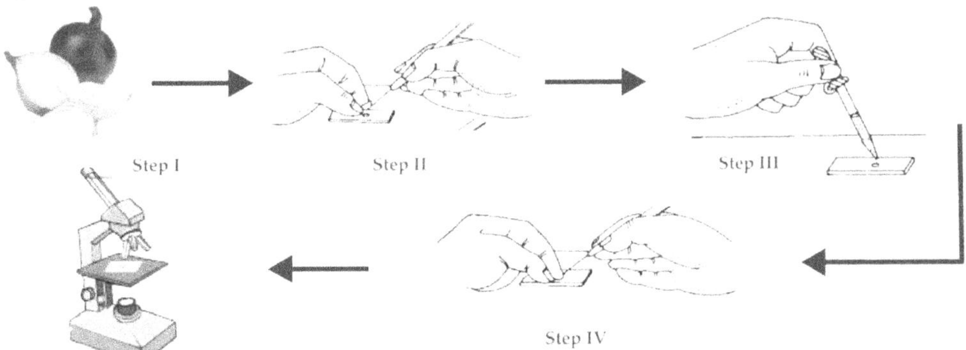

Observation :
You will see several small rectangular shaped cells. The boundary of each cell is covered by a cell membrane which in turn is covered by another thick covering called the cell wall. In the centre of cell, there is a dense round body called the nucleus. In between the nucleus and the cell membrane, there is a jelly like substance called cytoplasm. The large blank space inside the cytoplasm represents vacuoles.

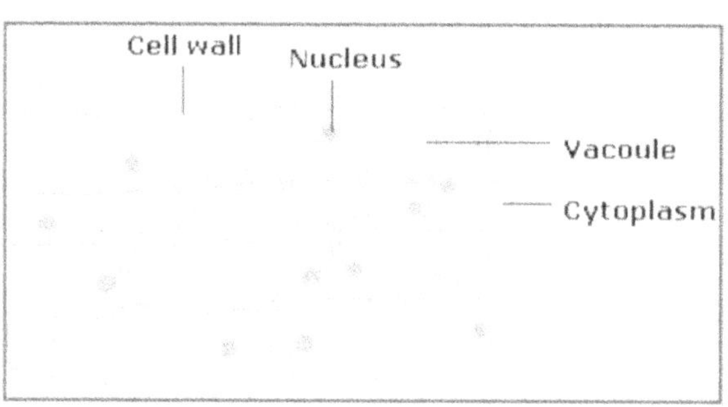

Cells observed in an onion peel

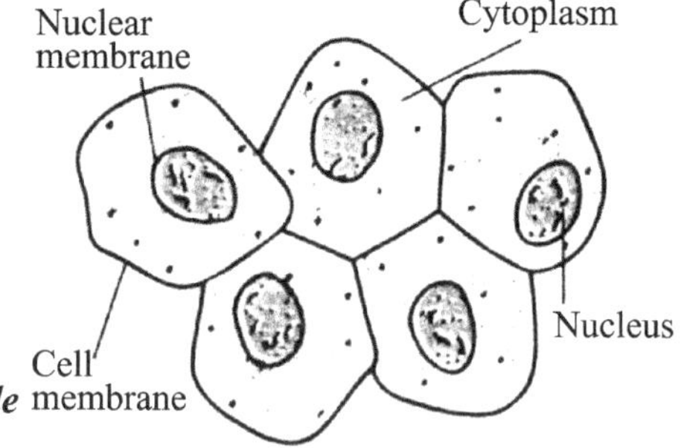

Human cheek cells

Part B : Animal cell (Cheek cells)
Procedure :

   (i)   *Take a clean glass slide and place a drop of water on it.*
   (ii) *Gently scrap the inside of your cheek with the blunt end of a clean toothpick.*
   (iii) *Then stir the material on the toothpick in the drop of water on the slide.*
   (iv) *Add a small drop of methylene blue stain to the slide.*
   (v)   *Now carefully place a coverslip over the slide and observe the slide under a microscope.*

Observation :
You can see large number of irregular shaped cells with a thin cell membrane. Cell wall is absent. In the center of cell, nucleus is present. It is stained dark blue.

PARTS OF A CELL

Cell has various components which have structural and functional importance. These components are *protoplasm* comprising of cytoplasm (having various organelles) and nucleus.

A unit mass of protoplasm present in a cell is called *protoplast*. Protoplast have four components.

I. Plasma membrane/Cell membrane	II. Cytoplasm
III. Nucleus	IV. Vacuole

CELL MEMBRANE

The cell membrane (plasma membrane) is the outer covering of every cell. It separates the cell from its environment and form distinct functional compartment (nucleus, organelles) in the cell. The outer cell membrane is called plasma membrane.

Note:

PROTOPLASM : (Proto = first and plasma = liquid.)
Purkinje (in 1839) coined the term protoplasm. Protoplasm is a liquid substance that is present inside the cell membrane. It includes cytoplasm, nucleus and other organelles. It is an aggregate of molecules of various chemicals. Most of these contain organic molecules like proteins, fats, carbohydrate etc.

Time to Check Your Knowledge

☞   **Can you tell or imagine how the plasma membrane keeps all the pieces inside.**

SOLUTION :

Plasma membrane appears like a big plastic bag with some tiny holes. This bag holds all of the cell pieces and fluids inside the cell. It also prevents the entry of unwanted foreign particles into the cell. The holes are there to let somethings move in and out of cells.

Cell membrane is a bilipid membranous layer composed of proteins, fats and carbohydrates. The phospholipid makes the basic bag. The proteins are found around the holes and helps to move molecules in and out of cells.

It protects the integrity of the interior of the cell by allowing certain substances into the cell, while keeping other substances

out. **Function of cell membrane :**
(i) It protect the cell from external injury.
(ii) It gives shape to the cell.
(iii) It controls the movement of substances 'into the cell' and 'out of cell'. Hence, it is also known as **selectively permeable membrane**.

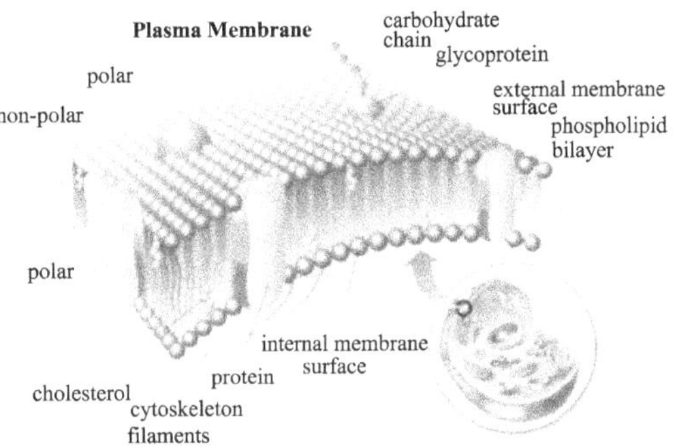

Structure of plasma membrane

CONNECTING TOPIC

Have you ever thought how does movement of substance take place inside the cell? Let us have a look.

Movement of carbon dioxide or oxygen : The movement of carbon dioxide or oxygen across the cell membrane occurs by a process called *diffusion*. **Diffusion** is the process of movement of molecules from a region of its high concentration to region of its low concentration. No energy is used in this process.

Differences between Diffusion and Osmosis

Diffusion	Osmosis
Can occur in any medium.	Occurs only in liquid medium.
Involves movement of solid, liquid & gas.	Involves movement of solvent molecules only.
Semipermeable membrane is not required.	Semipermeable membrane is necessary.

Movement of water across cell membrane : The movement of water across the membrane occurs by *osmosis*. **Osmosis** is the diffusion of water across a selectively permeable membrane from a region of high water concentration to a region of low water concentration.

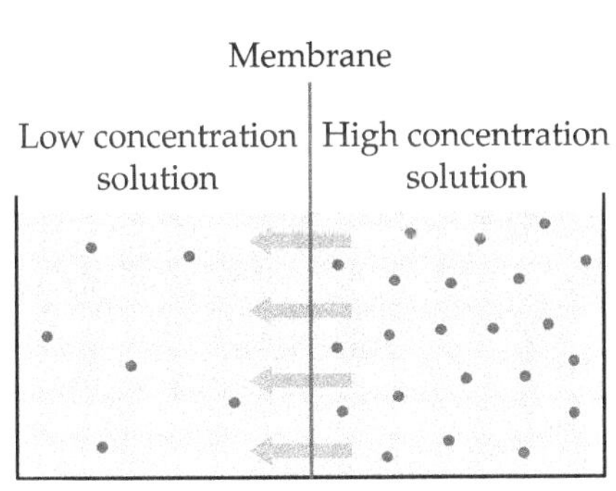

Diffusion

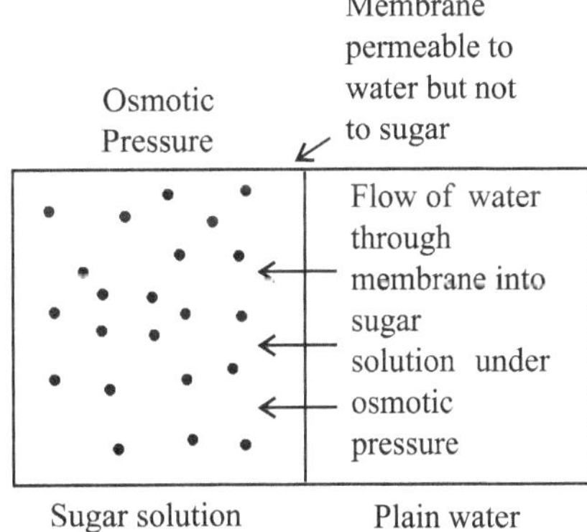

Osmosis

Let us perform an experiment to study plant and animal cells with a microscope.

Part A : Plant cells (Onion skin mount)

Let us perform an activity to understand the process of osmosis.

Take an animal or a plant cell and put it in three medium to observe.

(I) Medium that has higher water concentration than the cell.

> *What will happen? The cell will gain water by osmosis. Such type of solution are known as hypotonic solution. Since, water molecules are free to pass across the cell membrane in both directions, so when the cell is placed in a hypotonic solution, more water will enter into the cell than leaves it. As a result, the cell is likely to swell up.*

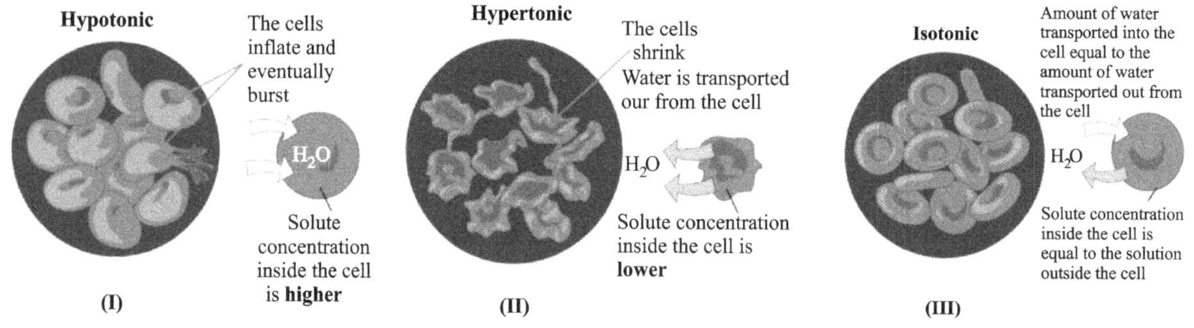

(II) Medium that has lower water concentration.

> *What will happen? The cell will lose water by osmosis. Such a solution is known as hypertonic solution. Since, water molecules are free to pass across the membrane, so when the cell is placed in hypertonic solution, it will lose water. As a result the cell will shrink.*

(III) Medium that has same water concentration as cell. What will happen?

> *There will be no net movement of water across the membrane. Such a solution is called isotonic solution. In isotonic solution, the amount of water entering into and leaving the cell is same. Hence, there is no net movement of water and thus the cell size remains the same.*

CYTOPLASM

Cytoplasm is a transparent, jelly like material (called cytosol or cytoplasmic matrix) that fills the cell between nucleus and cell membrane. Autonomic movement of matrix in the cytoplasm in a cell is called **cytoplasmic streaming** or **cyclosis**. The various structures present in the cytoplasm of a cell are called organelles. The most important organelles are the nucleus, endoplasmic reticulum mitochondrion, the ribosome, the golgi bodies, the lysosome, cell wall, cilia and flagella, pastids etc.

Function of cytoplasem -

(i)   It holds cell organelles in place.

(ii) It gives the shape to cell structure.

(iii) Most of the chemical reactions (which keeps the cell alive) takes place in cytoplasm.

NUCLEUS

The nucleus is a large, spherical organelle present in the cells. In animal cell, it is located at the centre of the cell, while, in plant cell, it is located at the periphery, near the edge. Nucleus controls the cell's function and is thus known as the brain of the cell.

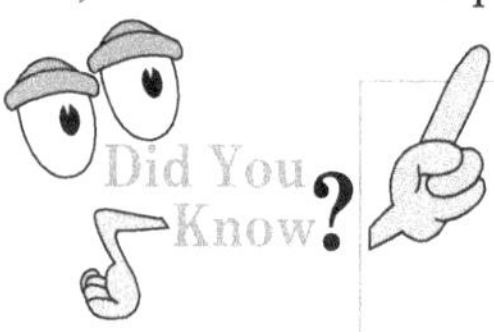

Nucleoid

The nucleoid is the dense region in the prokaryotic cell (bacteria) that contains the main DNA material. The nucleoid has an irregular shape compared to the nucleus of eukaryotic cells, which is circular. DNA in the nucleoid is circular, and may have multiple copies at any given time. Additionally, DNA in the nucleoid may be supercoiled, meaning it has twists in the circular shape that makes it more compact. As the cells grow, the DNA in the nucleoid may extend into the cytosol (cellular fluid).

Parts of Nucleus

The nucleus consists of *nuclear envelope, nucleous, chromatin* and *nucleoplasm.*

(i) **Nuclear envelope :** It is a double membranous structure with a fluid-filled space. It separates nucleoplasm from the cytoplasm. The outer membrane is connected with endoplasmic reticulum and its outer surface may contain ribosomes while the inner surface is smooth. The nuclear envelope is perforated by many *nuclear pores*. These pores provide a channel for the movement of important molecules between nucleus and cytoplasm.

(ii) **Nucleoplasm :** Nucleoplasm is a clear, non-staining fluid material in the nucleus. It contains raw materials, enzymes and metal ions for the synthesis of DNA and RNA. It supports the chromatin material and nucleoli.

(iii) **Chromatin :** Nucleus contains a fibrous material known as chromatin. Chromatin forms a long thread like structure called **chromosomes** during cell division. Each chromosome is made up of protein and a single molecule of DNA. Chromosomes contains genes that control cell metabolism and heredity. *Heredity* is the transfer of characters from parents to offspring.

(iv) **Nucleolus (or Nucleoli) :** Nucleolus is a naked round or slightly irregular structure which is attached to the chromatin at a specific region called nucleolar organizer region (NOR). It is responsible for protein synthesis and is the active site of the development of ribosomal RNAs.

Function of Nucleus are –

(i) The nucleus acts like the brain or the controlling centre of the cells.

(ii) It is responsible for ribosome synthesis.

(iii) It regulates cell metabolism by directing the synthesis of functional proteins.

(iv) It develops genetic variation that contribute to evolution.

(v) It also contains genetic information for reporduction, development and behaviour of the organisms along with their structure and metabolism.

Anatomy of the Nucleus

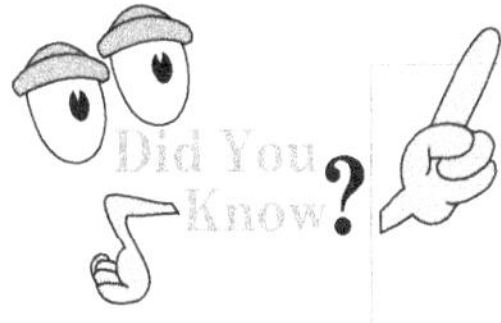

Cells which lack the nucleus
Red blood cells of humans and other mammals lose their nuclei which enables them to carry more haemoglobin & thus pickup more oxygen.
Phloem sieve tubes lose tubes nuclei which facilitates the flow of materials through them.

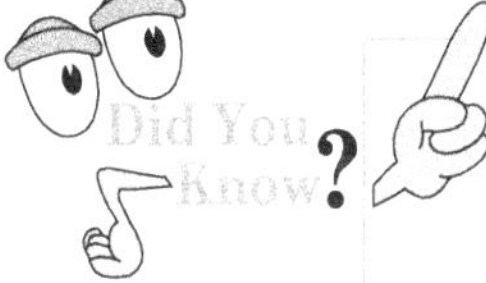

Chromosomes
Chromosomes are long stringy aggregates of genes that carry heredity information. Each chromosome is made up of DNA tightly coiled many times around proteins called histones that support its structure. Chromosomes can be seen visually through a light microscope during late interphase as well as during mitosis.
Gene
Gene is the unit of heredity. Gene gives an identity to each and every organism. It is the basic molecular unit of inheritance in living organisms. It controls the transfer of heredity characteristics from parents to the offspring.

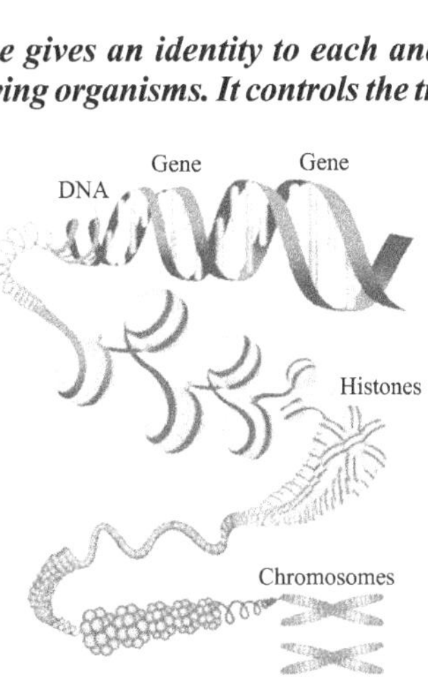

Structure of gene

Do all cells contain a well defined nucleus structure?

No. Not all cells contain a well defined nucleus. The nucleus of the bacterial cell is not well organised like the cells of multicellular organisms. They lack nuclear membrane. Such type of cells are known as prokaryotic cells. On the other hand, the cells that have well organised nucleus with a nuclear membrane are called eukaryotic cells.

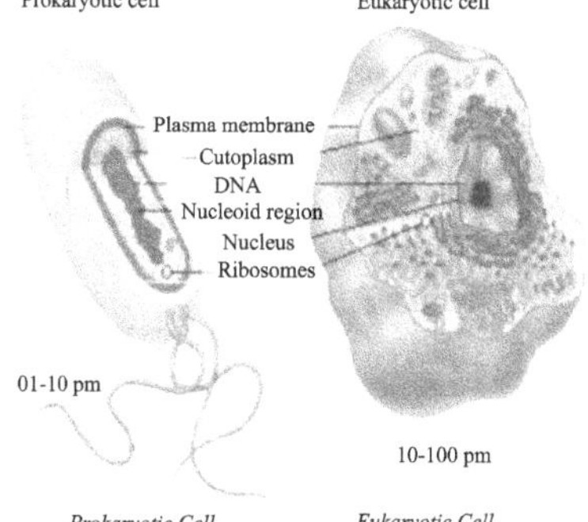

Table : Difference between Prokaryotic and Eukaryotic cell

	Prokaryotic cells	**Eukaryotic cells**
(i)	Prokaryotic cells are usually small $(0.1 - 5.0\ \mu)$ compared to other cells.	Eukaryotic cells are larger in size $(5 - 100\ \mu)$.
(ii)	They do not have organized nucleus. The DNA present is clumped in an area but there is no organized nucleus with a membrane.	They have an organized nucleus with a nuclear envelope. It means they have true nucleus. The DNA is found enclosed within the nucleus.
(iii)	They do not have any cell organelle except for ribosomes.	Eukaryotic cells usually have cell organelles such as endoplasmic reticulum, Golgi bodies, lysosomes etc.
(iv)	Examples–bacteria and blue green algae.	Examples–plant and animal cells.

☞ **Why nucleus is important?**

SOLUTION :

Nucleus is the cell's brain which controls all its activities. Nucleus contain DNA. DNA contains instructions needed for cell reproduction and also produces proteins that controls metabolism and other cell function.

DNA - The blueprint of life

DNA (Deoxyribonucleic acid) is a molecule that encodes the genetic instructions used in the development and function of all known organisms and many viruses. The DNA carries a complete blue print of the organism that transfers characteristics from one generation to the next.

DNA is the major store of genetic information. Watson and Crick Model shows that DNA is a double helix with sugar-phosphate backbones on the outside and paired bases on the inside. They proposed the three dimensional structure of DNA based on the X-ray diffraction photographs of DNA fibres taken by Rosalind Franklin and MHF Wilkins.

DNA contains the instructions needed for an organisms to develop, survive and reproduce. To carry out these functions, DNA sequences must be converted into messages that can be used to produce proteins which are the complex molecules that do most of the work in our bodies.

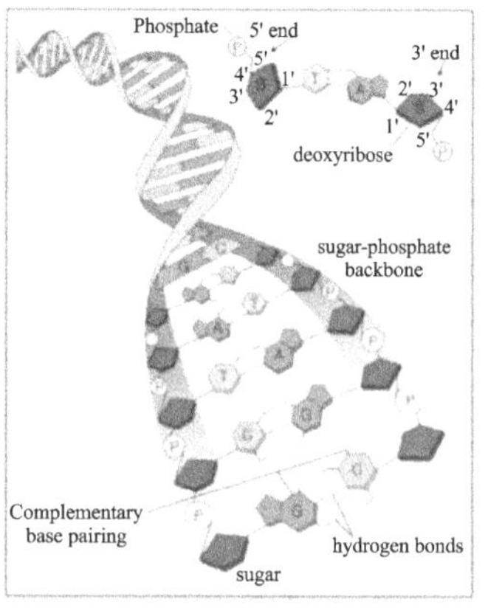

Structure of DNA

DNA is made of chemical building blocks called nucleotides. These building blocks are made of three parts: a phosphate group, a sugar group and one of four types of nitrogen bases. To form a strand of DNA, nucleotides are linked into chains, with the phosphate and sugar groups alternating.

The four types of nitrogen bases found in nucleotides are: adenine (A), thymine (T), guanine (G) and cytosine (C). The order, or sequence, of these bases determines what biological instructions are contained in a strand of DNA. For example, the sequence ATCGTT might instruct for blue eyes, while ATCGCT might instruct for brown.

We inherit our genetic material through DNA from our parents - half from our father and half from our mother that is why we often look like our parents.

Time to Check Your Knowledge

☛ **Why do we often look like our parents ?**

SOLUTION :

The way we grow and develop is determined by the genes present on our chromosomes which we recieve from our parents through the egg and sperm. The characteristics of individual human beings are passed from one generation to next in their chromosomes. Each of our parents gives us 23 chromosomes making 46 in all. Gene controls the transfer of hereditary characteristics which means that our parents pass some of their characteristics to us.

VACUOLES

Vacuoles are fluid filled organelles enclosed by a membrane (called **tonoplast**). It appears as an empty space under the microscope. Plant cells have a large vacuole. Their vacuole is filled with a liquid called "**cell sap**" that contains dissolved sugar and salts. The cell sap is generally neutral but at maturity it becomes acidic in nature.

Function of vacuole in plant cells –

(i)   It keeps the plant cell firm or turgid.

(ii) It stores various substances including waste products of the cell.

Animal cells may or may not have vacuole. If present, vacuoles in animals are much smaller than those found in plant cells.

Function of vacuole in animal cells –

(i)   In *Amoeba*, vacuoles contain food particles, hence, known as food vacuole.

(ii) They store materials such as food, water, sugar, minerals and waste products.

Vacuoles in plant cell

Endoplasmic Reticulum (ER)

ER is a network of membranous canals which encloses a fluid -filled lumen.

It is of two types – Rough endoplasmic reticulum (RER) and Smooth endoplasmic reticulum *(SER)*.

(i)   RER– It is lined with ribosomes and is rough in appearance.

(ii) SER– It contains no ribosomes and hence are smooth in appearance.

It is absent in prokaryotes but present in all the eukaryotes except germinal cells and mature mammalian erythrocytes

Function of endoplasmic reticulum:

(i)   The ER is the "transport system" of the cell. It transports chemical between cells and within cells.

(ii) It provides large surface area for the organization of chemical reactions and synthesis.

(iii) RER plays an important role in protein synthesis.

(iv) SER plays an important role in lipid synthesis.

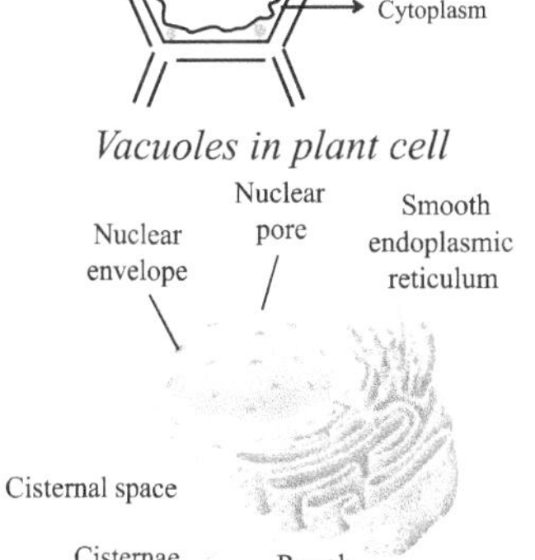

Endoplasmic reticulum

Ribosomes

Ribosome is a non-membranous, spherical body composed of RNA (ribonucleic acid) and protein enzyme. Ribosomes are also present separately in cytoplasm. It is the site of protein synthesis in a cell, hence, called protein factory.

Ribosomes are of two basic types – 70 S and 80 S ribosomes. The 70 S ribosomes are found in prokaryotes while the 80 S ribosomes are found in eukaryotes. S'refers to svedberg units of sedimentation coefficient. The 'S' is a measure of the speed of the sedimentation for a particular cell organelle in ultracentrifuge.

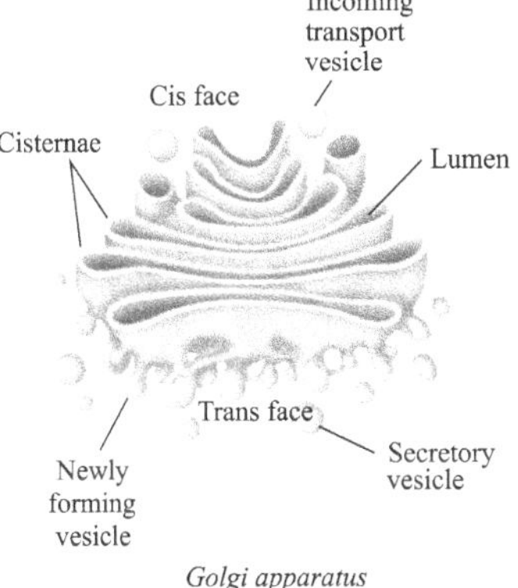

Golgi apparatus

Golgi Bodies

Golgi bodies are sacs of membrane bound cisternae, vesicle and vacuoles. These are usually stacked together in parallel rows. Golgi apparatus was discovered by Italian anatomist Camillo Golgi.

Function of golgi bodies :

(i) The golgi apparatus is responsible for taking the proteins which were created by ribosomes and package them. When the golgi apparatus is done, it releases the new proteins into the cell, where they can be used to strengthen and build up cells. It is also involved in formation of lysosomes and peroxisomes.

(ii) It plays an important role in modification, secretion and storage of chemicals.

Mitochondria

Mitochondria are rod shaped organelles bounded by double membranes. The outer and inner membrane are separated by a space called intermembrane space. The outer membrane is smooth whereas inner membrane folds over many times to form **cristae**. Cristae greatly increases the surface area of the inner membrane. The wide space between the cristae is called the **inner chamber** which is filled with a dense fluid (called **mitochondrial matrix**).

Mitochondria are the sites of energy production. They contain enzymes for cellular respiration in which energy is released. *You all must have learnt about cellular respiration in previous classes. Here,* is a brief overview.

During respiration, we inhale oxygen which the blood transports to all the cells in our body. During cellular respiration, using this oxygen, glucose gets oxidized to form ATP (adenosine triphosphate) molecules. ATP is a form of energy that our body can use.

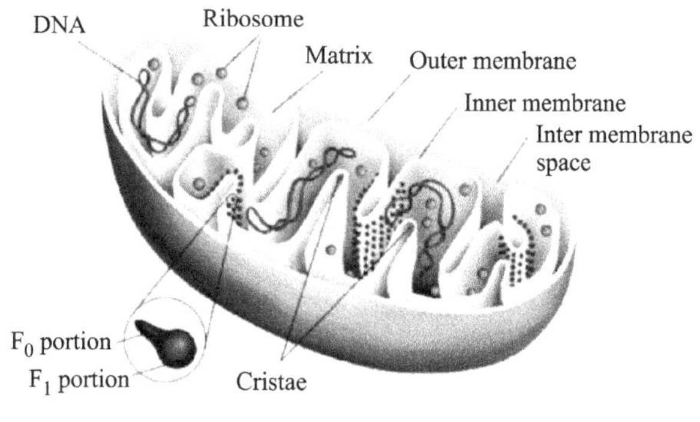

Mitochondria

$$\text{Glucose} + \text{Oxygen} \longrightarrow \text{Carbon dioxide} + \text{Water} + \text{Energy (ATP)}$$

Therefore, these organelles are called as the **powerhouse of the cell**. They take in nutrients, break them down, and create energy for the cell.

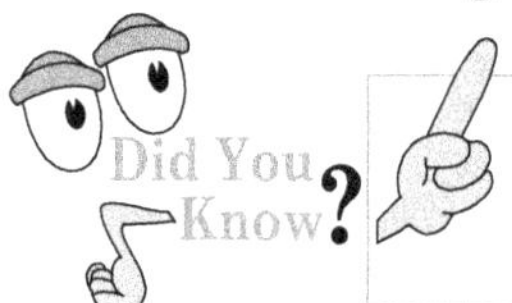

Note:

Mitochondria is the third largest organelle in plant cells and second largest organelle in animal cells. Mitochondria are able to make their own DNA and proteins, hence they are regarded as semi-autonomous organelle.

Lysosome

Lysosomes are present in animal cells only. They are sac-like structure surrounded by a single membrane. The membrane bound bag contains powerful digestive (hydrolytic) enzymes capable of either digesting or breaking down all organic materials. It act as a mini digestive system within the cell and is known as the "suicidal bag".

Lysosomes destroy any foreign materials that manages to enter the cell such as pathogens.

They also remove worn-out or poorly functioning organelles from the cell. They may even sometimes digest the entire damaged or dead cells containing them.

- *Lysosomes are also called as suicidal sacs/bags as they contain hydrolytic enzymes.*
- *In animals, lysosomes are abundant in leucocytes, macrophages, Kupffers cells and similar cells with phagocytic activity, prokaryotes lack lysosomes.*

Cilia and flagella

Cilia are short, hair like projections that occur in large numbers on the outside surface of certain animal cells. They cover the entire surface of the cell. For example, *Paramecium*, a single celled organism, has cilia on its surface. Cilia are the organs of locomotion.

Flagella are long, thread like structures at one end of the cell. There are usually a few flagella present on a cell. For example, *Euglena*, a single-celled organism, has flagellum at its mouth region. Like cilia, flagella also helps in movement of organism.

Cell Wall

The plant cells have a thick and rigid cell wall surrounding the cell membrane. It is composed of tough material called cellulose. Cell wall are found in plants, bacteria, fungi, algae and some archae. Animals and protozoa do not have cell wall.

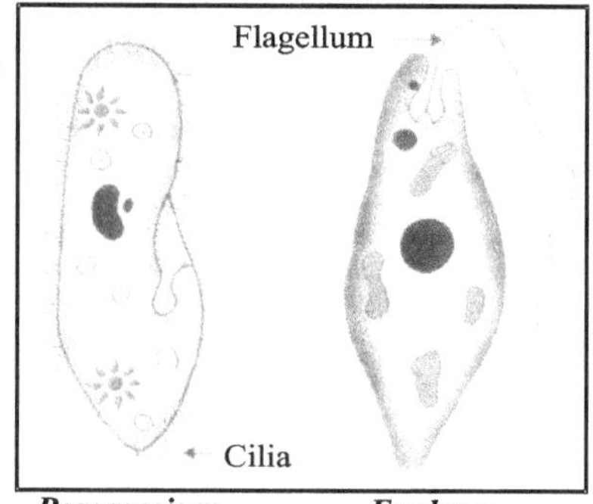

Cilia and flagella

Function of cell wall :
(i)   It gives shape and support to plant cell.
(ii)   It protects the cell from mechanical injury.
(iii) It contains pores that allow materials to pass in and out of the cell.

Time to
Check Your
Knowledge

1.   **Why do plants have cell walls, and not animals?**
2.   **What would happen if the cells in our body had cell walls?**
3.   **Why cell wall is absent in animals?**

SOLUTION :

1.   In order to provide plants strength and necessary support, the cells within the plant have this hard cell covering. If the trees were soft like an animal, they could not stand strong and upright. Plants require cell wall for protection against variations in temperature, high wind speed, atmospheric moisture, etc. that they are exposed to because they cannot move.
2.   If an animal's body were made of cell walls the animals would be very stiff and unable to move easily.
3.   Cell wall is incompatible with the way in which an animal moves and grows.

Plastids

Plastids are double membrane bound organelles. They occur in most plant cells and are absent in animal cells. Depending upon their pigment colour, they are classified into two main types : leucoplasts and chromoplast.

(i)   **Leucoplasts :** It is a colourless organelle that stores starch or other plant nutrients. For example – starch stored in potato. It occurs in large number in cells of fruits, seeds and rhizomes.

(ii)   **Chromoplast :** It contains differents coloured pigments. The most important type of chromoplast is **chloroplast**. Chloroplast are green–coloured organelles present in cytoplasm of plant cells. The process of food making by plants (known as *photosynthesis*) takes place in chloroplasts. Hence, chloroplasts are the food producers of the cell.

Like the mitochondria, plastids also have their own genome *i.e.,* DNA and ribosomes. They are self-replicating organelles like the mitochondria *i.e.,* they have the power to divide.

Chloroplast contains green colour pigment called *chlorophyll* which absorbs energy from the Sun and helps the plant in the process of photosynthesis.

CONNECTING TOPIC

Chloroplast

Each chloroplast is a double membranous structure with an inter-membrane space in between them. The space enclosed by inner membrane is called **stroma**. The stroma is an area where all chemical reactions occurs and starch (sugars) is synthesized. The stroma contains small cylindrical structures (called **grana**) in it.

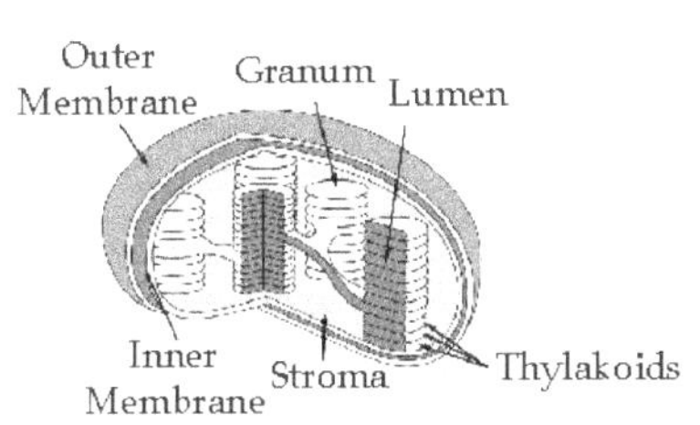

Outer Membrane
Granum
Lumen
Inner Membrane
Stroma
Thylakoids

Chloroplast

Grana consists of membranous or lamellar system. This lamellar system is made up of **thylakoid**. About 20–50 thylakoids are placed one above the other like a stack of coins to form a **granum**. Many membranous tubules called **stroma lamellae** interconnect thylakoids of different grana. Each thylakoid has chlorophyll molecules on their surface that traps sunlight and take part in the process of photosynthesis.

Therefore, chloroplast is called the **site of photosynthesis**. In chloroplast, carbon dioxide and water combines in the presence of sunlight to produce food such as glucose. Thus, chloroplasts help in synthesis of food in green plants.

$$CO_2 + H_2O \xrightarrow[\text{Sunlight}]{\text{Chlorophyll}} \textbf{Glucose + Oxygen}$$

CASE STUDY-1 : Cellular Organelle

An organelle is a specialised subunit, usually within cell that has a specific function.

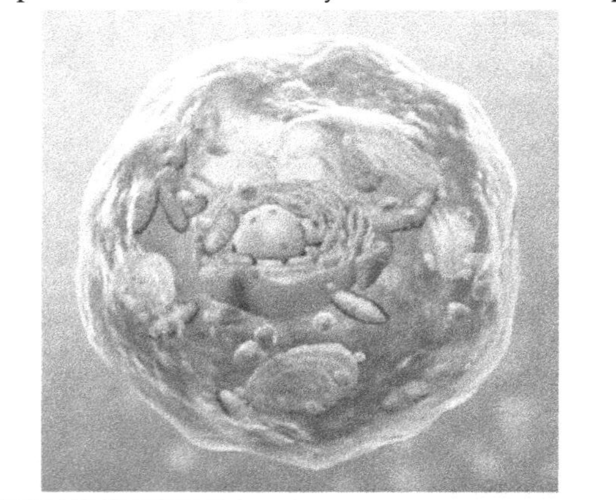

CASE I: *Mitochondrice is the power house of the cell.*

Mitochondrice is a double membraned, has ATP molecules and its own genetic material.

CASE II: *Lysosomes are the suicidal bag of the cell.*

Lysosome is single membraned has digestive enzymes which destroy any foreign material that enters inside the cell.

CASE III: *Chloroplast is the photo-synthetic site of the cell.*

Chloroplast is double membraned, has its own genome and carry out photosynthesis in plants.

CASE IV: *Nucleus is the heredity unit of the cell.*

Nucleus is double membraned and is the central centre of cell. It is also responsible for ribosome synthesis.
It has nucleoprotein and genetic material of the cell and regulates the cell divison.

 *T*hink **O**ut *of the* **B**ox

Q 1. Which organelle is connected to the outer membrane of nucleus and why?

Q 2. State two differences between eukaryotic and prokaryotic cell?

COMPARISION OF PLANT AND ANIMAL CELL

Now, we have studied that plants and animals are similar in many respects but they are also different in some respects. Plant and animal cells are a type of eukaryotic cells. Most of the organelles and other structures of cells are common in animals and plants. Let us now see the important similarities and dissimilarities between plant cells and animal cells.

Similarities between plant and animal cell

(i)   They both have a cell membrane or plasma membrane around them.

(ii)   Both the cells have cytoplasm.

(iii)   Both the cells have nucleus, endoplasmic reticulum ribosome, mitochondria and golgi apparatus.

Table : Difference between Plant and animal cell

	Plant Cells	**Animal Cells**
(i)	A plant cell has a rigid cell wall around it.	Cell wall is absent.
(ii)	Plastids are present	An animal cell does not have plastid in it.
(iii)	A plant cell has a centrally located large vacuole in it.	Vacuoles are either absent or smaller in size.
(iv)	It cannot change its shape.	It can often change its shape
(v)	Plant cells do not burst if placed in hypotonic solution due to presence of cell wall.	Animal cell usually bursts if placed in hypotonic solution unless and untill they possess contractile vacuole.

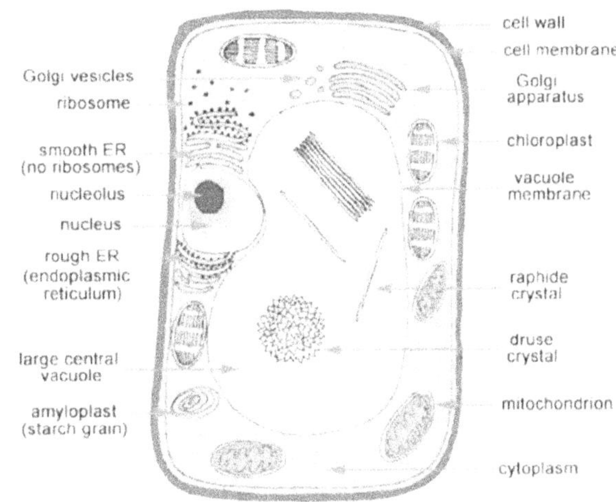

Plant Cell

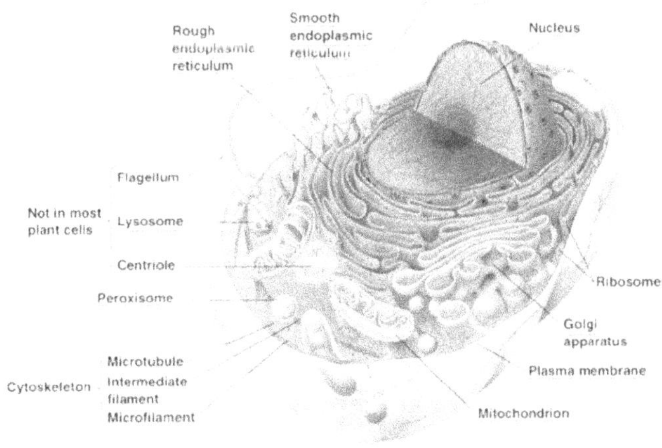

Animal Cell

Table : Summary of the functions of different parts of a cell

CELL	Functions
Cell membrane	1. It gives shape and support to the cell.
	2. It allows the entry and exit of cellular materials.
Nucleus	1. It controls all the activities of the cell.
	2. It is responsible for genetic characteristics.
	3. It synthesizes and stores proteins.
Endoplasmic reticulum	It is involved in the synthesis, storage, and transport of cell products.
Mitochondria	They act as sites of energy production. So they are also called the powerhouses of the cell.
Ribosomes	These granular structures act as sites of protein synthesis.
Golgi apparatus	They are responsible for the secretion of enzymes, hormones and proteins.
Lysosomes	They are capable of digesting damaged cells and a variety of extra- and intra-cellular materials.
Vacuoles	These fluid-filled spaces store excess water, useful minerals, salt, food substances, pigments and waste products.

The following table compares the presence of few features of plant, animal and bacterial cell. Tick (ü) mark the organelles present in plant, animal and bacterial cells.

Cell part	Plant cell	Animal cell	Bacterial cell
Cell membrane			
Cell wall			
Nucleus			
Nucleus membrane			
Cytoplasm			
Plastids			
Vacuole			

SUMMARY

- *Cell* is the basic structure and functional unit of life that can carry out all the processes of life.

- *Robert Hooke* was the first person to observe cells under a microscope.

- *Schleidan and Schwann* proposed the cell theory in 1838.

- *Tissue* is a group of cells that are alike and work together to perform a specific function.

- *Organ,* a relatively independent part of the body, is a group of tissue that carries out one or more specialized function.

- *Organisms* made of more than one cell are called *multicellular organisms.* Examples – plants and animals.

- Organisms made of single-cell are called *unicellular organisms.* Examples – *Amoeba, Paramecium.*

- The single cell of unicellular organisms performs all the basic functions performed by a variety of cells in multicellular organisms

- A white blood cell (WBC) in human blood is an example of single cell which can change its shape.

- The cell has four main parts –

  - Cell membrane

  - Cytoplasm

  - Nucleus

  - Vacuole

- Cells without well organised nuclei (*i.e.,* lacking nuclear membrane) are called *prokaryotic cells.* For example, bacterial cell.

- Cells having well organised nuclei with a nuclear membrane are called *eukaryotic cells.* For example, onion cells and cheek cells.

- Plasma membrane is a selectively permeable membrane. It regulates the movement of molecules in and out of the cell.

- Plant cells differ from animal cells in having an additional layer around cell membrane called *cell wall.*

- When a plant cell is put in a hypertonic solution, it losses water due to osmosis (exosmosis) and as a result, protoplast is shrinked away from the cell wall. This is called plasmolysis.

- Various membrane bound cell organelles present in eukaryotic cell are nucleus, endoplasmic reticulum, golgi apparatus, mitochondria, plastids, lysosomes etc.

- *Mitochondria* forms the powerhouse of cell. They use molecular oxygen and generate energy-rich compunds (ATP).

- *Chloroplasts* are chlorophyll containing green plastids. They use water and CO_2 and convert radiant energy of sunlight into chemical energy of carbohydrates.

- *Ribosomes* are sites of protein synthesis.

- *Endoplasmic reticulum* are of two types — SER and RER. SER synthesizes lipids and RER synthesizes proteins.

- *Golgi apparatus* is the site for the storage, processing and packaging of various cellular secretions.

- *Lysosomes* form the excretory system of animal cells.

- *Nucleus* contains thread like structure called chromosomes, which carry genes and helps in transmission of characters.

CASE STUDY-2 : Plant Cell and Animal Cell

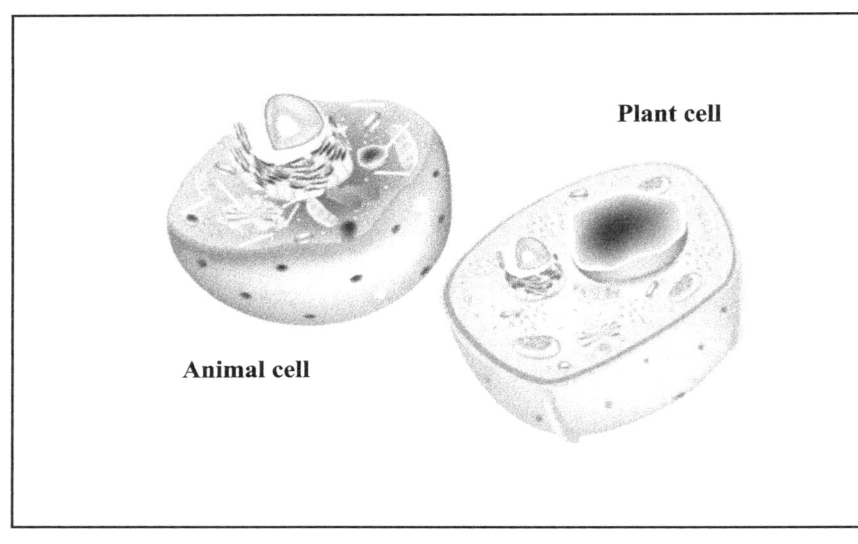

CASE I: *I am organelle 'A'. I am present in plant cell, but absent in animal cell I. I can store and produce food such as glucose. Who am I?*

Organelle 'A' are plastids.

CASE II: *I am a component of plant cell. It provide shape strength and support. I protect the plant cell from mechanical injuries. Who am 'I'?*

This component of plant cell is cell wall. It is absent in animal cells.

CASE III: *I am organelle 'B'. I am bigger in size in a plant cell. I keep the plant cells firm or turgid. I store various substances including waste products of the cell. Who am 'I'?*

Organelle 'B' is vacuole. Plant cells have a centrally located large vacuole. Which is filled with a liquid called 'Cell Sap'.

*T*hink *O*ut of the *B*ox

Q 1. What happens if a plant cell is kept in hypotonic solution?

Q 2. What would happen if animals have cell walls?

Q 3. Why are chloroplasts present in plant cells, but absent in animal cells?

Exercise 1 — Master Boards

Multiple Choice Questions

DIRECTIONS : This section contains multiple choice questions. Each question has four choices (a), (b), (c) and (d) out of which ONLY ONE is correct.

1. Nucleus is separated from cytoplasm by
   (a) Nucleus membrane   (b) Nudeoplasm
   (c) Organs   (d) Cell membrane
2. The coloured organelle which are found in plants only
   (a) Plastids   (b) Nucleus
   (c) Ribosome   (d) Endoplasmic Reticulum
3. The structural and functional unit of life called cell was discovered by
   (a) Robert Boyle   (b) Charles Darwin
   (c) Robert Koch   (d) Robert Hooke
4. The non-living part of a tomats cell is
   (a) Cell membrane   (b) Nucleus
   (c) Chloroplast   (d) Cell wall
5. The empty blank looking structures in the cytoplasm is
   (a) Vacoules   (b) Plastids
   (c) Plasma membrane   (d) Nucleus

Assertion & Reason

DIRECTIONS : Each of these questions contains an Assertion followed by Reason. Read them carefully and answer the question on the basis of following options. You have to select the one that best describes the two statements.

(a) If both **Assertion** and **Reason** are **correct** and Reason is the **correct explanation** of Assertion.
(b) If both **Assertion** and **Reason** are correct, but Reason is **not the correct explanation** of Assertion.
(c) If **Assertion** is **correct** but **Reason** is **incorrect**.
(d) If **Assertion** is **incorrect** but **Reason** is **correct**.

1. **Assertion :** Specialization of cells is useful for organism
   Reason : It increases the operational efficiency of an organism.
2. **Assertion :** The number of cells in a multicellular organism is inversely proportional to a size of body.
   Reason : All cells of biological world are alive.
3. **Assertion :** Cell is an open system.
   Reason : Cell receives a number of materials including energy containing nutrients from outside.
4. **Assertion :** Schleiden and Schwann were the first to observe the cells and to put forward cell theory.
   Reason : The cells are always living unit.
5. **Assertion :** Ribosome are non-membrane bound organelles found in the prokaryotic cells only.
   Reason : These are present only in the cytoplasm.

Fill in the Blanks

DIRECTIONS : Complete the following statements with an appropriate word / term to be filled in the blank space(s).

1. Cell theory was proposed by _________ and _________ .
2. _________ is considered as the biggest cell.
3. _________ is considered as the smallest cell.
4. One micron is _________ of a meter.
5. _________ controls all the activities of cell.
6. The process by which water enters through a selectively permeable membrane is called _________ .
7. Cellular respiration occurs in _________ of cell.
8. _________ is called suicidal bag of cell.
9. Genetic material of plant and animal cell is found in _________ .
10. _________ gives shape and support to the plant cell.
11. Plastids are present only in _________ cells.
12. _________ acts as the skeleton of chloroplast.
13. The 'cell sap' of vacuole contains dissolved _________ and _________ .
14. Nerve cells are known as _________ .
15. A group of cells performing a similar function is called a _________ .

True / False

DIRECTIONS : Read the following statements and write your answer as true or false.

1. Animal cells have cell wall followed by the cell membrane.
2. Chromosomes carry genes.
3. Plastids and chloroplasts are found in plant cells.
4. Onion cells and cheek cells are the examples of prokaryotic cell.
5. Pseudopodia is found in higher animals.
6. Nerve cells are long and have branches.
7. *Amoeba* is a multicellular organism.
8. Plant cells are made up of cellulose.
9. Xylem and phloem are example of tissue.
10. Energy is stored in the cell in the form of ADP molecules.

Match the Following

DIRECTIONS : Each question contains two columns which have to be matched. Statements/terms (A, B, C, D and E) given in column I have to be matched with statements/terms (p, q, r, s, t) given in column II.

1.

	Column-I (Functions)	Column-II (Organelles)
A.	Entry and exit of cellular materials	p. Vacuoles
B.	Transmission of genetic character	q. Mitochondria
C.	Production of energy	r. Nucleus
D.	Secretion of enzyme and proteins	s. Cell membrane
E.	Store excess water mineral, food substances and pigments	t. Golgi apparatus

2.

Column-I (Organelles)	Column-II (Definitions)
A. Endoplasmic reticulum	p. Spherical or rod shaped body which produces energy.
B. Prokaryotic cells	q. Contains cell organelles and found in both plant and animal cell.
C. Eukaryotic cells	r. A network of cytoplasmic tubes and channels.
D. Mitochondria	s. Cells having nuclear material without nuclear membrane.
E. Cytoplasm	t. Cells having well organized nuclei with a nuclear membrane

Passage Based Questions

DIRECTIONS : *Study the given paragraph(s) and answer the following questions.*

The cells have been present in the living organisms (plants and animals) since the origin of life. This cells were, however, not studied or observed for thousand of years. It was only when microscopes having high magnification power were made in the seventeenth century to magnify things greatly that cells could be seen in living organisms. Each cell has a number of smaller parts in it. Some of the parts are present in all type of cells. (plants cells as well as animals cells). But certain parts are found only in plant cells.

1. The basic similarity among all the living organism is that they are made up of
   (a) tissues   (b) organs
   (c) cells   (d) organ system
2. The parts which are not present in an animal cell are
   (a) Cell membrane   (b) Chloroplast
   (c) Cell wall   (d) Mitochondria
3. Which of the following is a plant cell?
   (a) Cartilage cell   (b) Neuron
   (c) Epidermal cell   (d) Epithelial cell

Very Short Answer Questions

1. What is cell?
2. Name the scientist who had first observed the free cell under microscope.
3. Where organelles are embedded in a cell?
4. What is the difference between unicellular and multicellular organisms.
5. Name the outer layer of an animal cell.
6. What is cytoplasm?
7. Which plastid stores starch and other plant nutrients?
8. Which two organelles are semi-autonomous?
9. Name the largest floating body generally found in the centre of cell?
10. Write a function of ribosome.
11. Who had developed the first microscope?
12. Which cell has the ability to change its shape?
13. Write the function of xylem and phloem cells.

14. Give one difference between rough endoplasmic reticulum and smooth endoplasmic reticulum.
15. In which part of the chloroplast all chemical reactions occurs.
16. What is protoplasm?
17. Which cell organelle regulates the process of cell division?
18. Give an example of unicellular organism.
19. Which cell organelle helps transport substances within the cell?
20. Which organelles contain hydrolytic enzymes?

Short Answer Questions

1. Why cell membrane is called selectively permeable?
2. Why chloroplasts are present only in plant cells?
3. State the difference between prokaryotic and eukaryotic cells.
4. Give an important characteristic of a muscle cell.
5. Why mitochondria is called the powerhouse of the cell?
6. Where are the ribosomes found? Write their functions?
7. How chromosomes carry genetic characters?
8. Write a short note on DNA.
9. Write the different levels of organization in multicellular organism.
10. What are plastids? How they are classified?
11. Give structure and functions of nucleolus.
12. How plant cell is different from animal cell with respect to the vacuoles?
13. How prokaryotic cell is different from eukaryotic cells?

Long Answer Questions

1. Discuss the main components of a typical cell.
2. Briefly explain the various components of a plant cell.
3. Explain the structure and function of nucleus.
4. Make a list of functions of all eukaryotic cell organelles.

Reasoning Basedm Questions

1. Why are plant and animal specimens usually stained with dyes before observing them through a microscope?
2. Why are nerve cells are long and have branches?
3. Why could cells not be observed and studied for thousand of years?
4. Why the tomatoes are red in color?
5. Why chloroplasts are found only in plant cells.
6. Why is it important to know about the cells?

Hots Questions

1. White blood cells have the ability to change its shape. Comment on this.
2. Cells of ants and elephants are same in size. Do you agree with this? Give reason.
3. "Cell is the structural and functional unit of life." Explain.
4. Bacteria have a region called nucleoid, in which their genetic material is located. Why, then bacteria are classified as prokaryotic cell and not eukaryotic.
5. Make a model of plant cell and animal cell by using household waste.
6. Refer the given figure and answer the following questions.

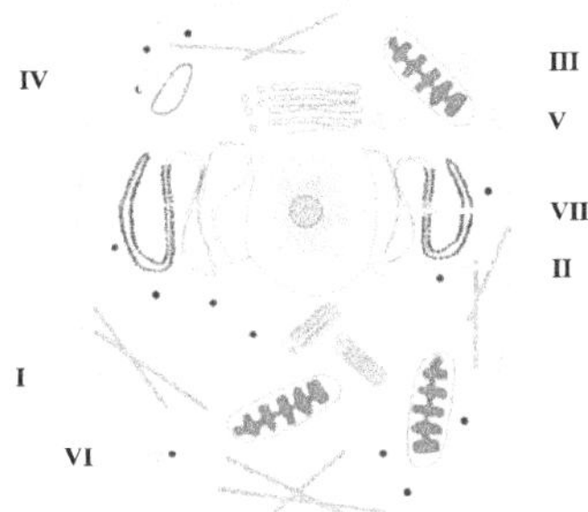

(i) Which organelle is called as suicidal bag?
(ii) Which organelle is called "engine of the cell"?
(iii) Which structure is called "Little nucleus"?
(iv) Which organelle is called the "powerhouse of the cell"?
(v) Which labelled area is known as selectively permeable membrane?

7. Give a term for the following processes.
(i) Swelling of resins in water.
(ii) Exchange of gases during respiration.
(iii) Crenation of erythrocytes.
(iv) Change of flaccid cell into turgid cell.

8. Complete the crossword-puzzle of cell structure and function:

Across	**Down**
1. A group of similar cells performing a specific function.	2. The organism which are made up single cell.

3. It helps in transfer of characters from the parents to their offsprings
4. The jelly like substance between the nucleus and the cell membrane.
5. The cell organelle present in plants which are mainly responsible for imparting colour.
6. An empty structure in the cytoplasm which performs storage function.
7. The green coloured plastids responsible for photosynthesis.

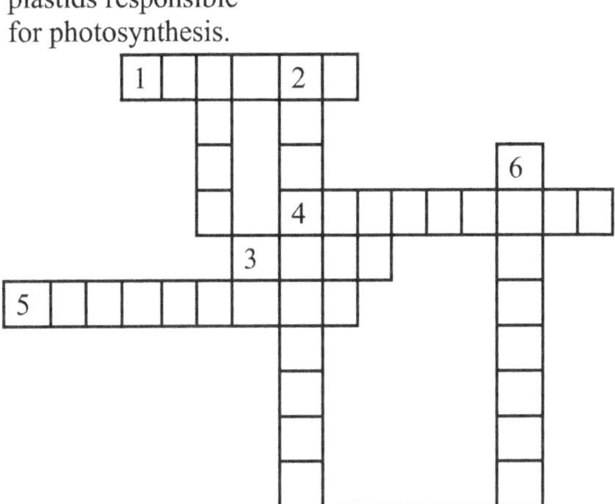

Exercise 2   ⭐ Master NCERT (Text–book & Exemplar)

Text-book Exercise

1. Indicate whether the following statements are True (T) or False (F).
(a) Unicellular organisms have one-celled body. (T / F)
(b) Muscle cells are branched. (T / F)
(c) The basic living unit of an organism is an organ. (T / F)
(d) *Amoeba* has irregular shape. (T / F)

2. Make a sketch of the human nerve cell. What function do nerve cells perform?

3. Write short notes on the following.
(a) Cytoplasm   (b) Nucleus of a cell

4. Which part of the cell contains organelles?

5. Make sketches of animal and plant cells. State three differences between them.

6. State the difference between eukaryotes and prokaryotes.

7. Where are chromosomes found in a cell? State their function.

8. 'Cells are the basic structural units of living organisms'. Explain.

9. Explain why chloroplasts are found only in plant cells?

10. Complete the crossword with the help of clues given below.

ACROSS
1. This is necessary for photosynthesis.
3. Term for component present in the cytoplasm.
6. The living substance in the cell.
8. Units of inheritance present on the chromosomes.

DOWN
1. Green plastids.

2. Formed by collection of tissues.
4. It separates the contents of the cell from the surrounding medium.
5. Empty structure in the cytoplasm.
7. A group of cells.

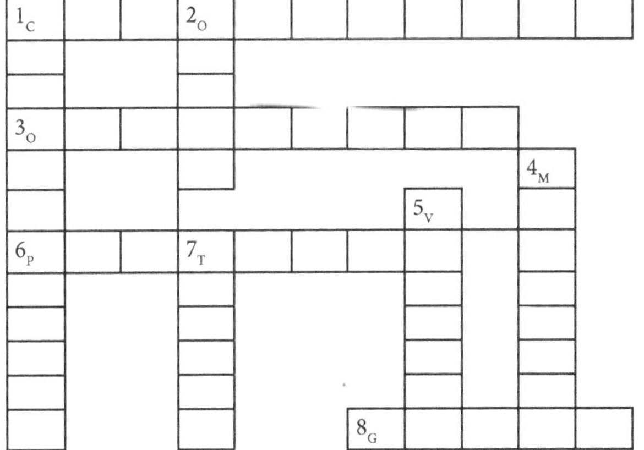

Exemplar Questions

1. We do not sense any pain when we clip our nails or cut our hair.
2. In a cell, where are the genes located.
3. Amoeba and Paramecium belong to which category of organisms?
4. What are the functions of cell wall in plant cells?

5. Is the following statement correct? If it is wrong, correct the statement
   Statement: "Unicellular organisms do not respire, only multicellular organisms respire"
6. Classify the following terms into cells, tissues and organs and write in the tabular column given below.
   RBC, WBC, Nerve cell, blood, muscle, blood vessels, brain, heart, hand

Cell	Tissue	Organ
....	....	....

....
....

7. Cells consist of many organelles, yet we do not call any of these organelles as structural and functional unit of living organisms. Explain.
8. Why do plant cells have an additional layer surrounding the cell membrane? What is this layer known as?
9. The size of the cells of an organism has no relation with the size of its body. Do you agree? Give reason for your answer.

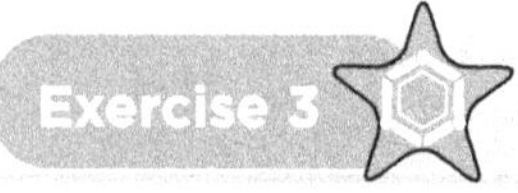

Exercise 3 — Foundation Builder

Multiple Choice Questions

DIRECTIONS : *This section contains multiple choice questions. Each question has four choices (a), (b), (c) and (d) out of which ONLY ONE is correct. Choose the correct option.*

1. Which of the following statement (s) is not correct?
   (a) In plant cells, vacuoles are absent.
   (b) Vacuole is bounded by a single membrane.
   (c) In *Amoeba*, contractile vacuole is important for excretion.
   (d) Flagellum is important for transport of bacteria.
2. Which of the following cell organelles are non-membranous and found in both prokaryotic and eukaryotic cells?
   (a) Lysosome (b) Vacuoles
   (c) Ribosome (d) Mitochondria
3. The main constituents of cytoplasm is C, N, O, H. These are derived from
   (a) protein (b) carbohydrate
   (c) water (d) none of these
4. How many cells are present in human body?
   (a) One million cells (b) One billion cells
   (c) One trillion cells (d) More than a trillion cells
5. The scientist who described cell as "many little boxes" was
   (a) Robert Hooke
   (b) Theodar Schwann
   (c) Anton Van Leeuwenhoek
   (d) Rudolf Virchow
6. The characteristic of a nerve cell that relates directly to its function is its
   (a) long extensions
   (b) flat shape
   (c) ability to change shape
   (d) ability to engulf bacteria
7. Which of the following statements is correct?
   (a) Prokaryotic cells are surrounded by a cell membrane.
   (b) Prokaryotic lysosome is bounded by tonoplast.
   (c) Protein synthesis takes place in mitochondria.
   (d) Eukaryotic cells have membrane bound organelles.
8. Old organelles, viruses, bacteria etc. that a cell can ingests are broken down in
   (a) ribosomes (b) RER
   (c) SER (d) lysosomes
9. Organelles that are surrounded by two membranes are
   (a) nucleus and mitochondria
   (b) nucleus and Golgi bodies
   (c) endoplasmic reticulum and lysosomes
   (d) endoplasmic reticulum and mitochondria
10. A cell that contains a cell wall, chloroplasts and a central vacuole is
    (a) plant cell (b) animal cell
    (c) yeast cell (d) bacterial cell
11. When a human RBC is placed in a hypotonic environment, it
    (a) undergoes turgidity
    (b) undergoes plasmolysis
    (c) is at equilibrium
    (d) experiences decreased turgor pressure
12. Cells that have a high energy requirement generally have many
    (a) ribosomes (b) nucleus
    (c) mitochondria (d) chloroplast
13. Which of the following statement (s) is correct about plasma membrane?
    (a) It allows all substances to pass into and out of cells.
    (b) It prevents all substances from passing into and out of cell.
    (c) It is composed mainly of a protein bilayer.
    (d) It is composed mainly of a lipid bilayer.
14. Which of the following organelles is found in plant cells but not in animal cells?
    (a) Nucleus (b) Mitochondrion
    (c) Chloroplast (d) Golgi apparatus
15. Smallest cell organelle is
    (a) mitochondria (b) ribosome
    (c) vacuole (d) lysosome
16. A function of golgi body is
    (a) excretion (b) ATP synthesis
    (c) secretion (d) RNA synthesis
17. Plasma membrane is
    (a) permeable (b) selectively permeable
    (c) impermeable (d) semi-permeable
18. When the concentration of water and solutes on either side of the cell membrane is same, the solution is said to be

(a) hypertonic   (b) isotonic
(c) hypotonic   (d) none of these

19. Cell organelle known as suicide bags :   **[JSTSE]**
(a) Golgi apparatus   (b) Plastid
(c) Endoplasmi reticulum (d) Lysosome

20. Mitochondria are strange organelles as they have their own: **[JSTSE]**
(a) Nucleus   (b) DNA
(c) Ribosome   (d) both (b) and (c)

21. Chromosomes are made up of :   **[JSTSE]**
(a) DNA   (b) Protein
(c) DNA and Protein   (d) RNA

22. The smooth endoplasmic reticulum helps in the manufacture of :   **[JSTSE]**
(a) Lipids   (b) Glycogen
(c) Sugars   (d) Proteins

23. Two sisters looked exactly same. This may be due to
(a) mitochondrial DNA (b) genes   **[NTSE]**
(c) nucleoli and nuclei (d) genes and RNA

24. A person with blood group 'A' can donate blood to the persons with blood group 'A' or 'AB' because it
(a) has both 'A' and 'B' antigens.   **[NTSE]**
(b) has only 'A' antigen and 'B' antibodies.
(c) has only 'B' antigen and 'A' antibodies.
(d) does not have any antigens and antibodies.

25. An animal cell, a plant cell and a bacterium share the following structural features :   **[NTSE]**
(a) Cell membrane, endoplasmic reticulum, vacuoles
(b) Cell wall, plasma membrane, mitochondria
(c) Cell wall, nucleus, cytoplasm
(d) Plasma membrane, cytoplasm, ribosomes

26. Suggest which among the following is NOT a function attributed to endoplasmic reticulum.   **[NTSE]**
(a) Detoxification of poisons and drugs
(b) Digestion/egestion of foreign materials outside the cell
(c) Manufacture of fat and lipid molecules
(d) Biogenesis of membranes

27. Cell organelles that are involved in the waste diposal system of the cell are :   **[NTSE]**
(a) Golgi apparatus.   (b) Lysosomes
(c) Chromosomes   (d) Ribosomes

28. Which of the following statements is NOT correct ?   **[NTSE]**
(a) Tendons are tissues with great strength and flexibility.
(b) Bones are connected to each other by tendons.
(c) Cartilage smoothens bone surface at joints.
(d) Tendons connect muslces to bones.

29. Which one of the following statements about cell organelles and their function is correct?   **[NTSE]**
(a) Mitochondria are associated with anaerobic respiration.
(b) Smooth endoplasmic reticulum is involved in protein synthesis.

(c) Lysosomes are important in membrane biogenesis.
(d) Golgi bodies are involved in packaging and dispatching of materials.

30. The organelle which is primarily associated with storage of starch, oil and proteins etc are   **[JSTSE]**
(a) Leucoplasts
(b) Inner membrane of Mitochondria
(c) Endoplasmic reticulum
(d) Ribosomes

31. The cell organelle involved in membrane biogenesis is :
(a) Ribosomes   **[JSTSE]**
(b) Golgi body
(c) Endoplasmic Reticulum
(d) Peroxisomes

32. The plasma membrane of the cells is mainly composed of :   **[JSTSE]**
(a) Sugars and lipids   (b) Proteins and sugars
(c) Proteins and Lipids (d) Sugas and fats

33. Eukaryotic organisms have different levels of organization. Select the combination where the levels are arranged in the descending order.   **[NTSE]**
(a) DNA, chromosome, cell, nucleus, tissue
(b) Tissue, cell, nucleus, chromosome, DNA
(c) Nucleus, cell, DNA, chromosome, tissue
(d) Tissue, cell, chromosome, nucleus, DNA

Assertion & Reason

DIRECTIONS : *Each of these questions contains an Assertion followed by Reason. Read them carefully and answer the question on the basis of following options. You have to select the one that best describes the two statements.*

(a) If both **Assertion** and **Reason** are **correct** and Reason is the **correct explanation** of Assertion.
(b) If both **Assertion** and **Reason** are correct, but Reason is **not the correct explanation** of Assertion.
(c) If **Assertion** is **correct** but **Reason** is **incorrect**.
(d) If **Assertion** is **incorrect** but **Reason** is **correct**.

1. **Assertion :** Mitochondria does not help in photosynthesis.
Reason : Mitochondria have enzymes for photosynthesis.

2. **Assertion :** Lysosomes have basic enzymes.
Reason : Lysosomes are called autophagosomes.

3. **Assertion :** A cell membrane shows fluid-mosaic behaviour.
Reason : A membrane is composed of lipids and proteins.

4. **Assertion :** Bacterial cell wall is more complex than plant cell wall.
Reason : Bacterial cell wall contains proteins and oligosaccharides.

5. **Assertion :** The true nucleus is generally absent in prokaryotes.
Reason : An undifferentiated, unorganised fibrillar nucleus is observed in prokaryotic cells.

6. **Assertion :** Mitochondria is called power house of cell.
Reason : Mitochondria produce ADP.

Exercise 4 — Foundation Builder +

Multiple Choice Questions

DIRECTIONS (Qs. 1-11) : *This section contains multiple choice questions. Each question has four choices (a), (b), (c) and (d) out of which ONLY ONE is correct. Choose the correct option.*

1. Which of the following nucleic acids is present in an organism having 7°S ribosomes only? **[NTSE]**
   (a) Double stranded circular DNA with histone proteins.
   (b) Single stranded DNA with protein coat.
   (c) Double stranded circular naked DNA.
   (d) Double stranded DNA enclosed in nuclear membrane.

2. Which of the following statements about inclusion bodies is incorrect? **[NTSE]**
   (a) These are involved in ingestion of food particles
   (b) They lie free in the cytoplasm
   (c) These represent reserve material in cytoplasm
   (d) They are not bound by any membrane

3. The term 'glycocalyx' is used for
   (a) A layer surrounding the cell wall of bacteria
   (b) A layer present between cell wall and membrane of bacteria
   (c) Cell wall of bacteria
   (d) Bacterial cell glyco-engineered to possess N-glycosylated proteins

4. Which is the important site of formation of glycoproteins and glycolipids in eukaryotic cells? **[NTSE]**
   (a) Peroxisomes   (b) Golgi bodies
   (c) Polysomes   (d) Endoplasmic reticulum

5. Which of the following cell organelles is present in the highest number in secretory cells? **[NTSE]**
   (a) Lysosome   (b) Mitochondria
   (c) Golgi complex   (d) Endoplasmic reticulum

6. Which of the following cell organelles is responsible for extracting energy from carbohydrates to form ATP?
   (a) Ribosome   (b) Chloroplast
   (c) Mitochondrion   (d) Lysosome

7. Which one of the following organelle in the figure correctly matches with its function?
   (a) Golgi apparatus, protein synthesis
   (b) Golgi apparatus, formation of glycolipids
   (c) Rough endoplasmic reticulum, protein synthesis
   (d) Rough endoplasmic reticulum, formation of glycoproteins

8. The Golgi complex plays a major role
   (a) in digesting proteins and carbohydrates
   (b) as energy transferring organelles
   (c) in post translational modification of proteins and glycosidation of lipids
   (d) in trapping the light and transforming it into chemical energy

9. A major site for synthesis of lipids is :
   (a) SER   (b) Symplast
   (c) Nucleoplasm   (d) RER

10. Which of the following type of plastids does not contain stored food material?
    (a) Amyloplasts   (b) Chromoplasts
    (c) Elaioplasts   (d) Aleuroplasts

11. Select the alternative giving correct identification and function of the organelle 'A' in the diagram

    (a) Endoplasmic reticulum-synthesis of lipids
    (b) Mitochondria-produce cellular energy in the form of ATP
    (c) Golgi body-provides packaging material
    (d) Lysosomes - secrete hydrolytic enzymes

Multiple Matching Questions

DIRECTIONS (Qs. 12-14) : *The following question contains statements given in two columns which have to be matched. Statements (A, B, C....) in column I have to be matched with statements (i), (ii), (iii).... in column II.*

12. Match the column I with column II. **[NTSE]**

Column I		Column II
(A) Golgi apparatus	(p)	Synthesis of protein
(B) Lysosomes	(q)	Trap waste and excretory products
(C) Vacuoles	(r)	Formation of glycoproteins and glycolipids
(D) Ribosomes	(s)	Digesting biomolecules

Choose the right match from options given below:
(a) (A)-(p), (B)-(q), (C)-(s), (D)-(r)
(b) (A)-(r), (B)-(s), (C)-(q), (D)-(p)
(c) (A)-(s), (B)-(r), (C)-(p), (D)-(q)
(d) (A)-(r), (B)-(q), (C)-(s), (D)-(p)

13. Match the columns and identify the correct option.

Column-I		Column-II
(A) Thylakoids	(p)	Disc-shaped sacs in Golgi apparatus
(B) Cristae	(q)	Condensed structure of DNA
(C) Cisternae	(r)	Flat membranous sacs in stroma
(D) Chromatin	(s)	Infoldings in mitochondria

	(A)	(B)	(C)	(D)		(A)	(B)	(C)	(D)
(a)	(r)	(s)	(p)	(q)	(b)	(r)	(p)	(s)	(q)
(c)	(r)	(s)	(q)	(p)	(d)	(s)	(r)	(p)	(q)

14. Match the column-I with column-II:

Column-I		Column-II
(A) Centriole	(p)	Infoldings in mitochondria
(B) Chlorophyll	(q)	Thylakoids
(C) Cristae	(r)	Nucleic acids
(D) Ribozymes	(s)	Basal body cilia or fiagella

	(A)	(B)	(C)	(D)		(A)	(B)	(C)	(D)
(a)	(s)	(q)	(p)	(r)	(b)	(p)	(q)	(s)	(r)
(c)	(p)	(r)	(q)	(s)	(d)	(s)	(r)	(p)	(q)

SOLUTIONS
(Brief Explanations of Selected Questions)

Exercise 1 — Master Boards

Multiple Choice Questions

1. (a)   2. (a)   3. (d)   4. (d)
5. (a)

Assertion & Reason

1. (a) Both Assertion and Reason is tone, and Reason is the correct explaination of Assertion.
   Specialisation of the cell increases the efficiency of the cell for a particular function.
2. (d) Both assertion and reason are false.
   The size and shape of cell in multicellular organism depends upon the location and function performed by them.
3. (a) Both Assertion and Reason are correct, Reason is the correct explaination of Assertion.
   Cell is an isothermal open system as all the parts of the cell at any given time maintains the same temperature and pressure.
   Cell is an open system in which materials and energy are transferred between organism and external environment.
4. (d) Both assertion and reason are false.
   They are credited with cell theory but the cells are not always living unit. Cells die and still remain functional such as horny cells in animals and xylem vessels in plants.
5. (d) Both assertion and reason are false.
   Ribosome are non-membrane bound organelle found in eukaryotic as well as prokaryotic cells. Within the cell, ribosomes are found not only in the cytoplasm but also within two organelles chloroplast in plants and on rough ER.

Fill in the Blanks

1. Schleiden and Schwann   2. Egg of Ostrich
3. *Mycoplasm* bacteria   4. 10^{-6}
5. Nucleus   6. Osmosis
7. Mitochondria   8. Lysosome
9. Nucleus   10. Cell wall
11. Plant   12. Lamella
13. Sugar and salt   14. Neuron
15. Tissue

True / False

1. False. Cell wall is not present in animal cell.
2. True
3. True
4. False. Onion cells and cheek cells are the examples of eukaryotic cells.
5. False. Pseudopodia is found in lower animals.
6. rue
7. False. *Amoeba* is a unicellular animal.
8. True
9. True
10. False. Energy is stored in a cell in the form of ATP.

Match the Following

1. A-s; B-r; C-q; D-t; E-p   2. A-r; B-s; C-t; D-p; E-q

Passage Based Questions

1. (c)   2. (b)   3. (c)

Very Short Answer Questions

1. A cell is the smallest unit of life which has a definite structure and a specific function.
2. Anton Van Leeuwenhoek
3. Cytoplasm
4. Unicellular organisms are organisms made up of a single cell that can perform all basic life activities whereas multicellular organisms are composed of many specialised cells, that carries different functions.
5. Cell membrane
6. A jelly like substance that makes up most of the inside of a cell.
7. Leucoplast
8. Mitochondria and chloroplast
9. Nucleus
10. Responsible for protein synthesis.
11. Anton Van Leeuwenhoek
12. White blood cells
13. Xylem transports water and minerals absorbed by the roots to the leaves while phloem transports the food made by the leaves to other parts of the plant.
14. Rough endoplasmic reticulum has ribosome attached to its surface, while smooth ER has no ribosomes attached.
15. Stroma
16. It refers to the substances of which cell is made and includes all parts of the cell.
17. Centrosome
18. *Euglena*
19. Golgi apparatus
20. Lysosomes

Short Answer Questions

1. Cell membrane is called selectively permeable because it protects the inside contents of the cell and regulates the passage of molecules in and out of the cell.
2. Chloroplast is the site of photosynthesis in which food (sugar) is prepared or synthesized using simple substances like carbon dioxide and water with the help of light energy. So, they are present only in plants which are autotrophs and not in animals who are heterotrophs.

3. Refer inside the chapter.
4. Muscle cells bring about the movement of body parts by contraction and relaxation. The contraction of muscle cells moves the body part (to which they are attached), and when these contracted muscle cells relax, they expand and increase in length, so that the body part comes back to its original position.
5. Mitochondria are called the power house of cells because their primary purpose is to manufacture ATP during cellular respiration which is used as a source of energy.
6. Ribosomes are small dense cytoplasmic particles which are found individually in the cytoplasm and also lining the membranes of the rough endoplasmic reticulum. Ribosomes are the site of protein synthesis.
7. Chromosomes carry genetic characters with the help of genes. Gene is an inherited factor that determines the biological character of an organisms and supplies the expression of a particular trait.
8. DNA is the genetic material and the major store of genetic information. It is found in nucleus and cytoplasm. Its double helical structure with sugar phosphate backbones on the outside and paired bases on the inside was proposed/discovered by Watson and Crick.
9. Levels of organization in multicellular organisms are–

   Cell $\longrightarrow$ Tissue $\longrightarrow$ Organ $\longrightarrow$ Organ system
   $$\downarrow$$
   Organism

   Cell – Structural and functional unit of life.

   Tissue – Group of cells having common origin and functions.

   Organ – Group of tissue having distinct structure with one or more distinct functions.

   Organ system – Two or more organs coordinate their activities towards a common activity.
10. Plastids are double membrane organelle found in all plants and some unicellular organisms (*Eugle*) of uncertain affinity. It is the largest organelle which is involved in the formation and storage of soluble and insoluble carbohydrate. Plastids are classified into two groups on the basis of presence of pigment–leucoplast (colourless plastid incapable of performing photosynthesis) and chromoplast (coloured plastids responsible for photosynthesis process).
11. Nucleolus is characterized by the absence of limiting membrane, presence of chromatin and granules and fibrils of RNA and protein. It is composed of DNA + RNA + protein. It helps in the development of ribosomal RNA and is the centre for the formation of ribosomes.
12. Vacuoles are large in plant cell, but in animal cell it is small in size.
13. Prokaryotic cells lack membrane bound organelles and definite nucleus as compared to eukaryotic cells.

Long Answer Questions

1. The main components of a typical cell are cell membrane, cytoplasm, nucleus and vacuoles.

   Cell membrane, also called as plasma membrane, it separates the inside contents of the cell from the surrounding medium. This membrane is porous and allows the movement of materials both inward and outward of the cell.

   Cytoplasm is the jelly like substances present between the cell membrane and nucleus. Various organelles are present in the cytoplasm. These are mitochondria, golgi bodies, ribosome, endoplasmic reticulum etc.

   Nucleus is an important component of living cell. It is spherical in shape and located in the centre of the cell. Nucleus is separated from the cytoplasm by a membrane called nuclear membrane. This membrane is porous and allows the movement of materials between the cytoplasm and the inside of nucleus.

   Vacuole is a large organelle usually in the centre of the plant cell, containing a liquid called cell sap. It is bounded by a differentially or selectively permeable membrane called tonoplast. It is used for osmotic pressure and storage. It is smaller in animal cell and present at the periphery.

2. In plant cells the cytoplasm is composed of many living and non-living parts called cell organelles. The important organelles are mitochondria, golgi apparatus, endoplasmic reticulum, vacuoles, ribosome, chloroplast etc.

   Mitochondria are tiny, spherical or rod like bodies. They are the sites of energy production, therefore also called as powerhouse of the cell. The energy production process is called cellular respiration. The energy is stored in the form of ATP.

   Golgi apparatus, also called golgi bodies, are made up of tubules and vesicles. They are responsible for secretion of chemical substances like enzymes, hormones and proteins.

   Endoplasmic reticulum is a network of tubules and channels. It is involved in the synthesis, storage and transport of cell products.

   Ribosomes are small granules scattered all over the cytoplasm. These granules act as a site for protein synthesis.

   Vacuoles are fluid-filled spaces enclosed in a membrane. They store excess water, useful minerals, pigments and many other substances. The size of vacuole is larger in plant cells.

   Plastids are present in plant cells only. The plastids contain certain pigments. *i.e.* chloroplast, chromoplast and leucoplast. Chloroplast contains chlorophyll, which helps in the process of photosynthesis.

3. Nucleus is a membrane bound structure that contains the cell's hereditary information and controls the cell's growth and reproduction. It is commonly the most prominent organelle in a cell. The cell nucleus is bound by a double membrane called the nuclear envelope. This membrane separates the contents of the nucleus from the cytoplasm. Like the cell membrane, the nuclear envelope consists of phospholipids that form a lipid bilayer. The envelope helps to maintain the shape of the nucleus and assists in regulating the flow of molecules into and out of the nucleus through nuclear pores.

Chromosomes are located within the nucleus. Chromosomes consist of DNA, which contains heredity information and instructions for cell growth, development, and reproduction. Contained within the nucleus is a dense structure composed of RNA and proteins called the nucleolus. The nucleolus helps to synthesize ribosomes by transcribing and assembling ribosomal RNA.

Structure	Function
Plasma Membrane	Control the exchange of materials between the cell and its environment
Nucleus	Large structure surrounded by double membrane; maintain the integrity of the genes and control the activities of the cell by regulating gene expression (therefore, the control centre of the cell)
Nucleolus	Granular body within nucleus; site of r-RNA synthesis
Endoplasmic reticulum	Site of membrane lipid & protein synthesis
Golgi Complex	Stacks of flattened membrane sacs; modifies, packages and secretes proteins
Lysosomes	Membranous sacs; contains enzymes to digest materials
Vacuoles	Membranous sacs; transport and store water and other materials
Mitochondria	Sacs containing two membranes; Produces energy for the cell through cellular respiration which can be stored in the form of ATP, hence called power house of the cell.
Plastids	Sac-like structures with internal thylakoid membranes; Takes part in photosynthesis
Ribosomes	Granular organelles composed of RNA & protein; synthesize proteins
Centrioles	Small hollow cylinders; involved in cell division and anchors flagellae & cilia
Cilia	Short hair-like structures; movement, food intake
Flagella	Long projections; cellular locomotion, usually 1-5 on a cell.
Cell wall	Multiple-layers of cellulose; provides structural support and strength

Reasoning Based Questions

1. Plants and animals specimens are stained with dyes before observing them through a microscope because cells appear transparent under the microscope and to make the internal organelle and other structures clearly visible, different stains or dyes are used for efficient parts of the cells. For example, saframin and methyline blue are used to stain the nucleus.

2. Nerve cells are long and have branches because they need more surface area to pass the signals to cell by cell.

3. Most of the cells are extremely small and cannot seen with naked eye, hence cells could not be observed and studied for thousands of years.

4. The red colour of tomato fruit is due to a carotid called Lycopene.

5. Chloroplasts are found in plant cells only because chloroplast contain chlorophyll which is essential for photosynthesis. Chlorophyll traps sunlight and use it to prepare food for plants by the process of photosynthesis.

6. Cells are building block of life, they give us energy in the form of ATP which we utilise to perform different activities. Therefore, cells are extremely important.

HOTS Questions

1. White blood cells have the ability to change the shape because white blood cells can squeeze themselves in between other cells, to reach other, infected cells. For example, if there is an infection somewhere in the body, they can squeeze themselves through the walls of the blood cells to an inter-cellular space, where the infection is taking place.

2. Yes, the cells of ant and elephant are same. All organisms are made up of cells that have different body designs, shapes and sizes. It is not the size of cells which makes such a big difference between an ant and an elephant but it is the number of cells which makes such difference in their body size.

3. Each organ in the system performs different functions such as digestion, assimilation and absorption. Different plant organs also perform specific functions.
Each organ is further made up of smaller parts called tissues. A tissue is a group of similar cells performing specific function. Hence "cell is the structural and functional unit of life".

4. Bacteria are classified as prokaryotic cell because the nucleus of bacterial cell is not well organised like the cells of multicellular organisms. There is no nuclear membrane. The cells having nuclear material without nuclear membrane are termed as prokaryotic cells. The organisms with these kinds of cells are called prokaryotes.

5. (i) IV (Lysosome) (ii) VI (Ribosome)
(iii) VII (Nucleolus) (iv) III (Mitochondria)
(v) I (Cell membrane)

6. (i) Endosmosis; (ii) Diffusion; (iii) Exosmosis; (iv) Deplasmolysis.

 **Master NCERT (Text-book & Exemplar)**

Exercise

Text-book Exercise

1. (a) (T)
   (b) (F) Muscle cells are spindle shaped.
   (c) (F) The basic living unit of an organism is cell.
   (d) (T)

2.

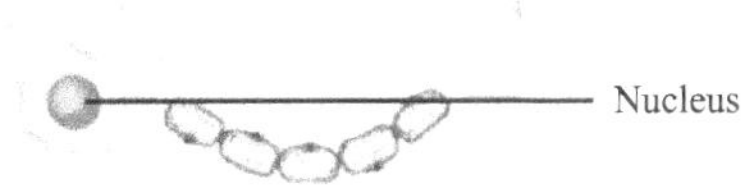

Nerve cell

Nerve cell is also known as neuron. Nerve cells send messages to the brain and then transfer these messages from the brain to the receptor organs. Thus, it controls the functions of different parts of the body.

3. (a) **Cytoplasm:** The fluid that occurs in between the plasma membrane and the nucleus occurs between the plasma membrane and the nucleus and fills the online cell is called cytoplasm. All the cell organelles like mitochondria, endoplasmic reticulum, ribosomes, Golgi bodies, etc. are suspended remain the cytoplasm. The cytoplasm also helps in the exchange of materials between cell organelles.

   (b) **Nucleus of a cell:** The nucleus is present at the centre of a cell and is generally spherical in shape. The nucleus is composed of the following components:

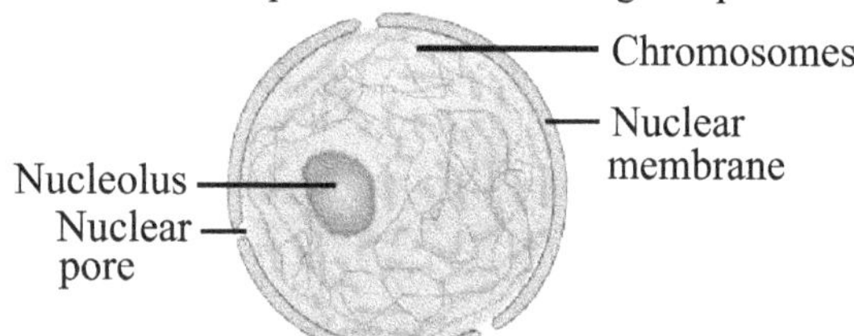

   (i) **Nuclear membrane:** The nucleus is bounded by a double-layered membrane called the nuclear membrane. It separates the contents of the nucleus from the cytoplasm. The nuclear membrane has nuclear pores that allows the exchange of materials between cytoplasm & nucleus.

   (ii) **Nucleolus:** It is a small spherical body present within the nucleus. It is not bounded by any membrane.

   (iii) **Chromosomes:** Chromosomes constitute the genetic material of the cell. They are thread-like structures that carry the genetic information. Chromosomes are made up of DNA which carries the information necessary for the transfer of characteristics from the parents to the offspring. Thus, chromosomes play an important role in the inheritance of characteristics.

4. Cytoplasm is the fluid part of the cell and various organelles such as mitochondria, ribosomes, Golgi bodies, etc are present within the cytoplasm. Entire space of the cell between the plasma membrane and the nucleus is present within the cytoplasm.

5.

Animal cell	Plant cell
They are generally small in size.	They are usually larger than animal cells.

Cell wall is absent.	A rigid cell wall is present which is made up of cellulose.
Vacuoles are many and one small in size.	Vacuoles are permanent centrally located large in size.
No other animal cell possesses plastids except for the protozoan Euglena.	Plastids are present.
Animal cells have centrosome and centrioles.	Plant cells lack centrosome and centrioles.

6.

Prokaryotes	Eukaryotes
Most of the prokaryotes are unicellular.	Most of the eukaryotes are multicellular.
Well defined Nucleus & nuclear membrane are absent.	The nucleus is well defined and is surrounded by a nuclear membrane.
Nucleolus is absent.	Nucleolus is present.
Cell organelles such as plastids, mitochondria, golgi bodies, etc. are absent.	Cell organelles such as plastids, mitochondria, golgi bodies, etc. are present.
Bacteria and blue-green algae are examples of prokaryotic cells	Fungi, plant, and animal cells are examples of eukaryotic cells

7. Chromosome are the thread-like structures intermingled with each other in the nucleus. They carry genes that help in the transfer of characters from the parents to the offspring and thus play an important role in the inheritance of characters.

8. A cell is the fundemental structural and functional unit of life. Cells are the building blocks of all living organisms. They can carryout all vital function of life. All cells vary in their shapes, sizes, and the functions they perform. In fact, the shape and size of the cell is related to the specific function it performs.

9.

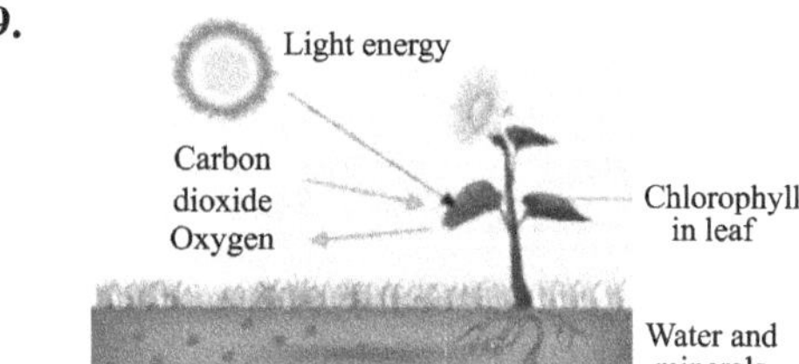

Chloroplast is a double membrane round organelle found in green plants. A green pigment called chlorophyll is present in the chloroplast. This chlorophyll pigment traps solar energy and utilizes it to manufacture food for the plant. The raw materials water is taken up by the roots of the plant & CO_2 is absorbed from the atmosphere through stomata. Animal cells do not have chloroplast hence can't perform photosynthesis. Animal cells do not have CO_2 also which is the main requirement for food synthesis.

10.

<table>
<tr><td>1C</td><td>H</td><td>L</td><td>2O</td><td>R</td><td>O</td><td>P</td><td>H</td><td>Y</td><td>L</td><td>L</td></tr>
<tr><td>H</td><td></td><td></td><td>R</td><td></td><td></td><td></td><td></td><td></td><td></td><td></td></tr>
<tr><td>L</td><td></td><td></td><td>G</td><td></td><td></td><td></td><td></td><td></td><td></td><td></td></tr>
<tr><td>3O</td><td>R</td><td>G</td><td>A</td><td>N</td><td>E</td><td>L</td><td>L</td><td>E</td><td></td><td></td></tr>
<tr><td>R</td><td></td><td></td><td>N</td><td></td><td></td><td></td><td></td><td></td><td>4M</td><td></td></tr>
<tr><td>O</td><td></td><td></td><td></td><td></td><td></td><td></td><td>5V</td><td></td><td>E</td><td></td></tr>
<tr><td>6P</td><td>R</td><td>O</td><td>7T</td><td>O</td><td>P</td><td>L</td><td>A</td><td>S</td><td>M</td><td></td></tr>
<tr><td>L</td><td></td><td></td><td>I</td><td></td><td></td><td></td><td>C</td><td></td><td>B</td><td></td></tr>
<tr><td>A</td><td></td><td></td><td>S</td><td></td><td></td><td></td><td>U</td><td></td><td>R</td><td></td></tr>
<tr><td>S</td><td></td><td></td><td>S</td><td></td><td></td><td></td><td>O</td><td></td><td>A</td><td></td></tr>
<tr><td>T</td><td></td><td></td><td>U</td><td></td><td></td><td></td><td>L</td><td></td><td>N</td><td></td></tr>
<tr><td>S</td><td></td><td></td><td>E</td><td></td><td></td><td>8G</td><td>E</td><td>N</td><td>E</td><td>S</td></tr>
</table>

ACROSS

1. Chlorophyll
3. Organelle
6. Protoplasm
8. Genes

DOWN

1. Chloroplasts
2. Organ
4. Membrane
5. Vacuole
7. Tissue

Exemplar Questions

1. Nails and hair are both made up of dead cells. They do not have nerve cells. Hence we don't feel the pain when they are cut.
2. Nucleus/chromosomes.
3. Unicellular and Eukaryotic/Protozoan.
4. Cell wall protects the cell contents, gives shapes to the cell.
5. No, the statement is wrong.
   Both unicellular and multicellular organisms respire/all organisms respire.

6.

Cell	Tissue	Organ
RBC	Blood	Blood vessels
WBC	Muscle	Heart
Nerve cell	Nerve	Hand
		Brain

7. Although cell organelles have specific structures and perform specific functions but they cannot be called structural and functional units of living organisms. This is so because they can perform their functions only when they are within a living cell. They cannot function outside the cell as an independent unit.

8. As plants cannot move they need protection against variations in temperature, high wind speed, atmospheric moisture, etc. Therefore, for protectoin plant cell ……… membrane. This layer is called the cell wall. Plant cells have an additional layer surrounding the cell membrane.

9. • I agree because the cells in body of an elephant is not necessarily bigger than those in a rat, it is not true that bigger organisms have cells of bigger size in their body.
   • The size of the cell in an organism is related to the function to performs. For example, the nerve cells in both, the elephant and the rat is are long and branched. They perform the same function, that of transferring messages.

Exercise 3   Foundation Builder

Multiple Choice Questions

1. **(a)** A vacuole is a membrane-bound organelle which is present in all plant and fungal cells and some protist, animal and bacterial cells. Vacuoles are essentially enclosed compartments which are filled with water containing inorganic and organic molecules including enzymes in solution, though in certain cases they may contain solids which have been engulfed.

2. **(c)** Ribosomes are cell organelles that consist of RNA and proteins. They are responsible for assembling the proteins of the cell. Depending on the protein production level of a particular cell, ribosomes may number in the millions. Ribosomes occur both as free particles in prokaryotic and eukaryotic cells and as particles attached to the membranes of the endoplasmic reticulum in eukaryotic cells.

3. **(c)** Cytoplasm is the cell substance between the cell membrane and the nucleus, containing the cytosol, organelles, cytoskeleton, and various particles. The main constituenvt of cytoplasm C, H, N and O is derived from water.

4. **(d)** More than one trillions cells are present in a human body.

5. **(a)** Robert Hooke observed cork cells under his microscope and found out some tiny compartments which he called cells.

6. **(a)** Nerve cells (neuron) are the primary cells in the nervous system. A typical neuron possesses a cell body (soma), dendrites, and an axon. The long threadlike extension of a nerve cell that conducts nerve impulses from the cell body is the characteristics which is directly related to its function. Neurons are responsible for relaying electrical messages to cells and tissues in other organ systems.

7. **(d)** All prokaryotes have cytoplasm surrounded by a cell membrane, also known as the plasma membrane. The cell membrane conforms to the fluid mosaic model, which means that its proteins float within a double layer of phospholipids.

8. **(d)** A lysosome is a membrane-bound cell organelle found in animal cells (they are absent in red blood cells). They are structurally and chemically spherical vesicles containing hydrolytic enzymes, which are capable of breaking down virtually all kinds of biomolecules, including proteins, nucleic acids, carbohydrates, lipids, and cellular debris. They act as waste disposal system of the cell by digesting unwanted materials in the cytoplasm, both from outside of the cell and obsolete components inside the cell. For this function they are popularly referred to as "suicide bags" or "suicide sacs" of the cell.

9. (a) Mitochondria and nucleus are double membrane organelles. Double membrane organelles are surrounded by two biomembrane layers, with an intermembranal space. Golgi bodies, lysosomes and endoplasmic reticulum are single membrane organelles.

10. (a) Plant cell are eukaryotic cells with a membrane-bound nucleus that differ in several key aspects from the cells of other eukaryotic organisms. Their distinctive features include: large central vacuole, cell wall, and chloroplast.

11. (a) When red blood cells are placed in hypotonic solution (pure water) it will undergo turgidity. Water will enter the cell by osmosis, causing the cell to swell and possibly even burst.

12. (c) Mitochondria are called the powerhouse of cell because it produces energy in the form of ATP. Therefore cells that have high energy requirements generally have many mitochondria.

13. (d) The plasma membrane (or cell membrane) is a biological membrane that separates the interior of all cells from the outside environment. The cell membrane is selectively permeable to ions and organic molecules and controls the movement of substances in and out of cells. The basic function of the cell membrane is to protect the cell from its surroundings. It consists of the phospholipid bilayer with embedded proteins.

14. (c) Chloroplasts are small organelles inside the cells of plants and algae. Chloroplasts contain chlorophyll pigment, which absorbs sunlight for the process of photosynthesis.

15. (b) Ribosome is the smallest cell organelle. A ribosome is a large complex of RNA and protein. Mitochondrion is the third largest and second largest organelle in plant and animal cell respectively.

16. (c) The Golgi complex, also known as the Golgi apparatus is a cytoplasmic organelle. It is found in eukaryotic cells, as in animals, plants, and fungi. The main function of the Golgi apparatus is to process and package macromolecules, such as proteins and lipids. The Golgi complex is especially active in processing proteins for secretion.

17. (b) The plasma membrane (or cell membrane) is a biological membrane that separates the interior of all cells from the outside environment. The cell membrane is selectively permeable to ions and organic molecules and controls the movement of substances in and out of cells. The basic function of the cell membrane is to protect the cell from its surroundings. It consists of the phospholipid bilayer with embedded proteins.

18. (b) An isotonic solution refers to two solutions having the same osmotic pressure across a semipermeable membrane. This state allows for the free movement of water across the membrane without changing the concentration of solutes on either side of the membrane.

19. (d) Cysosomes contains enzymes capable of digesting cellular contents.

20. (d) Mitochondria has both DNA and ribosomes.

21. (c) Chromosomes are made up of DNA and protein.

22. (a) SER are involved in the manufacture of lipids and steroids.

23. (b) Two sisters looked exactly same due to the similar genes present in them. Genes carry genetic informations or characters that passed on from parents to offsprings.

24. (b) A person with blood group 'A' can donate blood to the person with blood group 'A' or 'AB' because it has only 'A' antigen on RBCs and B-antibodies in plasma. In blood grup AB, there is no antibody in plasma so persons with 'AB' group can accept blood from persons with AB as well as the other groups of blood.

25. (d) Animal and plant cells are eukaryotic cells having cell membrane, cytoplasm, true nucleus, and various organelles (like ER, Golgi complex, ribosomes ((80S) etc.) Bacterial cell is prokaryotic cell in which plasma membrane, cell wall, primitive type of nucleus, ribosomes (70S) etc. present but cell organelles are absent. Animal cells lack cell wall. But there are some structural features which are common in these cells like plasma/cell membrane, cytoplasm and ribosomes.

26. (b) The function of endoplasmic reticulum is not related with digestion or egestion of foreign bodies but it detoxi fies harmful chemicals, manufactures fat and lipid molecules and helps in bio-genesis of membranes. It transports the synthesized proteins to different parts of cells and tissues.

27. (b) Lysosomes are found in cytoplasm of the cell. It acts as the waste disposal system by digesting unwanted or harmful substances in the cytoplasm. Due to this act, they are known as 'suicide bags'.

28. (b) Bones are connected to each other by ligaments which are tough band of tissues which attach the ends of bones together at a joint in the skeleton system of an animal.

29. (d) Golgibodies are involved in packaging and dispatching of materials. Mitochondria are the sites of aerobic respiration. Rough endoplasmic reticulum is involved in protein synthesis. Lysosomes contain hydrolytic enzymes.

30. (a) Leucoplasts associated with the storage of starch (Amyloplast) oil (Elaioplast) protein (Proteinoplast).

31. (c)

32. (c) Plasma membrane is a bilipid layer in which proteins are embedded.

33. (b)

Assertion & Reason

1. (c) Mitochondria are the energy factories of the cells or called the power house of the cell. The energy currency for the work that animals must do is the energy-rich molecule adenosine triphosphate (ATP) which is produced in the mitochondria using energy stored in food. Chloroplasts organelles are specialized subunits in plant and algal cells. Their main role is to conduct photosynthesis, where the photosynthetic pigment chlorophyll captures the energy from sunlight, and stores it in the energy storage molecules ATP and NADPH while freeing oxygen from water.

2. (d) Lysosomes are simple tiny spherical sac-like structures evenly distributed in the cytoplasm. Each lysosome is a small vesicle surrounded by a single membrane and contains powerful enzymes (acid hydrolase enzymes). These enzymes are capable of digesting or breaking down all organic materials. Lysosomes digest excess or worn-out organelles, food particles, and engulfed viruses or bacteria.

3. (a) Cell membrane can be defined as a biological membrane or an outer membrane of a cell, which is composed of two layers of phospholipids and embedded with proteins. It shows fluid mosaic behaviour. It is a thin semi permeable membrane layer, which surrounds the cytoplasm and other constituents of the cell.

4. (a) Cell wall is a tough, rigid layer that surrounds some types of cells. Cell wall is a characteristic feature to cells of plants, bacteria, fungi, algae and some archaea. The major function of the cell wall is to provide rigidity, tensile strength, structural support, protection against mechanical stress and infection. It also aids in diffusion of gases in and out of the cell. Cell wall composition varies from species to species and also depends on the developing stage of the organism. Bacterial cell wall is more complex than plant cell wall. In bacteria, peptidoglycan forms the cell wall. Peptidoglycan is a complex molecule composed of alternating units of N-acetylglucosamine (NAG) and N-acetylmuramic acid (NAM) cross-linked by short peptides.

5. (a) A prokaryote is a single-celled organism that lacks a membrane-bound nucleus, mitochondria, or any other membrane-bound organelles. Prokaryotic cells have a region in the cell, termed the nucleoid, in which a single chromosomal, circular, double-stranded DNA molecule is located.

6. (c) Mitochondria are the energy factories of the cells or called the power house of the cell. The energy currency for the work that animals must do is the energy-rich molecule adenosine triphosphate (ATP) which is produced in the mitochondria using energy stored in food.

1. (c) The organisms which have ribosomes of 70 S type are prokaryotes. Prokaryotes have double stranded DNA which is not enclosed in membrane.

2. (a) Inclusion bodies are nuclear or cytoplasmic aggregates which are stainable substances, usually proteins, and formed due to viral multiplication or genetic disorders in human beings these bodies are either intracellular or extracellular abnormalities and they are specific to certain diseases. These are not involved in ingestion of food particles.

3. (a) Glycocalyx or mucilage is the outermost coating of bacterial cells/cell wall which is rich in polysaccharides. A thick and tougher mucilage is called capsule which gives gummy or sticky trait to cells. It protects the cells from dessication, toxins and preventing attachment to foreign invaders.

4. (b) Golgi bodies are site of formation of glycoproteins and glycolipids in eukaryotic cells.

5. (c) The important function of Golgi apparatus is to process, package and transport the materials for secretion. Therefore secretory cells have Golgi apparatus in highest number.

6. (c) The site of aerobic oxidation of carbohydrates in cells to generate ATP are mitochondria.

7. (c) rough endoplasmic reticulum is a network or reticulum of tiny tubular structures scattered in the cytoplasm and bear ribosomes on their outer surface. These are involved in protein synthesis and secretion. They are extensive and continuous with the outer membrane of the nucleus.

8. (c) Golgi apparatus plays a major role in post translational modification of proteins forming glycoprotein and glycosidation of lipid forming glycolipids. A number of proteins and lipids synthesised on endoplasmic reticulum (rough and smooth respectively) are modified in the cisternae of the Golgi apparatus before they are released from the trans face.

9. (a) The smooth endoplasmic reticulum is the major site for synthesis of lipid. In animal cells lipid like steroidal hormones are synthesised in SER.

10. (b) Chromoplasts are non-photosynthetic coloured plastids which synthesise and store carotenoid pigmentes. They, therefore, appear orange red and yellow whereas amyloplast (store starch), aleuroplast (store proteins) and elaioplast (store oil droplets and fats) are leucoplasts colourless plastids.

11. (b) Fig., (A) shows the cell organelle mitochondria. The mitochondria are bounded by two membranes, *i.e.,* outer membrane and inner membrane. Mitochondria are referred as "powerhouse" of the cell as they produce 95% of ATP. This energy is produced during the break down of food

molecules which involve glycolysis, oxidative decarboxylation and oxidative phosphorylation (Kreb's cycle and respiratory chain).

12. (b) *Golgi apparatus* is involved in the formation of glycoproteins and glycolipids.

Lysosomes are membrane enclosed organelle. It contains digestive enzymes, which digest excess or worn out organelles, food particles etc.

Vacuoles is a membrane enclosed fluid filled sac which traps waste and excretory products.

Ribosomes is a minute particle consisting of RNA and associated proteins. They bind mRNA and tRNA to synthesise polypeptides and proteins.

13. (a) (A) → (r), (B) → (s), (C) → (p), (D) → (q)

14. (a) Centrosome is an organelle usually containing two cylindrical structures called centrioles. The centrioles form the basal body of cilia or flagella. In chloroplast a number of organised flattened membranous sacs called the thylakoids are present in the stroma. Chlorophyll pigments are present in the thylakoids. Each mitochondrion is a double membrane bound structure. The inner membrane forms a number of infoldings called the cristae towards the matrix. The cristae increase the surface area.

Think Out of the Box

Case study-1

1. The outer membrane of nucleus is in continuity with endoplasmic reticulum. This close association between these two organelles allow sharing of information in a very efficient manner.

2.

	Prokaryotic Cell		Eukaryotic Cell
1.	They lack a well-defined nucleus, have nucleoid instead	1.	Have a well defined nucleus enclosed into the neulear membrane
2.	Mitochondria is absent	2.	Mitochondria is present

Case study-2

1. Water will flow from the solution into the plant cell through the cell membrane and cell will swell up due to the uptake of water.

2. The animal would become stiff and would not be able to do usual activities like run, eat etc.

3. Chloroplasts are found in plant cell only because it contain chlorophyll which is essential for photosynthesis.

5 Reproduction in Animals

Build A Strong Foundation

CONCEPT MAP

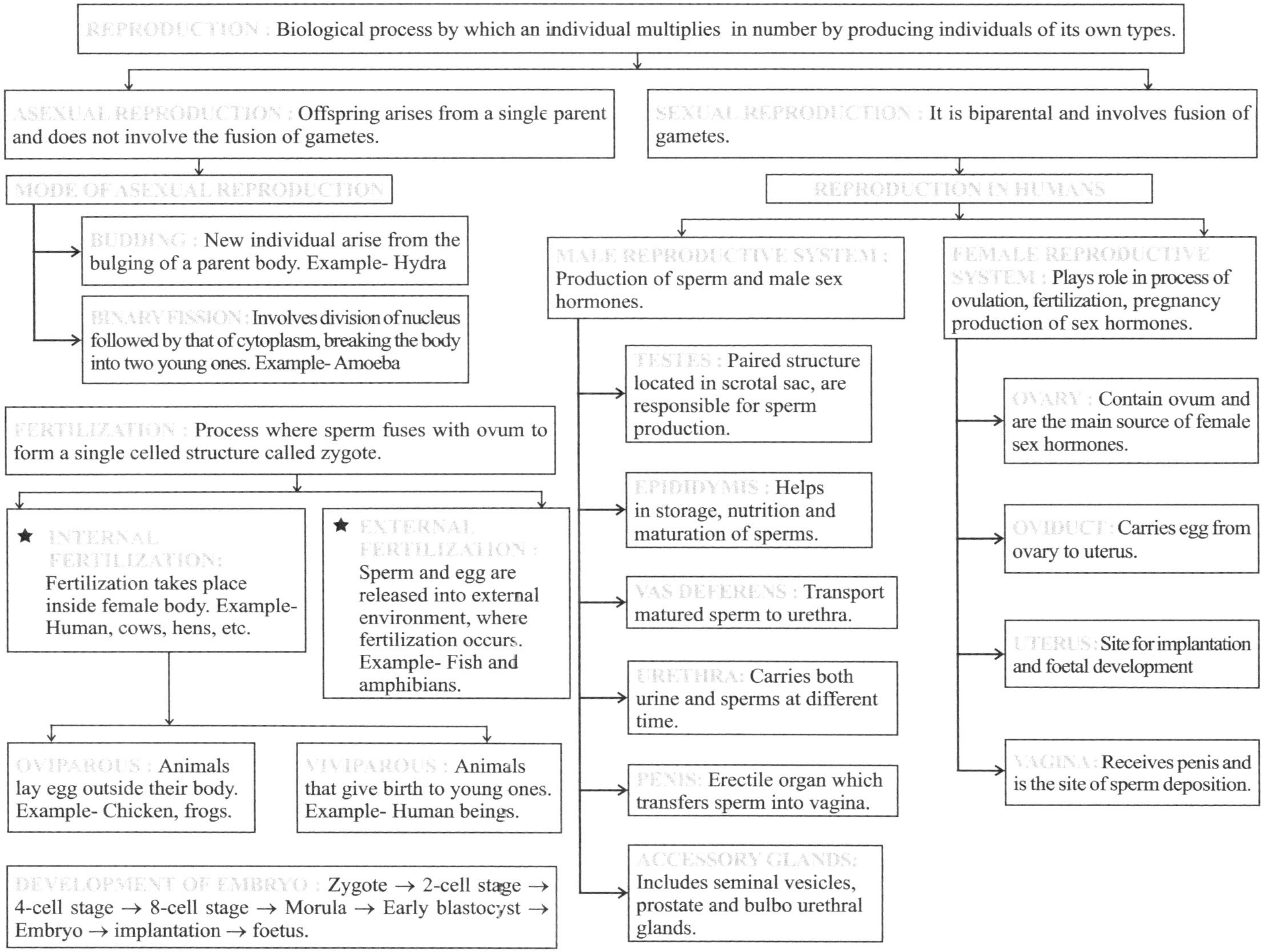

REPRODUCTION : Biological process by which an individual multiplies in number by producing individuals of its own types.
ASEXUAL REPRODUCTION : Offspring arises from a single parent and does not involve the fusion of gametes.
SEXUAL REPRODUCTION : It is biparental and involves fusion of gametes.
MODE OF ASEXUAL REPRODUCTION
BUDDING : New individual arise from the bulging of a parent body. Example- Hydra
BINARY FISSION : Involves division of nucleus followed by that of cytoplasm, breaking the body into two young ones. Example- Amoeba
REPRODUCTION IN HUMANS
MALE REPRODUCTIVE SYSTEM : Production of sperm and male sex hormones.
FEMALE REPRODUCTIVE SYSTEM : Plays role in process of ovulation, fertilization, pregnancy production of sex hormones.
TESTES : Paired structure located in scrotal sac, are responsible for sperm production.
EPIDIDYMIS : Helps in storage, nutrition and maturation of sperms.
VAS DEFERENS : Transport matured sperm to urethra.
URETHRA: Carries both urine and sperms at different time.
PENIS: Erectile organ which transfers sperm into vagina.
ACCESSORY GLANDS: Includes seminal vesicles, prostate and bulbo urethral glands.
OVARY : Contain ovum and are the main source of female sex hormones.
OVIDUCT : Carries egg from ovary to uterus.
UTERUS : Site for implantation and foetal development
VAGINA : Receives penis and is the site of sperm deposition.
FERTILIZATION : Process where sperm fuses with ovum to form a single celled structure called zygote.
★ INTERNAL FERTILIZATION: Fertilization takes place inside female body. Example- Human, cows, hens, etc.
★ EXTERNAL FERTILIZATION : Sperm and egg are released into external environment, where fertilization occurs. Example- Fish and amphibians.
OVIPAROUS : Animals lay egg outside their body. Example- Chicken, frogs.
VIVIPAROUS : Animals that give birth to young ones. Example- Human beings.
DEVELOPMENT OF EMBRYO : Zygote → 2-cell stage → 4-cell stage → 8-cell stage → Morula → Early blastocyst → Embryo → implantation → foetus.

★ ***Belongs to connecting topic.***

The ability to reproduce is one of the unifying characteristics of all living beings. They reproduce by various means – for example, human beings and other mammals reproduce by giving birth to babies, most birds reproduce by laying eggs and most plants reproduce through seeds.

Based on whether there is participation of one organism or two in the process of reproduction, it is of two types – sexual and asexual.

(I) **Sexual reproduction :-** Sexual reproduction involves fusion of male and female gametes and results in the formation of new organism genetically different from parent

(II) **Asexual reproduction :-** Asexual reproduction requires only one parent and does not involve the fusion of gametes. It is a reproduction by which offspring arise from a single parent and inherit the genes of that parent only.

Table : *Difference between Sexual and Asexual reproduction*

	Sexual Reproduction	Asexual Reproduction
(i)	Involves two parents	Involves only a single parent
(ii)	Individuals formed are not genetically identical but only resemble both the parents	Individuals formed are clone or genetically identical to the parents
(iii)	Slower mode of reproduction	Faster mode of reproduction
(iv)	Variation occurs	Variation does not occur.
(v)	Occurs by the formation of haploid gametes which fuse to form a diploid zygote	Occurs by budding, fission fragmentation etc.
(vi)	Occurs in higher invertebrates (earthworm, insect, prawn etc.) and all vertebrates	Occurs in lower organisms like *Amoeba, Paramecium, Sponges, Hydra Plararia* etc.

Note :

Gamete : It is a cell that fuses with another cell during fertilization in organisms that sexually reproduce. Gametes are of two types - male gametes (called sperm) and female gametes (called ovum or egg).

Offspring : It is the product of the reproductive processes of an animal or plant.

SEXUAL REPRODUCTION

Most of the animals reproduce sexually. Sexual reproduction is usually biparental *i.e.*, involves a male and female individual producing male and female gametes respectively. Such animals are called *unisexual* or *dioecious*. This process occurs during fertilization.

During fertilization, these gametes fuse to form a single celled structure *called zygote* which later develops into new individual. It is a slower mode of reproduction. Individuals formed are not genetically identical but resembles both the parents.

A special organ system *called the reproductive system* is responsible for carrying out the process of reproduction in humans. Let us now discuss about sexual reproductive organs in human beings.

In sex cell (male or female), the nucleus carries half of the information needed for reproduction in the form of chromosomes.

MALE REPRODUCTIVE SYSTEM

The male reproductive system consists of a number of sex organs that form a part of the human reproductive process. The organs of the male reproductive system are specialized for the following functions–

– To produce, maintain and transport sperms (male gamete) and protective fluid (semen).
– To discharge sperm within the female reproductive tract.
– To produce and secrete male sex hormones.

The male reproductive organs are –

1. A pair of testes (*singular*, testis)
2. Epididymis
3. Vas deferens
4. Urethra
5. Penis
6. Accessory sex glands – seminal vesicles, prostate gland and bulbourethral gland.

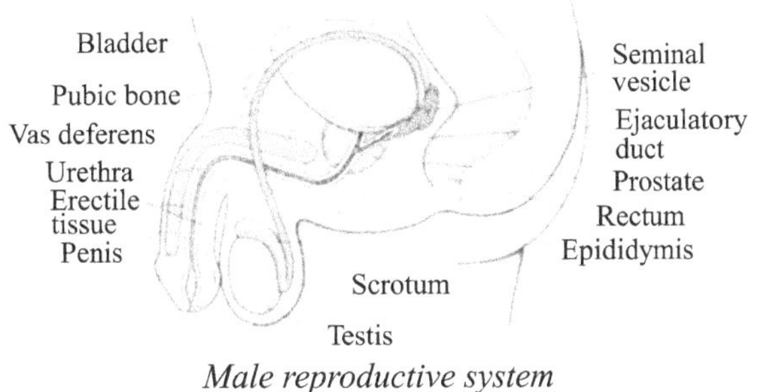

Male reproductive system

Testes

Testes (paired structure) are located outside the abdominal cavity to maintain a temperature lower than the body temperature within a sac called *scrotal sac or scrotum*. Within the testes are coiled masses of tubes called *seminiferous tubules*. These tubules are responsible for producing the sperm cells through a process called spermatogenesis.

Scrotum has a protective function and acts as a climate control system of the testes. It keeps the testes temperature at 2°C, lower than body temperature. The lower temperature is required for the normal development of sperms.

Each sperm is a single motile cell with a head, middle piece and a tail region.

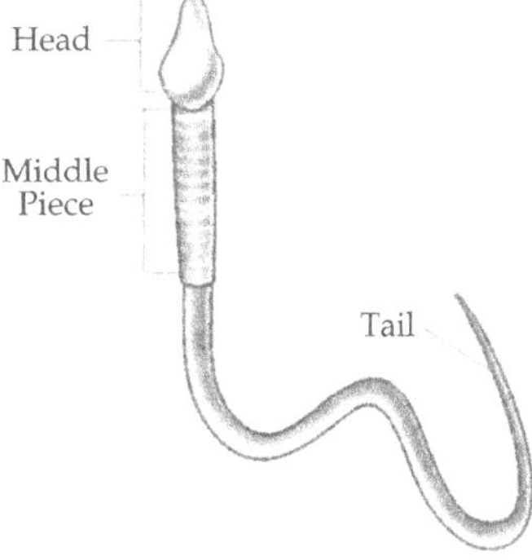

Structure of sperm

(i)   **Head :** The shape of head is oval and flat. It is the essential part of sperm as it contains nucleus and acrosome. Nucleus carries information about the cell-reproduction. Acrosome has chemicals which helps in breaking the ovum protective layers.

(ii)   **Middle piece :** The middle piece of a sperm is formed of numerous mitochondria. Mitochondria provides energy and strength for the movement of sperm.

(iii) **Tail :** It is fine, vibrating posterior portion of a sperm. It helps in the movement of sperm in the fallopian tube during the fertilization process.

The testes produce a hormone called *testosterone*. Testosterone is the male sex hormone that controls the development of male secondary sexual characters.

Note:

Acrosome is derived from the golgi complex and contains hydrolyzing enzymes that help in fertilization of the ovum.

Ejaculation

It is the release of sperm cells and seminal plasma from the male reproductive system.

Epididymis :

It is a long coiled tube that extends from the top of the testes along its side to its back. It collects and stores sperms temporarily. It helps in storage, nurturing and maturation of sperms.

Vas Deferens :

It is connected with epididymis at the tail end. It transports mature sperm to the urethra in preparation for ejaculation.

Urethra :

Urethra extends from penis to external opening. It helps in conduction of sperms, secretion of glands and carries urine to urinary bladder. The urethra, at different times carries both urine and sperms.

Penis :

Penis is a cylindrical, highly vascularized erectile organ. Its function is to transfer sperm into vagina of female reproductive system. The tip of the penis is called *glans penis*. The skin in this region is folded to form a retractable casing called the *foreskin* or *prepuce*.

Note:

Semen/Seminal plasma

It is a milky, viscous and alkaline fluid, ejaculated from the male reproductive system during orgasm. Seman contain sperms and the secretion of epididymis, seminal vesicle, prostate gland and bulbourethral (cowper's) gland.

Functions of semen

– Provides a fluid medium for sperm.

– Nourishes and activates sperm to keep them viable and motile.

– Its alkalinity protects the sperm from the acidity of the vagina.

Accessory or secondary sex glands :

The accessory or secondary sex glands includes seminal vesicles, prostate gland and bulbourethral gland.

(i) **Seminal vesicles** – These are sac like pouches, situated between the bladder. It secretes viscous fluid which constitute the main part of the ejaculate. It produces fructose (which provide nourishment for the activity of sperm), citric acid and prostaglandin.

(ii) **Prostate gland** – It s a walnut sized structure located below the urinary bladder in front of the rectum. Its fluid helps to nourish the sperm.

(iii) **Bulbourethral gland** – These are pea sized structure located on the side of the urethra just below the prostate gland. It secretes a clear, viscous mucous which is lubricating in function.

Female Reproductive System

The female reproductive system consists of organs that plays an important role in the production and transportation of gametes, process of ovulation, fertilization, pregnancy, birth and child care and production of sex hormones.

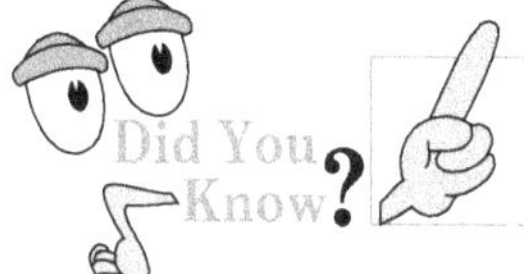

Human egg is about 50 times wider than a sperm cell.

The female reproductive organs are-

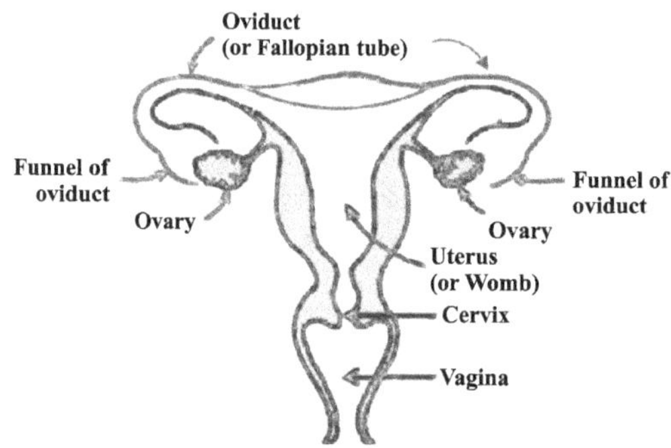

Female reproductive system

(1) Pair of ovaries   (2) Oviduct

(3) Uterus   (4) Vagina

Note:

The process of fertilization takes place in *ampulla isthimic junction* of fallopian tube.

Ovary :

Ovaries are oval shaped organs, located in the lower part of abdominal cavity.

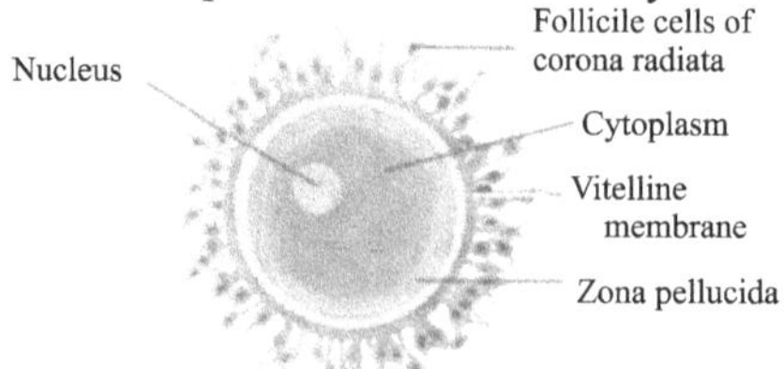

Human ovum

Each ovary contains thousand of eggs called *ovum*. Normally only one egg matures in each ovary every alternate month.

The ovum (or the female gamete) is much larger than the sperm in size. It is non - motile and laden with different types of energy rich materials like yolk, glycogen and proteins accumulated in its cytoplasm. It is enclosed by one on more egg envelops. Size of ovum varies in different animals and depends upon the amount of yolk present. The ovum travels from the ovary to the fallopian tube, where it may be fertilized before reaching the uterus.

The ovaries are the main source of female sex hormones, which control the development of female body characteristics, such as the breasts, body shape, and body hair. The main hormones are estrogen and progesterone. They also regulate the menstrual cycle and pregnancy.

Oviduct (also known as fallopian or uterine tube) :

It is a tube like structure that carries egg from the ovary to the uterus. Each oviduct is differentiated into four parts – infundibulum, ampulla, isthmus and uterine part.

Uterus or Womb :

It is a hollow pear shaped muscular organ that contains developing foetus. Uterus is the site for implantation of the pre-embryo and for the subsequent embryonic and foetal development. It has two regions-an upper wider portion which receives the two oviducts and smaller lower constricted part cervix.

Vagina :

It is the lowermost part of female reproductive system. It receives penis during sexual intercourse and is the site where sperms are deposited. The vagina is connected to the uterus at the cervix. Vagina forms the outer opening of female reproductive organ and is also known as the birth canal.

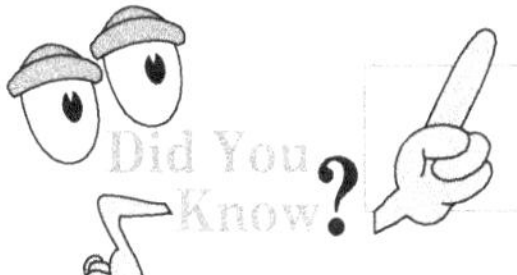

Vagina also serves as the birth canal by stretching to allow the delivery of the foetus during child birth. During menstruation, the menstrual flow exits the body via the vagina.

☞ **How is sperm different from ovum?**

SOLUTION :

Sperm is microscopic, motile and flagellated cell whereas ovum is larger, non-motile, spherical and food laden cell.

FERTILIZATION

Fertilization is the process where sperm (male gamete) fuses with ovum (female gametes) to form a single celled called **zygote.** In humans, the fertilization process most often occurs when sexual intercourse takes place during a woman's fertile or ovulation period. The sperms are released inside the vagina and they travel towards the uterus to the fallopian tube to seek out the egg. Hundreds of thousands of sperms may be released during ejaculation, but only one gets to penetrate the egg and start the fertilization process. Sperms are capable of staying alive for 48 to 72 hours inside the female reproductive tract, and can fertilize the egg as soon as ovulation takes place. *Hence,* the fusion of egg nuclei with the sperm nuclei is called fertilization.

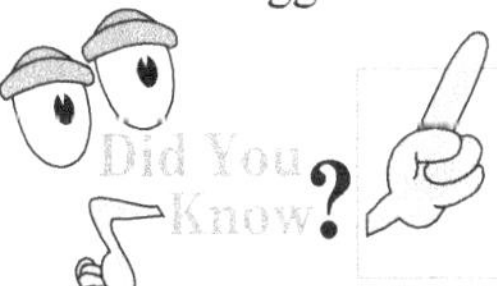

The zygote is a "fertilized ovum" or "fertilized egg". It is the beginning of a new individual. In multicellular organisms, it is the earliest developmental stage of the embryo and in single cell organisms, the zygote divides to produce offspring usually through the process of cell division.

This results in the formation of a fertilized egg or zygote. The zygote undergoes division and specific changes to grow into a new individual.

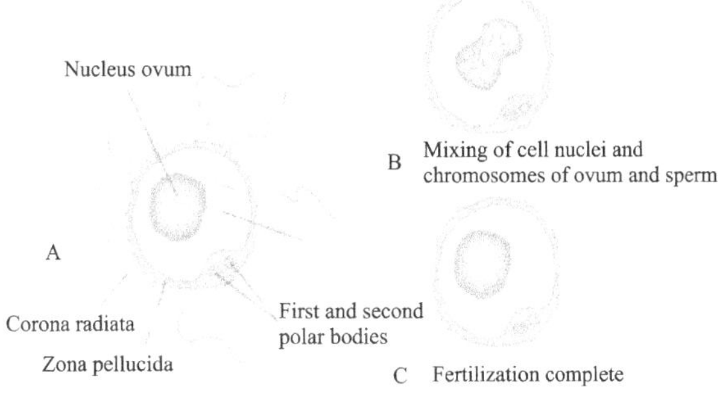

Process of fertilization

The new individual inherits some characteristics from the mother and some from the father. This is why children have some characteristics like father and some like mother.

☛ **Why all kinds of characteristics run in families?**

SOLUTION :

Every human body gets half of its genes from each parent, therefore it inherits some of the features from the mother and some from the father. That is why, all kind of characteristics, for example, height, run in families.

How are twins formed ?

Twins are two offsprings produced by the same pregnancy. The zygote or fertilized egg is a single cell. Sometimes, a single fertilized egg splits into two, each half developing into an embryo. This results in identical twins. If the fertilized egg splits into three or more parts, each of which develops into an embryo, then all the offspring produced will be identical.

If two eggs are fertilized by two sperms, this result in fraternal twins. They are also known as non-identical twins. Fraternal offspring may look alike, but they are genetically different and may not be all of same sex. On the contrary, identical offspring, are genetically same and are always of same sex.

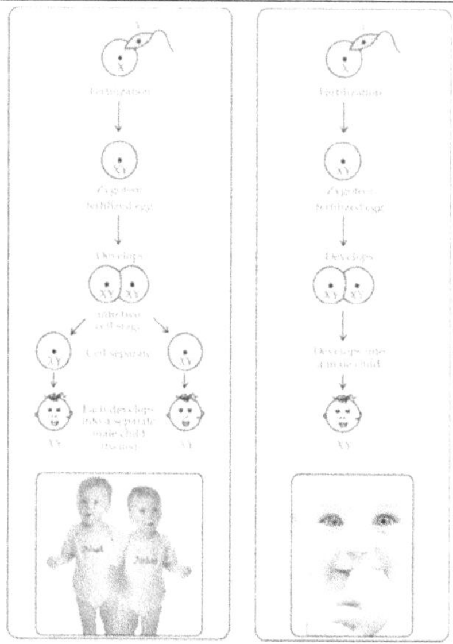

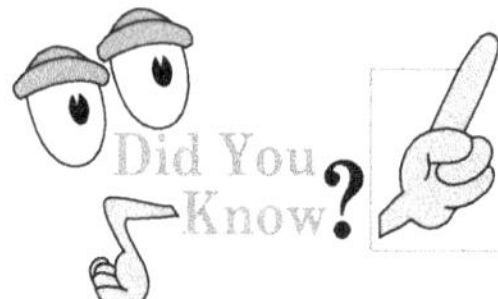

Conjoined twins joined at the hip, chest, back, face etc. are called Siamese twins.

CONNECTING TOPIC

Types of Fertilization

The process of fertilization might take place either outside the female body or inside the female body. *On the basis of this, fertilization is divided into two types* – external fertilization and internal fertilization.

External Fertilization

External fertilization is characterized by the release of both sperm and egg into an external environment. Sperm will fertilize the egg outside of the organism, as seen in spawning. External fertilization occurs mostly in wet environments and requires both the male and the female to release their

Eggs of frog in a layer of jelly

gametes into their surroundings (usually water). An *advantage* of external fertilization is that it results in the production of a large number of offspring. One *disadvantage* is that environmental hazards such as predators greatly reduce the chance of surviving into adulthood. Amphibians and fish are examples of animals that reproduce this way. It is very common in aquatic animals such as fish, starfish etc.

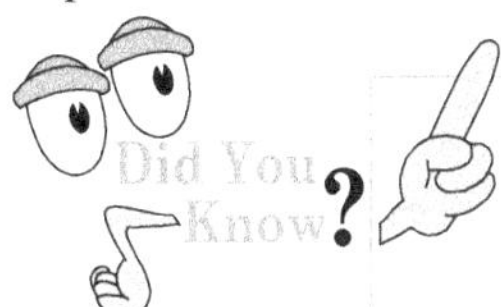

The main features of external fertilization

i. *Both the male and female parents interact only during a specific breeding period and spawning is observed.*

ii. *In some animals like fishes or certain frogs. the process differs a little where parental care is observed as far as care of the young are concerned.*

iii. *The eggs and the sperm are released together after a little span under appropriate conditions of temperature, light, rainfall etc.*

iv. *The sperms find their way to the ova by chemo-taxis involving specific chemicals.*

v. *The fertilized embryo develops inside the egg covered by thin shell, in certain cases, they may be carried by the mouth, or borne on the back.*

vi. *The developed embryo hatches into a larva which undergoes further development into fingerling, fry and then into adult.*

vii. *The matured larva can undergo progressive metamorphosis as the tadpole larva develops into a frog.*

Internal Fertilization

The fertilization that takes place inside the female body is called *internal fertilization*. In this sperm meets the egg while it is still attached to the female body. Humans, cows, hens etc are examples of internal fertilization. Animals that use internal fertilization specialize in the protection of the developing egg. *For example*, reptiles and birds secrete eggs that are covered by a protective shell that is resistant to water loss and damage. Internal fertilization protects the fertilized egg or embryo from predation and harsh environments, which results in higher survival rates than can occur with external fertilization.

Table : *Difference between Internal fertilization and External fertilization.*

S. No.	Internal fertilization	External fertilization
(i)	Fertilization that takes place inside the female body	Fertilization that takes place outside the female body
(ii)	Small number of eggs are produced.	Large number of eggs are produced
(iii)	Chances of survival of offsprings are more.	Chances of survival of offsprings are less.
(iv)	Examples : Humans, cows, hens etc.	Examples : Fish, frog, starfish etc.

The number of eggs that an individual produce for successful reproduction depends on two factors–
(i)   Chances of fertilization   (ii) Level of parental care
Hence, if there is low chance of fertilization and less care, then large number of eggs are produced. This is because some of eggs and sperms may get destroyed when exposed to water movement, wind and rainfall. These factors prevent the sperms from reaching the eggs. Thus, production of large numbers of eggs and sperms is necessary to ensure fertilization of at least a few of them.

In case of hen, development of embryo takes place inside the female body. The zygote divides repeatedly and move down to fallopian tube to form embryo. During development, embryo forms several protective layers around it. As a result a white colour hard shell is formed around developing embryo. After this, the hen lays a fertilized egg. The parent hen then sits and warms the eggs or keeps them safely in the warm place till they hatch. After three weeks, the chick is completely developed and it bursts open the egg shell.

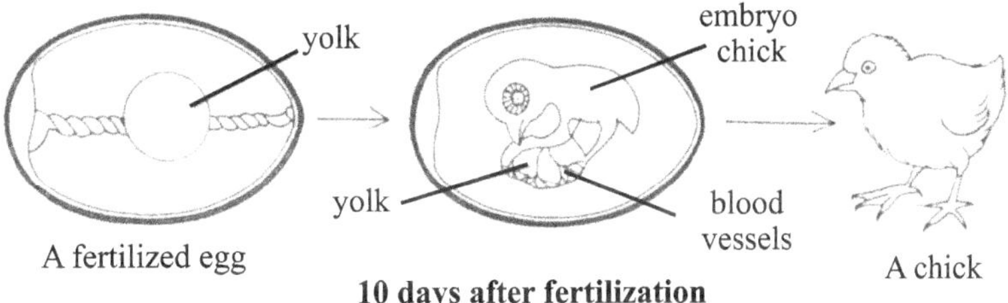

Stages of development in hen

CASE STUDY-1 : Fertilisation

Fertilization,is the union of a sperm, with an egg nucleus, to form the primary nucleus of an embryo. In all organisms the essence of fertilization is the fusion of the hereditary material of two different sex cells, or gametes, The most primitive form of fertilization, found in microorganisms and protozoans, consists of an exchange of genetic material between two cells.

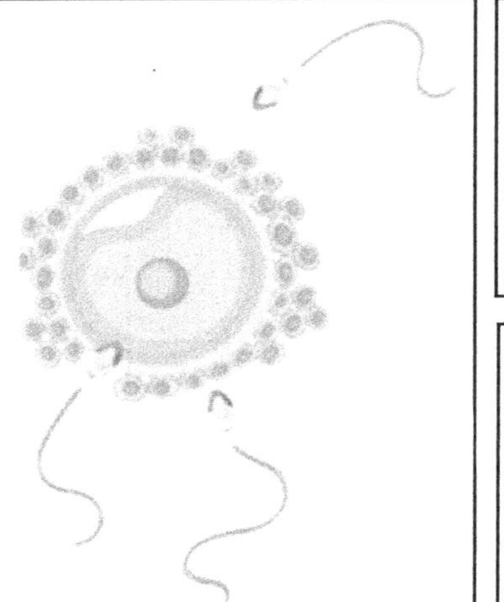

CASE I: *Siblings have some characters similar to their biological parents.*

The process of fertilization is the meeting of an egg cell from the mother and a sperm cell from the father . therefore the new individual inherits some characters from the father and some from the mother.

CASE II: *Internal and external fertilization are the two main type of fertilization process.*

Fertilization that takes place inside the female body is called as internal fertilization. It occurs in many animals like humans, cow and dogs. Fertilization in which fusion of the gamete takes place outside the body of the female is called external fertilization.it is very common in aquatic animals.

CASE III: *In vitro fertilization is the artificial technique of fertilization.*

In vitro fertilisation (IVF) is a process of fertilisation where an egg is combined with sperm outside the body.

If the fertilization occur the zygot is allowed to develop for about a week and then it is placed in the mother's uterus.

 **Think Out of the Box**

Q 1. What is the type of fertilization in hen ?

Q 2. What do you think would happen if multiple sperms fused with one egg?

Q 3. What is fertilized egg known as?

VIVIPAROUS AND OVIPAROUS ANIMALS

Now, you have learnt that humans give rise to young baby while chicken lays egg that eventually develops into young ones. The animals that give birth to young ones are called **viviparous animals.** The example includes dog, cat or man. The animals that lay eggs are called **oviparous animals**. Frog, butterfly and chicken.

Table : *Difference between Oviparous and Viviparous animals.*

S. No.	Oviparous animals (Egg bearing animals)	Viviparous animals (Live – bearers)
(i)	Animals that lays egg outside their body.	Animals that give birth to young ones.
(ii)	Development of embryo does not takes place within the mother's body.	Embryos develop inside the mother's body from which it gains nourishment.
(iii)	*Examples–* Chicken, frogs and butterfly.	*Examples–* Human beings, certain fishes etc.

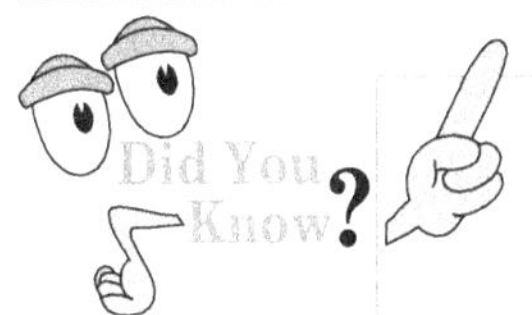

- *Snakes reproduce by producing eggs as well as young ones!!*
- *The animals that undergo external fertilization such as fish and frog lay egg in hundreds while a hen lays only one egg at a time. This is because these animals lay hundred of eggs and release millions of sperms, all the eggs do not get fertilized and develop into new individuals. The eggs and sperms get exposed to water movement, wind and rainfall. Also there are other animals in the pond which may feed on eggs. Thus production of large number of eggs and sperms are necessary to ensure fertilization of at least a few of them.*

Platypus is the only egg laying mammal.

In-vitro fertilization (IVF)

In-vitro fertilization is a process where fertilization of egg occurs outside the female body. It involves the removal of eggs from female ovaries. This egg is then allowed to fertilize with sperm in a fluid medium in a test tube. The fertilized egg cell then grows in the laboratory until it divides into eight cells. Then it is introduced into the mother's womb (uterus) so that it can develop normally. A baby conceived by fertilization that occurs outside mother's body is called test tube baby. Scientists usually perform this process to help the couples with infertility problems.

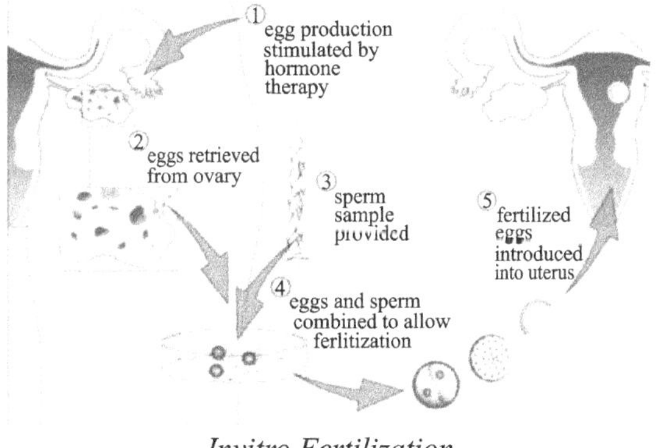

Invitro Fertilization

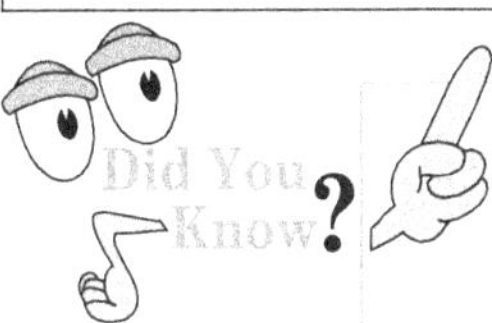

A foetus develops the sense of vision around the 26th week. At this time, the eyes open and even begin to blink.
Gestation Period
It is the period from fertilization to birth. In human beings, the gestation period is about nine months.

DEVELOPMENT OF EMBRYO

Fertilization results in the formation of zygote (a single diploid cell) that begins to develop into a multicellular embryo. The zygote divides repeatedly to give rise to a ball of cells. The cells then begin to form groups that develop into different tissues and organs of the body. This developing structure is called an **embryo**. The embryo gets embedded in the wall of uterus for further development. The close attachment of the embryo with the uterus is called **implantation** and it results in pregnancy.

The embryo continues to develop in the uterus. An unborn baby develops 'head first', starting from the brain and head, then the main body, then the arms and legs. Life begins when the fertilized egg divides into two cells, then four, eight and so on. After a few days, there are hundred of cells and after a few weeks, millions. These cells build up the various body parts. The unborn baby's heart begin to beat after only four weeks, although it has not yet taken on its full shape. Infact, by eight weeks all the main parts have formed, even the fingers and toes - yet the tiny body is only the size of grape. The stage of embryo in which all body parts can be distinguished easily is called a **foetus**. The embryo / foetus grows in the mother's uterus for about nine months.

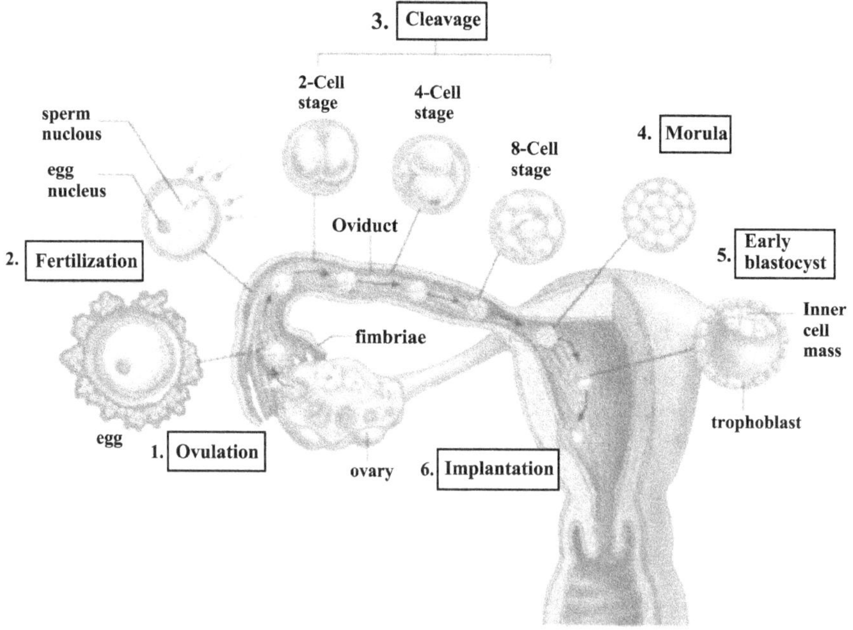

Development of embryo

After nine months, the baby is ready to give birth to young one. The birth of the fully developed foetus is termed as *parturition*. It occurs through the birth canal or vagina. Foetus requires following things for its development –

(i)   Nutrients   (ii)   Oxygen   (iii)   Protection

It also needs to remove waste materials such as carbon dioxide, metabolic wastes from its body. The embryo receives nutrition and oxygen from the mother's blood *via* placenta. **Placenta** is an organic connection between the foetus and the uterine wall to allow nutrient uptake, waste elimination and gas exchange etc. It is developed at the point of implantation. It is connected to the foetus by umbilical cord.

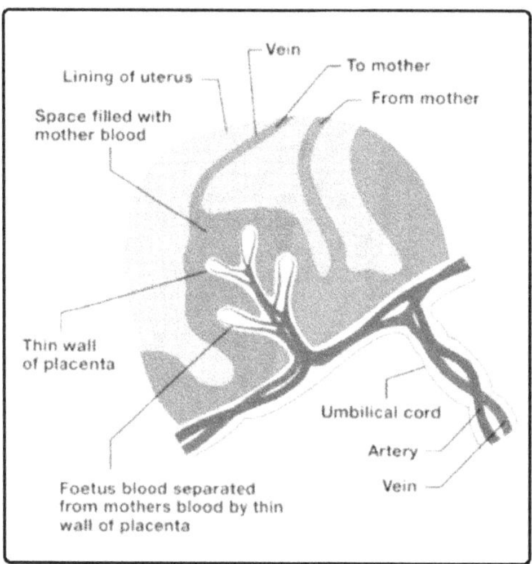

Placenta (Section)

Umbilical cord: The flexible cord that attaches an embryo or foetus to the placenta. The umbilical cord contains blood vessels that supply nutrients and oxygen to the foetus and remove its wastes, including carbon dioxide.

Function of placenta -
(i)   It prevents the entry of pathogen from mother's body to embryo/foetus.
(ii) It supplies oxygen from the mother to foetus and excretes CO_2 from foetus to the mother's blood.
(iii) It provides nutrients such as glucose, amino acids, lipid, vitamin etc. to the foetus from mother's blood.
(iv) It helps in excretion of metabolic wastes, CO_2 and urea from embryo into mother's blood.
      The developing foetus is protected by the uterus and a liquid called amniotic fluid. Amniotic fluid is present inside a bag called amnion.

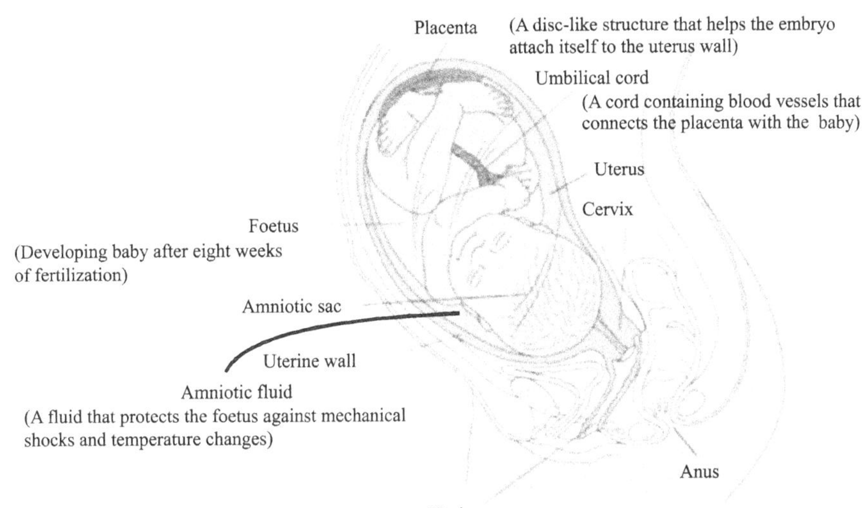

Foetus in the uterus

So far you have learnt what happens if the egg inside a female body gets fertilized. But have you ever thought, *what happens to the egg if it does not get fertilized.* An ovary releases an egg every month. The process of release of an egg by an ovary is called *ovulation* and the cycle of producing and releasing mature eggs or ova is called the *menstrual cycle.* In a normal, healthy girl, ovulation takes place on the 14th day of the beginning of menstrual cycle of 28 days. We have learnt that uterus prepares itself to receive the fertilized egg. During this, the inner lining of uterus get thickened and is supplied with blood from which growing embryo draws nutrition for its development. However, if an egg does not get fertilized, the inner lining of uterus breaks down slowly and is released out in the form of blood and mucous from the vagina. This process of releasing blood and mucous every month through the vagina is called *menstruation.* This is usually a 28 day cycle.

Note :

What about the changes that we observe in our body as we grow? Do you think that we also undergo metamorphosis?
No, we humans do not undergo metamorphosis. In human beings, body parts similar to the adults are present from the time of the birth. There is no drastic and abrupt change. Therefore, one can say that metamorphosis does not happen in the humans.

METAMORPHOSIS

Metamorphosis is a biological process of transforming larva into an adult. The process involves relatively abrupt changes in the animal's structure through cell growth and development.
Some insects, amphibians, molluscs crustaceans, cnidarians, echinoderms etc undergo metamorphosis. The silkworm is the larva or caterpillar of the domesticated silkmoth. Its life cycle includes : egs → Larva or caterpillar → pupa → audit.
This is already studied in previous class. Frog is such an another example. In its life cycle there is lot of changes that occur in tadpole which transform the latter into an adult frog.
Tadpole looks completely different from frog. The tadpole that emerges from the eggs contains gills, a tail and a small circular mouth. They can swim freely within the water. During its development, tadpole grows and undergo some abrupt changes in their structure and develops into mature frog. The metamorphosis of tadpole begins with the development of limbs, lungs development and finally the absorption of tail by the body. As a result of such changes, the tadpole gradually gets transformed into frogs. Thyroid hormones play a major role in the process of metamorphosis.

The tadpole is herbivorous, respires through gills and has tail.
The adult frog is insectivorous respires through lungs and skin (gills disappear) and the tail also disappears.
During metamorphosis the tongue of frog becomes long and highly mobile for catching preys.

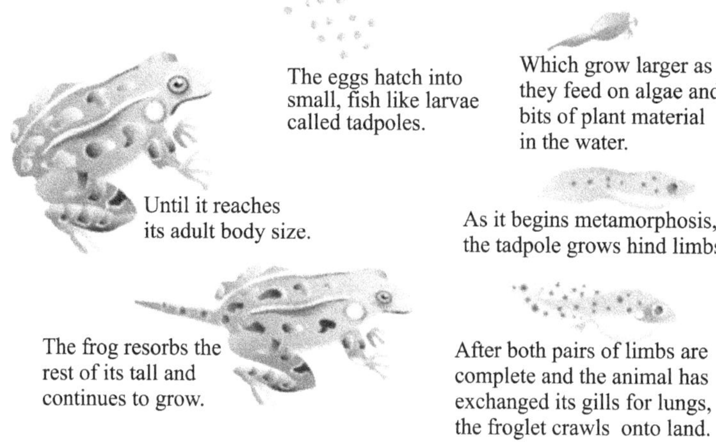

Life cycle of frog

In similar way, a beautiful butterfly emerges out of cocoon.

The caterpillar undergoes metamorphosis. It changes its colour and its body contracts. As a result the tissues become fluid and begin forming organs of adult butterfly. Within few days, once the development is complete a beautiful butterfly emerges out of the pupal shell. The adult will continue the cycle and reproduce.

ASEXUAL REPRODUCTION

Asexual reproduction is a mode of reproduction by which offspring arise from a single parent and inherit the genes of that parent only. It is a reproduction which does not involve meiosis or fertilization.

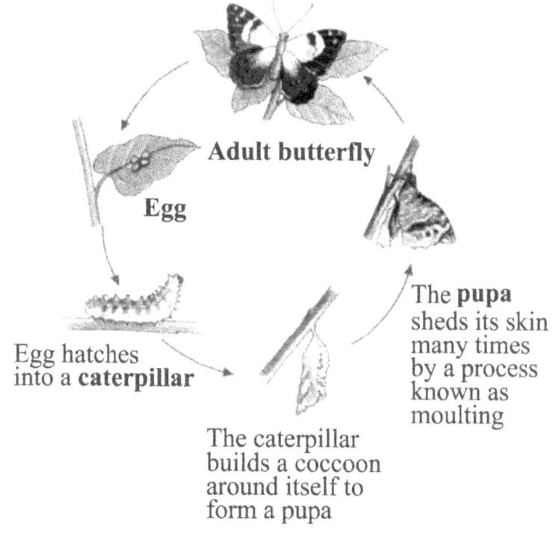

Life cycle of a butterfly

Animals such as *Hydra*, *Amoeba* etc. reproduces through asexual reproduction. Asexual reproduction does not involve fusion of male and female gamete. It requires only one parent. As a result, the offspring produced are genetically identical to each other and their parent. They are actually called clones. *Clones* are a group of genetically identical individuals.

MODE OF ASEXUAL REPRODUCTION

Various mode of asexual reproduction in animals are – budding and binary fission.

Budding

Budding involves the formation of a new individual from the bulging of a parent body. It is commonly seen in some plants, fungi and some animals such as yeast and *Hydra*. These bulges are actually buds. In *Hydra*, the cells divide rapidly at a specific site and develop as an outgrowth called bud. These buds, while still attached to the parent body, develop into smaller individuals. When these individuals become mature enough, they detach from the parent body and develop as an independent individual. This type of asexual reproduction is known as *budding*.

Yeast is a single-celled organisms that grows rapidly if sufficient nutrients are available to them. They reproduce through budding. When budding occurs in yeast cells, small bulb like projections protrudes out. This projection is called bud. The bud grows and detaches from parent cell to form new yeast cell. The yeast cell grows and produces more yeast cells through the process of budding.

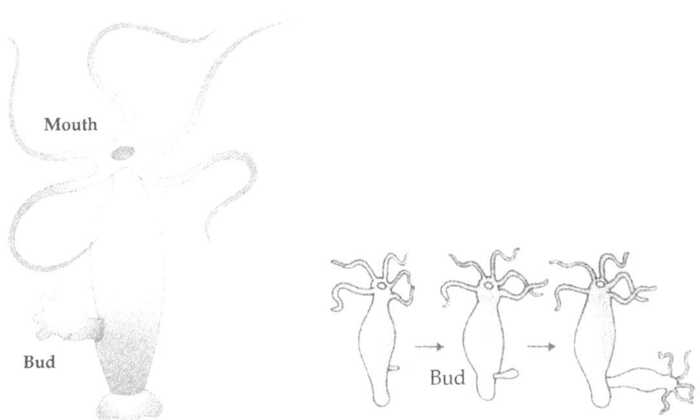

Budding in Hydra

Binary Fission

Binary fission is another type of asexual reproduction seen in bacteria and *Amoeba*. It involves the division of nucleus followed by that of the cytoplasm, breaking the body into two young ones. It occurs in unicellular organisms.

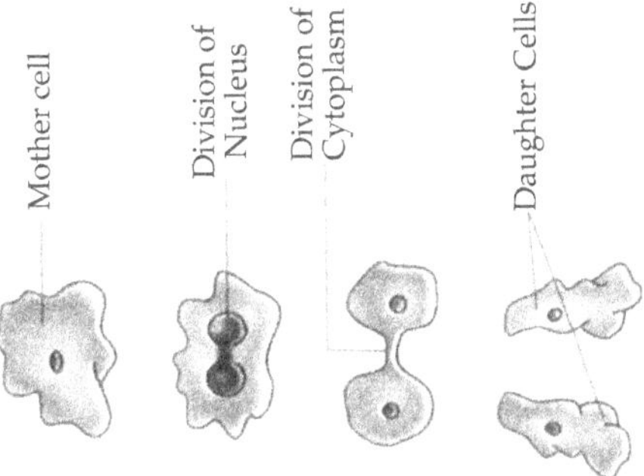

Binary fission in Amoeba

Amoeba is a single-celled organism. It begins the process of reproduction by the division of its nucleus into two nuclei. This is followed by the division of its body into two with each part receiving a nucleus. Finally, two *Amoebae* are produced from one *Amoeba*. The newly formed daughter *Amoeba* is genetically identical to each other and to the parent *Amoeba*.

Note :

Other form of asexual reproduction

Apart from budding and binary fission there are other method of asexual reproduction. ***Some common forms of asexual reproduction are –***

(1) **Gemmules (Internal buds)** – In this form of asexual reproduction, parent releases a specialized mass of cells that can develop into offspring. Sponges exhibit this type of reproduction.

(2) **Fragmentation** – In this, the body of the parent breaks into distinct pieces, each of which can produce an offspring. *Planaria* exhibit this type of reproduction.

Gemmules in sponges

Fragmentation in Planarians

(3) **Regeneration** – In regeneration, a piece from a parent body gets detached, which grows and develops into a completely new individual. Echinoderms exhibit this type of reproduction.

(4) **Parthenogenesis** – It involves the development of an egg that has not been fertilized into an individual. Animals like wasps, bees and ant reproduce by this process. If an egg gets fertilized, it will develop into a female. A non-fertilized egg may develop into a male.

ADVANTAGES OF ASEXUAL REPRODUCTION

Asexual reproduction is advantageous to certain animals that remains in one particular place like *Hydra*, *Planaria* and animals that are unable to look for mates. It also produces numerous offspring without costing the parent a great amount of energy or time.

DISADVANTAGES OF ASEXUAL REPRODUCTION

Asexual reproduction lacks genetic variation. All of the organisms that reproduces asexually are genetically identical and therefore share the same weaknesses. If the stable environments changes, the consequences could be deadly to all of the individuals, as the adaptation capacity is very low due to less variation.

Time to Check Your Knowledge

☛ **Why offspring are identical to one another and to their parent in asexual reproduction?**

SOLUTION :

In asexual reproduction, the offspring comes from the same parent. So, they are identical to one another and to their parent.

Cloning

Cloning is the process that is used to create an identical (exact) copy of a cell, tissue or a complete organism. It was successfully performed for the first time by Ian Wilmut and his colleagues at the Roslin Institute in Edinburgh, Scotland. They successfully cloned a Scottish sheep named Dolly. Dolly was born on 5th July 1996 and was the first mammal to be cloned from adult somatic cell. During the process of cloning of Dolly, somatic cells was collected from the mammary gland of a female Finn Dorsett sheep. Simultaneously, an egg was obtained from a Scottish black face ewe. Then they transferred the nucleus from the cell from Finn Dorsett sheep to the egg of the Scottish black face ewe. After few days, the egg with new nucleus started behaving like a normal fertilized zygote, which gradually developed into an embryo. This embryo was then surgically implanted into the uterus of a surrogate mother, which finally gave birth to a lamb called Dolly.

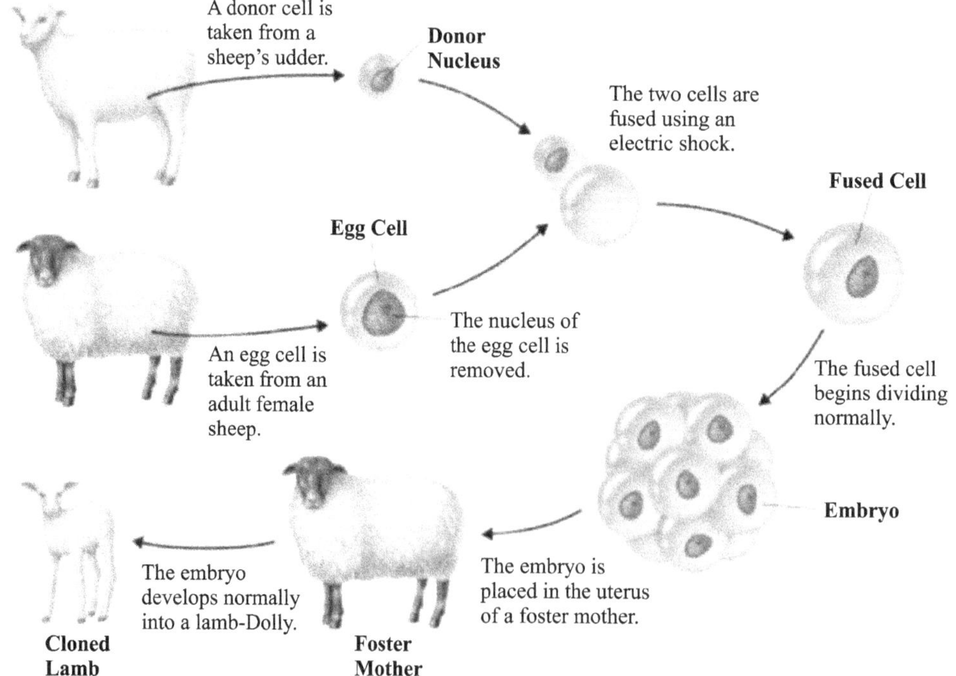

Though Dolly was given birth by the Scottish black face ewe, it was found to be identical to the Finn Dorsett sheep from which the nucleus was taken.

Dolly was a healthy lamb and produced several offspring of her own through sexual means. Unfortunately, Dolly died on 14th February 2003 due to certain lung disease.

CASE STUDY-2 : Cloning

Clonning is the process of manufacturing individuals with identical or virtually identical DNA, either naturally or artificially.

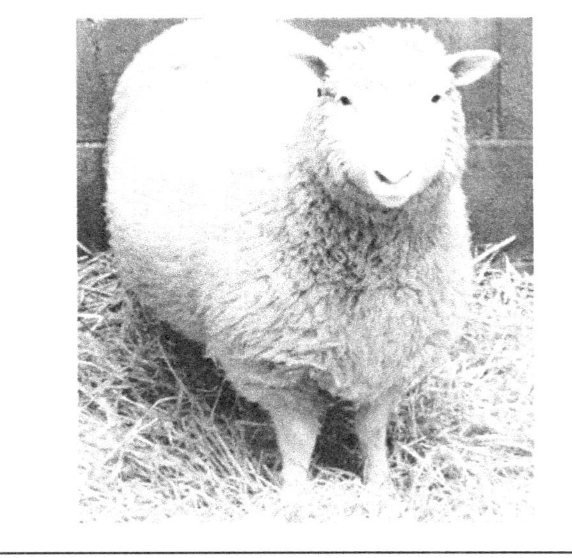

CASE I: The egg of Dolly sheep was obtained from a Scottish black face ewe. But Dolly has no resemblance to ewe. Why is it so?

White cloning dolly, the nucleus of the egg obtained from Scottish black face ewe was replaced by a nucleus from Finn Dorette sheep. Therefore, Dolly has resemblance to the sheep and not ewe.

CASE II: Dolly was given birth by the Finn Dorette sheep. Can this statement be justified?

This statement is not true as Dolly was born from the surrogate Black face.

CASE III: Dolly had three mothers and no father. How is it so?

Dolly sheep had three mothers: one provided the egg, another the nucleus or genetic material and a third carried embryo till birth Dolly had no father,

 **T**hink **O**ut of the **B**ox

Q 1. Why is Dolly considered to be a breakthrough in science?
Q 2. Why human clearing is unethical?

SUMMARY

- Reproduction is the biological process through which a living organism produces offspring that are similar to themselves.
- There are two modes of reproduction –
  - Sexual reproduction – Reproduction resulting from fusion of male and female gametes.
  - Asexual reproduction – Reproduction in which only a single parent is involved.
- The male reproductive organs includes testes, epididymis, vas deferens, urethra, penis and accessory glands like seminal vesicle, prostate gland and bulbourethral gland.
- The female reproductive organs include ovaries, oviducts, uterus and vagina.
- The testes produce male gametes called sperms while the ovary produces female gametes called ova.
- The process of fusion of male and female gamete is called fertilization.
- The fertilized egg is called zygote.
- There are two types of fertilization –
  - Internal fertilization – Fertilization that takes place inside the female body.
    Eg. – Human beings, hens, cows, dogs.
  - External fertilization – Fertilization that takes place outside the female body.
    Eg. – Frogs, fish and starfish.
- Animals such as humans, cow, etc., which give birth to young ones are called viviparous animals.
- Animals such as hen, frog, lizard, etc., which lay eggs are called oviparous animals.
- Placenta is a vascular tissue that is present in the inner lining of uterus. It is connected to foetus by umbilical cord.
- Umbilical cord is a cord containing blood vessels that connects the placenta with the foetus.
- The process of release of an egg by an ovary is called ovulation.
- The process of releasing blood and mucus every month through the vagina is called menstruation. It is usually a 28 day cycle.
- The transformation of the larva into adult through drastic changes is called metamorphosis.
- Clones are group of genetically identical organisms derived from a single individual by means of asexual reproduction.
- Budding in yeast and binary fission in Amoeba are two types of asexual reproduction.

Exercise 1 — Master Boards

Multiple Choice Questions

DIRECTIONS : This section contains multiple choice questions. Each question has four choices (a), (b), (c) and (d) out of which ONLY ONE is correct.

1. Reproduction is essential for living organisms in order to
   (a) keep the individual organism alive
   (b) fulfil their energy requirements
   (c) maintain growth
   (d) continue species forever
2. In asexual reproduction, two offspring having the same genetic material and the same body features are called:
   (a) callus   (b) twins
   (c) chromosomes   (d) clone
3. One of the following occurs in the reproductive system of flowering plants as well as that of humans. This is
   (a) ovary   (b) uterus
   (c) scrotal sac   (d) oviducts
4. By which method, asexual reproduction occurs in Ameoba.
   (a) fission   (b) budding
   (c) regeneration   (d) all of these
5. Which of the following is embedded in the uterine wall?
   (a) Placenta   (b) Embryo
   (c) Zygote   (d) Egg

Assertion & Reason

DIRECTIONS : Each of these questions contains an Assertion followed by reason. Read them carefully and answer the question on the basis of following options. You have to select the one that best describes the two statements.

(a) If both **Assertion** and **Reason** are **correct** and Reason is the **correct explanation** of Assertion.
(b) If both **Assertion** and **Reason** are correct, but Reason is **not the correct explanation** of Assertion.
(c) If **Assertion** is **correct** but **Reason** is **incorrect**.
(d) If **Assertion** is **incorrect** but **Reason** is **correct**.

1. **Assertion :** In asexual reproduction, only one parent is required to produce a new organism.
   Reason : Regeneration is a type of asexual reproduction.
2. **Assertion :** Asexual reproduction takes place in some unicellular and multicellular organisms
   Reason : Binary fission in *Amoeba*, budding in *Hydra*, regeneration in *Hydra* are some examples of asexual reproduction.
3. **Assertion :** Gametes are formed in gonads.
   Reason : Gonads are haploid in nature.
4. **Assertion :** In human male, testes are extra abdominal and lie in scrotal sacs.
   Reason : Scrotum acts as thermoregulator and keeps testicular temperature lower by 2°C for normal sperm formation.
5. **Assertion :** Individuals produced by asexual reproductions are known as clones.
   Reason : They are known as clones because they are genetically identical.
6. **Assertion :** Vagina is also called as birth canal.
   Reason : During birth baby passes through the vagina.
7. **Assertion :** Scrotum is present outside the abdominal cavity.
   Reason : It stores sperms which require lower temperature than the body temperature.
8. **Assertion :** Sexual reproduction plays a role in origin of new species.
   Reason : Sexual reproduction involves in the formation and fusion of gametes.
9. **Assertion :** Budding occurs in yeast.
   Reason : It is similar to fission process of bacteria.

Fill in the Blanks

DIRECTIONS : Complete the following statements with an appropriate word / term to be filled in the blank space(s).

1. The type of reproduction in which only single parent is involved is called _________ reproduction.
2. Animals which give birth to young ones are called _________ animals.
3. Egg laying animals are called _______ .
4. The type of reproduction in which both male and female animals are involved is called _________.
5. The fusion of ovum and sperm is called _________.
6. The fertilized egg is called a __________.
7. The male gamete is called _________.
8. The female gamete is called _______ .
9. The zygote divides repeatedly to form an ______.
10. The embryo gets embedded in the wall of _______ for its further development.
11. *Amoeba* reproduces by the process of ___ ______.
12. In humans, fertilization occurs in __________.
13. An ovum is ________ celled.
14. The process in which a bud appears on the body wall of certain organism that grows into a full organism is called _______.

True / False

DIRECTIONS : Read the following statements and write your answer as true or false.

1. In frog, fertilization occurs inside the body.
2. Fertilization is the process where sperm fuses with ovum to form a single cell called zygote.
3. In asexual reproduction the offsprings are not completely identical to the parent.
4. Fertilization of ova in human female occur in the vagina.
5. Placenta protects the embryo from entry of pathogen from mother's body.

6. In internal fertilization large number of eggs are produced.
7. Budding in *Hydra* is a process of asexual reproduction.
8. Umbilical cord connects placenta with the baby.
9. Head portion of human sperm carries genetic material for cell reproduction.
10. Binary fission is a type of sexual reproduction.

Match the Following

DIRECTIONS : *Each question contains terms (Given in column I) and their features or functions (given in columns II). Terms given in column I have to be matched with features given in column II.*

1.

Column-I (Terms)		Column-II (Features)
A.	Testes	p.	Produces tiny sperm cells
B.	Epididymis	q.	Transfer sperm to vagina of females
C.	Vas deferens	r.	Lubricates the sperm
D.	Urethra	s.	Storage and nourishes the sperm
E.	Penis	t.	Transfer sperm from epididymis to urethra
F.	Prostate gland	u.	Carries urine and sperm

2.

Column-I (Terms)		Column-II (Function)
A.	Ovary	p.	Produces ovum
B.	Oviduct	q.	Carries ovary to uterus
C.	Uterus	r.	Contains developing foetus
D.	Vagina	s.	Receives sperm from penis during sexual intercourse.

Passage Based Questions

DIRECTIONS : *Study the given paragraph(s) and answer the following questions.*

Passage

Rita was a month pregnant, she wanted to know how that foetus get delivered after the human pregnancy period. So, she asked her gynecologist to explain it to her. So that she can mentally prepared for her delivery. Her gynecologist explained the whole process in very precise manner. A typical pregnancy lasts 40 weeks from the first day of last menstrual period to birth of the baby. It is divided into three stages, called trimesters. The foetus undergo many changes throughout maturation.

1. What is the term given to the process of delivery of foetus.
   - (a) Fertilization
   - (b) Lactation
   - (c) Parturition
   - (d) Cloning
2. What is the average duration of human pregnancy?
   - (a) 7 months
   - (b) 8 months
   - (c) 9 months
   - (d) 10 months
3. Lactation starts at-
   - (a) at the end of pregnancy
   - (b) at the end of first trimester
   - (c) during pregnancy
   - (d) before partusition

Very Short Answer Questions

1. Define fertilization.
2. Where does internal fertilization occur?
3. In which type of asexual reproduction, an animal reproduces by dividing into two individuals?
4. Through which process a tadpole develops into an adult.
5. Name three reproductive organs found in females.
6. Name reproductive organs found in males.
7. What is zygote?
8. What is vasectomy?
9. What is ovulation?
10. What is a gestation period?
11. What is metamorphosis?
12. What is a test tube baby?
13. Expand IVF.
14. Define cloning.
15. What is the name of the young one of frog?
16. Name the process by which *Planaria* reproduce.
17. Name the process by which sponges reproduce.

Short Answer Questions

1. What is parthenogenesis? Give example of parthenogenesis.
2. What is parturition?
3. What is budding? Give two examples of budding.
4. What is the functions of testis?
5. What is implantation?
6. What do you understand by embryonic nutrition?
7. What are the disadvantages of asexual reproduction?
8. What is the main advantage of sexual reproduction over asexual reproduction?
9. What is the function of ovary?
10. Write about the development of butterfly.
11. What is cloning? Write the name of first cloned animal.
12. What do the sperms do after being released?
13. Write difference between external and internal fertilization.
14. Write the functions of placenta.
15. Write the differences between viviparous and oviparous.
16. Write a short note on menstruation.
17. Describe the path that sperm take while leaving the body.
18. Describe two structural differences between a mature sperm and a mature egg.

Long Answer Questions

1. Diagrammatically explain the development of embryo in uterus.
2. Describe the various types of asexual reproduction in animals.
3. Explain the life cycle of a frog with proper diagram.
4. Explain the process of fertilization in humans.

Reasoning Based Questions

1. Why is reproduction important?
2. Why does the embryo present in the hen's egg take time to develop into chick?
3. Why do some animals undergo metamorphosis others do not?
4. Why do some couple undergo in-vitro fertilisation?

5. Why umbilical cord is called as life line of developing baby?
6. If multiple sperm were combine to the ovum what will be the outcome?
7. Where does a fertilised egg develop into a baby in the human body?
8. Why do the offsprings formed as a result of sexual reproduction exhibit more variations?
9. Why do female frogs (or female fish) lays hundred of eggs?

Hots Questions

1. Collect information about first test tube baby of the world.
2. Why cows always produce one baby, whereas dog produces more than one puppies at a time?

3. Why most of the twins are similar?
4. Some twins are identical but some twins are non-identical. What is the reasons behind it?
5. How will you determine the sex of foetus while inside the mother's womb? Explain.
6. How does a leech do reproduction?
7. What is "parental care"? Give some idea about parental care with different examples?
8. Production of sperms requires low temperature. How is it accomplished in human body?
9. An ovum allows the entry of only one sperm at a time. Why?
10. Collect information about amniocentesis? Why it is necessary to ban amniocentesis?

Master NCERT (Text-book & Exemplar)

Text-book Exercise

1. Explain the importance of reproduction in organisms.
2. Describe the the process of fertilization in human beings.
3. Choose the most appropriate answer:
   (a) Internal fertilization occurs
      (i) in female body. (ii) outside female body.
      (iii) in male body. (iv) outside male body.
   (b) A tadpole develops into an adult frog by the process of
      (i) fertilization. (ii) metamorphosis
      (iii) embedding (iv) budding.
   (c) The number of nuclei present in a zygote is
      (i) none. (ii) one.
      (iii) two. (iv) four.
4. Indicate whether the following statements are True (T) or False (F):
   (a) Oviparous animals give birth to young ones.
   (b) Each sperm is a single cell.
   (c) External fertilization takes place in frog.
   (d) A new human individual develops from a cell called gamete.
   (e) Egg laid after fertilization is made up of a single cell.
   (f) Amoeba reproduces by budding.
   (g) Fertilization is necessary even in asexual reproduction.
   (h) Binary fission is a method of asexual reproduction.
   (i) A zygote is formed as a result of fertilization.
   (j) An embryo is made up of a single cell.
5. Give two difference between a zygote and a foetus.
6. Define asexual reproduction. Describe two methods of asexual reproduction in animals.
7. In which female reproductive organ does the embryo get embedded?
8. What is metamorphosis? Give examples.
9. Differentiate between internal fertilization and external fertilization.

10. Complete the cross-word puzzle using the hints given below.

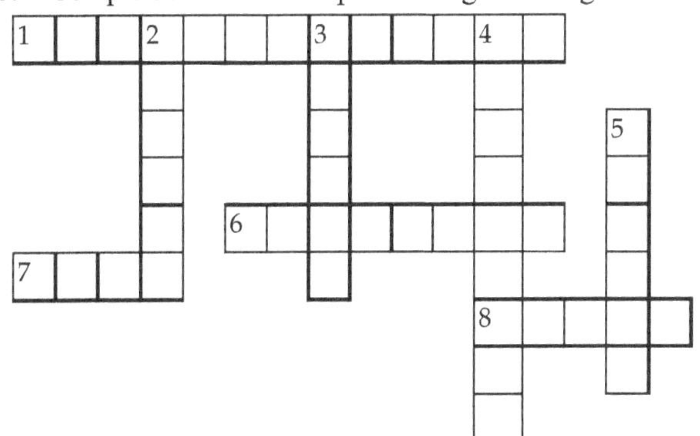

Across
1. The process of the fusion of the gametes.
6. The type of fertilization in hen.
7. The term used for bulges observed on the sides of the body of *Hydra*.
8. Eggs are produced here.

Down
2. Sperms are produced in these male reproductive organs.
3. Another term for the fertilized egg.
4. These animals lay eggs.
5. A type of fission in amoeba.

Exemplar Questions

1. What is the importance of reproduction?
2. In markets, eggs of birds are available but never eggs of dogs. Why?
3. The eggs of frogs do not have shells for protection, yet they are safe in water. How?
4. The term metamorphosis is not used while describing human development. Why?
5. Mother gives birth to a baby but the baby has characters of both parents. How is this possible?

6. How is reproduction in hydra different from that in amoeba?
7. How can we say that fish exhibits external fertilisation?
8. Hens and frogs are both oviparous exhibiting different types of fertilisation. Explain.
9. Observe the following figures

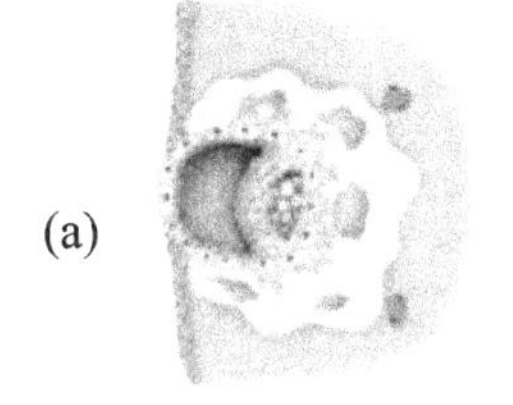 (a)

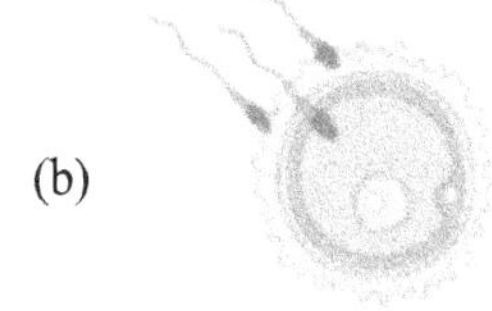 (b)

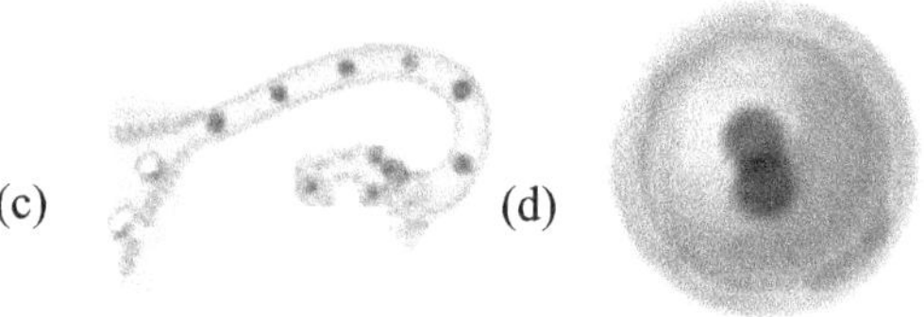
(c)   (d)

(i) Identify the stages a to d in Fig. during development of human baby.
(ii) Arrange the stages in correct sequence of development
(iii) Explain the development that takes place in any one stage.

Exercise 3   ⬡ **Foundation Builder**

Multiple Choice Questions

DIRECTIONS : *This section contains ultiple choice questions. Each question has four choices (a), (b), (c) and (d) out of which ONLY ONE is correct.*

1. Which of the following is hermaphrodite animal?
   (a) Bear   (b) Tiger
   (c) Leech   (d) Wolf
2. Which hormone is secreted by males?
   (a) Estrogen   (b) Progesterone
   (c) Testosterone   (d) Both (a) and (b)
3. A sperm is a
   (a) multicelled   (b) single celled
   (c) multilayered   (d) single layered
4. Which organ releases sperm?
   (a) Vas deferens   (b) Testes
   (c) Scrotum   (d) Urethra
5. Parthenogenesis occurs in which of the following animals?
   (a) Sheep   (b) Sponges
   (c) Ant   (d) *Hydra*
6. Which of the following is *not* a part of female reproductive system?
   (a) Uterus   (b) Vagina
   (c) Urethra   (d) A pair of ovaries
7. Which part of sperm provides energy for movement of sperm?
   (a) Head   (b) Middle piece
   (c) Tail   (d) All of these
8. The genetic information is carried by which part of the sperm?
   (a) Tail   (b) Middle piece
   (c) Head   (d) None of these
9. An ovary is large due to presence of
   (a) yolk   (b) water
   (c) air   (d) minerals
10. Which of the following hormone is responsible for secondary sexual characters in females?
    (a) Testosterone   (b) Estrogen
    (c) Thyroxine   (d) Pituitary
11. Another name for oviduct is
    (a) cervix   (b) seminal vesicles
    (c) prostate gland   (d) fallopian tube
12. Which of the following connects foetus with placenta?
    (a) Umbilical cord   (b) Amniotic fluid
    (c) Wall of uterus   (d) Fallopian tube
13. Which of the following is an unisexual animal?
    (a) Tiger   (b) Earthworm
    (c) Leech   (d) Tape worm
14. Which structure is cut and tied off in a vasectomy?
    (a) Penis   (b) Epididymis
    (c) Urethra   (d) Vas deferens
15. Where does fertilization occur in mammals?
    (a) Uterus   (b) Fallopian tube
    (c) Vagina   (d) Cervix
16. Which type of fertilization is found in frogs?
    (a) External, in water   (b) Internal, in abdomen
    (c) External, in uterus   (d) Internal, in epididymis
17. If an organism is a diploid (or $2n$) with 16 chromosomes, then how many chromosomes its sperm cells or egg cells will contain?
    (a) 8   (b) 16
    (c) 32   (d) 64
18. The vas deferens connects the epididymis to the
    (a) seminal vesicles   (b) urethra
    (c) testes   (d) prostate gland
19. After sperm move through the vas deferens, they enter the
    (a) seminal vesicles   (b) urethra
    (c) urinary bladder   (d) all of these
20. A sperm tail consists of
    (a) a nuclues   (b) mitochondria
    (c) flagellum   (d) golgi body
21. A zygote is a/an
    (a) implanted fertilized egg   (b) fertilized egg
    (c) ovulated egg   (d) blastocyst
22. How many chromosomes does a mature human sperm cell contain?
    (a) 1   (b) 2
    (c) 23   (d) 46
23. Which of the following is not a part of the female reproductive system in human beings?
    (a) Ovary   (b) Uterus
    (c) Vas deferens   (d) Fallopian tube

24. In the list of organisms given below, those that are reproduced by the asexual method are
(i) banana   (ii) dog
(iii) *Yeast*   (iv) *Amoeba*
(a) (ii) and (iv)   (b) (i), (iii) and (iv)
(c) (i) and (iv)   (d) (ii), (iii) and (iv)

25. The fertilized egg or the zygote gets implanted in the
(a) fallopian tube   (b) ovary
(c) uterus   (d) vagina

26. The following figures illustrate binary fission in *Amoeba*

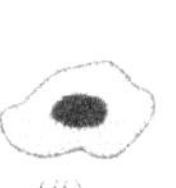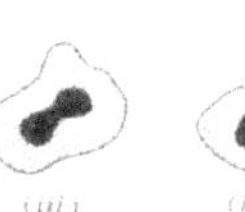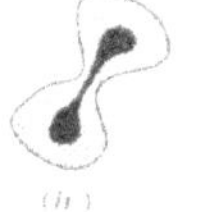

The correct sequence is
(a) (i), (iii), (iv), (ii)   (b) (ii), (iii), (iv), (i)
(c) (iv), (iii), (ii), (i)   (d) (iii), (iv), (ii), (i)

27. Which among the following is not the function of testes at puberty?
(i) Formation of germ cells.
(ii) Secretion of testosterone.
(iii) Development of placenta.
(iv) Secretion of estrogen.
(a) (i) and (ii)   (b) (ii) and (iii)
(c) (iii) and (iv)   (d) (i) and (iv)

28. Four students were asked to draw the diagram after viewing a prepared slide of 'Budding in Yeast' under a compound microscope. The diagrams are given below. Mark the correct diagram which is not depicting budding in yeast.

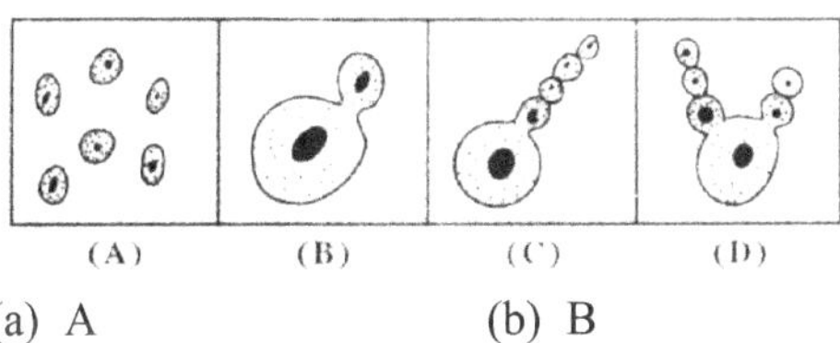

(a) A   (b) B
(c) C   (d) D

29. The human embryo gets nutrition from the mother blood with the help of a special organ called **[NTSE]**
(a) Zygote   (b) Ovary
(c) Oviduct   (d) Placenta

30. In the flowering plants sexual reproduction involves several events beginning with the bud and ending in a fruit. These events are arranged in four different combinations. Select the combination that has the correct sequence of events. **[NTSE]**
(a) Embryo, zygote, gametes, fertilization.
(b) Gametes, fertilization, zygote, embryo.
(c) Fertilization, zygote, gametes, embryo.
(d) Gametes, zygote, embryo, fertilization.

31. Which one of the following is correct route for passage of sperms? **[NTSE]**
(a) Testes - scrotum - vasdeferens - urethra - pennis
(b) Scrotum - testes - urethra - vasdeferends - pennis
(c) Testes - vasdeferens - urethra - seminal vesicles
(d) Testes - vasdeferens - urethra - penis

DIRECTIONS : Each question contains two columns which have to be matched. Statement/terms given in column I have to be matched with statement/terms given in column II.

32. Match the column I with appropriate items from column II. **[NTSE]**

Column I		Column II	
I.	Ginger	A.	Tuber
II.	Onion	B.	Grafting
III.	Potato	C.	Bulb
IV.	*Bryophyllum*	D.	Rhizome
		E.	Adventitious buds
		F.	Bulbil

Select the correct alternative.
(a) I-D, II-C, III-A, IV-E   (b) I-D, II-F, III-E, IV-C
(c) I-C, II-B, III-A, IV-D   (d) I-D, II-F, III-A, IV-B

Exercise 4 ★ Foundation Builder +

DIRECTIONS (Qs.1-9) : This section contains multiple choice questions. Each question has four choices (a), (b), (c) and (d) out of which ONLY ONE is correct.

1. A population of genetically identical individuals, obtained from asexual reproduction is **[NTSE]**
(a) Callus   (b) Clone
(c) Deme   (d) Aggregate

2. The "Eyes" of the potato tuber are **[NTSE]**
(a) root buds
(b) flower buds
(c) shoot buds
(d) axillary buds

3. Embryo sac occurs in **[NTSE]**
(a) Embryo
(b) Axis part of embryo
(c) Ovule
(d) Endosperm

4. Which is correct? **[NTSE]**
(a) Gametes are invariably haploid
(b) Spores are invariably haploid
(c) Gametes are generally haploid
(d) Both spores and gametes are invariably haploid

5. The shared terminal duct of the reproductive and urinary system in the human male is: **[NTSE]**
(a) Urethra   (b) Ureter
(c) Vas deferens   (d) Vasa efferentia

Biology

6. What is the correct sequence of sperm formation? **[NTSE]**
   - (a) Spermatogonia, spermatocyte, spermatozoa, spermatid
   - (b) Spermatogonia; spermatozoa, spermatocyte, spermatid
   - (c) Spermatogonia, spermatocyte, spermatid, spermatozoa
   - (d) Spermatid, spermatocyte, spermatogonia, spermatozoa

7. The part of fallopian tube closest to the ovary is **[NTSE]**
   - (a) isthmus
   - (b) infundibulum
   - (c) cervix
   - (d) ampulla

8. At the end of first meiotic division, male sperm differentiates into **[NTSE]**
   - (a) secondary spermatocyte
   - (b) primary spermatocyte
   - (c) spermatogonium
   - (d) spermatid

9. Freshly released human egg has **[NTSE]**
   - (a) one Y-chromosome
   - (b) one X-chromosome
   - (c) two X-chromosomes
   - (d) one X-chromosome & one Y-chromosome

Multiple Matching Questions

DIRECTIONS (Qs. 10-11) : *The following question contains statements given in two columns which have to be matched. Statements (A, B, C....) in column I have to be matched with statements (i), (ii), (iii).... in column II.*

10. Match the following columns and select the correct option. **[NTSE]**

Column-I		Column-II
(A) Placenta	(i)	Androgens
(B) Zona pellucida	(ii)	Human Chorionic Gonadotropin (hCG)
(C) Bulbo-urethral glands	(iii)	Layer of the ovum
(D) Leydig cells	(iv)	Lubrication of the Penis

	(A)	(B)	(C)	(D)
(a)	(i)	(iv)	(ii)	(iii)
(b)	(iii)	(ii)	(iv)	(i)
(c)	(ii)	(iii)	(iv)	(i)
(d)	(iv)	(iii)	(i)	(ii)

11. Match the items given in Column I with those in Column II and select the correct option given below : **[NTSE]**

Column I		Column II
A. Proliferative Phase	(i)	Breakdown of endometrial lining
B. Secretory Phase	(ii)	Follicular Phase
C. Menstruation	(iii)	Luteal Phase

	A	B	C
(a)	(iii)	(ii)	(i)
(b)	(i)	(iii)	(ii)
(c)	(iii)	(i)	(ii)
(d)	(ii)	(iii)	(i)

SOLUTIONS
(Brief Explanations of Selected Questions)

Exercise 1 — Master Boards

Multiple Choice Questions

1. (d)   2. (d)   3. (a)   4. (a)
5. (a)

Assertion & Reason

1. (b) Asexual reproduction is a mode of reproduction by which offsprings arise from a single organism, and inherit the genes of that parent only. The offsprings will be exact genetic copies of the parent. Regeneration is the ability of an organism to replace its lost or damaged body parts. *Hydra* has great power of regeneration.

2. (a) Asexual reproduction is the primary form of reproduction for single-celled organisms such as the archaebacteria, eubacteria, and protists. Types of asexual reproduction are budding, binary fission, fragmentation, regeneration etc. [For more refer answer 2 of long questions.]

3. (c) Gonads are the reproductive cells found in the testes in males and the ovaries in females. They produce gametes which are haploid in nature.

4. (a) Scrotum is a pouch of skin arising from the lower abdominal wall and hanging between the legs. The two testes lie in respective scrotal sacs. The scrotum acts as a thermo regulator and provides an optimal temperature for the formation of sperms. This temperature is 1-3 degree Celsius lower the temperature of the body. Failure of testes to descend into scrotum causes sterility. Because formation of sperms does not occur at abdominal temperature. It occurs at a temperature that is 2 degree centigrade lower than the body temperature.

5. (a) Both assertion and reason are true. Reason is the correct explanation of assertion.
   The new individuals produced after cell divisions in asexual reproduction are always genetically identical or clone to each other and their parents.

6. (a) Both assertion and reason are true. Reason is the correct explanation of assertion.
   Vagina is called as birth canal, because the baby passes through the vagina during birth.

7. (a) Both assertion and reason are true. Reason is the correct explanation of assertion.
   Scrotum a pouch containing testis is present outside the abdominal cavity because sperms require a lower temperature than the normal body temperature.

8. (a) Both assertion and reason are true. Reason is the correct explanation of assertion.
   Sexual reproduction involves two parents that results in the offsprings that are not identical to the parents. It causes variation, which are essential for evolution as well as survival of species under favourable conditions.

9. Assertion is true, but reason is false.
   Budding of vegetative cells is common in yeast. It is different from fission, in which cell divides in transverse plane into two cells.

Fill in the Blanks

1. Asexual
2. Viviparous
3. Oviparous
4. Sexual reproduction
5. Fertilization
6. Zygote
7. Sperm
8. Ovum
9. Embryo
10. Uterus
11. Binary fission
12. Fallopian tube
13. Single
14. Budding

True / False

1. False. It occurs outside the body.
2. True
3. False. Offsprings are completely identical to parents.
4. False. Fertilization in human female takes place in fallopian tube.
5. True
6. False. In external fertilization large number of eggs are produced.
7. True
8. True
9. True
10. False. Binary fission is a type of asexual reproduction.

Match the Following

1. A-p, B-s, C-t, D-u. E -q, F-r
2. A-p, B-q, C-r, D-s

Passage Based Questions

1. (c)   2. (c)   3. (a)

Very Short Answer Questions

1. The process by which sperm fuse with an ovum to form a single cell zygote is called fertilization.
2. Inside the female body.
3. Binary fission
4. Metamorphosis.
5. Ovary, Oviduct and Uterus.
6. Testes, Sperm duct and Penis.
7. Zygote is a single cell formed by fertilization of sperm and ovum.
8. The surgical procedure for male sterilisation.

9. The process of release of egg from ovary is called ovulation.
10. Duration of complete embryonic development starting from implantation up to the parturition.
11. Drastic change which takes place during the development of the larva into as adult is called metamorphosis.
12. Test tube baby is a baby developed from an egg that was fertilized outside the body and then implanted in the uterus of the biological or surrogate mother.
13. In vitro fertilization.
14. The process of forming an identical copy of cell, tissue or organism is called cloning.
15. Tadpole
16. Fragmentation
17. Budding or Gemmule formation inside the body.

Short Answer Questions

1. Parthenogenesis is a form of asexual reproduction in which growth and development of embryos occur without fertilization. Parthenogenesis occurs naturally in many plants, some invertebrate animal species (including nematodes, water fleas, some scorpions, aphids, some bees) and a few vertebrates.
2. The birth of the fully developed foetus is termed as parturition.
3. The process of developing a new individual from buds, is called budding. The examples are *Hydra* and *Yeast*.
4. The testis is a part of male reproductive system. The primary functions of the testes are to produce sperm (spermatogenesis) and to produce androgens, primarily testosterone hormone.
5. The attachment of the embryo with the uterus is called implantation.
6. Embryonic nutrition means the requirement of nutrients and oxygen by the embryo for its development.
7. The disadvantages of asexual reproduction include production of a less genetic variety that gives the offspring a lesser chance of survival in a varying environment and the fact that only identical individuals are produced. In asexual reproduction the offspring has identical genes and chromosomes of the parent.
8. Sexual reproduction brings about variation in individual. Also, it ensures survival of species in a population.
9. Function of ovary is to produce ovum and a hormone called estrogen.
10. The process of development of butterfly is known as metamorphosis. First the colour and body structure changes. The tissues become fluid and then development of adult butterfly starts.
11. Cloning is the process of creating genetically identical copies of biological matter. This may include genes, cells, tissues or entire organisms. Cloning from adult animals was introduced to the public in 1997 when scientists announced the birth of Dolly, the first animal cloned in this way.

12. The sperms swim in the oviduct to reach the egg. When they reach the egg one of the sperm may fuse the egg to form zygote.

13.

	External fertilization	**Internal fertilization**
(i)	External fertilization occurs outside the female body.	Internal fertilization occurs within the female body
(ii)	Examples- Frog, fish, starfish	Examples – birds, reptiles, mammals including human
(iii)	External fertilization desires water to facilitate their fertilization, therefore it happens in wet environments.	Internal fertilization protects the fertilized egg or embryo from predation and harsh environments, which results in higher survival rates than can occur with external fertilization.

14. Placenta is the mechanical and physiological connection between foetal and maternal tissues for the nutrition, respiration and excretion of the foetus.

15.

	Viviparous	**Oviparous**
(i)	Viviparous animals are those which give birth to young ones that have been nourished by the mother's body.	Oviparous animals are those which lay eggs. Fertilization may be internal or external and development takes place outside the female body.
(ii)	This includes all mammals except the egg-laying monotremes (the platypus and echidnas). Humans is an example of a viviparous animal.	Examples- birds, frog, reptiles

16. Menstruation, or period, is normal vaginal bleeding that occurs as part of a woman's monthly cycle. Every month, female body prepares for pregnancy. If no pregnancy occurs, the uterus, or womb, sheds its lining. The menstrual blood is partly blood and partly tissue from inside the uterus. It passes out of the body through the vagina.
17. Testes → Epididymis → Vas deferens → Urethra → Vagina → Cervix → Uterus → Fallopian tube
18. Sperm is microscopic, motile and flagellated while ovum is larger, non-motile, spherical and food-laden cell.

1. Diagrammatic representations of embryo in uterus.

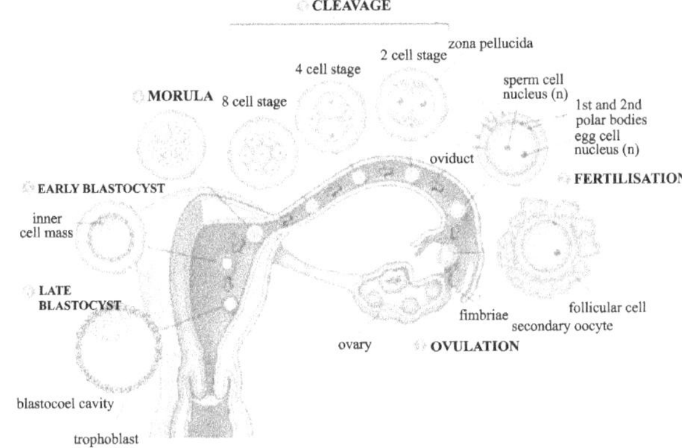

2. Asexual reproduction is a mode of reproduction by which offsprings arise from a single parent, and inherit the genes of that parent only. It does not involve meiosis, ploidy reduction, or fertilization.

The principal forms of asexual reproduction are as follows-

(i) **Binary fission:** In the process of binary fission, an organism duplicates its genetic material, or deoxyribonucleic acid (DNA), and then divides into two parts (cytokinesis), with each new organism receiving one copy of DNA.

Binary fission is the primary method of reproduction of prokaryotic organisms. In protists, binary fission is often differentiated into types, such as transverse or longitudinal, depending on the axis of cell separation. It may be irregular (*Amoeba*), longitudinal (*Euglena*), Transverse (*Paramecium* and *Planaria*), and oblique (Dinoflagellates).

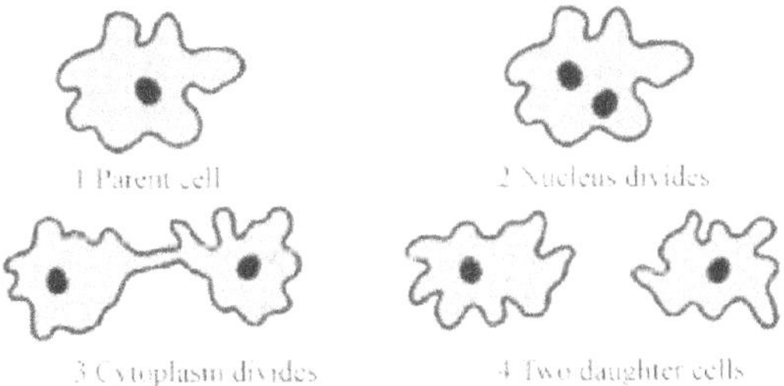

Fig: *Binary fission in Amobea*

(ii) Multiple fission: In this, the nucleus undergoes several mitotic divisions, producing a number of nuclei. After the nuclear divisions are complete, the cytoplasm separates, and each nucleus becomes encased in its own membrane to form an individual cell. It occurs in protozoa (*Plasmodium*)

(iii) Budding: During budding, a new organism starts growing from the parent's body. At first it looks like a bud. This bud later develops into a mature organism. Sometimes it stays attached to the parent's body and sometimes it breaks off. *Hydra* reproduces by budding. In *Hydra*, a bud develops as an outgrowth due to repeated cell division at one specific site . These buds develop into tiny individuals and when fully mature, detach from the parent body and become new independent individuals.

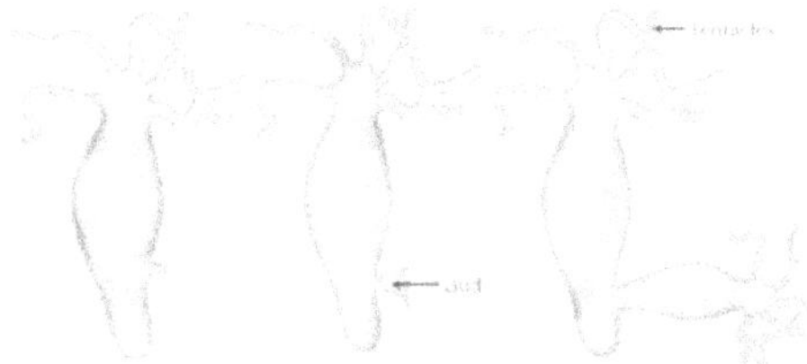

(iv) Fragmentation: Fragmentation is a form of asexual reproduction in which an organism is split into fragments. Each of these fragments develops into mature, fully grown individuals that are clones of the original organism. Fragmentation as a method of reproduction is seen in many organisms such as filamentous cyanobacteria, molds, *Spirogyra*, lichens, many plants, and animals like sponges, acoel flatworms, some annelid worms, and sea stars.

(v) Sporulation: Some types of mould reproduce through sporulation. They produce reproductive cells - spores - that are stored in special spore cases until they are ready to be released. After they are released they will develop into new, individual organisms. Bread mould reproduces by sporulation.

3. Life cycle of frog: There are three distinct stages in the life cycle of a frog - egg, tadpole and adult. During external fertilisation, the egg fuses with a sperm to form a zygote. The zygote further divides to form an early tadpole, which matures into a late tadpole. During metamorphosis, the tadpole transforms into an adult frog.

LIFE CYCLE OF A FROG

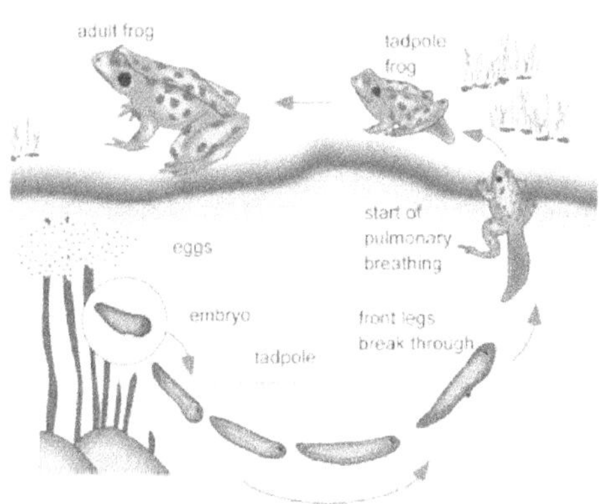

4. Human fertilization is a complicated process that results in a fertilized egg. The fertilized egg will mature in the womb of its mother until birth. The process of fertilization occurs in fallopian tube (Oviduct). The sperm that reached the egg in the Fallopian tube surround it and begin competing for entrance. The head of each sperm, the acrosome, releases enzymes that begin to break down the outer, jelly-like layer of the egg's membrane, trying to penetrate the egg. Once a single sperm has penetrated, the cell membrane of the egg changes its electrical characteristics. This electrical signal causes small sacs just beneath the membrane (cortical granules) to dump their contents into the space surrounding the egg. The contents swell, pushing the other sperm far away from the egg in a process called cortical reaction. The cortical reaction ensures that only one sperm fertilizes the egg. The other sperms die within 48 hours. The fertilized egg

is now called a zygote. The formation of zygote marks the beginning of new individual. The dividing zygote gets pushed along the Fallopian tube. Approximately four days after fertilization, the zygote has about 100 cells and is called a blastocyst. When the blastocyst reaches the uterine lining, it floats for about two days and finally implants itself in the uterine wall around six days after fertilization. This signals the beginning of pregnancy. The implanted blastocyst continues developing in the uterus for nine months.

Reasoning Based Questions

1. The process of reproduction ensures that a plant or animal species does not disappear from Earth. This process is very improtant in maintaining the stability in the ecosystem and for the continuation of life on earth.

2. The hen, sits on the egg to prouds sufficient warmth to the eggs for the development of the embryo into the chicks. The embryo normally take 3 weeks to develop into complete chick.

3. Metamorphosis is a type of animal development from one stage to another. However, unlike other types of development, the change is relatively fast. The animals body structure is significantly different from how its was in the previous stage. This is why there are no mammals which go through metamorphosis.

4. Some couples undergo in vitro fertilisation when male partner has - low sperm counts and female suffers from polycystic ovary syndrome, etc.

5. The umbilical cord (also called birth cord) attaches the placenta to the foetus. It is made up of three blood vessels: two smaller arteries (which carry blood to the placenta) and a larger vein (which returns blood to the foetus). It can grow to be 60 cm long, allowing the baby enough cord to safely move around without causing damage to the cord or the placenta. Umbilical cord development begins around the fifth week of the embryonic period of foetal development. The umbilical cord is derived from the yolk sac and allantois (which, in turn, were derived from the same zygote that the foetus develops from) and replaces the yolk sac as the foetus' source of nutrients. Umbilical cord blood contains stem cells that can be used to treat some immune disorders and cancers, so it is sometimes collected after the cord has been cut from the new born baby. Due to all these reasons umbilical cord is called the lifeline of the foetus.

6. If more than one sperm fuses - the condition called polyspermy is occured.

7. The fertilized egg (zygote) begin to develop into a hollow ball of cells called blastocysts.

8. Offspring produced from sexual reproduction shows more variation because sexual reproduction taken place between male and female of the same species and the genetic material will come from the both individual in the form of male and female gametes and there is a genetic recombination.

9. The female frogs (or female fish) lay hundred of eggs becasuse there are fewer chances of surviving in that environment. So from 100 even if 5 - 10 survive, their species will survive.

HOTS Questions

1. Test tube baby is a baby conceived through in vitro fertilization (IVF). On July 25, 1978, Louise Joy Brown, the world's first successful "test-tube" baby was born in Great Britain. Louise Brown was born as a result of natural cycle where no stimulation was made. Robert G. Edwards, the physiologist who developed the treatment, was awarded the Nobel Prize in Physiology or Medicine in 2010.

2. Dogs produce more than one egg at a time, hence more puppies are born to them at the same time whereas cows usually produce one egg at a time therefore produce one baby.

3. Most of the twins are similar because they share identical genes, who share half their DNA. Twins may be identical or non-identical. Identical twins arise when "one" egg is fertilized and the resulting embryo then splits to become two embryos, they contain the same genetic information and so develop in the same way. The same is not true for non-identical twins, in this case the ovaries release two eggs and both are fertilized and the pregnancy proceeds as normal, only there are two embryos instead of one, both embryos have their own different genetic material. Identical twins are genetically identical but this does not mean they will always look "exactly" the same, as they grow their environment, diet and physical activities will determine what they look like, for instance if one twin over eats they will put on weight, whereas if the other does not they will remain a healthy size. Many things determine what people look like not just genetic material.

4. The identical twins are produced when the embryo splits into two in the early stages of its development. This produces two identical children of the same sex. Some identical twins look so alike that they can only be differentiated by their finger prints. Only one in 83 pregnancies results in twins.

   Non-identical twins are produced when the two eggs are released at the same time and both are fertilized. They can be of same sex or different sex.

5. The sex determination of foetus can be done by the process called sonography. Sonography, also called ultrasound, is cyclic sound pressure with a frequency greater than the upper limit of human hearing. This limit varies from person to person, it is approximately 20 kilohertz in healthy, young adult. The production of sound is used in many different fields, typically to penetrate a medium and measure the reflection signature or supply focussed energy. The reflection signature can reveal details about the inner structure of the medium.

6. Leech has both male and female reproductive organ. It produces both testes and ovaries respectively. Leech reproduces by reciprocal fertilization and sperm transfer occurs during copulation. Leech use a organ called clitellum to hold their eggs and secrete the cocoon.

7. Parental care is the process of caring for child from infancy to childhood.

   Parental care mostly persists in amphibians, reptiles birds and fishes.

   Parental care is of 2 types.

   (i) Internal parental care

   (ii) External parental care

   In most of the egg laying organisms, the females give birth to eggs and male looks after the eggs. The parental care typically involves guarding the eggs from predators, fanning the eggs with increase oxygen supply and clearing the eggs to eliminate fungus. Reptiles like crocodile, turtles build nest for caring their child.

8. A low ambient temperature is essential for normal spermatogenesis (formation of sperms). Testicular temperature needs to be around 47°C cooler than core body temperature. This is why the testes are designed to drop out of the abdomen into the scrotal sac. Three mechanisms keep the scrotum cooler than the rest of the body are:

   1. Scrotal skin is thin, so the testes easily lose heat into the surrounding environment.

   2. Air circulating around the scrotum can cool the skin.

   3. The arteries bringing blood into the scrotum run alongside the veins taking blood away to form a sophisticated heat-exchange mechanism. Rather like a hot and cold water pipe running together, the hot arterial blood (coming from the abdomen) loses heat to the cooler venous blood (coming away from the testes), so blood is already partly cooled before entering the scrotum.

      Even if the testes heat up by as little as 2°C, sperm formation is adversely affected. Sperm count will drop, the number of normal sperm will fall and the number of abnormal sperm will increase.

9. An ovum allows the entry of only one sperm at a time because ovum has a layer of zona pellucida around itself. When a sperm enters the ovum, the cortical granules present in the ovum, causes the thickening of the zona pellucida. This prevents the entry of other sperms in the ovum and only one sperm is able to fertilize the egg.

10. Amniocentesis was developed by Richard Dedrick and can be used for prenatal sex discernment. Amniocentesis (also referred to as amniotic fluid test or AFT) is a medical procedure which is used in prenatal diagnosis of chromosomal abnormalities and foetal infections. It is also used for sex determination in which a small amount of amniotic fluid, which contains foetal tissues, is sampled from the amniotic sac surrounding a developing foetus, and the foetal DNA is examined for genetic abnormalities, like Down syndrome. Amniocentesis can diagnose these problems in the womb. Amniocentesis is usually done when a woman is between 16 and 22 weeks pregnant. As girl child was never accepted in many families, when a women got pregnant her family got amniocentesis done by which they could find the gender of the foetus and if the foetus was a girl the baby would be aborted. Seeing this reason amniocentesis is banned in India.

Master NCERT (Text-book & Exemplar)

Text-book Exercise

1. (a) Reproduction is necessary for the existence and maintainence of a species.

   (b) It is responsile for the continuation of similar kinds of individuals, generation after generation.

2. Male reproductive organs (testes) produce sperms (male gametes) while the female reproductive organs (ovary) produces eggs. Human beings reproduce by sexual process produce ova (female gametes). The sperms are released inside female bodies where they fuse with ovum and form zygote. Since this process takes place within the female body, it is called internal fertilization. The single celled zygote begins to develop into an embryo which further multiples into many cells and develops into a small baby.

3. (a) (i)   in female body.

   (b) (ii) metamorphosis.

   (c) (iii) One (diploid nuclei).

4. (a) False   (b) True   (c) True   (d) False

   (e) True   (f) False   (g) False   (h) True

   (i) True   (j) False

5.

Zygote	Embryo
Zygote is a single cell.	Embryo is multi-cellular.
No body parts.	Has well defined limbs and other body parts.
It is formed after fertilization when sperm fuses with ovum.	Embryo formation is a post fertilization process. The zygote multiples into multi-cellular body called embryo which ultimately gives rise to the baby.

6. Asexual reproduction is a mode of reproduction involving single parent to produce offspring. Thus, the offsprings produced are exact copies of their parents.

   It is generally observed in very small sized organisms for eg. *Amoeba*, *Hydra*. Binary fission, budding, fragmentation etc. are the examples of asexual reproduction.

   1. **Budding:** In this a small outgrowth starts bulging out from the parent body. Slowly it grows and detaches from the parents and finally develops into a separate individual. Examples: *Hydra*, yeast.

2. **Binary Fission:** It is a type of asexual reproduction in which the parent cell divides into two halves. Organisms that reproduce through binary fission are bacteria and *Amoeba*.

7. The embryo gets embedded in the walls of the uterus. Once attached to uterus the embryo, gradually develops various body parts such as hands, legs, head, eyes, etc.

8. Metamorphosis is a biological process of transformation of a larva into an adult. It involves sudden and abrupt changes in the body structure of the animal due to cell growth and differentiation. It is generally observed in amphibians (e.g. frogs) and insects (e.g. butterflies) etc.

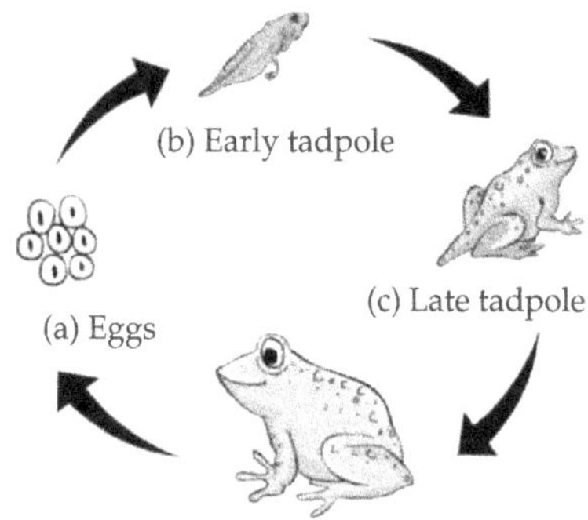

The life cycle of a frog has three life stages.

Egg >>>>> Tadpole >>>> Adult

1. **Eggs:** Eggs are the result of external fertilization and transform into fish like tadpoles.
2. **Tadpoles :** Tadpole has gills, small mouth and fish like tail to swim inside lakes and ponds. It is herbivorous and eats leaves.
3. **Frog:** Tadpoles grows and transform into a small frog which is amphibian by nature, respires though gills and skin and eats insects.

9.

Internal Fertilization	External Fertilization
Fusion of male and female gametes inside the female body.	Fusion of male and female gametes outside the female body.
High chances of survival of offspring, so less number of ova/eggs are produced. For e.g. Human Cows, Hens, Human beings.	Large number of eggs are produced because of low chances of survival. Examples: Fish, frog, starfish.

10.

<table>
<tr><td>¹F</td><td>E</td><td>R</td><td>²T</td><td>I</td><td>L</td><td>I</td><td>³Z</td><td>A</td><td>T</td><td>I</td><td>⁴O</td><td>N</td><td></td><td></td><td></td></tr>
<tr><td></td><td></td><td></td><td>E</td><td></td><td></td><td></td><td>Y</td><td></td><td></td><td></td><td>V</td><td></td><td></td><td></td><td></td></tr>
<tr><td></td><td></td><td></td><td>S</td><td></td><td></td><td></td><td>G</td><td></td><td></td><td></td><td>I</td><td></td><td></td><td>⁵B</td><td></td></tr>
<tr><td></td><td></td><td></td><td>T</td><td></td><td></td><td></td><td>O</td><td></td><td></td><td></td><td>P</td><td></td><td></td><td>I</td><td></td></tr>
<tr><td></td><td></td><td></td><td>I</td><td></td><td>⁶I</td><td>N</td><td>T</td><td>E</td><td>R</td><td>N</td><td>A</td><td>L</td><td></td><td>N</td><td></td></tr>
<tr><td>⁷B</td><td>U</td><td>D</td><td>S</td><td></td><td></td><td></td><td>E</td><td></td><td></td><td></td><td>R</td><td></td><td></td><td>A</td><td></td></tr>
<tr><td></td><td></td><td></td><td></td><td></td><td></td><td></td><td></td><td></td><td></td><td></td><td>⁸O</td><td>V</td><td>A</td><td>R</td><td>Y</td></tr>
<tr><td></td><td></td><td></td><td></td><td></td><td></td><td></td><td></td><td></td><td></td><td></td><td>U</td><td></td><td></td><td>Y</td><td></td></tr>
<tr><td></td><td></td><td></td><td></td><td></td><td></td><td></td><td></td><td></td><td></td><td></td><td>S</td><td></td><td></td><td></td><td></td></tr>
</table>

1. It ensures the continuation of species generation after generation.
2. Dogs do not lay eggs.
3. A layer of jelly covers the eggs of frog and provides protection.
4. In human beings, body parts of an adult are present from the time of birth itself. Whereas, in metamorphosis, the parts of the adult are different from those at the time of birth.
5. Although mother gives birth to child, fertilisatoin involves two gametes, one from the mother and the other from father. The zygote, therefore has both father and mother's contribution. Since the zygote develops into the baby it has characters of both parents.
6. Hydra reproduces by budding where an outgrowth arises from the parent and develops into a new individual. Amoeba reproduces by binary fission in which the division of nucleus is followed by division of the cell resulting in two individuals.
7. Female fish releases eggs into water and male fish releases sperms. Sperms swim randomly in water and comes in contact with the eggs. The nucleus of the sperm moves into the egg and fuses with it. Since fertilisaiton occurs in water, outside the female body, it is external fertilisation.
8. Hens are oviparous in which internal fertilisation takes place. The fertilised egg develops into an embryo inside the body. However, the development of chick from the embryo takes place outside the body.

   Frogs are oviparous in which both fertilisation and development of zygote to embryo and young ones occurs outside the body.

9. (i) (a) Embedding of the embryo in the uterus.
   (b) Fertilisation.
   (c) Zygote formation and development of an embryo from the zygote.
   (d) Zygote showing fusion of nuclei.
   (ii) The correct sequence is
   c, b, d, a
   (iii) Zygote formation
   The sperm and the egg nuclei fuses to form a single nucleus resulting in the fomation of a fertilised egg or zygote.
   (Note: One step is explained as an example. Students may explain any other step.)

Exercise 3   Foundation Builder

1. (c) Leech is a hermaphrodite. A hermaphrodite is an organism that has reproductive organs normally associated with both male and female sexes.
2. (c) Testosterone is a steroid hormone, secreted primarily by the testicles of males and the ovaries of females, although small amounts are also

secreted by the adrenal glands. It is the principal male sex hormone. In men, testosterone plays a key role in the development of male reproductive tissues such as the testis and prostate as well as promoting secondary sexual characteristics such as increased muscle, bone mass, and the growth of body hair.

3. (b) Sperm is a single celled gamete. It is smaller, usually motile male reproductive cell of most organisms that reproduce sexually. Sperm cells are haploid -they have half the number of chromosomes as the other cells in the organism's body). In male animals, sperms are normally produced by the testes in extremely large numbers in order to increase the chances of fertilizing an egg.

4. (b) Testes produces male gamete called sperm. For more refer answer 3.

5. (c) Parthenogenesis is a type of asexual reproduction in which a female gamete or egg cell develops into an individual without fertilization. Animals including most kinds of wasps, bees, and ants that have no sex chromosomes reproduce by this process.

6. (c) Urethra is not a part of female reproductive system. It is a tube that leads from the bladder and transports and discharges urine outside the body. In males, the urethra travels through the penis and carries semen as well as urine. In females, the urethra is shorter than in the male, and it emerges above the vaginal opening.

7. (b) Each sperm cell has three parts: a head, middle piece, and tail. An acrosome at the head tip produces enzymes that helps penetrate the female ovum (egg). During conception, chromosomes (genetic material) in the nucleus (cell control centre) join with chromosomes in the ovum. The middle piece contains mitochondria which provide energy for the sperm. The mitochondria are tightly spiralled around the axial filaments (contractile portion) of the flagellum (tail). Centrioles form the tail, which moves the sperm toward the ovum.

8. (c) The genetic information is carried by head part of the sperm for more refer answer 7.

9. (a) An ovary is large due to presence of yolk. Yolk is a yellow, usually spherical portion of an egg of a bird or reptile, surrounded by the albumen and serving as nutriment for the developing young.

10. (b) Estrogens are hormones that are important for sexual and reproductive development, mainly in women. They are also referred to as female sex hormones. In women, estrogen is produced mainly in the ovaries, but it is also produced by fat cells and the adrenal gland. Estrogen is involved in the onset of puberty, playing a role in the development of secondary sex characteristics, such as breasts, and pubic and armpit hair.

11. (d) Another name of oviduct is fallopian tube. The fallopian tubes, also known as the uterine tubes, are a pair of 4-inch (10 cm) long narrow tubes connecting the ovaries to the uterus. Ova (egg cells) are carried to the uterus through the fallopian tubes following ovulation. The ova may also be fertilized while in the fallopian tubes if sperm is present following sexual intercourse.

12. (a) The umbilical cord connects a baby in the womb to its mother. It runs from an opening in baby's stomach to the placenta in the womb. The average cord is about 50cm (20 inches) long.

13. (a) Unisexual animals are those organism or species which are capable of producing only male or female gametes (sex cells) but never both.

14. (d) Vasectomy is a surgical procedure for male sterilization and/or permanent birth control. During the procedure, the male vasa deferentia are severed and then tied/sealed in a manner so as to prevent sperm from entering into the seminal stream (ejaculate) and thereby prevent fertilization from occurring.

15. (b) Refer answer 11.

16. (a) In frog, fertilization is external in water. In almost all frogs, egg fertilization happens outside the female's body instead of inside. The female releases her eggs and the male releases his sperm at the same time. In order to make sure that the sperm reaches the eggs, the male and female get into a mating posture called amplexus.

17. (a) The number of chromosomes is 8.

18. (a) Vas deferens connects the epididymis to the seminal vesicles. The vas deferens is a muscular tube that passes upward alongside the testicles and transports the sperm-containing fluid called semen. The epididymis is a set of coiled tubes (one for each testicle) that connects to the vas deferens.

19. (b) After sperms move through the vas deferens they enter the urethra.

20. (c) Sperm tail consists of flagellum. Tail helps in swimming. This ability to swim is essential for the male fertility as the sperm has to swim up the vaginal canal, cervix, and uterine canal to reach the ovum.

21. (b) Zygote is a fertilized egg. It is the cell produced by the union of two gametes, before it undergoes cleavage.

22. (c) Mature human sperm cell contains 23 chromosomes.

23. (c)   24. (b)

25. (c) The fertilized egg or zygote gets implanted in the uterus after the process of fertilization.

26. (b) When Amoeba undergoes fission nucleus divides first and then the cytoplasm.

27. (c)

28. (a) There is no bud on the parent cell.

29. (d) It is a connecting link between mother and developing foetus, which provides nutrients and removes the waste from baby's blood.

30. (b)

31. (d) The correct route for passage of sperms is –
Testes → Vasdeferens → Urethra → Penis
Sperms are formed within testes and are ejaculated through penis into female reproductive tract vagina.

Match the following

32. (a)

Exercise 4   ★   Foundation Builder +

1. (b) Cloning is a technique by which genetically same individuals can be produced without including any sexual reproduction eg. Dolly sheep.

The term *clone* is derived from *Klon*, the *Greek* word for "twig", refering to the process, whereby a new plant can be created from a twig.

2. (d) The axillary buds of the potato tuber are called "eyes" in common language. They are found at the nodes of the stem tuber.

3. (c) Embryo sac is a female gametophyte which contains the egg apparatus.

4. (a) Spores are formed in lower plants by mitotic division and they may be diploid but gametes are always made by meiosis & they are always haploid.

5. (a) Urethra is a tube that connects the urinary bladder to the genitals for the removal of fluids from the body. The urethra travels through the penis, and carries semen as well as urine.

6. (c) In testis, the immature male germ cells or spermatogonia (2n) multiply by mitotic division and increase in number. Some spermatogonia (2n) known as primary spermatocytes divide by meiotic division to form secondary spermatocytes (n). The secondary spermatocytes undergo second meiotic division to produce spermatid which are transformed into spermatozoa (sperms) by the process called spermiogenesis.

7. (b) The part of fallopian tube closest to the ovary is infundibulum. Infundibulum possess finger-like projections called fimbriae that help in collection of ovum after ovulation. It leads to wider part of oviduct called ampulla. The last part of oviduct is isthmus that has a narrow lumen and joins the uterus.

8. (a) After first meiotic division primary spermatocyte (diploid) gives rise to two secondary spermatocytes (haploid).

9. (b) Human female has X X chromosomes. When eggs formed each egg carries 22 autosomes and one X chromosome. In human male each sperm carries 22 autosomes and either X or Y-chromosomes.

10. (c) The correct option is (c) because placenta secretes human chorionic gonadotropin (hCG). Zona pellucida is a primary egg membrane secreted by the secondary oocyte. The secretions of bulbourethral glands help in lubrication of the penis Leydig cells synthesise and secrete testicular hormones called androgens.

11. (d) In proliferative phase, the follicles start developing, called follicular phase. Secretory phase is also called as luteal phase mainly controlled by progesterone secreted by corpus luteum. Menstruation involves breakdown of overgrown endometrial lining.

Think Out of the Box

Case Study-1

1. Internal fertilization.

2. Polyspermy

3. zygote

Case Study-2

1. Dolly was the first mammal to be cloned from an adult cell. It was a proof that specialised cells can be used to produce clones of animals.

2. Human clearing violates personal identity freedom, individuality and uniqueness. Therefore, it is unethical.

6 Reaching the Age of Adolescence

Build A Strong Foundation

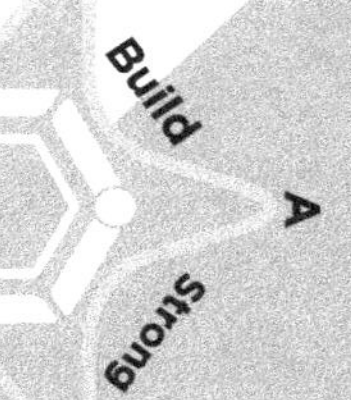

CONCEPT MAP

ADOLESCENCE : Period or stage of growing to maturity

PUBERTY : The process of physical changes by which a child becomes an adult.

CHANGES AT PUBERTY

- **Increase in height**
- **Change in Body shape**
- **Voice change**
- **Increased activity of sweat and sebaceous glands.**
- **Development of sex organs and secondary sexual characters.**
- **Reaching mental, intellectual and emotional maturity**

HUMAN ENDOCRINE SYSTEM

- **PITUITARY** – Influences the secretion of other glands.
- **THYROID** – Secrete thyroxine and calcitonin
- **PARATHYROID** – Regulate level of calcium by PTH
- **ADRENAL** – Secrete stress hormone
- **OVARY** – Secrete estrogen and progesterone
- **TESTES** – Secrete Testosterone

REPRODUCTIVE HEALTH : For rapid mental and physical growth during adolescence, individual needs to have a balanced diet, maintain personal hygiene, do regular exercise and say not to drugs.

ADOLESCENCE AND PUBERTY

Adolescence

Adolescence is a period or stage of growing to maturity. It occurs after childhood and before adulthood. It is characterized by a tremendous pace in growth and change that is second only to that of infancy. Growing up is a natural and ongoing process in one's life & growth begins from the day one is born. During adolescence, a young person begins to explore their sexuality making access to sexual and reproductive health education and services, a necessity for their well-being.

You must have seen a sudden increase in height in some of the boys or girls of your class. **OR** *You must have seen hairy line above the lips in boys? Have you ever wondered, what are these changes all about?*

These changes are all about due to phase of adolescence. Boys and girls are growing up during this phase. Upon crossing the age of 10 or 11, there is a sudden spurt in growth that becomes noticeable. Hence, the period of life, when the body undergoes certain noticeable changes, leading to reproductive maturity is called **adolescence**. It begins after the age of 11 and lasts upto 18 to 19 years of age. Adolescents are also called as "**teenagers**" because the period covers the teens (13 to 18 or 19 years of age). The human body undergoes several changes during adolescence. These changes mark the onset of *puberty*.

For girls, puberty generally begins sometimes between ages 9-13 and for boys between ages 10-15!!

☞ **Is puberty and adolescence the same thing?**

SOLUTION :

No. Puberty is the start of the time when a boy is biologically ready to become a father and a girl is biologically ready to become a mother. It basically refers to the bodily changes of sexual maturation during adolescence.

Puberty

Puberty is the process of physical changes by which a child's body becomes an adult and capable of reproduction. It occurs at about age 12 in girls and age 14 in boys. Puberty is characterized by maturing of the genital organs, development of secondary sex characteristics in boys, and in girls, onset of menstruation. Both sexes experience a swift increase in body size and changes in body shape and composition. Puberty marks the beginning of adolescence and ends when an adolescent reaches reproductive maturity.

Puberty attained before the normal age is called precocious puberty. Early puberty may result in short heighted female.

Changes at Puberty

Puberty involves all sorts of big and small changes to the body and brain. During puberty, body grows faster than at any other time in your life, except for when you were a baby.

The various changes that take place in adolescents during puberty are - increase in height, change in body shape, voice change increased activity of sweat and sebaceous glands, development of sex organs and reaching mental, intellectual and emotional maturity. Let us discuss each in detail.

1. Increase in Height

Increase in height is the most visible change during puberty. During this time, the long bones of the arms and the legs elongate and make a person tall. Epiphysis is a vital growth area near the end of a long bone, which later fuses with the main bone through ossification. Epiphyseal plates serve as the site of bone growth/elongation. Both boys & girls reach their maximum height by the time they reach the age of 18. The growth rate varies from individual to individual. *When you go through puberty, it might seem like your sleeves are always getting shorter and your pants are creeping up your legs. Why is it happening?* It is because your body is going through a growth spurt that lasts for about 2 to 3 years.

The other parts of body, especially feet, are growing faster than everything else. During adolescence, to ensure healthy growth of bones, muscles and other parts of body, correct nutrition is required.

Initially, girls grow faster than boys but by about 18 years of age, both reach their maximum height. Some children grow suddenly at puberty and then slow down, while some grow gradually.

Have you ever thought why do we stop growing after a period?

We stop growing after a period of certain age because we are genetically programmed to do so. Genes inherited from our parents are responsible for growth and development. Our genes start working at the moment of conception when a single cell becomes a complex organism in which billions of cells work in concert. Once we are born, we continue to grow and develop until the completion of puberty. At this point, our genetic program tells us to stop growing. The complex interaction of genes, nutrients and hormones cause bone cells to proliferate at the growth plate of long bones. The key hormones in this process are growth hormone, thyroxine, androgens and estrogen. They are secreted by the pituitary, thyroid and reproductive glands respectively. At the completion of puberty, the reproductive glands in both males and females increase the production of the hormone estrogen. It is the high concentration of estrogen in the blood that causes the growth plates of our bones to fuse. This fusion effectively closes the growth centres of long bones and renders them unable to respond to the hormones that initiate growth.

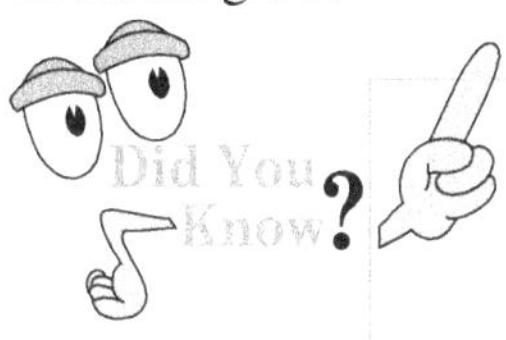

Growth spurt

Growth spurt is a period of rapid increase in growth or is a short burst of activity or something that happens in a hurry. When that growth spurt is at its peak, some kids grow 4 to more inches in a year. At the end of your growth spurt, you will reach your normal adult height or just about. The average growth spurts lasts 24–36 months.

We continue to grow, but only slightly after the age of 25 and we reach our maximum height at about the age of 35 or 40. After that we shrink about half an inch every ten years. The reason for this is the drying up of the cartilages in our joints and in the spinal column as we get older.

☛ **Why the height of an individual is more or less similar to their mother or father or other family members?**

SOLUTION :

The height of an individual depends on the genes inherited from parents. Genes provide instructions for making proteins and proteins determine the structure and function of each cell in the body. Genes are responsible for all the characteristics one inherits. Although, genetic help determines character, environmental influence has a considerable impact on shaping an individuals physical appearance and personality. So really, the way one's body looks and functions is a combination of genes and environment.

How can we calculate the full height of an individual?

The full height of an individual can be calculated by using the following formula.

$$\frac{\text{Present height (cm)}}{\%\ \text{age of full height at this age}} \times 100$$

The given table gives the average rate of growth in height of boys and girls with age. The figures in columns 2 and 3, give the percentage of the height a person has reached at the age given in column 1. For example, by the age 14, a boy has reached 92% of his probable full height, while a girl has reached 98% of her full height. These figures are only representative and there may be individual variations. Use the table for your friends and work out how tall they are likely to be.

Age of years	% of full height	
	Boys	Girls
8	72	77
9	75	81
10	78	84
11	81	88
12	84	91
13	88	95
14	92	98
15	95	99
16	98	99.5
17	99	100
18	100	100

Example: A girl is 10 years old and 124 cm tall. Calculate her full height (using the above formula) at the end of her growth period.

2. Changes in Body Shape

Human body shape is a complex phenomenon. The general shape or figure of a person is defined mainly by the moulding of skeletal structures as well as the distribution of muscles and fat. During puberty, differentiation of the male and female body occurs for the purposes of reproduction. In adult humans, muscle mass may change due to exercise, and fat distribution may change due to hormone fluctuations. Inherited genes play a large part in the development of body shape. During puberty, the following changes occur in boys and girls, like

In boys -
(i)   The shoulders become broader.
(ii) The chest becomes wider.
(iii) The body becomes more muscular.

In girls-
(i)   The pelvic region widens.
(ii) Hips get broaden.
(iii) Breasts develop and increase in size. The mammary glands (milk secretion glands) develop inside the breasts.

3. Voice Changes

Both boys and girls experience voice change as they grow older. *A boy's voice may change from sounding like a little bird to sounding like somebody's dad! Why it is so ?* This is due to changes in larynx.

The larynx (also known as *voice box*) is a part of respiratory system that holds vocal cords. Larynx helps the individual to talk, sing, hum, yell, cough and make all sort of noises. During puberty larynx gets bigger. When a boy reaches puberty his body starts secreting a hormone called testosterone. This testosterone causes the boy's larynx to grow and his vocal cords to get longer and thicker. Vocal cords are thin muscles that stretch across the larynx like rubber bands.

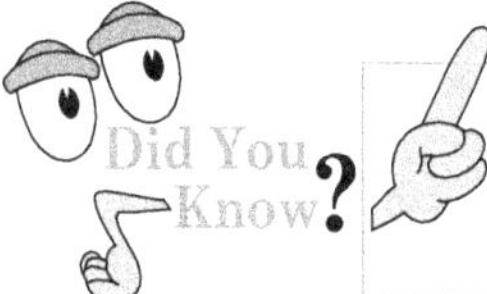

Larynx is also responsible for preventing food from entering the airway and controlling the airflow during breathing.

When you speak, air rushes from the lungs and makes vocal cords vibrate and produce the sound of your voice. Before you reach puberty, your larynx is small and your vocal cords are smaller and thinner. That is why your voice is higher than an adult's. As you go through puberty, the larynx gets bigger and the vocal cords get lengthened and thickened. This makes your voice deeper. As your body adjusts to this changing structure (larynx), your voice may 'crack' or 'break'. But this process lasts only for few months. Once the larynx has finished growing, your voice won't make those unpredictable noises. The growing voice box in boys can be seen as a protruding part of the throat called **Adam's apple**. When the larynx grows bigger, it tilts to a different angle and part of it sticks out inside the neck. It can be seen at the front of the throat.

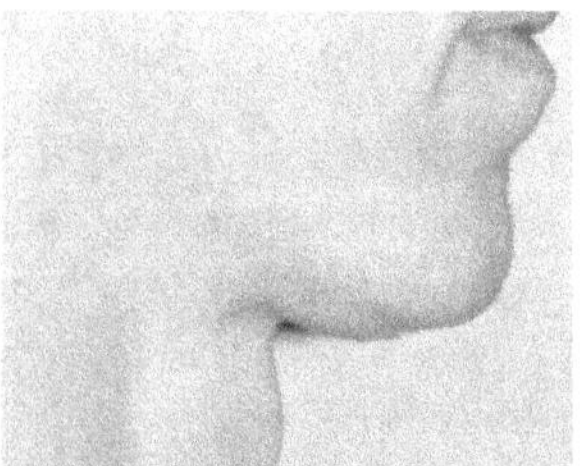
Fig.1: *Adam's apple in a grown-up boy.*

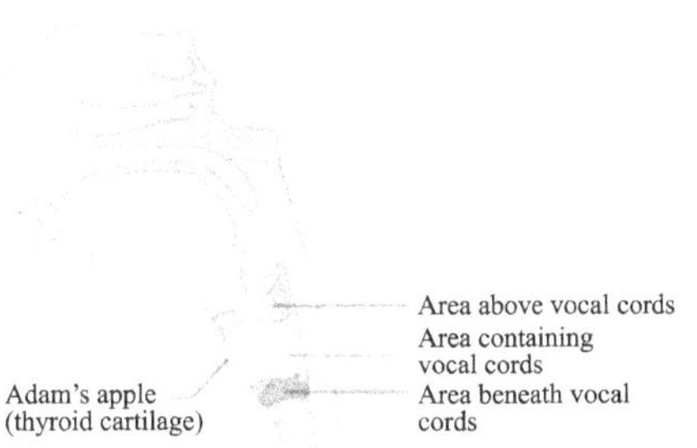

Fig.2: *Adam's apple*

For girls, the larynx also grows bigger but not as much as in boys. It means there is no Adam's apple in a women's neck. Generally, girls have a high pitched voice whereas the voice in boys, it is deep. Sometimes, the muscles of the growing voice box go out of control and voice becomes hoarse.

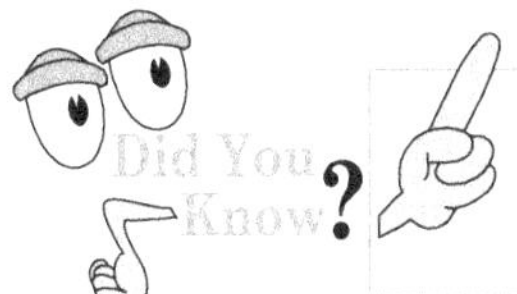

- *Adam's apple is the largest cartilage of the larynx and is named so because it looks like a small, rounded apple located in front of throat.*
- *The process of sound production in the larynx is known as phonation.*

Larynx

Larynx is a tube - shaped muscular and cartilaginous structure in the neck region between the pharynx (throat) and the trachea (breathing tube). The larynx houses the vocal cords and has cartilaginous skeleton and intrinsic and extrinsic muscles. Larynx consists of 3 main parts - supraglottis (the area above the vocal cords that contains the epiglottis cartilage); glottis (the area of the vocal cords); subglottis (the part below the vocal cords, containing the cricoid cartilage that continues down into the windpipe).

Larynx helps to carry out its primary functions, like

- voice production
- control of airflow (breathing)
- swallowing.

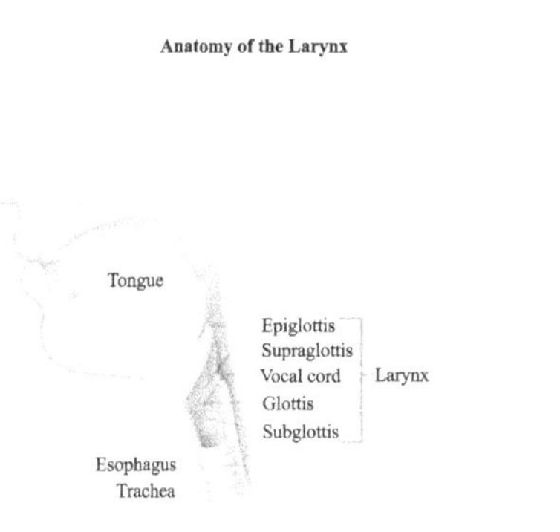

Fig.3: *Anatomy of larynx*

4. Increased Activity of Sweat and Sebaceous Gland

During puberty, the pubertal hormones stimulate the skin glands like sweat and sebaceous to become more active. During puberty sweat glands start producing more sweat. Sweat glands are used to regulate temperature and remove waste by secreting water, sodium salts, and nitrogenous waste (such as urea) onto the skin surface. The main electrolytes of sweat are sodium and chloride. The sweat is oily, cloudy, viscous, and odourless; it gains odour upon decomposition by bacteria.

Another thing that comes with puberty is acne. The increased secretion of sebum from sebaceous glands makes the skin oilier. Pimples usually start showing up and you may get them through out the teenage years. To help control pimples, wash your face twice a day with warm water and a mild soap or cleanser. Don't squeeze, pick, or pop your pimples.

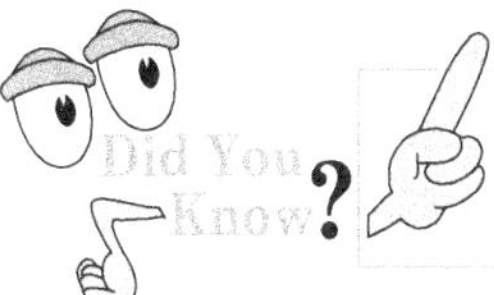

Sweat itself has no smell. The stinky smell of sweat arises when the sweat mixes with the bacteria that are present on our skin.

5. Development of Sex Organs

Though reproductive organs are present in infant stage, but they reach maturity and complete development during puberty. During this period the male sex organs like testes and penis develop completely. Also, the testes begin to produce sperm. In girls, the ovaries enlarge and eggs begin to mature. Also, ovaries start releasing matured eggs.

6. Reaching Mental, Intellectual and Emotional Maturity

During puberty, a child goes through many mental and emotional changes. You might feel confused or have strong emotions that you have never had before. You may feel overly sensitive or become upset easily. Some kids lose their tempers more often and get angry with their friends and families.

Intellectual development also occurs during adolescence to transform the individual from a child to adult. In fact, it is the time in one's life when the brain has the greatest capacity for learning. Hence during puberty :-

(i) There is mental growth of an individual. Individual is able to think in a more flexible and a logical way. The ability to see other's point of view, exploring ideas, developing concepts and memory skills improve.

(ii) There is an emotional growth. The individual is happy at one moment and the very next moment their mood changes. Interest in the opposite sex and desire for closeness arises.

(iii) There is a social growth. It includes developing a personal identity, accepting oneself, developing independence and preparing for a career. Sometimes, it is hard to deal with all these new emotions. But it is necessary for you to know that while your body is adjusting to the new hormones, so is your mind.

7. Secondary Sexual Characters

Secondary sexual characters are those features that help to distinguish the male from the female. In girls, during puberty, breasts begin to develop and in boys, facial hair like moustaches and beard begins to grow. As these features are used to distinguish male and female, hence they are called as *secondary sexual characters*.

Secondary sexual characteristics that develop in girls during puberty are –

(i) Development of breasts and increase in their size.
(ii) Development of hair under armpits and in the pubic region.
(iii) Widening of pelvic region and broadening of hips.
(iv) Start of menstrual cycle. (Discussed later).

Secondary sexual characteristics that develop in boys during puberty are –

(i) Growth of facial hair (beard and moustaches).
(ii) Voice becomes deeper.
(iii) Muscles develop and shoulders become broad.
(iv) Hair develop under the armpits, under chest and in the pubic region.
(v) Increase in weight.

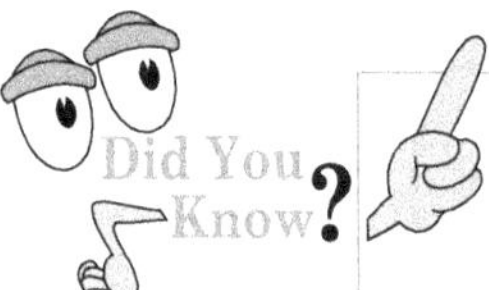

Laughter increases the amount of natural killer cells which destroys tumours and viruses, lowers blood pressure and increases oxygen in the blood.

But have you ever thought *what initiates changes at puberty?* The changes that occur at puberty or adolescence are controlled by hormones.

Hormones are chemical substances produced in the body that control and regulate the activity of certain cells or organs. They are secreted by endocrine glands (ductless) of endocrine system directly into the bloodstream. Each hormone has a definite function and acts on a particular tissue. Once a hormone is secreted, it travels through the bloodstream to the cells designed to receive its message. These cells are called **target cells**. The changes at puberty in males and females are triggered by secretion of male and female sex hormones from testes and ovaries respectively. Male hormone is called **testosterone** and female hormone is called **estrogen**. Testosterone and estrogen released by these glands is again released into the blood and reaches the target sites to trigger various body changes such as growth of facial/pubic hair and growth of breasts and mammary (milk producing) glands.

Hormones are primarily controlled by endocrine system. Endocrine system operates as a chemical communication system. They work closely with the nervous system in regulating certain activities of the body.

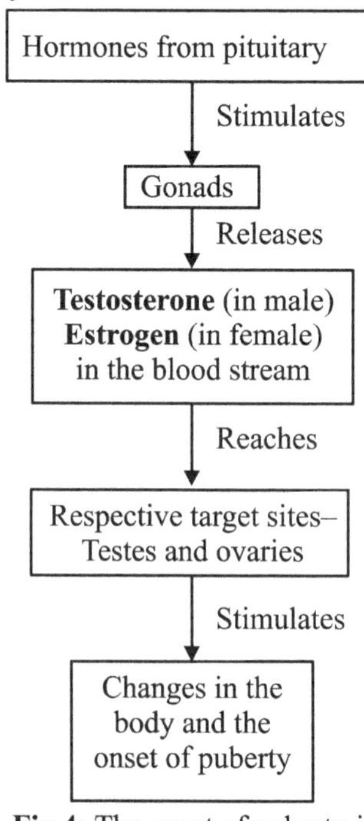

Fig.4: The onset of puberty is controlled by hormones.

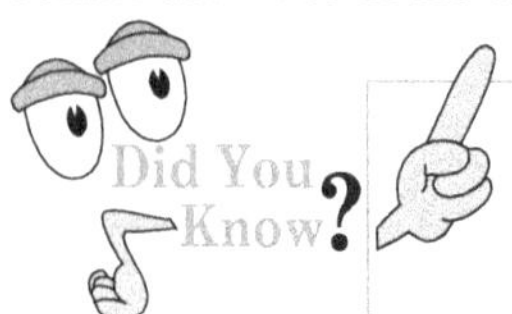

- *In 1902, Bayliss and sterling discovered first hormone called secretin.*
- *Types of hormones on the basis of their chemical composition:*
  - *Amine (Thyroxine, epinephrine, norepinephrine)*
  - *Steroids (Hormones of adrenal cortex, testis and ovaries)*
  - *Proteinaceous and peptides hormones (Hormones of hypothalamus, pancreas and pituitary)*

☛ **Why don't women have beards?**

SOLUTION :

The various glands and hormones in the bodies of female deliberately act to prevent the growth of beards in women. The female sex hormone estrogen works in such a way that growth of hair on the head is developed while the growth of beard and body hair is inhibited.

The male sex hormone, testosterone, on the other hand, works in such a way that beard and body hair are developed while the growth of hair on the head is inhibited or slowed down in the development.

GLANDS

Glands are specialized organ in an animal's body that synthesize a substance such as hormones that are released into the bloodstream (called endocrine gland) or into cavities inside the body or its outer surface (called exocrine gland).

Types of glands

Exocrine glands

The glands that release their secretions with the help of ducts at specific site are called **exocrine glands**. For example, the salivary gland secretes saliva in the mouth through salivary duct. Similarly, digestive glands four their secretions in the digestive tract with the help of ducts. Sweat gland is also an example of exocrine gland.

Endocrine glands

The glands that pour their secretions directly into the blood are called **endocrine glands**. Endocrine glands are also called ductless glands as they do not have ducts. The secretions reach their target through blood. The major endocrine glands that make up the human endocrine system are – pituitary gland, hypothalamus, thyroid glands, parathyroid glands, adrenal glands, pineal body and reproductive glands (that include testes in male and ovaries in female).

Heterocrine glands

Heterocrine glands are partly exocrine with duct and partly endocrine without duct. Exocrine part releases secretion in duct while endocrine part releases hormones in blood.

For example, pancreas and gonads.

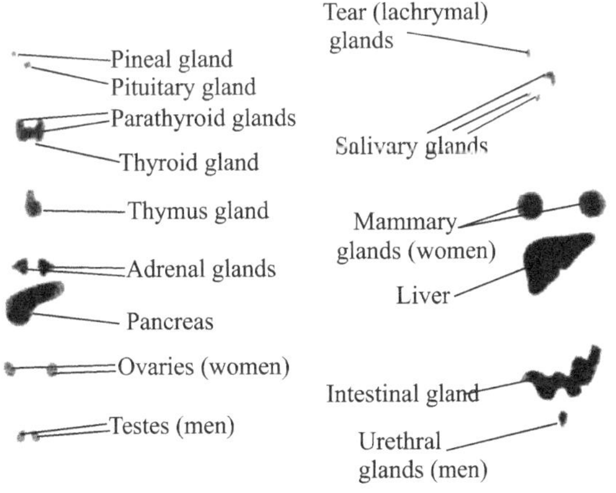

Fig. 5 : *Endocrine Glands*   **Fig. 6 :** *Exocrine Glands*

ROLE OF HORMONES IN INITIATING REPRODUCTIVE FUNCTION

Sex hormones control the onset of puberty and initiate the reproduction function. Body changes in male such as the growth of facial hair and cracking of voice, are initiated due to the secretion of testosterone. Body changes in females during puberty, such as breast development, are initiated by estrogen. During puberty, the testes begins to secrete the testosterone hormone. This hormones bring about the physical changes that make a boy look like an adult male. These changes are called male secondary sexual characteristics, which you have learnt in previous chapter. Similarly in girls, during puberty, the ovaries begin secreting the hormones called

estrogen and *progesterone*. These hormones develop female sexual features. The activity of testes and ovaries are under the control of hormones from another gland called the **master gland** or **pituitary gland**. This gland is located at the base of the brain. Pituitary gland is small (about 0.5 grams in weight) pea sized gland, present in brain. It secretes various hormones in blood which stimulate the target sites (testes and ovaries) to secrete their hormones. During puberty, the hypothalamus produces **gonadotropin-releasing hormone (GnRH)** which stimulates the anterior portion of the pituitary gland to produce **luteinizing hormone (LH)** and **follicle-stimulating hormone (FSH)**, these in turn induce cells of the ovary in girls and testis in boys to produce sex hormones that are necessary for ovulation and spermatogenesis and development of secondary sex characteristics.

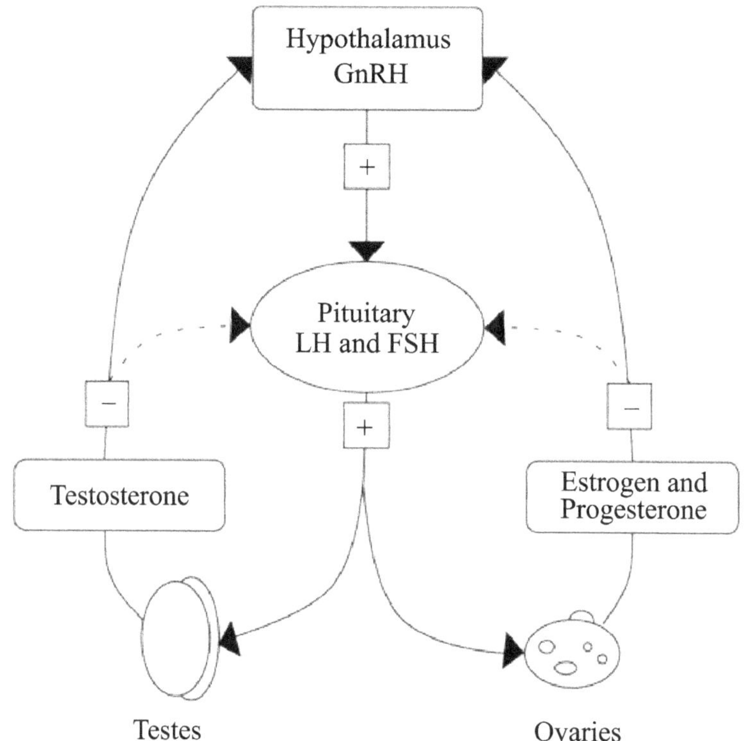

Fig.7: *Role of hormones on reproductive function*

REPRODUCTIVE PHASE OF LIFE IN HUMANS

The phase in individual's life during which there is production of gametes is called **reproductive phase**. In females, it is between 13 to 50 years and in males, it is from the age of 13, to life-long. The production of gametes starts earlier in females than in males. In females, the ova begins to mature with the onset of puberty. During this period, one ovum matures and is released by one of the ovaries once in about 28 days. The process of release of ovum is called **ovulation**. After ovulation, the egg lives for 24 hours. The wall of uterus passes through several phases that are controlled by two hormones, called estrogen and progesterone. The inner lining of uterus gets thickened and is supplied with blood from which growing embryo draws nutrition. This is a natural preparation to receive the egg in case it is fertilized and pregnancy occurs. If fertilization does not occur, the lining of uterus breaks down slowly and is released out in the form of blood and mucous along with the egg from the vagina. This loss of blood is called **menstruation**. Menstruation occurs once in about 28 - 30 days. The first menstrual flow begins at puberty and is called **menarche**. Around the age of 45 to 50 years, the menstrual cycle stops. The permanent stoppage of menstruation is called **menopause**. The menstrual cycle is controlled by a number of glands and a series of hormonal changes begin in the brain. A brain structure called the hypothalamus signals the pituitary gland to release hormones known as gonadotropins which prompt the ovaries to secrete the sex hormones, (estrogen and progesterone).

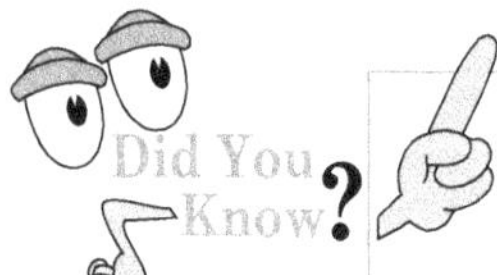

Periods (Menstrual cycle) usually come once in a month. But sometimes initially at the start of puberty it may become irregular and some girls may skip a month.

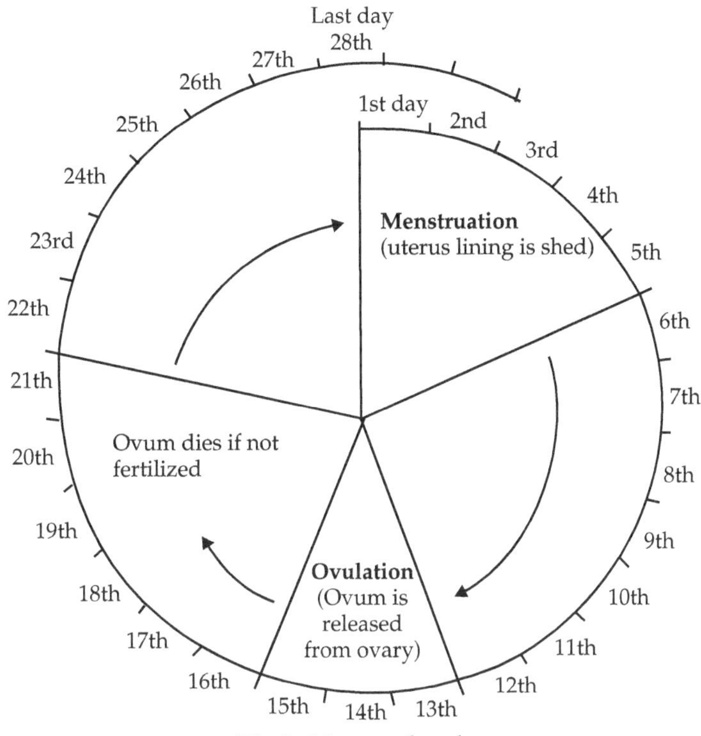

Fig.8: *Menstrual cycle*

CONNECTING TOPIC

Phases of the menstrual cycle

The follicular phase

The follicular phase is the time from the first day of menstruation until the moment of ovulation. During this phase, the pituitary gland releases a hormone which causes 10 and 20 follicles to develop within the ovary. These follicles bead on the surface of the ovary. Usually only one follicle will mature into an egg.

The growth of the follicles produces the hormone estrogen that causes the lining of the uterus (endometrium) become thick in preparation for the possible embedding of a fertilized egg.

Ovulation

Ovulation is the release of a mature egg from the ovary. During this phase, the pituitary gland increases production of a hormone (LH) which triggers the follicle and ovary to open up and release the mature egg. This occurs mid-way through the menstrual cycle, between days 12 and 16 for women with a 28 days cycle.

The luteal phase

The luteal phase is the time from ovulation until the first day of menstruation. During this phase, the follicle from which the mature egg was released transforms into a structure known as the **corpus luteum** and produces large amounts of the hormone progesterone as well as small amounts of estrogen. These hormones contribute to the further thickening and maintenance of the lining of the uterus in preparation for the embedding of a fertilized egg.

If fertilization of the egg does not occur, the corpus luteum dies and progesterone levels decline leading to the breakdown of the uterus lining, this shed through the vagina as a period (menstruation).

Menstruation

Menstruation occurs when the lining of the uterus breaksdown and flows from the body through the vagina. Menstruation generally lasts from 3 to 7 days. The length of a period can differ between women, and between cycles in individuals.

Important terms:

- Amenorrhea is the lack of a menstrual period.
- Dysmenorrhea is painful periods including severe cramps. Menstrual cramps in teens are caused by too much of a chemical called prostaglandin.

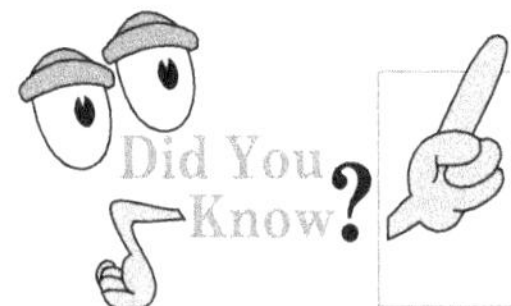

Many girls experience cramps before or during their periods (menstrual cycle). These cramps are caused by prostaglandins which is produced to make the muscles of the uterus contract. The constricting muscles help push the blood out through a girls vagina during her period.

SEX DETERMINATION – BOY OR GIRL

Sex determination is defined as the genetic mechanism by which sex is determined in all living organisms. *What determines whether the baby developing inside the mother's womb is a boy or a girl?* This is determined by a thread like structure called *chromosomes*. Chromosomes located inside the nucleus of zygote or fertilized egg carry heredity information in the form of **genes**. The chromosomes which carry genes for sex determination are called **sex chromosomes**. Sex chromosomes are also called **heterosomes or allosomes**. Human beings have 22 pairs of autosomes (chromosomes other than sex chromosomes) and one pair of sex chromosome. Chromosomes determine everything from hair colour and eye colour to sex. Whether you are a male or female depends on the presence or absence of certain chromosomes. There are two types of sex chromosomes- X and Y. Female cell contains two X chromosomes (XX) while male cells carry one X and one Y chromosomes (XY).

- If the sperm carrying X chromosome fertilizes the egg, it would be a girl, as the chromosome pair will be XX.
- If the sperm carrying Y chromosome fertilizes the egg, the baby will be a boy, as the chromosome pair will be XY.

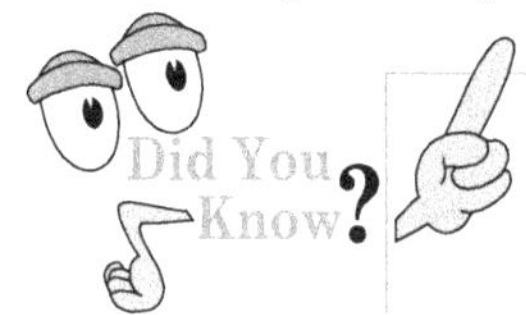

- *X chromosome was discovered by Henking (1891).*
- *Y chromosome was discovered by Stevens (1902).*
- *SRY gene (sex determining region): A gene for maleness found on the Y chromosome. It has a key role in development of the testes and determination of sex. The SRY gene provides instructions for making a transcription factor called the sex-determining region Y protein. A transcription factor is a protein that attaches (binds) to specific regions of DNA and helps control the activity of particular genes. The sex-determining region Y protein causes a foetus to develop as a male.*

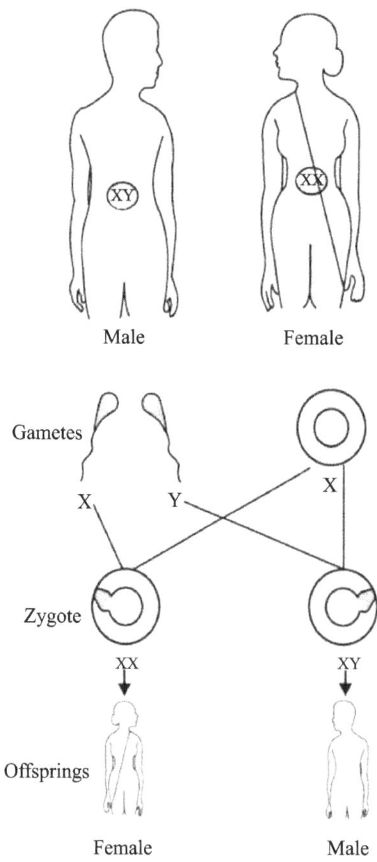

Fig.9: *Sex determination in humans*

Therefore, it is the Y chromosome that is essential for the development of the male reproductive organs, and with no Y chromosome, an embryo will develop into a female. This is because of the presence of the sex determining region of the Y chromosome, also known as the **SRY gene**.

Time to Check Your Knowledge

1. **The gender of the baby depends on the father's sperm and not on mother's egg cell. Many people blame the mother for the birth of a girl. Do you think it is scientifically true?**
2. **Is it possible to find out the sex of the baby while inside the mother's womb.**

SOLUTION :

1. No, this is not scientifically correct. Male gender is decided by the presence of Y chromosome. The sperm cell carrying either X or a Y chromosome determines the sex of the child because the egg cell from the mother (ovum) contains only X chromosomes.

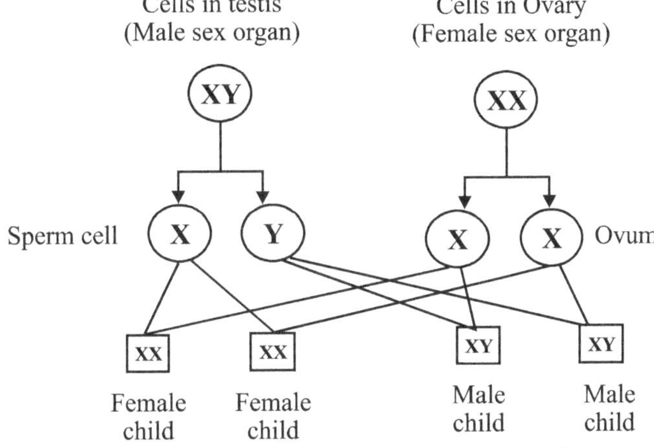

2. The sex of the child can be determined with the help of special techniques called sonography. Using the reflections of high-frequency sound waves to construct an image of a body organ (a sonogram) is called sonography. It is commonly used to observe foetal growth or study bodily organs. The process of killing foetus in mother's womb is called **abortion**. This killing of girl foetus is known as **female infanticide**.

HUMAN ENDOCRINE SYSTEM

Endocrine system is the system of glands (ductless) that produce endocrine secretions which help to integrate and control bodily metabolic activity. The secretions are called **hormones**. The endocrine system regulates development and growth (for example, puberty), metabolism, and sexual and reproductive processes. It includes the reproductive glands, adrenal glands, thyroid glands, hypothalamus, and pituitary glands. Although distinct from the nervous system, the endocrine system interacts with the nervous system through the hypothalamus, which regulates the pituitary gland. The nervous system and the endocrine system work together to help the body to function. The major glands that make up the human endocrine system are – pituitary, thyroid, adrenals, pancreas, the ovaries and the testes.

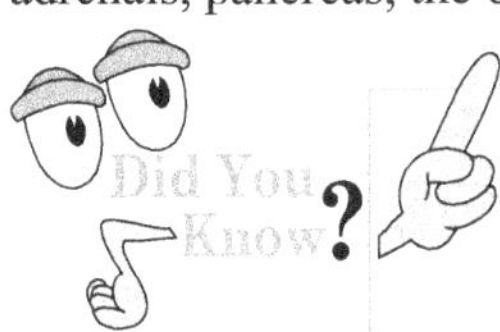

Did You Know?

The branch dealing with the study of endocrine glands and actions of thier hormones is called endocrinology.

How nervous system is different from endocrine system?

1. *Hormones are transported around (to their target organs) the body by the blood. Therefore, hormonal response are relatively slow as compared to the nervous responses.*
2. *Many hormonal responses (for example, growth) occur over relatively long period of time.*
3. *The main function of endocrine system is to maintain homeostasis within the body i.e. to keep the internal environment of body constant whereas the main function of nervous system is to receive and respond to stimulus.*
4. *Generally endocrine system is controlled by the nervous system through the hypothalamus mediated by pituitary gland.*

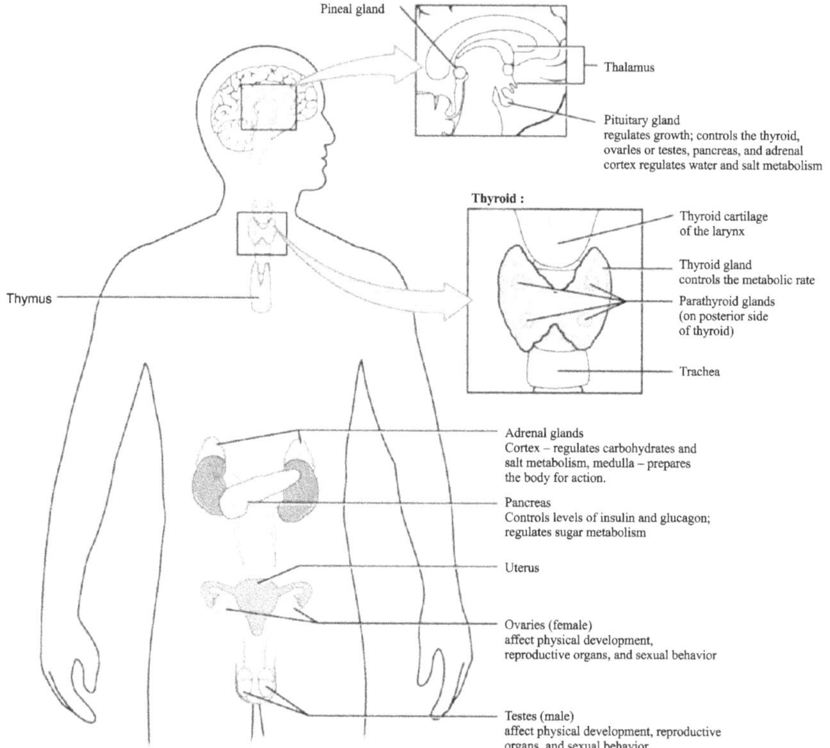

Fig. 10: *Human Endocrine System*

Hypothalamus

Hypothalamus is located in the basal part of forebrain and it regulates wide range of body functions. It contains neurosecretory cells that produces hormones. These hormones regulate the synthesis and secretion of pituitary gland. It is the main link between endocrine and nervous system.

Pituitary Gland

It is a small pea-shaped gland located at the base of the brain and is attached to hypothalamus by a infundibular stalk.

The pituitary gland is anatomically divided into an anterior pituitary and posterior pituitary gland.

The hormone secreted by pituitary gland influences the secretion of other glands. Therefore, they are known as **Trophic hormones**. Types of hormones secreted by pituitary glands are: thyroid stimulating hormone (TSH), luteinizing hormone (LH), follicle stimulating hormone (FSH), prolactin (PRL), growth hormone (GH), adrenocorticotropic hormone (ACTH), antidiuretic hormone (ADH)/vasopressin, and oxytocin.

Hormones and functions of pituitary gland.

Anterior Pituitary Gland

-   Growth hormone : Stimulates growth and development of body.
-   Prolactin : Stimulates milk production after giving birth.
-   ACTH (adrenocorticotropic hormone) : Stimulates the adrenal glands.
-   TSH (thyroid-stimulating hormone) : Stimulates the thyroid gland.
-   FSH (follicle-stimulating hormone) : Stimulates the ovaries and testes. LH (luteinizing hormone) : Stimulates the ovaries or testes.

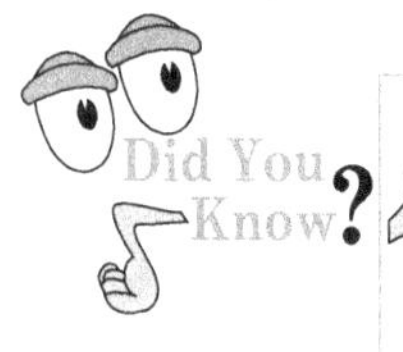

Pineal gland
The pineal gland is a small pine cone shaped gland of the endocrine system. The pineal gland is composed of cells called pinealocytes and cells of the nervous system called glial cells. It produces several important hormones including melatonin. Melatonin influences sexual development and sleep-wake cycles.

Posterior Pituitary Gland

- ADH (antidiuretic hormone) : It is produced in the hypothalamus, stored in the pituitary gland, and increases absorption of water into the blood by the kidneys.
- Oxytocin : Contracts the uterus during childbirth and stimulates milk production.

Table: *Types of pituitary hormones with their target tissue and function*

Endocrine gland	Hormone	Target tissue	Functions
Anterior pituitary	TSH	Thyroid gland	Stimulates release of thyroxine and tri-iodothyronine from the thyroid gland
	LH	Ovary/Testis	Females: Promotes ovulation of the egg and stimulates estrogen and progesterone production Males: Promotes testosterone release from the testis
	FSH	Ovary/Testis	Females: Promotes development of eggs and follicles in the ovary prior to ovulation Males: Promotes production of testosterone from testis
	GH	Bones, cartilage, muscle, fat, liver, heart	Acts to promote growth of bones and organs
	PRL	Breasts, brain	Stimulates milk production in the breasts and plays a role in sexual behaviour
	ACTH	Adrenal glands	Stimulates the adrenal glands to produce cortisol
Posterior pituitary	Vasopressin (anti-diuretic hormone, ADH)	Kidney, blood vessels, blood components	Acts to maintain blood pressure by causing the kidney to retain fluid and by constricting blood vessels
	Oxytocin	Uterus, milk ducts of breasts	Causes ejection of milk from the milk ducts and causes constriction of the uterus during labour

Pituitary gland is also called as master gland of the endocrine system. Because:

(i) The hormones it secretes play an active part in controlling the functions of other endocrine glands.

(ii) Its job is to receive messages about the need for a particular hormone and to secrete the hormones that cause the manufacture and release of the hormone.

Thyroid Gland

Thyroid gland is located in front of the neck below the larynx. The thyroid gland produces thyroxine and calcitonin hormones. Iodine is required for the production of thyroxine hormone. Thyroxine (also called T_4) regulates the body temperature and also plays a major role in growth and development of body.

The enlargement of thyroid gland due to deficiency of iodine in blood is termed goitre. This condition can be prevented by eating vegetables and fishes as they contain iodine in it. The abnormal secretion of thyroxine affects the body.

Hypothyroidism is a condition caused by underproduction of thyroxine. It is characterized by low energy production, slowing down of heart beat, loss of appetite and lethargy. *Hyperthyroidism* is a condition caused by over production of thyroxine. It is characterized by increased energy production, increased heart-beat, increased appetite, frequent sweating and shivering of hands. Apart from all these, it also causes a condition called cretinism which is characterised by

Thyroid Gland

the retardation of mental and physical development. In adult, the deficiency of thyroxine leads to a disease called *Myxoedema* while the over secretion of thyroxine leads to *exophthalmic goitre*.

Calcitonin, also called thyrocalcitonin, is a protein hormone and plays an important role in calcium and phosphorus metabolism. In particular calcitonin has the ability to decrease the blood calcium level at least in parts by effects on two well-studied target organs: bone and kidney.

Calcitonin along with parathormone, produced by parathyroid gland regulates the level of calcium ions in blood.

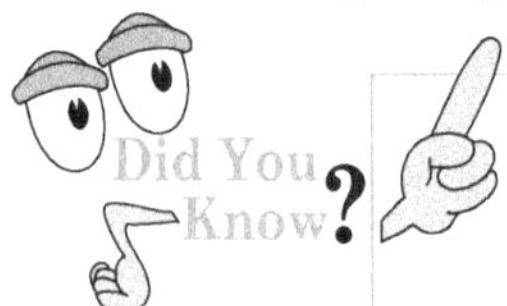

> *Thyroid gland is the largest endocrine gland in the human body. Thyroid gland is made up of two types of cells-*
> *(i) Follicular cells (secrete thyroxine, T4 and T3)*
> *(ii) Parafollicular: cells (also called G-cells, secretes calcitonin)*

Parathyroid Gland

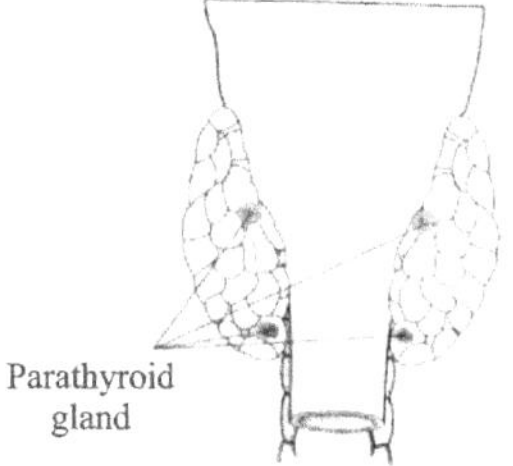

Parathyroid gland

Parathyroid Gland

Parathyroid glands are 4 small glands which are located on the posterior side of thyroid gland. They regulate the level of calcium ions in the blood by secreting parathyroid hormone (PTH). *What happens if there is increase production of parathormone in blood*? Calcium salts are absorbed from the bones and added to blood. As a result, bones become brittle. Also, the kidneys filter and excrete more calcium from the blood. This leads to stone formation in kidneys. The deficiency of parathormone leads to **tetany**. *Tetany* is abnormal increase in the excitability of nerves and muscles resulting in spasms of legs and arms.

Time to Check Your Knowledge

1. **How can deficiency of calcium in blood be rectified?**
2. **What is the role of thyroid gland in regulating the level of calcium ions.**

SOLUTION :

1. The deficiency of calcium in blood can be rectified by stimulating parathyroid to release parathormone. As a result, calcium is removed from bone, intestine and nephron to blood, there by increasing its quantity
2. When the level of calcium ions increases in blood, thyroid gland is stimulated to release calcitonin. Calcitonin, in turn causes the excess calcium to excrete through urine or to get accumulated in the bones.

Adrenal gland

Adrenal glands, which are also called **suprarenal glands**, are small, triangular glands located on top of both kidneys. An adrenal gland is made of two parts: the outer region is called the **adrenal cortex** and the inner region is called the **adrenal medulla**.

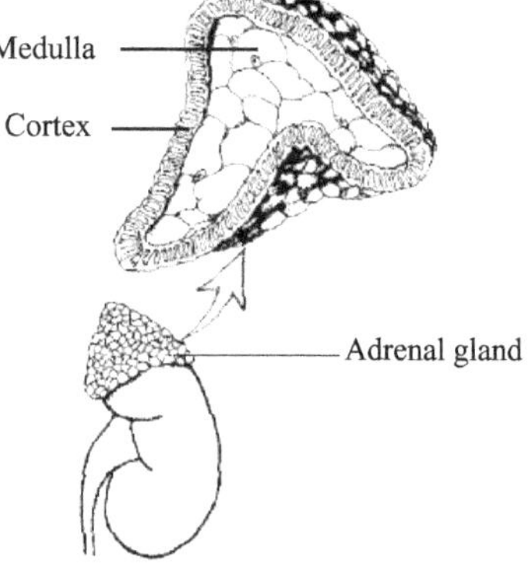

Medulla

Cortex

Adrenal gland

Adrenal gland

Adrenal Gland

Adrenal Cortex

The adrenal cortex secretes hormones that have an effect on the body's metabolism, on chemicals in the blood, and on certain body characteristics. The adrenal cortex secretes corticosteroids and other hormones directly into the bloodstream. The hormones produced by the adrenal cortex include:

(i) *Aldosterone* - Aldosterone helps to maintain the balance of salts and water in the blood, inhibits the sodium excrected into urine.
(ii) *Cortisol* - Cortisol stimulates the break down of proteins and fats. It also stimulates synthesis of glucose from amino acids. Continuous use of cortisol causes elevation of glucose level in blood.

Adrenal Medulla

The adrenal medulla helps a person in coping with physical and emotional stress. The adrenal medulla secretes the following hormones :

(i) *Epinephrine (also called adrenaline)* – This hormone increases the heart rate and force of heart contractions, facilitates blood flow to the muscles and brain, causes relaxation of smooth muscles, helps with conversion of glycogen to glucose in the liver and other activities.
(ii) *Norepinephrine (also called noradrenaline)* – This hormone has little effect on smooth muscles, metabolic processes and cardiac output, but has strong vasoconstrictive effects, thus increasing blood pressure.

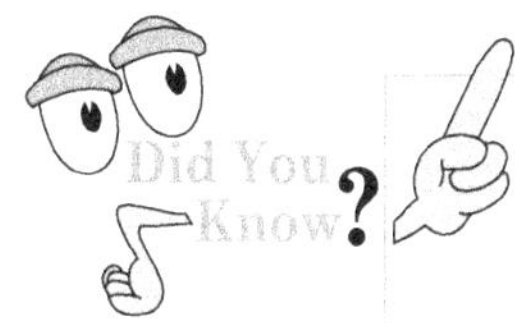

Adrenal gland is also called as 4s gland.
- *S-Source of energy*
- *S-Sex hormone*
- *S-Salt retaining*
- *S-Sugar metabolism*

ADRENALINE

Adrenaline is often known as the fight or flight hormone because it prepares the body to act, especially when the body encounters stress. Hence it is also termed as stress hormone because it helps to calm down when one is very angry, embarrassed or worried. It is released under emergency situations. Some of the physiological changes brought about by adrenaline are –
- The rate and intensity of heart beat increases.
- Blood pressure increases
- Blood flow to the limbs inncreases
- Hair of skin rises
- Blood glucose level increases
- Blood flow to alimentary canal and skin reduces.
- It results in overall increase in energy level in the body.

Pancreas

Pancreas is the **second largest** endocrine gland. It is located near the liver i.e. below the stomach. The pancreas is classified as a **heterocrine gland** because it contains both endocrine and exocrine glandular tissue. The exocrine tissue makes up about 99% of the pancreas by weight while endocrine tissue makes up the other 1%. The exocrine glands produce enzymes important to digestion. The endocrine tissue is arranged into many small masses known as **acini**. The endocrine portion of the pancreas is made of small bundles of cells called **islets of Langerhans**. Islet cells create and release important hormones directly into the bloodstream. Two of the main pancreatic hormones are insulin, which acts to lower blood sugar, and glucagon, which acts to raise blood sugar.

Deficiency of insulin leads to high level of sugar in body. This condition is called **diabetes**.

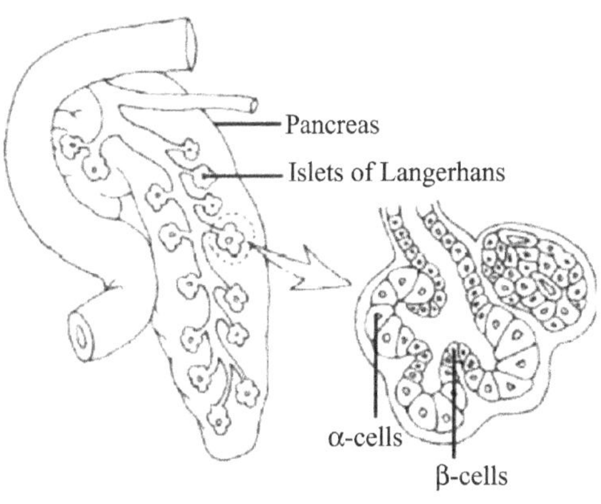

Pancreas

Ovaries

Ovaries are two in number and located in the pelvic region of female body. The hormones secreted are **oestrogen** and **progesterone**. Estrogen stimulates the growth and development of female seconedary sex organs and female secondary sexual characters (such as development of breasts).

Progesterone plays an important role in regulation of menstrual cycle and pregnancy.

During pregnancy, progesterone helps in attaching embryo to uterine wall, development of placenta and growth of secretory alveoli in mammary glands.

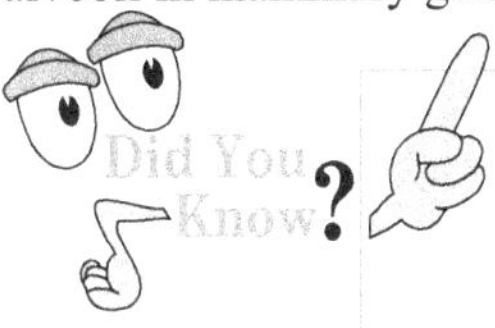

Islets of Langerhans contain four types of cells:
i.   alpha cells : Secrete glucagon
ii. beta cells : Secrete insulin and amylin
iii. delta cells : Secrete somatostatin, and
iv. gamma cells : Secrete pancreatic polypeptide.

Testes

Like ovaries testes are also two in number. The testes consists of two flat oval organs in the scrotum. Endocrine part of testes is formed of group of cells called interstitial cells or leydig cells. The hormone released by leydig cells is **testosterone**. Testosterone controls the development of secondary sexual characters in males such as facial hair, beard, moustaches etc. It stimulates spermatogenesis (formation of sperm).

CASE STUDY : Hormones

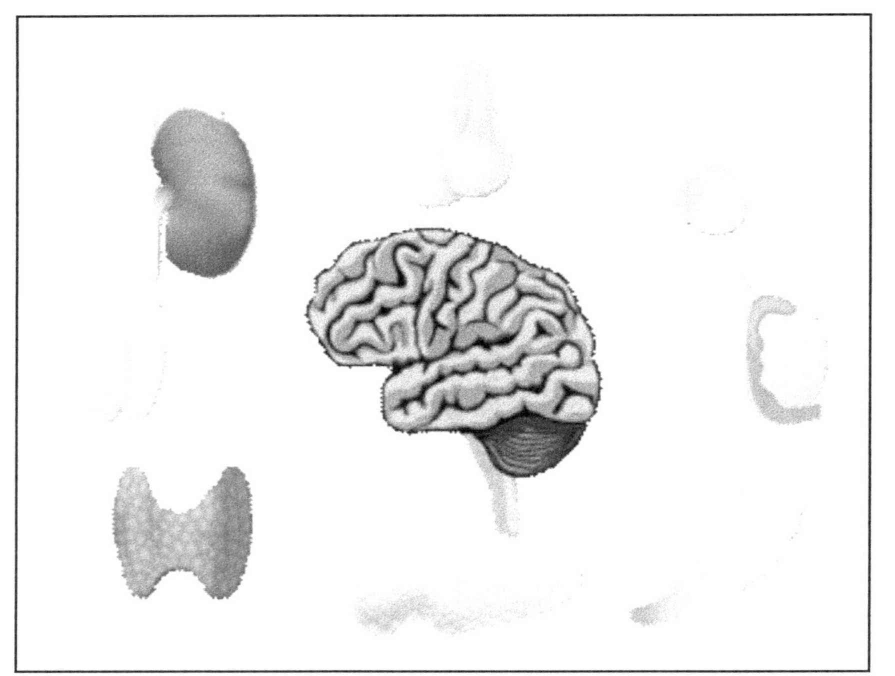

CASE - I : *A patient presents to the clinic with very big and bulging throat. What can be the probable disease this patient is suffering from?*

The patient is suffering from 'goitre'. It occurs due to the over secretion of thyroxine hormone from thyroid gland.

CASE - II : *If a person has spasms in legs and arms and brittle bones, what do you think is the probable reason for these symptoms?*

The person might be suffering from abnormal functioning of parathyroid gland. An increased secretion of parathormone in bloods leads to these symptoms in patients.

CASE - III : *Parents come to the clinic with their child who is 9 years old and is short heighted. What treatment can doctor prescribe to this patient?*

The best treatment in this case is administration of growth hormone as it controls the height in children.

CASE - IV : *A 15-year-old male presents to the clinic with delayed development of secondary sexual characteristics like beard, moustache and change in voice. What treatment can doctor prescribe to this patient?*

The best treatment in this case is to administer testosterone hormone in order to induce puberty.

Think Out of the Box

Q 1. Why is insulin given to patients suffering from diabetes?

Q 2. The levels of calcium in blood are completely controlled by parathormone secreted by parathyroid gland. Is this statement true? Why or why not?

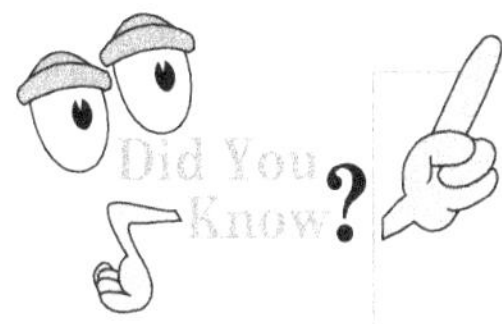

Diabetes
- *Diabetes is due to either the pancreas not producing enough insulin, or the cells of the body not responding properly to the insulin produced.*
- *The two types of diabetes are referred to as type 1 and type 2. Former names for these conditions were insulin-dependent and non-insulin-dependent diabetes, or juvenile onset and adult onset diabetes.*
- *Symptoms of diabetes include increased urine output, thirst, hunger, and fatigue.*
- *Diabetes is diagnosed by blood sugar (glucose) testing. A normal sugar level is currently considered to be less than 100 mg/dL when fasting and less than 140 mg/dL two hours after eating.*

Thymus Gland

Thymus gland is a ductless gland, which starts functioning in the embryonic stage itself, becomes active during childhood and undergoes regression and gradually stops functioning after adolescence.

Thymus produces hormone called thymosin that imparts resistance to diseases in children. However, it continues to be the production centre of lymphocytes.

Thymus is the first **developing lymphoid organ**. It reaches its greatest size at puberty.

Role of hormones in completing the life cycle of insects and frogs

In the previous chapter, we have learnt about the life history of a butterfly and a frog. Try to recall the stages of life history of the butterfly? In the life history of a butterfly the caterpillar has to pass through various stages to become adult. This process of change from larva to adult is called **metamorphosis**. In insects, the process of metamorphosis is controlled by insect hormones like Ecdysone. Similarly, in frog metamorphosis it is controlled by **thyroxine**. The presence of thyroxine causes the tadpoles to become adult frog. But do you know, thyroxine production requires the presence of iodine in water. If the water in which tadpoles are growing does not contain sufficient iodine, the tadpoles cannot get metamorphosed into adults.

REPRODUCTIVE HEALTH

During adolescence, there is rapid mental and physical growth. The physical and mental well being of an individual is regarded as an individual's health. Therefore for proper individual health, every human being needs –
(i)   To have a balanced diet.
(ii)   To observe personal hygiene and cleanliness regularly
(iii)   To undertake adequate regular exercise.

To have a balanced diet

A balanced diet contains the right amount of proteins, carbohydrates, fats, vitamins and minerals. The diet should contain adequate amounts of cereals for carbohydrate, pulses for proteins, controlled amount of butter and ghee for energy and fruits and vegetables for protection against diseases. Our Indian meal of roti/rice, dal (pulses) and vegetable is a balanced diet. Milk is a balanced diet in itself. Fast food is tasty but does not contain adequate nutrition. Hence, it should not be used as substitute for meals.

Personal Hygiene

The basic aim of maintaining personal hygiene is to keep the bacteria and microorganisms away from entering the body or infecting the food we consume. Personal hygiene is necessary for adolescents because the increased activity of sweat glands sometimes make the body smelly. Taking a bath every day and cleaning all parts of the body is essential, otherwise, there are chances of catching bacterial infections. Girls should keep track of their menstrual cycle and should be especially careful about hygiene during menstruation.

Regular physical exercise

Walking, playing and jogging etc. in the fresh air keeps the body fit and healthy. Since adolescence is a stage of insecurity and confusion, it is easy for the adolescent mind to get diverted by wrong company or advice and may fall prey to drug and alcohol abuse.

Say no to Drug

Adolescents are advised not to feel confused or insecure. You are just passing through a period of much activity in the body and mind, which is a normal part of growing up. So, if anybody suggests that you will get relief by taking some drugs just say 'No' to them. Drugs are actually addictive and once taken, there is a tendency to take them again and again. They harm the body in the long run, thereby ruining the health and happiness.

AIDS (ACQUIRED IMMUNODEFICIENCY SYNDROME)

AIDS is a fatal disease caused by HIV (Human immunodeficiency virus). HIV kills or damages cells of the body's immune system which slowly destroys the body's ability to fight infection and diseases. AIDS is the final stage of HIV infection.

Methods of transmission of virus are –
(i)   By sharing the syringes used for injecting drug between normal and infected person.

(ii) From infected mother to an infant through milk.

(iii) Through sexual contact with a person infected with HIV.

Preventing measures that can be taken to prevent spread of AIDS are -

(i) Do not share syringes or needles.

(ii) Avoid receiving infected blood during transfusion

(iii) Use sterilised surgical instruments

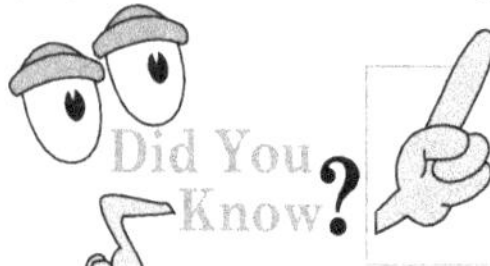

The first recorded case of HIV infection dates back to 1959 from Democratic Rebublic of Congo in Africa.

SUMMARY

- The period of life, when the body undergoes certain noticeable changes, leading to reproductive maturity is called *adolescence.*

- *Puberty* is the start of the time when a immature boy or girl becomes sexually mature and capable of reproduction.

- *Changes at puberty*
  - Both males and females rapidly become taller. But on average, boys grow more and so usually end up taller adults than girls.
  - Girls develop a more rounded body outline, especially on the shoulders and hips while boys become more angular with broader shoulders.
  - The reproductive or menstrual cycle begins in girls while reproductive organs in the male body begins to develop sperm cells.

- *Secondary sexual characters* are those features that help to distinguish the male from the female. In girls, breast begin to develop and boys begin to grow facial hair.

- The changes at puberty are controlled by hormones.

- *Hormones* are chemical messengers of the body that transfer information from one set of cells to another.

- *Glands* are group of specialised cells that produce and secrete hormones.

- *Glands are of two types* -

  (i) *Exocrine gland* release their secretions with the help of ducts at specific site. Ex- Salivary gland

  (ii) *Endocrine gland* release their secretions directly into blood. Eg Adrenal gland.

- The endocrine glands play a vital role in controlling and co-ordinating activities of life.

- The various hormones of pituitary gland control the secretion of hormones secreted from other endocrine gland.

- The pituitary and hypothalamus are connected by nerve fibres and blood vessels.

- *Various types of glands and their secretions are as follows :-*
  - *Pituitary* - Master gland of body
  - *Thyroid* gland - Thyroxine and calcitonin
  - *Parathyroid* - Parathormone
  - *Adrenal glands* — ┌ Cortex - Aldosterone and Cortisone
    └ Medulla - Adrenaline and nor- adrenaline
  - *Pancreas* - Insulin and Glucagon
  - *Gonads* — ┌ Testes - Testosterone
    └ Ovaries - Estrogen and Progesterone

Exercise 1 ⭐ Master Boards

Multiple Choice Questions

DIRECTIONS : This section contains multiple choice questions. Each question has four choices (a), (b), (c) and (d) out of which ONLY ONE is correct.

1. During menstrual bleeding, the fluid that comes out of the vagina contain __________ along with blood.
   (a) Embryo   (b) Ovum
   (c) Sperm   (d) Zygote
2. The time period when the body undergoes changes, leading to reproductive maturity is called.
   (a) growth   (b) senescence
   (c) adolescence   (d) puberty.
3. A human gamete has __________ sex chromosome
   (a) four   (b) half
   (c) two   (d) one
4. The pituitary gland is located below the __________.
   (a) thalamus   (b) medulla oblongata
   (c) vas deferens   (d) hypothalamus
5. Deficiency of iodine in our diet leads to a conditioned called.
   (a) Diabetes   (b) Goitre
   (c) Infertility   (d) Gignatism

Assertion & Reason

DIRECTIONS : Each of these questions contains an assertion followed by reason. Read them carefully and answer the question on the basis of following options. You have to select the one that best describes the two statements.

1. **Assertion :** In human being, growth is differential.
   Reason : Growth is rapid during pre-natal and puberty. While it slow down during juvenile and past adolescent period.
2. **Assertion :** Acne and pimple are very common among adults.
   Reason : This is due to increased production of sweat from sweat glands.
3. **Assertion :** Pituitary gland triggers shift of adolescence towards and adult stage by releasing hormone.
   Reason : Hormones are the chemical substance produced and secreted by the endocrine gland.
4. **Assertion :** Poor nutrition in adolescence can have adverse health consequences in adulthood.
   Reason : A balanced and healthy diet, during adolescence promotes proper growth and overall maturity.
5. **Assertion :** The spurt growth is more evident in girls between 11 – 13 years of age.
   Reason : The gills of this age become capable of reproduction.

Fill in the Blanks

DIRECTIONS : Complete the following statements with an appropriate word / term to be filled in the blank space(s).

1. When an adolescence reaches reproductive maturity, __________ ends.
2. The adolescence is also called as __________.
3. __________ is known as voice box.
4. __________ is absent in women's neck.
5. __________ glands make the skin oiler.
6. Follicle stimulating hormone is secreted by__________ gland.
7. Calcitonin is produced by __________ hormone.
8. __________ hormone maintains salt balance in the body.
9. The first period of a girl is called __________.
10. The __________ gland produces hormones which stimulate other gland to release their hormones.
11. Every sperm has __________ sex chromosomes.
12. __________ hormone regulates the amount of sugar in blood.

True / False

DIRECTIONS : Read the following statements and write your answer as true or false.

1. Exocrine glands are called ductless glands.
2. Thyroid stimulating hormone is responsible for the growth and development of body.
3. At puberty stage, mammary glands develop inside the breasts.
4. 23 pairs of chromosome is found in every normal human cell.
5. The stage at which the body becomes capable of reproduction is called menstruation.
6. Deficiency of insulin hormone may cause diabetes.
7. At adolescence stage, adolescents get mental, intellectual and emotional maturity.
8. Metamorphosis in insects is controlled by adrenaline hormone.
9. Female cells contain XX chromosome.

Match the Following

DIRECTIONS : Each question contains statements given in two columns which have to be matched. Statements terms (A, B, C, D) in column I have to be matched with statements terms (p, q, r, s) in column II.

1.

	Column-I		Column-II
A.	Master gland of body	p.	Thymus
B.	Stress hormone of body	q.	Pituitary gland
C.	Disease resistance hormone in child	r.	Goitre
D.	Deficiency of iodine causes	s.	Adrenaline

2.

	Column I		Column II
A.	Parathyroid	p.	Plays an important role in immune system
B.	Thymus	q.	Stimulate the function of thyroid gland
C.	Thyroxine	r.	Regulation of level of calcium level in blood
D.	Pancreas	s.	Maintain level of sugar in the body

Passage Based Questions

DIRECTIONS : Study the given paragraph(s) and answer the following questions.

Sohan was a very active and social child. He used to come forward for anybody help. One day he attended a blood donation camp and was ready to donate blood, but his blood test was done and he was **HIV** +ve. Therefore he was very upset and lost his interest in all activities and remained absent from school for long time. Rajiv his friend met him and consulted him. Sohan was back to school.

1. What is the full form of HIV?
   (a) Human Immunodeficiency virus
   (b) Herpes infection virus
   (c) Human infection virus
   (d) Human inferring virus
2. AIDS stands for ?
   (a) Acquired Immune deficiency syndrome
   (b) Acquired Infection defective system
   (c) Acquired Infectious deficiency syndrome
   (d) Acquired Immune defective syndrome

Very Short Answer Questions

1. Write the name of the medium by which endocrine gland release hormones?
2. What is a hormone?
3. Which hormone is responsible for maintenance of pregnancy?
4. Which organ is known as the sound box?
5. Which hormone is responsible for the change of vocal cord in boys?
6. Write the role of hypothalamus in the body?
7. What is the age of puberty in boys and girls?
8. Write the names of hormones secreted by pituitary gland?
9. Write the location of parathyroid gland?
10. What is the important role of adrenaline hormone?
11. Which hormone controls the metamorphosis in caterpillar?
12. Name the hormone secreted by thymus gland.
13. What developmental changes occur in uterus at the time of menstruation?
14. What is menopause?
15. How many pairs of sex chromosomes are found in human being?
16. Which hormone is responsible for the growth of bones?
17. Which technique determines the sex of the child?
18. What is the functions of aldosterone in human body?

Short Answer Questions

1. What is the difference between puberty and adolescence.
2. What is 'teenage"?
3. What are the secondary sexual characters in male and female?
4. What is infanticide?
5. What are tropic hormones?
6. What is the difference between hypothyroidism and hyperthyroidism?
7. What is the necessity of balance diet for adolescents?
8. Why personal hygiene is necessary for everyone?
9. What are drugs?
10. Expand AIDS? Write different methods of transmission of AIDS virus.
11. List the changes in male body that take place at puberty.
12. Write a short note on adrenal gland.
13. Write a short note on exocrine gland.
14. Write the name of two hormones secreted by the thyroid gland.
15. What is ductless gland?
16. What are the main functions of pituitary gland?

Long Answer Questions

1. Explain the structure and functions of different endocrine glands found in human body.
2. Explain the role of hormone in your body?
3. What is menstrual cycle?
4. Discuss the various habits that adolescents should acquire to have a proper physical health.

Reasoning Based Questions

1. Why do personal hygiene become more important during adolescent age?
2. Who is responsible for the sex of the unborn child, father or mother? Why?
3. Why is it more necessary for adolescents to take bath regularly (atleast one everyday)?
4. Why iron is needed in our body?
5. Why pimples are formed in our body?
6. What will happen if the water in which tadpoles are growing does not contain sufficient iodine?
7. Explain why people are advised to use iodised salt in cooking food.

HOTS Questions

1. Many adolescents do not grow according to their age. Can you give reason, why?
2. Why expecting mothers are advised not to do heavy work at the first phase of pregnancy?
3. Initially girls grow faster than boys but at 18 years of age, both reach their maximum height. Given reason, why?
4. What is dwarfism? What are the reasons of dwarfism?
5. "Some human female starts developing male characteristics like beard, degeneration of uterus and ovaries etc. in their growing period."
Give reason for the above statement.

6. During growth period, many adolescence get excessive growth, resulting into a symmetrically giant body. Why it happens so?

7. Why do most of the people get acne and pimples on the face during puberty?

8. What is the reason for irregularity in menstrution?

9. Heavy supplements are not good during physical exercise in adolescence

Do you agree. Give reason in support of your answer.

Exercise 2 ⭐ Master NCERT (Text-book & Exemplar)

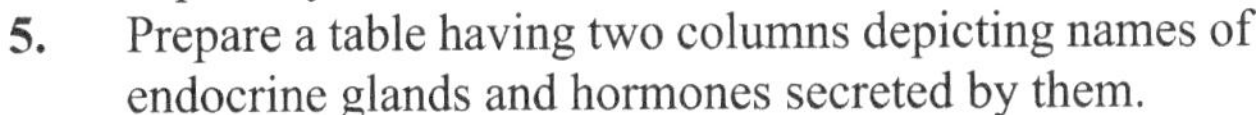

Text-book Exercise

1. What is the term used for secretions of endocrine glands responsible for changes taking place in the body?

Adolescents

2. Define adolescence.
3. What is menstruation? Explain.
4. List changes in the body that take place at puberty.
5. Prepare a table having two columns depicting names of endocrine glands and hormones secreted by them.
6. What are sex hormones? Why are they named so? State their function.
7. Choose the correct option.
    (a) Adolescents should be careful about what they eat, because
        (i)   proper diet develops their brains.
        (ii) proper diet is needed for the rapid growth taking place in their body.
        (iii) adolescents feel hungry all the time.
        (iv) taste buds are well developed in teenagers.
    (b) Reproductive age in women starts when their
        (i)   menstruation starts.
        (ii) breasts start developing.
        (iii) body weight increases.
        (iv) height increases.
    (c) The right meal for adolescents consists of
        (i)   chips, noodles, coke.
        (ii) chapati, dal, vegetables
        (iii) rice, noodles and burger.
        (iv) vegetable cutlets, chips and lemon drink.
8. Write notes on
    (a) Adam's apple.
    (b) Secondary sexual characters.
    (c) Sex determination in the unborn baby.
9. Word game : Use the clues to work out the words.
    Across
    3. Protruding voice box in boys
    4. Glands without ducts
    7. Endocrine gland attached to brain
    8. Secretion of endocrine glands
    9. Pancreatic hormone
    10. Female hormone
    Down
    1. Male hormone
    2. Secretes thyroxine
    3. Another term for teenage
    5. Hormone reaches here through blood stream
    6. Voice box
    7. Term for changes at adolescence

10. The table below shows the data on likely heights of boys and girls as they grow in age. Draw graphs showing height and age for both boys and girls on the same graph paper. What conclusions can be drawn from these graphs?

Age (years)	Height (cm) Boys	Height (cm) Girls
0	53	53
4	96	92
8	114	110
12	129	133
16	150	165
20	173	165

Exemplar Questions

1. Give a suitable word for each of the following statements.
    (a) The site which responds to a hormone.
    (b) Name of a gland which transports secretions through ducts,
    (c) Chemicals which control changes at adolescence stage.
    (d) It marks the beginning of reproductive period.
2. Name the hormone that is released by testes at the onset puberty.
3. Name the female hormone produced by ovaries that helps in development of mammary glands.
4. Mention any two features each that are seen in boys and girls each to distinguish them from each other at puberty.
5. We should avoid taking medicines/drugs unless prescribed by a doctor. Give reasons.
6. In human females, each time during maturation and release of egg the inner wall of uterus thickens. Is this thickening permanent? Give reasons.
7. Our government has legalised the age for marriage in boys and girls. Give reaons as to why one should get married after a certain age.
8. It is believed that height of a child depends upon the genes inherited from parents. However, it is often seen that tall parents may have short children and vice-versa. Are there factors other than genes, that can cuse these variations?

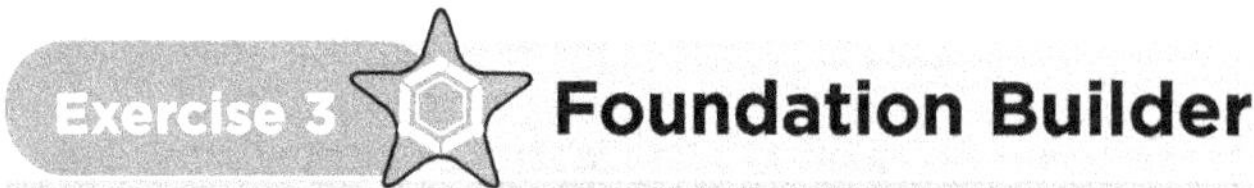
Exercise 3 — Foundation Builder

DIRECTIONS : *This section contains multiple choice questions. Each question has four choices (a), (b), (c) and (d) out of which ONLY ONE is correct. Choose the correct option.*

1. What is hormone?
(a) Organic complex substances
(b) Chemical messenger
(c) Glandular secretion
(d) Blood cells

2. Which of the following system exhibits body co-ordination?
(a) Blood vascular system
(b) Nervous system
(c) Brain
(d) Nervous and endocrine system

3. Which of the following flows directly into blood?
(a) Enzyme   (b) Hormone
(c) Minerals   (d) Proteins

4. Which of the following is not a gland?
(a) Pancreas   (b) Adrenal
(c) Pituitary   (d) Kidney

5. Endocrine glands
(a) do not possess ducts
(b) sometime have duct
(c) always have duct
(d) pour their secretion through ducts.

6. Which hormone regulates the process of spermatogenesis and sperm formation?
(a) Follicle stimulating hormone
(b) Growth hormone
(c) Thyroxine hormone
(d) Glucagon

7. Pituitary gland is found in
(a) pancreas   (b) brain
(c) gonads   (d) trachea

8. Which hormone controls secretion of estrogen?
(a) Progesterone   (b) Follicle stimulating hormone
(c) Aldosterone   (d) Adrenaline

9. Which one of the following is an endocrine disorder?
(a) Typhoid   (b) Jaundice
(c) Goitre   (d) Pneumonia

10. Which hormones regulates the growth of metamorphosis in frog?
(a) Adrenaline   (b) Insulin
(c) Thyroxine   (d) Cortisol

11. Which hormone is responsible for ovulation?
(a) LH   (b) Testosterone
(c) Estrogen   (d) FSH

12. Which hormone regulates calcium level in blood ?
(a) Glucagon   (b) Insulin
(c) Thyroxine   (d) Parathormone

13. Which hormone controls the blood pressure in emergency?
(a) Thyroxine   (b) Prolactin
(c) Insulin   (d) Adrenaline

14. Which hormone stimulates the stomach to secrete gastric juice?
(a) Gastrin   (b) Parathormone
(c) Thyroxine   (d) Insulin

15. Which hormone is associated with milk secretion in mammals?
(a) Estrogen   (b) Prolactin
(c) Adrenaline   (d) GH

DIRECTIONS : *Each of these questions contains an assertion followed by reason. Read them carefully and answer the question on the basis of following options. You have to select the one that best describes the two statements.*

(a) If both **Assertion** and **Reason** are **correct** and Reason is the **correct explanation** of Assertion.
(b) If both **Assertion** and **Reason** are correct, but Reason is **not the correct explanation** of Assertion.
(c) If **Assertion** is **correct** but **Reason** is **incorrect**.
(d) If **Assertion** is **incorrect** but **Reason** is **correct**.

1. **Assertion :** The dietary deficiency of iodine causes goitre.
Reason : Iodine is required for the formation of thyroid hormone.

2. **Assertion :** Prolactin is also called 'Milk ejection hormone'.
Reason : Prolactin stimulates contraction of smooth muscles of mammary glands.

3. **Assertion :** Adrenaline is known as fight, fright and flight hormone.
Reason : The hormone adrenaline helps the body to combat against stress and emergency condition.

4. **Assertion :** A tadpole deprived of thyroid gland fails to metamorphose into adult.
Reason : Thyroxine stimulates tissue differentiation therefore affects metamorphosis of tadpole into an adult.

5. **Assertion :** Excess amount of calcium is regulated by calcitonin.
Reason : Parathormone is produced by parathyroid gland.

6. **Assertion :** Sweat glands sometimes make body smelly.
Reason : It is due to infection by bacteria.

Exercise 4 ⭐ **Foundation Builder +**

Multiple Choice Questions

DIRECTIONS (Qs. 1-6) : This section contains multiple choice questions. Each question has four choices (a), (b), (c) and (d) out of which ONLY ONE is correct.

1. AIDS is caused by HIV that principally infects:
   (a) all lymphocytes
   (b) activator B cells
   (c) cytotoxic T cells
   (d) T_4 lymphocytes

2. A certain patient is suspected to be suffering from Acquired Immuno Deficiency Syndrome. Which diagnostic technique will you recommend for its detection?
   (a) ELISA
   (b) MRI
   (c) Ultra sound
   (d) WIDAL

3. Drug called 'Heroin' is synthesised by : **[NTSE]**
   (a) methylation of morphine
   (b) acetylation of morphine
   (c) glycosylation of morphine
   (d) nitration of morphine

4. Select the option including all sexually transmitted diseases. **[NTSE]**
   (a) Gonorrhoea, Malaria, Genital herpes
   (b) AIDS, Malaria, Filaria
   (c) Cancer, AIDS, Syphilis
   (d) Gonorrhoea, Syphilis, Genital herpes

5. Which of the following contraceptive methods do involve a role of hormone? **[NTSE]**
   (a) Lactational amenorrhea, Pills, Emergency contraceptives
   (b) Barrier method, Lactational amenorrhea, Pills
   (c) CuT, Pills, Emergency contraceptives
   (d) Pills, Emergency contraceptives, Barrier methods

6. In which of the following techniques, the embryos are transferred to assist those females who cannot conceive?
   (a) GIFT and ZIFT
   (b) ICSI and ZIFT **[NTSE]**
   (c) GIFT and ICSI
   (d) ZIFT and IUT

Multiple Matching Questions

DIRECTION (Qs. 7-8) : The following question contains statements given in two columns which have to be matched. Statements (A, B, C, D) in column I have to be matched with statements (p, q, r, s) in column II.

7. Given below are four methods (A-D) and their modes of action (p-s) in achieving contraception. Select their correct matching from the four options that follow:

Method		Mode of Action
A. The pill	(p)	Prevents sperms reaching cervix
B. Condom	(q)	Prevents implantation
C. Vasectomy	(r)	Prevents ovulation
D. Copper T	(s)	Semen contains no sperms

   (a) A-(p), B-(p), C-(s), D-(q)
   (b) A-(s), B-(p), C-(q), D-(r)
   (c) A-(r), B-(s), C-(p), D-(q)
   (d) A-(q), B-(r), C-(p), D-(s)

8. Match the following sexually transmitted diseases (Column-I) with their causative agent (Column-II) and select the correct option : **[NTSE]**

Column-I		Column-II
(A) Gonorrhea	(p)	HIV
(B) Syphilis	(q)	*Neisseria*
(C) Genital Warts	(r)	*Treponema*
(D) AIDS	(s)	Human papilloma-Virus

	(A)	(B)	(C)	(D)
(a)	(r)	(s)	(p)	(q)
(b)	(s)	(q)	(r)	(p)
(c)	(s)	(r)	(q)	(p)
(d)	(q)	(r)	(s)	(p)

SOLUTIONS
(Brief Explanations of Selected Questions)

Exercise 1 — Master Boards

Multiple Choice Questions

1. (b)   2. (b)   3. (d)   4. (d)
5. (b)

Assertion & Reason

1. (a) The growth rate is not uniform but is different at different periods of life, so growth is differential. Growth is rapid in the pre-natal and puberty period. It slow down in the juvenile and post adolescent period as there is no addition of living matter in this period.
2. (b) Both Assertion and Reason are true, and Reason is the correct explanation of Assertion.
   Acne and pimples is due to increased activity of sebaceous (oil) glands in the skin releasing sebum.
3. (a)
4. (a) Both Assertion and Reason are true and Reason is the correct explanation of Assertion. Poor nutrition in teenage age can result in undergrowth hence balanced diet is advised for proper growth and overall maturity.
5. (a) Both Assertion and Reason are true and Reason is the correct explanation of Assertion.
   Puberty starts when changes in child's brain cause sex hormone to start being released from the gonads. In girls puberty range from 8-13 years and various physical changes occur in girl body and become capable of reproduction.

Fill in the Blanks

1. Puberty
2. Teenage
3. Larynx
4. Adam's apple
5. Sebaceous gland
6. Pituitary gland
7. Thyroid
8. Aldosterone
9. Menarche
10. Pituitary
11. Two
12. Insulin

True / False

1. False. Endocrine glands are called ductless glands.
2. False. Thyroid stimulating hormone is responsible to produce T_3 and T_4 hormone from thyroid gland.
3. True
4. True
5. False. The stage at which the body becomes capable of reproduction is called puberty.
6. True
7. True
8. False. Metamorphosis in insects is controlled by ecdysone hormone.
9. True

Match the Following

1. A-q, B-s, C-p, D-r
2. A-r, B-p, C-q, D-s

Passage Based Questions

1. (a)   2. (a)

Very Short Answer Questions

1. Blood stream
2. Hormones are chemical messengers which regulate most of the metabolic and other activity inside the body.
3. Progesterone
4. Larynx
5. Testosterone
6. Hypothalamus regulates the synthesis and secretion of pituitary gland.
7. In girls, 11-14 years. In boys, 12-18 years
8. GH, TSH, LH, FSH, prolactin, ACTH
9. At the posterior side of thyroid gland.
10. Prepares body to act against stress.
11. Ecdysone
12. Thymosin
13. The inner lining of uterus gets thickened and is supplied with blood by which growing embryo gets nutrition.
14. Menopause is the stoppage of menstruation of woman at the age of 45 to 50 years.
15. 1 pair (XY)
16. Pituitary
17. Sonography
18. Aldosterone maintain balance of salt and water in human body.

Short Answer Questions

1. When the body undergoes certain noticeable changes, leading to reproductive maturity, it is called adolescence. These changes mark the onset of puberty.
2. The age of adolescence between 13 to 19 years is called teenage.
3. Secondary characters in male –
   (i) Growth of facial hair
   (ii) Shoulder become wider.
   Secondary character in females –
   (i) Breasts develops
   (ii) Pelvic region widens
   (iii) Mammary glands develop inside breast.
4. Infanticide is the killing of foetus inside the mother's womb.

5. Hormone which control activity of other endocrine glands or growth are called trophic hormones.

6. Hypothyroidism is caused due to underproduction of thyroxine hormone in the body. Hyperthyroidism is caused due to overproduction of thyroxine hormone in the body.

7. As the body is in a stage of rapid growth during adolescence, nutritional needs are also more. The diet during this period has to be a balanced diet. Balanced diet includes carbohydrates, fats, proteins and vitamins. Balance diet is important for adolescent because it provides nutrition to the body to function properly and helps in its proper growth and development.

8. Personal hygiene is necessary for everyone, because due to unhygiene, different bacteria may cause odour and infection in the body.

9. Drugs are chemical substances used in the treatment, cure, prevention, or diagnosis of disease or used to otherwise enhance physical or mental well-being.

10. AIDS: Acquired immune deficiency syndrome. AIDS virus can be transmitted by several methods like,
   (i) Sexual contact with an infected person.
   (ii) Transmission *via* donated blood or blood clotting factors.
   (iii) Sharing needles, syringes or other injection equipment with someone who is infected.
   (iv) Mother to child transmission

11. Changes that take place in male during puberty are:
   - Voice becomes deeper.
   - Increase in body weight.
   - Muscles develop and shoulder broadens.
   - Hair develops under armpit, on the chest and in the pubic region.
   - Facial hair such as beard and moustaches develops.

12. The adrenal glands, also called suprarenal gland, are small structures attached to the top of each kidney. Each gland consists of two parts: an inner medulla, which produces epinephrine and norepinephrine (adrenaline and noradrenaline), and an outer cortex, which produces steroid hormones (aldosterone, cortisol). The two parts differ in embryological origin, structure, and function. The hormones help control heart rate, blood pressure, the way the body uses food, the levels of minerals such as sodium and potassium in the blood, and other functions particularly involved in stress reactions.

13. Exocrine glands : The glands that release their secretions with the help of ducts at specific site are called *exocrine glands*. For example, the salivary gland secrete saliva in the mouth through salivary duct. Similarly, digestive glands secrete their secretions in the digestive tract with the help of ducts. Sweat gland is also an example of exocrine gland.

14. Thyroid gland secretes thyroxin and calcitonin hormone.

15. The gland which does not have duct and release the hormones directly into the blood stream, is called ductless gland.

16. Pituitary gland produces several hormones that control water balance, growth and also release of other hormones.

Long Answer Questions

1. **Different endocrine glands are:**
Hypothalamus: The hypothalamus is a part of the brain which serves many different functions in the nervous system. It is also responsible for the direct control of the endocrine system through the pituitary gland.

Pituitary gland: The pituitary gland is a pea-sized gland located in the centre of the skull, inferior to the hypothalamus of the brain and posterior to the bridge of the nose. The pituitary gland is made of 2 completely separate structures: the posterior and anterior pituitary glands. It is an important link between the nervous and endocrine systems and releases many hormones which affect growth, sexual development, metabolism and human reproduction.

Pineal gland: The pineal gland is a small mass of glandular tissue found just posterior to the thalamus of the brain. The pineal gland produces the hormone melatonin that helps to regulate the human sleep-wake cycle known as the circadian rhythm.

Thyroid gland: The thyroid gland is a butterfly-shaped gland located at the base of the neck and wrapped around the lateral sides of the trachea. The thyroid gland produces 3 major hormones: calcitonin, triiodothyronine (T3), thyroxine (T4). The thyroid plays an important role in regulating the body's metabolism and calcium balance.

Parathyroid glands: The parathyroid glands are 4 small masses of glandular tissue found on the posterior side of the thyroid gland. The parathyroid glands produce the hormone parathyroid hormone (PTH), which is involved in calcium ion homeostasis.

Adrenal glands: The adrenal glands are a pair of roughly triangular glands found immediately superior to the kidneys. The adrenal glands are each made of 2 distinct layers- the outer adrenal cortex and inner adrenal medulla. The adrenal cortex produces many cortical hormones in 3 classes: glucocorticoids, mineralocorticoids, and androgens. The adrenal medulla produces epinephrine and norepinephrine hormones. Both of these hormones help to increase the flow of blood to the brain and muscles to improve the "fight-or-flight" response to stress. These hormones also work to increase heart rate, breathing rate, and blood pressure while decreasing the flow of blood to and function of organs that are not involved in responding to emergencies.

Pancreas: The pancreas is a large gland located in the abdominal cavity just inferior and posterior to the stomach. The pancreas is considered to be a heterocrine gland as it contains both endocrine and exocrine tissue. The endocrine cells of the pancreas are called islets of Langerhans. Within these islets are 2 types of cells-alpha and beta cells. The alpha cells produce the hormone glucagon, which is responsible for raising blood glucose levels. Glucagon triggers muscle and liver cells to break down the polysaccharide glycogen to release glucose into the bloodstream. The beta cells produce the hormone

insulin, which is responsible for lowering blood glucose levels after a meal. Insulin triggers the absorption of glucose from the blood into cells, where it is added to glycogen molecules for storage.

Gonads: Gonads (ovaries in females and testes in males) are responsible for producing the sex hormones of the body. Testes are pair of ellipsoid organs found in the scrotum of males that produce the testosterone hormone. Testosterone controls the growth and development of the sex organs and body hair of males, including pubic, chest, and facial hair. The ovaries are a pair of almond-shaped glands located in the pelvic body cavity. The ovaries produce the female sex hormones progesterone and estrogen. Progesterone is most active in females during ovulation and pregnancy where it maintains appropriate conditions in the human body to support a developing foetus. Estrogen triggers the development of female secondary sex characteristics such as uterine development, breast development, and the growth of pubic hair.

Thymus: The thymus is a soft, triangular-shaped organ found in the chest posterior to the sternum. The thymus produces hormone called thymosine that helps to train and develop T-lymphocytes during foetal development and childhood. The thymus becomes inactive during puberty and is slowly replaced by adipose tissue throughout a person's life.

2. Hormones are chemicals naturally occurring within human bodies. They are produced by cells or glands and their role is to affect other organs. Hormones are responsible for simulation of growth, control of cell's life span, control of immune system, metabolism regulation, control of phases of life, self-preservation reactions, sexual functions, reproductive cycle. Human bodies need different hormones for various stages of life.

3. When the egg is released from the ovary, the lining of the uterus begins to become thicker. If the egg gets fertilized, it attaches itself to the wall of the uterus and receives nourishment. If the egg is not fertilized, the lining of the uterus is shed. This is known as **menstruation** or **periods.** Once the wall is shed, it begins to build up again. This contituous building and shedding of the inner wall of the uterus occurs during a **menstrual cycle**. In a mature female, normally one egg is formed during the menstrual cycle. The duration of one menstrual cycle is about 28 days. At the end of the cycle, the egg is released from the ovary.

4. Proper physical health in adolescents is a need.
   - Balanced diet : balanced diet contains the right amounts of proteins, carbohydrates, fats, vitamins and minerals
   - Fast food which is tasty but does not have adequate nutrition, such as chips or aerated drinking, should not be used as substitute for meals.
   - Personal hygiene due to increased activity of sweat and sebaceous glands, proper personal hygiene is very important for adolescents, otherwise body odour and bacterial infection may result. Girls should be especially careful about hygiene during menstruation.

   - Physical exercise like walking, jogging, aerobics, outdoor games, etc., are good for the growing adolescent body.

1. The basic aim of personal hygiene is to keep body heat and clear to avoid microbes like bacteria, virus entering our body. Otherwise these harmful body can infect us.

2. Father (male) is responsible for the sex of the child. Males carry two different type of chromosomes (XY) while the female carry two chromosome of single type XX.

3. It is more necessary for adolescents to take bath regularly (at least once everyday) because increased activity of sweat glands sometimes make the body smelly.

4. Our body uses iron to make hemoglobin, a protein in red blood cells that carries oxygen from lungs to all parts of the body.

5. As the body begins to mature and develop, though hormones stimulate the sebaceous gland to make more sebum. Pores become clogged if there is too much sebum and too many dead skin cells.

6. In a frog, it is controlled by thyroxine, the hormone produced by thyroid. Thyroxine production require the presence of iodine in water. If the water in which the tadpoles are growing does not contain sufficient iodine the tadpoles cannot become adults.

7. Iodine is needed by the thyroid gland for the production of thyroxine hormone. It the quantity of iodine in food is lesser than required, then the neck will swell up due to the enlargement of the thyroid gland. This deficiency disease is known as goitre. Therefore the iodized salt is advised.

1. Many adolescent do not grow according to their age. This is due to lack of balanced diet. A balanced diet gives your body the nutrition it needs to function properly.

2. The first phase of pregnancy is a period of major development for foetus and of profound physical and emotional changes for mother. Expecting mothers are not advice to do heavy work at the first phase of pregnancy because her centre of gravity and balance has changed and additionally because the hormones of pregnancy have caused her connective tissue, ligaments and tendons so soften. So, if she lifts a heavy load she can injure herself, but will probably do no harm to the pregnancy or the baby.

3. Initially, girls grow faster than boys but by about 18 years of age, both reach their maximum height. The rate of growth in height varies in different individuals.

4. Dwarfism is a condition of short stature. It is caused by deficiency of growth hormone. From early age growth of long bones and of the body stops prematurely, making the patient dwarf.

5. Excessive secretion of male hormone (androgen) in a female foetus before complete formation of ovaries causes abnormal development of muscles, beard and moustache. Sometimes it results in female sterility.

6. Many adolescents get excessive growth, which results into a giant body during its growing period. It is caused due to secretion of excess of growth hormone after adolescence. As a result, the bones like lower jaw and limb (arms, hands, legs) become abnormally large.

7. During puberty, there is an increased secretion of sweat and oil (sebaceous) glands. It is because of the increased secretion that many young people get acne and pimples on their faces.

8. Menstruation is the periodic blood that flows as a discharge from the uterus. Menstrual irregularities can be caused by a variety of conditions, like pregnancy, hormonal imbalances, infections, malignancies, diseases, excessive weight gain or loss, trauma, and certain medications.

9. Heavy supplement intake during physical exercise causes abnormal changes in growth of muscle, stiffness of muscle and maturity before age.

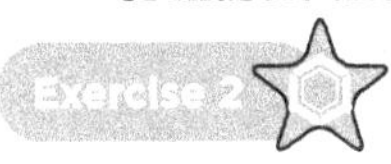 **Exercise 2** **Master NCERT (Text-book & Exemplar)**

Text-book Exercise

1. The are chemical messengers that transport signal from one cell(or gland) to another cell (or gland).

2. Adolescence is defined as that period of life, when the body undergoes changes, leading to reproductive maturity. It begins around the age of 11 and lasts upto 18 or 19 years of age. Since this period covers the 'teens' years of age (13 to 18 or 19), adolescents are also called 'teenagers'. In girls, adolescence may begin a year or two earlier than in boys. Also, the period of adolescence varies from person to person.

3. In a female ovaries, the ova begin to mature with the onset of puberty. There are 2 ovaries. One ovary releases one ovum once in about 28 to 30 days. During this period, the wall of the uterus becomes thick and gets ready to receive the egg in case of fertilization. If fertilization does not occur, the released egg, and the thickened lining of the uterus along with its blood vessels are shed off. This causes bleeding in women which is called menstruation. Menstruation occurs once in about 28 to 30 days.

4. Common changes that occur among boys and girls during puberty:
   1. Sudden increase in height.
   2. Change in body shape
   3. Change in voice. Voice becomes deep and harsh in boys whereas in girls it is high pitched voice.
   4. Increased activity of sweat and sebaceous glands.
   5. Reproductive organs begin to mature.
   6. Appearance of secondary sexual characteristics.

   Changes in Boys during puberty:
   (i) Development of facial hairs such as beard and moustaches.
   (ii) Development of hair under the armpit, under chest and in the pubic regions.
   (iii) Voice becomes deeper.
   (iv) Muscles develop, and shoulder becomes broad.
   (v) Increase in weight.

Changes in Girls during puberty:
(i) Development and enlargement of breasts.
(ii) Development of hair under the armpit and in the pubic regions.
(iii) Hips broaden and pelvic region widens
(iv) Initiation of menstrual cycle.
(v) Deposition of fat around hips.

5.

	Endocrine Glands	Hormones secreted
i.	Pituitary	Growth Hormones
ii.	Thyroid	Thyroxine
iii.	Adrenal Glands	Adrenalin
iv.	Pancreas	Insulin
v.	Testes	Testosterone
vi.	Ovaries	Estrogen, Progestrone

6. Hormones which regulate the secondary sexual characters are called sex hormones.

In general, hormones work instantly when they are released in the blood stream. Sex hormones are different because they start to work at later stages and gradually prepare the body for reproduction.

The sex hormones are responsible for the fundamental change in growth and development. They stimulate the development of secondary sexual characters. The testes and the ovaries are the reproductive Organs; both are stimulated by the pituitary during Puberty. That's the reason these are called *sex hormones*.

Functions of Sex Hormones:
1. In male the sex hormone is testosterone relased by testes. This hormone helps in the development and maintenance of the primary and secondary sexual characters as well as functions of sperms.

2. In female, the ovaries secrete estrogen and progesterone which are responsible for the primary and secondary sexual characters.

7. (a) (ii) proper diet is needed for the rapid growth taking place in their body.
   (b) (i) menstruation starts.
   (c) (ii) chapati, dal, vegetables.

8. (a) **Adam's apple:** It is the protruding part of the throat. It is the enlarged voice box or larynx which gets enlarged and becomes visible from outside in boys at the onset of puberty. This is why the voice of boys is hoarse.

   (b) **Secondary Sexual Characters** are those characters which distinguish a male from female. A few of these are descibed below:

   Boys:
   1. Facial hairs such as beard and moustaches develop.
   2. Hair develops under the armpit, under chest and in the pubic regions.
   3. Voice becomes hoarse.
   4. Muscles develop, and shoulder broadens.
   5. Weight increase.

Girls:

1. Development and enlargement of breasts.
2. Development of hair under the armpit and in the pubic regions.
3. Hips broaden and pelvic region widens
4. Initiation of menstrual cycle.
5. Deposition of fat around hips,

(c) **Sex determination in unborn baby:** 23 pairs of chromosomes are present in the nuclei. Each cell of a human body has these two chromosomes and the sex chromosomes, named X and Y. A female has two X chromosomes, while a male has one X and one Y chromosome. The gametes (egg and sperm) have only one set (23) of chromosomes. The unfertilised egg always has one X chromosome. But sperms are of two kinds. One kind has an X chromosome, and the other kind has a Y chromosome. When a sperm containing X chromosome fertilises the egg, the zygote would have two X chromosomes and develops into a female child. If the sperm having Y chromosome fuses with the egg the zygote would develop into a male child. This concludes that the sex chromosomes of the father determines the sex of an unborn baby.

9. See figure below.

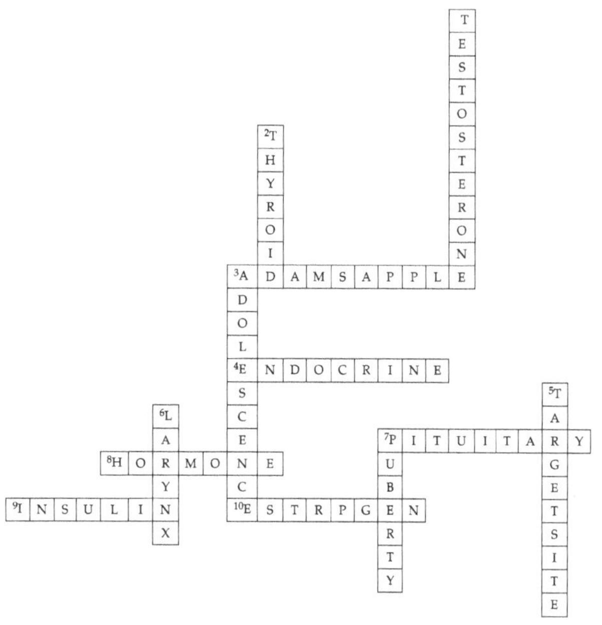

10. **Conclusion:**
    (i) Girls are taller than boys till they reach the age of 12 years.
    (ii) Till the age of 16 years, the height of both boys and girls remain the same.
    (iii) After 16, both boys and girls gain increase in height. In general, boys are taller than girls.

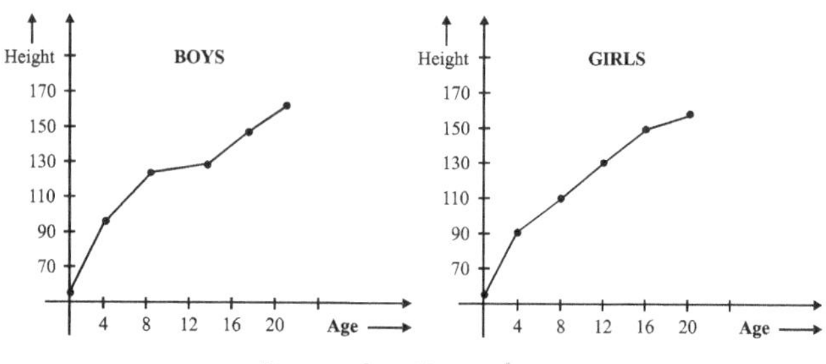

1. (a) Target site
   (b) Sweat glands/salivary glands/oil glands (any one)
   (c) Hormones
   (d) Puberty
2. Testosterone.
3. Estrogen.
4. Two features seen in boys at puberty are:
   (i) Growth of facial hairs
   (ii) Voice becomes hoarse.
   Two features seen in girls at puberty are:
   (i) Development of breasts.
   (ii) Region below the waist becomes wider.
5. Several medicines have adverse side effects and have specific dosage levels which if not followed may harm the body. Drug can be addictive too and can ruin our health and happiness.
6. No, this thickening of the uterine wall is not permanent. If the egg gets fertilised, it starts developing and gets embedded in the uterine wall resulting in preganancy. During pregnancy no more eggs are released and the thickened lining is discharged only when the baby is born. However, if fertilisation does not occur, the released egg and the thickened lining are shed off resulting in mensturation.
7. In our country, the legal age for marriage is 18 years for girls and 21 years for boys. This is because teenage mothers are not prepared mentally or physically for motherhood. Early marriage and motherhood causes health problems in both mother and the child. It also curtails employment opportunities for the young woman and may cause mental agony as she is not ready to shoulder responsibilities of motherhood.

   Also, the boys before that age may not be mentally matured and financially secure enough to take on the responsibilities of a family.
8. (Open Ended) students may write about the effects of nutrition, hormones, exercises, disease, etc. on the height.

1. (b) Hormone is a chemical substance produced in the body that controls and regulates the activity of certain cells or organs. Hormones are released directly into the body. Hormones are essential for every activity of life, including the processes of digestion, metabolism,

growth, reproduction, and mood control. Many hormones, such as neurotransmitters, are active in more than one physical process.

2. (d) Nervous and endocrine system exhibit body coordination. They both work closely in regulating certain activities of the body.

3. (b) Refer answer 1

4. (d) Kidneys are two bean-shaped organs, each about the size of a fist. They are located just below the rib cage, one on each side of the spine. The kidneys perform the essential function of removing waste products from the blood and regulating the water fluid levels.

5. (a) Endocrine glands are glands of the endocrine system that secrete their products, hormones, directly into the blood rather than through a duct.

6. (a) Follicle-stimulating hormone (FSH) is a hormone associated with reproduction and the development of eggs in women and sperm in men.

7. (b) The pituitary gland is a pea-sized structure located at the base of the brain, just below the hypothalamus and attached to it by nerve fibres. It is part of the endocrine system and produces hormones which control other glands as well as various bodily functions.

8. (b) Follicle stimulating hormone (FSH) control secretion of estrogen hormone. FSH is synthesized and secreted by anterior pituitary gland. Development of the ovarian follicle is largely under FSH control, and the secretion of estrogen from this follicle is dependent on FSH and LH. FSH regulates the development, growth, pubertal maturation and reproductive processes of the body.

9. (c) Goitre is an enlarged thyroid gland. It can develop as a result of numerous different conditions. It can be associated with over-function of the thyroid gland (hyperthyroidism, or excessive thyroid hormones) or with under-function of the gland (hypothyroidism, or inadequate levels of thyroid hormones).

10. (c) Metamorphosis (in an insect or amphibian) is the process of transformation from an immature form to an adult form in two or more distinct stages. Thyroxine regulates the growth of metamorphosis in frog.

11. (a) Ovulation is the release of egg from the ovary. In women, LH stimulates estrogen and progesterone production from the ovary. A surge of LH in the midmenstrual cycle is responsible for ovulation, and continued LH secretion subsequently stimulates the corpus luteum to produce progesterone.

12. (d) Parathormone (PTH) regulates calcium level in blood. PTH is released from the parathyroid glands when calcium ion levels in the blood drop below a set point. PTH stimulates the osteoclasts to break down the calcium containing bone matrix to release free calcium ions into the bloodstream. PTH also triggers the kidneys to return calcium ions filtered out of the blood back to the bloodstream so that it is conserved.

13. (d) Adrenaline and noradrenaline hormones help to increase the flow of blood to the brain and muscles to improve the "fight-or-flight" response to stress. These hormones also work to increase heart rate, breathing rate, and blood pressure while decreasing the flow of blood to and function of organs that are not involved in responding to emergencies.

14. (a) Gastrin is a hormone which stimulates secretion of gastric juice and is secreted into the bloodstream by the stomach wall in response to the presence of food.

15. (b) Prolactin (PRL) is hormone secreted by the pituitary gland that stimulates lactation (milk production). It also has many other functions, including essential roles in the maintenance of the immune system.

Assertion & Reason

1. (b) Goitre is an enlargement of the thyroid gland. The thyroid can't manufacture its hormones without sufficient dietary iodine.

2. (c) Prolactin is a hormone secreted by the pituitary gland that stimulates lactation (milk production). Prolactin levels rise during pregnancy and drop for a short period just before birth, then they rise once again a few hours after delivery, or immediately when the baby is put to the breast. It also has many other functions, including essential roles in the maintenance of the immune system.

3. (a) Adrenaline is known as an emergency hormone. Adrenaline and noradrenaline hormones help to increase the flow of blood to the brain and muscles to improve the "fight-or-flight" response to stress. These hormones also work to increase heart rate, breathing rate, and blood pressure while decreasing the flow of blood to and function of organs that are not involved in responding to emergencies.

4. (b) Thyroxine is secreted by thyroid gland. Hence, a tadpole deprived of thyroid gland fails to metamorphosize into adult. Metamorphosis in amphibians is regulated by thyroxine concentration in the blood because thyroxine stimulates tissue differentiation therefore affects metamorphoses of tadpole into adult.

5. (b) Calcitonin is released when calcium ion levels in the blood rise above a certain set point. Calcitonin functions to reduce the concentration of calcium ions in the blood by aiding the absorption of calcium into the matrix of bones. The parathyroid glands produce the hormone parathyroid hormone (PTH), which is involved in calcium ion homeostasis. PTH is released from the parathyroid glands when calcium ion levels in the blood drop below a set point.

6. (a) Sweat glands (also known as sudoriferous) are small tubular structures of the skin that produce sweat. There are two main types of sweat glands: eccrine sweat glands (distributed almost all over the body) and apocrine sweat glands (limited to the axilla (armpits) and perianal areas in humans). Sweat glands make body smelly due to infection of bacteria.

Exercise 4 — Foundation Builder +

1. (d) AIDS virus infects T_4 lymphocytes (also called Helper cells). Cytotoxic T cells called T_8 lymphocytes.

2. (a) ELISA is an fundamental tool of clinical immunology and is used as an initial screen for HIV detection.

3. (b) Heroin is synthesised by acetylation of morphine. Heroin, commonly called smack and is chemically diacetylmorphine is made from the resin of poppy (*Papaver somniferum*) plants. Milky, sap-like opium is first removed from the pod of the poppy flower. This opium is refined to make morphine, then further refined into different forms of heroin. The synthesis of heroin is a simple one step acetylation reaction, and typically is performed by the addition of a large excess of acetic anhydride directly to morphine followed by heating the resulting solution to, or near, boiling. Generally the final product is isolated by treating the cooled reaction mixture with sodium carbonate and collecting the heroin base by filtration.

4. (d) Gonorrhoea, Syphilis, Genital herpes are sexually transmitted diseases. Gonorrhoea is caused by a bacterium *Neisseria gonorrhoeae*. Syphilis is caused by a bacterium *Treponema pallidum*. Genital herpes is caused by a virus Type-II-Herpes simplex virus.

5. (a) In lactational amenorrhea, pills and emergency contraceptives methods, there is the involvement of hormones.

   Lactational amenorrhea (absence of menstruation) is based on the fact that ovulation and therefore the cycle do not occur during the period of intense lactation following parturition. Prolactin is the major hormone responsible for milk production and is present in sufficient quantities in almost all women to allow the establishment of normal lactation.

   Emergency contraception methods include emergency contraception pills (ECP), intrauterine device, e.g., LNG-20 (Levonor- gestrel) and ulipristal acetate.

   CuT and barrier method do not involve any hormonal role.

6. (d) Option (d) is the answer because ART in which embryos are transferred, include ZIFT and IUT i.e. Zygote Intrafallopian Transfer and Intra Uterine Transfer respectively, both are embryo transfer (ET) methods.

   Option (a), (b) and (c) are incorrect because in GIFT (Gamete Intrafallopian Transfer), gamete is transferred into the fallopian tube of female who cannot produce ova. ICSI is Intra cytoplasmic sperm injection in which sperm is directly injected into the ovum.

7. (a) A. The pill — Prevents ovulation
       B. Condom — Prevents sperm reaching cervix
       C. Vasectomy — Semen contains no sperms
       D. Copper-T — Prevent implantation.

8. (d)

Think Out of the Box

Case Study

1. Diabetes occurs when pancreas either do not produce insulin or they stop responding to insulin. In such cases, external administration of insulin hormone is necessary to treat disbetic patients.

2. This statement is not true as the levels of calcium in blood are also controlled by thyroid gland. When the level of calcium ion increases in blood, thyroid gland secretes calcitonin which excretes excess calcium through urine or to get accumulated in the bones.

7 Life Processes

Build A Strong Foundation

CONCEPT MAP

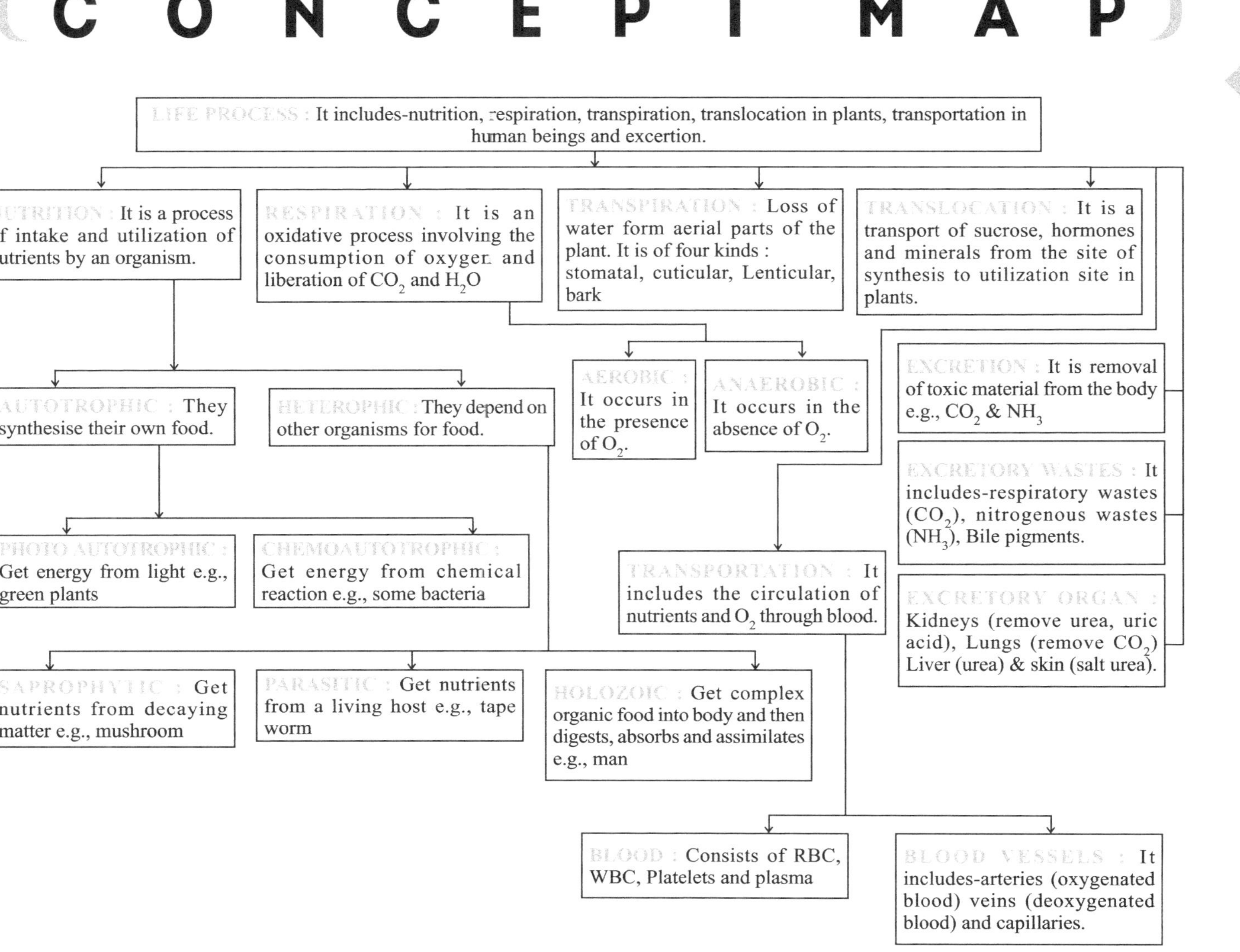

NUTRITION

Nutrition refers to all activities included in obtaining food and its utilization in the body. As we all know, all living organisms need food that provides energy for various activities of the body. Carbohydrates, proteins and fats are vital for energy or growth. They are called *nutrients*. Vitamins minerals and water are accessory food, that helps human body to work properly.

Different organism take food through different modes. *Based on the mode of food production, organisms can be classified as follows :-*

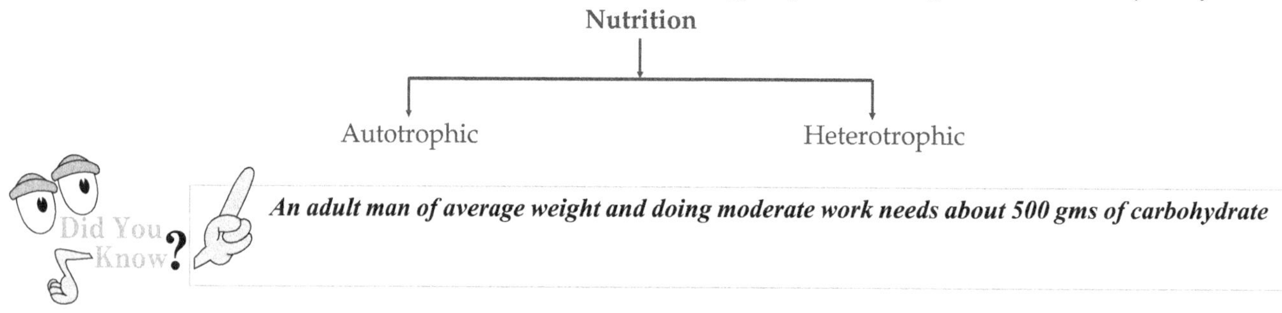

Did You Know?

An adult man of average weight and doing moderate work needs about 500 gms of carbohydrate

Nutrition in Plants (Autotrophs)

Plants are autotrophs. They prepare their own food by the process of photosynthesis.

Photosynthesis is the process by which plants can manufacture their own food. Leaves are the "food factories of plants". They can make food because they contain chlorophyll. Most leaves are green in colour.

How do leaves make food? Leaves make food by a process called photosynthesis. It takes place only when water, carbon dioxide, sunlight and chlorophyll are present. Water comes from the soil. It is absorbed by the roots. It travels up the fine tubes in the roots and the stem and the veins of the leaves. Carbon dioxide comes from the air which enters the leaves through the breathing pores. Chlorophyll is the green pigment found naturally in plants. It is most abundant in the leaves. Sunlight comes from the sun. When there is chlorophyll, water and carbon dioxide present in a leaf, a special chemical reaction takes place in the presence of sunlight. Water combines with carbon dioxide to form sugar and oxygen. The sugar is used by the plant as food. The oxygen passes out of the leaf through the breathing pores called stomata. Sunlight provides the energy for the chemical reaction.

This happens during photosynthesis :

Carbon dioxide + Water + Light energy → Sugar + Oxygen

Photosynthesis is the process by which green leaves in sunlight combine carbon dioxide and water to form sugar and oxygen.

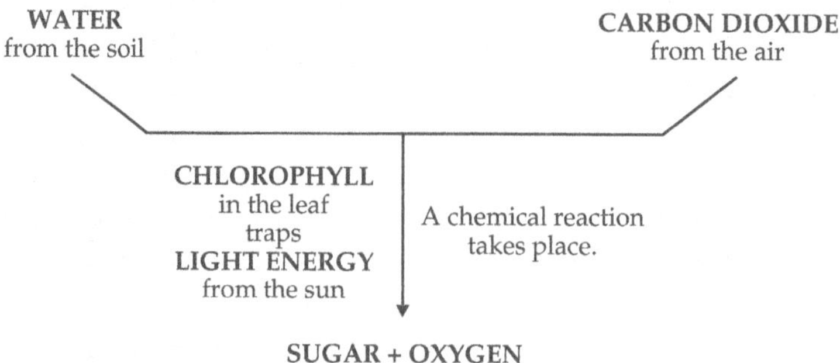

A small number of plants do not photosynthesize, they feed on living things.

1. **Parasites :-** A small number of plants are parasites. This means that they do not make their own food, but live and feed on other living things, called hosts. The dodder plant, for example, attaches itself firmly to its host plant by sending thread like structures called haustoria into it. Dodder stems then grow rapidly all over the host, which becomes completely covered and eventually dies.

2. **Saprotrophs :-** Some organisms feed on dead matter instead of living on a host or making their own food. They are known as saprotophic plants or saprotrophs. Fungi and some orchids are saprotrophs.

3. **Meat eaters or Insectivorous plants :-** Some plants can kill and digest small creatures, such as insects. They are called carnivorous plants. They attract their victims into deadly traps using colour or particular smell. Once inside, the insect is dissolved by powerful chemicals called enzymes.

Such plants grow in soil which contains few minerals. They absorb what they need from the bodies of their prey by digesting them. For example, pitcher plants catch animals in their jug like leaves called pitchers.

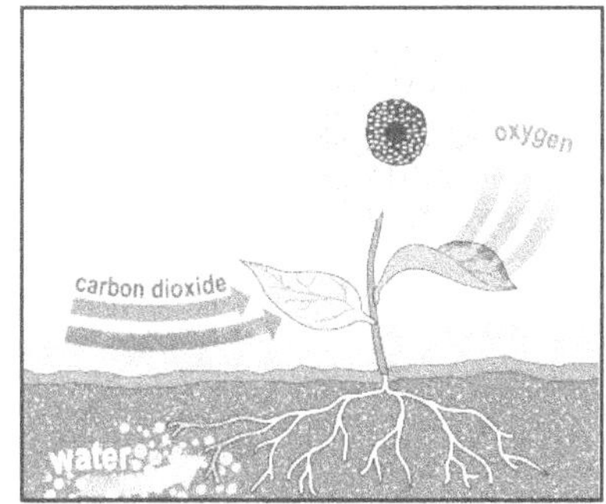

Plant Photosynthesis

Why is photosynthesis so important?

SOLUTION :

Photosynthesis is very important firstly because it makes food. All animals, whether they are plant-eaters or animal-eaters, ultimately depend on plants for food. There will be no food for the animals if there are no plants or no photosynthesis. Secondly, photosynthesis keeps the air fresh by removing carbon dioxide and replacing it with oxygen. This ensures that there is always enough oxygen in the air for plants and animals to breathe. Plants and animals will suffocate and die if the air does not have enough oxygen.

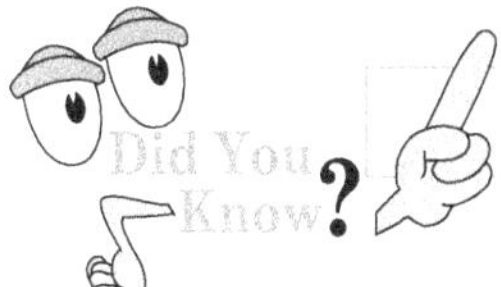

Some bacteria found in ocean depth do photosynthesis without sunlight

Autotrophs are divided into two types :

(i) **Photoautotrophs :** The autotrophs which do photosynthesis in the presence of sunlight, are called photoautotrophs. Examples include green plant, algae and some bacteria.

(ii) **Chemoautotrophs :** The autotrophs which do photosynthesis without sunlight, are called chemoautotrophs. Examples include certain bacteria found in deep sea. They use chemicals like H_2S.

What is the difference between autotrophs and heterotrophs.

SOLUTION :

Autotrophs :
1. They can make their own food from raw materials in presence of sunlight.
2. They take in simple inorganic substances and change it into complex organic food. e.g., all green plants.

Heterotrophs :
1. They cannot make their own food.
2. They take in complex food and break it into simple food e.g., all animals and fungi and non-green plants.

Biology

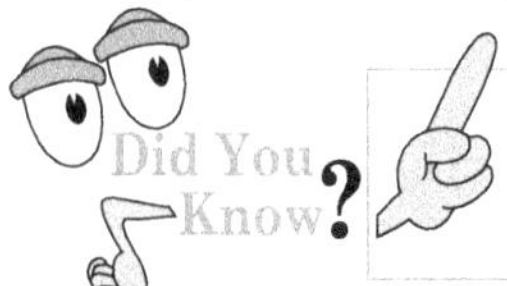

Nutrition in Animals (HeterotRophs)

Animals cannot make their own food. They depend on the food synthesized by plants. The food intake by animals is *holozoic*. Organisms which depend on other organisms for their food are called *heterotrophs*. Their mode of intake of food is called *heterotrophic nutrition*.

> **In adult the whole digestive tract is about 9m long.**
> **The longest part of the digestive system, is the small intestine, measuring 6m.**
> **The large intestine is 1.5 m long.**

DIGESTIVE SYSTEM IN HUMANS

Human body needs food which contain many substances, that is used to help the body grow and repair itself. It also provides energy to move about. Water is needed to continually replenish the supply of water in the blood stream. The process of taking in food and breaking it into tiny pieces, small enough to absorb into the body, is known as *digestion*. The human digestive system includes :-

Mouth, Teeth, Tongue, Oesophagus, Stomach, Small Intestine, Large In testine, Liver, Pancreas

Let us now discuss the process of digestion. As food passes through your body, it is broken down into pieces small enough to be dissolved in our blood. This process, called **digestion**, takes place in the **digestive tract** or **alimentary canal**. Alimentary canal is a tube that runs from your mouth to a hole in your bottom called the **anus**. Food is broken down physically by chewing and churning, and chemically by the action of **digestive juices**, made by organs called **glands**.

Stages of digestion :-

1. Food is chewed in the mouth and mixed with a digestive juice called *saliva*, which is made in your *salivary glands*. Saliva moistens the food so it slides down your throat easily by peristalised. It also starts to break down starch in the food into a sugar called *maltose* by the action of amylase.

2. Our throat muscles guide the food through the *pharynx* into a passage called the *gullet* or *oesophagus*. As you swallow, a flap called the *epiglottis* blocks off the top of your *windpipe* or *trachea*, so the food does not go down the wrong way.

3. Food travels down the gullet into your stomach. Muscles in the wall of the gullet contract to push the food along. This action, called *peristalsis*, takes place all along your digestive tract.

4. In the *stomach*, food is churned up with *gastric juices*. These start to digest protein and they also contain hydrochloric acid which kills germs in the food. Your stomach lining has folds called *rugae*, which flatten as it fills.

5. The food moves into a tube called the *small intestine*. This has three sections: the *duodenum*, the *jejunum* and the *ileum*. In the duodenum, digestive juices made by the liver and pancreas break down fats, protein and starch.

6. The small intestine, especially the *ileum*, is lined with tiny, finger-like projections called *villi* which increases its surface area. Each villus contains minute blood vessels, which absorb the digested food, and carry it to the liver for further processing before it is carried around the body.

Lichen

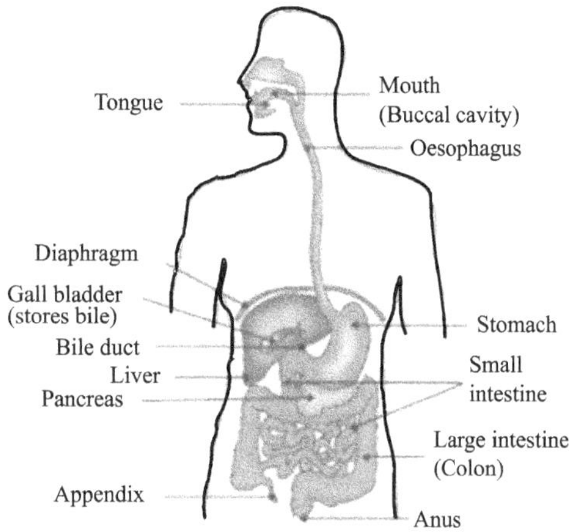

Human alimentary canal

Digestive Enzymnes : Sources, Effects		
Part/Organ	**Source**	**Enzymes**
Mouth	Salivary glands	Amylase
Stomach	Gastric glands	Pepsin
Pancreas	Pancreatic juice	Trypsin
		Carboxy
		peptidase
		Amylase
		Lipase
		Amino
		peptidase,
		Maltase

Respiration involves exchange of gases, i.e. breathing and oxidation of food to release energy. The oxygen taken in during breathing oxidises the food to release energy. Carbon dioxide is released during this process and is given out. The process of taking in oxygen (inhalation) and giving out carbon dioxide (exhalation) is called respiration. It is the most vital process that never stops in organisms.

Respiration in plants : Respiration or exchange of gases among plants takes place through the pores called stomata. *Stomata* are found in leaves and stems of plants, which allows oxygen, carbon dioxide and water vapour to move in or out of plants. The stomatal pores are enclosed by two guard cells which are surrounded by several subsidiary cells. Generally, more number of stomata are present on the lower surface of leaf.

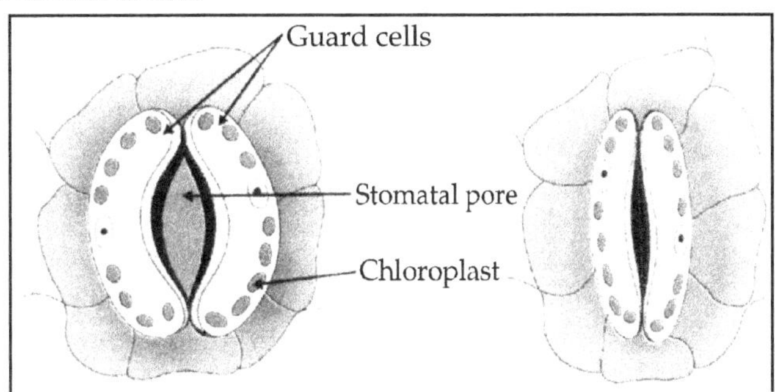

Stomata

Respiration in animals : Some unicellular animals such as *Amoeba* and *Hydra* take oxygen and give out carbon dioxide through cell membrane. Insects such as cockroach, mosquito take oxygen through the air holes (spiracle) present on the side of the body. Fishes respire through gills. The tadpoles take oxygen through gills but when they are metamorphosed into adult frog, gills are replaced by lungs.

Higher organisms like tigers, birds, rats, snakes, human have lungs as their respiratory system.

Respiratory system in humans :-

The *respiratory system* is made up of *lungs* and the passages that lead to them. Humans breathe air into lungs, and oxygen from the air passes into the blood, which carries it around whole body. Waste, carbon dioxide passes from the blood into the lungs and is breathed out.

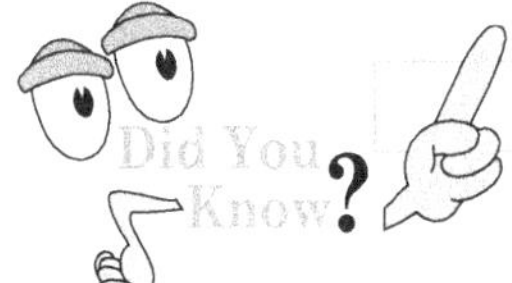

Sea anemone has the simplest type of respiratory surface and diffusion starts across a thin layer.

Why do we sneeze?

SOLUTION :

We sneeze to expel foreign particles from our nose. When pollens, dust or smoke enter our nose, they cause irritation. Sneezing involves a sudden and violent expiration of air through the nose and mouth. When the nerve endings in the nose lining detect any irritating substances, it controls involuntary actions. The brain then sends signals to the respiratory organs, like lungs and pharynx, to squeeze and then expel a gust of air with a loud blast.

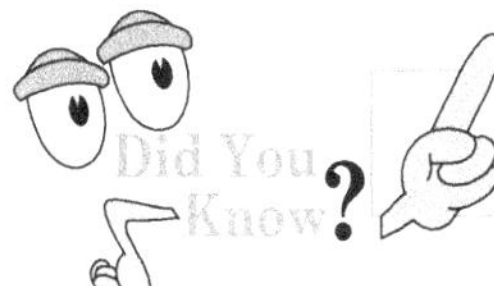

A sneeze usually starts with release of chemicals, such as histamine, by inflammatory cells in nose, signalling that there is urgent need to expel something out of the nose.

TRANSPORTATION

By now, we have learnt that every cell needs a regular supply of nutrients and oxygen to provide energy. The food that we eat is broken down into smaller components to be absorbed by the cells. The oxygen that we inhale is also absorbed by all the cells of the body. Our body also requires a constant removal of wastes materials such as carbon dioxide. *Have you ever thought how these nutrients and oxygen is transported in our body? OR How the oxygen is transported to all the body cells?* The oxygen is transported through blood and the blood is pumped to different parts of our body through an organ called heart. For the supply of useful materials and removal of wastes from the body cells, human body consists of a transport system called circulatory system. It is the transportation system of our body. *Transportation* is the movement of substances, especially oxygen, water, food molecules, carbon dioxide and waste products into or out of cell.

Circulatory System

The human circulatory system is composed of three major parts.
- *Heart:* A pumping organ to transport blood
- *Blood vessels:* Arteries, Veins, Capillaries
- *Blood:* Red blood cells (RBCs), White blood cells (WBCs), Platelets

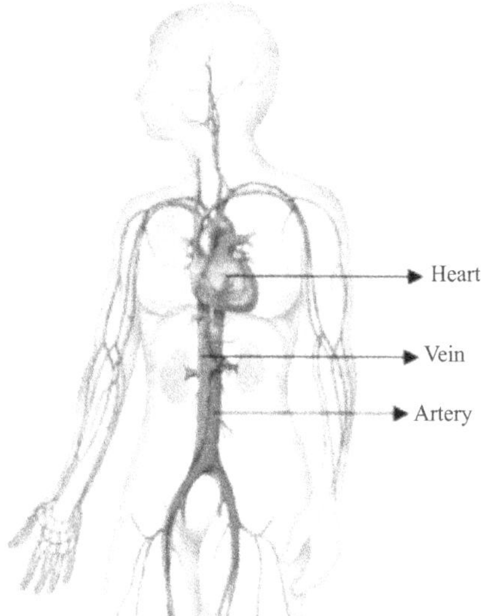

Circulatory system

Heart

Heart is a hollow muscular organ as big as your fist. It contracts and relaxes rhythmically to pump blood throughout the body. The heart beats approximately 70-90 times per minute.

Human heart consists of four chambers. The *upper two chambers* are called *atria* while the *lower two chambers* are called *ventricles*.

Hence, the human heart is four chambered. *The right atrium* receives carbon dioxide rich blood from the body. Blood from the right atrium then enters the *right ventricle*, which contracts and pumps the blood to the lungs. In the lungs the blood becomes oxygenated with the help of the oxygen present in the lungs as a result of breathing. On the other hand, oxygen rich blood from the lungs returns to the *left atrium*. From the left atrium, blood enters the *left ventricle*. The left ventricle contracts and pumps the blood to all parts of the body.

The rhythmic contraction and expansion of various chambers of the heart maintains the transport of oxygen to all the parts of the body.

Blood

What happens when your finger is pricked with a needle? A red colour fluid, called blood flows out. The main function of blood is to transport oxygen and nutrients to various parts of the body.

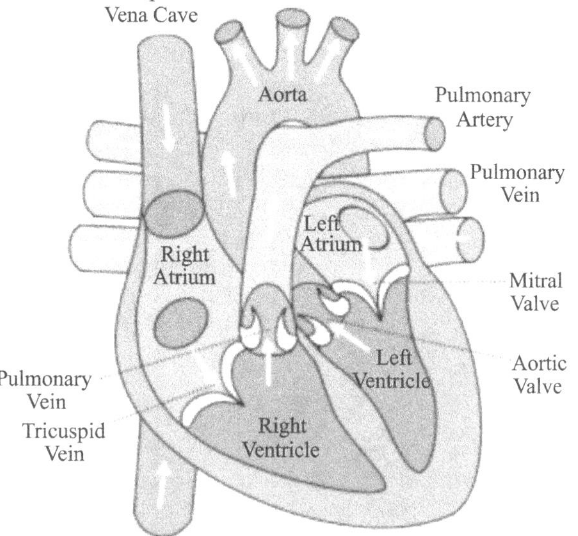

Human Heart

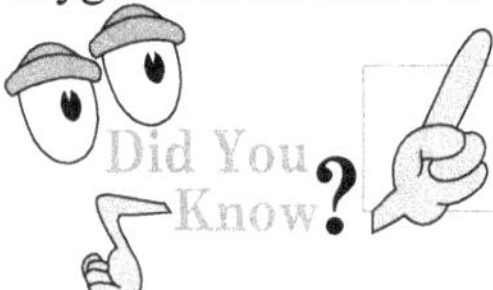

There is no substitute for human blood. It is known as river of life. A new born baby has about one cup of blood in his body.

The blood consists of liquid or fluid called *plasma* with red blood cells, white blood cells and platelets floating in it. *Plasma* is the colourless fluid of the blood. It helps in the transport of food, CO_2, wastes and salts.

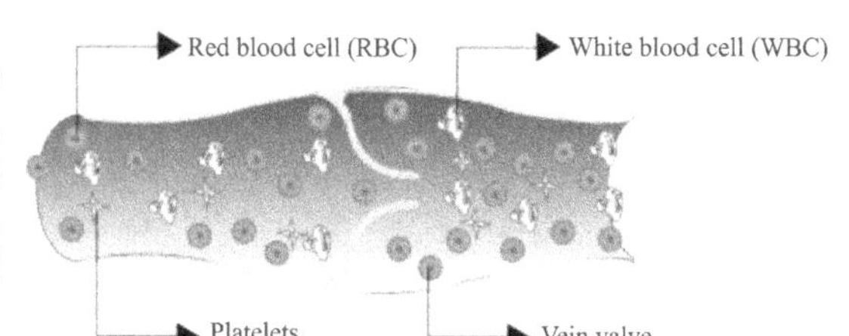

1. *Red blood cells (RBCs):* Red blood cells are the most abundant cells in the blood. These cells contain a red pigment called *haemoglobin*. It is the haemoglobin which carries oxygen and transports it to all parts of the body.
2. *White blood cells (WBCs):* WBCs are colourless cells without haemoglobin. They are the largest cell of the blood. They fight against infections and protect the body from foreign particles. The foreign particles include germs and bacteria. Basically, WBCs are like soldiers that protect the body from various infections.

3. *Platelets:* Platelets are small irregular bodies present in the blood. They contain essential chemicals that help in clotting. The main function of platelets is to prevent bleeding.

When you get injured, blood comes out from the site of injury. But within few minutes, the blood stops and a dark red colour clot appears.
How red colour clot is formed?

SOLUTION :

The clot is formed because of platelets. Platelets release blood clotting chemicals at the site of injury. These chemicals form a clot and prevent further bleeding.

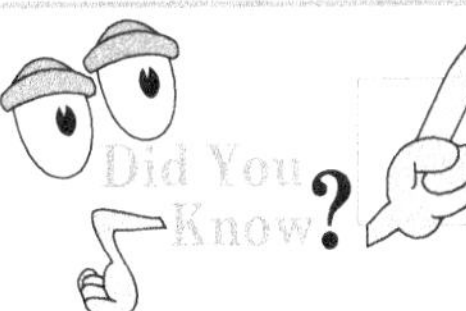

Our blood vessels (arteries, veins and capillaries) are over 60000 miles long which is long enough to go around the world more than twice!

Blood Vessels

Blood vessels are hollow tubes that carry blood to all parts of the body. They are located throughout the human body.
There are three types of blood vessels: Arteries, Veins, and Capillaries

1. **Arteries:** Arteries are tough, elastic tubes that carry blood from the heart to various organs of the body. They generally carry O_2 rich blood except for *pulmonary artery.* Pulmonary artery is the only artery that carries CO_2 rich blood from heart to lungs.

Gently place your middle and index finger of right hand on the inner side of your left wrist.
Observation: You will feel something beating strongly or violently. This is called your pulse.
Conclusion: Pulse arises due to rhythmic contraction and expansion of the arteries with each beat of the heart. The number of beats per minute is called the pulse rate.

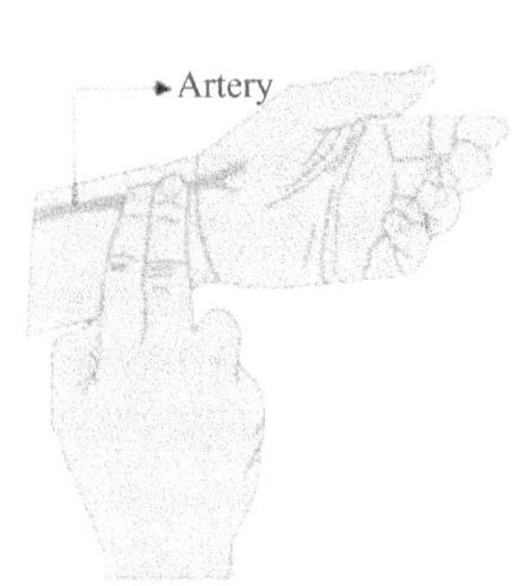

Pulse in wrist

2. **Veins:** Veins are thin walled, non-elastic blood vessels. They transport blood towards the heart from the various organs. Veins carry CO_2 rich blood except for pulmonary vein. Pulmonary vein carries oxygen rich blood from the lungs to the heart. Though veins are thin-walled but they possess valves. The valves are present to prevent the backflow of waste materials to the tissues.

3. **Capillaries:** As the arteries move away from the heart to the various organs and tissues, they divide into smaller vessels called capillaries. The wall of the capillaries is very thin. They form networks which reach every living cell of the body. These capillaries then join to form veins which carry blood to the heart.

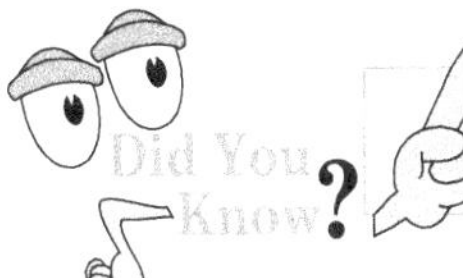

You can check your pulse rate where an artery comes close to the skin such as your wrist, neck, temple area behind the knee or top of your foot.

Count the number of beats of your pulse in 30 seconds by placing your middle and index finger of right hand on the inner side of your left wrist. Then double the count result to get the number of beats per minute. How many pulse beat could you count? A resting person usually has a pulse rate between 72 to 80 beats per minute.

BLOOD PRESSURE

The force that blood exerts against the wall of a vessel is called blood pressure. This pressure is much greater in arteries than in veins. The pressure of blood inside the artery during ventricular systole (contraction) is called systolic pressure and pressure in artery during ventricular diastole (relaxation) is called diastolic pressure. The normal systolic pressure is about 120 mm of Hg and diastolic pressure is 80 mm of Hg.

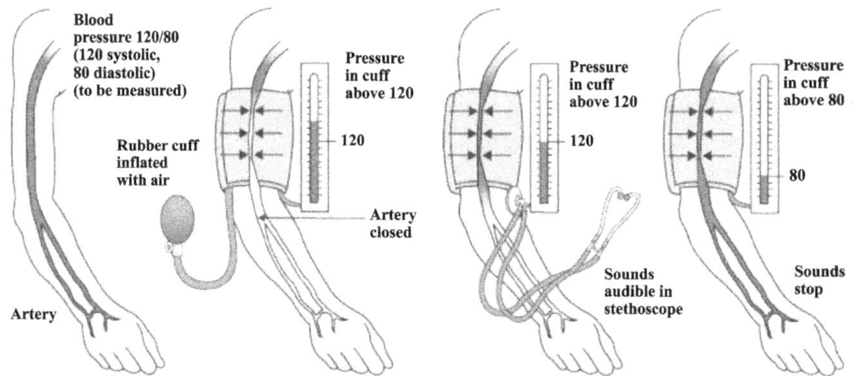

Blood pressure is measured with an instrument called sphygmomanometer. High blood pressure is also called hypertension and is caused by the constriction of arterioles, which results in increased resistance to blood flow. It can lead to the rupture of an artery and internal bleeding.

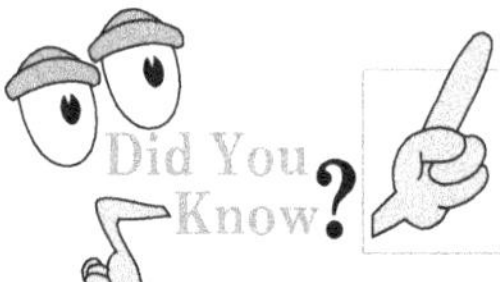

Doctors use a stethoscope for listening to the sound generated by heart inside your body.

Transportation of Substances in Plants

Plants have tube like vessels conducting tissues which transport water and minerals from the soil to the leaves and food from the leaves to all plant parts. The tissues involved in transport are collectively known as *vascular tissue*.

- *Xylem* takes up water and minerals from the soil via roots and transport (root hair) to rest of the plant body.
- *Phloem* transports food materials from the leaves to different parts of the plant body. Thus xylem and phloem transport water and food respectively.

EXCRETION

The waste products are usually toxic and they may prove to be fatal if retained inside the body. These wastes need to be removed. The biological process which removes these harmful metabolic wastes from the body into the surrounding, is called excretion.

Excretion in Plants

Plants use a variety of methods to get rid of waste materials. For example, they get rid of excess of water by transpiration. *Transpiration* is the evaporation of water from the plants. The water evaporates through the stomata, present on the surface of leaves. Some plants may store waste materials in the cell vacuoles as gum and resin. Also oxygen is excreted through stomata of leaves as a waste product during photosynthesis.

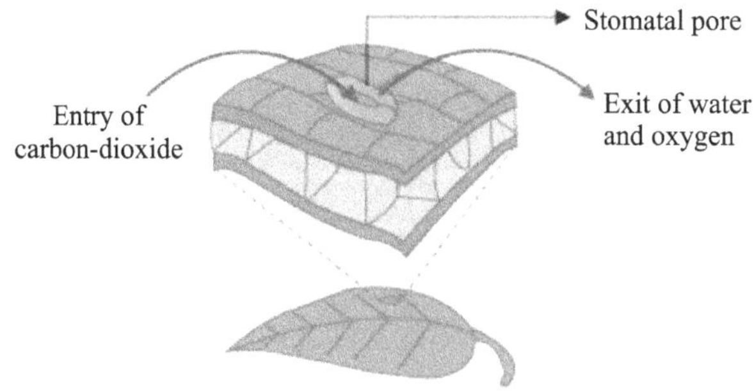

Excretion in Animals

The process of removing waste products produced in the cells of living organism is called *excretion*. It is an essential process in all forms of life.Different organisms have different kind of mechanism for excretion. In one celled organisms, wastes are discharged through the surface of cell. In humans, the main organs of excretion are the kidneys.

The organs involved in the process of excretion form the *excretory system*.

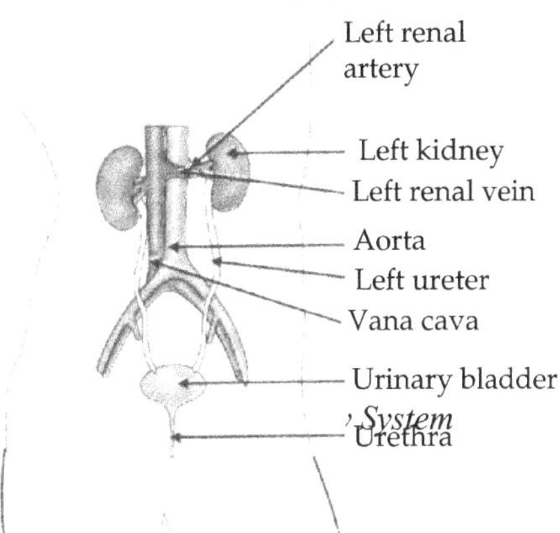

Excretion in Humans

The excretory system of humans consists of- a pair of kidneys, a pair of ureters, a urinary bladder and a urethra. The main excretory organs of the human body are the *kidneys*. They are connected via the ureter to the *urinary bladder*, which is then connected to *urethra*. The most important structure in the kidneys is the microscopic blood capillaries that filter the blood to produce urine.

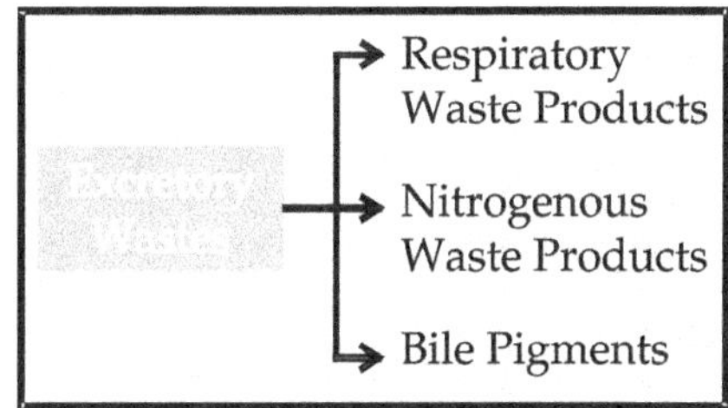

Excretory Wastes in Humans

Time to Check Your Knowledge

☛ **How urine is produced in body?**

SOLUTION :

During blood circulation the blood passes through the kidneys. This blood contains both useful and waste materials. The kidneys filter the wastes from the blood and produce urine. From the kidneys, the urine goes into the urinary bladder through two narrow tubes called the ureters. The urinary bladder stores the urine until it is forced out of the body, through an opening known as the urethra.

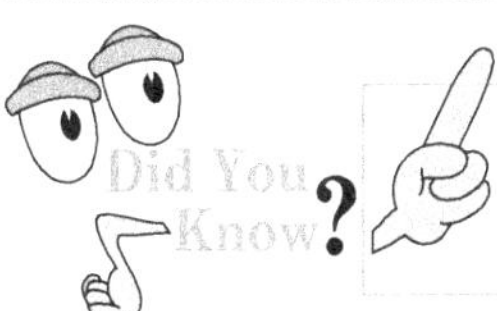

Did You Know ?

Kidney receives more blood for their size than any other body organ about 1.2 litres every minute. All the body's blood flows through the kidney more than 300 times a day.

SUMMARY

- The maintenance of life requires processes like nutrition, respiration, transportation of materials with in the body and excretion of waste products.
- Plants show autotrophic nutrition, wheras animals show heterotrophic mode of nutrition.
- The process of nutrition in animals includes ingestion, digestion, absorption, assimilation and egestion.
- Some plants are heterotrophic. Heterotrophs are divided as insectivorous, saprophytes, parasites and symbiotic.
- Transport of minerals and water takes place through xylem and phloem.
- In human beings, transport of material such as oxygen, carbon dioxide, food and excretory product is a function of the circulatory system. The circulatory system consists of heart, blood and blood vessels.
- Respiration may be aerobic or anaerobic. Aerobic respiration makes more energy than anaerobic respiration.
- In plants respiration takes place by stomatal pores.
- Plants do not have specialised excretory organ but remove waste through stomata.
- Human beings excrete sweat through skin, urea through kidney and carbon dioxide through lungs.

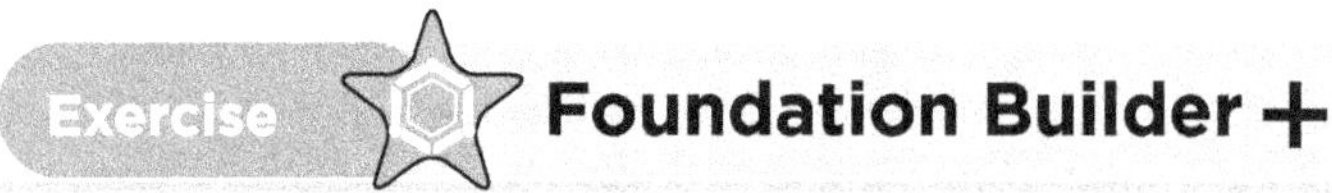

Multiple Choice Questions

DIRECTIONS (Qs. 1-37): This section contains multiple choice questions. Each question has 4 choices (a), (b), (c) and (d) out of which ONLY ONE is correct.

1. The major site of biological action of the human circulatory system is –
   (a) the arteries   (b) the veins
   (c) the capillary bed   (d) the heart

2. Which of the following is not an important function of the vertebrate circulatory system –
   (a) transport of nutrients and respiratory gases
   (b) regulation of body temperature
   (c) protection of the body by circulating antibodies
   (d) removal of waste products for excretion from the body

3. The exchange of gases in human beings takes place in–
   (a) in skin   (b) in mouth
   (c) in nostrils   (d) in lungs

4. The autotrophic mode of nutrition requires :
   (a) Carbon dioxide and water
   (b) Chlorophyll
   (c) Sunlight
   (d) All of the above

5. Plants are green in colour because –
   (a) they absorb green light only
   (b) they reflect green light
   (c) they absorb green light but reflect all other lights
   (d) none of the above are correct

6. Digestion of food in human starts from –
   (a) duodenum   (b) small intestine
   (c) mouth   (d) large intestine

7. Blood vessel carrying blood from lungs to heart is–
   (a) pulmonary artery   (b) pulmonary vein
   (c) coronory artery   (d) none of these

8. Excretion is removal of –
   (a) CO_2
   (b) Harmful and useless ingredients
   (c) Extra water
   (d) Metabolic waste

9. The by-products of photosynthesis are –
   (a) O_2 and H_2O (b) CO_2 and H_2S
   (c) O_2 and CO_2 (d) H_2O and H_2S

10. The process of carbon assimilation is known as –
    (a) transpiration   (b) respiration
    (c) photosynthesis   (d) excretion

11. Phloem transports –
    (a) Minerals   (b) Food prepared by leaves
    (c) Water   (d) All the above

12. Vessels that take blood to the heart from the body are called.
    (a) Arteries   (b) Veins
    (c) Capillaries   (d) None

13. Animals that only eat plant material for food are called
    (a) Carnivores   (b) Herbivores
    (c) Omnivores   (d) None of the above

14. Which of these is a part of your digestive system?
    (a) Stomach   (b) Pancreas
    (c) Rectum   (d) All of the above

15. What tube is used by both the digestive and respiratory systems ?
    (a) Esophagus   (b) Larynx
    (c) Pharynx   (d) None of these

16. Identify the correct statement with reference to human digestive system. **[NTSE]**
    (a) Serosa is the innermost layer of the alimentary canal
    (b) IIeum is a highly coiled part
    (c) Vermiform appendix arises from duodenum
    (d) IIeum opens into small intestine

17. Which of the following guards the opening of hepatopancreatic duct into the duodenum ? **[NTSE]**
    (a) Semilunar valve   (b) Ileocaecal valve
    (c) Pyloric sphincter   (d) Sphincter of Oddi

18. Which of the following statements is not correct? **[NTSE]**
    (a) Goblet cells are present in the mucosa of intestine and secrete mucus
    (b) Oxyntic cells are present in the mucosa of stomach and secrete HCl.
    (c) Acini are present in the pancreas and secrete carboxypeptidase
    (d) Brunner's glands are present in the submucosa of stomach and secrete pepsinogen

19. The enzyme enterokinase helps in conversion of **[NTSE]**
    (a) trypsinogen into trypsin
    (b) caseinogen into casein
    (c) pepsinogen into pepsin
    (d) protein into polypeptides

20. Which of the following options best represents the enzyme composition of pancreatic juice? **[NTSE]**
    (a) amylase, pepsin, trypsinogen, maltase
    (b) peptidase, amylase, pepsin, rennin
    (c) lipase, amylase, trypsinogen, procarboxypeptidase
    (d) amylase, peptidase, trypsinogen, rennin

21. In the stomach, gastric acid is secreted by the **[NTSE]**
    (a) gastrin secreting cells
    (b) parietal cells
    (c) peptic cells
    (d) acidic cells

22. Select the correct events that occur during inspiration.
    (i)   Contraction of diaphragm   **[NTSE]**
    (ii) Contraction of external inter-costal muscles
    (iii) Pulmonary volume decreases
    (iv) Intra pulmonary pressure increases
    (a) (iii) and (iv)   (b) (i), (ii) and (iv)
    (c) Only (iv)   (d) (i) and (ii)

23. Tidal volume and Expiratory reserve volume of an athlete is 500 mL and 1000 mL respectively. What will be his Expiratory capacity if the residual volume is 1200 mL?
    (a) 1500 mL   (b) 1700 mL   **[NTSE]**
    (c) 2200 mL   (d) 2700 mL

24. Lungs are made up of air-filled sacs, the alveoli. They do not collapse even after forceful expiration, because of: **[NTSE]**
    (a) Inspiratory Reserve Volume
    (b) Tidal Volume
    (c) Expiratory Reserve Volume
    (d) Residual Volume

25. Identify the wrong statement with reference to transport of oxygen.   **[NTSE]**
    (a) Partial pressure of CO_2 can interfere with O_2 binding with haemoglobin
    (b) Higher H^+ conc. in alveoli favours the formation of oxyhaemoglobin
    (c) Low pCO_2 in alveoli favours the formation of oxyhaemoglobin
    (d) Binding of oxygen with haemoglobin is mainly related to partial pressure of O_2

26. What is the time of rest in the heart?   **[NTSE]**
    (a) Never   (b) While sleeping
    (c) Between two beats   (d) While doing yogasan

27. Centre of hunger located in: **[JSTSE]**
    (a) Forebrain   (b) Midbrain
    (c) Hindbrain   (d) Spinal cord

28. Select the correct schematic representation of blood circulation in human from the followings: **[NTSE]**

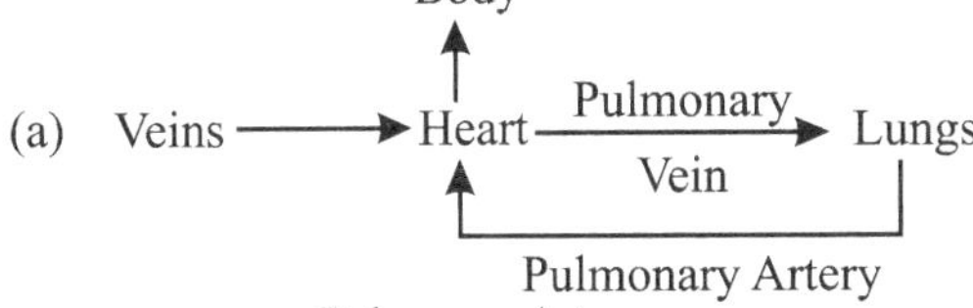

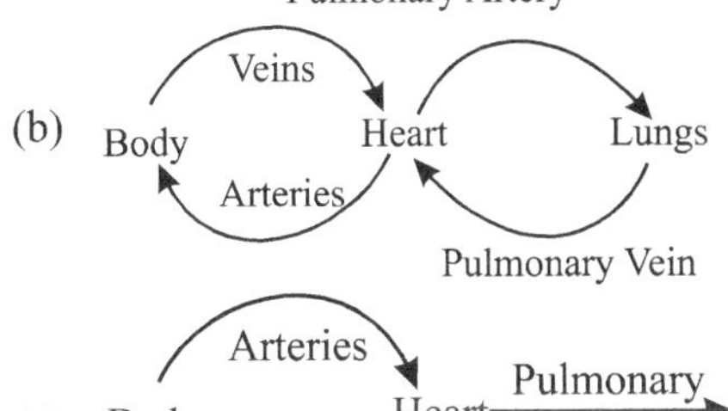

29. What would happen to the person if cerebellum of his brain is damaged?   **[NTSE]**
    (a) He will lose his memory power.
    (b) He will not be able to swallow food properly.
    (c) He will be unable to coordinate and stand properly.
    (d) He will lose his power of vision and hearing.

30. Which one of the following is known as energy currency of cell?   **[NTSE]**
    (a) Adenosine diphosphate
    (b) Adenosine triphosphate
    (c) Pyruvate
    (d) Glucose

31. Sequence of events which occured in a reflex action are   **[NTSE]**
    (a) Receptor - motor neuron - CNS - sensory neuron - effector muscle
    (b) Effector muscle - CNS - sensory nerve - sensory organ
    (c) CNS - sensory neuron - motor neuron - effector muscle
    (d) Receptor organ - sensory neuron - CNS - motor neuron - effector muscle

32. The phenomenon of normal breathing in a human being comprises.   **[NTSE]**
    (a) an active inspiratory and a passive expiratory phase.
    (b) a passive inspiratory and an active expiratory phase.
    (c) both active inspiratory and expiratory phases.
    (d) both passive inspiratory and expiratory phases.

33. Cow has a special stomach as compared to that of a lion in order to: **[NTSE]**
    (a) absorb food in better manner
    (b) digest cellulose present in the food
    (c) assimilate food in a better way
    (d) absorb large amount of water

34. Pancreas is composed of   **[NTSE]**
    (a) Only exocrine cells
    (b) Only endocrine cell
    (c) Both endocrine and exocrine
    (d) Nephrons

35. Hormones produced in one part of the organism reach the distantly located target via   **[NTSE]**
    (a) muscles   (b) bone
    (c) cartilage   (d) blood

36. From the given figure identify the part of human brain controlling most of the involuntary actions: **[NTSE]**

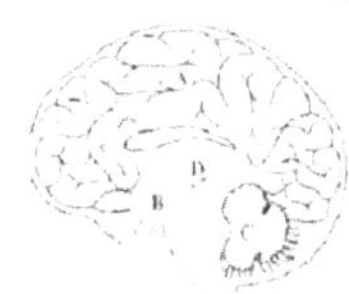

    (a) A & B   (b) B & C
    (c) C & D   (d) D & A

37. Pancreatic juice contains more than one enzyme. Which among the following combination is correct?   **[NTSE]**
    (a) Pepsin and Lipase   (b) Amylase and Pepsin
    (c) Pepsin and Trypsin   (d) Trypsin and Lipase

Assertion & Reason

DIRECTIONS (Qs. 38-43) : *Each of these questions contains an Assertion followed by reason. Read them carefully and answer the question on the basis of following options. You have to select the one that best describes the two statements.*

(a) If both **Assertion** and **Reason** are **correct** and Reason is the **correct explanation** of Assertion.

(b) If both **Assertion** and **Reason** are correct, but Reason is **not the correct explanation** of Assertion.

(c) If **Assertion** is **correct** but **Reason** is **incorrect**.

(d) If **Assertion** is **incorrect** but **Reason** is **correct**.

38. **Assertion :** ATP is the energy carrier of cell.

Reason : ATP is a nucleotide

39. **Assertion :** Thick layers of muscles are present in the wall of alimentary canal.

Reason : The muscles help in the mixing of food materials with the enzymes coming from different gland in the alimentary canal.

40. **Assertion :** Saliva is the secretion of salivary glands.

Reason : Saliva is a mixture of water and electrolyte derived from blood plasma.

41. **Assertion :** Fishes respire through gills.

Reason : Counter current flow occurs in gills.

42. **Assertion :** Arteries carry blood from various body organs to heart.

Reason : Veins carry blood from various body organ to heart.

43. **Assertion :** Cardiovascular system involves blood, blood vessels and heart.

Reason : The human circulatory system is composed of heart, vessels and blood.

Match the following

DIRECTIONS (Qs. 44-47): *Each question contains terms (Given in column-I) and their features or functions (Given in column-II). Terms given in column-I have to be matched with features given in column-II*

44.

Column-I		Column-II
A. Fungi	p.	Autotrophs
B. Animals	q.	Saprotrophs
C. Plants	r.	Heterotrophs
D. Bacteria	s.	Insectivorous plants
E. Pitcher plants	t.	Chemoautotrophs

45.

Column-I		Column-II
A. Salivary gland	p.	Transportation
B. Stomata	q.	Excretion
C. Heart	r.	Digestion
D. Kidney	s.	Circulation
E. Xylem	t.	Transpiration

46.

Column-I		Column-II
A. Salivary gland	p.	Bile salts
B. Gastric gland	q.	Trypsin
C. Pancreatic juice	r.	Amylase
D. Bile juice	s.	Pepsin

47.

Column-I		Column-II
A. Rennin	(i)	Vitamin B_{12}
B. Enterokinase	(ii)	Facilitated transport
C. Oxyntic cells	(iii)	Milk proteins
D. Fructose	(iv)	Trypsinogen

(a) (A)-(iii), (B)-(iv), (C)-(i), (D)-(ii)

(b) (A)-(iii), (B)-(iv), (C)-(ii), (D)-(i)

(c) (A)-(iv), (B)-(iii), (C)-(i), (D)-(ii)

(d) (A)-(iv), (B)-(iii), (C)-(ii), (D)-(i)

SOLUTIONS
(Brief Explanations of Selected Questions)

Exercise **Foundation Builder +**

1. (c) 2. (c) 3. (d) 4. (d)
5. (b) 6. (c) 7. (b) 8. (b)
9. (a) 10. (c) 11. (b) 12. (b)
13. (b)

14. (d) All of these choices are a part of your digestive system. Your digestive system has many other associated organs including the small intestine, large intestine, and liver. The stomach is an area of food digestion. The pancreas releases hormones that affects the digestive process. The rectum is the last place you store you food before the process of elimination (pooping).

15. (c) The pharynx connects the mouth to an area in your throat with a flap. The flap is the epiglottis. The flap moves to one side for food and the other side as you breathe. The branching point leads to the larynx or the esophagus.

16. (b) Option (b) is correct as ileum is a highly coiled tube. Serosa is the outermost layer of the alimentary canal, thus, option (a) is an incorrect statement.
    A narrow finger-like tubular projection, the vermiform appendix arises from caecum part of large intestine thus; option (c) is incorrect statement. Ileum opens into the large intestine, thus option (d) is also an incorrect statement.

17. (d) The sphincter of Oddi (or hepatopancreatic sphincter) is a muscular valve that controls the flow of digestive juices (bile and pancreatic juice) through the ampulla of Vater into the second part of the duodenum.

18. (d) Duodenum contains Brunner's glands which secrete mucus and digestive juices.

19. (a) The correct option is (a) because trypsinogen is activated by an enzyme, enterokinase, secreted by the intestinal mucosa into active trypsin. Trypsinogen is a zymogen from pancreas.

20. (c) Rennin and Pepsin enzymes are present in the gastric juice whereas Maltase is present in the intestinal juice.

21. (b) The main constituent of gastric acid is hydrochloric acid which is produced by parietal cells (also called oxyntic cells) in the gastric glands in the stomach.

22. (d) Inspiration is initiated by the contraction of diaphragm, which increases the volume of thoracic chamber in the anterio-posterior axis. The contraction of external inter-coastal muscles lifts up the ribs and the sternum causing an increase in the volume of the thoracic chamber in the dorso-ventral axis.

23. (a) Expiratory capacity is the total volume of air that a person can expire after a normal inspiration. this includes tidal volume and expirtory reserve volume (TV + ERV).
    Tidal volume of an athelete = 500 ml
    Expiratory reserve volume of an athelete = 1000 ml
    Expiratory capacity = TV + ERV
    = 500 + 1000
    = 1500 ml

24. (d) Volume of air present in lungs after forceful expiration as residual volume prevents the collapsing of alveoli.

25. (b) The correct option is (b) because higher H^+ concentration favours the dissociation of oxygen from oxyhaemoglobin in tissues. In the alveoli, high pO_2, low pCO_2, lesser $H+$ concentration and lower temperature favour formation of oxyhaemoglobin.

26. (a) 27. (b) 28. (b) 29. (c)
30. (b) 31. (d) 32. (a) 33. (b)
34. (c) 35. (d) 36. (c) 37. (d)
38. (c) 39. (a) 40. (b) 41. (a)
42. (a) 43. (d)

44.

	Column-I		Column-II
A.	Fungi	q.	Saprotrophs
B.	Animals	r.	Heterotrophs
C.	Plants	p.	Autotrophs
D.	Bacteria	t.	Chemoautotrophs
E.	Pitcher plants	s.	Insectivorous plants

45.

	Column-I		Column-II
A.	Salivary gland	r.	Digestion
B.	Stomata	t.	Transpiration
C.	Heart	s.	Circulation
D.	Kidney	q.	Excretion
E.	Xylem	p.	Transportation

46.

	Column-I		Column-II
A.	Salivary gland	r.	Amylase
B.	Gastric gland	s.	Pepsin
C.	Pancreatic juice	q.	Trypsin
D.	Bile juice	p.	Bile salts

47. (a) Rennin is a milk digesting proteolytic enzyme releted to pepsin that is synthesised by chief cells in the stomach of some animals.

Enterokinase, produced by cells of duodenum, is involved in digestion. It converts trypsinogen (a zymogen) into its active form trypsin, resulting in the subsequent activation of pancreatic digestive enzymes.

Fructose shows facilitated transport .

Oxyntic cells secrete HCl and intrinsic factors that are essential for absorption of vitamin B_{12}.

Tissues

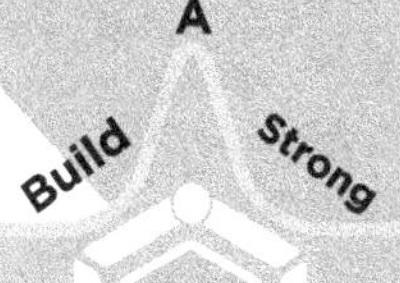

CONCEPT MAP

TISSUE : Tissues are group of cells that have a similar structure and act together to perform a specific function.

PLANT TISSUE

- **Meristematic Tissue**
  - Apical meristem
  - Lateral meristem
  - Intercalary meristem
- **Permanent Tissue**
  - Simple permanent tissue
    - Parenchyma
    - Collenchyma
    - Sclerenchyma
  - Complex permanent tissue
    - Xylem
    - Phloem
- **Protective Tissue**
  - Epidermis

ANIMAL TISSUE

- **Epithelial Tissue**
  - Squamous
  - Columnar
  - Cuboidal
  - Ciliated
  - ★ Glandular epithelium
  - ★ Pseudo-stratified epithelium
- **Muscular Tissue**
  - Striated
  - Unstriated
  - Cardiac
- **Connective Tissue**
  - Fluid
    - Blood
    - Lymph
  - Skeletal
    - Cartilage
    - Bone
  - Proper Connective Tissue
    - Loose connective
      - Areolar
      - Adipose
    - Dense connective
- **Nervous Tissue**

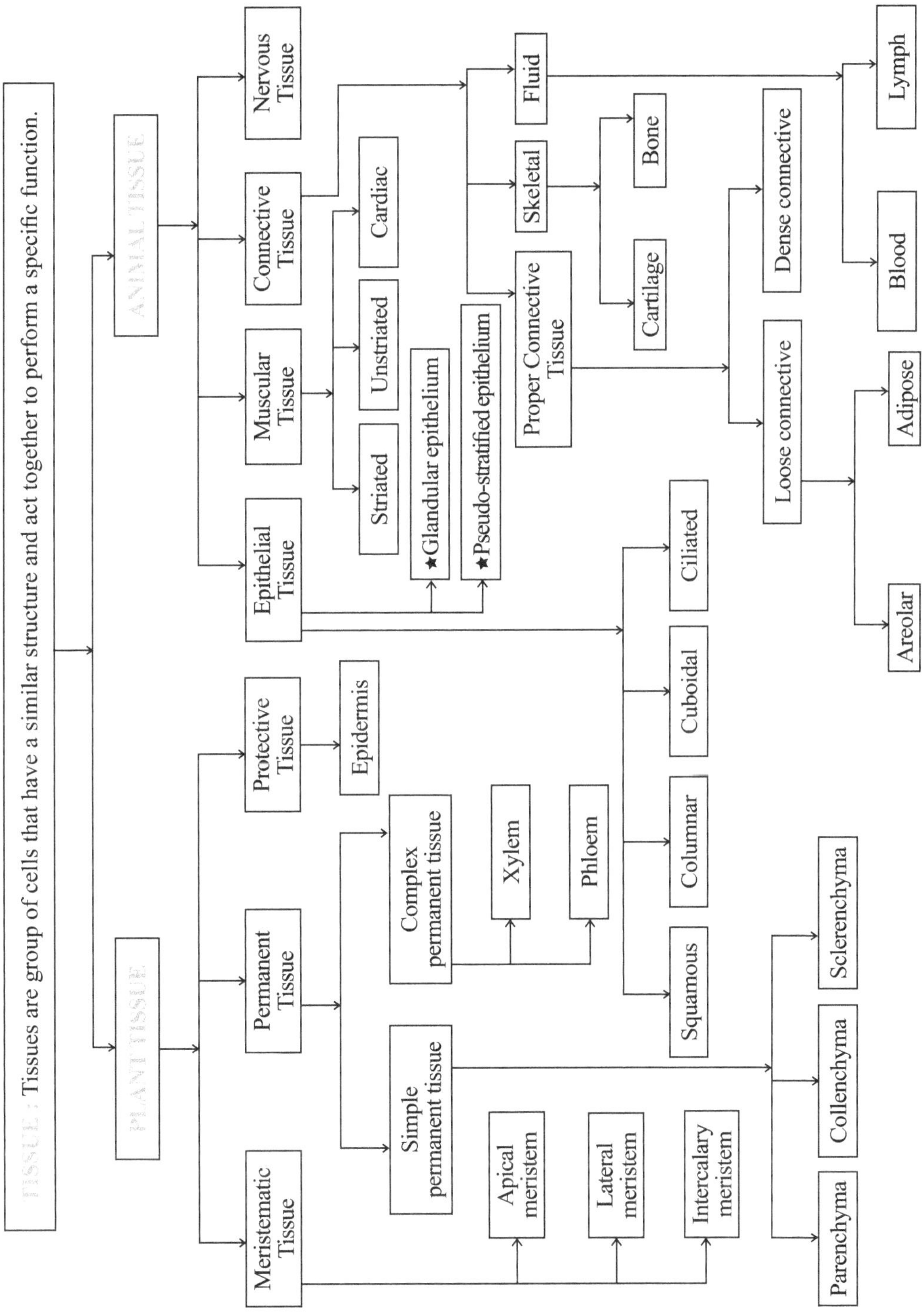

PLANT TISSUES

Plants are autotrophic organisms that prepare their own food by the process of photosynthesis. They are stationary organisms that need not have to move from one place to another in search of food. Most of the tissues of plants are supportive that provide them structural strength or support. Further, there are some tissues in plants that divide throughout the life. *Based on the ability of division in tissues, the various plant tissues can be classified as meristematic and permanent tissues.*

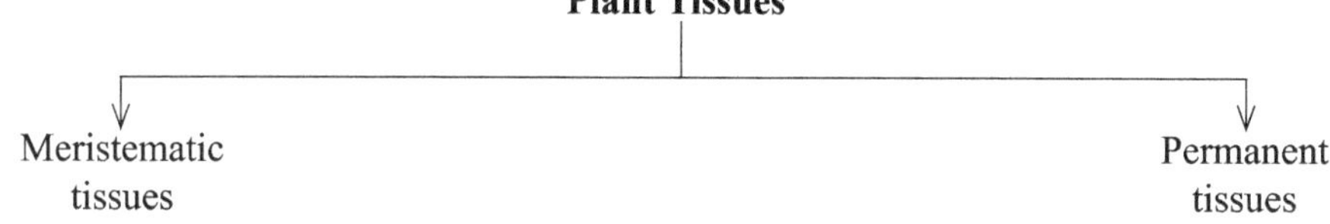

1. **MERISTEMATIC TISSUES :** Meristematic tissues are composed of cells that divide continuously. *These cells show the following characteristics :-*
   (i)   The cells may be spherical, oval, polygonal or rectangular in shape.
   (ii) The cells of meristematic tissue are similar in structure and have thin cell wall, made up of cellulose.
   (iii) The cells are compactly arranged without inter cellular spaces.
   (iv) The cells contain dense cytoplasm and prominent nuclei.
   (v)   Vacuoles are absent and if present, they are few in number.
   (vi) The cells of meristematic tissue are very active.

   Occurrence : Meristematic tissues are found in growing tips of root and shoot.
   Based on their position in the plants, meristems are divided into three types :
   (i) Apical meristem, (ii) Lateral meristem and (iii) Intercalary meristem
   (i)   *Apical meristems* are found at the growing tips of stems and roots. It helps to initiate growth in new cells of seedling. It results in increase in height of the plant.
   (ii) *Lateral meristems* are found beneath the bark. It increases the girth of the stem or root.
   (iii) *Intercalary meristem* are located at the base of leaves or internode. It increases the length of internode.

   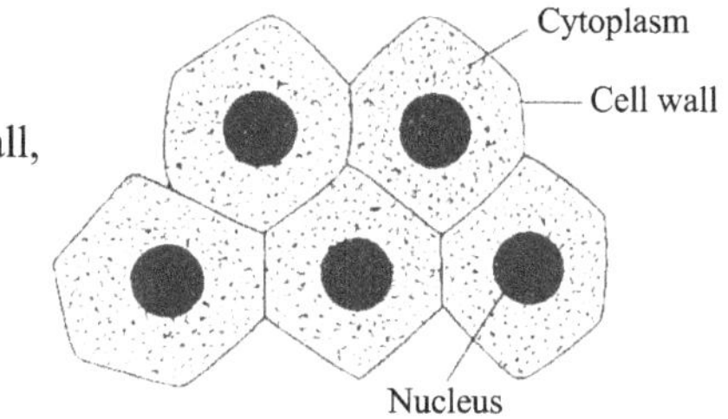

   Meristematic tissue

   The growth of plants occurs in certain specific region. New cells produced by meristem are intially like those of meristem itself, but as they grow and mature, their characteristics changes.

   Cells derived from division of meristematic tissues take up specific function and thereby lose the ability to divide. Thus, they form **permanent tissue**. The developmental process by which cells take up a permanent shape, size and a function is called *differentiation*.

2. **PERMANENT TISSUES :** Permanent tissues are tissues that are derived from meristematic tissues that have lost the power of division and have attained their definite forms. The process of differentiation leads to the development of various types of permanent tissues. They are classified into two main types –
   (A) Simple permanent tissue   (B)   Complex permanent tissue

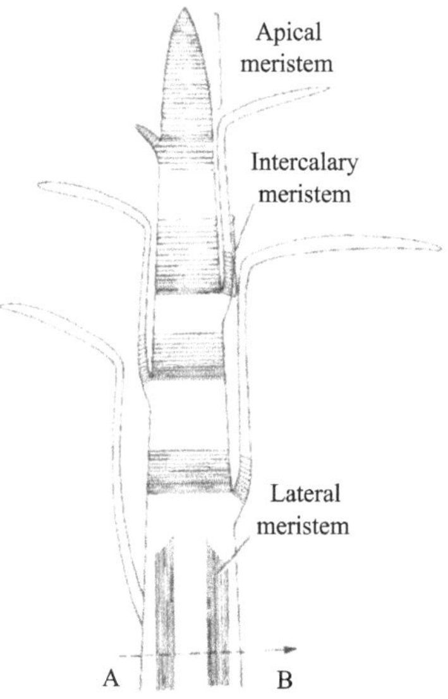

Shoot apex showing location of meristem and young leaves.

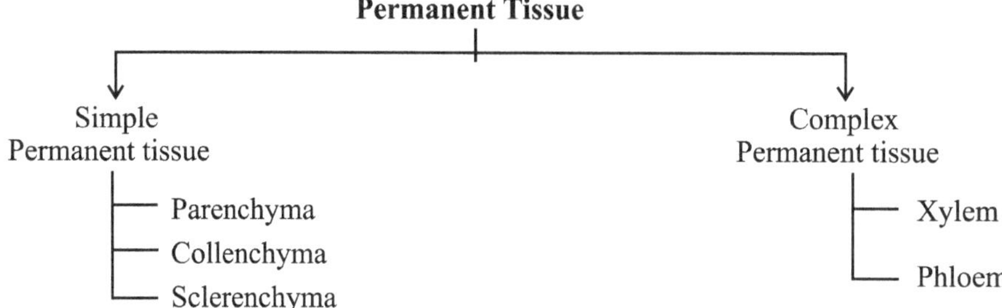

A. **Simple Permanent Tissues :** A simple permanent tissue is made up of one type of cells forming a uniform mass. *They are classified into three types* :

(i)   Parenchyma   (ii)   Collenchyma

(iii) Sclerenchyma

(i) *Parenchyma* **:** Parenchyma is widely distributed in plant body such as stem, root, leaves, flower. They are found in the cortex of root, ground tissue in stems and mesophyll of leaves.

- Parenchyma forms the bulk of the plant body. Hence, it is known as packing tissue.
- They are living and possess the power of division.
- Parenchymal cells are isodiametric, having equal diameters in all directions.
- They are oval, round, polygonal and elongated in shape.
- The cell walls are thin and are made of cellulose.
- Cytoplasm is dense with a single large vacuole.
- Parenchyma are loosely packed cells that make up the intercellular spaces.

Parenchyma that contain chlorophyll are called *chlorenchyma* while parenchyma specialised for gas exchange are called *aerenchyma*, generally present in aquatic plants.

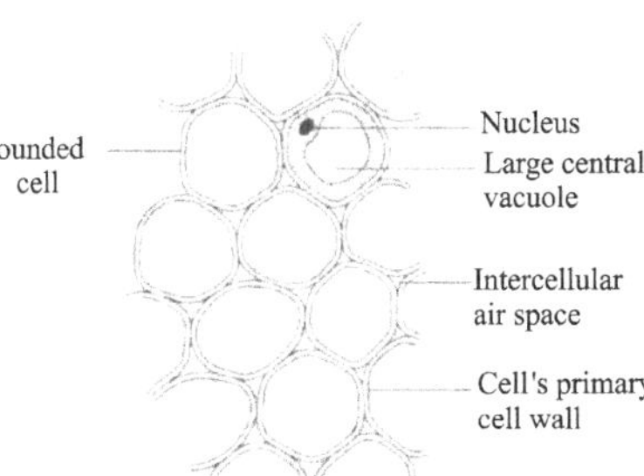

Parenchyma tissue

Functions :

1.   They store and assimilate food. They serve as food storage tissue.
2.   They give mechanical strength by maintaining turgidity.
3.   They perform photosysthesis if chlorophyll is present.
4.   They store waste products like tannin, gum, resins etc.

(ii) *Collenchyma* **:** Collenchyma are found below the epidermis of dicot stem and leaf stalk below epidermis.

- Collenchyma are characterised by the deposition of extra cellulose at the irregular thickened corners of the cells.
- The cells are elongated in shape.
- There is very little intercellular space.

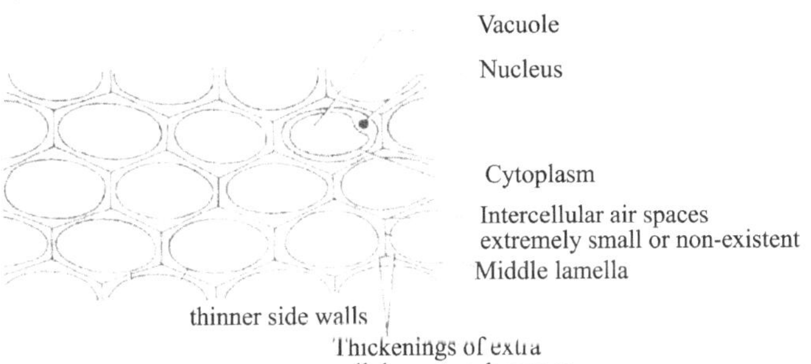

Collenchyma tissue

Functions :

1.   Collenchyma is a mechanical tissue. It provides mechanical support to the stem.
2.   They provide tensile strength with flexibility to those organs in which it is found, like tendrils and stems of climbers.

(iii) *Sclerenchyma* **:** Sclerenchyma are found abundantly in stems, roots, vein of leaves, and hard covering of seeds and nuts.

- These are dead cells that are devoid of protoplasm.
- The cell wall is evenly thickened with lignin. Due to excessive thickening of the wall of a sclerenchyma cell, its cell cavity or lumen becomes nearly absent forming long and narrow cells.
- A conspicuous middle lamella exists between two sclerenchymatous cells with no intercellular space.

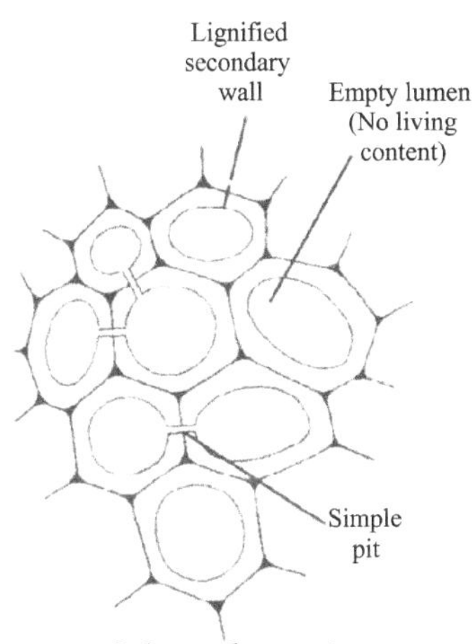

Sclerenchyma tissue

Cells of sclerenchyma are of two types :-

(i) *Fibres* **:** They are usually pointed at both ends and are clustered into strands. They consists of very long, narrow, thick and lignified cells.

(ii) *Sclereids* **:** Sclereids, also called stone cells, are irregular-shaped. They are found in the cortex, pith, phloem, hard seeds, nuts and stony fruits. Their function is to give firmness and hardness to the part concerned.

You most have noticed that flesh of pear and guava are sometimes gritty . Can you guess why it is so? It is due to the presence of sclereids. These cells are thick-walled, hard and strongly lignified.

Function : They give mechanical support to the plant by giving rigidity, flexibility and elasticity to the plant body.

Note

Lignin is a complex polymer that hardens cell wall. It makes the cell wall impermeable so that substances can not pass through it.

Difference table between parenchyma, collenchyma and sclerenchyma.

Parenchyma	Collenchyma	Sclerenchyma
Cell walls are relatively thin, and the cells in parenchyma tissues are loosely packed with large inter cellular space.	The cell wall is irregularly thickened at the corners and there is very little space between the cells.	The cell walls are uniformly thickened and there are no intercellular spaces.
The cell wall in this tissue is made up of cellulose	Pectin and hemicellulose are the major constituents of the cell wall.	An additional layer of the cell wall mainly composed of lignin is found.

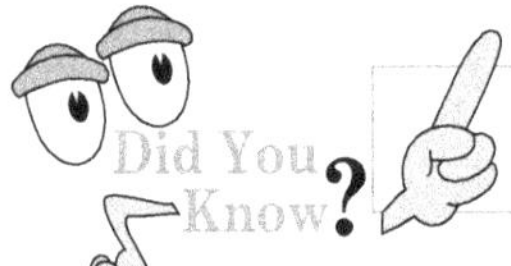

Did You Know?

Husk of coconut is made of sclerenchymatous tissue. It is present in the mesocarp of coconut fruit.

Protective tissue :

(i) *Epidermis* **:** These tissues are usually present in the outermost layer of the plant body such as leaves, stem and root. It includes epidermis and cork.

- Epidermal tissue form a continuous layer without intercellular.
- The outer and side walls are thicker than the inner wall making the cell relatively flat.
- It is one cell thick and covered with cutin and protects the underlying tissue present in plant body.

The main function of epidermis is to protect the plant from desiccation and infection. It also helps in exchange of gases through the stomata.

(ii) *Cork* **:** As roots and stems grow older with time, tissues at the periphery become cork cells.

- Cork cells are dead, they have no intercellular spaces and the cell walls are heavily thickened by the deposition of suberin. Making the cell impermeable to water and gases.
- Cork is protective in function. They prevent loss of water from plant body, protect plant from infection and mechanical injury.

Let's Do Activity

How epidermal cells help in gaseous exchange? Let us perform an activity :

Take a freshly plucked leaf of a Rhoe plant. Stretch it from upper side and breakit by applying pressure. While breaking it, stretch gently so that peel projects out. Place this peel in a petridish filled with a water. Add a few drops of safranine stain to it. Observe it under microscope. *What did you observe?* You will find tiny pores of stomata along with the epidermal cells. The stomata are bound by a pair of kidney shaped guard cells. Guard cells are the two curved cells on the either side of the pore. By changing their shape they can open or close the pore. When guard cells absorb water, they bend outwards, so that the pore between them opens up. When they lose water they go back to a less curved shape, closing the pore between them.

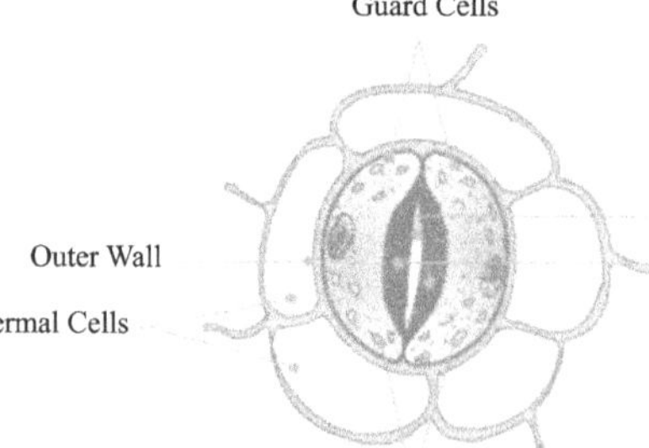

Functions of stomata :-

(i) Stomata helps in transpiration. Transpiration is the process of evaporation of water from the leaf surface.

(ii) Stomata allows the exchange of gases (CO_2 and O_2) with the atmosphere.

B. Complex Permanent Tissues : The complex permanent tissues consists of more than one type of cells. All these cells co-ordinate to perform a common function. They transport water, salt and prepared food materials to various parts of the plant body.

Complex tissues are of two types :-

I. Xylem   II. Phloem

They are both conducting tissues and constitute a vascular bundle. Vascular tissue is a distinctive feature of the complex plants which makes its survival in terrestrial environment possible.

(I) *Xylem* : Xylem is a conducting tissue that conducts water and minerals to various parts of the body. It is composed of four different types of cells.

Xylem

Vessels   Tracheids   Xylem parenchyma   Xylem fibres

(a) *Vessels* – Vessels consist of dead, hollow cells with widelumens. Cells are linked end to end in a drainpipe fashion. End walls have one or more perforations, which allows rapid transport of large volumes of water from roots up through the stem. Vessels have thick lignified walls that prevents the cells from collapsing, enabling them to withstand the negative pressure generated as water is pulled up through their lumens. Lignin also provides waterproofing.

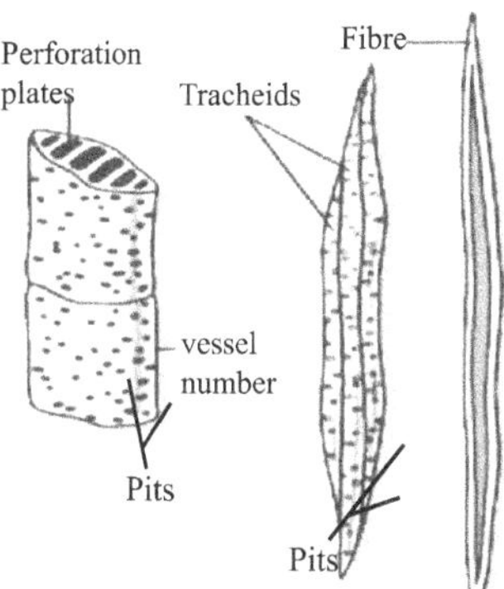

Components of Xylem

Side walls may have bordered pits (unlignified areas), which allows lateral movement of water. If for example, one xylem vessel becomes blocked, water moves sideways to another vessel and then moves upward again.

Vessels are the main conducting cells in angiosperms. Large diameter of vessels enables large volume of water to be moved throughout the plant.

(b) *Tracheids* – They have dead, hollow cells with narrower lumens than the vessels. Tracheids are connected vertically to each other via bordered pits. They conduct water in conifers which, have needles in place of leaves and do not lose much water. Narrower lumens encourage capillarity.

They are elongated cells with tapering ends. Their end walls are thickened with lignin which provides mechanical strength.

(c) *Parenchyma* – They are made up of parenchymal cells, with thin cellulose walls and living contents. They contribute support via turgidity.

(d) Fibres – They are sclerenchymal cells that form wood in older plants. These cells are dead and provide strength.

Note

Except for Xylem parenchyma, all other xylem elements are dead and bounded by thick lignified walls.

Functions :

(i) Xylem conducts water and minerals upward from the roots to the different parts of plant.

(ii) Cells that are lignified such as tracheids, vessels and parenchyma fibres are used to give mechanical strength to the plant body.

(iii) Xylem parenchyma stores food and helps in lateral conduction of water.

(II) *Phloem* : Phloem is also a conducting tissue that transports prepared food material from leaves to the other parts of plant. It is composed of four different types of cells.

Phloem

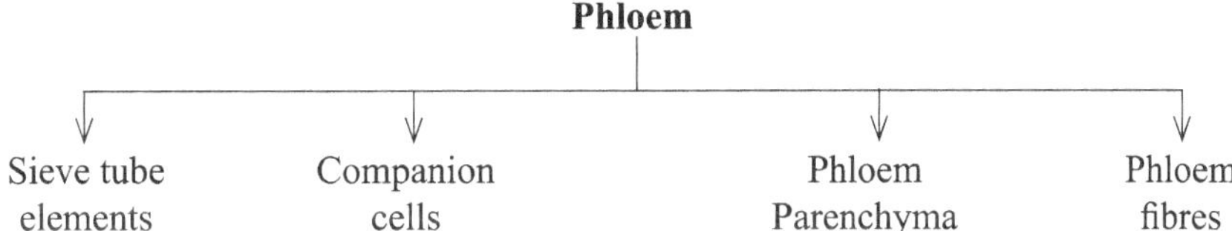

Sieve tube elements   Companion cells   Phloem Parenchyma   Phloem fibres

(a) **Sieve tube elements :** They are living, tubular cells linked end to end. Their end walls are perforated and form a sieve plate, which allows bidirectional flow of solutes and hormones. Cytoplasm of sieve tube element is thin and peripheral. They have cellulose cell walls, which allows exchange of substances across them.
Each sieve tube element is directly connected via strands of cytoplasm known as plasmodesmata to its own companion cell. The companion cell controls movement of solutes in the sieve tube element and allows selective exchange of substances between the sieve tube element and the companion cell.

(b) **Companion cell :** They are small cells containing large nucleus and abundant other organelles e.g., ribosomes, mitochondria and golgi body. Nucleus controls the activities of sieve tube element. Ribosomes allow production of enzymes while the mitochondria produces ATP for active transport in sieve tube element.

(c) **Phloem parenchyma :** Parenchyma provides support through turgidity.

(d) **Fibres :** They are sclerenchymal cells that provide support and some protection for delicate sieve tube elements.

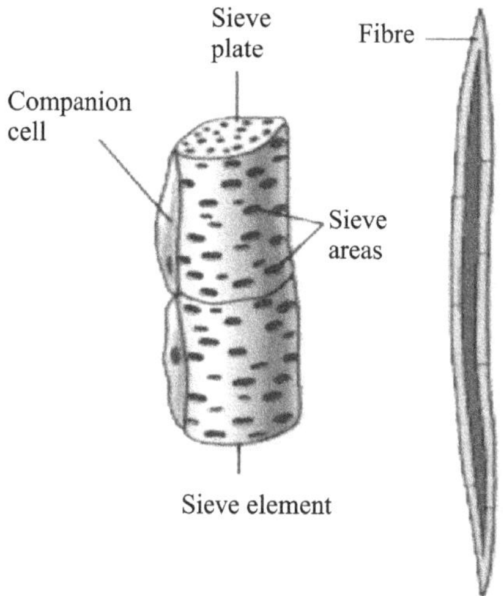

Components of Phloem

Note

Except for phloem fibres, other phloem cells are living cells.

Let us now summarise how Xylem is different from phloem.

Xylem	Phloem
Xylem is a complex tissue that comprises of mainly dead elements.	Phloem is a complex tissue that comprises of mainly living tissues.
Xylem conducts water and minerals from roots to other aerial parts of the plant.	Phloem conducts prepared food material from leaves to all the parts of the plant body.

Difference table between simple tissue and complex tissue.

Simple tissue	Complex tissue
These tissues consist of only one type of cells	These tissues are made up of more than one type of cells
The cells are more or less similar in structure and perform similar functions.	Different types of cells perform different functions. For example in the xylem tissue, tracheids help in water transport whereas parenchyma stores food
Three types of simple tissues present in plants are parenchyma, collenchyma and Sclerenchyma.	Two types of complex permanent tissues present in plants are xylem and phloem.

Difference table between meristematic tissue and permanent tissue.

Sl. No.	Meristematic Tissue	Permanent Tissue
1	Meristematic tissue are composed of cells that divide continuously	Permanent tissue are composed of cells that are derived from meristematic tissue that do not divide
2	The cells are undifferentiated	The cells are fully differentiated.
3	The cells are small in size and isodiametric	The cells are variable in shape and size
4	Intercellular spaces are generally absent	Intercellular spaces are present.
5	The cell walls are thin	Cell walls may be thin or thick.

ANIMAL TISSUES

Breathing is the most vital process that never stops. Along with the heart, it is the most essential activity of the body. When we breathe, we feel the movement of our lungs and diaphragm. Have you ever thought, *which part of our body helps us in moving?* For this we have specialised cells called muscle cells. The contraction and relaxation of these muscle cells result in movement. Every physical activity whether it is blinking an eyelid or turning a somersault, involves muscles into play. Muscle is a type of tissue in our body. *In higher animals like man, cells are organised into four types of tissues, based on their different functions.*

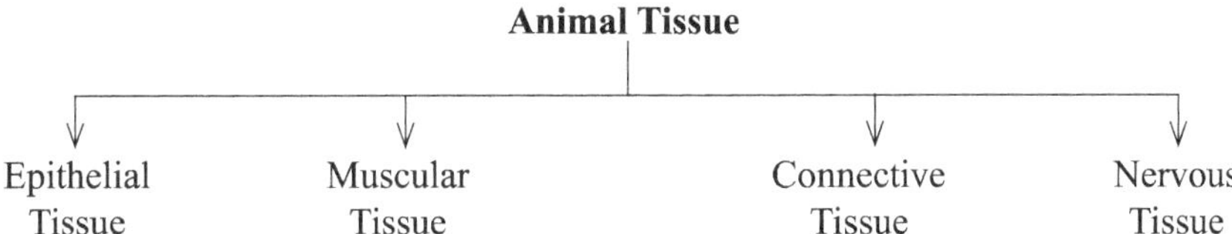

Let us now discuss, each of these tissues one by one.

1. **Epithelial Tissue :**

    It is the protective tissue of the animal body. Epithelium covers most organs and cavities within the body. It also forms a barrier to keep different body systems separate. The permeability of the epithelial cells play an important role in regulating the exchange of materials between the environment and the body. The cells are compactly packed with little or no intercellular matrix and have underlying basement membrane. *The epithelial tissue is of two types :-*

    (i)   Simple epithelial tissue.   (ii)   Stratified epithelial tissue

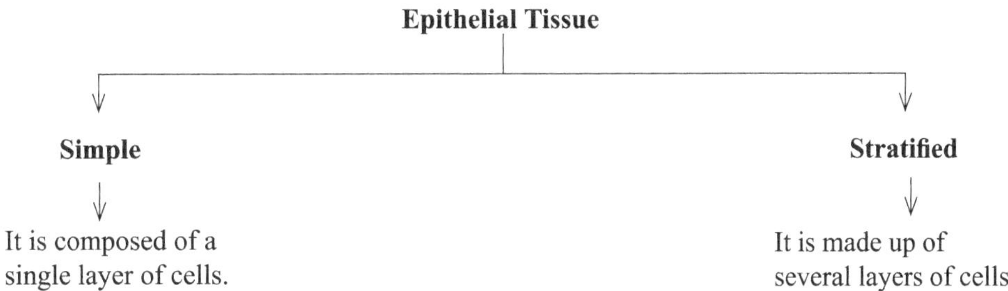

Depending upon the shape and function of the cells, the epithelial tissues are further divided into four types.

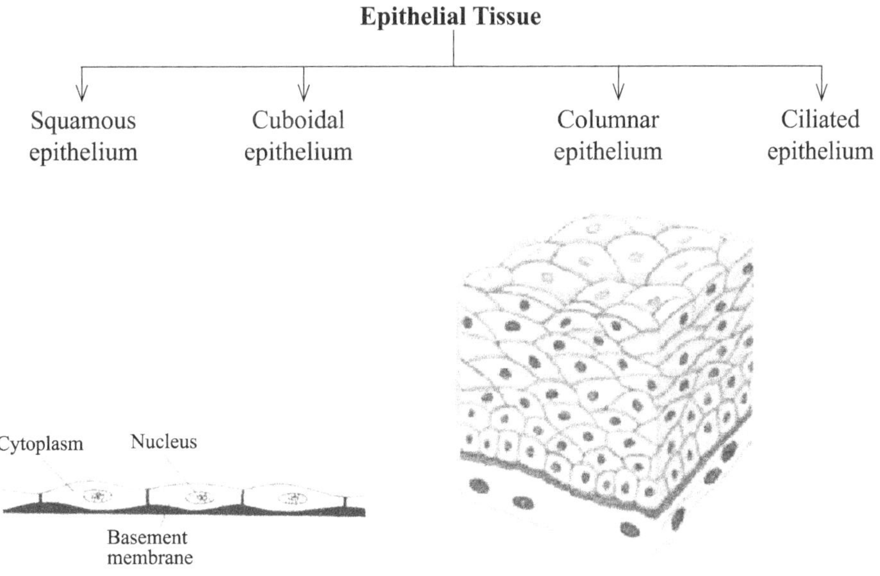

Squamous epithelium   *Stratified squamous epithelium*

(i)   ***Squamous epithelium*** : It is made of thin flat, irregular shaped cells that fit togetherto form a compact tissue.

•   It forms the delicate lining of cavities (like mouth, oesophagus, nose, etc.) lung alveoli and blood vessels.

•   *Function :* It protects the underlying parts of body from mechanical injury and entry of germs.

Stratified squamous epithelium :

- Unlike squamous epithelium, cells of this tissue are arranged in many layers.
- They are found in skin and cover the external dry surface of the skin.
- This epithelium is water proof and highly resistant to mechanical injury.

(ii) *Cuboidal Epithelium* **:** These comprises cube like cells.

- It is found in kidney tubules and in gland like salivary gland, sweat gland, pancreas etc.
- It forms germinal epithelium of testes and ovaries.

    Functions :

    (a) It provides mechanical support to the part where they are found.

    (b) It helps in absorption, excretion and secretion.

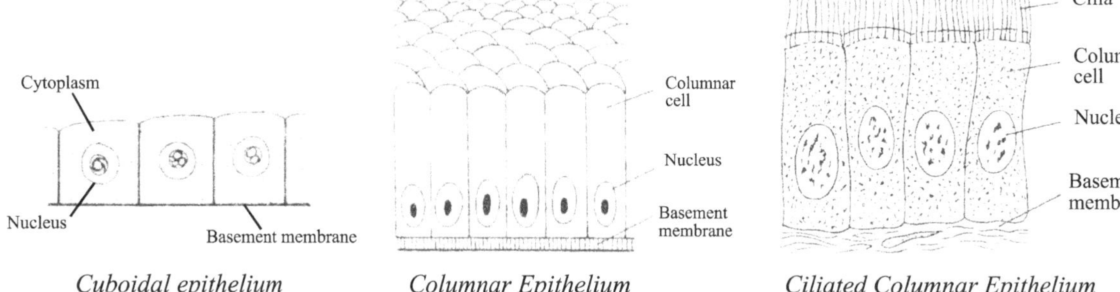

| Cuboidal epithelium | Columnar Epithelium | Ciliated Columnar Epithelium |

(iii) *Columnar Epithelium* **:** It consist of cells that are pillar-like (i.e. taller than broader). The nuclei are towards the base. The free ends of cells have a brush border containing microvilli. It forms lining of the stomach and small intestine, forming mucous membrane.

Functions :

(a) They help in absorption of digested food material from stomach and intestine.

(b) They help in secretion, for example, secretion of mucus by goblet cellsor mucous membrane.

(iv) *Ciliated Epithelium* **:** The cuboidal or columnar cells (have a free border) that bear thread-like cytoplasmic outgrowth called cilia, forms the ciliated epithelium. Ciliated epithelium lines the trachea, bronchi, kidney tubules and oviducts.

Function : The beating of cilia helps in movement of solid particles and mucus in one direction.

2. Muscular Tissue :

Muscle tissue helps in the movement of internal organs such as heart and alimentary canal in your body. It helps in contraction and relaxation of body organs. Every movement, every breathe, every mouthful you chew- all these actions and more are carried out by the body's muscle cells.

Structure of a muscle : A muscle contains bundles of long, thin muscle fibres called myofibres, about the width of human hair. Each fibre is made of even thinner parts called muscle fibrils (called myofibrils) which in turn contains even narrower parts called myofilaments. There are two kinds of filaments, made of different types of proteins.

(i) **Actin** which is thin and

(ii) **Myosin** which is thick.

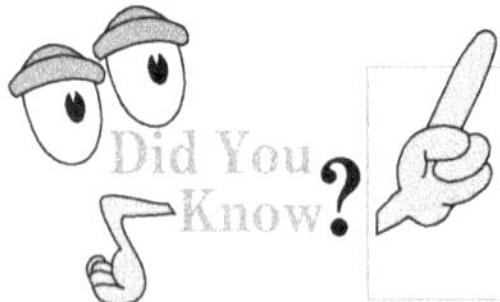

Over time the appearance of skin changes in our body. It becomes more wrinkled and creased. It is because as people change, the collagen fibres in their skin weaken, causing the skin to become loose.

These slide past each other to shorten the fibrils causing the whole muscle to contract.

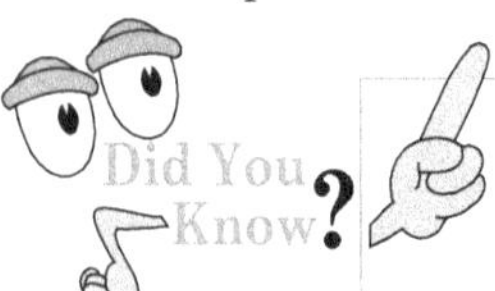

By weight, muscles make up more than 40 percent of our body. They include most of what we call our flesh, and they also form the main part of all our internal organs. Altogether, the body has about 650 separate muscles.

Muscle tissues are made of muscle cell that are elongated and large-sized. A single muscle can do only one task that is to get shorter to pull on body parts. But by working together in a very precise and co-ordinated way, hundreds of muscle in our body carry out thousands of different activities every day.

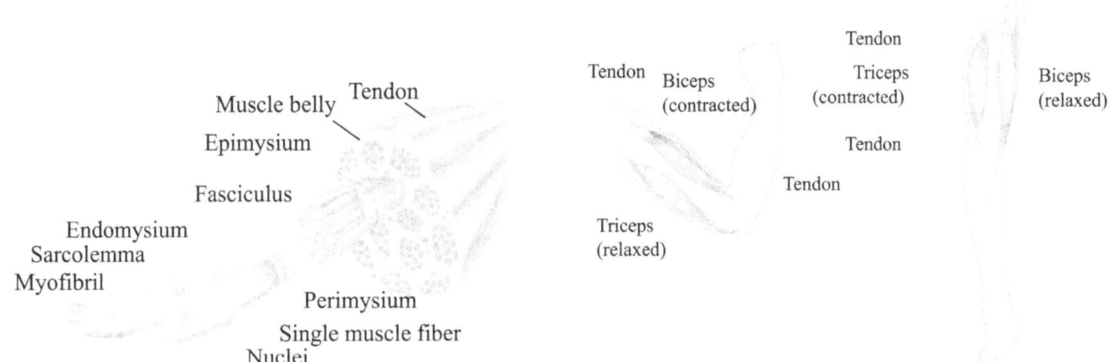

Movement of Muscle

Can you recall from your previous knowledge, how does a muscle work?

Muscles are attached to the bones of the skeleton by cords called **tendons**. If you want to lift your arms, your brain sends a signal to your arm muscles through nerves. Thus muscles contract (get smaller) and pull the bones of the forearm up.

When a muscle works (contracts or relaxes), it uses energy. This energy comes fromchemical action between glucose (stored in muscle) and oxygen from the blood. The chemical action forms lactic acid. As the acid builds up, the muscle begins to feel tired. However, when the muscle rests, the acid is reconverted to glucose.

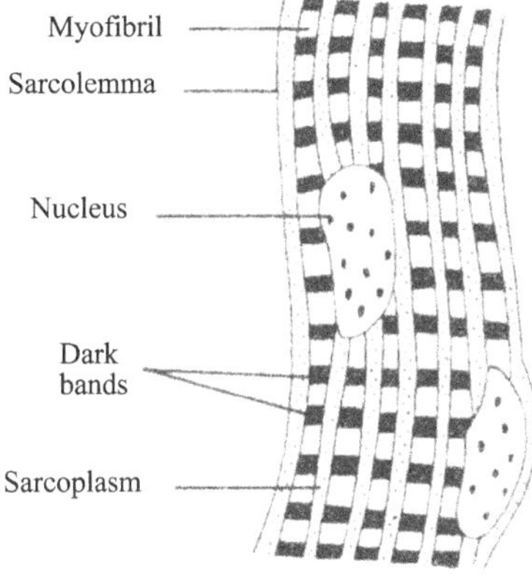

Striated muscles

On the basis of their location structure and function, there are three types of muscle fibres :

(i)   Skeletal muscles

(ii) Smooth muscles

(iii) Cardiac muscles

(i)   Skeletal muscle : The muscle that allows you to move around from one place to another is called *skeletal muscles*. They are called so because, they are attached to bones and are responsible for body movement. They are also known as *striated muscle* because of light and dark parts of the muscle fibre that make them look striped. They are also *voluntary muscles* as these are the muscles that are under the control of our will. They are long, cylindrical, unbranched cells with many nuclei, situated towards the periphery of muscle fibre.

How do skeletal muscle allows movement of body?

Our skeletal muscle is attached to a tendon which in turn is attached to our bone. This tendon allows us to move our body. A tendon is a tough cord that attaches muscle to bone. Striated muscles are located in muscles of limbs, body wall, face, neck etc.

Function : Striated muscles provide the force for locomotion (movement) and all other voluntary movements of the body.

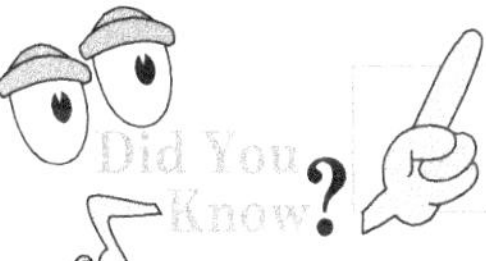

Striated muscles are powerful and undergo rapid contraction. Hence, these muscles can easily get tired and therefore, needs rest.

(ii) **Smooth muscles :** These are smooth and involuntary muscles. You cannot control movements ofthis type of muscles as they work involuntarily. This means that your brain and body tell these muscles what to do without you even thinking about it. Each muscle fibre is long, narrow with spindle shaped tapering ends and are uninucleate.

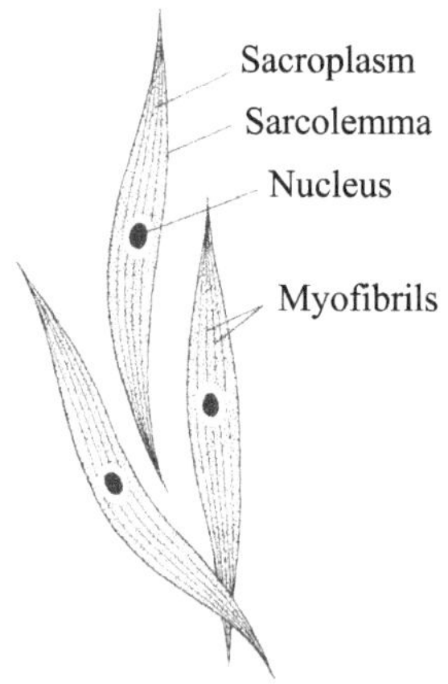

Smooth muscle cells (fibres)

Now *can you guess what causes the movement of food in alimentary canal?* Yes, it occurs by contraction and relaxation of smooth muscle, found in the wall of alimentary canal. Smooth muscle helps to push food from your stomach into your small intestine and contribute in contraction or relaxation of blood vessels. They do not bear any stripes across the muscle, hence, called *unstriated or smooth muscles.*They are found in visceral organs except heart. That is why they are also called *visceral muscles.* They are found in walls of alimentary canal, urogenital duct, blood vessels, iris of eye, bronchi of the lungs etc.

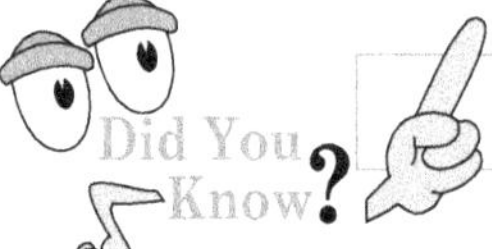

Smooth muscles contract slowly but can remain contracted for long period of time.

Function : In alimentary canal, they cause movement of food and in blood vessel they help the blood to flow.

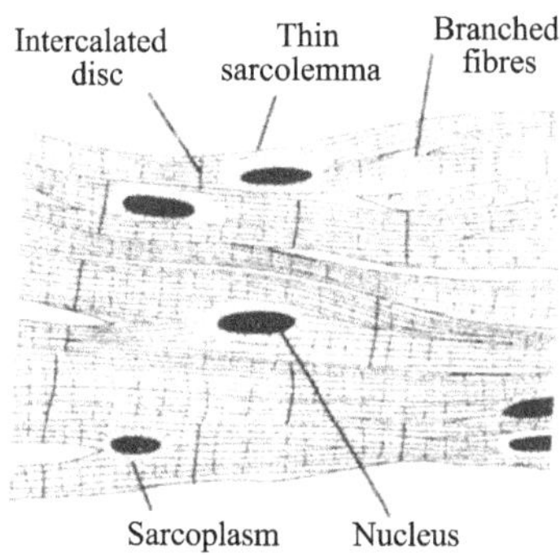

Cardiac muscle

(iii) **Cardiac muscles :** They show the characteristics of both smooth and striated muscles. They are composed of non-tapering cells with faint cross-striations. Like striated muscles, cardiac muscles have stripes of light and dark bands. While like smooth muscles, they are involuntary. Cardiac muscle works all by itself with no help. The cells are cylindrical, branched and uninucleate.

Function : They are found in the walls of heart. Cardiac muscle causes the heart to contract and to pump blood out. Then it relaxes to let blood back in after it has circulated through the body. This means, cardiac muscles contract and relax rapidly rhythmically and tirelessly throughout the life. This contraction and relaxation of heart muscle helps to pump and distribute blood to various parts of the body.

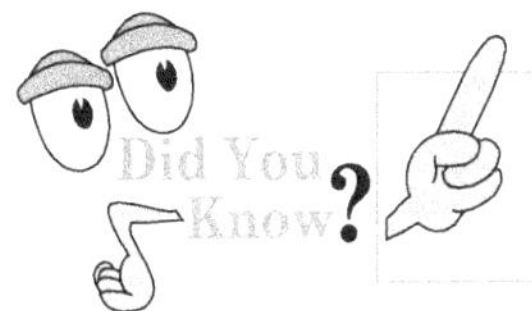

- *The muscles used to smile are called voluntary muscles because we can control how and when we use them to express how we are feeling.*
- *More than 50 muscles work in each arm when playing sports such as volleyball.*

VOLUNTARY AND INVOLUNTARY MUSLCES

There are two main kinds of muscles, voluntary and involuntary.

Voluntary muscle are those that we can deliberately use. For example, the muscles that come into use when we walk or talk. Involuntary muscles are those muscles over which we have no control. They do their work without any knowledge on your part. For example, Breathing in and out of air.

Heart muscles look like voluntary muscles, but act as involuntary muscles.

Difference table between striated muscle, unstriated muscle and cardiac muscle.

Striated muscle	Unstriated muscle	Cardiac muscle
On the basis of structure :		
Cells are cylindrical	Cells are long	Cells are cylindrical
Cells are not branched	Cells are not branched	Cells are branched
Cells are multinucleate	Cells are uninucleate	Cells are uninucleate
Alternate light and dark bands are present	There are no bands present	Faint bands are present
Its ends are blunt	Its ends are tapering	Its ends are flat and wavy
On the basis of location :		
These muscles are present in body part such as hands, legs, tongue etc.	These muscles control the movement of food in the alimentary canal, the contraction and relaxation of blood vessels, etc.	These muscles control the contraction and relaxation of the heart.

Identify the type of muscle shown in each of the given illustrations.

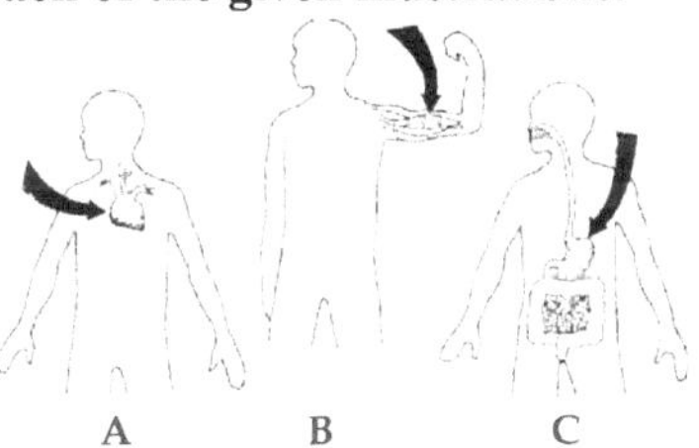

SOLUTION :

A – Cardiac muscle; **B** – Skeletal muscle; **C** – Smooth muscle.

3. **Connective Tissue :**

   Have you ever thought how various body organs are connected to each other? OR *Why organs do not get displaced during body movements?* This happens because of connective tissues. The connective tissue is specialised to connect and anchor various body organs. It also gives support to various parts of body forming packing around organs preventing organs displacement by body movements. The main functions of connective tissues are :

   (a) It helps in binding of tissues

   (b) It helps in supporting various parts of body.

   (c) It helps in packing different organs of the body.

   Structure : The cells of connective tissue are living, loosely spaced and very less in number. Homogenous, gel-like substances called matrix forms the main bulk of connective tissue. The non-living matrix can be solid as in case of bone and cartilage and fluid as in blood. Matrix is fibrous in nature and bind other tissues. The nature of matrix decides the function of connective tissue.

Note

When a muscle is very active, it needs much greater supplies of glucose. So the heart beats faster than normal and the blood vessels connected to the muscles widen, supplying the muscle with three times more blood than it has when it is at rest.

There are five types of connective tissue.

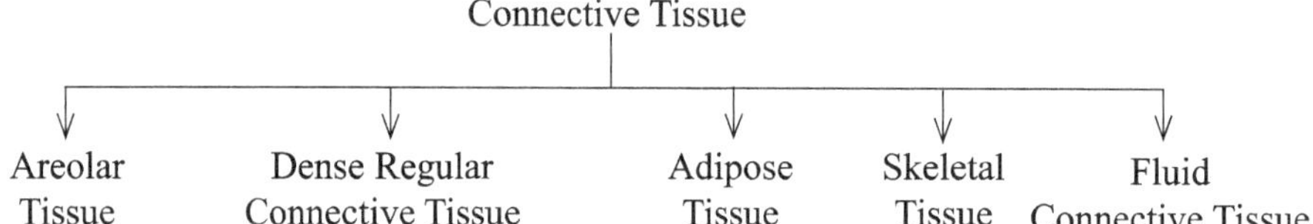

(a) **Areolar tissue :** It is a loose connective tissue. The tissue has a matrix that consists of scattered special cells and fibres that may be yellow or white.

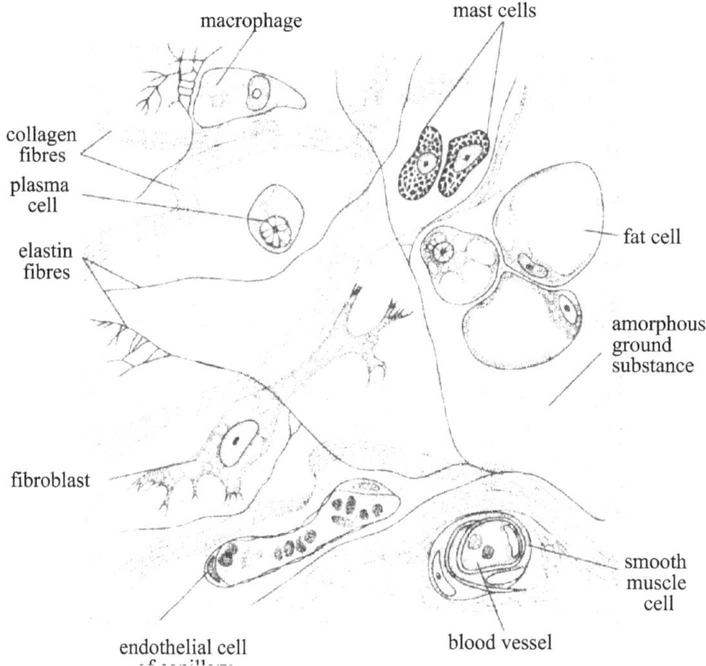

Aerolar connective tissue

It is the widely distributed connective tissue that joins skin to muscles. It is also found around muscles, blood vessels and nerves and fills the space inside the organs.

Functions :

(i)   It helps in supporting internal organs.

(ii) It helps in repairing the tissues of the skin and muscles.

(iii) It also helps in preventing infections.

(b) **Dense Regular Connective Tissue :-** It is a fibrous connective tissue, characterized by densely packed collection of fibres and cells. The principle components of dense regular connective tissue are tendons and ligaments

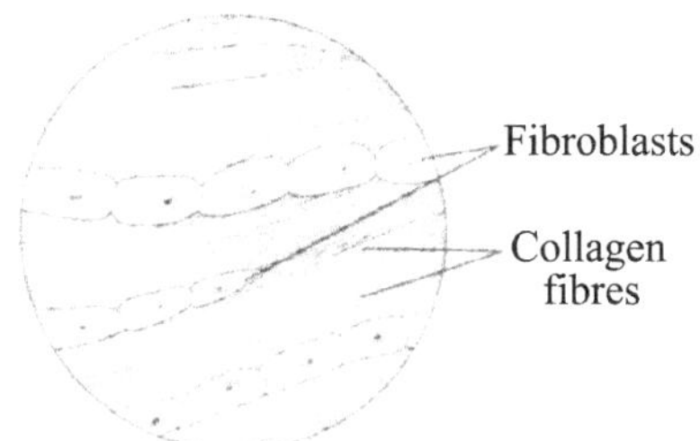

(i)   *Tendons* are strong, inelastic structure that join skeletal muscles to bones. It has a great strength but its flexibility is limited.

(ii) *Ligaments,* on the other hand, are elastic structure with very little matrix that connects bones to bones. It is highly elastic and has great strength. *Ligaments* strengthen the joint and permit normal movement of bone but prevent over-flexion and over-extension.

Dense regular connective tissue

(c) **Adipose Tissue :** These are basically oval in shape filled with fat droplets. It is found below the skin between internal organs and in the bone marrow.

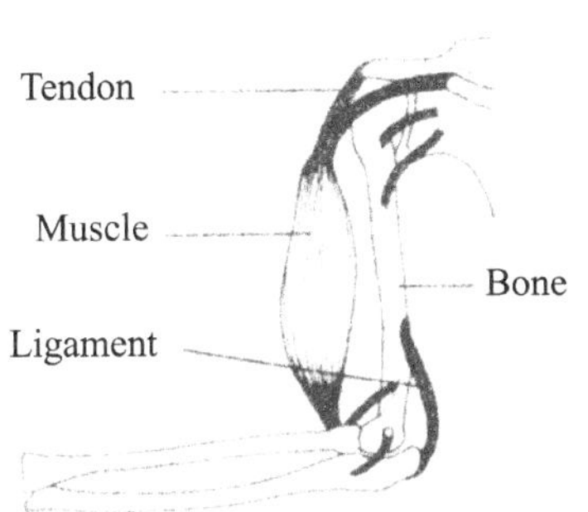

Attachment of tendons and ligaments

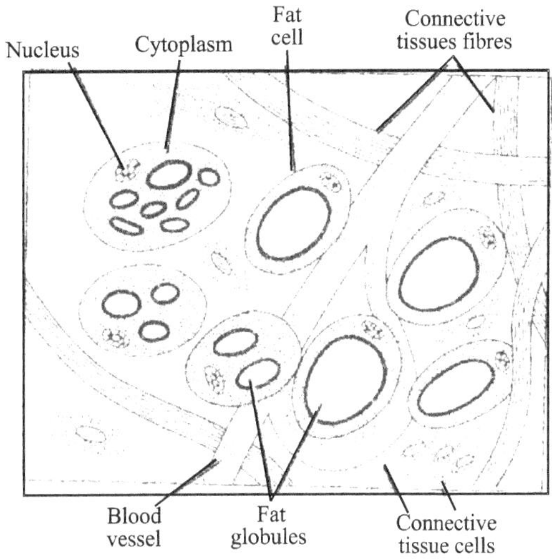

Adipose tissue

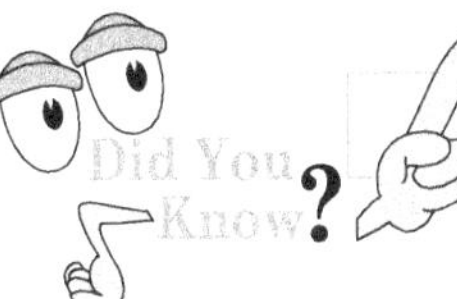

Sprain is caused by excessive pulling of ligaments.

Functions :

(i)   It act as a fat reservoir.

(ii) It acts as an insulator. It reduces loss of heat from the body, that is, it regulates body temperature.

(d)   Skeletal Tissue : It is a connective tissue whose matrix is composed of elastin. It is of two types – bone and cartilage.

There are 206 bones in the average skeleton of human body, but a baby's skeleton has over 340 bones. This is because as the baby grows, some separate bones fuse together to form a single bone.

(i)   Bone : *Touch your limbs or fingers. Do you feel something hard inside. What is it?* The hard parts in the body are the bones. 206 bones form the body's internal supporting frame work, called the skeleton. Bones are strong and stiff, giving the body its shape, protecting internal organs and holding together the soft parts such as blood vessels, nerves etc.

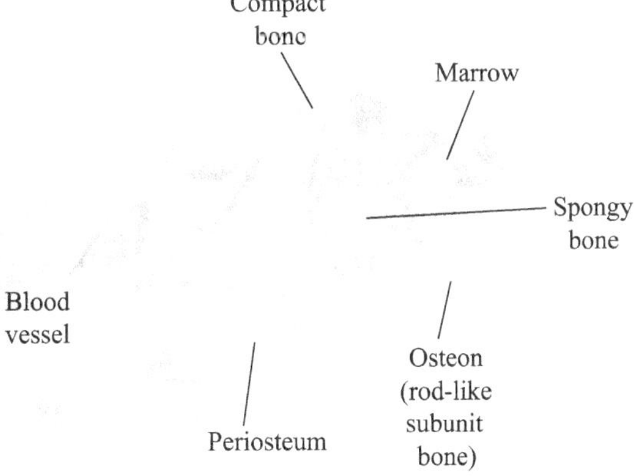

Structure of a bone

A single bone is rigid and tough and can hardly bend. But the whole skeleton can move because its bones are linked at flexible joints, designed to reduce wear and tear. Bones are very strong, yet they are also very light weighted.

Structure of Bone : Most bones are not solid bone throughout. They have three layers. Outside is a shell of *hard or compact* bone, which is strong and stiff. Inside this is a layer of *spongy bone* with tiny holes for lightness. In the middle is the marrow, a soft and jelly like substance that makes new red and white cells for the blood. The whole bone is covered by an outer tough skin-like layer called the *periosteum.*

Bones form endoskeleton of human beings. *The main functions of bones are :*

(a) They provide shape to the body.

(b) They provide skeletal support to body.

(c) They serve as storage site of calcium and phosphate.

(d) They anchor the muscles.

Have you ever thought, what happens if a bone breaks ? It starts to repair itself. Bones are actually made of living tissues, so if they break, microscopic cells called osteoblast begin to make new bone that fills the break or gap. After a few months the gap is joined and the bone is repaired.

(ii) Cartilage : *Touch your ear pinna, or your nose tip. Do you feel something hard but flexible. What is it?* It is specialized connective tissue that is compact, vascular and very flexible. It is commonly known as cartilage. Cartilage has widely spaced cells. The solid matrix is composed of proteins and sugars. It is found in joints, nose, trachea, larynix and discs between vertebrae.

Functions :

(i) Cartilage provides support and flexibility to body parts.

(ii) It also smoothens surface at joints.

What will happen, if there are no bones in the body?

SOLUTION :

Bones provide the strong framework that supports the whole body and holds its parts together. Without bones you would flop down in the floor like a jellyfish.

(e) Fluid connective tissue : This type of connective tissue links different parts of body and forms a continuity in the body. It includes, blood and lymph.

(i) Blood : Blood is a fluid connective tissue, as cells move in a fluid or liquid matrix called blood plasma. The blood plasma contains proteins, salts, hormones and three types of blood cells. These blood cells are:

1. Red blood cell or Erythrocytes that carry oxygen.

2. White blood cells or Leucocytes to fight diseases.

3. Platelets to help blood to clot and seal a wound.

One cubic mm of blood (the size of a pinhead) contains 5 million red cells, 8000 white cells and 350,000 platelets.

Functions of Blood : Blood has more than hundred jobs to do.

(i) They transport oxygen, nutrients and hormones to the tissues.

(ii) They transport excretory products from tissues to the liver and kidney.

(iii) The red blood cells (RBCs) carry oxygen to tissues for breakdown of food.

(iv) White blood cells (WBCs) play an important role in engulfing and destroying foreign bodies and contribute to our immunity system.

(v) Platelets help in the clotting of blood.

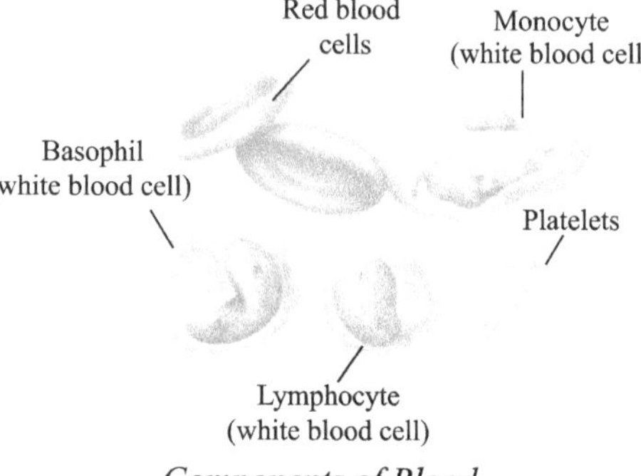

Components of Blood

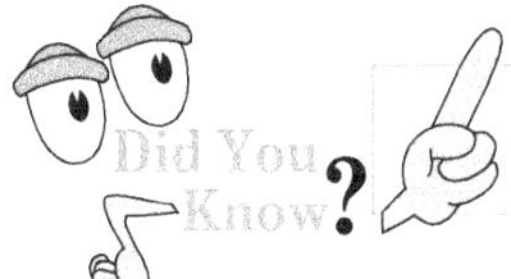

About one twelfth of the body's weight is blood.

HOW PENICILLIN WAS DISCOVERED?

How does blood fight against germs or foreign organisms?

When germs enter the body, millions of white blood cells leave the blood stream and enter the infected tissue to attack and digest them. During the process, dead germs and cells are seen as pus.

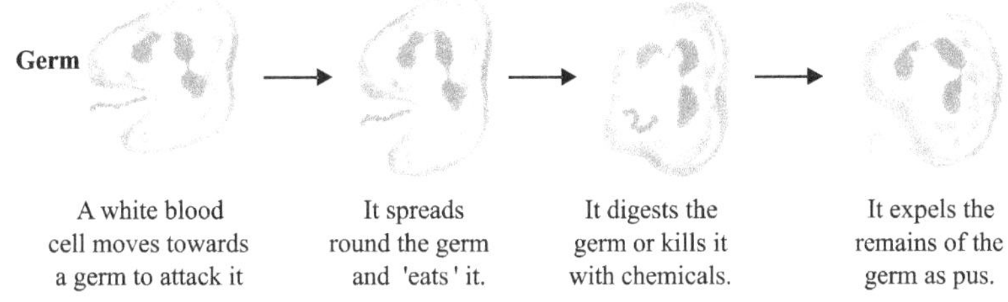

A white blood cell moves towards a germ to attack it

It spreads round the germ and 'eats' it.

It digests the germ or kills it with chemicals.

It expels the remains of the germ as pus.

(i)   Take a drop of blood on a clean slide.

(ii) Then observe it under microscope.

You will observe different types of blood cells in it. Identify them and write their functions.

(ii) Lymph : Lymph is a colourless fluid that has filtered out of blood capillaries. It is similar to blood but does not have RBCs looks and some blood proteins. White blood cells forms the major component of the lymph. Lymph flows in special vessels called lymph vessels.

Functions :

1.   They transport nutrients that have filtered out of blood capillaries back into heart to be circulated again in body.

2.   It brings waste products from tissue fluid to blood.

3.   Lymph also protects the body against infection. It forms the immune system of the body.

The lymphatic system helps in the absorption of fats and fat-soluble vitamins from the digestive system.

An adult has about 5 liters of blood. It is roughly enough blood to fill seven wine bottles. More than half is plasma.

Why blood is considered a vital fluid?

SOLUTION :

Without blood, the cells that make up the body's tissue could not live. Blood carries food and oxygen to them nourishing them and enabling new cells to develop. It also removes carbon dioxide and other waste products, so that they can be expelled harmlessly from the body. Blood also carries hormones, the chemical substance that controls many of the body's activities. Its other function includes fighting infection and helping to control temperature by carrying excess heat to skin surface.

Biology

4. Nervous Tissue :

Close your eyes and feel things. *Can you recognize the object?* Yes, you can. *But have you ever thought, how do you remember things?. Do sense organs help you remember things?* No, the sense organs only collect information from your surroundings. It is the nervous system that helps you to remember and feel things. A tissue that is specialised to transmit messages in our body is nervous tissue. Cells of the nervous tissue are highly specialised for being stimulated and then transmitting the stimulus very rapidly from one place to another within the body. Like a computer network, it sends tiny electrical signals to and fro, carrying information from one part of body to another. The electrical signals are called nerve messages and they travel along wire-like nerves, which spread in a vast network through the entire body. The control of the whole nervous system and the also whole body comes from the brain while the nervous tissues are present in the spinal cord.

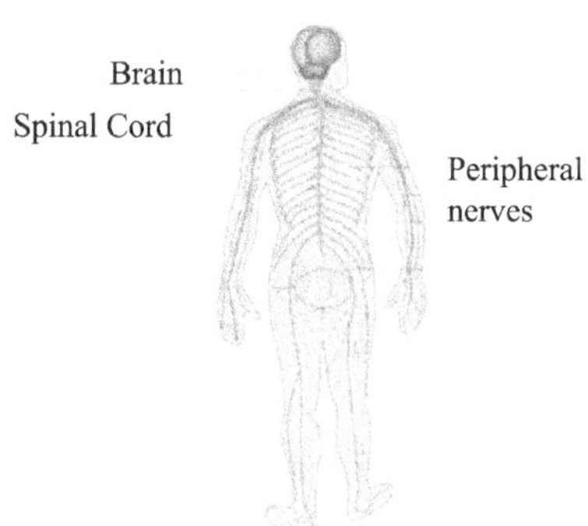

Human Nervous Tissue

The nervous system has three main parts —

1. Brain;   2. Spinal cord;   3. Peripheral nerves

The *brain* consists of billions of nerve cells and other tissue in top half of the head. Its lower end merges into the spinal cord. *Spinal cord* is the body's main nerve. The spinal cord is inside a tunnel formed by the row of holes inside the vertebrae of the backbone (or spine). *Peripheral nerves* branch out from the spinal cord and brain and reach out to every body part.

Neuron : The nervous system is built up of billions of very specialised cells called nerve cells or neurons. *Neuron* is the basic functional unit of the nervous system. They are unique and the only type of cells that stop reproducing shortly after birth. So, when the neurons die, they cannot be replaced. They have specialised structure called axon and dendrites that send and receive information. Our body has more than 100 billion neurons.

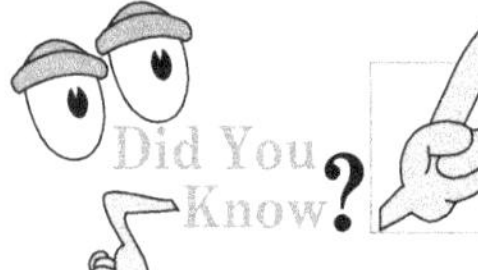

Different types of nerve fibres carry signals at different speeds. The fastest signal travels at more than 120 m/sec. The slowest signals travel at 1-2 m/sec.

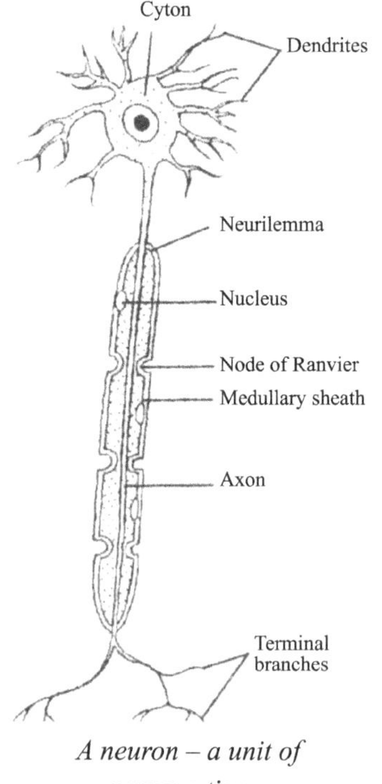

A neuron – a unit of nervous tissue

Each neuron consists of :-

(1) *Cell body* or *cyton* has a nucleus and cytoplasm. Cell body has two extensions known as axons and dendrites.

(2) An *axon* is a long thread like extension of the nerve cells that transmits impulses away from the cell body.

(3) *Dendrites,* on the other hand, are thread like extensions of the cell body that receives nerve impulse.

Thus, axon transmits impulses away from the cell body while dendrites receive nerve impulses. This coordinated function helps in transmitting impulses very quickly.

Nervous tissue exhibits two unique properties :-

(i) **Irritability :** It is the capacity of tissue to respond to the stimulus.

(ii) **Conductivity :** It is the capacity to transfer the response from one region to another.

FACTS ABOUT BRAIN

A new born baby's brain grows almost three times during the course of its first year. The left side of the human brain controls the right side of the body and the right side of the brain controls the left side of the body.

SUMMARY

- *Tissues are group of cells similar in structure that work together to perform a particular function.*
- **Plant tissues are of two types :**
  - *Meristematic* - Cells that are capable of cell division.
  - *Permanent* - Mature cells that are incapable of cell division
- *Meristematic tissues are further classified as - Apical, lateral and intercalary meristems*
- *Permanent tissues are classified as simple and complex tissue.*
- *Parenchyma, collenchyma and sclerenchyma are three types of simple tissues while xylem and phloem are two types of complex tissues.*
- **Animals tissues are of four types**
  - *Epithelial tissue* - It comprises of squamous, cuboidal, columnar and glandular epithelium.
  - *Muscular tissues* - It comprises of striated, unstriated and cardiac muscles.
  - *Connective tissue* - It comprises of areolar tissue, adipose tissue, bone, cartilage, tendon, ligament and bone
  - *Nervous tissue* - It is made up of neurons that receive and conduct impulses
- *Neuron is the basic functional unit of the nervous system. Each neuron consists of the cell body, axon and dendrites.*

Exercise ⬡ Foundation Builder +

Multiple Choice Questions

DIRECTIONS (Qs.1-28) : *This section contains multiple choice questions. Each question has four choices (a), (b), (c) and (d) out of which ONLY ONE is correct.*

1. Which type of tissue forms glands?
    (a) Epithelial   (b) Connective
    (c) Nervous   (d) Uterus

2. Which tissue provides flexibility to plants?
    (a) Parenchyma   (b) Collenchyma
    (c) Sclerenchyma   (d) Aerenchyma

3. Which of the following are the components of xylem?
    (a) Sieve tube   (b) Sclereid
    (c) Companion cells   (d) Tracheid

4. Which of the following tissue is composed of dead cells?
    (a) Phloem   (b) Epidermis
    (c) Xylem   (d) Endodermis

5. Which of the following are simple tissues?
    (a) Parenchyma, xylem and phloem
    (b) Parenchyma, collenchyma and sclerenchyma
    (c) Parenchyma, xylem and sclerenchyma
    (d) Parenchyma, xylem and sclerenchyma

6. In which of the following, growth is sub-apical in nature?
    (a) Root   (b) Shoot
    (c) Petiole   (d) Pedicle

7. Which of the following tissue first evolved in animals?
    (a) Muscular tissues   (b) Skeletal tissues
    (c) Epithelial tissues   (d) Connective tissues

8. Which of the following helps in maintaining the body temperature ?
    (a) Sweat glands   (b) Connective tissues
    (c) Adipose tissues   (d) Hair

9. Which of the following tissue is more elastic in nature?
    (a) Bone   (b) Cartilage
    (c) Ligament   (d) Adipose tissue

10. Which of the following cells are associated with immune system of our body?
    (a) Platelets   (b) WBC
    (c) Blood proteins   (d) RBC

11. Which of the following is not a part of nervous tissue?
    (a) Cyton   (b) Axon
    (c) Dendrites   (d) Nephron

12. Pseudo stratified epithelium is present in
    (a) Urinary bladder   (b) Nephron
    (c) Larynx   (d) Trachae

13. Which type of permanent tissue helps in storing food in plants.
    (a) Parenchyma   (b) Collenchyma
    (c) Xylem   (d) Phloem

14. Skin has
    (a) Stratified squamous epithelium
    (b) Simple squamous epithelium
    (c) Columnar epithelium
    (d) Cuboidal epithelium

15. Ciliated columnar epithelium is found in the lining of
    (a) Respiratory tract   (b) Nephron
    (c) Oesophagus   (d) Mouth

16. Smooth muscles are likely to be found in
    (a) Muscles of legs   (b) Muscles of arms
    (c) Stomach   (d) Heart

17. Which connective tissue helps in storing fats?
    (a) Tendon   (b) Ligament
    (c) Adipose   (d) Areolar tissue

18. The product of Photosynthesis is transported from source of production to the storage organs through
    (a) Palisade tissue   (b) Phloem tissue
    (c) Spongy tissue   (d) Xylem tissue

19. Which one is not a tissue?   **[JSTSE]**
    (a) Blood   (b) Muscle
    (c) Nucleus   (d) Xylem

20. The tissue present in aquatic plants which enables them to keep floating by giving buoyancy is :   **[JSTSE]**
    (a) Collenchyma   (b) Aerenchyma
    (c) Sclerenchyma   (d) Chlorenchyma

21. Which of the following are characteristic feature of cells of meristematic tissue?   **[NTSE]**
    (a) Actively dividing cells with dense cytoplasm, thick cell wall and prominent nuclei
    (b) Actively dividing cells with dense cytoplasm, thin cell wall and no vacuoles
    (c) Actively dividing cells with little cytoplasm, thin cell wall and prominent nuclei
    (d) Actively dividing cells with thin cytopalsm, thin cell wall and no vacuoles.

22. The fibrous tissue having great strength but limited flexibility are :   **[JSTSE]**
    (a) Ligaments   (b) Areolar Tissue
    (c) Adipose Tissue   (d) Tendons

23. The element of xylem which help in sideways conduction of water is: **[JSTSE]**
    (a) Trachied   (b) Xylem Parenchyma
    (c) Vessels   (d) Xylem fibres

24. Regeneration of damaged growing grass following grazing is largely due to: **[NTSE]**
    (a) Secondary meristem
    (b) Lateral meristem
    (c) Apical meristem
    (d) Intercalary meristem

25. Xylem translocates: **[NTSE]**
    (a) Water only
    (b) Water and mineral salts only
    (c) Water, mineral salts and some organic nitrogen only
    (d) Water, mineral salts, some organic nitrogen and hormones
26. Which of the following is made up of dead cells?
    (a) Collenchyma   (b) Phellem   **[NTSE]**
    (c) Phloem   (d) Xylem parenchyma
27. Transmission tissue is characteristic feature of: **[NTSE]**
    (a) Solid style   (b) Dry stigma
    (c) Wet stigma   (d) Hollow style
28. Casparian strips occur in   **[NTSE]**
    (a) Epidermis   (b) Pericycle
    (c) Endodermis   (d) Cortex

Multiple Matching Questions

DIRECTION (Qs.29-30) : The following question contains statements given in two columns which have to be matched. Statements (A, B, C, D, E) in column I have to be matched with statements (p, q, r, s, t) in column II.

29. Match Column I with Column II

Column I		Column II
A.	Parenchyma	(p) Shoot apex
B.	Sclerenchyma	(q) Mechanical tissue
C.	Xylem	(r) Water conduction
D.	Apical meristem	(s) Universal tissue
E.	Phloem	(t) Sieve cells

    (a) A → (r); B → (s); C → (q); D → (p); E → (t)
    (b) A → (s); B → (r); C → (q); D → (p); E → (t)
    (c) A → (s); B → (r); C → (p); D → (q); E → (t)
    (d) A → (s); B → (p); C → (r); D → (q); E → (t)
30. Match the followings and choose the correct option from below.

A.	Meristem	(p) photosynthesis, storage
B.	Parenchyma	(q) mechanical support
C.	Collenchyma	(r) actively dividing cells
D.	Sclerenchyma	(s) stomata
E.	Epidermal tissue	(t) sclereids

    (a) A-(p), B-(r), C -(t), D-(q), E-(s)
    (b) A-(r), B-(p), C-(q), D-(t), E-(s)
    (c) A-(q), B-(s), C-(t), D-(p), E-(r)
    (d) A-(t), B-(s), C-(r), D-(q), E-(p)

Assertion & Reason

DIRECTIONS (Qs.31-36): Each of these questions contains an Assertion followed by reason. Read them carefully and answer the question on the basis of following options. You have to select the one that best describes the two statements.

(a) If both **Assertion** and **Reason** are **correct** and Reason is the **correct explanation** of Assertion.

(b) If both **Assertion** and **Reason** are correct, but Reason is **not the correct explanation** of Assertion.

(c) If **Assertion** is **correct** but **Reason** is **incorrect**.

(d) If **Assertion** is **incorrect** but **Reason** is **correct**.

31. **Assertion :** Muscle cells are also called myofibrils.
    Reason : Muscle cells are very thin and elongated.
32. **Assertion :** Epithelial tissues protect the under lying and over lying tissues.
    Reason : Materials are exchanged between epithelial cells.
33. **Assertion :** Permanent tissue is composed of mature cells.
    Reason : Meristematic tissue is a group of actively dividing cells.
34. **Assertion :** Xerophytic leaves may contain sunken stomata.
    Reason : Spongy parenchyma is more in xerophytic plants.
35. **Assertion :** Tendon is present in all bone joints.
    Reason : Tendon connects the bones at the joints & hold them in position.
36. **Assertion :** Ciliated epithelium helps in movement of particles.
    Reason : Cilia helps in movement.

SOLUTIONS
(Brief Explanations of Selected Questions)

Exercise ⬠ **Foundation Builder +**

Multiple Choice Questions

1. (a)	**2.** (b)	**3.** (d)	**4.** (c)
5. (b)	**6.** (a)	**7.** (c)	**8.** (c)
9. (b)	**10.** (b)	**11.** (d)	**12.** (d)
13. (a)	**14.** (a)	**15.** (a)	**16.** (c)
17. (c)			

18. (b) Phloem is a vascular tissue helps in transportation of food. The end product of photosynthesis is glucose $[C_6H_{12}O_6]$ synthesized in leaves and transported to the various storage organs like flowers, fruits, seeds and tubers etc. through phloem tissue.

19. (c) Nucleus is a part of a cell.

20. (b) Aerenchyma tissues helps in floating because of the presence of air spaces.

21. (b) Meristematic tissue actively dividing cells contains dense cytoplasm, their cell wall and no vacuoles.

22. (a) Ligaments connects bone to bone it has limited flexibility and great strength.

23. (b) Xylem parenchyma are living cells and they store food material and also help in the conduction of water and mineral.

24. (d) Intercalary meristems are capable of cell division and they allow for rapid growth and regrowth of many monocots. Intercalary meristem, found in grasses, help to regenerate the parts removed by the grazing herbivores.

25. (d) Xylem is a type of complex tissue. It translocates water, mineral salts, organic nitrogen and hormones.

26. (b) Cork cambium undergoes periclinal division and cuts off thick walled suberised dead cells towards outside i.e. phellem (cork) and it cuts off thin walled living cells i.e., phelloderm on inner side.

27. (a) A solid style has transmission tissue which has large intercellular spaces. It allows growth of pollen tube in pistil.

28. (c) Casparian strip is a band of cell wall material deposited in the radial and transverse walls of the endodermis. Casparian strip is made of suberin and sometimes lignin.

29. (b)   **30.** (b)

Assertion & Reason

31. (b)	**32.** (b)	**33.** (b)	**34.** (a)
35. (c)	**36.** (a)		

9 Diversity in Living Organisms

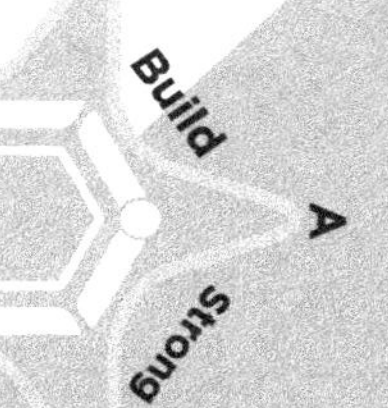

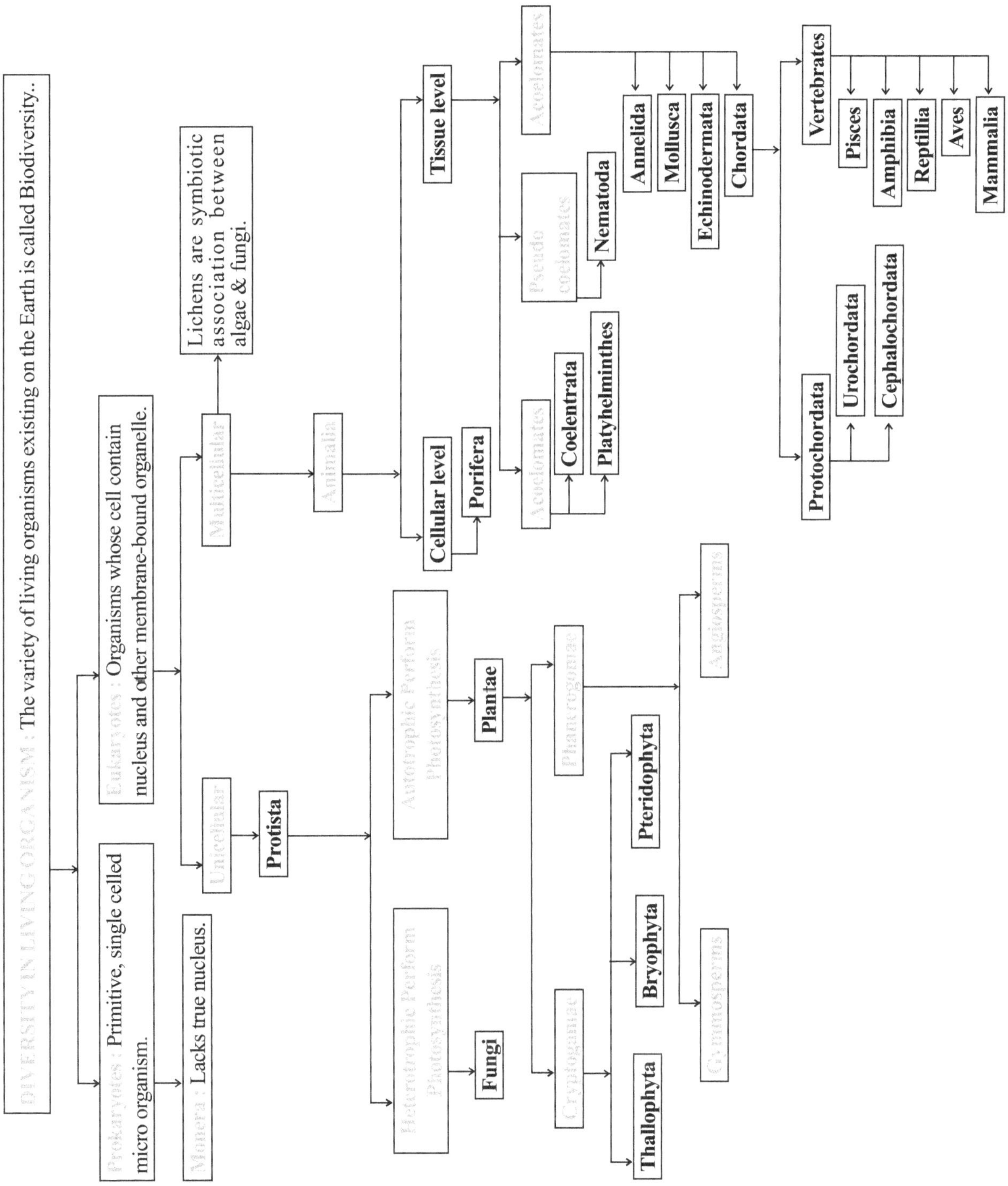

DIVERSITY AND CLASSIFICATION

There are variety of living organisms in terms of size, which ranges from microscopic bacteria to tall trees of 100 metres. The life span of different organisms is also quite varied. For example, a crow lives for only 15 years, whereas a parrot lives for about 140 years. Such huge range of these life forms makes it very difficult to study them one by one. Therefore, we look for similarities among them and classify them into different classes to study these different classes as a whole. Thus, classification makes our study easier. Classification is a system of categorizing living things.

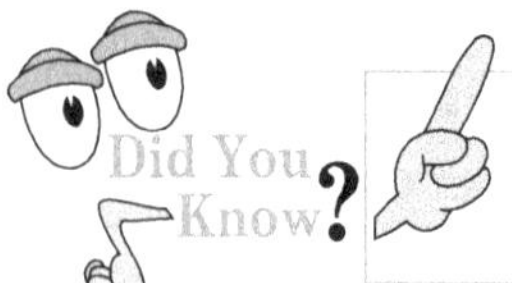

Biodiversity refers to variety of life forms found in a particular region.

Importance of classification:
(i)   It determines the methods of organizing the diversity of life on Earth.
(ii) It helps in understanding millions of life forms in detail.
(iii) It helps in understanding the interrelationship among different groups of organisms.
(iv) It also helps in predicting the line of evolution. Evolution is a complex process by which the characteristics of living organisms change over many generations.

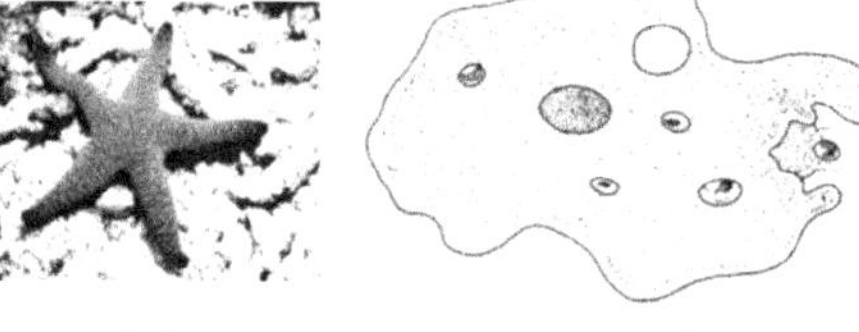
starfish   amoeba

Based on evolution, organisms can be divided into two types: Primitive and advanced organisms. A *primitive organism* or lower organism is the one which has a simple body structure and ancient body design or features that have not changed much over a period of time. An *advanced organism* or higher organism has a complex body structure and organization and has evolved over a period of time. For example, an *Amoeba* is more primitive as compared to a starfish. *Amoeba* has a simple body structure and primitive features. So, it is considered more primitive than a starfish. Thus classification helps in predicting the line of evolution.

BASIS OF CLASSIFICATION

Organisms are classified on the basis of their characteristics. It could be in terms of appearance or behaviour. These characteristics give clues about how species evolved.

The broadest divisions are based on the most basic characters. For example, the primary characteristic on which the first division of organisms is made is the nature of the cell. It is considered to be the fundamental characteristic for classifying all living organisms. Nature of the cell includes the presence or absence of membrane-bound organelles. Therefore, on the basis of this fundamental characteristic, we can classify all living organisms into two broad categories of eukaryotes and prokaryotes. Then, further classification is made on the basis of cellularity or modes of nutrition.

Some basic characters used in classification are-
1. Prokaryotes and eukaryotes
2. Unicellular and multicellular organisms
3. Autotrophs and heterotrophes
4. Level of organization of organisms
5. Type of body development.

BINOMIAL NOMENCLATURE

Nomenclature is the process of giving scientific names to plants and animals. Carl Linnaeus devised a binomial system of nomenclature (naming system) in which an organism is given two names:
(i)   A generic name which it shares with other closely related organisms which has features similar enough to place them in the same group.
(ii) A specific name which distinguishes the organism from all other species. No other organism can have the same combination of genus and species.

The scientific name derived by using the system of nomenclature is followed all over the world as they are guided by a set of rules stated in the International Code of Nomenclature.

Certain conventions are followed while writing the scientific names:
1. The name of the genus begins with a capital letter.
2. The name of the species begins with a small letter.
3. When printed, the scientific name is written in italics.
4. When written by hand, the genus name and the species name have to be underlined separately to indicate their latin origin.

For example, Humans are referred to as *Homo sapiens*. Similarly, mango is referred to as *Mangifera indica*.

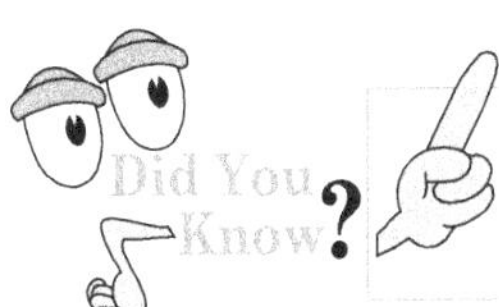

> *Carl Linnaeus was the father of modern botany. He was a Swedish naturalist who laid the foundation of modern classification and nomenclature in 1758.*

HIERARCHY OF CLASSIFICATION

For developing a hierarchy of classification, we choose the fundamental characteristic among several other characteristics. For example, plants differ from animals in the absence of locomotion, chloroplasts, cell wall, etc. But, only locomotion is considered as the basic or fundamental feature that is used to distinguish between plants and animals. This is because the absence of locomotion in plants gave rise to many structural changes such as the presence of a cell wall for protection, and the presence of chloroplast for photosynthesis (as they cannot move around in search of food like animals). Thus, all these features are the result of locomotion. Therefore, locomotion is considered to be a fundamental characteristic. By choosing the basic or fundamental characteristic, we can make broad divisions in living organisms as the next level of characteristic is dependent on these. This goes on to form a hierarchy of characteristics.

R.H. Whittaker proposed a five kingdom classification of living organisms on the basis of Linnaeus' system of classification. The five kingdoms proposed by Whittaker are Monera, Protista, Fungi, Plantae, and Animalia. These groups are formed on the basis of their cell structure, mode and source of nutrition and body organisation.

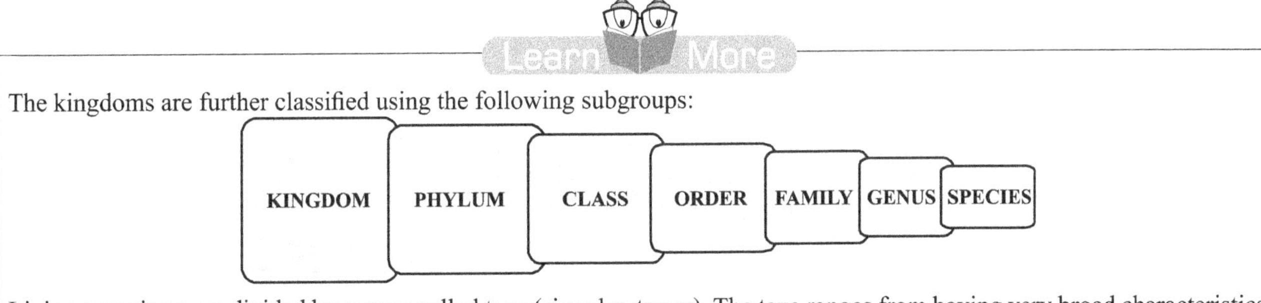

The kingdoms are further classified using the following subgroups:

Living organisms are divided by groups called taxa (singular, taxon). The taxa ranges from having very broad characteristics to much more specific characteristics. The smallest taxon is species. At the species level, organisms look alike and are able to breed with one another. The next largest taxon is genus. At the genus level, there is a group of similar species that are closely related.

As you can see from the figure, a species is the most specific group. A genus is a group of similar species. A family is a taxon of similar genera. Take an example, Lion (Panthera leo) and tiger (Panthera tigris) are different species but they belong to the same genus. This genus (Panthera) and another genus (Felis) which includes the domestic cat, also share some common characteristics. Therefore, there is the larger cat-family (Felidae) which includes the genus of lion and tiger, and the genus of the domestic cat. An order is a taxon of similar families. For example, the family of cats (lions, tigers, cats) and the family of dogs (dogs, foxes, jackals, etc.) possess some common features and so they make an order. In the example cited here the order is "Carnivora". A class is a taxon of similar orders. For example, the orders of different animals like those of dogs, cats, bats, whales, monkeys etc., have some common features such as hairy skin and milk-glands. The particular class of the animals mentioned here is "Mammalia". A phylum is a taxon of similar classes. For example, the classes of different animals like the mammals, birds, reptiles, frogs, fishes, etc., together constitute the phylum chordata. (Plant taxonomists use the taxon division instead of phylum). A kingdom is a taxon of similar phyla (plural for phylum). The Plant Kingdom consists of all kinds of plants. The Animal Kingdom consists of all kinds of animals.

MNEMONIC

Classification of human beings:
Kingdom- Animalia
Phylum- Chordata
Class- Mammalia
Order- Primates
Family- Hominoidea
Genus- Homo
Species- sapiens
Try this memory tool to help you remember the order of the groups from kingdom to species : Keep Putting Chocolate Out For Goodness Sake. The first letter of each word stands for one of the taxa.

Try to make the similar classification for DOG, TIGER, and CAT.

The basis for grouping organisms into five kingdoms is as follows:

(i) On the basis of the presence or absence of membrane-bound organelles, all living organisms are divided into two broad categories namely the eukaryotes and the prokaryotes. This division led to the formation of kingdom *Monera*, which includes all prokaryotes.

(ii) Then, eukaryotes are further divided as unicellular and multicellular organisms, on the basis of cellularity. Unicellular eukaryotes form the kingdom *Protista*, and multicellular eukaryotes form kingdom *Fungi*, *Plantae*, and *Animalia*.

(iii) *Animals* are then separated on the basis of presence or absence of a cell wall.

(iv) Since *fungi* and *plants* both contain a cell wall, they are separated into different kingdoms on the basis of their modes of nutrition. *Fungi* have saprophytic mode of nutrition, whereas *plants* have autotrophic mode of nutrition. This resulted in the formation of the five kingdoms.

Let us now study each of these kingdoms one by one in detail.

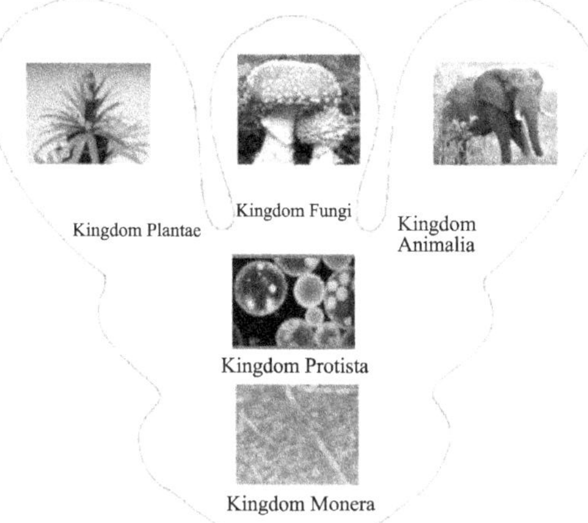

I. KINGDOM MONERA

- The organisms belonging to this group are unicellular prokaryotes.
- The mode of nutrition may be autotrophic or heterotrophic.
- Cell wall may or may not be present.
- *Examples:* Bacteria and Blue green algae

II. KINGDOM PROTISTA

- The organisms belonging to this group are unicellular eukaryotes.
- The mode of nutrition may be autotrophic or heterotrophic.
- Cell wall, like monerans, may or may not be present.
- *Examples*: Diatoms, Protozoans (*Amoeba*).

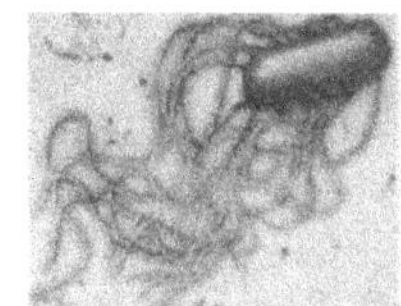

Bacteria   Blue Green Algae

Monera

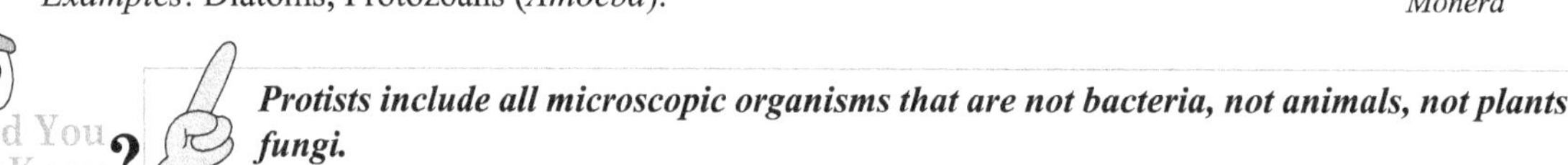

Protists include all microscopic organisms that are not bacteria, not animals, not plants and not fungi.

III. KINGDOM FUNGI

- They are unicellular or multicellular eukaryotes.
- Cell walls in fungi are made of chitin.
- These do not contain chlorophyll and hence are heterotrophic. They may be saprophytic (depend on dead or decaying organic matter for their food) or may be parasitic (depend on living organisms for their food).
- *Examples:* Yeast, Mushrooms, Bread mould (*Mucor*), Lichen etc.
- Lichen is a group which has two varieties of plants, an alga and a fungus living together. They co-exist for mutual benefit. This relationship is known as *symbiosis*. The fungus absorbs water and mineral salts and supplies it to the alga. The alga prepares food and supplies it to the fungus.

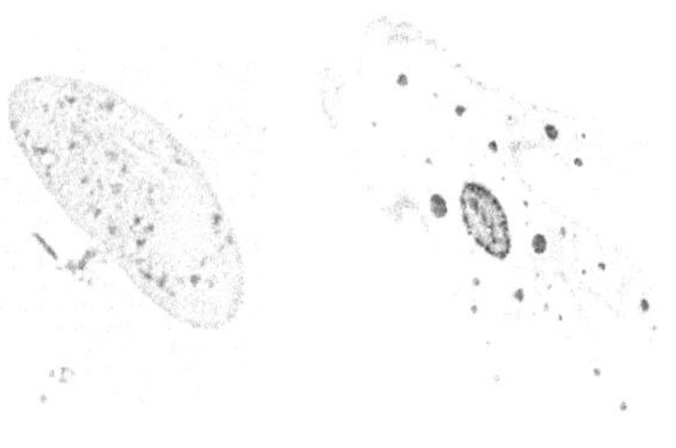

Paramecium   *Ameoba*

Protista

IV. KINGDOM PLANTAE:

- They are multicellular eukaryotes.
- They are usually autotrophic. They prepare their own food by the process of photosynthesis.
- Their cells have cell wall is made up of cellulose.
- They do not move from one place to another. They are stationary.
- *Examples:* Moss, *Riccia*, Pinus, Mango etc.

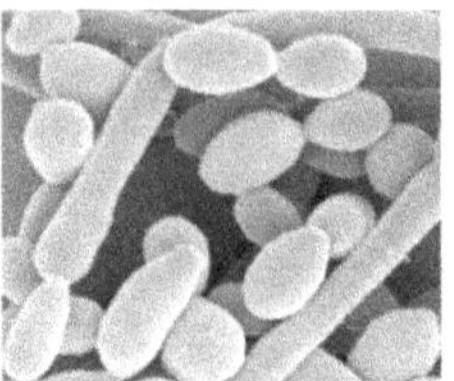

Yeast   **Mushroom**

Fungi

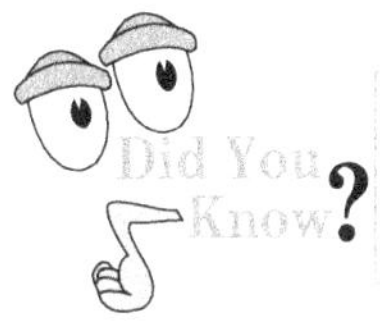

With over 250,000 species, the plant kingdom is the second largest kingdom. Plant species range from the tiny green mosses to giant trees

Pinus

Cedar

Plantae

☞ **List two ways in which fungi and plants are different.**

SOLUTION :

The cell wall in fungi are made of chitin, a complex carbohydrate while the plants have cell wall made of cellulose. Also fungi do not contain chlorophyll and hence are heterotrophic. They may be saprophytic (depend on dead or decaying organic matter for their food) or may be parasitic (depend on living organisms for their food). Plants, on the other hand, are autotrophic. They prepare their own food by photosynthesis.

The classification of kingdom Plantae depends on the following criteria:

(i) **Differentiated/ Undifferentiated plant body :** The first level of classification depends on whether a plant body is well differentiated or not. A group of plants that do not have a well differentiated plant body are known as *Thallophyta*.

(ii) **Presence /absence of vascular tissues :** Plants that have well differentiated body parts are further divided on the basis of the presence or absence of vascular tissues. Plants without specialised vascular tissues are included in division *Bryophyta*, whereas plants with vascular tissues are known as *Tracheophyta*.

(iii) **With/without seeds :** Tracheophyta is again sub-divided into division *Pteridophyta*, on the basis of absence of seed formation.

(iv) **Naked seeds/ seeds inside fruits :** The other groups of plants having well developed reproductive organs that finally develop seeds are called *Phanerogams*. This group is further sub- divided on the basis of whether the seeds are naked or enclosed in fruits. This classifies them into gymnosperms and angiosperms. *Gymnosperms* are seed bearing, non-flowering plants, whereas *angiosperms* are flowering plants in which the seeds are enclosed inside the fruit.

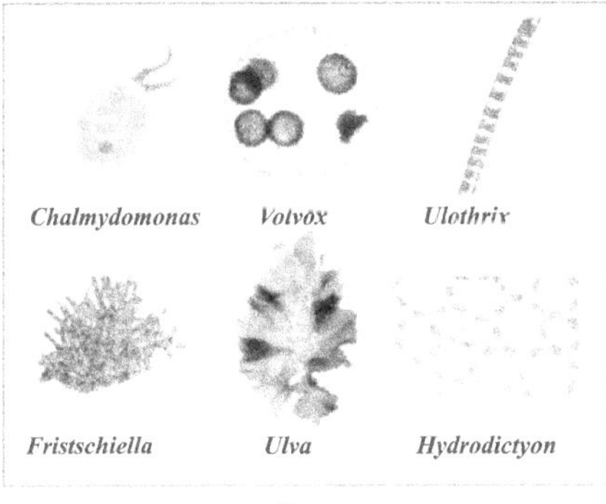

Chalmydomonas   *Volvox*   *Ulothrix*

Fristschiella   *Ulva*   *Hydrodictyon*

Algae

(1) **Division: Thallophyta (Thallus-undifferentiated, Phyta-plant)**
- It includes the simplest organisms.
- This group includes plants that do not contain a well differentiated plant body.
- Their body is not differentiated into stem, root and leaves but is in the form of thallus.
- They are commonly known as algae.

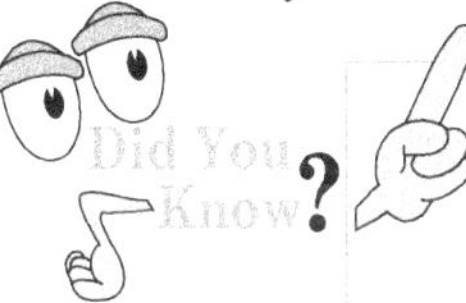

Eichler in 1883 suggested a system to classify the plant kingdom which is well accepted. He said that the plant kingdom is subdivided into two subkingdoms: Cryptogamae and Phanerogamae The plant kingdom is broadly divided into two groups on the basis of reproductive organs and embryo structure.

(2) **Division Bryophyta**
- These are the simplest forms of land plants. The plant body is flat and lack true leaves and roots. These are called the amphibians of the plant kingdom. They do not have any specialised tissue for the conduction of water. *Example: Riccia, Marchantia, Funaria*

Riccia

Marchantia

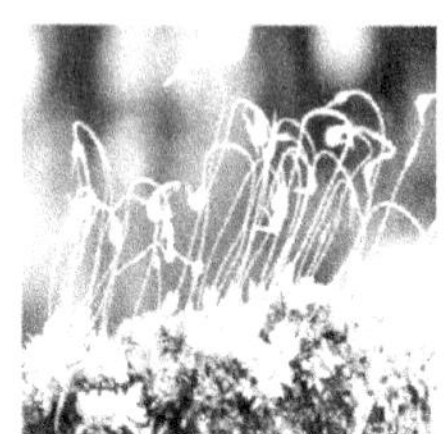

Funaria

Bryophytes

(3) Division Pteridophyta
- They grow in damp cool shady places.
- The plant body is differentiated into stem, leaves and roots.
- Vascular system is present.
- They have inconspicuous or less differentiated reproductive organs, therefore called cryptogaus.
- They produce naked embryos called spores.
- *Example:* Ferns

(4) Division Gymnospermae
- Gymnosperms are intermediate between cryptogams and angiosperms.
- They have well developed reproductive organs.
- The male flower is a cone which produces pollen. The female flower is much larger and consists of a rosette of carpels which bear ovules along the two margins.
- *Example: Cycas*, *Pinus* and Coniferous trees.

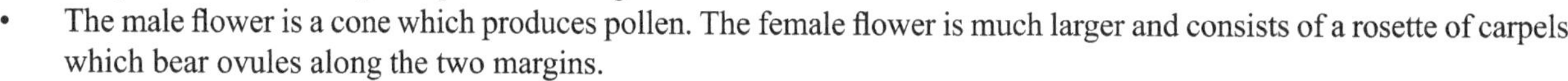

Ferns

Pteridophyta

Cycas

Pinus

Gymnosperms

(5) Division Angiospermae
- This group constitutes the largest group of plants.
- Seeds are produced inside an ovary which later modifies to become a fruit.
- These are highly evolved group of plants and are flowering plants.
- The plant body is distinctly differentiated into roots, stem and leaves.
  Based on the number of cotyledons (seed-leaves) that form the seed, this group is divided into:
  (i)   *Monocotyledons:* Example: Rice, Wheat
  (ii) *Dicotyledons:* Example: Beans, Mango

The plant with the largest flower is Rafflesia, which grows up to 1 m across.
The Welwitschia plant of the southern African scrub has two leaves, each many metres long, which lasts for hundreds of years.

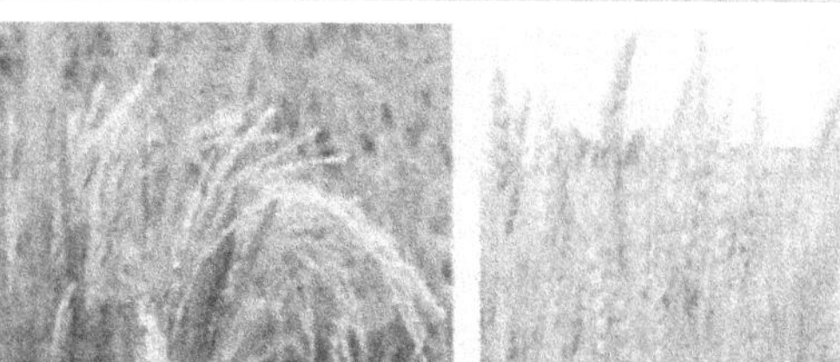

Rice

Wheat

Mango

Fig. 9.11 : *Angiosperms*

☛ **How gymnosperm is different from angiosperms?**

SOLUTION :

Gymnosperm	Angiosperm
They are non-flowering plants	They are flowering plants
They have naked seeds not enclosed inside fruits.	They have seeds enclosed inside fruits.
Examples include, Pinus, Cedar, Cycas, etc	Examples include, Coconut, mango etc.

CRYPTOGAMAE AND PHANEROGAMAE

(I) **Sub Kingdom Cryptogamae :** (Crypto-hidden, Gammous-marriage)
These are lower plants that do not bear flowers or seeds. Their reproductive organs are inconspicious. They have naked embryos called spores.
Thallophyta, Bryophyta and Pteridophyta belong to Cryptogams.

(II) **Sub Kingdom Phanerogamae :** This division is made up of plants that bear flowers and seeds and make up the majority of the larger plants. The body is differentiated into true stem, leaves and roots. Propagation of the plant takes place with the help of seeds. Seeds are formed as a result of sexual reproduction. The male and female gametes (sex cells) fuse together inside the ovary (female part of the flower) and develop into the seed. In some plants seed is not produced inside an ovary.
Phanerogamae is further directed into two divisions: Gymnosperms (naked seeded plants) and angiosperms (Seed borne within a fruit).

V. **KINGDOM ANIMALIA**
- They are multicellular eukaryotes
- They have heterotrophic mode of nutrition.
- Cell wall is absent.
- *Examples:* Round worm, Tape worm, House fly, Man etc.

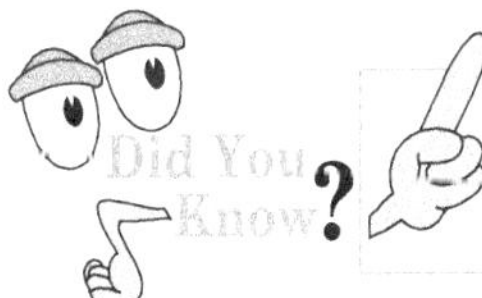

The animal kingdom is the largest kingdom with over 1 million known species.

Animals are arranged progressively from simple single-celled protozoans to highly complex mammals. *Kingdom Animalia is divided into two major groups on the basis of presence or absence of a notochord.*
Non-chordates do not possess a notochord, while all members of the phylum chordates possess a notochord.
Non-chordate is further divided into subgroups on the basis of the following features:
True tissue- Absent or Present
Body cavity- Absent or Present
Type of body symmetry- Radial or Biradial
Type of coelom development- Acoelom, Pseudocoelom or True coelom.
Type of true coleom- Enterocoelom or Schizocoelom
On the basis of the above features, non-chordates are divided into the following subgroups: Porifera, Coelenterata, Platyhelminthes, Nematodes, Annelids, Molluscs, Arthropoda, and Echinodermata.

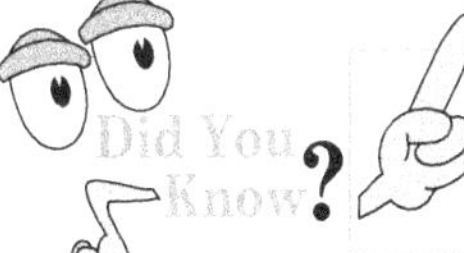

Members of the animal kingdom are found in the most diverse environments in the world.

(1) **Phylum Porifera (Sponges):** These are simplest multicellular animals. They are mostly marine, non-motile and found attached to the rocks. The cells are loosely held together and do not form tissues. They have 'pores' all over their body that leads to canal system that helps in circulation of food and oxygen. *Example, Spongilla* and *Euplectella.*

(2) **Phylum Coelenterata (Cnidaria):** They are exclusively marine animals that either live in colonies like corals or have a solitary life span like hydra. *Example* includes Jelly fish, sea anemones.

(3) **Phylum Platyhelminthes (Flatworms) :** Body is dorsoventrally flat and leaf like or ribbon-like with bilateral symmetry. The body cavity has only one opening which serves as both the mouth and the anus. Example *Planaria, Taenia, Fasciola.*

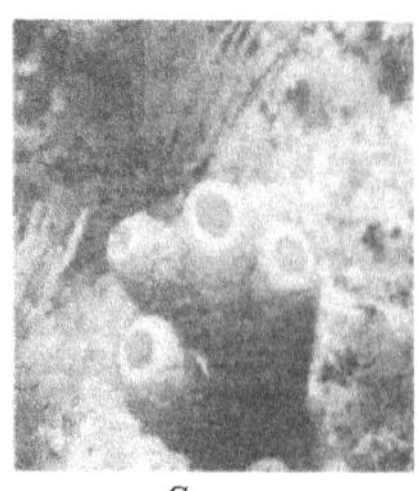

Sycon
Poriferans

Jellyfish
Coelenterates

Palanaria
Platyhelminthes

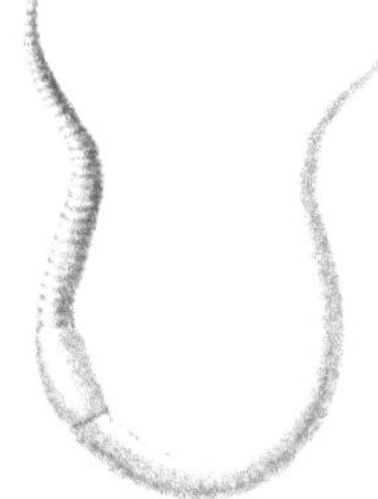

Earthworm
Annelids

(4) **Phylum Aschelminthes (Round Worm):** They have triploblastic cylindrical body showing bilateral symmetry. Alimentary canal begins with the mouth and ends with the anus. Example *Ascaris*

(5) **Phylum Annelida (Segmented Worms) :** Body is covered by a non-chitinous cuticle which may have chitinous setae, or parapodia. The body is divided into several identical segments. Example Earthworm, Leech.

(6) **Phylum Arthropoda (Animals with jointed legs):** This is the largest phylum with almost 80% of the animal's kingdom in these phyla. Body is bilaterally symmetrical, segmented and have open circulatory system. It is divided into head, thorax and abdomen.

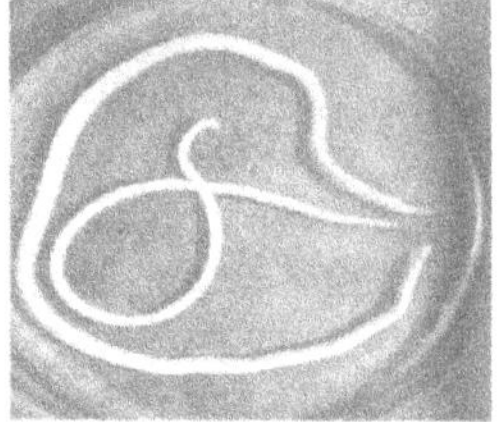

Aschelminthes

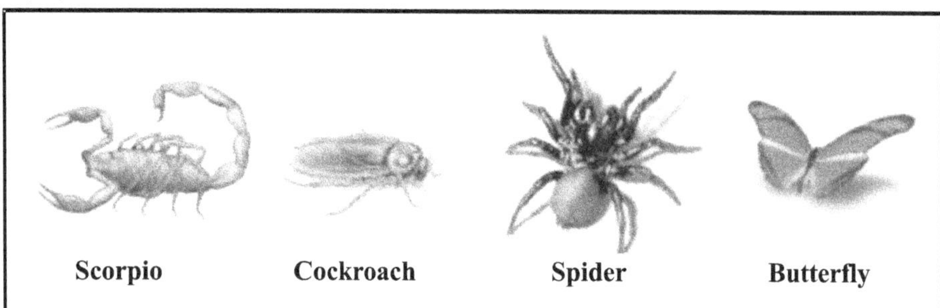

Arthropoda

(7) **Phylum Mollusca :** They are aquatic in habitat but some land forms are also seen. Body is soft and divided into three regions- head, dorsal visceral mass and ventral foot. They have an open circulatory system and kidney-like organs for excretion. Example Snail, Slugs, *Octopus*

(8) **Phylum Echinodermata:** Body is radially symmetrical, star shaped, spherical or elongate. Exoskeleton is spiny. Head is absent and five radially arranged arms are present. They also have peculiar water-driver tube system that they use for moving around. They have hard calcium carbonate structures that they use as a skeleton. Example Starfish, Sea urchin

Pila
Mollusca

(9) **Phylum Hemichordata :** They have characteristics of both invertebrate and chordate. Body is divided into proboscis, collar and trunk.

(10) **Phylum Chordata :** All members of the phylum chordata possess

    (i)   A notochord

    (ii) A dorsal nerve cord

    (iii) Paired gill pouches

    (iv) Post anal tail

Starfish
Echinoderms

However, some animals such as *Balanoglossus*, *Amphioxus*, *Herdmania*, etc. have a notochord, which is either absent or does not run the entire length of the animal's body. Therefore, these animals are kept in a separate sub-phylum called *Protochordata*, and the rest of the chordates are included in the sub-phylum *vertebrata*.

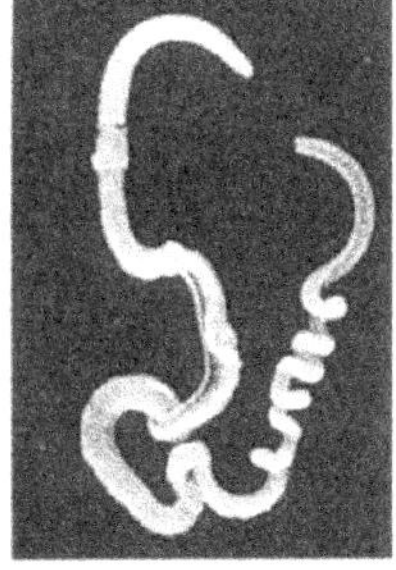
Phylum Hemichordata

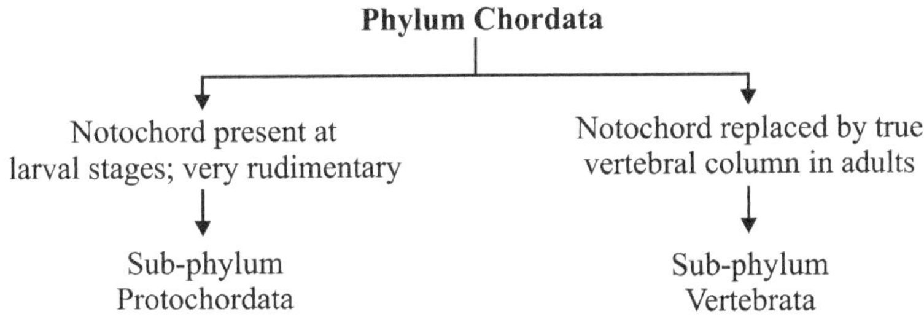

The members of the sub-phylum vertebrata are advanced chordates. They are cold blooded with two chambered heart. Some fish have skeleton made up of cartilage only, such as shark, while others have skeleton made up of both bone and cartilage, such as Tuna or Rohu. *They are divided into five classes:* Pisces, Amphibia, Reptilia, Aves, and Mammalia.

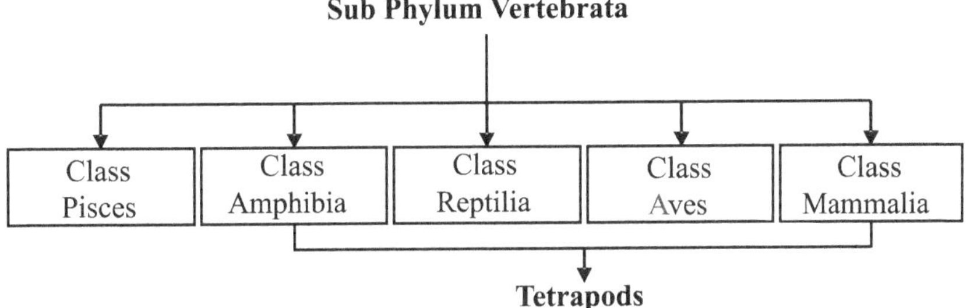

(i) **Class Pisces:** This class includes fishes such as Scoliodon, Tuna, Rohu, Shark, etc. These animals are exclusively aquatic. Hence, they have special adaptive features such as a streamlined body, presence of a tail for movement, gills, etc. to live in water. Vertebrates are bilaterally symmetrical, triploblastic, coelomic, segmented with a true vertebral column and internal skeleton

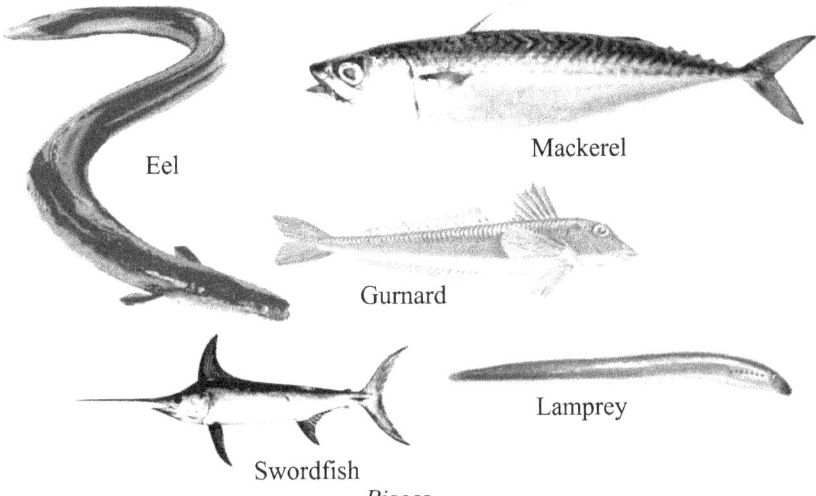

Pisces

(ii) **Class Amphibia:** It includes frogs, toads, and salamanders. These animals have a dual mode of life as they are found both in water and on land. In the larval stage, the respiratory organs are gills, but in the adult stage, respiration occurs through the lungs or skin. They lay eggs in water. *Examples:* Frogs, toads and salamanders are amphibians.

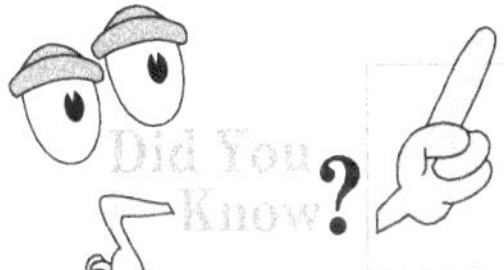

Amphibians were the first animals to venture onto land. They emerged from the oceans over 300 million years ago.

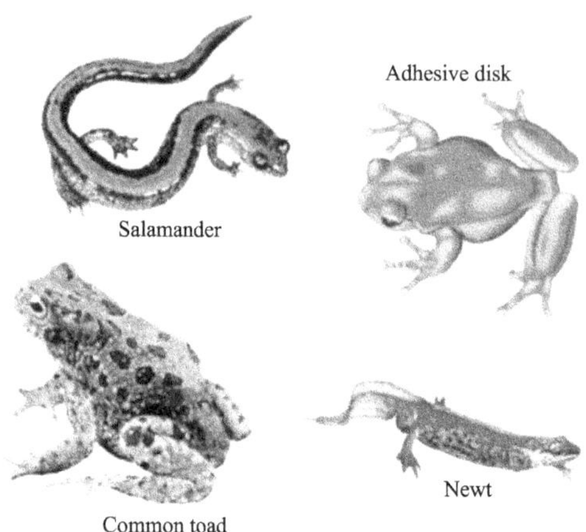

Amphibians

(iii) Class Reptilia: It includes reptiles such as lizards, snakes, turtles, etc. They usually creep or crawl on land. The body of a reptile is covered with dry and cornified scaled skin to prevent water loss. They lay eggs on land, which have tough coverings.

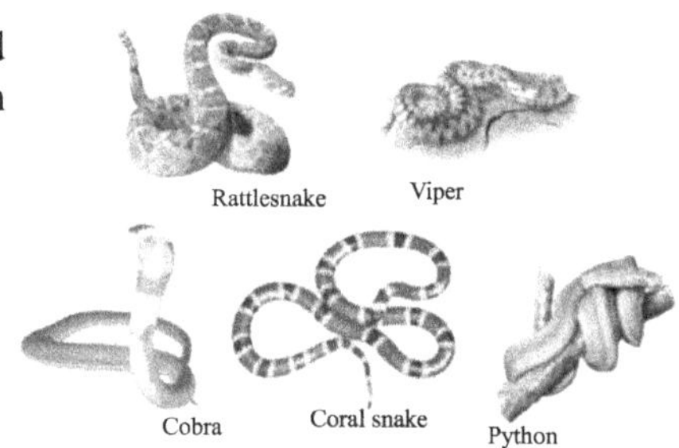

Reptiles

(iv) Class Aves: It includes all birds such as sparrow, pigeon, crow, etc. Most of them have feathers. Their forelimbs are modified into wings for flight, while hind limbs are modified for walking and clasping. They lay eggs.

(v) Class Mammalia: It includes a variety of animals which have milk producing glands to nourish their young ones. Some lay eggs and some give birth to young ones. Their skin has hair as well as sweat and oil glands to regulate their body temperature.

Aves

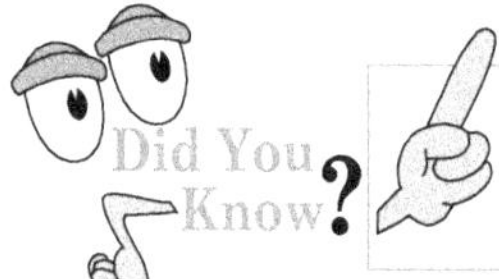

Blue whale is the largest mammal and water shrew is the smallest mammal.

Mammals

SUMMARY

- Living world is rich in variety of plants and animals.
- In order to facilitate the study of kinds and diversity of organisms, biologists have evolved certain rules and principles for identification, nomenclature and classification of organism.
- *Nomenclature* is defined as system of naming objects (plants and animals).
- *Identification* determines the exact place or position of an organism in the set plan of classification.
- Generic and specific names have Latin origin. First letter of the generic name starts with capital letter and of the species name with a small letter.
- *Taxonomy* is the branch of biology that deals with the framing of laws and principles of classifying the organisms on the basis of their evolutionary relationship.

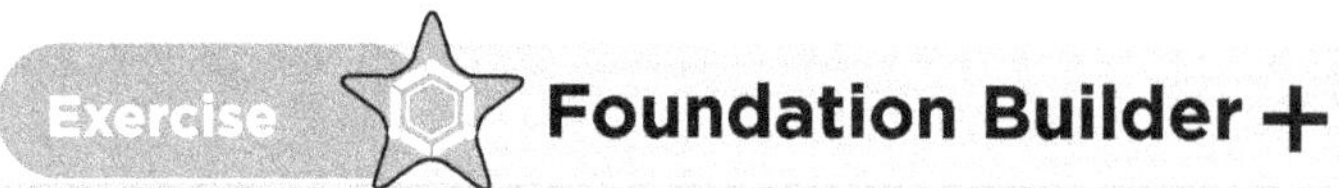

Multiple Choice Questions

DIRECTIONS (Qs.1-53) : *This section contains multiple choice questions. Each question has four choices (a), (b), (c) and (d) out of which ONLY ONE is correct. Choose the correct option.*

1. A kingdom of unicellular eukaryotes is
   - (a) Monera
   - (b) Protista
   - (c) Fungi
   - (d) Plantae

2. A diverse group of eukaryotic organisms separated from other plants by lack of chlorophyll is
   - (a) Algae
   - (b) Fungi
   - (c) Protista
   - (d) Monera

3. Who gave the term binomial nomenclature?
   - (a) Linnaeus
   - (b) Whittakar
   - (c) Aristotle
   - (d) Robert Hooke

4. Which of the following statements is correct about yeast?
   - (a) It lacks chlorophyll
   - (b) It lacks nucleus
   - (c) It lacks cell wall.
   - (d) It lacks cytoplasm

5. Which is the highest category of taxonomy?
   - (a) Kingdom
   - (b) Phylum
   - (c) Genus
   - (d) Species

6. A group of related genera are classified as
   - (a) Family
   - (b) Order
   - (c) Genus
   - (d) Species

7. The scientific name of mango is written as
   - (a) *Mangifera Indica*
   - (b) *Mangifera indica*
   - (c) *mangifera Indica*
   - (d) *mangifera indica*

8. In *Solanum tuberosum*, *Solanum* is
   - (a) *Species*
   - (b) *Genus*
   - (c) *Order*
   - (d) *Class*

9. A plant that produces seed but not fruit is
   - (a) *Cycas*
   - (b) *Riccia*
   - (c) Mango
   - (d) *Spirogyra*

10. Notochord is present in
    - (a) Star fish
    - (b) Earthworm
    - (c) Pila
    - (d) Shark

11. The difference between algae and protozoan is that algae are
    - (a) Heterotrophic
    - (b) Always multicellular
    - (c) Photosynthetic
    - (d) Always unicellular

12. Unlike animals, fungi
    - (a) Ingest their nutrients before digesting them.
    - (b) Secrete enzymes and then absorb the digested nutrients through their cell wall.
    - (c) Have cell walls made of cellulose without chitin.
    - (d) Do not store energy in the form of glycogen.

13. Ferns are a type of
    - (a) Bryophyta
    - (b) Pteridophyta
    - (c) Gymnosperm
    - (d) Angiosperm

14. The body of an organism "X" is covered with dry and cornified skin to prevent water loss. They lay eggs on land. The animal "X" belongs to which class of Chordata?
    - (a) Amphibian
    - (b) Reptilian
    - (c) Avian
    - (d) Mammalian

15. Which of the following organisms belongs to Phylum echinoderm?
    - (a) Starfish
    - (b) Earthworm
    - (c) Sponges
    - (d) Butterfly

16. Which of the following characteristics is unique to avians?
    - (a) Presence of lungs
    - (b) Presence of feathers
    - (c) Presence of scales
    - (d) Presence of mammary glands

17. The scientific name of humans is *Homo sapiens*. It belongs to the genus
    - (a) *Homo*
    - (b) *sapiens*
    - (c) Man
    - (d) Humans

18. Which of the following correctly represents the correct order of various levels of classification?
    - (a) Species→Genus→Family→Order→Class→Phylum
    - (b) Phylum→Genus→Order→Family→Class→ Species
    - (c) Species→Family→Class→Order→Genus→Phylum
    - (d) Class→Family→Order→Genus→Phylum→Species.

19. Which of the following produces seeds which are enclosed in fruits?
    - (a) Gymnosperms
    - (b) Angiosperms
    - (c) Pteridophytes
    - (d) Bryophytes

20. Which of the following is absent in ferns?
    - (a) Flowers, fruits and seeds
    - (b) Roots, leaves and stems
    - (c) Vascular tissues
    - (d) Spores

21. *Ulothrix* belongs to **[JSTSE]**
    - (a) Thallophyta
    - (b) Amoeba
    - (c) Bryophyta
    - (d) None of the above

22. Starfish belong to phylum : **[JSTSE]**
    - (a) Mollusca
    - (b) Coelenterate
    - (c) Arthropoda
    - (d) Echinodermata

23. System of scientific naming included **[JSTSE]**
    - (a) Phylum and genus
    - (b) Class and species
    - (c) Genus and species
    - (d) Genus and class

24. Which type of food is stored in Fungi? **[JSTSE]**
    - (a) Starch
    - (b) Maltose
    - (c) Protein
    - (d) Glycogen

25. What is the basic Unit of classification? **[JSTSE]**
    - (a) Species
    - (b) Genus
    - (c) Family
    - (d) Class

26. Who was the writer of the book 'Systema Naturae' : **[JSTSE]**
    - (a) Robert Whittaker
    - (b) Carolrus Linnaeus
    - (c) Charles Darwin
    - (d) Robert Brown

27. The figure given below shows as Electric Ray (Torpedo). The part Labelled as 'F' called : **[JSTSE]**

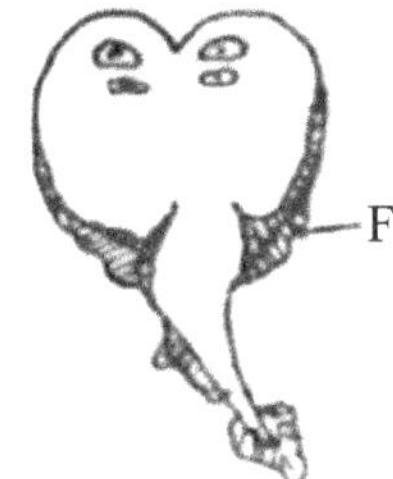

(a) Pelvic fin
(b) Candal fin
(c) Dorsal fin
(d) Pectroal fin

28. The part labelled as 'D' in the figure of Paramecium given below is called as **[JSTSE]**

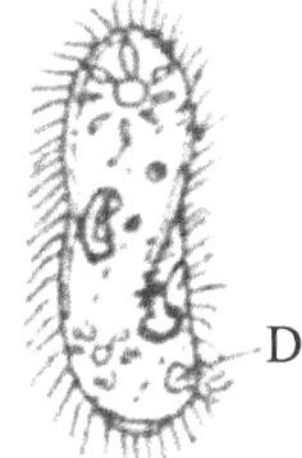

(a) Cytosome
(b) Oral groove
(c) Cytopyge
(d) Eye spot

29. Mushroom belongs to : **[JSTSE]**
(a) Algae
(b) Fungi
(c) Plantae
(d) Protozoa

30. Open vascular system is found in: **[JSTSE]**
(a) Prawn (b) Snakes (c) Fish (d) Man

31. Which one of the following is not a eukaryote: **[JSTSE]**
(a) Euglena
(b) Anabaena
(c) Spirogyra
(d) Agaricus

32. The excretory units of Annelids are: **[JSTSE]**
(a) Uniferous tubule
(b) Flame cells
(c) Nephridia
(d) Malpighian tubule

33. Which of the following is an example of a single cell that does not function as a full-fledged organism? **[NTSE]**
(A) White blood cell (WBC)
(B) *Amoeba*
(C) WBC and *Amoeba*
(D) *Paramecium*
(a) (B) only
(B) (B) and (D)
(c) (A) only
(D) (C) and (D)

34. Select the correct statements with respect to migration in animals. **[NTSE]**
(A) The same Siberian Crane can be seen in Bharatpur in two consecutive winters.
(B) Some fish lay eggs in rivers and the fingerlings gradually swim to sea.
(C) Some fish migrate from cold climate to a warmer climate to escape cold weather.
(D) Some butterflies migrate up to 10,000 kilometres to escape cold weather.

Which of the following alternative has the correct statements?
(a) (A) and (B)
(b) (B) and (C)
(c) (C) and (D)
(d) (A) and (D)

35. A plant that has well differentiated body, special tissues for transport of water and other substances, but does not have seed or fruits is a (n) : **[NTSE]**
(a) Bryophyte
(b) Angiosperm
(c) Gymnosperm
(d) Pteridophyte

36. You are observing a non-chlorophyllous, eukaryotic organism with chitinous cell wall under a microscope. You shall describe the organism as a **[NTSE]**
(a) fungus.
(b) alga.
(c) protozoas.
(d) bacterium.

37. Which of these organisms the body is bilaterally symmetrical? **[JSTSE]**
(a) Sea anemone
(b) Liver fluke
(c) Sycon
(d) Hydra

38. Plants having well differentiated reproductive tissue that ultimately make seeds are called: **[JSTSE]**
(a) Cryptogams
(b) Phanerogams
(c) Pteridophytes
(d) Bryophytes

39. Which one of the following animals is different from other in not having the paired gill pouches? **[NTSE]**
(a) Whale
(b) Water snake
(c) Star fish
(d) Sea horse

40. You discover a new species of a plant. You also discover that it produces motile sperms and dominant generation has diploid cells. It belongs to **[NTSE]**
(a) Bryophyte
(b) Angiosperm
(c) Gymnosperm
(d) Pteridophyte

41. The leaves of lotus plant float on water due to the presence of : **[JSTSE]**
(a) Chlorenchyma
(b) Collenchyma
(c) Sclerenchyma
(d) Aerenchyma

42. The record of all endangered plants and animals is called as: **[JSTSE]**
(a) Flora
(b) Monograph
(c) Manual
(d) Red Data Book

43. Select the **correctly** written scientific name of Mango which was first described by Carolus Linnaeus: **[NTSE]**
(a) *Mangifera indica* Car. Linn.
(b) *Mangifera indica* Linn.
(c) Mangifera indica
(d) *Mangifera Indica*

44. Nomenclature is governed by certain universal rules. Which one of the following is contrary to the rules of nomenclature? **[NTSE]**
(a) Biological names can be written in any language
(b) The first word in a biological name represents the genus name, and the second is a specific epithet
(c) The names are written in Latin and are italicised
(d) When written by hand, the names are to be underlined

45. One scientist cultured Cladophora in a suspension of Azotobacter and illuminated the culture by splitting light through a prism. He observed that bacteria accumulated mainly in the region of : **[NTSE[**
(a) Blue and red ligh (b) Violet and green light
(c) Indigo and green light (d) Orange and yellow light

46. Which among the following is not a prokaryote? **[NTSE[**
(a) Saccharomyces (b) Mycobacterium
(c) Oscillatoria (d) Nostoc

47. Which of the following is correct about viroids? **[NTSE]**
(a) They have free RNA without protein coat
(b) They have DNA with protein coat
(c) They have free DNA without protein coat
(d) They have RNA with protein coat

48. Which of the following pairs is of unicellular algae?
(a) *Gelidium and Gracilaria* **[NTSE]**
(b) *Anabaena and Volvox*
(c) *Chlorella and Spirulina*
(d) *Laminaria and Sargassum*

49. Floridean starch has structure similar to **[NTSE]**
(a) Amylopectin and glycogen
(b) Mannitol and algin
(c) Laminarin and cellulose
(d) Starch and cellulose

50. Bilaterally symmetrical and acoelomate animals are exemplified by **[NTSE]**
(a) Platyhelminthes (b) Aschelminthes
(c) Annelida (d) Ctenophora

51. Which of the following animals are true coelomates with bilateral symmetry ? **[NTSE]**
(a) Annelids (b) Adult echinoderms
(c) Aschelminthes (d) Platyhelminthes

52. Consider following features: **[NTSE]**
(A) Organ system level of organisation
(B) Bilateral symmetry
(C) True coelomates with segmentation of body
Select the correct option of animal groups which possess all the above characteristics.
(a) Annelida, Arthropoda and Chordata
(b) Annelida, Arthropoda and Mollusca
(c) Arthropoda, Mollusca and Chordata
(d) Annelida, Mollusca and Chordata

53. If the head of cockroach is removed, it may live for few days because **[NTSE]**
(a) the cockroach does not have nervous system.
(b) the head holds a small proportion of a nervous system while the rest is situated along the ventral part of its body.

(c) the head holds a $1/3^{rd}$ of a nervous system while the rest is situated along the dorsal part of its body.
(d) the supra-oesophageal ganglia of the cockroach are situated in ventral part of abdomen.

Assertion & Reason

DIRECTIONS (Qs.54-55) : Each of these questions contains an Assertion followed by reason. Read them carefully and answer the question on the basis of following options. You have to select the one that best describes the two statements.

(a) If both **Assertion** and **Reason** are **correct** and Reason is the **correct explanation** of Assertion.
(b) If both **Assertion** and **Reason** are correct, but Reason is **not the correct explanation** of Assertion.
(c) If **Assertion** is **correct** but **Reason** is **incorrect**.
(d) If **Assertion** is **incorrect** but **Reason** is **correct**.

54. **Assertion :** Bacteria are prokaryotic.
Reason : Bacteria do not possess true nucleus and membrane bound cell organelles.

55. **Assertion :** The science of classifiying organisms is called taxonomy.
Reason : Systematics and taxonomy have same meaning.

Match the following

DIRECTIONS (Qs.56-58): Each question contains terms (Given in column I) and their features or functions (Given in column II). Terms given in column I have to be matched with features given in column II

56.

	Column I		Column II
A.	Monera	p.	Mango
B.	Protista	q.	Lichens
C.	Fungi	r.	Volvox
D.	Algae	s.	Diatoms
E.	Angiospermae	t.	Blue green algae

57.

	Column I		Column II
A.	Porifera	p.	Segmented worm
B.	Cnidaria	q.	flat worm
C.	Platyhelminthes	r.	round worm
D.	Aschelminthes	s.	canal system
E.	Annelida	t.	corals

58.

	Column I		Column II
A.	*Mangifera indica*	p.	Potato
B.	*Homo sapiens*	q.	Dog
C.	*Solanum tuberosum*	r.	Lion
D.	*Panthera leo*	s.	Mango
E.	*Canis familiaris*	t.	Human

SOLUTIONS
(Brief Explanations of Selected Questions)

Exercise ★ **Foundation Builder +**

1. (b)	2. (b)	3. (a)	4. (a)
5. (a)	6. (a)	7. (b)	8. (b)
9. (a)	10. (d)	11. (c)	12. (b)
13. (b)	14. (b)	15. (a)	16. (b)
17. (a)	18. (a)	19. (b)	20. (a)

21. (a) *Ulothrix* is an alga and placed in a division thallophyta.

22. (d) Star fish are placed in a phylum Echinodermata.

23. (c) Scientific name comprise of Genus + species.

24. (d)

25. (a) Species is the basic unit of classification. Because the members of the same species are Reproductive isolates.

26. (b) Carolus linnaeus is the author of 'Systema Naturae'.

27. (a) In the given diagram the labelled part 'F' is Pelvic fin.

28. (c) Cytopyge: Egestion of undigested flood takes place through cytopyge. Which is temporarily formed Anus.

29. (b) Mushroom is the only edible fungi.

30. (a)   31. (b)   32. (c)

33. (c) WBCs are blood corpuscles involve in defending the body against both infectious diseases and foreign materials but they are not able to survive independently unlike *Amoeba* and *Paramecium*, which are acellular protozoans and complete their life processes like digestion, respiration, circulation, excretion etc. within a single cell.

34. (d)   35. (d)

36. (a) Fungus have eukaryotic cellular organisation with cell wall made up of chitin. They are heterotrophic because of absence of chlorophyll

37. (b) Live fluke is the member of phylum - platyhelminthes and their body is bilaterally symmetrical.

38. (b) Flowers are the reproductive parts of plant and they are phanerogams.

39. (c) Starfish is not having paired gill pouches. It respires through its tube like appendages i.e. tube feet.

40. (d) Pteridophytes include the ferns, horsetails and spike musses etc. These have motile sperms and dominant generations has diploid cells.

41. (d) Aerenchyma are the parenchyma cells filled wet air, which gives buoyancy to the plant.

42. (d) Red Data Book have the record of all endangered plants and animals.

43. (b) According to rules of binomial nomenclature, correctly written scientific name of mango is Mangifera indica Linn.

This system of nomenclature was given by Carl Linnaeus. The scientific name of mango is given as *Mangifera indica Linn. Mangifera* indicates the 'genus' while *indica* represents a particular species or 'specific epithet' and Linn indicates the Biologist Linnaeus who first described the species of mango.

44. (a) Binomial nomenclature is a formal system of naming species of living things by giving each a name composed of two parts, both of which use Latin grammatical forms, although they can be based on words from other languages.

45. (a) *Azotobacter is aerobic bacteria.* and *Cladophora* is green alga.

Engelmann used a prism to split light into its spectral components, and then illuminated a green alga, *Cladophora*, placed in a suspension of aerobic bacteria. The bacteria were used to detect the sites of oxygen evolution.

He observed that aerobic bacteria accumulated mainly in the region of blue and red light of the split spectrum thus giving the first action spectrum of photosynthesis.

46. (a) Saccharomyces i.e. yeast is an eukaryote (unicellular fungi). Mycobacterium is a bacterium. Oscillatoria and Nostoc are cyanobacteria.

47. (a) Viroids have free RNA without protein coat. Viroid, an infectious particle smaller than any of the known viruses, an agent of certain plant diseases. The particle consists only of an extremely small circular RNA (ribonucleic acid) molecule, lacking the protein coat of a virus.

240

Biology

48. **(c)** *Chlorella* and *Spirulina* are unicellular algae. *Gelidium, Gracilaria, Laminaria* and *Sargassum* are multicellular. *Volvox* is colonial.

49. **(d)** Floridean starch is stored food material in red algae. Its structure is similar to Amylopectin and Glycogen.

50. **(a)** Platyhelminthes are bilaterally symmetrical, triploblastic and acoelomate animals with organ level of organisation.

51. **(a)** Annelids exhibit bilateral symmetry with metameric segmentation where external segments correspond to internal segments.
Adult echinoderms are bilaterally symmetrical. Aschelminthes are pseudocoelomates and platyhelminthes are acoelomates.

52. **(a)** Organ system of organisation, bilateral symmetry and true coelomates with segmented body are found in annelid, arthropoda and chordates.

53. **(b)** Cockroaches breathe passively through a network of pipes connected to holes called spiracles along the length of their body. They are independent of blood circulation to move oxygen around and their body fluids are at a much lower pressure. The sensory input from the eyes and antennae, along with many other behaviours, are transmitted and handled by their brain such as running and reacting to touch, handled by 'mini brains' called ganglia in each body segment. A decapitated cockroach will eventually starve to death but this can still take few days.

54. **(a)**   **55.** **(c)**

56.

	Column I		Column II
A.	Monera	t.	Blue green algae
B.	Protista	s.	Diatoms
C.	Fungi	q.	Lichens
D.	Algae	r.	Volvox
E.	Angiospermae	p.	Mango

57.

	Column I		Column II
A.	Porifera	s.	canal system
B.	Cnidaria	t.	corals
C.	Platyhelminthes	q.	flat worm
D.	Aschelminthes	r.	round worm
E.	Annelida	p.	segmented worm

58.

	Column I		Column II
A.	*Mangifera indica*	s.	Mango
B.	*Homo sapiens*	t.	Human
C.	*Solanum tuberosum*	p.	Potato
D.	*Panthera leo*	r.	Lion
E.	*Canis familiaris*	q.	Dog

10 Genetics

Build A Strong Foundation

CONCEPT MAP

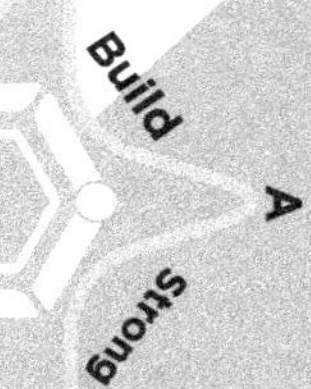

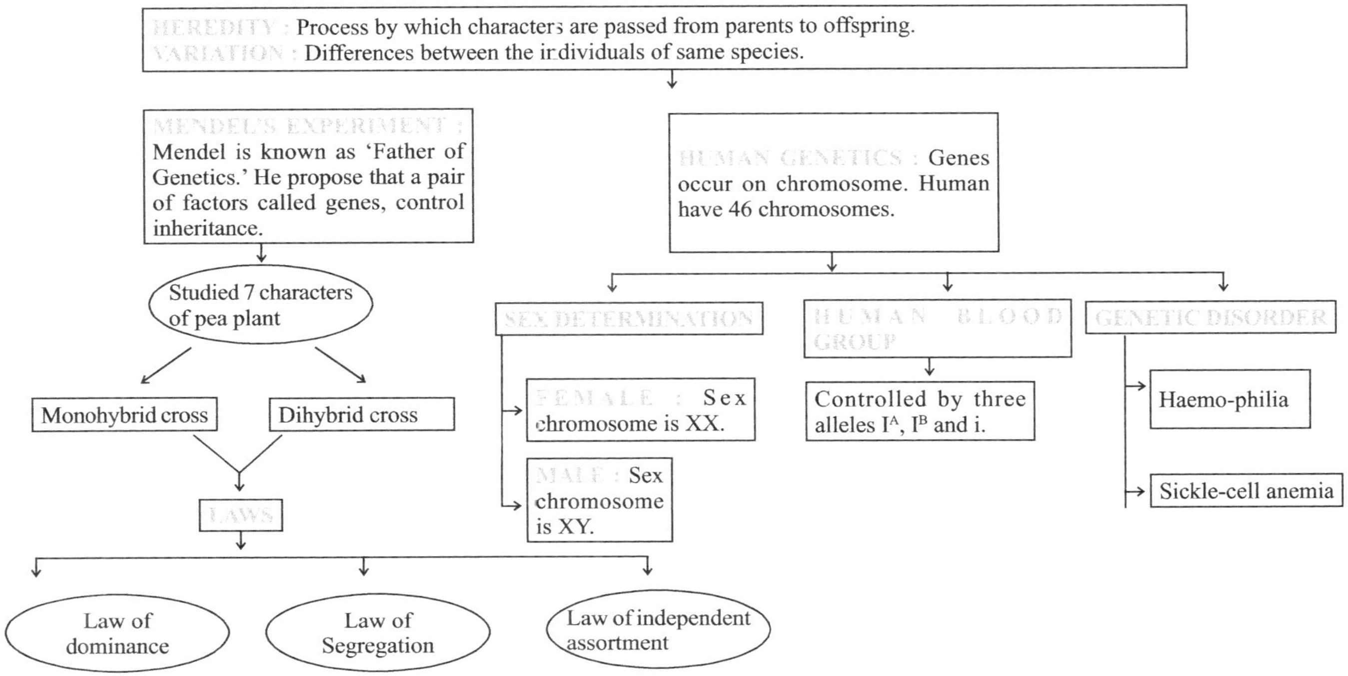
HEREDITY : Process by which characters are passed from parents to offspring.
VARIATION : Differences between the individuals of same species.
MENDEL'S EXPERIMENT : Mendel is known as 'Father of Genetics.' He propose that a pair of factors called genes, control inheritance.
Studied 7 characters of pea plant
Monohybrid cross
Dihybrid cross
LAWS
Law of dominance
Law of Segregation
Law of independent assortment
HUMAN GENETICS : Genes occur on chromosome. Human have 46 chromosomes.
SEX DETERMINATION
FEMALE : Sex chromosome is XX.
MALE : Sex chromosome is XY.
HUMAN BLOOD GROUP
Controlled by three alleles I^A, I^B and i.
GENETIC DISORDER
Haemo-philia
Sickle-cell anemia

The puzzle of how characteristics are passed on from one generation to the next, or even why some characteristics skip a generation, was solved by an Austrian monk called Gregor Mendel (1822-1884). Mendel grew garden peas, and studied its various characters. By recording how these characteristics were passed on from one generation to the next, he worked out on a set of the basic rules of genetic inheritance.

Note

Hybrid : A plant and animal produced by parents that have different hereditary characteristics.

MENDEL'S WORK ON HEREDITY

Gregor Mendel was the first scientist to study the pattern of inheritance. He did this by using different characters of pea plants (*Pisum sativum*) which he grew in his garden. Mendel choose pea plants for studying inheritance because pea plants had many contrasting characters with clear cut difference to identify them. For example, some pea plants were tall while others were dwarf. Some pea plants produce round-yellow seeds while others produced wrinkled-green seeds.

The advantage of using plants are :
(i)   Life cycle in the pea plant is very short.
(ii)   Pea plant produce a large number of seeds.
(iii) Pea plants exhibit natural self-pollination, because the petals of flowers remain closed.
(iv)   It was possible to conduct cross-pollination by transforming pollen grain from one flower to another.
(v)   Pea plants have many visible contracting characters.

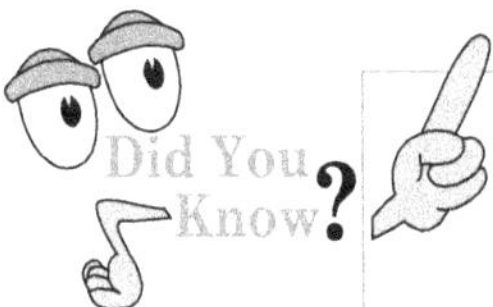

Mendel appeared in 1850 for passing a teaching certificate. Though he studied little science in school and had never attended a university, he succeeded in passing the examination in physics but failed in Geology and classification of mammals. He spent his last day in a conflict of church and died in 1884, without even knowing that he will be father of genetics in future.

MENDEL'S EXPERIMENT

Mendel performed experiments in three stages :
(i)   Selection of pure or true breeding parents.
(ii)   Hybridisation and obtaining first (F_1) generation.
(iii) Self-pollination of hybrid to get generations like F_2 and F_3 and so on.

(i)   Selection of Parents:

Note

A pure breeding variety produces offspring having similar characterstics. For example : white flower plant produces white flowered offsprings etc.

Mendel selected fourteen pure breeding variety of peas as the material for his experiments. The pure breeding nature of each variety was insured through self-pollination. He eliminated the plants which did not form similar offsprings. The true breeding plants formed the **parent (P) generation.**

Mendel employed seven characters with easily distinguishable contrasting forms. The characters were seed colour, seed shape, flower colour, pod colour, pod shape, flower position and plant height.

The following table represents the contrasting characters:-

	Parameters	Contrasting characters
1	Length of stem	Tall and dwarf
2	Position of flower	Axial and terminal
3	Pod shape	Inflated and constricted
4	Pod colour	Green and yellow
5	Colour of seed	Grey and white
6	Shape of seed	Round and wrinkled
7	Colour of flower	Purple and white

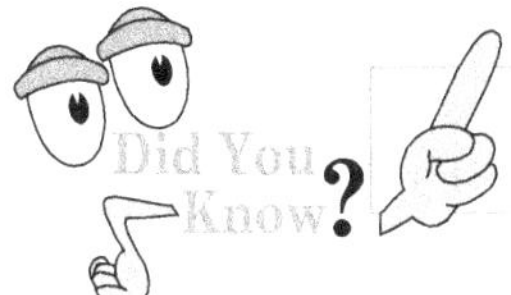

An organism is homozygous for a trait, when it has two copies of same allele. An organism is Heterozygous for a trait when it has two different alleles.

Character	Dominant trait	Recessive trait	Character	Dominant trait	Recessive trait
Seed shape	Spherical	Wrinkled	Flower position	Axial	Terminal
Seed color	Yellow	Green			
Flower color	Purple	White			
Pod shape	Inflated	Constricted	Stem height	Tall	Dwarf
Pod color	Green	Yellow			

(ii) Hybridization and obtaining first generation :-

Mendel selected true breeding tall (TT) and dwarf (tt) pea plants. Then, he crossed these two plants. The seeds formed after fertilization were grown and these plants that were formed represent the first filial progeny or F_1 generation. All the F_1 plants obtained were tall.

Note

In genetics, genes are represented by letters. A capital letter shows that a gene is dominant, and a small one represents a recessive gene.

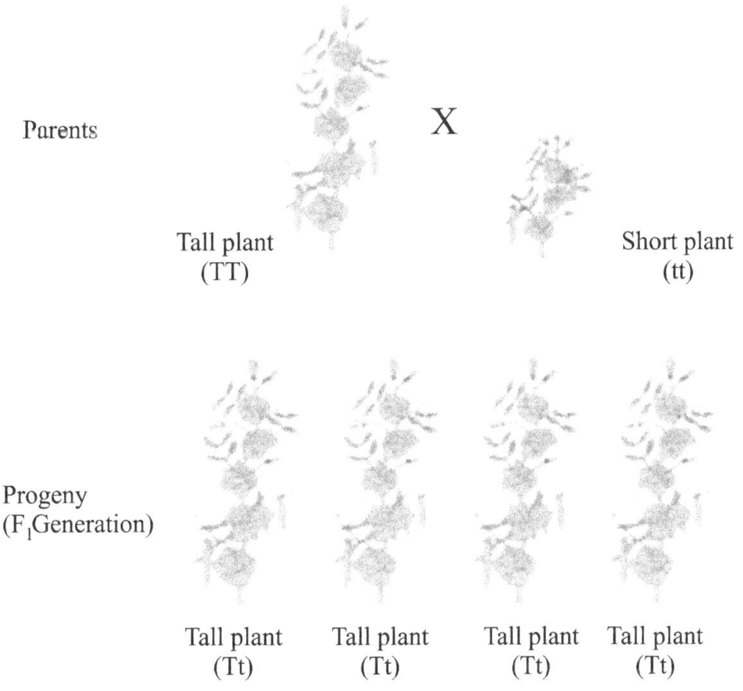

Cross pollination of tall and short plant

Biology

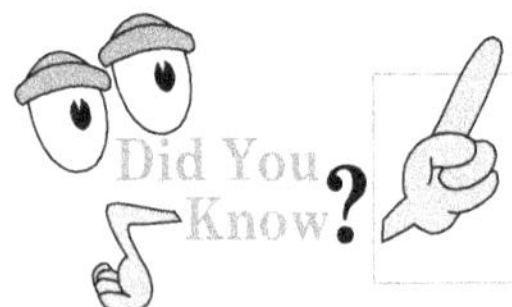

> *The gene which decides the appearance of an organism even in the presence of an alternative gene is known as dominant gene. On the other hand, the gene which can decide the appearance of an organism only in the presence of another identical gene is called a recessive gene.*

(iii) Self-pollination of hybrids to get generations like F_2 and F_3 :

Then, Mendel self-pollinated the F_1 plants and observed that all plants obtained in the F_2 generation were not tall. Instead, one-fourth of the F_2 plants were short.

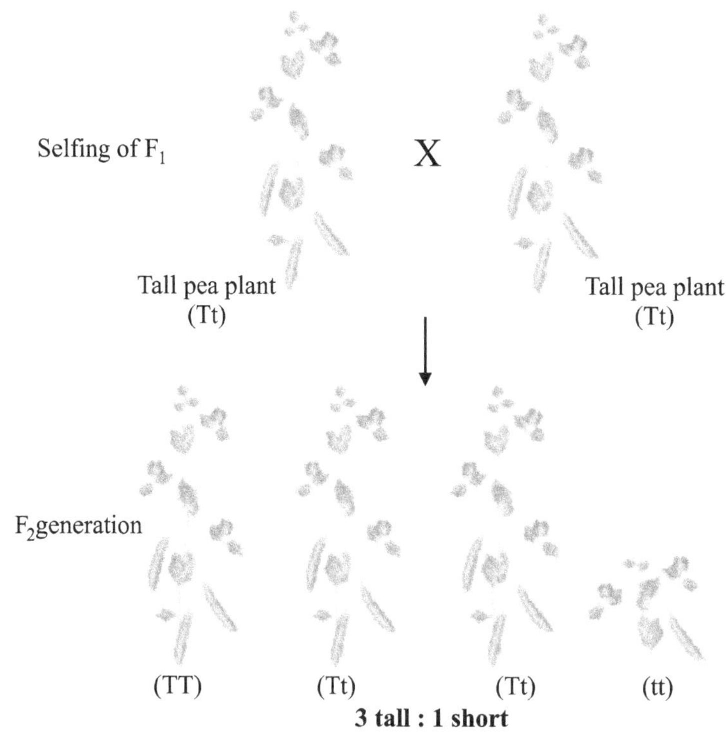

Self-pollination of F_1 plants.

From this experiment, Mendel concluded that the F_1 tall plants were not true breeding. They were carrying traits of both dwarfness and tallness. They appeared tall only because the tall trait is dominant over the dwarf trait.

Note

Genotype is the description of the genetic composition in an organism. For example, TT, tt or Tt.

Phenotype is the characteristic which is visible in an organism. For example, tall or dwarf are phenotypes of a plant.

MENDEL'S OBSERVATION

(i) The F_1 hybrids always showed one of the parental forms of the trait.

(ii) Both the parental forms of the trait (contrasting forms of the trait) appeared without any change in the F_2 generation.

(iii) The two contrasting forms in a trait did not show any blending either in the F_1 generation or in the F_2 generations.

(iv) The form of the trait that appeared in the F_1 hybrids is called *dominant* form and it appeared in the F_2 generation about three times in frequency as its alternate (recessive) form.

MENDEL'S FINDINGS

On the basis of his experiment, Mendel postulated three laws which are known as Mendel's law of heredity. These are:

(i) Law of dominance

(ii) Law of segregation

(iii) Law of independent assortment.

(1) Law of Dominance

This law has its basis from the monohybrid cross. According to this law "when a cross is made between two homozygous (pure line) individuals considering contrasting alleles of same character, then the allele that appears in F_1 hybrid is called dominant and the other is recessive".

(2) Law of segregation or law of purity of gamete

According to this law "In F_1 hybrid the dominant and recessive character though remain together for long time but they do not mix with each other and separate or segregate at the time of gamete formation such that a gamete receives only one of the two factors. Thus the gamete formed, receives either dominant or recessive character out of them. This law is called law of purity of gametes i.e., a gamete when formed is always pure for a particular trait, just because of the fact that they always contain the factors which determines single trait pertaining to a particular character.

Note

Monhybird cross: It involves cross between two parents that differ only in one heritable character. For example : Tallness and dwarfness (height).

Dihybrid cross: It involves cross between two parents that differ in two heritable characters. For example, round-yellow seeds and wrinkled green seeds (seed shape and colour).

Mendel crossed pea plants having round green seeds (RRyy) with pea plants having wrinkled yellow seeds (rrYY).

Since the F_1 plants are formed after crossing pea plants having green round seeds and pea plants having yellow wrinkled seeds, it will have both these characters in them. However, as we know that yellow seed colour and round shape of seeds are dominant characters, therefore, the F_1 plants will have yellow round seeds. For F_2 generation, F_1 plants were self-pollinated.

(3) Law of independent assortment

In dihybrid cross the phenotype observed were round yellow, wrinkled yellow, round green and wrinkled green and appeared in the ratio of 9 : 3 : 3 : 1. Such a ratio was observed for several traits.

Based on this dihybrid cross, Mendel proposed the law of independent assortment, which states that when two pairs of traits are combined in a hybrid, segregation of one pair of characters is independent of the other pair of characters.

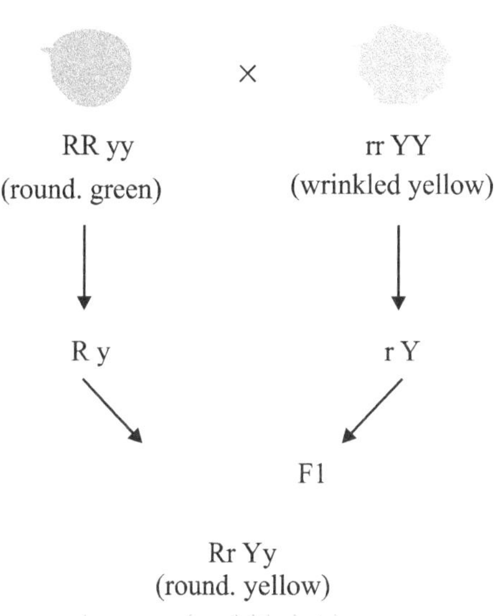

An example of dihybrid crosses

CHROMOSOMES - THE CARRIERS OF HEREDITY

Chromosomes are only visible when a cell nucleus is about to divide. The chromosome number is constant for the individuals of a species and every cell has the same number. Humans have 46 chromosomes.

In 1915, T.H. Morgan noted peculiar similarity between chromosomal behaviour and Mendelian factors and supported the chromosomal theory of inheritance propounded by N.S. Sutton in 1902. *According to the chromosomal theory of inheritance*, the Mendelian factors came to be known as 'genes'. Genes occur on the chromosome in a linear fashion. Each characteristic or trait seems to be controlled largely by gene.

The paring and separation of a pair of chromosomes would lead to the segregation of a pair of factors they carried.

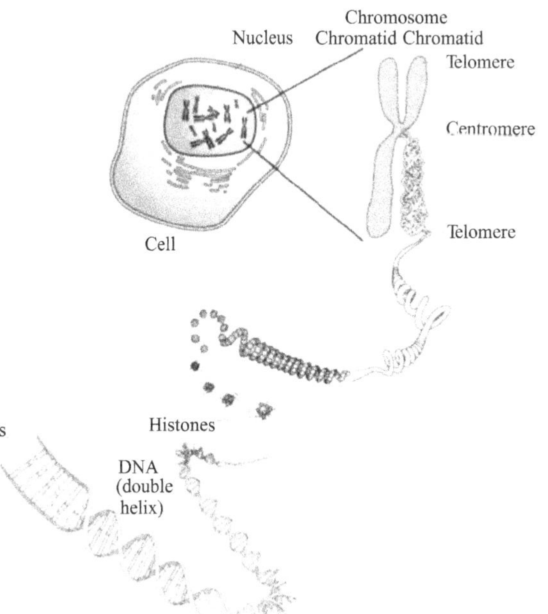

Chromosome

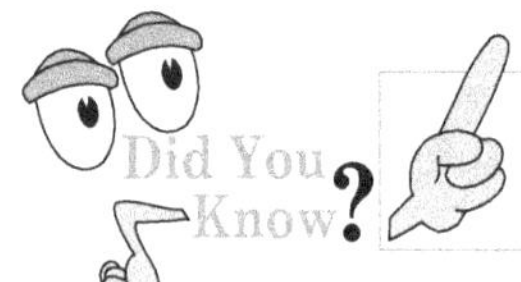

Chromosomes are thread like bodies found in the nucleus of a cell. We have a total of 46 chromosome in our cell.

Deoxyribonucleic Acid (DNA)

Watson and Crick (1953) at Cambridge proposed the double helical structure of DNA. The X-ray photographs showed that the DNA was a helix and the width of the helix is 2nm. The purine and pyrimidine base were stacked 0.34 nm apart in a ladder. The helix made one full turn every 3.4 nm. Thus, there are 10 layers of bases stacked in one turn. Since the width of the helix is 2 nm it can accommodate only two stands and not three.

They found that the best model, which satisfied all the X-ray data, was a double helix with the sugar phosphate chain on the outside and the bases on the inside. The two chains run in an antiparallel fashion with one chain having a 5' – 3' orientation and the other has 3' – 5' In DNA the, adenine (A) pairs with thymine (T), and guanine (G) pairs with cytosine (C) The two strands of DNA are held together by hydrogen bonds.

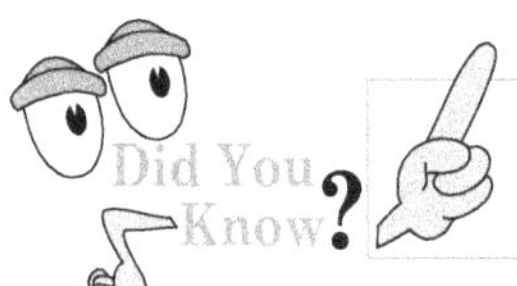

Frederick Meisher was the first who proved that DNA is a genetic material.

Note

Autosomes: The chromosomes other than the sex chromosome. Each member of an autosome pair (in diploid organisms) is similar in length and in the gene it carries. There are 2 pairs of autosomes in human.

☛ **Why are genes important?**

SOLUTION :

Genes are important as they are responsible for transmitting traits, characteristics, diseases and all other hereditary information from one generation to another. Genes are the basic chemical units of DNA molecules found in chromosomes. Our behaviour and personality traits are determined by our genes. Each gene carries instruction for specific characteristic such as curly or straight hair, eye colour, or albino skin.

You must have noticed that brothers or sisters often look alike. Have you ever thought, how it happens?

It is the inherited traits that makes their physical appearance so similar. An inherited trait is a particular genetically determined characteristic that distinguishes a person. The traits of children are determined by the traits that are passed on from their parents. Some traits are obvious in a family, a child's nose is shaped like their mother's nose, but some traits are less obvious. You may have similar traits to many of your classmates even though you are not related to them. For example you roll tongue but your brother may not.

There are numerous traits in humans, but some traits occur more frequently than others. About 70-90% of the human population have free-hanging earlobes and can roll their tongue. The traits which occur more commonly are called dominant and those which are less are called recessive trait.

HUMAN GENETICS

The process of creating new life is called reproduction. A man's body makes male sex cells, which are called sperms while woman's body produces ova, which are female sex cells. When a sperm (fuses) with an ovum, a new cell is formed. This cell contains all the information needed to build a unique human being and is called zygote.

The instructions that tell the body how to develop genes, and the study of genes is called genetics. Genes are sections of a long thread like structure are called DNA (Deoxyribonucleic acid), which is packed in bundles forming structure called chromosomes. Chromosomes are packed inside a control unit called nucleus. Human cells have 46 chromosomes, which are inherited from parents.

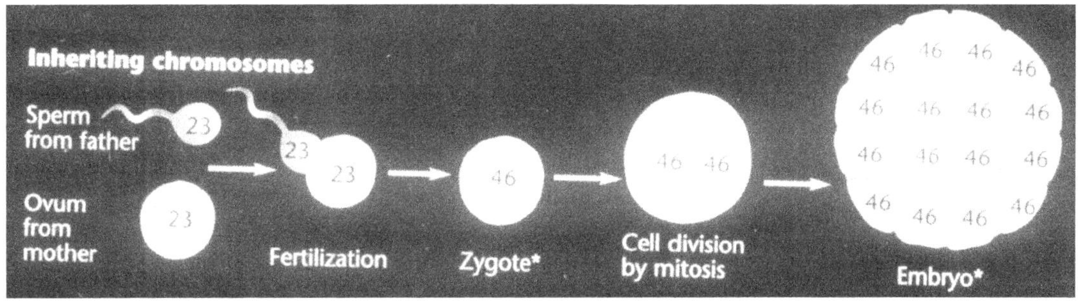

Let us discuss, how these genes work?

Humans have 23 pairs of homologous chromosomes. Each gene, or gene group, on one of these chromosomes, act together with its partner on the other paired chromosome. This gives an instruction to create or control characteristics.

Genes for certain features, such as eye or hair colour, or blood group, have different forms, called *alleles*. So a gene pair might be made up of alleles giving identical instructions, or alleles giving different instructions.

HUMAN BLOOD GROUP

The blood group character is controlled by a set of three alleles. I^A, I^B and i. Genes I^A and I^B both are dominant over gene I^O or i, but not over each other.

- For blood group B, the genotype would be $I^B I^B$ or I^Bi.
- For blood group AB, the genotype would be $I^A I^B$.
- For blood group O, the genotype would be ii.
- For blood group A, the genotype would be $I^A I^A$ or I^Ai.

SEX DETERMINATION (GIRL OR BOY)

In human beings, the females have two X chromosomes and the males have one X and one Y chromosome. Therefore, the females are XX and the males are XY.

The gametes, as we know, receive half of the chromosomes from each parent. The male gametes have 22 autosomes and either X or Y sex chromosome.

Type of male gametes: 22+X OR 22+ Y.

However, since the females have XX sex chromosomes, their gametes can only have X sex chromosome along with 22 autosomes.

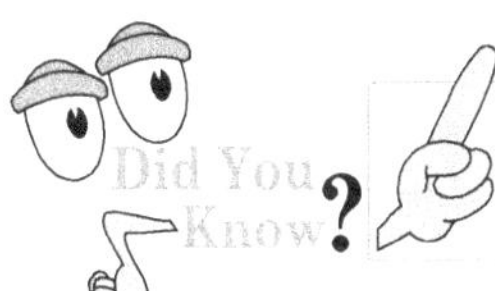
DNA is a double-straned coiled molecular chain held together by linearly held nucleotide. They make gene.

Type of female gamete: 22+X

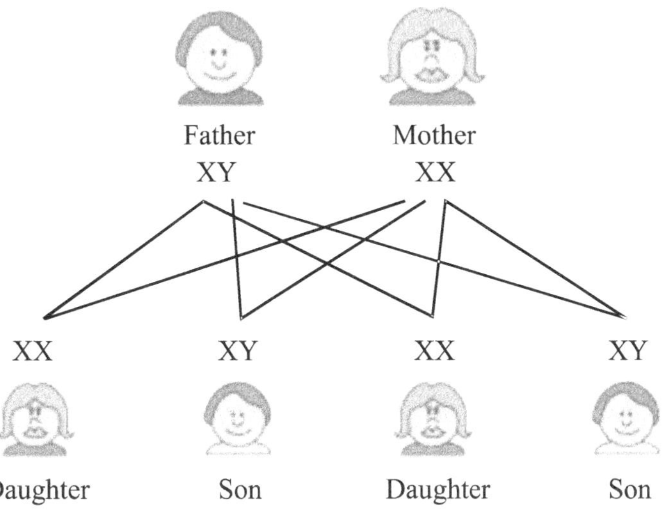

Sex determination in Human

Thus, the mother provides only X chromosomes. The sex of the baby is determined by the type of male gamete (X or Y) that fuses with the X chromosome of the female.

GENETIC DISORDERS

A large number of diseases are known to be inherited from the parents to the offspring. Such diseases are known as genetic disorder. Most of these diseases are caused by the expression of recessive genes.

Most common and prevalent disorders are haemophilia, cystic fibrosis, sickle cell anaemia, colour blindness, thalassemia etc.

Some genetic diorders are discussed below :

(i) Haemophilia:
- It is a sex linked recessive disease. It transmits from unaffected carrier female to some of the male progeny.
- In this disease a single protein that is a part of the cascade of proteins involved in the clotting of blood is affected. Due to this, in an affected individual a simple cut will result in non-stop bleeding.
- The heterozygous female (carrier) for haemophilia may transmit the disease to sons.
- The possiblity of a female becoming a haemophilic is extremely rare because mother of such female has to be at least carrier and father should be haemophilic. It is called royal disease, because of its relevance in the royal family pedigree which shows a number of haemophilic descents as queen Victoria was a carrier of the disease.

Cross between haemophilic carrier female and normal male :

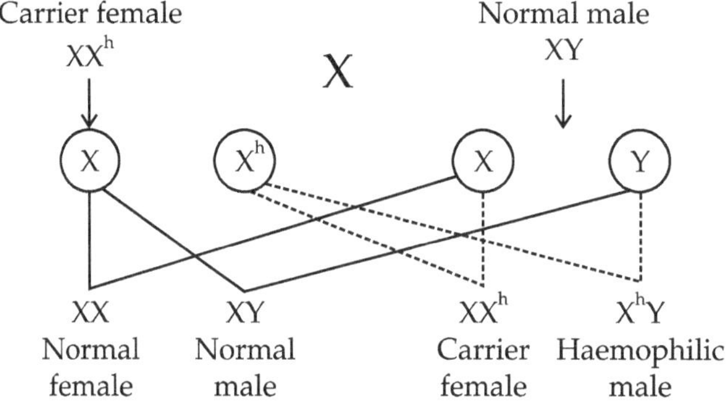

(ii) Sickle cell anemia
- This is autosome linked recessive trait that can be transmitted from parents to the offspring when both the partners are carrier for the gene.
- The substitution of amino acid is the globin protein of haemoglobin causes the change in the shape of the RBC into elongated sickle like structures.

☞ **When was haemophilia discovered in the royal line?**

SOLUTION :

Haemophilia is an inherited deficiency whereby the substance necessary for blood clotting is missing. The transmission of this condition is sex linked, being present mostly in males but carried solely by females. Sons of a haemophilic male are normal, but daughters, although outwardly normal, may transmit this deficiency to half of their sons. The existence of haemophilia in certain royal families of Europe is well known. Working from family trees it seems probable that Queen Victoria naturally produced the gene for haemophilia and is the carriers of the disease.

Genetic Engineering

Scientists have discovered how to extract genes and use them in different ways, for instance in medicine, farming and industry. This manipulation of genes is known as genetic engineering.

The main technique used in genetic engineering is called gene splicing. Chemicals called restriction enzymes are used to cut specific genes out of DNA. Other enzymes, called ligases, are used to splice, or join, the genes with DNA taken from a suitable organism.

This modified DNA, known as recombinant DNA (rDNA), can then be used in different ways. For example, it may be placed in a fast-breeding bacterium. This reproduces very quickly to create lots of bacteria, each containing the rDNA with the specific gene.

SUMMARY

- If a forest area is left undisturbed for a long time, it restablishes itself.
- The process by which characters or traits are passed from the parents to the offspring is called heredity.
- Variations means differences between the individuals of the same species.
- The science which deals with the study of heredity and variations is known as genetics.
- An Austrian monk named Gregor Johann Mendel was the first person to study genetics. He is known as the 'Father of Genetics'.
- Mendel proposed that a pair of factors which are now called genes, control inheritance.
- Genes were found to occupy specific position on thread like structure called chromosome.
- The paired condition is known as diploid.
- DNA is the most important constituent of a chromosome.
- DNA is a macromolecule which is made up of a large number of nucleotide units.
- The females carry two X-chromosomes as sex chromosome.
- The males carry one X and one Y chromosome as sex chromosome.

Multiple Choice Questions

DIRECTIONS (Qs.1-10): *This section contains multiple choice questions. Each question has four choices (a), (b), (c) and (d) out of which ONLY ONE is correct.*

1. Which among the following genotype characteristics of an organism is heterozygous for two genes?
(a) RRYy (b) RrYY
(c) RRYY (d) RrYy

2. Which one is a sex–linked disorder?
(a) Leukemia (b) Cancer
(c) Night Blindness (d) Colour blindness

3. Which of the following is considered as a recessive character by Mendel?
(a) Round seed (b) Wrinkled seed
(c) Axial flower (d) Green pod

4. Which is the functional unit of inheritance?
(a) Chromosome (b) Gene
(c) Cistron (d) Allele

5. Which of the following is not true for haemophilia?
(a) Royal disease
(b) Bleeder's disease
(c) X-linked disease
(d) Y-linked disease

6. Which of the following is not a hereditary disease?
(a) Cretinism (b) Cystic fibrosis
(c) Thalassaemia (d) Haemophilia

7. The genetic component of an organism is called its
(a) DNA (b) Genotype
(c) Phenotype (d) Chromosome

8. In how many chromosomes were the seven characters chosen by Mendel located?
(a) 5 (b) 7
(c) 4 (d) 1

9. The structure of DNA is
(a) linear (b) cystic twisted
(c) double helical (d) spiral

10. Sections of DNA are called
(a) Chromosomes (b) Genes
(c) Nucleus (d) None of these

11. Which one of the following genetic phenomena is represented by the blood group *AB*?
(a) Codominance
(b) Dominance
(c) Overdominance
(d) Semidominance

12. In a diploid organism, when the locus X is inactivated, transcription of the locus Y is triggered. Based on this observation, which one of the following statements is CORRECT?
(a) X is dominant over Y
(b) X is epistatic to Y
(c) Y is dominant over X
(d) Y is epistatic to X

13. If the genotypes determining the blood groups of a couple are $I^A I^O$ and $I^A I^B$, then the probability of their first child having type O blood is:
(a) 0 (b) 0.25
(c) 0.50 (d) 0.75

14. A cross was carried out between two individuals heterozygous for two pairs of genes. Assuming segregation and independent assortment, the number of different genotypes and phenotypes obtained respectively would be
(a) 4 and 9 (b) 6 and 3
(c) 9 and 4 (d) 11 and 4

15. According to Watson-Crick model, hydrogen bonding in a double-stranded DNA occurs between
(a) adenine and guanine (b) adenine and thymine
(c) cytosine and adenine (d) guanine and thymine

16. Considering ABO blood grouping system in humans, during blood transfusion some combinations of blood groups are compatible ($\checkmark$), whereas the others are incompatible ($\times$). Which one of the following options is correct?

(a)

		Recipient			
		O	A	B	AB
Donor	O	×	×	×	✓
	A	✓	×	✓	×
	B	✓	✓	×	×
	AB	✓	✓	✓	✓

(b)

		Recipient			
		O	A	B	AB
Donor	O	×	×	×	×
	A	✓	×	✓	×
	B	✓	✓	×	×
	AB	✓	✓	✓	×

(c)

		Recipient			
		O	A	B	AB
Donor	O	✓	×	×	×
	A	✓	✓	×	×
	B	✓	×	✓	×
	AB	✓	✓	✓	✓

(d)

		Recipient			
		O	A	B	AB
Donor	O	✓	✓	✓	✓
	A	×	✓	×	✓
	B	×	×	✓	✓
	AB	×	×	×	✓

17. A couple has two sons and two daughters. Only one son is colourblind and the rest of the siblings are normal. Assuming colourblindness is sex-linked, which one of the following would be the phenotype of the parents?
(a) Mother would be colourblind, father would be normal
(b) Father would be colourblind, mother would be normal
(c) Both the parents would be normal
(d) Both the parents would be colourblind

18. What is the length of human DNA containing 6.6×10^9 bp?
(a) 22 nm
(b) 0.22 mm
(c) 2.2 m
(d) 22 m

19. If a *ds*DNA has 20% adenine, what would be its cytosine content?
(a) 20%   (b) 30%   (c) 40%   (d) 80%

20. What is the number of chromosomes in an individual with Turner's syndrome?
(a) 44   (b) 45   (c) 46   (d) 47

21. Restriction endonucleases are enzymes that are used by biotechnologists to
(a) cut DNA at specific base sequences
(b) join fragments of DNA
(c) digest DNA from the 3' end
(d) digest DNA from the 5' end

22. A person with blood group AB has
(a) antigen A and B on RBCs and both anti-A and anti-B antibodies in plasma
(b) antigen A and B on RBCs, but neither anti-A nor anti-B antibodies in plasma

(c) no antigen on RBCs but both anti-A and anti-B antibodies are present in plasma
(d) antigen A on RBCs and anti-B antibodies in plasma

23. Considering the average molecular mass of a base to be 500 Da, what is the molecular mass of a double-stranded DNA of 10 base pairs?
(a) 500 Da
(b) 5 kDa
(c) 10 kDa
(d) 1 kDa

24. Experimental verification of the chromosomal theory of inheritance was done by **[NTSE]**
(a) Sutton
(b) Boveri
(c) Morgan
(d) Mendel

25. In *Antirrhinum* (Snapdragon), a red flower was crossed with a white flower and in F_1 generation, pink flowers were obtained. When pink flowers were selfed, the F_2 generation showed white, red and pink flowers. Choose the incorrect statement from the following: **[NTSE]**
(a) This experiment does not follow the principle of dominance.
(b) Pink colour in F_1 is due to incomplete dominance.
(c) Ratio of F_2 is $\frac{1}{4}$ (Red): $\frac{1}{2}$ (Pink): $\frac{1}{4}$ (White)
(d) Law of Segregation does not apply in this experiment.

26. A woman has an X-linked condition on one of her X chromosomes. This chromosome can be inherited by
(a) Only daughters   **[NTSE]**
(b) Only sons
(c) Both sons and daughters
(d) Only grandchildren

27. Which of the following characteristics represent 'Inheritance of blood groups' in humans?   **[NTSE]**
A. Dominance   B. Co-dominance
C. Multiple allele   D. Incomplete dominance
E. Polygenic inheritance
(a) B, C and E
(b) A, B and C
(c) A, C and E
(d) B, D and E

28. The genotypes of a husband and wife are $I^A I^B$ and $I^A i$. Among the blood types of their children, how many different genotypes and phenotypes are possible? **[NTSE]**
(a) 3 genotypes ; 4 phenotypes
(b) 4 genotypes ; 3 phenotypes
(c) 4 genotypes ; 4 phenotypes
(d) 3 genotypes ; 3 phenotypes

29. Among the following characters, which one was not considered by Mendel in his experiments on pea? **[NTSE]**

    (a) Trichomes – Glandular or non-glandular

    (b) Seed – Green or Yellow

    (c) Pod – Inflated or Constricted

    (d) Stem – Tall or Dwarf

30. Which one from those given below is the period for Mendel's hybridisation experiments? **[NTSE]**

    (a) 1840 - 1850

    (b) 1857 - 1869

    (c) 1870 - 1877

    (d) 1856 - 1863

31. A tall true breeding garden pea plant is crossed with a dwarf true breeding garden pea plant. When the F_1 plants were selfed the resulting genotypes were in the ratio of **[NTSE]**

    (a) 1 : 2 : 1 :: Tall homozygous : Tall heterozygous : Dwarf

    (b) 1 : 2 : 1 :: Tall heterozygous : Tall homozygous : Dwarf

    (c) 3 : 1 : : Tall : Dwarf

    (d) 3 : 1 : : Dwarf : Tall

32. How many pairs of contrasting characters in pea plants were studied by Mendel in his experiments? **[NTSE]**

    (a) Six   (b) Eight

    (c) Seven   (d) Five

33. Alleles are **[NTSE]**

    (a) true breeding homozygotes

    (b) different molecular forms of a gene

    (c) heterozygotes

    (d) different phenotype

34. In his classic experiments on Pea plants, Mendel did not use **[NTSE]**

    (a) Pod length   (b) Seed shape

    (c) Flower position   (d) Seed colour

35. A man with blood group 'A' marries a woman with blood group 'B'. What are all the possible blood groups of their offsprings ? **[NTSE]**

    (a) A,B and AB only

    (b) A,B,AB and O

    (c) O only

    (d) A and B only

36. Which of the following carry hereditary characters to the offspring in the organism? **[NTSE]**

    (a) Ribosome   (b) Chromosome

    (c) Plasma   (d) Lysosome

37. A pea plant with round green (RRyy) pea seed is crossed another pea plant with wrinkled yellow (rrYY) seeds. What would be the nature of seed in the first generation (F_1 generation)? **[NTSE]**

    (a) Round green   (b) Wrinkled green

    (c) Wrinkled yellow   (d) Round yellow

38. The gene for hemophilia is present on X chromosome. If a hemophilic male marries a normal female, the probability of their son being hemophilic is **[NTSE]**

    (a) nil   (b) 25%

    (c) 50%   (d) 100%

39. In the experiment conducted by Mendel, RRyy (round green) and rrYY (wrinkled, yellow) seeds of pea plant were used. In the F_2 generation 240 progeny were produced, out of which 15 progeny had specific characteristics. What were the characteristics? **[NTSE]**

    (a) round and green   (b) round and yellow

    (c) wrinkle and yellow (d) wrinkle and green

40. The production of gametes by the parents, the formation of zygotes, the F1 and F2 plants, can be understood using **[NTSE]**

    (a) Wenn diagram   (b) Pie diagram

    (c) A pyramid diagram (d) Punnet square

Match the following

41. Match the terms in Column-I with their description in Column-II and choose the correct option. **[NTSE]**

Column-I		Column-II
(A) Dominance	(p)	Many genes govern a single character
(B) Codominance	(q)	In a heterozygous organism, only one allele expresses itself
(C) Pleiotropy	(r)	In a heterozygous organism, both alleles express themselves fully
(D) Polygenic inheritance	(s)	A single gene influences many characters

	(A)	(B)	(C)	(D)
(a)	(q)	(p)	(s)	(r)
(b)	(q)	(r)	(s)	(p)
(c)	(s)	(p)	(q)	(r)
(d)	(s)	(r)	(p)	(q)

42. Match the items of Column-I with Column-II :

Column-I	Column-II
(A) XX-XO method	(p) Turner's syndrome of sex determination
(B) XX-XY method	(q) Female heterogametic of sex determination
(C) Karyotype-45	(r) Grasshopper
(D) ZW-ZZ method of sex	(s) Female homogametic determination

Select the correct option from the following :

(a) (A)-(s), (B)-(q), (C)-(p), (D)-(r)

(b) (A)-(q), (B)-(s), (C)-(p), (D)-(r)

(c) (A)-(p), (B)-(s), (C)-(q), (D)-(r)

(d) (A)-(r), (B)-(s), (C)-(p), (D)-(q)

Assertion & Reason

DIRECTIONS (Qs. 43-47) : Each of these questions contains an Assertion followed by reason. Read them carefully and answer the question on the basis of following options. You have to select the one that best describes the two statements.

(a) If both **Assertion** and **Reason** are **correct** and Reason is the **correct explanation** of Assertion.

(b) If both **Assertion** and **Reason** are correct, but Reason is **not the correct explanation** of Assertion.

(c) If **Assertion** is **correct** but **Reason** is **incorrect**.

(d) If **Assertion** is **incorrect** but **Reason** is **correct**.

43. **Assertion :** Workers prior to Mendel could not work on the principles of inheritance

   Reason : They considered the individuals as a whole complex of characters.

44. **Assertion :** The law of segregation is one of the most important contribution to biology.

   Reason : It introduced the concept of hereditary factors as discrete physical entities which do not blend.

45. **Assertion :** The genetic complement of an organism is called genotype.

   Reason : Genotype is the type of hereditary properties of an organism.

46. **Assertion :** Mendel successed to know the process of inheritance.

   Reason : He considered a single character at one time

47. **Assertion :** Mendel's seven characters are confined to only four chromosome.

   Reason : Test cross is a cross between F1 hybrid and recessive parent.

SOLUTIONS
(Brief Explanations of Selected Questions)

Exercise ⬡ Foundation Builder +

1. (d)   **2.** (d)   **3.** (b)   **4.** (b)
5. (d)   **6.** (a)   **7.** (b)   **8.** (c)
9. (c)   **10.** (b)

11. (a) Codominance occurs when both alleles show dominance, as in the case of the AB blood type ($I^A I^B$) in humans. It is a relationship between two versions of a gene. Individuals receive one version of a gene, called an allele, from each parent. If the alleles are different, the dominant allele usually will be expressed, while the effect of the other allele, called recessive, is masked.

12. (d) A gene is said to be epistatic when it's presence suppresses the effect of a gene at another locus, so here X is suppressing Y. Hence, X is epistatic to Y.

13. (a) The genotypes of offspring of parents having $I^A I^O$ and $I^A I^B$ blood groups are:

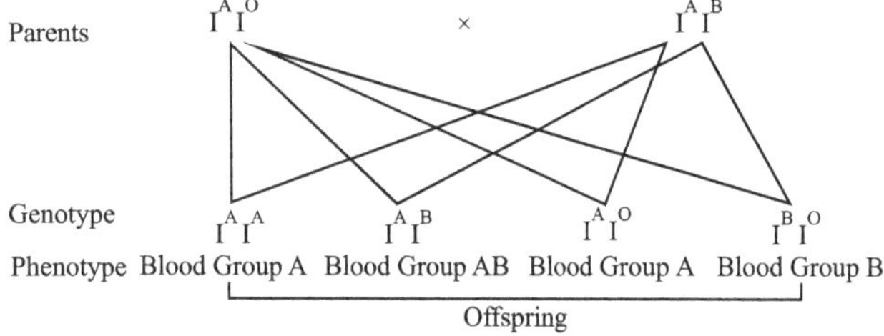

From the above cross, it is shown that none of the offspring will be of blood group O.

∴ The probability of their first child having type O blood is zero.

14. (c) In the given question, both parents are heterozygous for two pairs of genes. This means the cross is a dihybrid cross.

Let us assume a dihybrid cross,

Pure breeding – Yellow round   ×   Wrinkled green
traits   seeds   seeds
              (YYRR)   (yyrr)

F_1 – Yellow round seeds
           (YyRr)

↓ Gametes

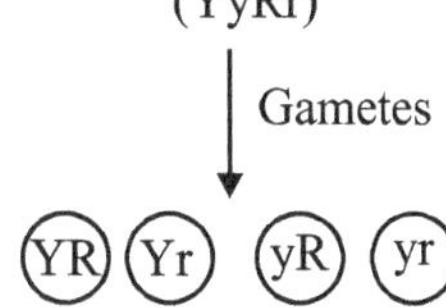

♀ \ ♂	YR	Yr	yR	yr
YR	YYRR yellow round	YYRr yellow round	YyRR yellow round	YyRr yellow round
Yr	YYRr yellow round	Yyrr yellow wrinkled	YyRr yellow round	Yyrr yellow wrinkled
yR	YyRR yellow round	YyRr yellow round	yyRR green round	yyRr green round
yr	YyRr yellow round	Yyrr yellow wrinkled	yyRr green round	yyrr green wrinkled

The genotype ratio is 1 : 2 : 1 : 2 : 4 : 2 : 1 : 2 : 1
The phenotypic ratio is 9 : 3 : 3 : 1

∴ The number of different genotypes and phenotypes obtained would be 9 and 4, respectively.

15. (b) In 1953, JD Watson and FHC Crick proposed a 3-D model of physiological DNA. They proposed that DNA is a double-stranded helical molecule. It consists of two sugar-phosphate backbones, spirally arranged and held together by hydrogen bonds which are present between pairs of nitrogenous bases. The base adenine (A) always pairs with thymine (T) by two hydrogen bonds and guanine always pairs with cytosine (C) by three hydrogen bonds. This complimentarity is known as the base pairing rule.

16. (d) Blood group-O individuals are called universal donor as they can give blood to person having blood groups A, B, AB and O. Individuals having blood group AB can only give blood to persons with blood group AB but can receive blood from all other blood groups.

Therefore, the correct table for the blood transfusion compatibility for ABO blood group system in human is

		Recipient			
		O	A	B	AB
Donor	O	✓	✓	✓	✓
	A	✗	✓	✗	✓
	B	✗	✗	✓	✓
	AB	✗	✗	✗	✓

17. **(c)** Colourblindness is a X-linked recessive disease. A carrier mother (heterozygous) does not show the disease as she has two X-chromosome. So matter would be normal while a father cannot be a carrier of the disease as he has single X-chromosome.

In the given question, the son is colourblind which means he had inherited X-chromosome from the mother. But another son is normal. This shows that the mother is heterozygous for the disease.

The expected cross for the question will be

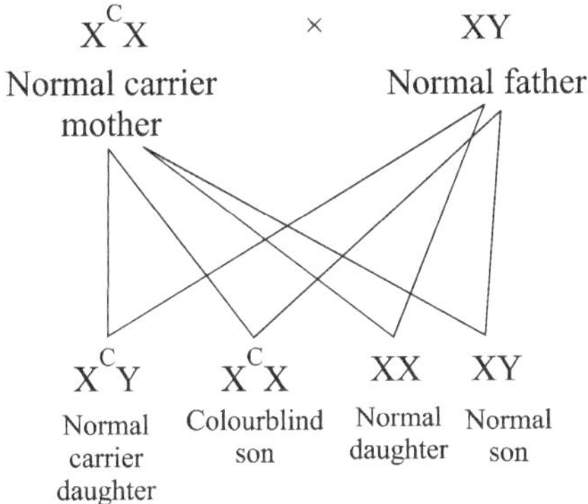

This shows that both the parents would be normal if they have one colourblind son and one normal son.

18. **(c)** The distance between 2 nucleotides/nitrogen bases is 0.34×10^{-9} m or 3.4 Å.

Therefore, the length of human DNA containing 6.6×10^9 bp would be

$= 0.34 \times 10^{-9}$ m $\times 6.6 \times 10^9$ bp

$= 2.2$ m

19. **(b)** According to Chargaff's Rule,

% Adenine = % Thymine and

% Guanine = % Cytosine

If dsDNA has 20% of adenine, then according to the law, it would have 20% thymine.

Thus, percentage of A + T content = 40%

The remaining 60% represents both G + C molecule. So, the percentage of cytosine content molecule is 30%.

20. **(b)** The people with Turner's syndrome have 44 + XO chromosomes, so there are a total of 45 chromosomes only in each cell. Such persons are sterile females who have rudimentary ovaries, undeveloped breasts, small uterus, short stature and abnormal intelligence.

21. **(b)** Excessive salt inhibits the bacterial growth in pickles by exosmosis because external medium become hypertonic. It results in drawing water out of the cells of microbe through osmosis (more specifically exosmosis). Due to this bacteria will die by the process of plasmolysis.

22. **(b)** Person with blood group AB have both A and B antigen on the surface of red blood cells but blood plasma does not contain any antibodies against either A or B antigen. Due to this reason, blood group AB is called universal recipient.

23. **(c)** Molecular mass of a base = 500 Da

Number of base in a dsDNA = 10 bp or 20 bases

Thus, molecular mass of a dsDNA with 20 bases = 20 × 500 = 10 kDa

24. **(c)** Experimental verification of the chromosomal theory of inheritance was done by Morgan. Sutton and Boveri proposed chromosomal theory of inheritance but it was experimentally verified by T.H. Morgan.

25. **(d)** Genes for flower colour in snapdragon shows incomplete dominance which is an exception of Mendel's first principle (*i.e.* Law of dominance), whereas Law of segregation is universally applicable. Incomplete dominance is a process when a dominant allele, or form of a gene, does not completely mask the effects of a recessive allele, and the organism's resulting physical appearance shows a blending of both alleles.

26. **(c)** Woman acts as a carrier. Both son & daughter inherit X-chromosome. Although only son would be the diseased one.

$$X^c X \times XY$$
$$\downarrow$$
$$X^c X \quad X^c Y \quad XX \quad XY$$

27. **(b)** IAIO, IBIO - Dominant-recessive relationship

$I^A I^B$ - Codominance

I^A, I^B & I^O - Three different allelic forms of a gene (multiple allelism)

28. **(b)** Husband × Wife

$I^A I^B$ $\quad$ $I^A i$

$\female$ \ $\male$	I^A	I^B
I^A	$I^A I^A$	$I^A I^B$
i	$I^A i$	$I^B i$

Number of genotypes = 4

Number of phenotypes = 3

$I^A I^A$ and $I^A i$ = A

$I^A I^B$ = AB

$I^B i$ = B

29. **(a)** During his experiments Mendel have taken seven characters in a pea plant. Among these, nature of trichomes i.e., glandular or non-glandular was not considered by Mendel.

30. **(d)** According to NCERT, Mendel conducted hybridisation experiments for 7 years on Pea plant between 1856 to 1863 and his data was published in 1865.

31. **(a)**

Parents – TT × tt
(Tall) (Dwarf)

F_1 generation — Tt (Heterozygous Tall)

On Selfing

	T	t
T	TT Tall	Tt Tall
t	Tt Tall	tt Dwarf

Phenotypic ratio : 3: 1 (Tall :Dwarf)

Genotypic ratio: 1:2:1 (Homozygous Tall : Heterozygous Tall : Dwarf)

32. **(c)** Seven pairs of contrasting characters were selected in pea plant and studied by Mendel in his experiment.

33. **(b)** Alleles are defined as alternative forms of the same gene.

34. **(a)** Mendel did not use pod length for his experiment.

35. **(b)** Possible × Possible
genotype genotype
of man with blood of woman with
group A blood group B
$I^A I^A$, $I^A i$ × $I^B I^B$, $I^B i$
If the genotype is
$I^A i$ × $I^B i$

The possibility of resultant blood group may be A, B, AB and O.

36. **(b)** Chromosomes carry genes, which are the hereditary characters to the offspring.

37. **(d)**

Round Green X Wrinkled yellow
(RRyy) (rrYY)
Ry – Ry rY – rY
..... F_1

RrYy RrYy RrYy RrYy
(Round (Round (Round (Round
yellow) yellow) yellow) yellow)

Thus, in the first generation (F_1), all seeds would be round and yellow.

38. **(a)**

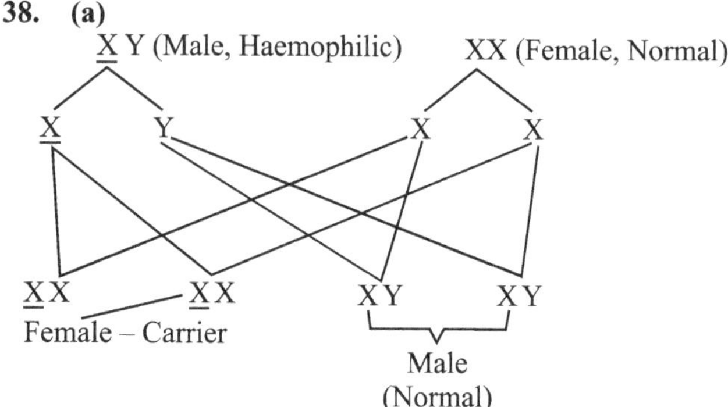

Since all the male progeny will get the X chromosome form their mother, they will all be normal.

39. **(d)**

40. **(d)** Punnett square is a graphical representation of the possible genotypes of an offspring arising from a particular cross or breeding event. With the help of Punnett square the production of gametes, the formation of zygotes and the F1 and F2 plants can be understood.

41. **(b)**

42. **(d)** XX- XO type of sex determination is seen in crickets, grasshoppers, and some other insects. In all these organisms the female is XX and is the homogametic sex. The male is the heterogametic sex but only has one sex chromosome. The male in XX-XO systems produce gametes with (X) or without (O) a sex chromosome.

In XX -XY method of sex determination, the sex of an individual is determined by a pair of sex chromosomes. Females typically have two of the same kind of sex chromosome (XX), and are called the homogametic sex. Males typically have two different kinds of sex chromosomes (XY), and are called the heterogametic sex. Turner's syndrome is also known as 45, X or 45, X,. It is a condition that affects only females, and results when one of the X chromosme (sex chromosomes) is missing or partially missing.

ZW-ZZ method of sex determination can be seen in some birds, butterflies, moths, and other organisms. Instead of X and Y chromosomes, they have Z and W chromosomes. The female is the heterogametic sex. In all these organisms female has a pair of dissimilar ZW chromosomes and male has two similar ZZ chromosomes.

43. (a)   **44.** (b)   **45.** (b)   **46.** (b)

47. (b)

www.ingramcontent.com/pod-product-compliance
Lightning Source LLC
LaVergne TN
LVHW080558210726
843508LV00017BC/1506